Hancock County, Indiana
Civil War Soldiers

Plus Related Facts

Sue Baker

HERITAGE BOOKS
2006

HERITAGE BOOKS
AN IMPRINT OF HERITAGE BOOKS, INC.

Books, CDs, and more—Worldwide

For our listing of thousands of titles see our website
at
www.HeritageBooks.com

Published 2006 by
HERITAGE BOOKS, INC.
Publishing Division
65 East Main Street
Westminster, Maryland 21157-5026

Copyright © 2002 Sue Baker

Other books by the author:

Hancock County, Indiana Court Records: Will Indexes, 1828-1950, Probate Indexes, 1828-1948, Births-Court Recorded, 1867-1919

Hancock County, Indiana Tombstone Inscriptions: One Hundred Years, 1833-1933

All rights reserved. No part of this book may be reproduced or transmitted in any form or by any means, electronic or mechanical, including photocopying, recording or by any information storage and retrieval system without written permission from the author, except for the inclusion of brief quotations in a review.

International Standard Book Number: 978-0-7884-2181-6

Dedication

To Hancock County's Civil War soldiers…..
ordinary men who had extraordinary courage

Hancock County Indiana Civil War Soldiers

Table of Contents

Key vi

Preface vii

Call to Arms 1

Home Guards 17

Union Guards 21

Morgan's Raid 23

Mississippi Marines 27

Soldiers 29

Regiments 423

Prisons 467

Sultana 475

Letters 485

Grand Army of the Republic 501

Newspapers This 'N' That 511

Bibliography 525

Index 527

Hancock County Indiana Civil War Soldiers

Key to Abbreviations

Reg	Regiment
NOD	no other data in primary Hancock County sources
HC	Hancock County
s/o	son of
d/o	daughter of
c/o	children of
y	years
m	month
d	day

Hancock County Indiana Civil War Soldiers

Preface

This volume is the culmination of nearly fifteen months of researching and writing to document as many soldiers as possible who resided in Hancock County, Indiana, before, during or after the United States Civil War, 1861-1865. I have collected more then 2,000 men from primary military sources, official public records, newspapers of the era, and twenty secondary sources of published books and compiled material concerning the Civil War. All sources are public records.

Having done genealogical research in Hancock County for thirty-five years, I could not record names of soldiers and their units only, therefore, brief biographies of as many men as possible are included. I have spent hours and hours deciphering names that had been transcribed from original regiment records kept by an army company clerk whose fancy flourishes of penmanship and phonetic spelling constantly became cantankerous puzzles for me.

I have relied, but not too heavily, on county histories with their glowing biographies, which are notorious for inaccuracies, but often used them only as a compass to point in another direction for sources when a piece of evidence was needed to verify conflicting statements. Even with its outdated syntax, the soldiers' edition of *Presidents, Soldiers and Statesmen,* published in 1899, has been valuable in constructing the lives and military experiences of many Hancock County Civil War veterans.

I have attempted to relate the details of several regiments' engagements, but in no stretch of the imagination am I a military historian. Wrestling with conflicting evidence, the mortal enemy of genealogists, I have striven for accuracy, however, no compilation is without error. Additions and corrections are welcome.

This book about the Hancock County Civil War soldiers could not have been written without the assistance of many kind

Hancock County Indiana Civil War Soldiers

and generous people. I am grateful to the Hancock County Public Library for their collections and Inter-Library-Loans; the Reference Desk, Diana Hoy, Joy Summers and Marcia Hunt for their patience during long hours of research and to staff member, Raylene McCreery, for allowing me to use not only her knowledge but her books concerning the Sultana disaster; also Pam Baker and Karen Lindsay of the Hancock County Health Department for assistance in locating official Death Records.

Many thanks to descendants who shared files, stories and letters of their Hancock County Civil War ancestors. To Jonzees Photography, Pendleton, Indiana, for their many hours in printing photos.

Colonel (retired) Robert Fischer, Military Historian, answered my endless questions about the Civil War era army. The Indiana State Archives' collections were invaluable, thanks to archivists Steve Towne and Vickie Casteel for sharing their insight into the Civil War.

I am grateful to the Park Rangers at Chickamauga and Chattanooga National Military Park for their expertise; especially to Kennesaw Mountain Park Ranger, W.R. Johnson and his staff for the stories of the 57th Indiana, and the research done for me concerning the Battle of Sulphur Trestle, Alabama, in which many Hancock County soldiers were engaged.

My thanks to National Park Ranger, Joan Stibitz, and staff at the Andersonville Historic Site and library; Tommy Coleman, Old Cahawba (Alabama) State Park Ranger for answering my questions about the prison site; and the helpful staffs of the National Cemeteries at Marietta, Georgia; Nashville and Chattanooga, Tennessee.

This book would have been impossible without the computer knowledge of my niece, Joy Wesseler, and my nephew and niece, Ron and Gloria Jones—and absolutely impossible without my right-hand-husband, Jim, for his long hours and untiring efforts on my behalf.

Hancock County Indiana Civil War Soldiers

Call To Arms

After the attack on Fort Sumter 12 April 1861, the call to arms echoed across the land. Hancock County answered Lincoln's call for Union volunteers adding its share to the 259,000 volunteers ultimately supplied from Indiana, more than any other state. Hancock County quickly called a citizens meeting and on 20 April 1861, adopted resolutions concerning "appropriation of men and means of the vigorous prosecution of the war now existing by the act of the so-called Southern Confederacy," and elected the following men as officers: James Tyner, President; Robert Barr and James Foley, Vice Presidents; and Thomas Bedgood and William Frost, Secretaries.

Full of military fervor, a fife and drum corps was organized by Reuben Riley and Henry Snow to make rounds of the county communities to boost patriotic emotion and volunteer enlistment. On 22 April 1861 Reuben Riley, a Greenfield attorney, organized the first volunteers who were mustered in at Indianapolis and known as Company G, attached to the 8th Indiana Infantry Regiment for a term of three months. These first recruits were also known as Union Guards of Hancock County and are named in this volume.

The newly-trained soldiers left 19 Jun 1861 for western Virginia where they were victorious in the battle of Rich Mountain, saving many counties for the Union which later became known as West Virginia. (See details of the battle on the pages for the 8th Regiment.) The three months regiment was mustered out 6 Aug 1861 and was quickly reorganized into a three year unit that left Indianapolis for St. Louis, Missouri.

Published in the *Hancock Democrat*, mid-August 1861: "On Monday last Captain Walls left for Indianapolis with a company of Hancock County boys to enter the service of the United States for a term of three years or during the war. It will be part of the

Hancock County Indiana Civil War Soldiers

Eighth Regiment as reorganized, and will retain its former position in the regiment. The scene at the depot as the boys passed through, the large number of men, women and children who gathered in from all points of the county to witness the departure, was sad and sorrowful in the extreme. God bless the noble-hearted boys, and preserve and protect them in the patriotic hazardous duties they have voluntarily taken upon them selves! May they all safely return at the expiration of a term of service to receive the warm embrace of mothers, fathers, sisters, brothers and kind friends left behind."

Hancock County men enlisted in 31 Indiana Regiments with the bulk being members of three cavalry units, the 5th, 9th and 13th; and eleven infantry units, 8th; 11th 12th; 18th ;19th ; 51st; 53rd; 57th; 79th and 99th.

The examining physician filled in the blanks on: Form For Examining A Recruit A volunteer was given a physical examination of head, ears, face eyes, nose, organs of mastication and voice, neck, chest, abdomen, genital and urinary organs, vertebral column, superior extremities, inferior extremities; and asked ten questions: Have you ever been sick; Have you any diseases now, and what; Have you ever had fits; Have you ever received an injury or wound upon the head; Have you ever had a fracture, a dislocation, or a sprain; Are you in the habit of drinking or have you ever had the horrors; Are you subject to piles; Have you any difficulty in urinating; and Have you been vaccinated or had small pox?

Fathers, sons, brothers, nephews and cousins often volunteered the same day, served in the same company, wounded in the same battle and even died the same day. Patriotism turned a deaf ear to the thundering apocalypse of war, pestilence, famime and death.

No matter the unit, the enlistees were in both the western and the eastern theaters of war and were in the bloody battles of Pea Ridge, Arkansas; Vicksburg, Mississippi; Shiloh, and Stone's River and Missionary Ridge in Tennessee; Antietam and Manassas in Virginia; and Kennesaw Mountain in Georgia, and

Hancock County Indiana Civil War Soldiers

Atlanta, Sherman's march to the sea plus others. A cavalry unit often fought dismounted, the soldiers moved in squads of four with three on foot as the fourth held their horses safely out of range.

Music helped to relieve the boredom of camp life. Singing, fiddle playing, strumming a banjo and twanging a Jews harp with the popular tunes of "When This Cruel War Is Over." "Yankee Doodle;" "Tenting Tonight On The Old Campground" and strains of "Lorena" were heard from both the Blue and the Gray camps. Physical contests were a daily part of the soldier's camp life, boxing, broad-jumping, wrestling matches, foot races and a free-for-all. Letter writing was important to soothe lonely hours, but reading letters from home was the all-time favorite pastime.

Soldiers were often on a special detail in the Pioneer Corps. Attached to the Corps of Engineers, the Pioneers went in advance of the regiment to build roads, bridges and pontoons across rivers where and when necessary for artillery, supply wagons, and to clear any unusual and/or dangerous obstacles that might slow the regiments' progress. Among others who served as Pioneers from Hancock County were John Davis and Samuel Roney, Daniel Burk, plus Lt. William Hill of Hancock County was commander of a Brigade's Pioneer Corps.

Also, soldiers were on a special detail as Sharpshooters and were just what the name implies, expert marksmen, used as special skirmishers who could hit any target. Requirements were to place ten shots in a 10-inch circle from 200 yards using any long gun. Among others were Wesley Catt, Thomas Hiday, Richard Lamb and Nevil Reeves of Hancock County; Lamb was killed "while sharpshooting."

Naturally in war, cannons, rifles, muskets, pistols and sabers take their toll but for every man killed in action during the Civil War, two died behind the lines of illness and disease. Not only did two armies clash, but more sophisticated weapons and lack of medical knowledge also were doing battle. Blood-splattered surgeons labored in make-shift field hospitals near the front lines

Hancock County Indiana Civil War Soldiers

where they employed three basic procedures. They probed to remove shot and pieces of shell, sewed torn arteries and flesh to control hemorrhaging, but most of the surgeon's time was spent in amputation of mangled arms and legs which were tossed onto a nearby pile. A sight such as this nightmare was never forgotten by any soldier who saw it and especially if a part of it.

Soldiers were plagued with fleas, flies, dysentery, chronic diarrhea from poor diets, measles developing into pneumonia, ague, and add hemorrhoids to the cavalryman's sufferings. Among the medications of the day to treat such afflictions were calomel, strychnine, belladonna, castor oil and opium. The castor oil was often given to relieve diarrhea. Is it any wonder that so many died of wounds, illness and disease? A total of 700,000 Americans lost their lives in the Civil War. Sir Winston Churchill once said of Civil War soldiers: "with them, uncommon valor became a common virtue."

The 99th Regiment History states the following about the burial of a soldier: "The burial of a soldier is one of the sad tasks of his comrades. When in camp it was always attended with more formality than after a battle, and in camp we could usually get a plain coffin. His shroud was his martial suit of blue, for how better could a soldier rest than with his soldier outfit on him. He was borne from his quarters to the grave by four of his comrades , usually his messmates, the body preceded by the regimental band, and there are few echoes that wake the air with more doleful melody than the 'dead march' as its minor cadences come from the roll of muffled drums.

"Following the band at the head of the coffin came the chaplain , and behind the coffin came the comrades of the departed one, often as devoutly as ever dropped their tears upon the cold and silent clay. Arriving at the grave the body is lowered into the tomb, when the chaplain with a few words of scripture, usually the twenty-third Psalm, begins a short address based upon the promises of God that inspire hope, pointing out the fact that God was too wise to err, and that death is the only way by which we come to life eternal. A few words in regard to

Hancock County Indiana Civil War Soldiers

the life and character of the deceased, and a verse or two of a familiar hymn, usually "Jesus Lover of My Soul" is sung. The chaplain closes with prayer, especially remembering the loved ones far away, who will sorrow at their soldier boy who will never come to his home again.

"The firing squad then fire three rounds over the grave and the company goes back to take up the duties of life again, feeling in their hearts that the flag of their country is more dear to them because another comrade had died in its service." Fallen heroes may have been interred and reinterred more than one time, having been buried where they fell and then moved to a National Cemetery. One sad story of unidentified graves is that during the removal, coffin lids were marked with chalk as identication, left in the weather too long that caused the markings to run and disappear.

In the first years of the war, disabled soldiers were given an honorable discharge but in April 1863, to ease the shortage of men, the War Department created the Invalid Corps. Soldiers, unfit for field duty but fit for light duty, were enlisted to serve as guards, clerks, nurses and cooks. The disabled officers and men were formed into companies and regiments but found the name, Invalid Corps, offensive and in March 1864, it was changed to Veteran Reserve Corps.

A private's pay was $13 a month. Frequently, Hancock County soldiers at the front would send money in one amount to a trustworthy friend at home to give to their families. By July 1862 the war progressed and more soldiers were needed. To encourage volunteers to fill the county's quota and escape the draft, Hancock County Commissioners authorized a bounty of $25 to "each and every citizen who would volunteer for three years."

The county quota increased in the fall of 1863 and the following is abstracted from the *Hancock Democrat*, 31 Dec 1863: "Attention Recruits Under the late call of the President for '300,000' more soldiers and to every Veteran Volunteer Recruit, that is, to every recruit who has served at least nine months in the

Hancock County Indiana Civil War Soldiers

army, and who has been honorably discharged from the service for other cause than that of disability, a bounty and premium of **Four Hundred and Two Dollars** will be paid. To all accepted recruits, not veterans, in addition to one month's pay in advance a bounty and premium of **Three Hundred and Two Dollars** will be paid. Capt. John G. Dunbar, of the 79th Indiana is authorized to recruit for Hancock County and may be found at the Dunbar House, Greenfield (northeast corner of State and Main Streets). To the above bounties, the County Commissioners have generously added one hundred dollars."

A bounty of $502 to serve your country was an attractive amount of money for people who earned very little "cash money." Frederick C. Kreft (Kraft), a shoemaker at New Palestine "was induced to enter the army as a substitute for a man who had been drafted, receiving for such service the sum of $900 to serve in Company G, 148 Indiana Regiment." It was the grand total of Federal, State and Local bounties.

Hancock County Commissioners not only set the amount of bounty paid by the county but in March 1863, they also set the following to assist soldiers' families, "relative to supplying soldiers' families with clothing and food, agents shall be restricted to the following specified articles: muslin cotton prints; common clothing for children, shoes, socks or stockings when necessary; food items were, flour; meal; pork or bacon or beef; molasses; salt; soda and pepper. Allow physicians for medicine, the cost being standard price of the druggist."

In 1862 the United States government launched a pension program to benefit disabled soldiers. It required they be disabled as a direct result of military duty or "developed after combat from causes which can be directly traced to injuries or disease contracted while in military service." The amount of each pension was determined by the military rank of the soldier and level of disability. Pensions granted to widows, orphans and other dependents of deceased soldiers were calculated at the total disability rate. In 1873 the Government added an extra benefit to

Hancock County Indiana Civil War Soldiers

widows in that they received money for each dependent child in their care.

On 27 June 1890 the Dependent Pension Act was notably revised as a result of the lobbying effort of the Grand Army of the Republic. The new law allowed any veteran to receive a pension who was honorably discharged and disabled for manual labor. In 1906 another addition was made that old age alone was sufficient to receive a Government pension for military service in the Civil War.

Following is a required 1890 form with questions to be answered by the veteran to determine disability: "I) Did you have Camp or Chronic Diarrhea in the army from the bad food and water? Where and When contracted?; II) Did you have Rheumatism or Lumbago of the Back in the army from laying on the cold and damp ground? Where and When contracted? III) Did you have in the army, Malarial Poisoning (chills and fever) from laying in the swamps and drinking water of the South? Where and When contracted?

"Upon the return of this letter with the questions properly answered, you will be advised further. Give this your immediate attention, as the present Liberal policy of the Pension Bureau may not always continue.

It seems the army did have lighter moments. *Hancock Democrat*, 12 May 1864: "From the 99th Regiment, Scottsboro, Alabama, 29 Apr 1864: All is quiet in the 'moving column' since our return from Dalton (Georgia). Our new division commander, being very strict, attempted to confine the boys to their regiments quarters by the imposition of strong camp guards, but the boys, not being used to so small an area, were not to have their usefulness thus limited, and the attempt failed. Double duty was inflicted, but the boys were used to that.

"Finally, a large wooden horse was erected in town; patrols thrown out; and every man caught outside his regiment without a pass, was sentenced to two hours ride on the artificial animal of 'Trojan antiquity.' It was most strange to see two or three on at a time, and our division was in a very fair way to become efficient

Hancock County Indiana Civil War Soldiers

in equestrianship ; but unfortunately one morning, this celebrated *animule* was not to be found, but on every post and building in town was seen the following notice.

"**$600 Reward** Strayed or stolen. A fine Potomac Stallion disappeared on the night of 20 April 1864. Any person returning the same to these Headquarters will be entitled to above reward, and one free ride. Signed, Brig. Gen. William Harrow, Commanding 4th Division. Information was immediately communicated to the General, who acknowledged that instead of teaching the 4th Division, he had become their pupil. No one ever applied for the reward, and the fine Potomac Stallion, no doubt, yielded up his existence as a *burnt offering* on the altar of our country. signed J.M. Alley, Company B, 99th Indiana."

Boys, who were too small to lie about their age and just could not wait for their eighteenth birthday to join the adventure of war knew the easiest way to get in the army was to be a musician. Can you imagine the excitement when boys would read an ad in the *Hancock Democrat*, Wanted: Young men who like to get up early, make noise all day, love exercise and excitement. If interested, please see the nearest Union Army Recruiter.

The excitement of war enticed 16-year-old Levi Thayer, a student in Greenfield, to join the army as a drummer in June of 1861. He was paid $13 a month, same as a private, and was wounded at Shiloh and Fort Donelson while drumming for the 11th Indiana Zouaves. Dressed in flashy uniforms, they relied on him for calls: wake up, sick, breakfast, drill, dinner, tatoo, get ready for bed, lights out, the long roll, readiness for battle, and set the pace for marching.

Not only drums but bugles told the soldiers what to do and where to be all day, and were a vital role on the battlefield as their calls amplified officers' orders. Even over the roar of cannons, buglers often intercepted the orders of the enemy giving a battlefield advantage.

Regimental colors were the focal point on the battlefield. A color bearer was usually a tall, muscular man who was calm under fire and who could hold the flag aloft to keep it visible

Hancock County Indiana Civil War Soldiers

through battle smoke. Courage was likewise required to carry a flag into battle, the colors "drew lead like a magnet." Andrew J. Fuller, Hancock County, was a color bearer for Company B, 8th Regiment and was wounded in the ankle during a charge at Vicksburg.

Hancock Democrat, 24 Sep 1885: "**Return of a Flag** Dallas Texas, 8 Sep 1885, Parson's Confederate brigade had its reunion and a flag was given to the Department of Texas Grand Army of the Republic. It was the battle flag of the 57th Indiana Regiment captured by Corporal Crook who now lives in Cleburne (Texas). The Texas G.A.R. offered to return it to the Indiana G.A.R."

The 57th Indiana Regiment accepted the return of its colors at the reunion 22 and 23 Sep 1885, at Kokomo, Indiana. The Texas delegation was invited, "no pains will be spared to make the return of the colors as impressive as possible and if Corporal Crook could come he would be certain to receive a grand ovation. The delegation during its sojourn, will be the guests of the Department of Indiana and the regiment. It will be a gala time and Indiana and Texas will join hands in fraternal greeting."

Hancock County had its share of Union brothers, cousins and nephews and Confederate brothers cousins and nephews spilling blood against each other, due to the fact that people migrating from southern states a decade or so before the war left family members whose loyalties were to the Confederacy. Following are three families recorded in Hancock County sources.

Two Hancock County brothers, Captain Robert Preston Andis and Alexander Andis enlisted for the Union but their brother, Earl Carson Andis enlisted for the Confederacy in a Virginia unit known as the Grayson Daredevils. See sentiments expressed between them in the letter section of this volume.

David H. Baity of Hancock County enlisted in the Union army and his three brothers enlisted in the Confederate army: Alexander was a prisoner for eighteen months at Point Lookout, Maryland; and Henry, "who left Confederate service and came through the lines and got to Greenfield where he lived until his death;" and William, "served in the Confederate army."

Hancock County Indiana Civil War Soldiers

Garrett Wiggins migrated to Indiana and was the father of four sons: Phillip, the oldest, remained in Kentucky and was a soldier in the Confederate army; three sons enlisted from Hancock County in the Union army, George, who was never heard from after the war; John and Lawson (Loss) both returned to Hancock County after the war.

Early in the war capture meant parole and exchange, for prisoners to return to their regiment but that process unraveled (details on Prison pages) and prison pens became a dreaded horror. Ever so many Hancock County soldiers were captives at Andersonville, Cahaba and Libby where they lived, and died, in unspeakable conditions. Among them are recorded: James W. Cass, wounded and captured at Dallas, Georgia, a prisoner in Andersonville, plus, he died in the Sultana disaster; and 16-year-old Christopher Hugh (Kip) Sears was captured at Sulphur Branch Trestle, Alabama, imprisoned at Cahaba, Alabama, survived the Sultana disaster only to die two months later from the harsh effects of war's rigors. The three happenings, wounded in battle, a Prisoner of War and on the Sultana, were a triple challenge of a soldier's life.

In the scorching Georgia summer of 1864, fierce fighting and bloodshed continued as the Billy Yanks pushed the Johnny Rebs across Kennesaw Mountain south to Atlanta, where the Yanks nearly surrounded the city, especially with the battles at Peach Tree Creek and Jonesboro. Atlanta was finally captured on 2 Sep 1864.

On 12 November 1864, and with all colors flying, General Sherman led 60,000 soldiers from Atlanta, beginning the infamous "March to the Sea." Hancock County was well represented and recorded soldiers in five infantry regiments, 12th; 38th; 48th; 53rd; and 99th. In two columns the overpowering Yankees slashed across Georgia in a sixty-mile-wide path of destruction and arrived at Savannah on 10 Dec 1864. Sherman hoped the appalling wake of desolation would break the South's will to continue the war.

Hancock County Indiana Civil War Soldiers

The 10,000 man Confederate garrison at Savannah, unable to withstand an attack from such a large Union force, evacuated the city. On 22 Dec 1864 General Sherman sent a dispatch to President Lincoln, "I beg to present to you as a Christmas gift, the city of Savannah with 150 heavy guns, plenty of ammunition and also about 25,000 bales of cotton." Sherman's army rumbled northward and on 17 Feb 1865, captured Columbia, South Carolina, and burned two-thirds of the city. The Union soldiers had a special dislike for South Carolina because in their minds that State was responsible for the war, having been the first state to withdraw from the Union and attacked Ft, Sumter in 1861.

President Lincoln could see the imminent close of the war, and gave General Grant the surrender terms to be carried out: "I want no one punished, treat them liberally all around. We want these people to return to their allegiance to the Union and submit to laws." Dudley D. Hudson and Salem Shumway were among the few Hancock County soldiers who were recorded as having earned a furlough and went home to vote in the 1864 election. Did they vote for Abraham Lincoln and Andrew Johnson or for former General George B. McClellan and George Pendleton? Fifteen-year-old William H. Power told of casting his first vote in the field for Abraham Lincoln.

Hancock Democrat, 13 April 1865: "Grant's Terms of Surrender Appomatox Court House, 9 April 1865. To Gen R.E. Lee, Com'ding C.S.A.: In accordance with the substance of my letter to you of the 8th inst., I propose to receive the surrender of the Army of Northern Virginia on the following terms, to-wit: Rolls of all officers and men to be made in dulpicate, one copy to be given to an officer designated by me, the other to be retained by such as you desnigate .

"The officers to give their individual paroles not to take arms against the Government of the United States until properly exchanged; each company or regimental commander to sign a parole for the men of their commands.

"The arms, artillery and public property, to be parked and stacked and turned over to the officers appointed by me to

Hancock County Indiana Civil War Soldiers

receive them. This will not embrace the side-arms of the officers nor their private horse or baggage. This done, each officer and man will be allowed to return to their homes, not to be disturbed by the United States authorities so long as they observe their parole, and the laws in the force where they may reside. Signed, Very Respectfully, U.S. Grant, Lieutenant General."

Hancock Democrat, 13 April 1865   Lee Accepts Grant's Terms   9 April 1865: To Lieut-Gen U.S. Grant, Com'd'g, U.S.A. General: I have received your letter of this date, containing the terms of surrender of the Army of Northern Virginia, as proposed by you. As they are substantially the same as those expressed in your letter of the 8t^h inst., they are accepted. I will proceed to designate the proper officers to carry the stipulations into effect. Signed, Very Respectfully, your ob't servant, R.E. Lee, General." The Southern soldiers also were allowed to keep their horses/mules for without them crops could not be planted.

April 1865 was the month of several surrenders, one assassination and one marine disaster.. Sherman and his large Union force were in merciless pursuit of Johnston and his smaller Confederate force into North Carolina. When the news of the surrender of General Lee's Army of Virginia was announced to the troops on 14 April 1865, there was jubilant celebration in all camps, however, three days later the somber announcement of the assassination of President Lincoln put an abrupt end to the festivities.

The assassination and surrenders shoved the marine disaster to the end of telegraph messages and back pages of newspapers. On 27 April 1865 the steamship, Sultana, overloaded with returning Union prisoners of war, exploded without warning and burned in the middle of the Mississippi River; with more loss of life than the Titanic. The names of Hancock County soldiers are listed on the pages about the Sultana disaster and also the narrative of James H. Kimberlin of Hancock County who survived.

With Lees army gone, General Johnston requested terms to surrender his Confederate Army of North Carolina, on the same

Hancock County Indiana Civil War Soldiers

terms granted to Lee, and did so on 26 April 1865, at Bennett's house, near Durham, North Carolina. Confederate General Richard Taylor (son of President Zachary Taylor) surrendered his forces in Alabama and Mississippi on 4 May 1865. It was not until 26 May 1865 that Confederate General E. Kirby Smith surrendered the Trans-Mississippi Department, excepting one regiment, the 1st Cherokee Mounted Rifles, commanded by Cherokee lawyer, Stand Waites (Wayt-ee), who held out until 23 June 1865 when he surrendered near Fort Towson in the Indian Territory.

Hancock Democrat, 13 April 1865: "The reception of the news of the surrender of General Lee and his rebel hordes, in our town, early on Monday last, was the occasion of great and lasting joy. Bells were rung, bonfires were built, powder was freely used, and all business suspended for the day. Men women and children thronged the streets and greeted each other as they had not greeted each other before.

"The dark hours were passed; the day began to dawn, and all was safe. The country, in spite of rebels, and rebel sympathizers, at home and abroad, and difficulties that cannot be told, was redeemed, regenerated and disenthralled, and stood up among the nations of the earth, more powerful than when the great struggle began.

"At night a large number of the houses, along the principal street, business as well as private, were beautifully illuminated. Martial music paraded the street, followed by a mass patriotism of either gender. A stand was extemporized at Walker's corner, and the crowd gathered round to hear the speeches. Messrs. Hough, Judge Gooding, Ballenger, Riley, Hall, Col. Gooding, Mason, White, and others spoke to the crowd."

On 10 May 1865 the nations new president, Andrew Johnson, declared that all armed hostilities were "virtually at an end," and plans began for an immense victory parade of the Union's main fighting forces. It was a two-day spectacle that would make all other parades pale in comparison. General William Tecumseh Sherman's Army of Georgia, having completed a grueling 2,000-

Hancock County Indiana Civil War Soldiers

mile march through Georgia and North Carolina, and General George Gordon Meade's Army of the Potomac arrived in Washington for the Grand Review. Being camped on opposite sides of the Potomac River did not shackle the customary rivalries as the soldiers met in the evening in downtown Washington for fun and frolic and fisticuffs.

The first day of the parade was 23 May 1865, General Meade's force marched down Pennsylvania Avenue before thousands of cheering spectators. They stepped smartly passed the reviewing stand in front of the White House where sat President Johnson, General-in-Chief, Ulysses Grant and top Government officials. Meade's army of 80,000 infantrymen marched 12 abreast, one source said 60 abreast, curb to curb, in perfect precision, plus hundreds of artillery pieces; and a seven-mile long line of cavalrymen that alone took an hour to pass.

If there would be added excitement at the reviewing stand, who would the culprit be but the flamboyant General George Armsrtrong Custer? Whether by accident or design of the expert cavalry commander, Custer lost control of his horse and in gaining control rode by the reviewing stand twice. Continuing from his days at West Point, he always looked for ways to gain notoriety.

The second day of the Grand Review, 24 May 1865, was equally as bright as the first when Sherman's 65,000-man force passed in review for six hours. Listening to the band music of "Marching Through Georgia," his lean, tattered and sunburned troops, marched with less precision than Meade's but brought just as many cheers as they passed through the crowds with their mixture of hospital wagons, laborers, black families who were fleeing slavery, the "bummers" who scavenged for army supplies and livestock captured from Georgia and Carolina farms. Many of the regiment's colors were evidence of fierce battles as the tattered and ragged flags waved in the breeze. Sherman recalled years later that leading his victorious troops on that day, "was the happiest and most satisfactory moment of my life."

Hancock County Indiana Civil War Soldiers

There were countless Hancock County soldiers who marched in the Grand Review and within days were in Indianapolis being greeted by Governor Morton on the lawn of the Capital. When discharged the soldiers were allowed to buy their weapons paying $6 for muskets; $10 for Spencer's carbines; $8 for revolvers and $3 for sabers.

After enduring the thundering horsemen of the apocalypse, war, pestilence, famine and death—the Hancock County warriors eagerly welcomed the reality of home—ending the Call To Arms.

Hancock County Indiana Civil War Soldiers

Home Guards

The Legion of Indiana was organized early in the War for protection on the home front and their companies became known as Home Guards. Each community usually had their own company and their own place to drill, such as a common area or school grounds. The Hancock Guards marched and drilled on a large pasture that adjoined Greenfield in the area of Grant and East Street, east of the branch (Potts Ditch). (Where the current Post Office is located.) Imagine the excitement they must have caused on Saturday afternoons as they stepped in cadence on the field of bluegrass.

Two Home Guard companies, Hancock and Anderson, were called into active service to defend Indiana against General Morgan and his raiders.

Anderson Guards, New Palestine organized 13 Sep 1861, Thomas Tuttle, Captain; Conrad Shellhouse, 1st Lt.; George Stineback, 2nd Lt.

Brandywine Guards, organized 26 Aug 1861, Robert Andis, Captain; Ezra Fountain, 1st Lt.; John M. Dixon, 2nd Lt.

Buck Creek organized but no officers given.

Fortville Guards, organized 4 Jun 1861, James H. Perry and P. Bond, Captains; John K. Faucett, 1st Lt.; Charles Doty, 2nd Lt.

Greenfield, boys too young for service, were organized as the Greenfield Union Cadets, Hamilton Dunbar (whose father and two brothers were in active service), Captain; James W. Knight, 1st Lt.; James Gapen, 2nd Lt.; and Oscar Thomas, 3rd Lt.

Hancock Guards, organized 10 Jun 1861, Alexander K. Branham and Henry A. Swope, Captains; William E. Hart, 1st Lt.; William E. Duncan, William Lindsey; George H. Walker; and Joshua Edwards, 2nd Lt.

Hancock County Indiana Civil War Soldiers

Jackson Guards, organized 1863, John A. Craft and Joseph H. McKown, Captains; John M. Davis, 1st Lt.; Asa H. Allison, 2nd Lt.

New Palestine had a company of forty German boys, organized by Dr. Buchel, a German physician. This unit disbanded because nearly all the members enlisted for active service.

Union Hancock, Cavalry, organized 1863, Taylor W. Thomas, Captain; Solomon Kauble, 1st Lt.; William E. Henry, 2nd Lt.;

Vernon Township Guards, organized 1863, Sylvester Gaskins, Captain; Thomas J. Hanna, 1st Lt.; Perry J. Brinegar, 2nd. Lt.

Hancock Democrat, 4 Apr 1861: "The Hancock Guards will parade on Saturday morning next at ten o'clock. Persons who have or desire to attach themselves to this Company are requested to present themselves at that time. By order, A.K. Branham, Capt.; William Mitchell, O.S."

Hancock Democrat, 1 May 1861: " The Hancock Guards opened their roll on Saturday last receiving a large accession. The vacancies were filled. The Company is officered as follows: A.K. Branham, Captain; H.A. Swope, 1st Lt.; William A. Lindsey, 2d; J.K. Sloan, 3d; John Rardin 4th; William Mitchell 1st Sergeant; S.H. Dunbar 2d; John Dennis 3d; F.H. Crawford 4th; Wm. J. Foster 5th; William E. Hart 1st Corporal; L.W. Gooding 2d; A.R. Wallace 3d; John Osborn 4th; Wm. R. West Quartermaster; and George H. Walker, Treasurer. The Company drills every morning at 5 o'clock and each Saturday afternoon."

Hancock Democrat, 25 Sep 1861: "Attention, Hancock Guards! In pursuance of orders from the Adjutant General of Indiana, you are hereby ordered to meet at your Armory, on Saturday next, at 9 o'clock, A.M., fully armed and equipped for business and parade. Those having no muskets, must substitute private arms and to such as have not procured uniforms, the requirements of the law will be waived until further notice. The

Hancock County Indiana Civil War Soldiers

law will be fully enforced upon all absentees. signed, A.K. Branham, Capt.

Hancock Democrat, 25 Sep 1861: "On Saturday last the Hancock Guards were mustered into the Indiana Legion by Capt. Austin H. Brown. The following gentlemen were elected as officers of the Company: Capt, A.K. Branham; 1st Lt. H.A. Swope; 2nd Lt. Wm. C. Lindsey; Orderly Sergeant S.T. Kauble; 1st Sgt S.H. Dunbar; 2nd Wm. E. Hart; 3rd F.H. Crawford; 4th J.V. Hinchman; 1st Corporal John Sloan; 2nd Thomas Samuels; 3rd A.R. Wallace; 4th W.H. Gooding; Company Clerk H.B. Thayer; and Quartermaster Wm. R. West. The ceremony of swearing into the Legion was an interesting scene, and was witnessed by many of our citizens. The Company may now be considered as part and parcel of the troops of the country, ready and willing, at a reasonable notice, to quit the joys and comforts of home for the stirring scenes of active service in defense of the State and the Nation. It is a fine looking Company. and will no doubt give a good account of itself."

Hancock County Indiana Civil War Soldiers

Union Guards of Hancock County

by Dorothy June Williams
The Ad News, 26 January 1994

Roster of the Union Guard of Hancock County, and eventually was sworn in as Company G of the 8th Indiana Infantry Regiment: Reuben A. Riley, Captain; Henry Raridan, 1st Lieutenant; George W.H. Riley, 2nd Lieutenant; William R. Wall, Sr. 3rd Lieutenant; 1st Sergeant, John M. Stevenson; Sergeants, Pelatiah Bond, John S. Edwards; and Marion M. Stephenson; Corporals, John S. Chittenden; Ebberlee S. Duncan; John H. Duncan; Samuel Marsh; and Henry Snow; Musicians, Jacob Mullin; Sylvester S. Shorn; and George P. Stevenson; Privates, William W. Alexander; John W. Allison; Lucellus Anderson; Jacob T. Barrett; Benjamin Bond; Arthur V. Brown; James Buchanan;

William Campbell; Martin V. Chapman; James L. Clayton; Thomas Day; Charles Dipper; Jesse D. Dobbins; Martin Dunn; Frederick Dye; John Dye Jr.; Samuel Dye; Benjamin Elliott; Orlando Ellis; Alfred Gapen; William Gappen; Jabez E. Harrison; Charles Hartner; William G. Hill; Aaron Hutton; Milton Jackson; George W. Johnson; Henry Jones; Isaac T. Jones; Thomas S. Jones; Miller Laporte; George L. Lipscomb; John A. Lynam;

Seth Marsh; Lot W. Martin; Jasper C. McElvey; George McNamee; Henry Merket; John A. Morford; Marion Philpot; John Pope; Newton Pope; James S. Reeves; Nicholas Remeshart; Jasper Rollins, George Rynierson; William H. Scott; William J. Scott; Conrad H. Shellhouse; Joseph T. Short; William H. Short; Aaron A. Sleeth; Lafayette Slifer; Levi Slifer; George W. Smith; Andrew Stutsman; Calvin Sullivan; George W. Travis; David N. True; Elijah Tuttle; David Ulrey; and John Wolf.

Hancock County Indiana Civil War Soldiers

Morgan's Confederate Raid Into Indiana

The Civil War had been raging for two years when on a sultry day, 8 July 1863, Indiana fluttered briefly in the pages of Civil War history. The bold, Confederate general, John Hunt Morgan, disobeying orders, led 2,500 cavalrymen across the Ohio River from Kentucky into Indiana and provoked an adventure that lasted five days.

Without a doubt, Morgan had a daring reputation, was dismissed from college for boisterous behavior but did distinguish himself in 1847 during the Mexican War. As a businessman who was born in Kentucky, he had strong ties to the economy of the Confederacy and when his state remained with the Union, he moved deeper into the South. In 1861 at age 36 years, Morgan took his oath to the Confederacy as a captain in the cavalry.

He became well-known as a commander who used stealth, surprise and mobility to gain his objectives, therefore, his command traveled light, discarded their sabers and often fought on foot as mounted infantry using rifles and Colt repeating pistols. Due to his lightning methods, he became known as the "Thunderbolt of the Confederacy." Adding to the haughty aura of Morgan and his men, their wide-brimmed hats were adorned with plumes.

There are intriguing questions about why Morgan disobeyed orders and crossed the Ohio River. Many at the time thought he was on a foraging expedition to increase dwindling Southern supplies. It's possible the rumors that Indiana was a stronghold for the Knights of the Golden Circle, a secret society whose members pledged loyalty to the South, influenced Morgan's decision in the expectation of bringing Indiana into the Confederacy, by force if necessary. Then, too, Robert E. Lee

Hancock County Indiana Civil War Soldiers

was heading toward Gettysburg in the very week of the raid; recent historians believe that Morgan may have hoped to ride across Ohio and join Lee in Pennsylvania

No matter his reasons for invading Indiana, it caused a great disturbance. Governor Oliver Morton issued a proclamation ordering "all able-bodied male citizens in the counties south of the National Road to form companies and arm themselves with such arms as they could procure." The first fight on Hoosier soil was at Corydon, ironically the first capitol of Indiana, then the raiders galloped to Salem then east to Vienna, Lexington, North Vernon, Dupont, Versailles and Osgood before crossing into Ohio at Harrison.

Two Companies from Hancock County were ordered into active service for a week during the July 1863 raid in Indiana by Morgan and his men. They were the Hancock Guards, commanded by Captain A.K. Branham and the Anderson Guards, commanded by Captain Thomas Tuttle.

Captain Branham's Company E of 105th Regiment of Indiana Volunteers was mustered in 11 Jul 1863, and after reaching Indianapolis was ordered to the southern part of the State. The Indiana Adjutant General's report states the following: "After Morgan had left Indiana it was reported he was returning to capture Lawrenceburg (Dearborn County)."

The 105th Regiment moved out to check him, and getting into position a lamentable indiscriminate firing took place among the men, on 14 Jul 1863, resulting in the following casualties: Ferdinand Hafner and John Porter were killed; William E. Hart wounded and later died of wounds; Captain Branham, David S. Gooding, Samuel Duncan and Benjamin T. Rains were wounded and recovered.

Captain Tuttle's Company D, 106th Regiment of Indiana Volunteers, was mustered in 10 Jul 1863, went as far as Cincinnati, Ohio, without having been in any engagements and was mustered out 17 Jul 1863.

Morgan continued his roving assault across Ohio with Union regiments in pursuit. The Confederates attempted to cross the

Hancock County Indiana Civil War Soldiers

Ohio River at Buffington Island ford (near Pomeroy, Ohio), but the rebels were soundly defeated and scattered by the Yankees and river gunboats. Sleeping in the saddle, the Southern troops fled into northeastern Ohio, always looking for a place to cross the Ohio River and return to friendly territory. The hit and run tactics of the raid took their toll not only with spent horses but with weary troopers. Morgan and about 300 remaining men surrendered on 26 Jul 1863, near New Lisbon, Ohio.

Morgan and several of his senior officers were imprisoned at the Ohio Penitentiary, Columbus, Ohio, but, after only four months, 27 Nov 1863, perfected an escape and returned to the South. Confederate General John Hunt Morgan was killed in Sep of 1864, as he led a raid at Greenville, Tennessee.

Hancock Democrat, 3 Sep 1863: "About John Morgan It may not be a matter of consequence to the public to know any further status of Morgan except that he is in safe custody, in the Ohio Penitentiary under the care of our vigilant and inflexible Warden N. Merton, Esq. where he will remain in all security till removed by the proper authority. There are sixty-eight of Morgan's officers in the prison. They are locked up separately in cells at seven o'clock in the evening and are unlocked at about seven in the morning.

"Morgan's valuables amounted to twenty-three dollars and a butternut breast pin. The amount of our Government and postal currency found on the persons of other officers was not large. They had considerable sums in Confederate money.

"Morgan and his men are all shaved and trimmed in accordance with the rules of the institution. They do not attend chapel service as it would bring a crowd of visitors attracted by curiosity. All who desire Bibles are supplied by the Warden from the prison library.

"In appearance Morgan looks like a man addicted to worldly pleasures. He is full six feet high, straight and well built, with an elastic step, and something of a commanding presence. His upper lip is short and somewhat sunken so that his front teeth are

Hancock County Indiana Civil War Soldiers

slightly exposed. His complexion is sandy and the hair quite thin on the top of his head. (At this time he is 38 years old.)

"Colonel Cluke is three or four inches taller than Morgan, very slender, with a thin, sharp face and resolute eyes. I suppose from his appearance he has more dash and daring than Morgan.

"Brig. General Basil Duke is a small man, firmly built and muscular. His complexion is dark and his eye and head indicate some mind and a bad heart. He is much the most intelligent looking man of the crowd.

"I only speak of them as they *appear*. I have no intercourse with any of them, except as I have met three or four in the hospital. I see and talk with them there, as I do with the other sick. Signed, J.L. Grover, Chaplain, O.P., Columbus, O., 15 Aug 1863."

Hancock County Indiana Civil War Soldiers

Mississippi Marine Brigade and Ram Fleet

Early in the Civil War, with the approval of Secretary of War Edwin Stanton, Charles Ellett formed the Ram Fleet, including the Mississippi Marines, unique organizations to operate on the western waters of the United States. The new unit was ignored as folly until 6 Jun 1862 when the Ram Fleet defeated the Confederate ironclads at Memphis where the founder, Charles Ellett, was mortally wounded. His brother, Alfred, was an officer and assumed command. Indecision reigned as this strange fleet who was initially unwanted by the Army and the Navy, seemingly, it was an orphan.

The western waters of the United States were important highways for both the Union and Confederate armies to move men and supplies. They fought over supremacy of the Mississippi and all its tributaries like two dogs with one bone. The Union ultimately controlled the rivers themselves but the surrounding countryside was scattered with bands of Confederate guerilla fighters who would harass military steamers. The soldiers on board would return the fire and chase them away but it was only temporary as the guerillas quickly disappeared into dense woods awaiting another opportunity to strike.

To overcome the hit-and-run tactics of the rebels and to patrol the rivers, there was an idea for a special gunboat to be attached to the orphan Ram Fleet. Colonel Alfred Ellett, USA and Rear Admiral David Porter, USN, gained permission from Washington to organize a gunboat unit. On 1 Nov 1862, it was authorized to include one infantry regiment, four cavalry squadrons and one light artillery battery to be permanently assigned aboard steamships, under the command of Ellett with the Mississippi Ram Fleet.

The Mississippi Marine Brigade was born 1 Nov 1862. Recruiting was a problem because nearly all volunteers wanted

Hancock County Indiana Civil War Soldiers

to muster in a unit with friends and relatives, not strangers. The new unit began to persuade men with recruiting posters boasting "a Marine Brigade, to act in concert with the invincible Ram Fleet, is to be raised immediately, all under the command of Brig. Gen. A.W. Ellett. Large steamboats are engaged to carry the troops down into the heart of Rebeldom, and open the Mississippi and her tributaries to the navigation of the Northwest. There will be very little marching for any of the troops. There are good quarters on transports fitted expressly for them where they will keep all their valuables, clothing, stores, etc. There will be no long hard marches, camping without tents or food, carrying heavy knapsacks, but good, comfortable quarters and good facilities for cooking at all times.

"There will be plenty of active service in keeping the rivers clear of rebel guerrillas, and securing the safe navigation of the great highways. Every soldier reenlisting in this Brigade is entitled to a final settlement, and all pay in arrears will be paid promptly, besides $2 premium, one month's pay in advance, and $25 bounty."

Men wore the uniform of their respective units. Caps, however, were different than those of a Navy officer with a wide green band edged with gold lace. Cap badges for officers were two tangled anchors, a bugle for infantrymen and crossed cannon for artillery. The Mississippi Marines were disbanded in late summer of 1864.

Samuel Newton Shelby allied with this select crew of brown water sailors...he related stories to his grandson, Charles Hull of Greenfield, Indiana, about his Civil War duty with the Mississippi Marines on a gunboat with a mobile force of soldiers who went ashore to do battle with rebels and return to the boat. Shelby also told of firing guns on towns along the river.

HC newspaper article, 4 Jun 1931: "Samuel Shelby and other members of his company were ordered by boat down the Mississippi River and were provided with only swamp water for drinking purposes. Practically all of the men became ill of fever and died. Mr. Shelby survived."

Hancock County Indiana Civil War Soldiers

Soldiers

◄ A ►

Abney, Eli; 12 Reg Co.B; 15 May 61-19 May 62; applied for a pension, 11 Jan 1869 #138549. Married 25 Nov 1871 Lydia Whelchel, HC Bk 6-65.

Acker, Daniel; 105 Reg Co E, 11 Jul 63-18 Jul 63. NOD.

Adams, David; 8 Reg Co B, 25 Aug 61-died Oct 62 St Louis, Missouri.

Adams, Harrison; 12 Reg Co B, 15 Aug 61-19 May 62. Applied for a pension 27 Jan 1887 #595153.

Adams, James W.; 66 Reg Co H, 19 Aug 62-16 Jun 65. A James Adams married 17 Apr 1866 Susan Wishmire HC Bk 5-51.

Adams, Dr Marcellus M.; 3 Cav Co I, 19 Aug 62-Mar 64, discharged. He was living at Freeport, Shelby County, Indiana, following his profession of medicine when he enlisted Company I, 3rd Indiana Cavalry. He served until 19 Sep 1863, when he was discharged by reason of expiration of service. He reenlisted the same day, in the 116th Indiana Volunteers, and received a commission as Assistant Surgeon of the regiment.

He served his company faithfully in this capacity, in numerous instances protesting against the amputation of limbs of wounded comrades, thus often saving limb and life. His battle list includes Walker's Ford and Tazwell, besides the extreme suffering, incident to that cold winter of the historic Burnside campaign in East Tennessee.

He received his honorable discharge in March, 1864, and enjoys the distinction of being a "Persimon," a name that clings to the Brigade that the regiment was in. "In 1863 when the 116 Reg. was ordered home, he was left in charge of the sick and ordered to bring home those that he could. He started with thirty-four men, 139 horses and four mules, but without saddles or bridles. They traveled 114 miles to Camp Nelson, Kentucky, over almost impassable roads. So many horses and mules died that it was said a bridge to Knoxville could have been made out of the carcasses."

Dr. Adams, born 12 Nov 1834, s/o Isaac and Nancy (Polk) Adams, married 1) 20 Oct 1858 Miranda Bailey of Freeport, Shelby County, Indiana, who died 11 Jul 1873, children, Clara; Fannie; and Nettie. Dr. Adams married 2) 12 Mar 1874 Nancy Hinchman, (HC Book 6-262), children Olive; Mary; and Ellen. Nancy was the daughter of John and Charlotte (Blackledge) Hinchman. Dr. Adams' wife's brother, J. Vincent Hinchman, saw service in the 9th Indiana Cavalry." Dr. Adams buried Park Cemetery: 1834-1909.

Adkins, John; 1 Heavy Artillery Co K, no dates. John died 26 Feb 1886 age 56, his body plus three other family members (not named) were moved from the Old Greenfield Cemetery to Park Cemetery 10 Jun 1894. NOD.

Akeman, Martin; 13 Cav Co I, 23 Dec 63. died of wounds 19 Dec 64. Federal Pension data: Martin's widow, Hester Akeman applied for pension 1 Mar 1865, #173717. HC Muth Cemetery: Martin Akeman Co I 13 Ind Cav, died 19 Dec 1864; Hester Akeman 2 Jan 1837-27 Mar 1913; infant d/o M and H Akeman died 1 Apr 1863; Zora d/o M and H died 17 Sep 1884 20y 4m 2d. Hester (Gardner) Akeman married Daniel Muth 3 Jan 1869 HC Bk 5-273.

Allee, Oliver; 19 Ind Light Artillery roster at Chickamauga National Battlefield, residence or place of enlistment, Wilkinson, Indiana, mustered 1 Jun 64-19 Jun 65. HC courthouse burial list: Oliver Allee, occupation, carpenter; died 9 May 1904; burial, Knightstown, Henry County, Indiana.

Alexander, Benjamin F.; 12 Reg Co B, 15 May 61-19 May 62, 19 Jul 62 promoted Sgt. same Reg Co G. "discharged 1 Jan 63 at Indianapolis, Indiana, by reason of crippled condition of the back from a cannon ball 30 Aug 62 at Battle of Richmond, Kentucky. "Born Madison Co, Indiana, 5' 10," dark complexion, dark eyes, dark hair, farmer when enrolled."

Hancock County Indiana Civil War Soldiers

Married 30 Oct 63 Ann Amick; HC Book 4-410. Benjamin applied for a pension 22 Feb 1869 #140103, his widow, Ann Dewitt (remarried) applied for a pension 29 Aug 1877 #323984, his minor child, Morgan Chandler, applied for a pension 10 Jun 1886 #340541. Benjamin died 26 Oct 1873, 33y 4m 17d; Ann E. died 28 Mar 1881, 33y 5m 0d; both buried HC Cook Cemetery.

Alexander, William; 8 Reg Co B, 25 Jul 61-died 26 Jul 63 at Memphis, Tennessee, from severe arm wounds received May 63 near Vicksburg, Mississippi.

Alfont, Reuben M.; 12 Reg Co G, 6 Jul 62, musician-8 Jun 65. Reuben M. Alfont married 8 Nov 1874 Catherine Wynn, daughter of John Wynn, HC Book 6-317. Reuben applied for a pension 2 Oct 1891 #1066903, widow, Catherine, applied for pension 15 Jun 1924 #1168390. HC obit 23 Dec 1920 "Milton R.(euben) Alfont, born 22 Jul 1844, son of William (born France) and Elizabeth (Freeburn) Alfont (born N.Y.) died 14 December 1920, age 76 at his home near Fortville of heart trouble. Survived by wife, Catherine, and six sons." HC Wynn Cemetery: Reuben M(ilton) Alfont 1844-1920, Catherine, 1852-1930. The facts seem to indicate that Reuben M. and Milton R. are the same man. Additions /corrections?

Alfont, Richard; 12 Reg Co G; 8 Aug 62-8 Jun 65. Applied for pension 25 Mar 1869 #141294. NOD.

Alfont, Robert; 12 Reg Co B, 15 May 61, musician-19 May 62; 12 Reg Co G, 12 Aug 62, 2nd Lt.; promoted 4 Mar 64 First Lt.; 17 Oct 64 promoted Captain. Robert applied for pension 21 Mar 1866 #105111; his widow, Amelia, applied for pension 30 Sep 1873 #212273. Robert Alfont married 16 Aug 1862 Amelia Brown HC Bk 4-345.

Alford, George H.; 5 Cav Co B, 16 Aug 62-15 Sep 65. Born Monroe County, Virginia, 5' 7," fair complexion, blue eyes, light hair, carpenter when enrolled." He was captured three times, a prisoner in Andersonville, Georgia; in a stockade at Florence, S.C. and Libby Prison at Richmond, Virginia. Each time after being released he returned to his regiment and company, was honorably discharged a Sergeant. Upon returning home followed the cabinet maker's trade. Married twice: Phoebe Lemmons and Jennie Wade; no children. George died 11 Jun 1911, buried HC Park Cemetery.

Alford, William H.; 7 Reg Co B, 30 Aug 61-20 Sep 64. "Born Preble County, Ohio, age 20, 5' 10," fair complexion, blue eyes, light hair, farmer when enrolled." He applied for pension 27 Jul 1890 #847704, his widow, Lizzie E. Alford, applied pension 23 Mar 1891 #505370. William H. Alford married 8 Jun 1865 Elizabeth Burns, place not stated. A William H. Alford died 2 Nov 1890, aged 52y 3m 2d, buried HC Caldwell Cemetery; a William Alford buried HC Curry's Chapel Cemetery, no dates.

Alfrey, Isaac; 75 Reg Co I, 14 Jul 62-15 Nov 62. He applied for pension 30 Jun 1879 #295105, widow, Sarah J. Alfrey applied for pension 1 Dec 1905 #838923.

Allen, Elijah; 79 Reg Co C, 24 Feb 65-10 May 65,drafted, unassigned. "Born Rush County, Indiana, age 41, 5' 9," light complexion, gray eyes, light hair; farmer when enrolled." An Elijah Allen married 25 Sep 1847 Sarah Wilson HC Bk 2-257; also an Elijah Allen married 28 Jun 1865 Sarah Peacock HC Bk4-520. Parents of Elijah; Adam and Sarah (Thompson) Allen. HC Gilboa Cemetery: Elijah 18 Jan 1825-14 Oct 1891, Sarah w/o E. died 18 Apr 1864, 40y 6m 28d, Sarah 24 Nov 1828-5 May 1901. Elijah died HC, age 66, of Lagrippe.

Allen, Henry; 5 Cav Co G, 24 Aug 64-12 Jun 65. Applied for pension 1 Aug 1890 #822810. NOD.

Allen, John; 99 Reg Co B, 13 Aug 62, Sgt.; 1 Mar 65 1st Lt.; out5 Jun 65. A John Allen married 1 Jan 1874 Eliza Dunwoody HC Bk 6-248.

Allen, John; 79 Reg Co G, 11 Aug 62, died 3 Apr 63, Murfreesboro, Tennessee. A John Allen married 20 Jan 1847 Elizabeth Dennis HC Bk 2-221. John's widow, Elizabeth Allen, applied for pension 6 Jun 1863 #23830; John's minor child, Elizabeth Lemay, applied for pension 23 Apr 1867 #446073.

Hancock County Indiana Civil War Soldiers

Allen, Richard; 13 Aug 62-5 Jun 65. "Age 20, 5' 10," dark complexion, blue eyes, black hair, farmer when enrolled." 99 Regiment History states: "Richard Allen was born 5 Jun 1842 HC, married 1) 1 Jan 1866 Sarilda Catt (HC Bk 5-18); six children. Moved to Coles County, Illinois in 1881, Sarilda died 23 Mar 1900. Married 2) 18 Oct 1905 Julia England. " Richard applied for pension 23 Jun 1871 #166760. HC obit, 21 Dec 1905: "Richard Allen died at his home in Oakland, Illinois, being a brother of George and Wilson Allen of Greenfield and son-in-law of Jacob Catt."

Alley, George H.; 99 Reg Co B, 13 Aug 62-22 May 65. Married 23 Feb 1866 Martha Cox, HC Bk 5-35. George applied for pension 3 Jan 1879 #264418, his widow, Martha L. Crane applied for pension 7 Sep 1917 #1106847. 99 Regiment History states: "George H. Alley, was born Rush Co, Indiana, 17 Nov 1841, wounded 28 May 1864 at Dallas, Georgia, but recovered. Since the War has lived in California, Oregon and Washington. In 1900 lives in Goldendale, Washington with wife and five children."

Alley, John M.; 99 Reg Co B as 1st Lt. no dates given.; aka Marshall Alley. A John Alley married 4 Mar 1866 Martha Curry HC Bk 5-39. NOD.

Alley, Samuel D.; 99 Reg Co B, 13 Aug 62, wounded 28 May 64 Dallas, Georgia, died 4 Sep 64 from those wounds at Rome, Georgia. His mother, Sarah Alley, applied for pension 4 Feb 1870 #184347.

Allison, Asa; 105 Reg Co E, 11 Jul 63-18 Jul 63; also 147 Reg Co H, 6 Mar 65-20 Jun 65. An Asa Allison married 14 Sep 1860 Eliza Blessinger HC Bk 4-207.

Allison, Calvin; 8 Cav Co M, 1 Jan 64-15 May 65. Applied for pension 19 May 1868 #133423. A Calvin Allison, carpenter, died 15 May 1902 age 76, buried HC Park Cemetery. NOD.

Allison, John S.; 8 Reg Co G, 22 Apr 61-6 Aug 61. John applied for pension 30 Aug 1890 #945008; his widow, Elizabeth E. Allison applied for pension 10 Aug 1916 #1070318. NOD.

Hancock County Indiana Civil War Soldiers

Allison, Richard; 12 Reg Co G, 5 Aug 62-8 Jun 65. Richard applied for pension 23 Mar 1885 #535497, his widow, Nancy Allison, applied for pension #854994, no date.

Allison, Samuel B.; 12 Reg Co G, 28 Jul 62-8 Jun 65 He applied for pension 11 Nov 1879 #320971. NOD.

Allison, Thomas G.; 11 Ohio Inf Co G, 9 Jul 61-discharged disability 7 Apr 63. He applied for pension 15 Feb 64 #61358; his mother, Eunice Allison applied for pension 29 Aug 1898 #681534. Thomas died 30 Jun 1864, 18y 3m 27d, Unis Allison 11 Nov 1811-2 Dec 1901 both buried HC Gilboa Cemetery.

Allman, Fred; 105 Reg Co E, 11 Jul 63-18 Jul 63. NOD.

Alyea, Aaron; Enlisted 8 Reg Co B, died 15 April 1865, Vicksburg, Mississippi, buried National Cemetery at Vicksburg. He was born 5 Jan 1832, Hamilton County, Ohio s/o James and Hannah (Abbott) Alyea. Aaron had two brother who also served in the Civil War: John Abbott Alyea, who survived; and Andrew Jackson Alyea who died 1862, at St. Louis, Missouri. Aaron was unmarried.

Alyea, Albert; 13 Cav Co I, 11 Jan 64, Sgt.-18 Nov 65. He applied for pension 28 Sep 1891 #1062578; his widow, Hannah Alyea, applied for pension 23 Dec 1915 #1058165. HC obit, 18 Nov 1915: "Albert Alyea was born 6 Oct 1845, Hamilton Co., Ohio and died at his home in New Palestine. Survived by his wife, Hannah, daughter of James H. Smith, of Shelby County, Indiana,." HC New Palestine Cemetery: Albert Alyea 1845-1915, Hannah Alyea 1846-1931.

Alyea, (Andrew) Jackson; 8 Reg Co B, 25 Aug 61; married 4 Oct 1861 Sarah (Evelyn) Barrett HC Bk 4-292. "(Andrew) Jackson Alyea has gone to War with John Scott, Charles Gunn and John Alyea." (Andrew) Jackson Alyea died of disease at a Government hospital 10 Dec 62, St. Louis, Missouri. Andrew and Evelyn had one child, Mary, died 24 Sep 1864, 1y 8m 11d. Andrew Jackson's widow, Sarah Alyea, applied for pension 2 Sep 1864 #63593. Andrew Jackson Alyea was born 1 Nov 1835, s/o James and Hannah (Abbott) Alyea. HC newspaper,

Hancock County Indiana Civil War Soldiers

18 Dec 1862: "The remains of Jackson Alyea, a private in Co B 8th Indiana, arrived at this place. Deceased died at St. Louis on the 10th inst. He was about 25 years of age, and leaves a wife and many relations and friends to mourn his untimely end." (Andrew) Jackson Alyea is buried HC Mt. Lebanon Cemetery.

Alyea, John Abbott; 8 Reg Co B, 8 Aug 62-14 Jun 65. "Born Hamilton County, Ohio, parents, James and Hannah (Abbott) Alyea. When enrolled John A. Alyea was age 27, 5' 9," fair complexion, hazel eyes, fair hair, farmer." Company B, 8th Regiment report states: John A. Alyea was reported as absent, sick, twice during his enlistment; he was mustered out at Indianola. Texas 31 Dec 63; enlisted as Veteran Volunteer at same place 7 Feb 64; absent on leave 22 Apr 64; mustered out, Darien, Georgia, 28 Aug 65.

Married 25 Aug 1867 Frances Jane Sexton, of Shelby County, Indiana. John applied for pension 7 Apr 1883 #478800. HC newspaper obit 20 Feb 1915: John A. Alyea in his 81st year, committed suicide Saturday evening (20 Feb 1915) at his home. one mile west of the Scott schoolhouse in Brandywine Township by shooting himself through the head with a twenty-two rifle after he had tried to kill himself by bleeding to death from a self inflicted wound in the arm. About 3 pm his daughter-in-law, Mrs. Charles Alyea, residing close by, went to his home to take him some food she had prepared for him.

Mr. Alyea was living alone. As she entered the house she found him on the floor and his clothes were covered with blood from the wound on the arm. She said, "Grandpa, what are you doing?" He answered saying, "I am fixing to end it all now." At this. Mrs. Alyea became badly frightened. She turned and ran to her home to notify her husband. They returned as fast as they could but not in time. They found him badly wounded, having shot himself. The bullet entered the left temple, ranging upward, passing above and back of the right temple, and entered the wall. Dr. W.A. Justice, of Greenfield, was called and did everything for the wounded man. He, however, was

Hancock County Indiana Civil War Soldiers

beyond medical skill, death relieving him about 6 pm. It is stated that his mind had been deranged for several days before he committed the deed. He was well known in his township. He lived here several years. Mrs. Alyea preceded him in death some six years ago. Funeral services were held Monday last. The interment was at the Low Cemetery (Little Sugar Creek). HC Little Sugar Creek/Low Cemetery: John 8 Mar 1834-20 Feb 1915; Frances Jane 8 Nov 1846-12 Jul 1910. Contributed by Dicie Niggl, Bolton, Massachusetts. See pages for his brothers, Aaron Alyea and Andrew Jackson Alyea.

Amos, William T.; 13 Cav Co I, 23 Dec 63, wagoner-18 Nov 65. He applied for pension 25 Aug 1887 #320437. HC obit 12 Apr 1923: "William T. Amos died 10 Apr 1923, Central Indiana Hospital. Mr. Amos was a soldier in the Civil War and was more than eighty years old. Survivors, two sons, Thomas E., Greenfield and Clinton, Shelby Co Indiana".

Anderson, Asbury; 9 Cav Co B, 13 Nov 63-13 Jun 65, Sgt. An Asbury Anderson married 23 Mar 1866 Angie McCarty, HC Bk 5-47. NOD.

Anderson, David L.; 100 Reg Co K, 15 Aug 62-31 Dec 64. NOD

Anderson, Henry; 53 Reg Co A, 24 Feb 62-21 Jul 65 Corp'l. NOD.

Anderson, James D.; 9 Cav Co B, 9 Dec 63-2 Aug 65, Corp'l.; James applied for pension 11 Feb 1867 #122097; his widow, Electa, applied 12 Sep 1896 #640448. "A James Anderson's daughter, Mary, was fishing, fell in Blue River and drowned, 29 May 1875."

Anderson, John B.; 8 Reg Co B, 20 Aug 61-4 Sep 64. "Born Winchester, Ohio, age 21, 5' 5", dark complexion, black eyes, black hair, farmer when enrolled." HC obit, 4 Aug 1910: "John B. Anderson, age 66, born 12 April 1844, died at his home, St. Petersburg, Florida, 29 July 1910, where he and his wife lived the past few years, hoping the change in climate would be beneficial to his health. The body was brought here to the home of Mr. and Mrs. B.S. Johnson. Interment HC Park Cem."

Hancock County Indiana Civil War Soldiers

Anderson, Lucellus Lusettus; 8 Reg Co G, 22 Apr 61-6 Aug 61; 53 Reg Co A, 24 Feb 62-no out date. NOD.

Anderson, Samuel P.; 3 Cav Co I, 23 Dec 63-13 May 65. "Born HC, age 31, 6' 1," fair complexion, blue eyes, dark hair, farmer when enrolled, residence, Carrollton, Indiana." Married 29 Dec 1853 Julia Barrett HC Bk 3-195. Applied for pension 2 Mar 1876 #215114, his widow, Julia Ann Anderson, applied 15 Feb 1910 #935999.

Anderson, William; 51 Reg Co K, 22 Feb 62-13 Dec 65. There is a William Henry Anderson HC obit, 18 Apr 1918: "Lived in Indianapolis, Indiana, died 14 Apr 1918, age 78 Funeral at the home of his daughter, Mrs. Leona Thompson, three miles south of Greenfield. Interment Asbury Cemetery, Shelby County, Indiana.

Andis, Alexander; 5 Cav Co G, 16 Aug 62-15 Sep 65. Born 18 Feb 1827, Washington Co., Virginia, farmer when enrolled, age 35, 5' 6", fair complexion, hazel eyes, light hair; parents, William and Sara Ann (Gray) Andis. Alexander married 26 Jul 1855 America Linder HC Bk 3-293. HC obit, 16 Feb 1899, "Alexander Andis, aged 74, died 14 Feb at the Central Hospital, Indianapolis, Indiana. Mr. Andis enlisted 8 Oct 1847 in Company D 5th Indiana Volunteers during the Mexican War; also a member of the 5th Cavalry in the army of the Rebellion. Funeral and burial HC Mt Lebanon Church. Contributed by Richard Andis, Greencastle, Indiana.

Andis, Oliver; 148 Reg Co C, 17 Feb 65-5 Sep65. NOD.

Andis, Robert Preston; Born 21 Mar 1830, Washington Co. Virginia, s/o William and Sarah (Gray) Andis; enlisted Mexican War HC Co D 5 Indiana Volunteers, served 8 Oct 1847-28 Jul 1848. "Civil War Enlistment 13 Aug 62, 99 Reg Co B as 2nd Lt; 9 Apr 63 promoted 1st Lt.; 20 Mar 64 promoted Captain. He commanded the Company until the battle of 22 Jul 64 in front of Atlanta, when as the enemy advanced, he fell with his skull pierced by a rifle ball. He was taken to the hospital senseless and speechless where the surgeons saw the ball had entered the brain and gave him up to die. They took

Hancock County Indiana Civil War Soldiers

out the ball from the lower skull bone. He could understand everything but could not reply or put a sentence on paper. After untold suffering he was brought home and recovered so that he was able to do business".

99th Regiment History states: "He was discharged 14 Dec 1864. The scar and effects of the wound remained with him all his life. He married 12 Aug 1852 Phoebe Low, and had five children. He left HC for Bourbon Co. Kansas in 1881;" HC newspaper 22 Dec 1864: "Captain Robert P. Andis has been honorably discharged from the service for disability, and that means wounded in battle.

"The Captain is a true and brave soldier, and we rejoice that though bearing the marks of honorable wounds, he is still living and enjoying the comforts of a quiet home. His company is deprived of a most excellent officer by his discharge, but none can regret the necessity for the step more than Capt. Andis." He applied for a pension 1 Mar 1865 # 62361.

Andrick, Jacob; 19 Reg Co D, 29 Jul 61-no out date. Applied for pension 13 Jul 1867 #127268. HC obit 27 Aug 1891: "Jacob Andrick died at his home in Charlottesville of liver and kidney trouble, age 71. He was born in Germany 20 Oct 1819 and died 27 Aug 1891. He was the father of seven children, he leaves a wife, three daughters, one son and one sister. The funeral was preached at his home and his body was laid to rest in the Hinchman graveyard. His worn out and tired body was placed in the tomb, but his soul is safe in Heaven."

Andrick, George S.; 5 Cav Co G, 16 Aug 62-19 May 65. "Born Green Co. Ohio, age 25, 5' 8", fair complexion, gray eyes, dark hair, cooper when enrolled." George Andrick married 23 Aug 1862 Rachel Price HC Bk 4-337. He applied for pension 3 Feb 1888 #683417, his widow, Rachel J. Andrick applied 6 Oct 1892 #561008. HC obit 15 Sep 1892, "George Andrick passed away peacefully 13 Sep 1892, age 57, after an illness of several days duration from heart trouble. He was a soldier in the late

Hancock County Indiana Civil War Soldiers

War and is survived by the wife and several children. Interment HC Hinchman Cem."

Andrick, Perry H.; 5 Cav Co G, 16 Aug 62-15 Sep 65, Corp'l. "Born 12 Apr 1840, Green Co. Ohio, age 22, 5' 9," fair complexion, dark eyes, dark hair, farmer when enrolled. Father Jno Andrick, born Germany, mother Getty (sic) born Ohio." Perry married 18 Sep 1862 Mary Ann Hatch, HC Bk 4-349. He applied for pension 15 Sep 1888 #672367; his widow, Mary Ann Andrick, applied for pension 6 Apr 1908 #888650. Perry died 31 Mar 1908, cause apoplexy, retired farmer." Both buried HC Park Cemetery: Andrick, P.R. Co G 5 Cav, Mary Ann 1841-1916.

Apple, Henry; 11 Reg Co K, 31 Aug 61-no out date; "died in Civil War; parents, William H. and Julia (Gardner) Apple."

Apple, John H; no units given; HC obit, 6 Jul 1922, "One of the old residents of the County died at the home of Nolie Sanford north of Philadelphia. Mr. Apple was born 9 Sep 1838, Ohio, 83 years old, and a soldier of the Civil War. He will be laid to rest with full military honors at the National Soldier's Home, Dayton, Ohio."

Applegate, Samuel; 12 Reg Co H, 5 Aug 62-8 Jun 65. Married 23 Sep 1854 Nancy Camp HC Bk 3-237. Samuel applied for a pension 22 Nov 1875 #210652, his widow, Nancy Applegate applied for a pension 29 Dec 1900 #732229.

Armstrong, John P.; 100 Reg Co K, 15 Aug 62-3 May 65. Married 27 Nov 1859 Eliza Anderson HC Bk 4-165. HC obit, 6 Apr 1899: "J.P. Armstrong, a prominent Mason, old soldier and citizen, died, 3 Apr 1899, age, 64 of kidney disease at his home in New Palestine. He was a plasterer and son of John Armstrong." New Palestine Cemetery: Armstrong, J.P. 1834-1899, Eliza J. 1841-1921.

Hancock County Indiana Civil War Soldiers

Arnold, Omer; 18 Reg Musician, 16 Aug 61-20 Aug 62. NOD.

Asbury, Elijah; 12 Reg Co H, 17 Aug 62-8 Jun 65. An Elijah Asbury married 27 Jan 1865 Nancy Hamilton HC Bk 4-523.

Ash, Henry; 144 Reg Co E, 2 Feb 65-5 Aug 65. His widow, Mary Ash, applied for a pension 16 Jan 1873 #207368. NOD

Ashcraft, George Washington; 79 Reg Co B, 9 Aug 62-7 Jun 65. "Born Hancock Co Indiana, 5' 8", age 18, fair complexion, blue eyes, dark hair, farmer when enrolled..." George received a slight gunshot wound in the arm at the battle of Chickamauga, Tennessee, 19 Sep 1863; he evidently recovered enough to return to duty as the Company roster reports him as absent 25 Nov 1863, from the effects of severe gunshot wound in the left shoulder and breast received at Chattanooga, Tennessee. Reported Nov 1863 to Mar 1864, absent, sick, wounded and left Chattanooga, Tennessee, 28 Nov 1863; July and Aug 1864, absent, sick in hospital; Sep 1864, on extra duty, Orderly; Oct 1864 to April 1865, absent on detached service as 3rd Brigade cattle guard. George Washington Ashcraft, s/o Amos and Sarah (Brandenburg) Ashcraft, was born 28 Mar 1844; died 8 Jul 1867; married Jane Dye 2 Nov 1866 HC Bk 5-96. Contributed by Dicie Niggl, Bolton, Massachusetts.

Ashcraft, Henry B.; 13 Aug 62-5 Jun 65, Sgt. Applied for pension 1 May 1883 #485303. Born 30 Oct 1837, parents, John and Sophia (Bennett) Ashcraft; brother Salem Ashcraft; Henry died 30 Sep 1913, buried HC Philadelphia Cemetery. History of 99 Regiment states: "Henry B. Ashcraft, Sgt., is a resident of Indianapolis, Indiana in 1900." Contributed by Retta Livengood, Greenfield, Indiana. Company B 99 Regiment reports state: Henry B. Ashcraft was present from 13 Aug 62 to muster out 5 Jun 65, Washington, D.C.; he was promoted from Corporal to Sergeant 28 Apr 65; last paid to 31 Aug 64; clothing account last paid 31 Aug 64, drawn since, $61.52; bounty paid $25, due $75, born Butler County, Ohio; married to Martha. Contributed by Dicie Niggl, Bolton, Massachusetts.

Hancock County Indiana Civil War Soldiers

Ashcraft, Salem; There was a Salem Ashcraft who served in Company B, 99th Regiment. I believe he is a brother to Nancy Ann Ashcraft, wife of David Nelson True and a brother to Phoebe Ashcraft, wife of Harvey True. Contributed by Retta Arbuckle Livengood, Greenfield, Indiana. 99 Reg Co B, 13 Aug 62-5 Jun 65. 99 Regiment History states: "Salem was born 27 Jan 1836, Ohio; blue eyes, black hair, 6' tall, when enrolled and served throughout the War. He married 12 Sep 1858 Martha A. Morford (HC Bk 4-97) who died 16 Aug 1877. Six children living. Residence in 1900, Philadelphia, Indiana." The following contributed by Dicie Niggl, Bolton, Massachusetts: Salem, s/o John and Sophia (Bennett) Ashcraft; brother Henry B. Ashcraft. Salem died 2 Apr 1902, 66y 2m 3d, cause chronic nephritis, burial Philadelphia Cemetery.

Askins, William; 8 Reg Co B, 25 Aug 61-died 13 Oct 63, Georgetown, Missouri. NOD.

Atkison, Joseph B.; 53 Reg, 21 May 62 1st Lt.-5 Oct 62, wounded Hatchie Bridge, Tennessee, died from wounds 17 Nov 62. Buried HC Park Cemetery.

Ayres, William S.; 59 Reg Co G, 16 Aug 62-15 Sep 65, Corp'l. NOD.

Hancock County Indiana Civil War Soldiers

Aaron Alyea

Courtesy of Dicie Niggl

Robert P. Andis

Courtesy of 99th Regiment History

George W. Ashcraft

Courtesy of Dicie Niggl

Hancock County Indiana Civil War Soldiers

◄ B ►

Bailey, George S.; 106 Reg Co D, 10 Jul 63-17Jul 63; 9 Cav Co B, 13 Nov 63-16 Jun 65. NOD.

Bailey, Lemuel; 26 Reg Co H, 24 Sep 64-6 Sep 65. A Lemuel Bailey married 4 Feb 1866 Mary Ann Blanton HC Bk5-31. HC obit 30 Nov 1905: "Lemuel Bailey, well-known citizen of Vernon Twp. died 25 Nov 1905 at his home near Woodbury, funeral at Mt. Zion Church."

Bailey, Shelton; 26 Reg Co H, 24 Sep 64- 6 Sep 65. NOD.

Baity, David H.; 147 Reg Co F, 10 Feb 65-4 Aug 65. He applied for pension 26 Jul 1890 #921120, widow, Rachel Baity applied for pension 18 Jul 1931 #1703582. HC obit 13 May 1931: "David H. Baity was born in North Carolina, 18 June 1842, one of thirteen children born to Isom and Nancy Baity, natives of North Carolina. David came to Hancock County at age 18 to live with an uncle, soon enlisted under the last call of volunteers in 1876, served seven months. He returned to Hancock County where he bought a farm in GreenTownship and resumed farming. He married 19 Jan 1870 Rachel L. Wilson (HC Bk 5-351) The widow, Rachel, and son, Orville, survive. Interment HC Eden Church Cemetery. Mr. Baity had three brothers who were in the Confederate Army: Alexander was a prisoner at Point Lookout, Maryland, and was furnished money and provisions by the family of his Union brother, David; Henry left Confederate service, came through the lines and got to Greenfield where he lived until his death; and William, 'who served in the Confederate army' "

Baker, James; 5 Reg Co E,11 Jul 63-18 Jul 63; 148 Reg Co C, 17 Feb 65-5 Sep 65. Applied for pension 2 Aug 1888 #666519

Hancock County Indiana Civil War Soldiers

Baker, John; 8 Reg Co G, 5 Sep 61-8 Aug 65. A John Baker married 5 Jul 1853 Hetty Thomas HC Bk 3-170. NOD.

Baldwin, Garriott; 99 Reg Co B, 23 Mar 64; transferred to 48 Reg, 30 Mar 64-15 Jul 65. A Garriott Baldwin married 31 Oct 1861 Mary Ann Sample HC Bk 4-293. 99 Regiment History stated: "Garriott Baldwin reported dead in 1900."

Baldwin, Jonathan; 99 Reg Co B, 23 Mar 64; transferred to 48 Reg 23 Aug 64-15 Jul 65. 99th Regiment History states: "Jonathan Baldwin was wounded, Dallas, Georgia, 28 May 64." A John Baldwin married 9 Sep 1868 Martha Crabb HC Bk 5-244.

Baldwin, Joseph; 99 Reg Co B, 13 Aug 62-wounded Dallas Georgia, 28 May 64, discharged 5 Oct 63. HC obit 28 Apr 1891: "Joseph Baldwin, one of our best known citizens died 25 Apr 1891, at age 47 of heart failure. He was the son of Jackson and Rainey (Scott) Baldwin. His mother died shortly after his birth, 6 March 1844, and he was left in charge of his grandmother. His father, Jackson Baldwin, joined Capt. James R. Bracken's Company D 5th Indiana Volunteers of the Mexican War and died in Mexico in 1847. Joseph married 9 May 1867, Evaline Fuqua (HC Bk 5-134). Joseph's funeral procession comprised the Greenfield Cornet Band, Greenfield Light Artillery, Masons from around the County, the minister, the hearse, relatives in carriages, Presbyterian Church Choir and a long retinue of vehicles containing citizens, friends and visitors. Interment HC Park Cemetery."

Bales, Abijah; 8 Reg Co B. 25 Aug 61-no out date. HC obit, 7 Mar 1912: "Abijah Bales, born and reared in Hancock County, where he joined the Army. His leg was splintered with a minie ball in battle, causing it to be amputated. He secured a position in the pension department at Washington and died at his country home in Virginia, just across the District of Columbia line. He had many warm friends in this city and County."

Ball, Isaac; 116 Reg Co E, no dates. An Isaac Ball married 25 Aug 1864 Mary A. Cass HC Bk 4-467. He died 20 Dec 1896,

Hancock County Indiana Civil War Soldiers

age 54, occupation, barber; buried HC Eden Church Cemetery: Isaac Ball 25 Sep 1842-20 Dec 1896.

Ball, William; 9 Cav no Co #. HC Death Bk RH6-p12: William Ball, born in Indiana, son of Henry and Nancy (Taylor), died 12 Dec 1888, age 43, of consumption." Buried, HC Curry's Chapel Church Cemetery. NOD.

Ballenger, N.B.; 105 Reg Co E, 11 Jul 63-18 Jul 63. NOD

Banks, Andrew J.; 105 Reg Co E, 11 Jul 63-18 Jul 63. HC obit: 10 Oct 1912: "Andrew J. Banks. age 82, a resident of Greenfield for almost fifty years, died at his home on North Pennsylvania Street. He was born 26 Aug 1830, Wayne Co Indiana, s/o Adam and Susanna (Koff) Banks. On his arrival in Greenfield about 1858, he became the junior member of the firm of Banks, Wallace and Banks, general merchants. At the time of his death, he and his son, Luman, were in the contracting business. On 24 Jul 1859 he married Viola Harvey of near Milton, Wayne Co. Indiana. They were the parents of six children, four of whom are living: Rosalind Corcoran, Lina Gant, Viola Spencer and Luman Banks. Andrew J. Banks died 7 Oct 1912 and is buried at HC Park Cemetery with his wife, Viola 6 Jan 1839-5 Feb 1910."

Banks, James K.; 51 Reg Co D, 16 Feb 64-no out date. A James K. Banks married 28 Oct 1869 Mary Ann Arbuckle HC Bk 5-334.

Bannon, Abraham;12 Reg Co G, 20 Jul 62-died 25 Jan 64, Fortville. HC Wynn Cemetery: Abraham Bannon died 25 Jan 1864, 27y 11m 18d. NOD.

Bannon, John H.;12 Reg Co G, 19 Jul 62-12 Jan 63, discharged wounds, date and place of wounds not given. A John Bannon married 23 Oct 1856 Margaret Weldon HC Bk 3-363.

Bannon, William C.;12 Reg Co G, 8 Oct 62, transferred to 48 Reg, out 8 Jun 65. NOD.

Bannon, William R.; 26 Reg Co H, 24 Sep 64-6 Sep 65. A William R. Bannon married 23 May 1861 Mary Caudell HC Bk 4-266. NOD.

Hancock County Indiana Civil War Soldiers

Banta, Albert; 9 Reg Co D, 24 Feb 64-28 Sep65. NOD.

Barnard, Charles; No unit given; HC newspaper, 26 Aug 1926: "Charles Barnard, former Hancock County man, and now a resident of the National Soldiers and Sailors Home in Virginia, had a comrade visitor from the Soldiers and Sailors Home at Dayton, Ohio, Jesse (Teedy) Barrett. Sadly, during the visit, Mr. Barrett, became ill and died."

Barnard, James W.; 12 Reg Co G, 12 Jan 61-died 28 Jan 64, Scottsboro, Alabama, age 22. "He was born 19 Nov 1840, s/o Robert Y. and Polly (Hopper) Barnard." His body must have been was brought home and as he has a marker at HC Wynn Cemetery."

Barnett, Samuel Warsaw; 18 Reg Musician, 16 Aug 61-20 Aug 62; 105 Reg Co E, 11 Jul 63-18 Jul 63. HC obit 5 Mar 1885: "Samuel Warsaw Barnett died 1 March 1885, after a painful and lingering disease of consumption, aged 44. He was born 8 April 1840 in Harrison County, Kentucky, son of Jack and Amanda Barnett. Samuel's occupation was a tinner and he married 16 Feb 1869 Mary J. Wood d/o Hiram Wood, HC Bk 5-280. Due to failing health, Mr. Barnett moved to Colorado three years ago hoping the change in climate would improve his condition, but all efforts to arrest the progress of his disease proved in vain and he returned to Greenfield. He was buried HC Park Cemetery by the Masonic fraternity, assisted by Dunbar Post GAR."

Barr, Henry; 147 Reg Co H, 14 Feb 65-11 Aug 65. NOD.

Barr, John; 134 Reg Co K; 24 May 64-Jun 65. HC obit: 16 Jan 1930: "John A. Barr, age 85 years, a Civil War veteran and highly esteemed citizen, passed away, 12 January 1930, at his home on East Main Street, Greenfield. He was born 6 October 1844 in Ohio, the son of Robert and Elizabeth (Crockett) Barr and was married 31 December 1868 to Mary E. Wiggins (HC Bk 5-272). He was a partner and bookkeeper in the blacksmithing and wagon business with Taylor Morford. He is survived by the wife and one daughter, Miss Lenna Barr and one granddaughter, Mrs. Marie Dornfield of New York, two

Hancock County Indiana Civil War Soldiers

half brothers, George and Frank Barr of Kansas. Interment Hancock Co Park Cemetery."

Barrett, Augustus; 99 Reg Co B, 13 Mar 62-31 Dec 63. 99 Regiment History states, "Augustus Barrett, dead in 1900." NOD.

Barrett, Jacob T.; 8 Reg Co G, 22 Apr 61-6 Aug 61; 9 Cav Co B, 13 Nov 63-21 Jul 65, Sgt. "born HC, age 29, 5' 6," dark complexion, black eyes, black hair, farmer when enrolled." A Jacob T. Barrett married 17 Sep 1856 Sarah Ross HC Bk3-359. HC newspaper, 3 Aug 1865: "J.T. Barrett arrived at home and has been honorably discharged."

Barrett, (Teedy) Jesse; 8 New Hampshire Reg Co E, 21 Dec 61-16 Feb 64. discharged disability. After the War he lived in HC and at the Soldiers and Sailors Home, Dayton, Ohio. He died while visiting a comrade, Charles Barnard, at Soldiers and Sailors Home in Virginia. Jesse Barrett buried at Soldiers and Sailors Home in Dayton.

Barrett, Dr Jonathan J.;HC newspaper article, 10 Sep 1863:"Dr. Jonathan J. Barrett, formerly of this County, has been appointed Assistant Surgeon of the 4 Cav."

Barrett, Richard J.;99 Reg Co B, 13 Aug 62-5 Jun 65. "born HC, age 20, 5' 8", dark complexion, blue eyes, dark hair and farmer when enrolled." Married 4 Sep 1866 Eliza Martin HC Bk 5-80. HC Curry's Chapel Church Cemetery: Richard J. Barrett 1842-1899, Eliza A. 1850-1929.

Barrett, Sylvester W.; 79 Reg Co G, 11 Aug 62-died 2 Feb 1863, Nashville, Tennessee. Sylvester W. Barrett married 27 Mar 1862 Martha A. Roberts HC Bk 4-318A.

Barrett, William R.; HC newspaper obit 15 Oct 1863: "We regret to learn that William R. Barrett, son of John Barrett, Esq., is dead. He died 10 Sep1863 at New Orleans of flux. Mr. B. entered the service of his country about one year ago as a volunteer member of the 54 Reg and enjoyed excellent health until about one month before his demise. It seems hard that our young friend and fellow citizen should pass unharmed through all the perils of the Mississippi Campaign, and fall a victim of disease a few weeks before the expiration of his term of service. We are not advised whether his remains will be sent home." HC Gilboa Cemetery: William Barrett, soldier, died Sep 1863, 30y 7m 25d.

Bartlow, Cornelius; 134 Reg Co K, 24 May 64-4 Aug 65. A Cornelius Bartlow married 9 Dec 1865 Julia Franklin HC Bk 5-11.

Bartlow, Joseph F.; 9 Reg Co C, 14 Feb 64-28 Sep 65. A Joseph F. Bartlow married 13 May 1847 Minerva Barrett HC Bk 2-239.

Bartlow, Oliver W.; 57 Reg Co A, 13 Dec 61-5 Nov 62, discharged disability; also 38 Reg Co A 11 Nov 64-_ Jun 65. An Oliver Bartlow married 30 Aug 1860 Esther Ann Stewart HC Bk 4-203.

Barton, Robert D.; No units; HC obit 13 Sep 1930: "Robert D. Barton, age 86, a Civil War veteran, died 12 Sep 1930 at his home in Philadelphia (Indiana), where he had lived for four years. Mr. Barton was born 28 Apr 1844, Michigan, son of David Barton, and is survived by the widow, Anna, and a son. Mr. Barton was a member of the Grand Army of the Republic and the burial service will be conducted by the American Legion." A Robert D Barton married 12 Jun 1918 Anna Pyles HC Bk13-180.

Barton, W.; Recorded as a member of 5 Cav Co G, who survived Andersonville Prison, Pencase 22 Apr 1865. Code #50166 NOD.

Barwick, W.D.; 5 Cav Co G no dates. HC newspaper 11 Aug 1864: "W.D. Barwick was taken prisoner during the disastrous expedition commanded by Gen. Stoneman." Survived prison at Andersonville, Georgia, and exchanged April 1865. Code #50169. NOD.

Basey, Charles William Ferdinand; 148 Reg Co C, 1 Feb 65-5 Sep 65 "age 31, blue eyes, fair hair, fair complexion, 5' 7", shoemaker, entitled to Bounty when enrolled." Married 8 Jun 1856 Anna E. Fauldt HC Bk 3-343. Charles was born 4 Oct 1833, Prussia, died 4 Nov 1890 and both he and Anna (1840-

Hancock County Indiana Civil War Soldiers

1917) are buried HC New Palestine Cemetery. Contributed by Irene Basey, New Palestine, Indiana.

Basey, Christian; 25 Reg Co G, no dates; brother of Charles W. Basey, above. Christian Basey died 1870, 29y 3m 22d. Buried HC New Palestine Cemetery. NOD.

Beachman, Henry; 9 Cav Co B, 9 Dec 63-18 Jul 65.

Beaver, Perry; 53 Reg Co A, 17 Feb 64-31 May 65.

Bedford, Nelson F.; 105 Reg Co E, 11 Jul 63-18 Jul 63. Married 1 May 1861 Lorissa Matlock HC Bk 4-262. HC obit 5 Feb 1920: "Mrs. Nelson F. Bedford, age 79, formerly of Greenfield, passed away at Bishop, California, primarily due to old age. When the Civil War broke out, her husband, N.F. Bedford, entered the war and Mrs. Bedford was prominent in war work. In 1907 they moved to Bishop California. Survived by seven children.".

Bedgood, Stephen; 11 Reg Co F, 31 Aug 61-30 Aug 64. "born Perquimans Co., North Carolina; age 23 5' 8", hazel eyes, light complexion, brown hair, teacher when enrolled." NOD.

Bedgood, Thomas M.; 105 Reg Co E, 11 Jul 63-18 Jul 63. A Thomas Bedgood, s/o Penuel, married 11 Nov 1849 Elizabeth J. Brooks HC Bk2-355. Thomas 10 Oct 183-21 Jul 1879, Elizabeth Julia w/o Thomas M. died 28 Oct 1881 52y 6m 2d, both buried HC Park Cemetery.

Beeler, Lorenzo D.; 106 Reg Co D, 10 Jul 63-17 Jul 63.

Beeler, Thomas J.; 106 Reg Co D, 10 Jul 63-17 Jul 63.

Beeson, Amos C.; 79 Reg Co G, 12 Aug 62-5 Feb 65. Amos was born 29 Jul 1842, Randolph County, Indiana, came to HC 1856, son of Mahlon Beeson and older brother of Jesse W. Beeson. HC newspaper article, 7 Jul 1864: "Amos C. Beeson, formerly of this office was wounded in the left hand at Kennesaw Mountain and are sorry to learn of his misfortune; participated in battles of Chickamauga, Lookout Mountain, Knoxville, Tunnel Hill, Dalton, Resaca, Cassville, Lost Mountain and Kennesaw Mountain." Married 10 Oct 1867 Margaret E. Marsh, d/o William and Martha Marsh, HC Bk 5-168. Amos Beeson died May 1903, no place given. HC death

Hancock County Indiana Civil War Soldiers

notice, 16 Oct 1913: " Word was received here of the death of Mrs. M.E. Beeson, widow of the late Amos Beeson, at her home in Winchester, Indiana. She was well known here, being the sister-in-law of J.W. and Jesse Beeson of Blue River Township. Funeral services at her late home."

Beeson, Daniel; 79 Reg Co B, 26 Aug 62-15 May 63. NOD.

Beeson, Isaac N.; 3 Cav Co G, 5 Sep 61-27 Sep 64. "born Randolph Co., Indiana, age 29, 5' 8," light complexion, blue eyes, light hair, carpenter when enrolled." An Isaac Beeson married 21 Nov 1875 Adaline Brock HC Bk 6-405.

Beeson, John C.; 79 Reg Co G, 20 Jul 64-5 Sep 65. NOD.

Bell, George M.(N); 97 Reg Co D, 20 Aug 62-9 Jun 65. Died 11 Nov 1896, 70y 5m 9d, occupation brick molder, buried HC Gilboa Cem.

Bell, Samuel

36 Reg Co A, no dates. He was born 21 Aug 1837, Indiana, son of Vinson and ___Kizar Bell; died HC 2 Sep 1906, 69y 0m 11d. buried HC Simmons Cemetery.

Belville, E.; 5 Cav Co G, 6 May 62-16 Jun 65. HC newspaper 11 Aug 1864: "Taken prisoner during disastrous expedition commanded by Gen. Stoneman." Recorded as prisoner at Andersonville, survived and exchanged Apr 1865, #50301.

Belville, Granville; 9 Reg Co E, 24 Feb 65-28 Sep 65. NOD.

Belville, Landon; 5 Cav Co G, 6 May 62-16 Dec 62. NOD.

Bellville, Seth; 53 Reg Co A, 24 Feb 62-21 Jul 65. NOD.

Bennett, Calvin; 148 Reg Co C, 17 Feb 65-5 Sep 65. HC obit, 15 Sep 1898: "Calvin Bennett died 1 Sep 1898, age 69. A cabinetmaker, Mr. Bennett was born 25 Sep 1829, Taylor Co., West Virginia, came to Hancock County in 1853 and has been a resident ever since that time except two years spent in Marion and Montgomery Counties. He was married 26 Apr 1860 Amanda Hawkins (HC Bk 4-189). They were the parents of five children, three living." Wife, Amanda 2 May 1840-24 Dec 1926, both buried HC New Palestine Cemetery.

Bennett, David O.; 100 Reg Co K, 11 Aug 62-20 Jun 65. David O. Bennett married 10 May 1868 Mina Anderson HC Bk 5-

Hancock County Indiana Civil War Soldiers

222. See page for John Davis. See page for Christian Wishmeier.

Bennett, George; 105 Reg Co E, 11 Jul 63-18 Jul 63.

Bennett, George W.; 148 Reg Co C, 17 Feb 65-5 Sep 65. A George Bennett died 8 Jan 1895, place not given.

Bennett, John; 9 Cav Co B, 13 Nov 63-died 10 Feb 65, Gallatin, Tennessee. NOD.

Bennett, Samuel H.; HC Courthouse burial list: 54 Reg Co H; died 17 Jan 1898; 52 years; occupation, shoemaker; burial, HC Gilboa.

Berry, George W. 53 Reg Co A, 24 Oct 62-21 Jul 65. Survived Andersonville Prison, exchanged at Atlanta, Georgia, 19 Sep 1864, code #50349. NOD.

Berry, Harrison 53 Reg Co A, 24 Feb 62-29 May 65. Survived Andersonville Prison, exchanged at Atlanta, Georgia 19 Sep 1864, code #50350. NOD.

Berry, James M.; 132 Reg Co I, 18 May 64-no out date.

Berry, John G.; 53 Reg Co A, no dates. NOD.

Berry, William R.; 53 Reg Co A, 24 Feb 62-19 May 65. Married 9 Jan 1858 Emily Jane Smith HC Bk 4-60; 1860 HC census: William R. Berry, age 23, farm laborer, born Ohio, Emily J, age 20 born Indiana, Sarah J. age 2 born Indiana. NOD.

Bevil, Henry; 134 Reg Co K, 24 May 64-no out date. NOD.

Bills, Aaron; 12 Reg Co H, 7 Aug 62-8 Jun 65. NOD.

Bills, Josephus; 12 Reg Co H, 16 Aug 62 as 2nd Lt.-resigned 8 Aug 63. Married 18 Dec 1859 Elizabeth Camp HC Bk 4-168; Madison County, Indiana, Gravel Lawn Cemetery: Bills, Joseph, 1835-1905; Elizabeth, his wife, 1840-1924.

Bills, Nelson; 12 Reg Co H, 17 Aug 62-28 Jul 65. Married 4 Mar 1860 Rachel Crossley HC Bk 4-181.

Bird, Adam; 148 Reg Co I, 17 Feb 65-5 Sep 65. NOD.

Bixler, David; 105 Reg Co E, 11 Jul 63-18 Jul 63; 148 Reg Co C, 17 Feb 65-5 Sep 65. Died, age 80, 16 Jun 1910, buried HC Park Cemetery.

Hancock County Indiana Civil War Soldiers

Bixler, Noah; 8 Reg Co B, 25 Aug 61-26 Dec 61, died Otterville, Missouri. NOD.

Black, Eli; 134 Reg Co K, 24 May 64-term expired. NOD.

Black, George H.; 8 Reg Co B, 25 Aug 61-28 Aug 65, Lt. A George H. Black married 9 Nov 1866 Dorcas Welling HC Bk 5-4. HC newspaper 11 Jun 1863: "George H. Black was slightly wounded in the shoulder. He did not leave the field though, in too much pain to reload and shoot, but carried water from the spring to the boys while they fought."

Black, Harrison; 53 Reg Co A, 24 Feb 62-21 Jul 65, Sgt. NOD.

Black, Jesse; 79 Reg Co B, 9 Aug 62-7 Jun 65. NOD.

Black, Richard Alexander; recorded as a Charter member of Greenfield Dunbar Post G.A.R. as a member of 118 Reg Co D. Richard A. Black, born 24 Aug 1847, died 28 Oct 1900, married 1884 to Ione Brown, no places given for data. One of nine children, he was the s/o Rev. Michael and Jane Black, both natives of County Sligo, Ireland. Richard A. Black is the brother of Dr. John P. Black who practiced medicine in Greenfield about 1890. "Rev. Michael Black recruited a company for the Civil War but no call for muster. About 1870 he left Hancock County for Florida where he was a missionary." HC Park Cemetery: Richard A. Black 1847-1900; Jane Black, died 15 Aug 1866, 50y, born Ireland; w/o R.M. Black of the Ind. Conf. M.E. Church.

Blakely, Pvt. A.; 5 Cav Co G, no dates. HC newspaper 11 Aug 1864: "taken prisoner during disastrous expedition commanded by Gen. Stoneman." NOD.

Blakely, George W.; 99 Reg Co B, 13 Aug 62-31 Dec 63. 99 Regiment History states: "George W. Blakely is dead in 1900." NOD.

Blakely, Nathaniel; 99 Reg Co B, 13 Aug 62-died 13 Feb 63 at Fort Fowler. NOD.

Blanton, John; 79 Reg Co C, 15 Aug 62-7 Jun 65. NOD.

Blessinger, Frederick; 9 Cav Co B, 7 Jan 64-died 27 Apr 65. 9th Cavalry History states: "Frederick Blessinger was captured at Sulphur Branch Trestle in Alabama and lost by explosion and

Hancock County Indiana Civil War Soldiers

burning of the steamer, Sultana, 27 Apr 1865." A Frederick Blessinger married 9 Feb 1854 Mary McCorkhill HC Bk 3-202.

Bodkin, James T.; 124 Reg Co D, 17 Dec 63-31 Aug 65. "born Marion Co Indiana, age 19, 5' 3," light complexion, blue eyes, dark hair, farmer when enrolled" A James T.(homas) Bodkin married 14 Jun 1866 Martha Thornton (d/o Dr. Jacob Thornton), no place given. HC obit 28 Nov 1918: "James T(homas), son of J.T. and Mary Bodkins, age 73, died 28 Nov 1918 and buried HC Park Cemetery. "HC newspaper, 5 Dec 1918:"One of the characteristics of the late (James) Thomas Bodkins whose remains were laid to rest in this city was the fact he posted his farm, known as "Cozy Corner" farm as follows: "Hunt all you please on "Cozy Corner" farm; be careful of livestock and you are welcome to the house for dinner" By this act he made many warm friends among men who liked the sport of hunting." The dates of these facts seem to indicate that James T. and Thomas are the same man. Additions/corrections?

Bogart, Dr. Henry K.;139 Reg, 8 Jun 64. Married 3 Jun 1866 Sarah Shipman HC Bk 5-65. HC obit 2 Jun 1898: "After an illness of only a few days, Dr. H.J. Bogart, a physician of this city, died at his residence on East Main Street, of hemorrhage of the stomach. He was a Union soldier in the late War and was a surgeon in the 139 Indiana Volunteers and was a member of Dunbar Post GAR. He was sixty-four years of age and leaves a wife to mourn his loss. Interment at Knightstown."

Bogg, John; 100 Reg Co K, 11Aug 62-29 Jun 65. NOD.

Bolander, Henry; 11 Reg Co K, 22 Oct 62-26 Jul 65, Corp'l; A Henry W. Bolander married 4 Mar 1873 Nancy Davidson HC Bk 6-184. Henry Bolander buried HC McCordsville Cemetery: 28 Dec 1838-27 Apr 1903, soldier.

Bolander, John W.; 9 Reg Co D, 24 Feb 64-died 18 Apr 65, Shield's Mill, Tennessee. NOD.

Bolander, William H.; 12 Reg Co H, 17 Aug 62-8 Jun 65. "He was born 30 Nov 1841, Indiana, son of Henry Bolander (born

Hancock County Indiana Civil War Soldiers

Ohio) and Elizabeth Vanzant (born Indiana). Surviving is wife, Margaret." William died 16 Sep 1916, age 74 and is buried HC McCordsville Cemetery.

Boles, Harman W.; 79 Reg Co G, 15 Aug 62-7 Jun 65. "born 21 Apr 1841, Bracken Co., Kentucky, age 22, 5' 10", dark complexion, gray eyes, dark hair and farmer when enrolled." Married 4 Jun 1861 Harriett Johnson HC Bk 4-268; Harman died 20 Oct 1913, Dora d/o Harmon and Harriett 1873-17 Mar 1890, both are buried HC Mt Lebanon Cemetery.

Boles, John W.; 79 Reg Co G, 12 Aug 62-7 Jun 65. A John W. Boles married 28 Jan 1866 Mary E. Colwell HC Bk 5-29.

Boman, Joseph H.; 99 Reg Co B, 8 Apr 64, wounded 28 May 64, Dallas Georgia; transferred to 48 Reg, out 15 Jul 65. NOD.

Boman, William H.; 53 Reg Co A, 24 Feb 62-no out date. NOD.

Bond, Benjamin; 8 Reg Co G, 22 Apr 61-6 Aug 61. NOD.

Bond, Petitia (Pelatiah); 8 Reg Co G, 22 Apr 61-6 Aug 61. NOD.

Boone, John B,; 12 Reg Co G 19 Jul 62-died 12 Aug 63, Camp Sherman, Mississippi. NOD.

Bowers, Jacob, 8 Reg Co B, 25 Aug 61-died 12 Jan 62, Otterville, Missouri. *Hancock Democrat*, 5 Feb 1862: "letter from Lt. Samuel Dunbar, of 8 Reg: Jacob Bowers has died. He was sick since coming from Springfield. His death is another, among hundreds of similar cases testimony of the folly, or at least destructive effects, of that ever to be remembered march."

Boyce, Alfred; 79 Reg Co B, 9 Aug 62-7 Jun 65, Corp'l. An Alfred Boyce married 4 Sep 1869 Rachel Phillips HC Bk 5-318.

Boyce, Nelson; 79 Reg Co B, 9 Aug 62-died 3 Dec 62, Nashville, Tennessee. NOD.

Boyce, James G.; 26 Reg Co I, 24 Sep 64-6 Sep 65. James G. Boyce was born 25 Nov 1831, Indiana, son of Daniel Boyce, born Penn. and Julia Kitchen, born Virginia. Daniel married 3 Aug 1854 Sarah Elliott (1836-1906) HC Marriage Bk 3-226.

Hancock County Indiana Civil War Soldiers

James, occupation lumberman, died 6 Oct 1905, age 73, and buried HC Philadelphia Cemetery.

Boyce, James M.; 79 Reg Co B, 9 Aug 62-7 Jun 65. NOD.

Boyer, Jeremiah; 57 Reg Co A, 13 Dec 61-12 Jan 62. NOD.

Boyer, Samuel; 105 Reg Co E, 11 Jul 63-18 Jul 63; 57 Reg Co A 9 Apr 64-14 Dec 65, Corp'l. A Samuel Boyer married 28 Jan 1835 Sylvia Gibbs no place given (daughter of Eusebus and Electa Gibbs). HC Caldwell Cemetery: a man named Samuel Boyer died 8 Mar 1882, 76y, Sylvia w/o Samuel 12 Feb 1818-31 Dec 1882, 64y 10m 19d.

Boyer, William; 57 Reg Co A, 13 Dec 61-13 Aug 65. A William Boyer married 19 Mar 1864 Rebecca Barnes HC Bk 4-441. HC obit 6 Jun 1907: "William Boyer, of Anderson (Indiana), died of cancer. Funeral and burial at Harlan's Church. He leaves a wife and eight children. Mr. Boyer was formerly postmaster at Wilkinson, this County." HC Harlan Cem, William Boyer, 1844-1907, soldier.

Bracken, James R.; 1 Cav Co K, 21 Jun 61, 1 Mar 62, resigned. Also he organized Company D of the 5th Indiana Volunteers of foot soldiers in Hancock County for service in the Mexican War from Sep 1847 until mustered out 28 Jul 1848. James married Josephine Gapen 17 Oct 1847 HC Bk 2-260; Josephine died 13 Jun 1849 and is buried HC Baptist Cemetery.

Hancock Democrat, 1 Sep 1864: "A dispatch was received announcing the death of Capt. James R. Bracken in a railroad accident at Lawrenceburg, Indiana, where he had gone for an appointment. He was connected with the Indiana State Sentinel where he was assistant editor when he raised the first cavalry company that went from Indiana, called the Bracken Cavalry. Never when duty called was he found wanting; in all associations with him he proved himself to be the noblest work of God.

"James R. Bracken was born in Cincinnati in 1808 and when quite a youth, having fine health and a roving disposition, went abroad. He obtained a responsible position in the Dublin Bank, Ireland. Afterwards he went to the East Indies and served in

Hancock County Indiana Civil War Soldiers

the English Army. He returned to this country and served throughout the Mexican War, acquitting himself with honor and to the approbation of his countrymen. But his most genial characteristic is that he never came in contact with anyone who did not respect his integrity and acknowledge his worth. Our friend is dead. Our tribute to his memory is our tears, and not what we have written. *State Sentinel, 30 August 1864.*

Bracken, William; 148 Reg Co C, 17 Feb 65-5 Sep 65. NOD.

Braddock, James Richard, 3 Cav Co I, 24 Sep 62-8 Jun 65. Was in battles of Stone's River, Shelbyville, Franklin and capture of Atlanta; transferred to Co M 39 Reg, and to Hilton Head, South Carolina, embarked by boat from there to Raleigh, North Carolina, then to a camp at Greensborough, North Carolina until the end of the War. He was born 8 Jul 1835, HC, never married and was the son of Moses and Nancy Braddock. HC Park Cem, Braddock, James Richard 1835-1904, Moses 1795-1840, Nancy 1795-1870.

Bragg, James M.; 9 Reg Co C, 14 Feb 65-28 Sep 65; NOD.

Brandenburg, Andrew; 9 Reg Co F, no dates. He married 25 Dec 1878 Sarah Martin HC Bk 6-575. Occupation, farmer, died 2 Mar 1891, age 55, buried HC Jackson/Maple Grove Cemetery, Sarah died 13 Dec 1894, 41y 10m 7d., also buried there.

Branham, Major Alexander K.; 105 Reg Co E, 11 Jul 63-18 Jul 63. HC obit 16 Aug 1907: "Major Alexander K. Branham, age 80, died at his home, 333 East North Street. He was one of the old gentlemen of Greenfield, always well dressed with an unlit cigar in his mouth and a familiar figure on the streets. He was born 20 Feb 1825 in Georgetown, Kentucky, son of Tavner and Fannie Branham, the mother died in 1828 and the father of cholera three years later.

Having learned blacksmithing, A.K. emigrated to Indiana, in March, 1846 and married 1)16 Aug 1847 Amanda Malvina Sebastian d/o William and Elizabeth Sebastian HC Bk 2-249, Mrs. Branham died 1875. A.K. married 2) 7 Jun 1882 Mary J. Woodhall (sister of E.P, Lee and Hollis Thayer) HC Bk 7-366.

Hancock County Indiana Civil War Soldiers

Major Branham was a merchant and one of the founders of the Greenfield Christian Church and in 1854 raised a subscription of $600, donated thirty-five feet of ground for the church and bought the brick from the old Court House, using it to build the church. He served as an elder for forty-five years and was a leader in the erection of the new church and laid the first brick as he had done forty years before in the old church.

In 1859, Major Branham organized a militia company that was attached to the 105 Regiment of Indiana Legion. On 9 July 1863 he was ordered to lead his Company to southern Indiana to help drive Confederate General John Morgan from the State. He and his Company were present at the lamentable disaster of friendly fire at Lawrenceburg on the night of 14 Jul 1863 when three of his Company were killed and two wounded.

Major Branham died 16 Aug 1905 of Bright's disease and is the last of a large family: Eliza A. Glass, Cornelia Lineback, Thomas H. Branham, Irene Branham, Ellen E. Branham, Benjamin O. Branham and Mary J. Hodges. Survivors are the widow and one child, Amelia, the wife of Roy Robinson of Greenfield. Interment HC Park Cemetery."

Branson, William; 8 Reg Co B, 25 Aug 61. NOD.

Brantlinger, Jacob; 9 Reg Co D, 24 Feb 64-28 Sep 65. A Jacob Brantlinger married 17 Mar 1864 Mary Wallsmith, HC Bk 4-441.

Brantlinger, John; 12 Reg Co G, 22 Feb 64-8 Jun 65 transferred to 48 Reg Co I, out 15 Jul 65. NOD.

Brantlinger, William, 12 Reg Co H, 17 Aug 62-8 Jun 65. A man named William Brantlinger married 22 Mar 1862 Martha Crossley HC Bk 4-320; also a William Brantlinger married 5 May 1882 Nancy Whelchel HC Bk 7-361.

Breece, John, 5 Cav Co G, 18 Aug 62-died 5 May 63, Louisville, Kentucky. NOD.

Breece, Martin; 79 Reg Co B, 9 Aug 62-15 Feb 63. HC obit 21 May 1914; "Martin Breece, age 72, a well known veteran of the Civil War, died 15 May 1914, at his home in Philadelphia.

Hancock County Indiana Civil War Soldiers

He was born 27 Sep 1842, son of Ephraim Breece (born Ohio) and Lavinia Berry. He married 21 Apr 1864 Martha Walker (HC Bk 4-450, died 18 Sep 1871 24 y, buried beside Martin). He was a carpenter and for many years a tiemaker and said to have been, with the late Andrew Dudding, among the best in this part of the State. He made and sold thousands of railroad cross ties to what is now the Peoria and Eastern Railroad, which runs through Mohawk, Maxwell, etc He was a member of Company B, Seventy-ninth Indiana Volunteers. The funeral service and burial were at Maple Grove Church.".

Brewer, Christian; 79 Reg Co D, 25 Aug 62-7 Jun 65. NOD.

Bridges, Andrew J.; 53 Reg Co A, 1 Feb 62-21 Jul 65. "As a musician and fifer, he was promoted to Corporal and First Duty Sergeant later on. His early exposure to rain and cold caused sickness, and after recovery was sent to Memphis where he joined his regiment. He served in the entire Vicksburg campaign and was in the battles of Jackson, Rome, Kingston, in the Atlanta campaign, Big Shanty (Marietta, Georgia), Kennesaw, Peach Tree Creek siege of Atlanta, besides many minor engagements. On 23 Feb 1864, he reenlisted as a veteran, in the same command, and was detailed on special provost duty at Col. Duncan's Headquarters, Natchez, Mississippi.

Andrew Bridges has been twice married, 1) Euphemia Curry October 1865, two children, Walter and Orlando, Euphemia died 29 Aug 1872; Andrew married 2) Martha C. Foster, daughter of John Foster, one of the earliest settlers of Hancock County and was elected the first sheriff of the County. Andrew Bridges' maternal uncle, George Tague, was a Captain in the 99th Indiana Regiment, and was discharged due to permanent disability.

Martha (Foster) Bridges' brother, Willaim J. Foster, veteran of the Mexican War and Civil Wars, died at Castle Morgan Prison, Cahaba, Albama John T. Foster was a Pioneer in the 30th Missouri Infantry; and Thomas Foster was a musician in

Hancock County Indiana Civil War Soldiers

the 18th Indiana. A fraternal uncle, Alexander Foster, served in the Confederate Army and was captured at Fort Donelson."
Hancock Democrat obit 11 Sep 1919: "Son of William and Mahala (Tague) Bridges, Andrew J. Bridges was born 27 Jun 1840 in Virginia and died in Greenfield at his home 5 Sep 1919 after suffering fourteen years from paralysis. He was married 1) 9 Nov 1865 Euphemia Curry (HC Bk 5-2); married 2) 29 Aug 1872 Martha C. Foster (HC Bk 6-125). One son, Walter Bridges survives from the first marriage. The second wife and with their three children survive: Anna Bridges, Mrs. Alvin Wales of Greenfield and William H. Bridges, New York." HC Curry's Chapel Church Cemetery: Euphemia Bridges w/o Andrew J. died 23 Oct 1870; HC Park Cemetery: Bridges, Andrew J. Co A, 53 Ind Inf 1st Sgt.; Martha A. Foster 1844-1923.

Bright, Smith; also recorded on roster Bright as first name and Smith as last name 99 Co B 13 Aug 62-2 Jun 64 killed New Hope Church, Georgia. NOD.

Bright, William F.; 12 Reg Co B, 15 May 61-28 Sep 65; NOD.

Brinegar, Thomas J.; 79 Reg Co C, 15 Aug 62-killed 29 Jan 65, Huttonville, Alabama. NOD.

Brizendine, Francis M.; 5 Cav Co G, 28 Dec 63-15 Jun 65. *Hancock Democrat* 11 Aug 1864: "Francis Brizendine taken prisoner during disastrous expedition commanded by Gen. Stoneman" Captured near Macon, Georgia, sent to Millen, Georgia, 11 Nov 1864, from there to Andersonville Prison, survived and exchanged April 1865, code#50756. A Francis M. Brizendine married 29 Oct 1871 Rodosco Ramsey HC Bk 6-62. HC Sugar Creek Cem: Brizendine, Francis M. 1845-1911 Co G 5 Cav, Rodosco 1849-1911.

Brock, Alfred; 79 Reg Co B, 9 Aug 62-24 Mar 63. An Alfred Brock married 8 Jan 1866 Mary Breese HC Bk 5-24; and an Alfred Brock married 30 May 1870 Jane Cruey HC Bk 5-378.

Brock, John; 8 Reg Co H, 5 Sep 61-26 Aug 65. NOD.

Hancock County Indiana Civil War Soldiers

Brooks, John; 12 Reg Co H 17, Aug 62-died 21 Apr 64, Scottsboro, Alabama; father Samuel Brooks, mother not named.

Brooks, Joseph; 57 Reg Co A, 17 Oct 61-killed 31 Dec 62 Stone's River Tennessee. "Joseph Brooks was born in Hancock County, Indiana; age 25 when he enlisted as a private in Captain Allison's Co A 57 Indiana Infantry Volunteer Regiment for three years. Joseph was a tall, dark and handsome farmer as he stood 6' ½". The 57th left Indianapolis 23 Dec 1861 for duty at Bardstown and Lebanon, Kentucky. On to Nashville, Tennessee, from Feb 62 until 13 Mar 62. He was in the battle of Shiloh, and Stone River, Tennessee, 30-31 Dec 62.

Times were hard for the family in Indiana while Joseph served in the Union army. His name appeared on the Company muster roll as wounded in action at Stone's River, Tennessee, and his name appeared on a casualty sheet as wounded in the arm but from then on he is listed as missing and presumed dead. The family received a letter from Joseph saying he was going into battle--but he was never heard from again.

Joseph's nine-year-old sister, Margaret, felt the anguish as the family waited and waited for the news that never came about their loved one and she kept his memory alive by repeating the heartbreaking story to her descendants. Joseph Brooks' body is one of the identified burials in the Stone's River Cemetery, Section K #4281. A popular Civil War song, "Was My Brother in the Battle," must have been on their lips and in their hearts as they waited and watched for their soldier to return. Contributed by Frances Vander Weide, Jenison, Michigan

Brooks, Melvin, 75 Reg Co I, 14 Jul 62-8 Jun 65. NOD.

Brooks, Nehemiah; 75 Reg Co I, 14 Jul 62-3 Feb 63, Sgt. NOD.

Brooks, Samuel; 8 Reg Co B, (commanded by Captain Samuel Dunbar) 20 Aug 61-28 Jul 65, discharged disability. The 8 Regiment was subsequently attached to Fremont's Army of the West, Department of Missouri, and 13 Corps, Army of

Hancock County Indiana Civil War Soldiers

Tennessee until 1864. Having served his three years enlistment, Private Brooks reenlisted and was assigned to the 3 Brigade. While attached to General Phillip Sheridan's XIX Corps in the Shenandoah Valley Campaign in Virginia, Private Brooks was wounded 19 Oct 1864 at the Battle of Cedar Creek, Virginia, resulting in amputation of his left leg below the knee. The Battle of Cedar Creek was a rousing Union victory and credited with breaking the back of the Confederate Army in the Shenandoah Valley.

Private Brooks returned to Mohawk, Hancock County, Indiana, where he resided the remainder of his life and received forty dollars a month pension #61405. He was born 6 Jun 1839, son of Henry and Maria (Fuller) Brooks. Married Christena Maroska, children: Maggie May, Gertrude and John Logan Brooks. Samuel died 21 Jun 1905, buried HC Mt. Gilead/Reeves Cemetery and his grave is marked by a Government monument. Contributed by Linda L. Campbell, Greenfield, Indiana.

Brooks, Thomas L.; 38 Reg Co A, 5 Nov 64-15 Jul 65. A Thomas Brooks married 27 Mar 1869 Cally Evans HC Bk 5-292.

Brooks, William; 132 Reg Co I, for 100 days discharged 25 Aug 65, had not taken part in any battles. HC obit 29 Dec 1898: "William Brooks, born 16 Dec 1835, son of Samuel Brooks. William died at age 70 years, 23 December 1898 at his home Funeral at Walnut Ridge, Rush County, Indiana." A William Brooks, married 10 Aug 1877 Margaret Stansbury d/o Jonathan and Polly Stansbury, HC Bk 6-533.

Brown, Abner; 12 Reg Co H, 17 Aug 62-died 4 Feb 63, Memphis, Tennessee. NOD.

Brown, Adam Trees; 52 Reg Co E, 1 Feb 62-21 Jun 62, discharged disability. HC History: Adam Trees Brown was born 25 Feb 1839, in Rush County, Indiana, son of George and Elizabeth (Trees) Brown. He enlisted in Company E, 52nd Indiana Infantry and soon after went to the front in Grant's campaign against Forts Henry and Donelson; also the noted battles of Shiloh and Corinth. While on the field he had to withstand exposure of snow, and cold weather without a tent or blankets which caused extreme sufferings from rheumatism.

He had hospital care and in June 1862 went home on furlough to regain his health but did not recover sufficiently enough and was discharged. Adam Brown married 1) Cynthia Haford who died in 1866; married 2) Mary J. Wright. He continued to farm his place in Shelby County until 1868 when he invested in a farm in Brandywine Township, HC. Adam T. Brown died 6 Jul 1910 and is buried HC Mt. Lebanon Cemetery: Trees, Adam T. 1839-1910 Co C 52 Ind Inf; Mary J. 1847-1922.

Brown, Andrew; 79 Reg Co C, 15 Aug 62-7 Jun 65. Andrew Brown married 22 Apr 1885 Eliza Beaver HC Bk 7-603; They are buried in Madison county, Indiana, Gravel Lawn Cemetery: Brown, Andrew 21 Nov 1842-25 Feb 1930 Co C 79 Ind Inf; Eliza his wife 20 Feb 1844-7 May 1923.

Brown, Arthur; 8 Reg Co G, 22 Apr 61-6 Aug 61. NOD.

Brown, Benjamin; 12 Reg Co H, 17 Aug 62-killed 25 Jun 64, Kennesaw Mountain, Georgia. NOD.

Brown, David; HC McCordsville Cemetery: David Brown 20 May 1830-8 Jun 1906, soldier. A David Brown married 17 Apr 1872 Sarah A. Catt HC Bk 6-101. NOD.

Brown, Eli; 26 Reg Co E, 19 Dec 63-15 Jan 66. "born HC, age 27, fair complexion, gray eyes, light hair and farmer when enrolled." NOD.

Brown, Sgt. James R.; 99 Reg Co B, 6 Aug 62, as private, promoted steadily to Corp'l to 1st Lt. Wounded badly in the body at Dallas, Georgia, 28 May 1864. 99 Regiment History states: "he was a resident of Cleopatra, Missouri, in 1900."

Brown, Lewis; 148 Co I, 17 Feb 65-5 Sep 65. NOD.

Buchanan, Ezra; 79 Reg Co D, 7 Aug 62-1st Lt. 1 Mar 65, out 7 Jun 65. NOD.

Buchanan, James; 8 Reg Co G, 22 Apr 61-6 Aug 61; wounded 11 Jul 61, Rich Mountain, Virginia. NOD.

Buchel, Jacob; enlisted 9 Cav Co B but never mustered; also 1st Indiana Heavy Artillery; 17 Sep 64-no out date. HC New

Hancock County Indiana Civil War Soldiers

Palestine Cemetery: Buchel, Jacob 1827-12 Jun 1899, Hospital Steward 1st Ind HV Arty; wife, Mary 1831-1900.

Bucy, Amos; 12 Reg Co H, 17 Aug 62-died 14 Nov 63, Anderson, Tennessee. NOD.

Bundy, Jonathan; 9 Reg Co C, 14 Feb 64-28 Sep 65. NOD.

Bundy, Thomas M.; 16 Reg Co G, 1861-13 Jun 65. HC obit 10 Mar 1927: "Thomas M., son of Rex and Penelope Bundy, was born 12 Sep 1835, Pasquotank Co., North Carolina. Not being in sympathy with slavery, Thomas left the South in 1859, at age 24 years and came to the free state of Indiana. He married 10 Feb 1864 Adline Pool (no place given); twelve children of whom eight are living (1927): Florence Hiatt and Molly Wisler, Leisure; Mable Gray, Muncie; William, Greenfield; James, Williamsburg; Charles, Richmanod; Jesse, Grant Co. and Arna, Rush Co. He moved his family to the vicinity of Elwood in 1880 and lived there until the death of his wife, November, 1918 at Orestes; since then has lived with his children. Thomas M. Bundy died 10 Feb 1927 at his residence, 436 West North Street, Greenfield, buried, Elwood, Indiana."

Buntrum, Homer L.; 12 Reg Co B, 15 May 61-28 Sep 65. NOD.

Burdette, James L.; 105 Reg Co E, 11 Jul 63-18 Jul 63. HC Park Cemetery: James L. Burdette, died 17 Jan 1873, 32y 6m 14d. NOD.

Burk, Daniel; 57 Reg Co A, 13 Dec 61-14 Dec 65, Sgt; He took part in Atlanta Campaign and at the engagement of Pumpkin Vine Ridge, 18 Jun 63, was shot through the left foot; recovered and rejoined his regiment at Pulaski, Tennessee, then to Nashville and ordered to Texas where he served until the end of the War.

At enlistment, Daniel Burk was age 18, 5' 8 1/2", born Wayne Co. Indiana, light complexion, blue eyes, dark hair and occupation, blacksmith and mechanic. Due to his occupation, he was often attached to the Pioneer Corps, a unit which was the advance of the Regiment, to scout the terrain and find the best route. They were to clear the way not only for the soldiers

Hancock County Indiana Civil War Soldiers

but heavy artillery, build bridges where necessary and make travel as simple as possible whenever and wherever possible.

Daniel Webster Burk was born 13 Mar 1843, Wayne Co., Indiana; s/o George Burk Sr. and Susanna Armstrong. Daniel married 1) 30 Aug 1864 Mary M. Weaver HC Bk 4-468; she died 29 Mar 1879; married 2) 10 Sep 1882 Margaret Goddard Reynolds HC Bk7-381. Henry Co. obit Mar 1909: "Daniel Burk, age 66, a well-known citizen of Charlottesville, died after a week's illness of pneumonia and congestion of the brain. He made his home in Charlottesville for many years, plying his trades of shoemaking and barbering (he also was a Justice of the Peace of Hancock County, Indiana, in 1906.). Five children survive, Charles, Chicago; Jennie Edwards, Indianapolis; Gertrude Gray, Ft. Wayne; Mrs. Claude Lane, Charlottesville and Maude Stinger, Knightstown. Interment (HC) Six Mile Cemetery." Contributed by Ron Burk, Salinas, California.

Burk, Joseph; 134 Reg Co K, 24 May 64-2 Sep 64; born 1842, Wayne Co., Indiana, second son of George Burk, Sr.and Susanna Armstrong, and brother, Daniel Burk. Joseph married 24 Jul 1864 Margaret Jerauld HC Bk 4-522, died 1918 at Soldier and Sailor Home at Lafayette, Indiana. Contributed by Ron Burk, Salinas, California.

Burke, Samuel; 106 Reg Co D, 10 Jul 63-17 Jul 63; also 26 Reg Co I, 24 Sep 64-6 Sep 65. A Samuel Burke married 31 Jul 1862 Mary E. Everson HC Bk 4-341. See page for John Davis.

Burns, Conde; 53 Reg Co A, 21 Jan 64-21 Jul 65. NOD.

Burns, James; 21st Indiana Heavy Artillery Co B, 7 Oct 64-7 Oct 65. HC History: "James was born 28 Mar 1842, Ohio, s/o Harvey and Catherine (McKinney) Burns. Living in Marion County, Indiana, he enlisted in Company B, 21st Indiana Heavy Artillery and saw active fighting in the bombardment of Fort Spanish at Mobile where he slightly injured by an exploding shell and was discharged 7 Oct 1865. After his return to civil life, and first marriage 1 Mar 1866 to Catherine (Ruddesel) Delaney (HC Bk 5-37), he took up residence on his

Hancock County Indiana Civil War Soldiers

wife's farm and soon bought out the other heirs and took possession of the entire farm. Mrs. Burns died 1901 and a year later he married Ollie Lyons, born in Decatur County, Indiana." HC New Palestine Cemetery: Burns, James A. died 28 Feb 1916 73y 11m 0d, Catherine died 23 May 1901 71y 2m 22d.

Burnwick, John; 5 Cav Co G, 6 May 62. NOD.

Burris, Charles H.; 79 Reg Co D. 1860 Hancock Co. census records a Charles Burris, age 16, with family of Moses and Elizabeth Burris, siblings, John age 18, Taylor age 13, two young girls and one young boy.

Burris, Eden; 57 Reg Co A, 13 Dec 61-9 Mar 65. Married 12 Aug 1850 Rebecca Pauley HC Bk 3-2.

Burris, Elisha; 19 Reg Co A, 8 Jul 61-28 Jul 64. "Born Greene County, Ohio, s/o Moses and Hannah (Done) Burris, Elisha chose the blacksmith trade as a vocation and was living near Warrington when in 1861, the call came to save the Union. He enlisted as above and in a short time experienced the realities of war, fighting in the battles of Lewsinville, Cedar Mountain, Gaines Mill, Bull Run, South Mountain, Antietam, Gettysburg and numerous minor engagements.

"At the battle of Gettysburg, the regiment lost in killed or wounded fifty-five percent, or more than half of the number engaged in that awful struggle. Elisha was in the very thickest of that rain of shot and shell, and faced the pointed steel of the rebel bayonets, while bullets tore through his clothes and his haversack strap was shot off. He shared the labors, privations and hardships and well earned laurels with his comrades in that famous "Iron Brigade," receiving his discharge 28 Jun 1864, at Petersburg, Virginia.

"Upon returning home he married 14 Jul 1865 Mary A. Johns, of Knightstown, d/o Matthew and Ellen Johns. HC obit, 2 May 1907: "Elisha Burris died at his home near Shirley, aged 71. He was a blacksmith at Shirley in 1899. He was a soldier in the famous 19 Indiana Volunteer Infantry known as the Iron Brigade during the Civil War, and a member of Dunbar G.A.R. at Greenfield. Funeral at Friends Church at Wilkinson."

Hancock County Indiana Civil War Soldiers

Buried HC Simmons Cemetery: Burris, Elisha 10 Jul 1835-24 Apr 1907, Co A 19 Ind Inf; Mary A. 1849-1930.

Burris, Henry; 8 Reg Co G, 5 Sep 61-died of disease 3 Apr 63, Miliken's Bend, Louisiana. At enlistment: age 21, blue eyes, red hair, light complexion, 5' 11', born HC." HC Scotton Cemetery: Henry Burris died 3 Apr 1863 21y 0m 1d; on same stone with Johnson Burris died 23 Apr 1863 22y 5m 1d.

Burris, James; 9 Cav Co B, 9 Dec 63-28 Aug 65. NOD.

Burris, John C.; 12 Reg Co B, 15 May 61-28 Sep 65. A John Burris married 3 Jan 1861 Elizabeth Blakely HC Bk 4-232.

Burris, Johnson; 8 Reg Co G, no dates; HC Scotton Cemetery: Burris, Johnson died 23 Apr 1863 22y 5m 1d; on same stone with Henry Burris. See a letter written by him to his sweetheart a month before he died in that section of this volume.

Burris, Marion; 5 Cav Co G, 12 Aug 63-15 Sep 65. NOD

Burris, Moses; 51 Reg, Co D, 14 Dec 61-died 28 Nov 62, Nashville, Tennessee. Buried Nashville National Cemetery: private, Indiana, died 28 Nov 1862, section B, grave #6971.

Burris, Taylor M.; 51 Reg Co D, 14 Dec 61-discharged 25 Jun 62. NOD.

Burris, Thomas; 38 Reg Co D, 24 Sep 64-29 Jun 65. HC Burris/Hendricks Cemetery: Burris, Thomas died 1 May 1900 68y 6m 9d; Cecilia w/o T. died 7 Apr 1924 79y.

Bush, Henry; 8 Reg Co B, 25 Aug 61-4 Sep 65. A Henry Bush married 25 Jun 1868 Sarah B. Wharton HC Bk 5-229. HC Park Cemetery: Bush, Sarah B. w/o Henry M. died 25 Feb 1878 29y 8m 15d.

Bush, James; 8 Reg Co B 5 Sep 61-28 Aug 65. A James Bush married 4 Apr 1857 Elizabeth Hagens HC Bk 4-16. James buried Cass Co., Indiana.

Bush, John; 8 Reg Co B, 25 Aug 61-4 Sep 64. A John W. Bush (18 Jan 1841-11 Feb 1897), married 1 Jan 1878 Lila Willett HC Bk 6-570.

Hancock County Indiana Civil War Soldiers

Bush, Leroy; 105 Reg Co E 11 Jul 63-18 Jul 63; 9 Cav Co B, 13 Nov 63-28 Aug 65. HC Old Greenfield Cemetery: Bush, Leroy 9 Ind Cav Co B. NOD.

Bussell, James; 99 Reg Co B 13 Aug 62-died from disease 10 Nov 62, Moscow, Tennessee, s/o John Bussell born Miami Co., Ohio, and Mary Moore (Moon) born Crab Orchard, Kentucky; parents buried HC Bussell/BarrettCem: John died 16 Jul 1880 69y 2m 17d, Mary w/o John died 20 Jun 1873 63y.

Butcher, Isaac; 12 Reg Co B, 15 May 61-28 Sep 65. NOD.

Butcher, John L.; 99 Reg Co B, 13 Aug 62-5 Jun 65. 99 Reg History states: "1900 residence HC Warrington." NOD.

Butterfield, Loran; 99 Reg Co B, 13 Aug 62-9 Aug 65. 99 Regiment History states: "Loran Butterfield, HC Warrington, wounded 20 Aug 1864, Atlanta; dead 1900."

Butts, Wiley W; 152 Ohio Co B, enlisted at age 26 8 May 64-2 Sep 64. *Hancock Democrat*, obit 21 Mar 1907: "Wiley W. Butts, age 69 died at his home on Mill Street. He was born 3 Oct 1837, s/o Otto and Elizabeth (Jones) Butts. Mr. Butts was feeling much better and was out on the street in the morning. On hearing of the death of his comrade, Samuel Grigsby, he became worse at once and died a few minutes thereafter. For years he was the gentlemanly custodian of Park Cemetery, survivors, son, Eugene, Union City, and Mrs. Ralph Fuller, Greenfield." Wiley buried HC Park Cemetery.

Byers, William T.; 57 Reg Co A, 13 Dec 61-died 28 Jul 64 of wounds received at Kennesaw Mountain. NOD.

Byfield, Frederick W.; 9 Cav Co B, 13 Nov 63-29 Jun 65. NOD.

Byrkitt, Dr. William S.; HC Gilboa Cemetery, Byrkitt, William S., soldier, 1836-1872, Lafayette R. s/o W.S. died 23 Apr 1866 6y 2m 3d, Infant d/o W. and Charlotta died 1 Mar 1867. NOD.

Hancock County Indiana Civil War Soldiers

Alexander K. Branham

Courtesy of Hancock Democrat

Hancock County Indiana Civil War Soldiers

Joseph Brooks

Courtesy of Frances Vander Weide

Hancock County Indiana Civil War Soldiers

Wiley Butts

Courtesy of Hancock Democrat

Hancock County Indiana Civil War Soldiers

◀ C ▶

Cady, Thomas; 9 Cav Co B, 16 Sep 64-21 Jul 65.
HC newspaper 3 Aug 1865: "Thomas Cady arrived home and has been honorably discharged;" A Thomas Cady married 13 Oct 1864 Mary. Loehr HC Bk 4-481.

Cahill, John; 26 Reg Co H, 24 Sep 64-discharged 6 Sep 65. "an apt penman, he held position of Company clerk from Feb-Aug 65. Took part in battles of Mobile Harbor, Alabama, and at Fort Spanish for thirteen days, his unit was under constant fire from the fort.

Son of John and Hannah (Cunningham) Cahill, the soldier was born 15 Mar 1819, Ireland and was a resident of HC by 1850; where he married 6 Dec 1853 Jane Wilson HC Bk 3-193. Jane Wilson Cahill was born 29 Nov 1828 Brown Co., Ohio, the daughter of Isaac and Ann (Griffith) Wilson.

Mr. and Mrs. Cahill live on the farm they own near Mohawk (HC), where they have spent thirty-seven years of the battles of life, and he enjoying the proud satisfaction of having served his country as a loyal defender." HC obit 28 Feb 1907: "John Cahill, aged eight-two years, died at his home near Mohawk of old age and la grippe, Interment Sugar Creek Cemetery: John died 21 Feb 1907; Jane w/o John died 17 Dec 1907."

Calder, Angus; Born in Canada, 20 Oct 1836, s/o Alexander and Catharine (Campbell) Calder. Came to Madison County, Indiana 1877. He married 28 Feb 1865 at Williamsburg, Ohio, Mary C. Van Horn. Angus is buried HC Willow Branch Cemetery: Angus Calder, 27 Ohio Inf, Co K.

Caldwell, Benjamin; 2 California Inf. Co A, enlisted San Francisco, Calif. 26 Dec 64-discharged disability 17 Oct 65, at Drum Barracks, Calif. Born 1835 HC, married 23 Aug 1855 Lucinda Liming HC Bk 3-300; two children, Sophrona and Eliza. Benjamin died 1875, Powellville, Eureka Co., California. Contributed by James Brown, Venice, Florida.

Camp, George; 12 Reg Co H, 17 Aug 62-deserted 9 Nov 62. NOD.

Hancock County Indiana Civil War Soldiers

Camp, Joseph; 12 Reg Co H, 17 Aug 62-dischg 16 Jun 64.
A Joseph Camp married 20 Aug 1857 Elizabeth Enoch HC Bk 4-27.

Camp, Nicodemus; 12 Reg Co H, 17 Aug 62-8 Jun 65. Married 5 Apr 1866 Clarissa Vanzant, HC Bk 5 49. HC McCordsville Cemetery: Camp, Nicodemus, soldier, 7 Dec 1841-25 Apr 1906, C.A. w/o Nicodemus 31 Mar 1847-22 Mar 1916.

Camp. William; 12 Reg Co H, 7 Aug 62-8 Jun 65. A William Camp married 5 Aug 1858 Mary Jane Enoch HC Bk 4-90.

Campbell, Charles W.; 5 Cav Co G, 16 Aug 62-15 Sep 65. HC newspaper 11 Aug 1864, "Private C. W. Campbell taken prisoner during disastrous expedition commanded by General Stoneman." Private C.W. Campbell, 5 Cav Co G, prisoner, Andersonville, Georgia, code #51124, survived and was exchanged 5 Apr 65. (He is not listed as a passenger on the steamship, Sultana.)

Campbell, William; 8 Reg Co G, 22 Apr 61-6 Aug 61. NOD.

Campbell, William M.; 7 Reg Co K, 10 Sep 61-20 Sep 64. "born Shelby Co., Indiana, age 22, 5' 10", fair complexion, blue eyes, auburn hair, farmer when enrolled. NOD.

Cannon, Isaac; 53 Reg Co A, 24 Feb 62-7 Jul 65. An Isaac Cannon married 6 Aug 1866 Mary Blessinger HC Bk 5-75.

Cantwell, James; 13 Reg Co K, 15 Mar 65, substitute, unassigned. NOD.

Card, Captain Phineas Albertson; 21 Illinois Reg Co D. HC obit, 17 and 24 May 1923: "Captain Card was born 26 Jun 1840 in Rush County, Indiana, s/o John W. and Miriam Card; at the age of eight, he and his twin brother were orphans and grew to manhood in the home of their uncle, Henry Henley of Orange County, Indiana.

Phineas was visiting in Illinois when the first call of volunteers was made and he volunteered in Company D of the 21st Illinois Infantry. This Regiment was organized, drilled by that matchless military genius, Ulysses Grant, and participated in some of the hardest fought battles. Among them being the

Hancock County Indiana Civil War Soldiers

siege of Corinth, battles of Stone's River, Chickamauga, Nashville and Atlanta.

While on furlough in Rush County, Indiana, he married 1 May 1864, Myla Hasket. Capt. Card died at his home southwest of Greenfield, age 83, following complications arising from influenza and infirmities of old age. The body will be laid to rest beside Mrs. Card at Park Cemetery." HC Park Cemetery: Capt. Phineas Co D 21 Ill Inf, Miley A. w/o P.A. 1842-1919.

Carmichael, John C.; 148 Reg Co C, 17 Feb 65-5 Sep 65. A John C. Carmickle (sic) married 3 Nov 1870 Melinda Ogle HC Bk 5-420.

Carr, Captain James Harvey; organized Co B 99 Reg mustered 20 Aug 62. He was with his Company until 21 Jan 63 when he resigned due to failing health. HC obit 1 Dec 1910: "Captain James H, Carr, age 84, died, 28 November 1910, at his home, 107 Walnut Street, Greenfield, from the effects of a stroke of paralysis. He was born 8 March 1826, Floyd County, Indiana, son of North Carolina natives, John and Phoebe (Tague) Carr. Captain Carr was one of the oldest and best known business men in this County, He was appointed commissioner by the Hancock County Circuit Court and as such assisted in driving the fever and ague from the County.

At age 21, he enlisted in Company D Fifth Indiana Regiment under Captain James R. Bracken and served during the entire War with Mexico. At age 36 he organized Company B 99 Indiana Infantry Volunteers, mustered 20 August 1862, and served with his Company until 21 January 1863 when he resigned due to failing health.

He married 28 October 1849 Mary Catherine Huntington (HC Bk 2-353). Five children survive: George, William and Walter of Greenfield; Mrs. John Arnett and John Carr of Fortville. Funeral service in charge of Masons and GAR." Burial HC Park Cemetery: Carr, James H. 1826-1910, Mary C. 1833-1905.

Carr, George W.; 106 Reg Co D, 10 Jul 63-17 Jul 63; 53 Reg Co A, 2 Feb 64-died 28 Jun 64 from wounds received 27 Jun

Hancock County Indiana Civil War Soldiers

64, Kennesaw Mountain, Georgia. HC newspaper 7 Jul 1864: "We are sorry to learn that George Carr, youngest son of James Carr (and Mary Guymon) of this place, was wounded in the right breast, in one of Sherman's recent engagements, from the effects of which, he died the next day. He was a few months over fifteen years of age." Brothers, Thomas J. served in 79 Reg Co B; and Noah served in 53 Reg Co A.

Carr, Noah; 53 Reg Co A, 2 Feb 64-21 Jul 65. HC obit, 22 Apr 1915: "Noah Carr, almost a lifetime resident of Greenfield, a son of Mr. and Mrs. James (Mary Guyman) Carr died at the Soldier's Home at Marion, Indiana, The remains being taken to the home of his sister, Mrs. Samuel Williams, of Fortville (HC). He was a brother of the late Thomas Carr. Two daughters survive in the South, he having married there after the close of the Civil War. His wife preceded him in death a number of years ago." Madison Co., Indiana, Gravel Lawn Cemetery: Carr, Noah Co A 53 Ind Inf, 13 Feb 1847-18 Apr 1915.

Carr, Thomas J.; enlisted age 17, 79 Reg Co B, 9 Aug 62- promoted 1864 duty Sgt. and served until 7 Jun 65. Took part in battles of Richmond, Kentucky, Stone River, Tennessee, Atlanta, Dalton, Kennesaw Mountain, Franklin and Nashville; received two gunshot wounds at Chickamauga, chin and clavicle. Brother, George 53 Reg, was killed at Kennesaw Mountain, Georgia, 1864. Brother, Noah W., also served in 53 Reg.

"HC obit 8 Aug 1912: "Thomas J. Carr, son of James and Mary (Guymon) Carr, one of the best known veterans of the Civil War in this city, and known throughout the County as "Tube," so named because of his playing the Tuba in the Greenfield Band for many years, was found dead beside his bed Mr.Carr had returned home from Winchester, where he had been visiting with a granddaughter. His brother, Noah Carr, came down to this city to assist in swearing Mr. Carr to his pension papers. He was badly crippled some years ago suffering from tuberculosis of the bone resulting in one arm and one leg being amputated, after which he used a hand-crank cart to propel himself. There was a special Senate pension bill passed on his behalf." Thomas J. married 3 Mar 1872 Selena Tyner HC Bk6-91. HC Park Cemetery, Carr, Thomas J. 19 Nov 1844-7 Aug 1912, Selena 28 Feb 1841-20 May 1900.

Carroll, Henry; 57 Reg Co A, 13 Dec 61-12 Aug 62; reenlisted into 38 Reg 4 Nov 64-24 Jun 65. A Henry Carroll married 15 Aug 1860 Luvinia Niles HC Bk 4-202. HC Six Mile Cemetery, Carroll, Henry died 3 Mar 1889 53y 6m 19d, Lavinia w/o Henry 4 Apr 1840-11 Oct1927.

Carroll, George; 26 Reg Co H, 22 Sep 62-9 Sep 65, Sgt. NOD.

Carroll, John W.; 26 Reg Co H, 22 Sep 62-died 8 Aug 63, Port Hudson, Louisiana NOD.

Carroll, Wesley; 134 Reg Co K, 24 May 64-term expired, no date given. NOD.

Carson, David; 148 Reg Co C, 17 Feb 65-5 Sep 65. A David Carson married 6 Jun 1849 Sophia E. Church HC Bk 2-332.

Carson, John S.; 21 Penn. Cav, bugler, Co B, 3 Feb 64-discharged 8 Jul 65 and enlisted in the Regular Army. HC obit, 22 Mar 1906: "John S. Carson about age 60, died at his home on East Main Street, Greenfield, after a lingering illness of Brights disease. Mr. Carson was married twice, his first wife having been dead a number of years, one son, Harry. He married 2) 5 Nov 1882 Amanda Pauley (HC Bk 7-412). HC Park Cemetery, Carson, John S. Co B 21 Penn Cav 1845-1906, Amanda w/o John S. 1852-1918.

Carson, Oliver; 53 Reg Co A; 24 Feb 62-no out date. NOD.

Cartwright, Jonathan; 5 Cav Co G, saddler, 16 Aug 62-10 Mar 63. NOD.

Cass, James Washington; 99 Reg Co B, 13 Aug 62-28 May 64, missing in action. Born about 1839 in Hancock County, s/o Aaron and Elizabeth (Mitchell) Cass. James married 25 Oct 1860 Elizabeth Cook (HC Bk 4-218) and two children: Sarah Adaline Cass born 25 Dec 1861 and James Lewis Cass born 2 Apr 1863. He was captured near Dallas, Georgia, and sent to Andersonville, Prison, code #43036, released Apr 1865. He

Hancock County Indiana Civil War Soldiers

survived the horrors of prison only to die on the steamer, Sultana, as it exploded and burned on the Mississippi River near Memphis, 27 April 1865. His widow, Elizabeth Cass married 6 Mar 1866 (HC Bk 5-41) Alfred McKinsey and they moved to Kansas in 1873. Contributed by Richard Cooper, Greenfield, Indiana.

Casto, Richard; 53 Reg Co A, 24 Feb 62-no out date. NOD.

Casto, William; 53 Reg Co A, 9 Mar 64- 21 Jul 65. NOD.

Catlin, Davis; 12 Reg Co G, 21 Jul 62-discharged 11 Oct 63, wounds. NOD.

Catt, Edmond; 9 Reg Co G, 5 Sep 61-died Mound City, Illinois, no date. Buried Greenfield Old Cemetery, no dates. NOD.

Catt, Milton; 105 Reg Co E, 11 Jul 63-18 Jul 63. A Milton Catt married 1 Jan 1867 Angeline Keefer HC Bk5-109; HC obit, 13 Nov 1919: "Angeline Catt, formerly of Greenfield, died at her Terre Haute (Indiana) home at age 75; survived by her husband, Milton and two daughters of Terre Haute; funeral at Flanner and Buchanan, Indianapolis."

Catt, Nathan; enlisted at age 18 in 79 Reg Co G. HC newspaper, 19 Feb 1863: "We regret to learn that Nathan Catt, son of Solomon Catt, (and Serena Pickering Catt) of this County, died recently at Murfreesboro, Tenn. His Regiment fought through the battles resulting in the capture of Murfreesboro and came out unscathed. Due to fatigue and exposure he had gone through during and after the battle, he was attacked with the camp fever (one account says "typhoid fever") and diarrhea, and died, as many other manly and noble young men have done. He was a brave and gallant young soldier and energetic in the discharge of his duty." See data on his brother, William.

Catt, Wesley Smith; 99 Reg Co B, 13 Aug 62-5 Jun 65. "born HC, age 21, 5' 9", light complexion, blue eyes, light hair, farmer when enrolled; brother, William F. Catt; he was in many hard-fought battles: Vicksburg, Black River, Jackson, Missionary Ridge, Dalton, Kennesaw Mountain, Atlanta and on to the sea." 99 Reg. History states: Wesley S. Catt was born

Hancock County Indiana Civil War Soldiers

9 Feb 1841, HC. He was with Regiment in all battles from the beginning to the Grand Review in Washington. Married 1 Sep 1865 Mary L. Clark and has a family of four children; lived in HC since the War and by occupation a farmer. His address is Cleveland (1900)."
HC obit 4 Aug 1924: "The death of Wesley Smith Catt occurred at Carthage (Rush Co. Indiana) 29 Jul 1927, age 86. He was a Civil War veteran and formerly resided in Jackson Township (HC), his wife died thirteen years ago at Carthage." Burial Simmons Cemetery: Catt, W.S. 9 Feb 1841-29 Jul 1927, Mary L. 26 Mar 1846-30 Mar 1913.

Catt, Wesley Smith; 99 Reg Co B, 15 Aug 62-5 Jun 65. "born HC age 27, 5' 7" tall, dark complexion, black eyes, black hair, farmer when enrolled...wounded 31 Aug 64 at Jonesboro, Georgia, by a gunshot in the right arm, and has the bullet which was taken out, and keeps it as a trophy of that memorable event. He was detached from his Company a while as sharpshooter and marched in the Grand Review at Washington, D.C.

Married 1) name and date not given, ten children; married 2) 30 Sep 1891 Ruth Ella Gray HC Bk 8-357; six children." HC newspaper 4 Feb 1915: "William Catt, a Civil War veteran and aged man of East Greenfield, while on his way to the City proper Monday morning was run down by a horse and buggy. One of his shoulders was considerably injured." HC obit, 22 Feb 1922: "William F. Catt, born 6 Oct 1834, passed away, age about ninety, at his home on North A Street, East Greenfield following a long illness. Mr. Catt leaves a widow and several children and grandchildren. He was a soldier in the Rebellion. Burial Mt Lebanon Church Cemetery." See data on his brother, Nathan.

Catt, Wilson; 134 Reg Co K, 24 May 64-term expired, no date. NOD.

Chambers, Hiram; HC Courthouse soldier burial list, 11 WS Reg Co F; occupation, blacksmith; died 8 Jun 1899; age 70 years; burial HC Cooper Cemetery. NOD.

Hancock County Indiana Civil War Soldiers

Chancery, Michael; 9 Cav Co B, 13 Nov 63-died 4 Mar 65, Vicksburg, Mississippi.

Chandler, George L.; 10 Sep 62-13 Oct 63. A George L. Chandler married 11 Aug 1867 Thena Garten HC Bk 5-151.

Chapman, John Joseph; 5 Cav Co G, at age 42 enlisted 16 Aug 62-discharged 20 Jan 63. John Chapman also served in the Mexican War: mustered into Co D Fifth Indiana Volunteers, 15 Jun 1847 at Fort Clark by Colonel Churchill; mustered out with Regiment 28 Jul 1848. John was born 1823, Coshocton County, Ohio, married Margaret Hays 4 Aug 1842, Wayne County, New York. John and Margaret (Fanny) had six children: one died young; at John's death two of the other three were under age sixteen. John J. Chapman is buried HC Curry's Chapel Church Cemetery: stone simply says, Johnny died 22 Apr 1865, 44y. Contributed by Patti Vahary, Battle Creek, Michigan.

Chapman, Joseph; 5 Cav Co G, 16 Aug 62-15 Sep 65. NOD.

Chapman, Martin; 8 Reg Co G, 22 Apr 61-6 Aug 1; also Martin Chapman, Sr. 110 Reg Co I 10 Jul 63-15 Jul 63. NOD.

Chapman, William; 134 Reg Co K, 24 May 64-term expired, no date given. A William Chapman married 29 Mar 1849 Margaret Jay HC Bk 2-319.

Chappel, Isaac; 79 Reg Co C, 15 Aug 62-died 27 Apr 65, on steamboat, Sultana, when it exploded and burned on Mississippi River near Memphis. An Isaac Chappel married 2 Aug 1860 Nancy Paxton HC Bk4-200.

Chappell, James A.; 2 Cav Co B, 20 Sep 61-discharged 1 Nov 62. "A James A. Chappell, son of George and ___(Halcomb) Chappell, died 10 Feb 1892, of Lagrippe, age 70, at Maxwell (Indiana); married 6 Jun 1846 Ann Kingery HC Bk 2-197. HC Alford Cemetery: Chappell, James A. Co B 2 Ind Cav."

Chappell, John W.; 51 Reg Co K, 2 Feb 62-13 Dec 65. HC Maple Grove/Jackson/Olvey Cemetery: Chapple, John W. died 7 Aug 1878 38y 2m 18d, Angeline w/o J.W. died 4 Jun 1889. A John Chappell married 27 Feb 1861 Anna Talkington HC Bk

Hancock County Indiana Civil War Soldiers

4-246; and a John Chappell Jr married 1 Oct 1861 Sara Ann Powers HC Bk 4 p287. One of these could be Angeline??

Chappell, William; 51 Reg Co K, 2 Feb 62-13 Dec 65. "A William Chappell, born 1 Apr 1833 Indiana, son of John (born Carolina) and Mary Benge (born Indiana), died 19 Dec 1915. A retired plasterer, he was 82y 8m 18d. Wife, Ellen, survives. Burial Eden Church Cemetery."

Childers, John; HC Courthouse soldier burial list: died 17 Mar 1906; occupation, farmer; burial, HC Hays Cemetery.

Chittenden, Charles Edward; at age 17 enlisted 22 Reg Co G, 6 Jul 61-9 Jun 65. "He was wounded Mar 62 at Pea Ridge, Arkansas, by a falling limb shot from a tree by Confederate Artillery, remained with Regiment and rode in an ambulance until he recovered. He was wounded by a rifle bullet at the battle of Chickamauga, and at the battle of Kennesaw Mountain, received a gunshot in the left shoulder; he was at once captured, and held at Libby Prison for a while, then taken to Andersonville Georgia where he was for six months." He is not listed in their database but that doesn't mean he wasn't there for a short time. The National Park Service at Andersonville will add any soldier with proper military proof.

He was discharged from his first enlistment at Blaine's Cross Roads, Tennessee, 22 Dec 1863, and immediately reenlisted as a veteran in the same command, with which he served until the final muster out at Camp Chase, Ohio 9 Jun 1865. The son of Charles Giles and Roena (Bird) Chittenden, Charles Edward, was born 7 Sep 1843, St. Louis, Missouri; and married 3 Nov 1867 Lydia Hendren HC Bk 5-173; Lydia was born 14 Jan 1848 and her brother, Jeremiah Hendren, served in the Mexican War." HC Park Cemetery Charles E. Chittenden, died 27 Jan 1897, Co G 22 Ind Inf.

Chittenden, Daniel B.; 105 Reg Co E, 11 Jul 63-18 Jul 63. NOD.

Chittenden, John; 8 Reg Co B, 25 Aug 61 as Sgt.-no out date. HC newspaper, 4 Dec 1862: "Our young friend and townsman, John S. Chittenden, was duly elected and commissioned a

Hancock County Indiana Civil War Soldiers

Lieutenant of Captain Riley's Cavalry Company (Co B 8 Reg). This is a good selection and it will enhance the unity of the Company." HC newspaper, 11 Aug 1864: "Lt. John S. Chittenden of Co G 5 Cav was killed in the recent expedition of General Stoneman; was instantly killed by the explosion of a shell hitting him in the head." See data on his brother, Charles Edward Chittenden.

Chitwood, Robert; 12 Reg Co G, 23 Jul 62-8 Jun 65. NOD.

Christian, Francis M.; 148 Reg CO I, 9 Feb 65-5 Sep65. NOD.

Church, Charles E.; 9 Cav Co B, 13 Nov 63-27 Apr 65, missing and presumed drowned on steamship, Sultana. 9 Cav History states: "Charles E. Church was captured at Sulphur Branch Trestle, Alabama, and lost by the explosion and burning of the steamboat, Sultana, on the Mississippi River, a few miles above Memphis, 27 April 1865."

Church, Xenas K.; 105 Reg Co E, 11 Jul 63-18 Jul 63. Married 28 Sep 1847 Ida Shiperd HC Bk 2-255; HC Park Cemetery: Xenas K. Church died 27 Mar 1887 70y 1m 10d.

Clampett, Edward; 12 Reg Co B, 15 May 61-19 May 62. NOD.

Clapper, Charles H.; 8 Reg Co B, 25 Aug 61-4 Sep 64. "born HC, age 23, 5' 8," fair complexion, gray eyes, fair hair, farmer when enrolled." HC newspaper, 11 Jun 1864: "reported wounded slightly in the arm near Vicksburg, Mississippi." He died 21 Nov 1917, Missouri.

Clark, Calvin; 9 Cav Co B, 13 Nov 63-died 21 Apr 64, Indianapolis, buried at Old Greenfield Cemetery: Calvin Clark, s/o J. and E., 16y 2m 12d, Co B 9 Ind Cav.

Clark, David; 148 Reg Co I, 9 Feb 65-5 Sep 65. NOD.

Clark, Frank W.; 150 Pa Reg Co A, Corp'l, 19 Sep 62-23 Jun 65. "Frank W. Clark, retired veteran, died 19 Aug 1931, age 83. He was born 22 Feb 1848, England, son of Joe Clark (born England). Widow Christina, New Palestine, survives. Interment HC New Palestine Cemetery.

Clark, George W.; 12 Reg Co B, 15 May 61-19 May 62. NOD.

Hancock County Indiana Civil War Soldiers

Clark, Henry; 155 Reg Co E, 21 Mar 65-8 Jul 65. A Henry Clark, age 74y 7m 0d, died 25 Nov 1911, Fortville. He was born 8 Apr 1837, s/o Thomas Clark (born N.C.) and Mary Ann Coleman (born N.C.) survived by widow, Lucinda. Burial HC Simmons-Caudell Cemetery. A Henry Clark married 15 May 1901 Lucinda Lemsford HC Bk 10-184.

Clark, John; 12 Reg Co G, 23 Jul 62-23 Jun 65. NOD.

Clark, John; 26 Reg Co H, 24 Sep 64-6 Sep 65; HC obit, 17 Feb 1898; "Mr. John Clark, an old soldier, was sitting at the home of his son in East Greenfield, conversing with some young people, when he fell over dead. He never fully recovered from injuries received from a fall a few months ago in a runaway accident. It is thought his death was due to the rupture of a blood vessel. He was seventy years of age, and leaves a number of children to mourn his sudden death." HC Park Cem; Jno Clark Co H 26 Ind Inf.

Clark, Thomas; 49 Ohio Inf Co F, 16 Aug 61-23 Feb 63. "He was wounded 2 Oct 62 in a skirmish from Louisville to Perryville. The son of Andrew (born Ireland) and Elizabeth (Clever) Clark, Thomas was born 26 Oct 1837, Freemont, Ohio, lived in Fortville, Hancock County, Indiana; married 1) in Sandusky County, Ohio, 5 Mar 1863 Mary J. Ferrell; married 2) 28 Sep 1870 Mary E. Shafer HC Bk 5-402. Thomas died 19 Dec 1919 at Fortville and buried Madison County, Indiana Gravel Lawn Cemetery." Contributed by Sue Ferrell, Fortville, Indiana.

Clayton, James; 8 Reg Co G, 16 Apr 61-6 Aug 61. He came to HC about 1845 with his parents, Joseph and Ruth (Roberts) Clayton, both born Penn. A James S. Clayton married 22 Mar 1860 Christina Cooper HC Bk 4-85; a James L. Clayton married 19 Jul 1863 Rebecca Hamilton HC Bk 4 395.

Clements, Lansford; 148 Reg Co C, 17 Feb 65-5 Sep 65. NOD.

Clevenger, Isaac; 9 Cav Co B, 9 Dec 63-25 Jul 65. NOD.

Cliff, Charles; 105 Reg Co E, 11 Jul 63-18 Jul 63. NOD.

Clifford, Burr N.; 19 Reg Co F, 29 Jul 61-18 Oct 64 transferred to 20th Reg. NOD.

Hancock County Indiana Civil War Soldiers

Cline, John H.; 79 Reg Co G, 19 Aug 62-7 Jan 63. NOD.

Cloud, Francis. M.; 2 Ky Inf Co E, 6 Jun 61-19 Jun 64. "age 21, 5' 9", fair complexion, black eyes, brown hair, farmer when enrolled." HC obit 24 Jul 1919: "Francis M. Cloud, son of James T. and Laura (Tebbs) Cloud was born in Dearborn County, Indiana, 10 May 1840 and died 16 Jul 1919, aged 79y 2m and 6d. He gained the rank of First Sergeant and was in the battles of Shiloh, Chickamauga, Lookout Mountain and other important engagements of the war. With great personal risk, he saved his Company's flag from being lost at the battle of Chickamauga. On 10 Dec 1868 he married Sarah Jane Radley, (1847-1923) of near Sunman, Indiana. He moved to New Palestine (HC) May 1873, where he followed his trade as tinner, retiring from business about 1890. Survived by the wife and five children, Ralph, George, Mrs. William Moffitt, Mrs. Edward Ayers, Mrs. C.M. Reeves; and one sister, Elizabeth Tompkins. Francis and Sarah buried HC New Palestine Cemetery.

Cly, Abraham M.; 19 Reg Co F, 29 Jul 61-18 Oct 64 transferred to 20 Reg; HC newspaper 19 May 1864: "A.M. Cly of the 19th wounded in the shoulder in the recent battles across the Rapidan." Abraham M. Cly married 1 Apr 1869 Martha L. Ray HC Bk 5-292; HC Burris/Hendricks Cemetery: A.M. Cly Co F 19 Ind Inf, Martha Cly 1852-1928; three c/o A.M. and M.L. Cly: George d 30 Mar 1874, 1y 8m 23d; Laura 5 Sep 1873-17 Mar 1896; and Zacherias d 4 Apr 1874, 2y 11m 15d.

Cly, John; 19 Reg Co F, no dates given. NOD.

Cochran, Oliver P.; 148 Reg Co C, 17 Feb 65-5 Sep 65. NOD.

Cochran, William; HC Harlan Cemetery: William Cochran Corp'l Co F 18 L A, 1840-1920. NOD.

Coffey, Isaac; HC Courthouse soldier burial list: 3 Kentucky Reg Co 76; died 30 Sep 1906; 74 years; occupation, laborer; burial, Park Cemetery.

Coffey, Thomas; 51 Reg Co F, no dates. HC newspaper, 29 Jun 1922: "Mr. and Mrs. Thomas Coffey celebrated their fiftieth

Hancock County Indiana Civil War Soldiers

wedding anniversary at the home of their daughter, Mrs. E.E. Hamilton, Greenfield. Mr. Coffey was soldier in the Civil War." HC obit 8 Jul 1926: "Thomas Coffey, eighty-two years of age and a Civil War veteran, passed away at his home on West Sixth Street (Greenfield) following years of poor health and an accident that resulted in a broken limb. He was born 30 Sep 1843, Shelby County, Indiana, son of James and Sarah (Carter) Coffey. Mr. Coffey saw long and hard service during the Civil War, being a survivor of the famous Stone River battle. His wife died fifteen months ago, son, Noble, a year ago. HC Park Cemetery: Coffey, Thomas H. 1834-1926, Cynthia A. w/o Thomas 1852-1925.

Coffin, (Squire) Edward Starbuck; 134 Reg Co K, 24 May 64- time expired, no date given. HC obits, 27 Aug and 3 Sep 1925: "E.S. Coffin, age 78, a veteran of the Civil War, died at his home on Center Street (Greenfield). He was born 17 Dec 1846, at Westland (HC), the son of John and Matilda (Walker) Coffin. After education at Friends Academy of Spiceland, Ind., he taught school, afterward studying law and was admitted to the bar at Greenfield, Ind., where he practiced; served one term as Justice of the Peace and was on his second term at the time of his death. He departed this life 23 August 1925, leaving a widow and two daughters by a former wife." Burial HC Park Cemetery.

Coffin, Elihu; no units for this man, however, HC Westland Church Cemetery records an Elihu Coffin, soldier, 24 Feb 1817-14 Jul 1899. HC death notice 20 Jul 1899: " Elihu Coffin, age 82, died at his late home near Westland of peritonitis. Services at Western Grove Church, interment at Westland Cemetery. (No mention of having been a soldier.)" A man named Elihu Coffin is a son of Zacharias and Phoebe (Starbuck) Coffin, whose other children are Abigail; Cyrena; Harvey; Alfred; John; Maria; Nathan Dix; and Phoebe.

Coffin, Elisha D.; 6 Cav Co L, 15 Aug 63-13 Jun 65. HC obit 3 Dec 1885: "Elisha Coffin, age 41, died 2 Dec 1885, of Bright's disease. He was born HC (no date), son of John and Matilda

Hancock County Indiana Civil War Soldiers

(Walker) Coffin. He was an old soldier and will be buried by the Samuel Dunbar Post G.A.R. at (HC) Gilboa Cemetery " An Elisha Coffin married 11 Oct 1865 Hannah Peacock HC Bk 4-549.

Coffin, Zachariah; 19 Reg Co F Sgt., 29 Jul 61-1 Jun 64 wounded Cold Harbor, Virginia. "born HC, age 19, 5' 10," light complexion, blue eyes, dark hair, farmer when enrolled." A Zachariah Coffin married 4 Oct 1870 Josephine New HC Bk 5-404.

Cohee, Isaac N.; 12 Reg Co A, 16 Jun 62-25 Nov 62. Isaac Cohee, age 69, died 17 Oct 1911, of liver disease. He was born 15 Nov 1841, son of William and Eliza (Willis) Cohee, and has a brother, Benjamin. HC Park Cemetery, Cohee, Isaac N. 1841-1912, Catherine w/o I.N. 1855-1905.

Colburn, Manley; 38 Reg Co D, 10 Nov 64-15 Jul 65. NOD.

Cole, James M.; 14 Ky Cav Co K, 2 Jan 63-no out date, listed as absent, sick. HC Mt. Gilead Cemetery: J.M. Cole Co K 14 Ky Cav. died 14 Nov 1895.

Coleman, Archibald; 53 Reg Co A, 10 May 64-21 Jul 65. NOD.

Collyer, Tilghman Howard; 99 Reg Co B, Corp'l, 13 Aug 62-5 Jun 65. HC obit 18 Mar 1926: "A veteran of the Civil War, Tilghman Howard Collyer, aged 81 years, died at the home of his daughter, Mrs. Rebecca Wagoner, New Palestine. He was born 10 Feb 1842, son of Wellington and Rebecca (Lyming) Collyer. He married 7 Sep 1865 Martha J. Hawk (1840-1909) HC Bk 4-532. Survived by seven children: Rebecca Wagoner, Arizona James, Mary Hook, Cynthia Reasoner, Wellington, Adam and George Collyer. He was a brother of Philander Collyer, Greenfield, Mrs. John Gardner and Mrs. Henry Pentland." Tilghman and Martha buried HC Philadelphia Cemetery.

Collins, Alpheus; 38 Reg Co E, 24 Sep 64-died 4 May 65, New Bern, N.C. An Alpheus Collins, married 12 Dec 1844 Mary Ruley HC Bk 2-139. NOD.

Hancock County Indiana Civil War Soldiers

Collins, Christopher C.; 19 Reg Co F, no dates given. HC death notice 24 Jan 1929: "Christopher C. Collins, born 9 Jan 1847, died 21 Jan 1929, age 82, in Cadiz, at the home of Mr. and Mrs. Ora Thomas. Funeral and burial at Mt Comfort Church and Cemetery."

Collins, Cornelius; 79 Reg Co C, 15 Aug 62-19 Nov 63. NOD.

Collins, Henry; 9 Reg Co G, 18 Mar 65-no out date. A Henry Collins married 21 Feb 1864 Lucretia Smith HC Bk 4-434.

Collins, Darius; 12 Reg Co B, 15 May 61-19 May 62. NOD.

Collins, John Henry; 99 Reg Co B, 13 Aug 62-died 18 May 64, Huntsville, Alabama. He was born 16 Aug 1843, son of Thomas and Sarah (Bray) Collins. John Henry's brother, Thomas J. Collins, died 29 Mar 1863 near Chattanooga.

Collins, Levi; 8 Reg Co B, 25 Aug 61-4 Sep 64. HC newspaper 28 May 1863: " Levi Collins of Co B 8 Regiment wounded slightly in the shoulder." NOD.

Collins, Rezin D.; 5 Cav Co G. HC newspaper 11 Aug 1864: "Sgt. R.D. Collins of Co G 5Cav was taken prisoner during the disastrous expedition of General Stoneman." Rezin D. Collins died 8 Jan 1865, Andersonville, Georgia, Prison of Scorbutus (scurvy); grave #12415.

Collins, Samuel; 13 Cav Co I, 23 Dec 63-18 Nov 65. Three HC marriages for a Samuel Collins: 14 Feb 1856 Mary Jane Armstrong Bk 3-323; 11 Feb 1866 Mary E. Hastings Bk 5-33; 25 Dec 1866 Caltha Bennett Bk 5-14. NOD.

Collins, Thomas J.; 99 Reg Co B, 13 Aug 62-died 29 Mar 63 LaGrange, Tenn." His brother, John Henry Collins died 16 May 1864, Huntsville, Alabama.

Collins, William; 79 Reg Co D, 8 Aug 62-7 Jun 65, Corp'l. "William F. Collins, carpenter, died 2 Aug 1906, of tuberculosis. He was born 29 Oct 1844, son of William and Elizabeth (Snyder) Collins. Burial HC Mt. Comfort Cemetery

Comstock, James; 79 Reg Co G, 23 Aug 62-resigned 24 Sep 62. HC newspaper 27 Nov 1862:"Lieut. James Comstock, of Company G 79 Regiment Indiana Volunteers, reached home on Friday last. Lieut. C. has been very sick and has tendered his

Hancock County Indiana Civil War Soldiers

resignation. He is of the opinion that he cannot stand service. He reports the health of the regiment as bad. He left the regiment at Silver Springs, 16 miles from Nashville, Tennessee. James E. Comstock, age 84, 303 North Swope Street, Greenfield; died 16 Jul 1930, of a cerebral hemorrhage. He was born 18 Nov 1845, son of Joseph and Faith (Benton) Comstock. He is survived by the wife. Burial HC Park Cemetery."

Comstock, Dr James Alico; 33 Reg Co D, Aug 61-1 Oct 64. "..born Greenfield, Indiana, age 17, sandy complexion, blue eyes, red hair, farmer when enrolled." 21 Oct 62 engagement at Wild Cat, Kentucky; from October 62 to June 63 was in engagements in eastern Kentucky and Tennessee. "5 Mar 63 received a gunshot wound in the right knee at Thompson Station, Tennessee; captured 7 Mar 63 at Spring Hill and liberated by Sheridan's men. Received care in hospital until spring 1864; rejoined his Reg't and participated in campaigns in and around Atlanta.

Became ill again, sent to Chattanooga and was honorably discharged 1 Oct 1864. He applied for a disability pension 28 June 1869, aged 25 years, resident of Marietta, Shelby County, Indiana, while in battle received a gunshot wound in the right knee. The ball remains in the said knee causing stiffness of the joint and weakness of his entire leg and causes general debility that he is unable to perform manual labor a portion of his time. Pensioner dropped from rolls as he died 9 Dec 1912 and was last paid 4 November 1912 at the Rate of $30.00."

HC newspaper obit: "Dr. James A. Comstock, aged 67 years, died 9 Dec 1912, at the Deaconess Hospital in Indianapolis, following a surgical operation a few days prior, for the relief of a bladder affliction from which he had suffered for many years. Including the last one, he had undergone eight surgical operations in the hope of relief. Dr. Comstock was born 8 January 1844 at Greenfield, s/o Dr. Hiram Bull Comstock and Rebecca Jane Golladay Mills, James married 19 Sep 1872, Shelby County, Indiana, Mary Emily Anderson (9 Apr 1855-25

Hancock County Indiana Civil War Soldiers

Mar 1909). At age seventeen James A. Comstock was not accepted into the service at once due to his youth, but in August 1861 the age limit was waived and he enlisted and was honorably discharged 1 October 1864.

Returning from the Army, Mr. Comstock commenced the study of medicine and was a graduate of the Ohio Medical College in Cincinnati and Rush Medical College in Chicago. On 12 March 1867, Dr. Comstock began the practice of his chosen profession at Marietta, Shelby County, Indiana. He came to Greenfield in 1889 and engaged in the practice of medicine until failing health caused him to retire. He is survived by two daughters, Lucy Caraway and Frankie Spannuth, and three sons, William D, John C., and J. Russell Comstock" James and Mary E. buried HC Park Cemetery. Contributed by Linda Comstock-Teel, Nashville, Indiana.

Conger, Gersham Wiley; 19 Reg Co B, 27 Jul 61-no out date. HC obit 6 May 1926: "The death of Gersham Wiley Conger, age 85, occurred at his home in Fortville, after an illness of only one week. Mr. Conger was a member of the 19th Indiana Infantry, Company B, and served four years in the Civil War. He participated in the Battle of Lookout Mountain and other major engagements. He was born 13 May 1841, son of Gershom and Mahala (Daniels) Conger. Burial Madison County, Gravel Lawn Cemetery."

Conner, Benjamin F.; 79 Reg Co G,21 Aug 62-discharged for promotion to 1st Lt. in 9 Reg. NOD.

Conner, Joseph; 9 Cav Co B, 9 Jan 64-28 Aug 65. A Joseph Conner married 16 Sep 1865 Maria Brown HC Bk 5-85. NOD.

Conner, Moses; 106 Reg Co D, 10 Jul 63-17 Jul 63 and 38 Reg Co D; 24 Sep 64-15 Jul 65. A Moses Conner married 1) 5 Sep 1853 Maria Leachman HC Bk 3-178; married 2) 8 May 1858 Allison Hawk HC Bk 4-81.

Connett, David; 9 Cav Co B, 13 Nov 63-24 Dec 64. NOD.

Cook, Charles W.; 79 Reg Co G, 18 Aug 62-7 Jun 65. A Charles Cook married 29 Oct 1865 Martha Lineback HC Bk 4-555.

Hancock County Indiana Civil War Soldiers

Cook, George; No units given. "George Cook, cousin of John Davis, received a gunshot wound in the shoulder crippling him for life." See page for John Davis.

Cook, James A.; 99 Reg Co B, 23 Mar 64-died 27 Apr 64. HC newspaper, 24 May 1864: "Scottsboro, Alabama, James A. Cook died at the hospital, his disease was measles."

Cook, William; No units given. "William Cook, cousin of John Davis, served throughout the Civil War." See page for John Davis.

Cooper, Benjamin Thomas; enlisted 22 Aug 1862 at Indianapolis in Company C, 79 Regiment Indiana Infantry, mustered in 27 Aug 1862. He deserted near Silver Springs, Tennessee, 18 Nov 1862 but voluntarily returned 14 April 1863 at Murfreesboro, Tennessee. He was "wounded in hand, slight," 25 Nov 1863, at the battle of Missionary Ridge, and was detailed a nurse at Chattanooga Army Hospital sometime about May 1864 and remained there until Sep 1864. From there he returned to his unit to face desertion charges. On 12 Feb 1865 he was tried by a General Court Martial and found not guilty of desertion, but was found guilty of being absent without leave and sentenced to forfeiture of one month's pay. He was age 26, 5' 6," light complexion, gray eyes, dark hair and a farmer when enrolled. He was mustered out at Nashville, 7 Jun 1865. He married 1) 28 Dec 1854, Martha Jane Cass; married 2) 12 Feb 1877 Mary Jane Watts. His widow applied for a pension in 1886 based on disease of consumption he contracted in the Army. Benjamin Thomas Cooper was born 1836, died 6 Jun 1878 HC, s/o Vincent and Amany (Mattocks) Cooper. Contributed by Richard Cooper, Greenfield, Indiana.

Cooper; Ezekiel; 12 Reg Co G, killed Missionary Ridge, 25 Nov 1863. NOD

Cooper, Francis M.; 135 Reg Co K, 24 May 64-term expired. NOD.

Cooper, James William; "He was born 29 Jul 1825, Kentucky, s/o Vincent and Amany (Mattocks) Cooper, married 15 Sep 1850 to Jemima Cass (HC Bk 3-7). James was drafted 24 Feb

Hancock County Indiana Civil War Soldiers

1865, into Company D 9 Indiana Infantry, Indianapolis. The Union must have been desperate for men as he was 39 years old with five children Less than four months later, he was sent to the army hospital in Nashville, Tennessee, on 12 Jun 65, where he was reported as unfit for duty due to consumption (tuberculosis) He was furloughed on 6 Jul 65, entered an army hospital in Indianapolis 4 Aug 65 and was mustered out 4 Sep 1865 at Indianapolis. He lived another four years and died, 16 Jul 1869, from consumption. He had one additional child during this time." "I knew Mr. Cooper (James William) before and since the war, lived within one mile of him, He was a rugged hard working man before the war. I saw him once in the army, he was sick then and had all indications of consumption. I was with him frequently after the war on until he died about four years after the war closed. He was never well and never worked, his cough grew gradually worse and consumption ended his life, he told and so did the physician, Dr. J.J. Carter, that the service ruined his health. Dr. J.J. Carter was his physician during his last sickness. I don't think he ever done a full days work after he came home from the army. Signed, Sidney Moore, Eden, Hancock County, Indiana, 30 April 1884."

"James W. Cooper came under my care and treatment about 22 January 1869, suffering as follows: chronic lung condition, could not speak above a whisper, complete loss of voice, almost constant cough. Bronchial tubes inflamed. Hepituration of left lung. When he began coughing he would vomit. The patient was quite emaciated. He was under my treatment from 22 January to 6 April, all in 1869. I pronounced the disease fatal and withdrew from the case 6 April 1869.

That said soldier died at Eden, Indiana, 16 July 1869 and the cause was __, I was not present at his death. Signed Samuel Milliken, M.D. 30 April 884." Jemima (Cass) Cooper, widow of James William Cooper, received a pension of $8 per month from Jun 1883 until her death in June 1887, based on James'

Hancock County Indiana Civil War Soldiers

service connected death. Contributed by Richard Cooper, Greenfield, Indiana.

Cooper, John W.; 6 Reg Co C, 20 Sep 61-22 Sep 64, promoted Corp'l and Sgt.; HC Park Cem: Jno Cooper Sgt. 6 Ind Inf, died 9 Aug 1910, age 72.

Cooper, John Wesley; 79 Reg Co C, 5 Aug 62-deserted 18 Nov 62. He was on muster out roll at Nashville, 7 Jun 65. John Wesley was born HC 11 Nov 1843, s/o Vincent and Amany (Mattocks) Cooper; married Sarah Elizabeth Jackson 7 Nov 1860. He abandoned his family and left HC; his wife divorced him in 1876 and later remarried. Contributed by Richard Cooper, Greenfield, Indiana.

Copeland, Daniel; 79 Reg Co G, 21 Aug 62-7 Jun 65. "..born HC, age 19, 5' 5," dark complexion. blue eyes, dark hair, farmer when enrolled..." NOD.

Copeland, John; 5 Cav Co G, 16 Aug 62-20 Nov 63, deserted.

Copper, Alexander; 9 Cav Co B, 13 Nov 63-8 Jun 65. An Alexander Copper married Nov 1886 Francis M. Lawson, place not given. "Alexander Copper was born 18 Jun 1846, Penn, died 7 Sep 1926, 79y 2m 19d. Wife, Frances M. Copper. Burial Wynn Cemetery.

Copper, Ezekiel; 12 Reg Co G, 15 May 61-killed 25 Nov 63, Missionary Ridge, Tennessee. An Ezekiel Copper married 30 Jul 1856 Almira Brown HC Bk 3-350.

Cotton, Thomas D.; HC Courthouse soldier burial list: 19 Kentucky Reg Co I; died 22 Mar 1898; 56 years; burial, New Bethel, Marion County, Indiana.

Cottrell, Samuel; 5 Cav Co G, 15 May 61-10 Apr 64. HC Wynn Cemetery: Sarah d/o Samuel and Nancy died 1863 10y.

Cottrell, Samuel P.; 12 Reg Co B, 15 May 61-19 May 62. NOD.

Cottrell, Thomas; 12 Reg Co G, 23 Jul 62-27 Jan 64 discharged disability. NOD.

Courtney, John; 148 Reg Co F, 3 Feb 65-5 Sep 65. NOD.

Cox, Philander W.; 79 Reg Co C, 15 Aug 62-died 19 Jul 63, Louisville, Kentucky. NOD.

Hancock County Indiana Civil War Soldiers

Craft, Homer; 57 Reg Co A, 10 Sep 62-discharged 5 Feb 63. "Born 28 Mar 1830, died 9 May 1881, parents, Abraham and Margaret Althans, brother Captain John A. Craft. An Homer Craft married 5 Mar 1866 Lucinda Broomfield HC Bk 5-38, Buried HC Gilboa Cemetery.

Craft, Captain John A.; 57 Reg Co A, 13 Dec 61-Aug 62 promoted 1st Lt. Was in engagements of Pittsburg Landing, Corinth, Tuscumbia, Alabama. Feb 63 promoted, Captain; 29 Mar 63 resigned by reason of ill health and on returning home was not expected to live. He was born 1 Sep 1824,Trumbull Co. Ohio, s/o Abraham and Margaret (Althans) Craft; about 1836 came with parents to HC. Learned the trade of plane maker at Cincinnati and came to Charlottesville where he carried on the same trade. Captain John married 29 Jul 1849 Elizabeth Fries (5 Jun 1825-1 Jul 1908) d/o Daniel Fries. John and Elizabeth buried HC Six Mile Cemetery.

Craining, Joseph; 9 Cav Co B, blacksmith, 9 Dec 63-30 May 65. NOD.

Crane. William E.; 5 Cav Co A, 6 Aug 62-22 May 65. "..born Franklin County, Indiana, gray eyes, light hair, 5' 11" tall, light complexion, age 36, farmer when enrolled.." His regiment participated in the siege of Knoxville, pitting against Longstreet in that famous campaign, following Morgan in his raid through Indiana and Ohio, and took part in the capture. "Applied for military pension 5 Aug 1870, age 44, resident of Willow Branch; on or about 1 May 1864, he was sent to the hospital at Camp Nelson, Kentucky, in consequence of physical disability resulting from piles, contracted while upon duty scouting in East Tennessee and southern Kentucky, being the result of constant duty in the saddle. Was ordered to the hospital, treated for piles and billious fever, and suffered from diarrhea Remained in hospital at Camp Nelson until furloughed home for fall elections of 1864 after which he returned to his Company at Louisville, Kentucky and remained with Company until about 1 Mar 1865 was discharged. Was treated for piles constantly and that said disability has

Hancock County Indiana Civil War Soldiers

continued; he has been able to do some work but is frequently entirely disabled.

4 March 1898, Certificate #114772: current wife is Winnie (Pilkenton) Crane, married 31 Mar 1886 at Maxwell, Indiana; previous wife was Eunice Bunker who died 21 Aug 1875, Greenfield, Indiana; names and dates of birth of children: Charles, 1850; Silas, 1852; William, 1854; John, 1856; Sarah, 1858; Tobias, 1860 and Amanda, 1868."

HC obit, 26 Nov 1914: "William E. Crane, was born 5 Jun 1826, Franklin County, Indiana (another source said Jennings County, Indiana), son of Caleb and Anna (Kidd). At age 88 years, he had been in poor health for more than a year when his son, John, came from Trinidad, Colorado, to live with him. A few weeks ago his grandson-in-law, Jack Chapman, and wife came to keep house for him. Mr. Crane was a tanner by trade and operated a tanyard at (HC) Nashville. During his latter years, he followed farming and gardening and had an income from the Government in the way of a pension. He leaves a number of children. He had been married eight times. The funeral was in charge of the Grand Army of the Republic, interment Park Cemetery. " Contributed by Irene Shireman, Greenfield, Indiana.

Cravens, Junius (James) E.; 18 Reg, musician, 16 Aug 61-20 Aug 62. NOD.

Crawford, Francis M.; 18 Reg musician, 16 Aug 61-20 Aug 62; 105 Reg Co E 11 Jul 63-17 Jul 63. A Francis M. Crawford married 7 Nov 1865 Susan. Offutt HC Bk 5-1.

Creviston, Cyrus W.; 51 Reg Co D, 14 Dec 61-19 Apr 65. Married 25 Sep 1851 Cinda Chapman HC Bk 3-61.

Crews. George W.; 9 Cav Co B, 13 Nov 63-29 Jan 65. NOD.

Crosley, Abner V.; 8 Reg Co K, 5 Sep 61-19 Oct 64, Corp'l, wounded at Cedar Creek Virginia. "Abner Vanmeter Crosley, age 75, died 11 Dec 1916, HC. He was born 18 Mar 1841, son of William and Elizabeth (Vanmeter) Crosley. Widower of Rosanna J. Crosley (15 Mar 1848-19 Oct 1911). Abner and Rosanna buried HC McCordsville Cemetery.

Hancock County Indiana Civil War Soldiers

Crosley, Joseph L.; 11 Reg Co K, 31 Aug 61-died 16 May 64 New Orleans, accidentally wounded, no date given.

Cross, Ebenezer; 51 Reg Co D. 14 Dec 61-died 20 Mar 62 Nashville, Tennessee. Married 14 Mar 1853 Catherine Gray HC Bk 3-147. Contributed by Retta Livengood, Greenfield, Indiana.

Cross, Joseph; 57 Reg Co B, 18 Dec 61-14 Dec 65. Buried HC Six Mile Cemetery: Co B 57 Ind Inf, no dates. See page for his brother, William H. Cross.

Cross, Warren; "joined Company G, 79th Regiment as a Private on 21 August 1862, Indianapolis, Indiana and was mustered in on 1 September 1862, for a term of three years. At the time of his enlistment, is described as being age 33, 6 feet tall, fair complexion, blue eyes light hair and farmer. In September the 79 Regiment was moved to Louisville and attached to the 11th Brigade, 5th Division, Army of the Ohio. September, 1862, sick at Louisville; November 1862, injured and sent to Nashville Hospital; 25 June 1863 sent to convalescent camp at Murfreesboro, Tennessee; 28 April 1864 transferred to Veterans Reserve Corps. 7 June 1865 muster out from Nashville, Tennessee, with the final accounting: Warren was paid $33.47 for clothing in kind or money advanced, paid $25 bounty with a balance of $75 owed. Warren was born 1829, Shelby County, Indiana, son of Ebenezer (born Virginia) and Eleanor (Davis born Pennsylvania) Cross. Warren married 5 Jan 1853 Clystia Miller. Contributed by Retta Livengood, Greenfield, Indiana.

Cross, William H.; 9 Cav Co B, 13 Nov 63-8 Jun 65. Took part in engagements of Mission Gap, Wilson's Pike, McMinnville, Franklin, Spring Hill, Columbia plus numerous skirmishes and minor engagements. In one of the engagements, a horse that he was riding fell, throwing him to the ground, injuring his back, causing a disability that clung to him the rest of his life. The son of Alfred and Hattie (Andrick) Cross, William was born 1844, Boston, Indiana, but greater part of his life spent in HC. William's brother, Joseph, and his wife's father, Jacob Andrick,

Hancock County Indiana Civil War Soldiers

were volunteers in Indiana regiments. William married 16 Sep 1868 Anna Elizabeth Andrick HC Bk 5-246. HC newspaper 8 Jun 1899: "William H. Cross, age 56, died at his home in East Greenfield of consumption, deceased was a member of Knightstown Post G.A.R."

Crossley, James H.; substitute, 12 Reg Co G, 22 Feb 64, transferred to 48 Reg; NOD.

Crossley, Ross; 5 Cav Co A, 6 Aug 62-15 Jun 65. Buried HC Gillium Chapel Cemetery.

Crossley, William; 70 Reg Co K. 25 Jun 62-20 Jan 63. Buried HC Gillium Chapel Cemetery: William Crosley h/o Elizabeth, rest illegible.

Crowder, James; 18 Reg Musician, 16 Aug 61-20 Aug 62. NOD.

Cummins, Thomas; 8 Reg Co K, 22 Apr 61-6 Aug 61. "Thomas Cummins, age 57, son of William Cummins, died 7 Apr 1889, of pneumonia. Buried HC Gillium Chapel Cemetery. A Thomas Cummins married 21 Nov 1865 Olive Steel HC Bk 5-6.

Cunningham, James D; 38 Reg Co D, 24 Sep 64-15 Jul 65. A James Cunningham married Eva Martin 6 Apr 1891 HC Bk 8-321. NOD.

Curry, Allen; 134 Reg Co K, 24 May 64-term expired no date. Married 27 Oct 1859 Elizabeth Jane Alford HC Bk 4-158. Allen died 22 Aug 1915, Great Bend, Kansas.

Curry, Andrew; 99 Reg Co B, musician, fife,13 Aug 62-died 15 Mar 63, La Grange, Tennessee. Buried HC Barrett/Bussell Cemetery: Andrew Curry s/o J.H. and S. died 15 Mar 1863, Musician, Co B 99 Ind Inf, enlisted 13 Aug 1862.

Curry, Captain Isaiah A.; 99 Reg Co B, Aug 62 as Private, gained successive promotions, Sgt., 2nd Lt.,1st Lt. and Captain. HC obit, 17 Jul 1902: "Captain Isaiah Curry , age 67, died at his home on North State Street, 12 Jul 1902. On 28 June he was taken with a severe attack of flux and lumbago, from which he never recovered. Captain Curry was born in Center Township, HC, 16 Jul 1835, the son of Morgan and Sophia

Hancock County Indiana Civil War Soldiers

(Haney) Curry. At age 16 his father died leaving him to care for his mother and several small brothers and sisters.
He married 31 Dec 1857 Mary Catherine Thomas (1840-1921) HC Bk 4-58. He saw active service with the 99th about Corinth, Memphis, Vicksburg, Chattanooga and Knoxville campaigns with Grant, being at Lookout Mountain and Missionary Ridge. He made the memorable forced march for the relief of Knoxville, was with Gen. Sherman in the Atlantic campaign, and on the famous march to the sea.. He was elected treasurer of Hancock County in 1880 and 1882 on the Democratic ticket. Funeral services were held at the Bradley M.E. Church, interment (HC) Park Cemetery."

Curry, Milton; 12 Reg Co G, 19 Jul 62-killed 30 Aug 62 Richmond, Kentucky. NOD.

Curry, Rossville; 9 Cav Co B, 9 Dec 63-26 Aug 65, Corp'l. NOD

Curry, William; 51 Reg Co D, 14 Dec 61-31 Jul 63. "William Curry, age 59, died 21 Feb 1892, buried HC Willow Branch Cemetery. He was born 1833, son of Nathaniel (born Kentucky) and Eliza (Winters born Kentucky) Curry.

Curry; William 99 Reg Co B, 15 Aug 62-5 Jun 65. ..."born Franklin Co., Ind., age 22, 5' 6," light complexion, blue eyes, light hair, farmer when enrolled. HC obit 20 Aug 1891: "William Curry was born at Bloomington, Franklin County, Indiana 24 August 1839 and died 12 August 1891. He was married to 29 Sep 1866, Nancy H. Thomas (1845-1921) The fruits of this marriage were eight children, five of whom survive him. William Curry was the son of Harrison and Susan Curry, who moved to this county when the deceased was quite young. He served a faithful servant to his country during the late war. He volunteered in 1862 in Company B, 99th Regiment and served until the close of the war.

"William Curry (better known as Billy) was of a jovial nature always ready for a joke. He left his home the evening of 12 August, stopping and chatting with the neighbors along the route to willow Branch, as was his custom to do, seeming to be

Hancock County Indiana Civil War Soldiers

in good health and spirits as usual, not complaining of any ailment. At the time of his death he was in the store of Henry Johnson, of Willow Branch, until the last moment of his life. He was in the act of buying a pair of overalls and as Mr. Johnson turned to get a second pair, Mr. Curry fell and gasped about three times for breath and was dead. He died of heart disease and was removed to his home, two and one-half miles west of Willow Branch. He was buried the next day at the Willow Branch graveyard." 99 Reg History states: "William Curry, Sgt., dead in 1900."

Curry, William Riley; 99 Reg Co B, 15 Aug 62-5 Jun 65, as musician, drummer. "born HC, age 21, 5' 11," dark complexion, black eyes, dark hair, farmer when enrolled." William R. Curry was born about 1841, son of Morgan and Sophia (Haney) Curry and brother of Captain Isaiah Curry. William R. married 12 Oct 1862 Sarah Tague HC Bk 4-353. William R. died 24 Dec 1868, age 27y 5m 9d, buried HC Curry's Chapel Cemetery.

Curry, Zachariah; 99 Reg Co B, 23 Mar 64-died 25 Apr 64. NOD.

Custer, Daniel; 4 Ind Inf, no dates; HC Death notice, 28 Jun 1900: "Mr. Daniel Custer, age 72, of Eden, died of cancer of the face. He was born in Virginia, son of Daniel (born Virginia) and Susan (Burger, born Virginia) He was a good citizen and leaves a large circle of relatives. His remains were laid to rest at Eden Church Cemetery."

Hancock County Indiana Civil War Soldiers

Dr. James A. Comstock

Courtesy of Linda Comstock Teel

Hancock County Indiana Civil War Soldiers

William Crane

Courtesy of Irene Shireman

Hancock County Indiana Civil War Soldiers

◄ D ►

Dailey, John; 105 Reg Co E, 11 Jul 63-18 Jul 63. A John Dailey married 25 Sep 1847 Anna Marsh HC Bk 2-257. A John Dailey died 16 Jan 1879, buried HC Park Cemetery

Dangler, Tunis; 79 Reg Co C, 22 Aug 62-18 Oct 62. Married 22 Mar 1860 Mary A. Cass HC Bk 4-184.

Darter, Marion; 139 Reg Co D, 18 May 64-8 Oct 64. "He was born 25 Mar 1845, Fayette County, Indiana, s/o David and Mary (Price) Darter. He participated in the siege and battle of Atlanta where comrades fell all around him; While on a foraging expedition with comrades, they were fired upon by the enemy, a bullet cut the strap of his haversack and it was lost but he made an escape. He was twice married, first to Belle Brown, afterwards marrying Sarah A. Tyner (born 31 Jan 1843) d/o Samuel G. and Mary (Stevens) Tyner.

Theodore Darter, brother of Marion saw service in the 16th Indiana; Mrs. Darter's brother James Tyner was in the 2nd Indiana Cavalry. John Tyner served in same command with Marion Darter." "Marion J. Darter died from a gunshot wound in the right temporal region of the head. His last will and testament leaves as joint tenants, his sister-in-law, Emma Gooding and her daughter, Maude Sanders. The Fortville Bank is named as executor. The will was made 5 April 1922, witnessed by John F. Wiggins and O.H. Cook."

Davidson, David; 12 Reg Co H, 17 Aug 62-died 10 Mar 63 at Grand Junction, Tennessee of typhoid fever. A David Davidson married 13 Jul 1854 Sarah Clouser HC Bk 3-22. See page for his brother, Henry S, Davidson.

Davidson, George M.; 8 Reg Co B, 25 Aug 61-28 Sep 64. See page for his brother, Henry S. Davidson.

Davidson, Henry S.; 11 Reg Co A, 31 Aug 61-2 May 62. "Henry was born 15 Dec 1825, Clermont County, Ohio, s/o John and Fanny (Murphy) Davidson. He was in the battles of Fort Henry, Fort Donelson and Shiloh, at the latter he was detailed as an ambulance driver and assisted in gathering up the

Hancock County Indiana Civil War Soldiers

wounded and burying the dead. He was married 1848 1) Jensie Philpott who died 3 Feb 1850, age 18, and is buried HC Mt Comfort Cemetery; he married 2) Celia Philpott; married Henry County, Indiana, 3) Margaret (Fletcher) Bill 27 Sep 1866. Member of Sol. D. Kempton Post G.A.R., Fortville. Henry's four brothers served: George, Jonas, David and James."

Davidson, James; 9 Reg Co D, 24 Feb 65-2 Jan 66. A James Davidson married 14 Aug 1860 Frances Knox HC Bk 4-202. HC Gilium Chapel Cemetery: A James Davidson of Co C 25 Ind Inf.

Davidson, Jonas; 5 Cav Co G, 20 Aug 62-died 19 Jul 63, "killed at Buffington Bar (near Pomeroy), Ohio, during Confederate General John Morgan's Raid into Indiana and Ohio and buried where he fell." (See page for his brother, Henry Davidson). HC newspaper 15 Jun 1865: "Married on Monday, 12 June 1865, by Rev. G.W. Bowers, Mr. Joseph Wilson from the Province of Upper Canada, to Mrs. Mary Ellen Davidson, of this place, and widow of the late Jonas Davidson, Company G, 5th Indiana Cavalry, who was killed at the Battle of Buffington Bar."

Davis, George W.; HC Gilboa Cemetery, George W. Davis, soldier, died 2 Aug 1869, 33y 8m 3d. NOD. See page for Jacob Davis who had a brother, George W. having served in an Indiana Regiment.

Davis, Jacob; 99 Reg Co B, 13 Aug 62-8 Apr 64. "He was born 1 Mar 1837, in Hancock County, s/o Pleasant and Rebecca (Hendricks) Davis. His Regiment experienced hard marching, exposure to extreme heat and cold, the fatigue of camp life and the horrors of the battlefield. They fought at Big Black River, second battle of Jackson and marched nine days and nights between Lagrange and Holley Springs, Tennessee, on three days rations, and lost fifteen pounds.

"Jacob's brothers, Nimrod, served in the 99 Reg, John S. in the 8 Reg and George W. in an Indiana Reg. and his wife's brother, Henry McCorkhill, served in the 8 Reg. Jacob married 1) 29

Hancock County Indiana Civil War Soldiers

Aug 1861 Nancy McCorkhill HC Bk 4-280, deceased; married 2) 13 Aug 1873 Jennie Caton. ..he was age 25, 5' 8" tall, light complexion, blue eyes, light hair and farmer when enrolled." HC obit 9 Jul 1925: " Jacob H. Davis, age 87, a veteran of the Civil War, died 5 July 1925, at the home of his daughter, Mrs. Charles Brammer. Interment HC Park Cemetery.

Davis, John; 26 Reg Co I, 17 Sep 62-6 Sep 65. "He was born 12 Aug 1841, HC, s/o Robert and Mary (Parrish) Davis. He married 17 Feb 1861 Harriett Bennett HC Bk 4-243. He served for a time on special detail with the Pioneer Corps, a unit attached to the Corps of Engineers that went in advance of the Regiment to build roads and bridge where and when necessary for artillery, supply wagons, and to clear any unusual and/or dangerous obstacles that might detain the regiments going into battle. And for three months was in charge of mail for the Regiment. He was in the fourteen day siege of Fort Spanish and was wounded on the left ankle. His cousins, George and William Cook, Joseph Parrish, David and John Snodgrass all served through out the War. Harriett (Bennett) Davis' cousins, Salem and Henry Ashcraft served in the 99 Reg, Samuel Burke in the 26 Reg and David O. Bennett also served in an Indiana Regiment. John Davis, died 23 Sep 1917 and buried HC Park Cemetery."

Davis, John S.;8 Reg Co B, Musician, 25 Aug 61-4 Sep 64. HC Gilboa Cemetery, John S. Davis data on stone same as above. "John Sylvester Davis, son of Pleasant Davis, was born 25 Nov 1842, widowed, Anna R. Davis, deceased, retired farmer, died 29 Sep 1917, buried (HC) Gilboa Cemetery." HC obit 6 Sep 1917: "John Sylvester Davis, a veteran of the Civil War and known to hundreds of men and children of this city and county, as the peanut man who had his car at the corner of Main and State Streets for a number of years, died quite suddenly but had not been well for many months. He became ill during the night and called a neighbor, Noble Curry, who summoned a physician, however, death claimed him in a few minutes. The body was taken to the home of his son, Emory, in

Hancock County Indiana Civil War Soldiers

Charlottesville." John Sylvester Davis married 1) 29 Jul 1865 Isabelle Morris HC Bk 6-338; married 2) 7 Jan 1875 HC Bk Reason A. Reed HC Bk 6-338. See page for his brother, Jacob H. Davis.

Davis, John W.; 9 Cav Co B, enlistment date unknown, never joined Regiment. NOD.

Davis, John W.; "Patent Office Hospital, Washington, D.C., 22 May 1862, To Captain Commanding Co B 12 Reg Ind Volunteers. Sir, I have to inform you that John W. Davis, Company B, 12th Indiana Regiment Volunteers, died at this hospital, Wednesday, 21 May 1862. The following is a list of his effects: one overcoat, one blanket, one shirt, one rubber blanket, one blouse, one pair pants, one hat, one pair shoes, one portfolio and $41.30 cash. Very Respectfully Yours, J.C. _____, assistant surgeon in charge of the Hospital.

Davis, Joseph; 8 Reg Co B, 25 Aug 61-22 May 64. NOD

Davis, Lewis C.; 9 Reg Co D, 24 Feb 65-2 Jan 66. HC Simmons Cemetery: Davis, L.C. 1 Sep 1816-7 Apr 1888, Nancy w/o L.C. died 28 Aug 1884 63y. A Lewis C. Davis married 17 Sep 1835 Nancy Maggard HC Bk 1-83.

Davis, Madison P. 106 Reg Co D, 10 Jul 63-17 Jul 63. NOD.

Davis, Nimrod; 99 Reg Co B 13 Aug 62-22 Sep 63 to Veteran Reserve Corps. See page for his brother, Jacob Davis

Davis, William; 54 Reg, Musician Co H, 8 Nov 62-no out date. "William Davis was born 25 Sep 1846, Ohio, s/o Jarred Davis (born Pennsylvania). William, occupation, baker, died 12 May 1913, buried HC Park Cemetery, also a Mary J. Davis 1855-1922. HC obit 15 May 1913: "Death came to William Davis, of North Swope Street (Greenfield), this morning after many weeks of illness. Mr. Davis was born in Cincinnati, Ohio, in 1847. He was a soldier of the Civil War, and was drummer boy in Company I, 54th Indiana Regiment, being in the same company as Dr. Morris Hinchman.

"Mr. Davis was at one time a steward on a steamer on the Ohio River, running from Cincinnati to New Orleans. He was united in marriage to Miss Mary Weymer. To this union were

Hancock County Indiana Civil War Soldiers

born four children: Miss Zella Davis; Ross and Clarence of Greenfield; and Leslie Davis of Illinois, all of whom survive. Mr. Davis was connected with the restaurant business in this city for almost five years. He was a member of the Christian Church."

Dawson, Henry L.; 148 Reg Co C, 17 Feb 65-5 Sep 65. A Henry Lee Dawson married 30 Mar 1867 Mary F. Vanlaningham HC Bk 5-137.

Dawson, John; 57 Reg Co A, 17 Oct 61-12 Nov 64. "born HC, age 22, 5' 10' tall, sandy complexion, blue eyes, sandy hair, farmer when enrolled." NOD,

Day, John; 5 Cav Co G, 20 Aug 62, died 1863. The 5th Cavalry saw action in Kentucky and Tennessee during 1862 and 1863 but the roster does not detail John's death. John Day, 1810-1863, married Nancy Dixon and they were the parents of eight daughters, Saphrony; Cassie; Elizabeth; Basha; Cynthis; Lavancha; Virginia and Mary Alice; and one son, Sylvester, served in the 2nd Indiana Cavalry, drowned 29 Nov 63 at Caney's Fork, Virginia. John Day's father was Mark Day who is buried on land that once was Ft. Harrison, Marion County, Indiana. Contributed by Irene Shireman, Greenfield, Indiana.

Day, Sylvester; 2 Cav Co B, 20 Sep 61- 29 Nov 63, drowned Caney's Fork, Virginia. See data on his father, John Day. A letter Sylvester Day wrote 20 Jan 1862, three miles from the Green River in Kentucky, is in the letter chapter of this volume. Contributed by Irene Shireman, Greenfield, Indiana.

Day, Thomas; 8 Reg Co G, 22 Apr 61-6 Aug 61. NOD.

Dearmin, James Monroe; 100 Reg Co K, 21 Aug 62, "wounded slightly in the left hip, 25 Nov 63, at Missionary Ridge during the battle of Chattanooga, Tennessee. On 19 Feb 1864, he was admitted to a general hospital at Madison, Indiana; 31 May (Mar) 1864 he was transferred to Veteran Reserve Corps in New York; began to develop hypertrophy of the heart while on march between Jackson and Vicksbug, Mississippi in Jul 1863 and on 29 Jun 1865 he was mustered out Louisville, Kentucky. When enrolled James received a

Hancock County Indiana Civil War Soldiers

bounty of $25, was age 40, 5' 7 ½ " tall, blue eyes, auburn hair, floria (tinged with red, ruddy) complexion, born Rockingham County, North Carolina, occupation, farmer. He married 26 Jan 1843 Matilda Elizabeth Muth in Hancock County, Indiana, Bk 2-68. James was born abt. 1822; s/o Matthew A. and Susan (Sookey) (Kallam) Dearmin; James died 17 Nov 1895, Shelby County, buried Pleasant View Cemetery, Shelby County, Indiana. Contributed by Dan Judd, Rochester, Minnesota.

DeCamp, Samuel; 75 Reg Co I, 14 Jul 62-8 Jun 65. "Samuel DeCamp was born 24 Oct 1841, Butler County, Ohio, s/o William and Mary (Richardson) DeCamp. 'age 22, 5' 8" tall, light complexion, blue eyes, auburn hair, farmer when enrolled.' The exposure to extreme heat and the hardships of the march and camp life, brought on sickness resulting in typhoid fever. Upon recovery he was in the battles of Murfreesboro, Stone River, Chickamauga, Missionary Ridge, and with Sherman at Resaca, Dalton, Atlanta, Jonesboro, Savannah and others. He was twice married, 1) 1 Sep 1868 Annie Coffman; married 2) 19 Oct 1871 Annie Armfield (8 Apr 1846-9 Dec 1926). Samuel died 7 Mar 1917. Two of his brothers served in the War, Joseph in an Ohio Regiment, William in the 155 Indiana. Annie DeCamp's brother served in the Confederate Army and died of yellow fever. Samuel and Annie buried HC Eden Church Cemetery."

Deck, John E.; 57 Reg Co A, 17 Oct 61-14 Dec 65. HC obit, 14 Dec 1922: "John E. Deck was born 27 Mar 1839, Fayette County, Ohio, s/o John and Nancy Deck. On 26 Feb 1868 (HC Bk 6-205), he was united in marriage to Minerva Tygart of Charlottesville. He was a Civil War veteran, departed this life 1 Dec 1922 and was one of twelve children who had all preceded him in death. Mr. Deck was laid to rest at Glencove Cemetery, Knightstown."

Deel, John W.; HC obit 18 Jun 1925: " John W. Deel, the second son of Hugh and Anna Deel, was born 16 May 1846, Botetourt County, Virginia and departed this life 8 Jun 1925. He was drafted into the Confederate army at the age of sixteen

Hancock County Indiana Civil War Soldiers

years and served under Major General Robert E. Lee until he surrendered. Three years after the close of the War, he came north to Indianapolis in 1868. In 1871 he married Elizabeth Settle who died in 1872. He then married 1 Sep 1875 (HC Bk 6-386) to Missouri Dunn of Mt. Comfort. Mr. Deel was buried in Memorial Cemetery in Indianapolis."

Delbert, Stephen; 26 Reg Co I, 30 Aug 61-7 Jan 64. HC newspaper 29 Sep 1906: " Stephen W. Delbert is attending a reunion of the 26th Indiana Regiment at Indianapolis. It is also the forty-third anniversary of the fight at Bayou Teche, Louisiana, where he received the shot that almost took his life. The shot went into the back of his neck, removing two vertebras and laying open the jugular vein. The track of the bullet is plainly seen as two great holes in the neck." HC obit 19 Nov 1914: "Stephen Delbert died at his home north of Morristown.. It will be remembered he formerly lived in Greenfield where he operated a photograph gallery. He was 70 years old, leaves a widow and step-son. He was an old soldier and highly respected by everyone."

Dennis, James L.; 105 Reg Co E, 11 Jul 63-18 Jul 63. A James L. Dennis married 10 Feb 1876 Mary Hendrickson HC Bk 6-429; A James L. Dennis was born 30 Jul 1824 and died 30 Nov 1886, no place given. NOD.

Dennis, Simeon; 9 Reg Co C, 14 Feb 64-28 Sep 65. A Simeon Dennis married 27 Mar 1856 Sarah Johns HC Bk 3-332. HC Shiloh Cemetery: Simeon Dennis h/o Sara 19 Sep 1834-14 Oct 1891.

Denny, Alphonso; 20 Iowa Inf Co F, 21 Aug 62-13 May 65, disability. "born HC, age 20, 5' 7" tall, light complexion, blue eyes, brown hair, carpenter when enrolled." An Alphonso Denny married 21 Jun 1868 Elizabeth Stager HC Bk 2-225.

Denny, Enos; 79 Reg Co C, 15 Aug 64-7 Jun 65. NOD.

Denny, George; 12 Reg Co G, 3 Aug 62-8 Jun 65. "born HC, age 16, 5' 7" tall, light complexion, dark eyes, dark hair, farmer when enrolled." He was born 24 Jun 1844, married 19 Oct 1865 Tabitha Jackson HC Bk 4-551.

Hancock County Indiana Civil War Soldiers

George died age 65y 0m 28d, (s/o Wyatt and Lydia (Moore) Denny), and is buried HC Mt Gilead/Reeves Cemetery.

Denny, Phillip; 147 Reg Co H, 14 Feb 65-4 Aug 65. NOD.

Denny, William P.; 2 Cav Co B, 20 Sep 61-15 Feb 64; also recorded as member of Company A, 11th Regiment of Zouaves in obit of Samuel Hook. HC obit 12 Mar 1925: "William P. Denny, one of the well-known and highly respected veterans of the Civil War, son of Wyatt and Lydia (Moore) Denny, died at the home of his son, Ransom R. Denny, 618 North Swope Street. Mr. Denny was born 11 Jun 1840 in Vernon Township, this County, married 14 Oct 1864 HC Bk 4-480 Angeline Martin (21 Feb 1841-25 Apr 1912), d/o Thomas Martin. William P. and Martha A. Denny are buried HC Park Cemetery."

Deppery, Charles; 8 Reg Co B, 25 Aug 61-28 Aug 65. NOD.

Derry, Alexander; 8 Reg Co B, 25 Aug 61-4 Sep 64. HC obit 31 Jan 1924: " Alexander Derry, a Civil War soldier, was born 18 Feb 1840, Hancock County and died at his home in Greenfield 21 Jan 1924. Mr. Denny married 1) 27 Sep 1865 Roberta Trees HC Bk 4-540; married 2) 16 Sep 1883 Amanda Beeson (1857-1921) HC Bk 7-476. Alexander and Amanda buried HC Park Cemetery."

Derry, James; 8 Reg Co B, 20 Aug 61-13 Aug 62, discharged by reason of injury to right ankle. "born HC, age 20, 5' 8" tall, fair complexion, hazel eyes, fair hair, farmer when enrolled." A James Derry married 4 Oct 1862 Nancy Kingen HC Bk 4-351.

Deshong, Amos; 79 Reg Co D, 12 Aug 62-7 Jun 65. An Amos Deshong married 5 Dec 1866 Phoebe Roney HC Bk 5-103.

Despo, Odell; 105 Reg Co E, 11 Jul 63-18 Jul 63; 9 Cav Co B, 23 Dec 63-28 Aug 65. NOD.

Dexter, S. Newton; 12 Reg Co B, 15 May 61-19 May 65. NOD.

Dickerson, Stephen; 105 Reg Co E, 11 Jul 63-18 Jul 63. died Jan 1893 Medicine Lodge, Kansas.

Hancock County Indiana Civil War Soldiers

Dickerson, James; HC newspaper article 15 May 1913: "James Dickerson, of Eldorado, Missouri, is visiting relatives in this city. He taught school in this community more than fifty years ago, and was a soldier in the Civil War, serving four years. It has almost been forty years since Mr. Dickerson left Greenfield. He is an uncle of Mrs. William Davis, of Lincoln Street, and a brother of Mrs. Amos Gambrel of this city. Mr. Dickerson was on the streets today receiving the glad welcome of his old comrades and Greenfield friends."

Dickey, Thomas; 132 Reg Co I, 18 May 64-no out date. NOD.

Dille, George J.; 147 Reg Co H, 14 Feb 65-4 Aug 65. NOD.

Dillman, James F.; 79 Reg Co D, 18 Aug 62-died 30 Nov 63 at Battle of Lookout Mountain, Tennessee. James F. Dillman was born Ohio, s/o Daniel and Margaret Dillman, married 19 Aug 1855 Mary Wright HC Bk 3-299.

Dillman, Oliver; 9 Reg Co E, 24 Feb 65 died of disease at Knoxville, Tennessee, no date given. NOD.

Dillman, Samuel H.; 8 Reg Co B, 25 Aug 61-no out date. HC newspaper 5 Feb 1862: " Samuel H. Dillman has been discharged on account of physical disability induced by the inclemencies (sic) of camp life." A Samuel Dillman married 18 Sep 1862 Lucy Wright HC Bk 4-349.

Dinkle, Jacob; 8 Reg Co B, 25 Aug 61-deserted, 6 Aug 64; returned 15 Sep 64, discharged 6 Aug 65. Jacob Dinkle married 4 Jan 63 Christina Knoop HC Bk 4-369. Both buried HC New Palestine Cemetery: Jacob 10 Jul 1831-11 Jun 1904, Christina 28 Nov 1844-22 Feb 1877.

Dinkle, Thomas; 8 Reg Co B, 25 Aug 61-28 Aug 65. NOD.

Dipper, Charles; 8 Reg Co G, 22 Apr 61-6 Aug 61. NOD.

Dixon, George W.; 8 Reg Co B, 25 Aug 61-28 Aug 65. A George W. Dixon married 5 Sep 64 Minerva Hawkins HC Bk 4-472; and married 26 Dec 1869 Nancy Nixon HC Bk 5-346.

Dixon, Milo; 148 Reg Co C, 17 Feb 65-5 Sep 65. NOD

Dobbins, Albert; 12 Reg Co G, 3 Aug 62-22 Jun 65. "..born HC, age 19, 5' 11' tall, light complexion, dark hair, dark eyes, farmer when enrolled. NOD.

Hancock County Indiana Civil War Soldiers

Dobbins, Jesse D.; 8 Reg Co G, 22 Apr 61-6 Aug 62. NOD.

Dobbins, John; 8 Reg Co B, no dates. HC newspaper 19 Nov 1863: "John Dobbins, son of Daniel, the great pump maker, has volunteered in Capt. Wall's Cavalry Company. Pump makers are dangerous men in the army, for they will be continually devising ways and means "to suck the rebels in"—Bully for John! He'll make a brave soldier boy, fighting for the Union and the Constitution." NOD.

Dobbins, Martin; HC McCordsville Cemetery, Martin Dobbins, soldier, no dates; Rebecca w/o Martin died 8 Jun 1893 72y 6m 13d. NOD.

Domanget, Perry; 70 Reg Co A, 19 Jul 62-killed 15 May 64, Resaca, Georgia. HC Philadelphia Cemetery: Perry A. Domanget 1842-1864 Co A 70 Ind Vol Inf. NOD.

Dorman, James; 51 Reg Co D, 14 Dec 61-14 Dec 64. NOD.

Dorman, John; 8 Reg Co B, 25 Aug 61-24 Sep 62, discharged disability; also 106 Reg Co D, 10 Jul 63-17 Jul 63. HC newspaper: 14 Aug 1862: "John Dorman left in a hospital boat a few days ago." A John Dorman married 6 Nov 1862 Martha James HC Bk 4-359; a Martha James died 27 Jun 1867, 32y 6m 15d, and buried HC Park Cemetery. A John Dorman married 25 Aug 1867 Nancy Lake HC Bk 5-158.

Doty, John; 132 Reg Co I, 18 May 64-7 Sep 64. John Doty married 8 Aug 1888 Nancy Elizabeth Hiday HC Bk 8-76. John is the brother of Thomas Doty, see page for Thomas.

Doty, Thomas J.; 2 Cav Co B, 13 Sep 61-4 Oct 64. "Thomas J. Doty was born 25 August 1838, Madison County, Indiana, son of John and Jane (Parsels) Doty. He was captured by Morgan's command at the battle of Hartsville, Kentucky, 28 Nov 1862, held prisoner for three days when he was exchanged. At the battle of Gallatin, Kentucky, his command was captured but he made his escape by out riding his pursuers. He also was in the battles of Chickamaugua and Missionary Ridge, Tennessee, plus numerous skirmishes. On 1 Feb 1864 he was stricken with chronic diarrhea and sent to the hospital at Knoxville, Tennessee, where he received a furlough to go home. The

Hancock County Indiana Civil War Soldiers

disease clung to him and he was discharged at Indianapolis. His brother, John Doty, served in 132 Reg, Co I., and his wifes' brother, Benjamin F. Davis saw service in the 8th Ind. Cav. Thomas married Sarah A. Davis 28 Feb 1878 Madison County, Indiana, d/o Baily and Charity (Pritchard) Davis. Thomas 25 Aug 1838-11 Apr 1924, and Sarah 23 Jan 1847-2 Sep 1918, are buried at Madison County, Indiana, Gravel Lawn Cemetery."

Dougherty, William; 5 Cav Co G, 20 Aug 62-15 Sep 65. HC Harlan Cemetery: a W.H. Dougherty died 8 Dec 1892 45y 3m 18d. NOD

Dove, David; 8 Reg Co B, 25 Aug 61-no out date. HC newspaper 25 Sep 1861:"David Dove is sick but one of the first in the ranks." NOD.

Dove, William; 8 Reg Co B, 25 Aug 61- 28 Aug 65. NOD.

Dowling, James; 12 Reg Co B, 4 Jul 61-19 May 62. NOD.

Downing, Thomas E.; 36 Ohio Inf Co B, no dates. "Thomas E. Downing, age 37, born Brown County, Ohio, s/o James and Indiana (Wiley) Downing, died 19 May 1886, of Bright's disease, buried HC Philadelphia Cemetery."

Drake, John; 134 Reg Co K, 24 May 64-term expired. John Drake married 3 Sep 1874 Eliza A. Dye HC Bk 6-298. HC newspaper 12 Jul 1894: "Eliza A. Drake, age 37, died from pistol wounds inflicted by her husband, John Drake, before he turned the gun on himself. Two sons, aged twelve and sixteen survive. Mr. Drake was a former resident of Greenfield, and is a nephew of Mrs. Charles Wiggins. Mrs. Drake is a step-daughter of Mrs. William Porter, of near Phildelphia (Indiana). Graveside funeral at Philadelphia Cemetery."

Dubois, Charles M.; 53 Reg Co A, 7 Oct 64 as substitute-27 Jul 65. NOD.

Dubois, John W.; 53 Reg Co A, 10 Oct 64 as substitute-21 Jul 65. NOD.

Dugan, George W.; 134 Reg Co K, 24 May 64-term expired. NOD.

Hancock County Indiana Civil War Soldiers

Dunbar, Jonathan; residence/place of enlistment, Greenfield, at age 51 years, he was commissioned as 1st Lieut. 51 Reg Co K, 22 Feb 62, resigned 20 Mar 63. 1850 Federal Census Hancock County, Indiana records Jonathan Dunbar, age 39, merchant, born Pennsylvania; Mary R., age 36, born Kentucky; Samuel, age 13, born Indiana; John, age 11, born Indiana; Hamilton, age 4, born Indiana. Jonathan was a tailor and in early Greenfield had a shop in the same building as Jeremiah Meek's tavern. In this Dunbar family, the father and two of his sons, Samuel and John G., served in the Civil War.

HC newspaper, 10 Nov 1870: "Jonathan Dunbar, an old citizen of this place (Greenfield), died today of carbuncles on the back of his neck and base of the brain." HC newspaper 17 Nov 1870: The funeral of Jonathan Dunbar, whose death was announced in our paper last week, took place on Sunday last. The funeral services were eloquently and impressively conducted by Rev. H.J. Lacey, at the house of the deceased and at the grave." The Greenfield GAR Post was named for Samuel Dunbar, s/o Jonathan.

Dunbar, John G.; 79 Reg Co B, residence/place of enlistment, Greenfield, enlisted 9 Aug 62, as 1st Liuet.; promoted to Captain, 29 Jan 63; promoted to Major, 25 Aug 64; transferred from Company B to Field and Staff, 13 Nov 64; mustered out 7 Jun 65. John G. Dunbar, s/o Jonathan and Mary Dunbar, married Julia Hammond, 1 Dec 1863, no place given. HC newspaper, 28 Aug 1862: "A handsome sword and sash were presented to Lieut. John G. Dunbar, of the 79th Regiment, one day last week. by his friends in Greenfield. The presentation speech was made by Judge Gooding. The reply of Lieut. D. was eloquent and stirring."

HC newspaper 23 Feb 1865: "We are sorry to learn that Maj. John G. Dunbar, 79th Indiana Infantry, was seriously injured by a fall at Nashville a few days since. His lower jaw-bone was broken." HC newspaper 2 Mar 1865: "We are happy to note the safe arrival of Major John G. Dunbar, 79th Indiana Infantry. He was much more seriously injured than we supposed; but is

Hancock County Indiana Civil War Soldiers

recovering slowly. The Major is a most excellent officer, and though glad to see him at home, we are sorry that his regiment is deprived of the presence of so good a commander. His stay will be determined by his recovery." See page for his father, Jonathan, and brother, Samuel.

Dunbar, Samuel; residence/place of enlistment, Greenfield, enlisted 19 Aug 61 as 2n^d Lieut., commissioned into Co B 8 Reg 25 Aug 61; promoted 1st Lieut. 30 Dec 61; promoted Captain, 18 Jan 63; died of disease 9 Jul 64. HC newspaper, 28 July 1864: "Death of Capt. S.H. Dunbar. A deep shade of gloom was thrown over our citizens by the announcement of the death of our friend and fellow-townsman, Capt. S.H. Dunbar, of Company B, 8th Regiment Veteran Volunteers, who departed this life at Terre Bonne, Louisiana, a small village on the New Orleans and Brashear Railroad, and about 55 miles west of New Orleans.

"He had not been in good health for many months past and on the morning of the 8th inst. was taken with a congestive chill, from the effects of which he died at 1 o'clock on the following morning. The regiment being under marching orders for the Army of the Potomac, time could not be had for the preparation necessary to send his remains, so he was buried, as became an officer of the army at Terre Bonne. It was a sad day for the brave boys of company B, to thus part with their best friend and officer, and one, too, that stood the highest among the gallant officers of that regiment, in every quality that made him the officer and the gentleman.

"Capt. Dunbar entered the service of his country from a high sense of duty and was placed by his company as 2nd Lieutenant. By the resignation of his superiors, Capt. Walls and Lieut. Kauble, he was placed in command of the company, which position he filled to the day of his death, with satisfaction to officers and men. He shared all the fortunes and misfortunes of his regiment, having traveled about 10,000 miles and over 3,000 on foot. Capt. Dunbar was a graduate of Greencastle College and had commenced the study of law which he

Hancock County Indiana Civil War Soldiers

abandoned in the breaking out of the rebellion. His remains will be brought home at the earliest practical day." HC newspaper 24 Nov 1864: "The remains of Capt. Samuel H. Dunbar reached this place (Greenfield) on Friday last, and were interred with Masonic honors on Sunday following. Prof. John W. Lock, of Asbury University, Greencastle, delivered an eloquent and appropriate address and eulogium on the occasion. A very large number of our citizens, from town and country, participated in paying the last sad tribute to the departed soldier and citizen. many an eye glistened with the tear of manly sorrow, as the clouds of the valley closed over the form of him, who in life, was the center of a cluster of warm and devoted friends."

HC Park Cemetery: Samuel H. Dunbar s/o J. and M.R., died 9 Jul 1864, 24y 3m 20d; Was Capt. in Co B 8 Ind Vol, enlisted in 1861 and was in constant service until his death which occurred in camp at Terre Bonne, Louisiana; other side of this stone records: sons and daughters of J. and M.R. Dunbar, Thomas J. died 20 May 1839, 6y 5m 12d; Francis A. died 26 Sep 1836, 1y 3m 3d; Ruth died 1 Jun 1845, 2y 1m 12d. These young children were all buried at Greenfield's Old Cemetery, and were reinterred in the New (Park Cemetery when it was established in April 1865. The Greenfield GAR Post was named for Samuel Dunbar, a gallant officer.

Duncan, Dr. Benjamin F.; HC newspaper 8 Jan 1863: "Drs. Howard and Duncan, of Greenfield, are the among the Physicians dispatched by Gov. Morton to look after wounded at Murfessboro (Tennessee). Dr. Duncan is recorded as one of the first doctors in Greenfield. The Old Greenfield Cemetery: Dr. Benjamin Duncan 1812-1865, Susan, his wife 1815-1869.

Duncan, Elberlee; 8 Reg Co G, 22 Apr 61-6 Aug 61 discharged disability. NOD.

Duncan, Ephraim; 105 Reg Co D 11 Jul 63-18 Jul 63; also 9 Cav Co B 23 Jul 63-28 Aug 65. "Ephraim Duncan was born 24 Feb 1846, HC, s/o Robert and Serena (Powell) Duncan. He took part in the battles of Mission Gap, McMinnville

Hancock County Indiana Civil War Soldiers

(Tennessee), Hollow Tree Gap, Spring Hill and numerous others. In the summer of 1864, He was sick and confined to the hospital at Pulaski, Tennessee, then at Vicksburg before returning to his comrades at Port Gibson, Mississippi. He married Arminda Gorman, 12 Oct 1870, a native of Clinton County, Ohio. HC obit 8 Jun 1911: Ephraim C. Duncan, aged 65, died 5 Jun 1911 at his home in Greenfield after an illness of kidney trouble. Mr. Duncan was a Civil War veteran of the Ninth Cavalry, of which George Parker and John Manche were also members. He leaves a widow and four children. Burial HC Park Cemetery."

Duncan, George W.; 5 Cav Co G, 5 Jan 64-1May 65. HC Democrat newspaper obit: 6 Feb 1913.:"George W. Duncan, 69 years, died (4 Feb 1913) at his home on West North Street (Greenfield) from a complication of diseases. Two years ago he fractured his ankle, injured it again and then fell from a ladder while picking cherries which laid him up again and he never fully recovered. He was born 23 Jan 1844, HC, s/o Washington and Lucinda Duncan.

"He enlisted in the Fifth Cavalry and on 31 Jul 1864, was 'taken prisoner in the disastrous expedition of General Stoneman' and placed in Andersonville Prison (Georgia), later he was transferred to a stockade at Savannah, Georgia. Making an escape some months later, he rejoined his Regiment, and at the close of the War was given an honorable discharge.

He attended Adrian (Michigan) College, taking the theological course but did not take a charge. He commenced the study of law with the firm of Dunbar and New and made this his profession. In 1876 he married Emma Pennington of Adrian, Michigan. He was elected prosecuting attorney Hancock and Henry Counties; and in 1894 was elected Mayor of Greenfield, serving two terms. Burial HC Park Cemetery."

HC Republican newspaper obit, 6 Feb 1913: Much the same data as above with the following additions: "He was elected Mayor of Greenfield in 1894, over A.J. Herron, the Democratic candidate, to succeed himself, and served until 1898. At the

Hancock County Indiana Civil War Soldiers

close of his official term, he resumed the practice of law, which he continued until his appointment as Postmaster in 1910, that would not have expired until July 1914. He saw with General Sherman on his march to the sea. In general hard service during his army career in the Civil War, was in Stoneman's raid 31 July 1864, and taken prisoner, together with Jefferson Willett; Marshall Meek; Morris Meek, James Hudson; Henry Gant; Frank Brizendine and John Samuels, all of this county and members of Company G, 5th Indiana Cavalry. He made his escape from the stockade at Savannah, Georgia, after eleven months, while a transfer of prisoners was being made. He is survived by, one son, William Clare, Greenfield; two brothers, James M. Duncan, Mohawk; and M.T. Duncan, Greenfield; two sisters, Mrs. William Piles and Mrs. Hudson Smith."

Duncan, Henry C.; 51 Reg Co D, 14 Dec 61-died 8 Jun 62, at Greenfield. A Henry Clay Duncan married 7 Jan 1858 Sarah Linder HC Bk 4-59. HC Mt. Lebanon Cemetery: Henry C. Duncan died 8 Jun 1862 28y 4m 25d.

Duncan, James N.; "Henry and Clarissa Duncan came to HC about 1834 and were the parents of seven children, the oldest was James N., a soldier in the fifth Illinois Cavalry during the late Rebellion, who entered the service in August, 1861, and died Mar 63, at Helena, Arkansas" NOD.

Duncan, John H.; 8 Reg Co G, 2 Sep 62 as 2nd Lt.-dropped as supernumerary. HC obit 26 May 1921: "John Hayes Duncan, age 82 years and a Civil War veteran passed away at his home 535 North State Street (Greenfield) following an illness of several months. Mr Duncan is survived by the widow, four sons, Charles, Frank, Arch and Hayes; two daughters, Mrs. Luther Newhouse and Mrs. George Wiggins all of this city. His four sons and two sons-in-law were the pallbearers. Interment HC Park Cemetery,"

Duncan, John L.; 51 Reg Co K, 13 Dec 61-died 3 Jan 62 at Bardstown, Kentucky. A John Duncan married 13 Dec 1860 Maria Jane Pope HC Bk 4-228.

Hancock County Indiana Civil War Soldiers

Duncan, Samuel E.; 105 Reg Co E, 11 Jul 63-18 Jul 63. "Samuel Duncan was born 6 June 1837, Indiana, s/o Joshua and Nancy (Smith) Duncan, both born Virginia. Samuel married 9 Sep 1875 Amanda Lace HC Bk 6-387. Samuel died 31 Jul 1907, 70y 1m 25d, buried HC Mt. Lebanon Cemetery.

Dunham, George; 12 Reg Co G, no dates. "George Dunham was born in Hancock County, 25 Nov 1842, s/o Franklin and Dorcas (Ellingwood) Dunham. George was in the battles of Richmond, Kentucky, Missionary Ridge, Dallas, Resaca, New Hope Church (where he received a gunshot wound in the chin), Kennesaw Mountain, Atlanta and Savannah. George married 10 Dec 1868 Virginia Cook, d/o of Daniel and Elizabeth (Walker) Cook and was prosecuting attorney when he died at Lapel, Indiana, 23 Jan 1899. His brother, James, served in the same Company and Regiment, was captured and held in a Confederate prison."

Dunham, Jesse; HC Courthouse Soldier Burial List Book: no unit given; died 18 Feb 1905; 75 years; lived at Lafayette Soldiers' Home; burial Mt. Zion, no location given. NOD.

Dunham, James; 12 Reg Co G, 7 Mar 64 transferred to 48 Reg-out 17 Jul 65. A James Dunham died 7 Jun 1888 42y 11m 29d and is buried at HC Gillium Cemetery. See page for George Dunham.

Dunlap, Robert M; 148 Reg Co I, 18 Feb 65-11 May 65. NOD.

Dunn, Andrew; 9 Cav Co B, 2 Jan 64- died 18 Sep 64, Pulaski, Tennessee. NOD.

Dunn, Martin; 8 Reg Co G, 22 Apr 61-6 Aug 61; also 2 Cav Co D, 22 Oct 62-22 Jul 65. "..born Shelby County, Ohio, age 17, 6' tall, light complexion, blue eyes, black hair, farmer when enrolled." Martin Dunn married HC Bk 5-116, 9 Feb 1877 Sophia Drischel (20 Feb 1843-24 Sep 1905). Both buried HC Sugar Creek Cemetery.

Dunn, Michael; 79 Reg Co D, 25 Aug 62-died 30 Nov 62 at home. HC Dunn Cemetery: Michael Dunn died 29 Nov 1862. NOD.

Hancock County Indiana Civil War Soldiers

Dye, Frederick; 8 Reg Co G, 22 Apr 61-6 Aug 61. A Frederick Dye married 12 Jun 1862 Harriett Tice HC Bk 4-334.

Dye, John E.; 8 Cav Co G, 22 Apr 61-6 Aug 61; also 5 Cav Co G, 20 Aug 62-1 Jul 63. HC obit 15 Jun 1916: " John E. Dye, 71 years, died at his home west of Philadelphia (Indiana) of cancer of the stomach. (He married 23 Aug 64 S. Henrietta Vanlaningham HC Bk 4-458.) He was born 21 Jun 1845, Indiana, s/o John and Mary Ann (Carson) Dye and was known for many years as Doc while he was engaged in the drug business at Philadelphia. He was state champion of trap shooting and won a diamond-studded badge. He leaves a widow and five children. Burial HC Philadelphia Cemetery: John E. Dye 1845-1916, h/o S. Henrietta."

Dye, Samuel; 8 Reg Co G 22 Apr 61. HC newspaper 22 May 61: "At Camp Morton, near Indianapolis, on 19 May 1861, Samuel Dye of this County, died of lung fever. He was a private in Capt. Riley's company of the 8th Regiment, aged about 30 years. The remains were brought to his late residence by Lieut. Walls and a squad of four men. He died in the cause of his country, and sleeps in an honorable grave. Peace to his remains."

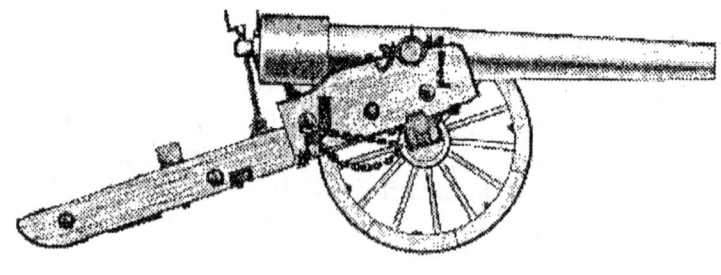

Hancock County Indiana Civil War Soldiers

John Day

Courtesy of Irene Shireman

Hancock County Indiana Civil War Soldiers

Sylvester Day

Courtesy of Irene Shireman

Hancock County Indiana Civil War Soldiers

◄ E ►

Eakes, Andrew J. 79 Reg Co C, 15 Aug 62-died 25 Jan 63, Nashville, Tennessee, from wounds received at Battle of Stone River 30 Dec 1862; buried Nashville National Cemetery, grave #766. He served in the war with his brother, Joseph Robert Eakes, and his brother-in-law, Andrew Jarrett. Volunteer Descriptive List records the following: Andrew J. Eakes; private; age 21; gray eyes; dark hair; dark complexion; 5' 6" tall; Hancock County, Indiana; occupation, farmer when enrolled 15 Aug 62 at Fortville; mustered 27 Aug 62 at Indianapolis; bounty paid $25; bounty due $75; remarks, died 25 Jan 1863 at Nashville, Tennessee, from effects of a wound received at the Battle of Stone River, 30 Dec 1862, copied from company record books, Chattanooga, Tennessee, 13 Nov 1863 The original of this document is in the possession of Jack Rapp, a descendant, Fortville, Indiana. Andrew James Eakes was born 7 Apr 1841, s/o Levi Eakes (1814-1849) and Martha Roberds (1803-1882). Andrew Eakes married 23 Oct 1856 Mariam (Mary) Jane Jarrett HC Bk 3-366. Contributed by Charles Murdoch, Jr., Prescott, Arizona.

Eakes, Joseph R. 79 Reg Co C, 15 Aug 62-8 Apr 65. "..born Hancock County, Indiana, age 23, 5' 9", light complexion, blue eyes, and light hair, a farmer when enrolled; surgeon's certificate of disability states: physically unfit to enter or reenlist in V.R.C. In April of 1865, the Office of Military Commander, Indianapolis, Indiana, the following remarks were made by his Captain: Joseph R. Eakes was wounded at Missionary Ridge, Tennessee, on 25 October. He was a good soldier and in a very healthy condition when wounded."

The son of Levi and Martha (Robberds, Roberds, Roberts), Joseph was born 31 Jan 1839, five miles south of Fortville and died 18 Mar 1923. The maiden name of Joseph Eakes' mother, Martha, is recorded as, Robberds, Roberds and Roberts. Joseph R. Eakes fathered 18 children with three wives; the first two died as a result of childbirth; wife 1) 1 Sep 1859 Amanda

Hancock County Indiana Civil War Soldiers

Brock HC Bk 4-148; Amanda H. Eakes w/o J.R. died 17 Nov 1869, 27y 9m 4d, buried HC Mt Carmel Cemetery, also buried there is Mittie Eakes, d/o J.R. and A.H., died 2 Oct 1880, 13y 1m 12d.

Joseph married 2) 22 Dec 1870 Mary E. Bristow HC Bk 5-434;Mary E. Eakes w/o J.R. died 4 Feb 1884, 31y 5m 24d, buried HC Mt. Carmel Cemetery, also buried there is Myrtle Eakes, d/o J.R. and M.E. died 9 Mar 1895, 14y 4m 0d. Joseph married 3) 17 Jul 1884 Elizabeth Aletha Banks HC Bk 7-539.

HC obit 22 Mar 1923: "Joseph R. Eakes, age 84 years, an old resident of Fortville and father of William Eakes of Greenfield, passed away at his home in Fortville. A few years ago he disposed of his farm near Greenfield and went to Fortville. Mr. Eakes was a soldier in the Civil War and is survived by the widow and a large family of children" Joseph and Elizabeth Eakes are buried Madison County, Indiana, Cemetery, Gravel Lawn: Joseph R. 1839-1923; Elizabeth A. 1862-1935. Research by Pamela Forth Lynch, Sharon Kingen, Barbara Pence, Eldon Apple and Charles Murdoch, Jr.; contributed by Charles Murdoch, Jr., Prescott, Arizona.

Earl, Isaac; 57 Reg Co A, 13 Dec 61-promoted to 1st. Lt. 19 Mar 65. An Isaac Earl married 19 Nov 1871 Harriett Griffith HC Bk 6-64.

Earl, John J.; 11 Reg Co I, 28 Feb 65-26 Jul 65. NOD.

Eastes, F.M.; 79 Reg Co D, 8 Aug 62-7 Jun 65. A Freemont Eastes married 4 May 1884 Rosa Russell HC Bk 7-528.

Eastes, James A.; 79 Reg Co D, 8 Aug 62-25 Mar 63. "James M. Eastes was born 24 April 1839, Indiana, s/o John N. and Charlotte (Woods) Eastes; James was a farmer, died 11 Mar 1913, 73y 10m 17d, widow, Julia." HC Mt. Comfort Cemetery: James A. Eastes 24 Apr 1839-11 Mar 1913 GAR, Julia A. Eastes 22 Oct 1839-13 Oct 1930.

Eaton, Bluford; 106 Reg Co D 10 Jul 63-17 Jul 63. NOD.

Eaton, Charles W.; 106 Reg Co D, 10 Jul 63-17 Jul 63. NOD.

Eaton, Henry; 79 Reg Co C, 13 Aug 62-22 Dec 62 transferred to U.S.Army 18th Infantry. "Henry H. Eaton , born Indiana, died 16 Feb 1896, at age 56, of an injury causing blood poison, causing septic fever for 19 days duration." HC New Palestine Cemetery: Henry Eaton 1840-1896.

Eaton, John W.; 106 Reg Co D, 10 Jul 63-17 Jul 63. NOD.

Eaton, Leland; 106 Reg Co D, 10 Jul 63-17 Jul 63. NOD.

Eaton, Lewis; 106 Reg Co D, 10 Jul 63-17 Jul 63. NOD.

Eaton, Thomas; 106 Reg Co D, 10 Jul 63-17 Jul 63. NOD.

Eaton, William T.; 106 Reg Co D, 10 Jul 63-17 Jul 63. "William T. Eaton, born 16 Nov 1842, Kentucky, s/o B. and Nancy (Phipps) Eaton. A William T. Eaton married 3 Mar 1878 Mary C. Kirkoff HC Bk 6-583. William T. Eaton died 29 Jun 1903 and is buried HC New Palestine Cemetery."

Edmunds, Henry; 132 Reg Co I, 18 May 64-time expired. NOD.

Edwards, Henry; 12 Reg Co G, 14 Jul 62-28 Sep 63, discharged disability. NOD.

Edwards, John; 8 Reg Co G, 22 Apr 61-6 Aug 61, Sgt. HC Mt. Gilead Cemetery: A Jonathan Edwards died 2 Nov 1875, 50y. Only one other Edwards buried Mt. Gilead: Kiziah, died 8 Mar 1896 68y 7m 2d.

Edwards, John S.; recorded as Major, 2 Cav. NOD.

Edwards. Joshua; 105 Reg Co E, 11 Jul 63-18 Jul 63, Sgt. A Joshua Edwards married 6 Sep 1861 Margaret Ann Noland, no location given.

Edwards, Theodore; 53 Reg Co A, 14 Feb 62-21 Jul 65. NOD.

Egger, John; 5 Cav Co G, 18 Aug 62-25 Nov 62; also 105 Reg Co E 11 Jul 63-18 Jul 63. A John Egger married 24 Mar 1857 Julia Bultel (sic) HC Bk 6-13/213.

Eikman, Henry William; 79 Reg Co D; 16 Aug 62-7 Jun 65, Corp'l. A Henry W. Eikman married 23 Nov 1866 Martha Koentler HC Bk 5-100. HC obit 19 Mar 1931: "Another one of the community's oldest citizens and Civil War veterans, Henry William Eikman, passed away at the home of his daughter, Mrs. John Harting, Indianapolis. Mr. Eikman had lived hie entire life in Sugar Creek Township, northwest of New Palestine. Interment HC Lutheran Cemetery: Eikman, Henry

Hancock County Indiana Civil War Soldiers

13 Jan 1841-15 Mar 1931, Mathilde, w/o H.W. 5 Dec 1848-24 Feb 1895."

Ellingwood, Cyrus; 39 Reg Co I, Aug 61-22 Jun 65. "Cyrus was born 6 Jan 1846, Hancock County, s/o Caleb and Mary (Lewis) Ellingwood. He took part in the battles of Shiloh, Stone River, Chickamauga, Buzzard Roost, Missionary Ridge, Atlanta, Savannah and numerous other engagements. In February of 1863, he was injured on the head by a falling part of a bridge; 16 Mar 65 he received a gunshot wound in the left thigh. At the battle of Stone River, he was captured and with 400 others sent to Libby Prison, then to Castle Thunder, held there three weeks, then paroled. He married 9 Aug 1868, Lou Girard in Marion County.. He settled in Marion County in 1888 and receives his mail at Castleton."

Ellingwood, William H.; 12 Reg Co G, 24 Feb 64-tranferred to 48 Reg, no date. NOD.

Elliott, Benjamin; 8 Reg Co G, 22 Apr 61-6 Aug 61; enlisted 38 Reg Co D, discharged 3 Jul 65. Took part in Chickamauga and Nashville battles. "Benjamin was born 14 Aug 1839, Pike County, Ohio, s/o James and Nancy (Townsend) Elliott. Benjamin married 4 Mar 1866 Ann Welling HC Bk 5-38, she was the d/o Hamilton and Rachel Welling. HC obit 17 Mar 1912: "Benjamin Elliott, 72 years, died of pneumonia at the home of his son, Ernest Elliott. For years he was one of the well-known Christian men of Sugar Creek Township. Interment HC Philadelphia Cemetery: Elliott, Benjamin 14 Aug 1839-3 Mar 1912, Ann Elizabeth 25 Dec 1842-11 Apr 1904." Also a Benjamin Elliott married 1 Jan 1863 Elizabeth Adams HC Bk 4-371 and Elizabeth Elliott w/o Benjamin died 23 Mar 1863 buried HC Griffith Cemetery.

Elliott, James M.; 79 Reg Co B, 9 Aug 62, 7 Sep 63 transferred to V.R.C. out 27 Jun 65. Fought in battles of Perryville, Kentucky and Stone River, Tennessee. James was born 27 Oct 1840, Hancock County, s/o James and Nancy (Townsend) Elliott. HC Philadelphia Cemetery: Susan E. w/o James M. 17

Hancock County Indiana Civil War Soldiers

Feb 1849-2 Dec 1875; and Elizabeth J. w/o James M. 1849-1929. No HC marriages.

Elliott, John; 106 Reg Co D, 10 Jul 63-17 Jul 63. NOD.

Elliott, William; 18 Reg as Musician, 16 Aug 61-20 Aug 62. NOD.

Ellis, John W.; 8 Reg Co H, 5 Sep 61-28 Aug 65. NOD.

Ellis, Orlando; 8 Reg Co G, 22 Apr 61-6 Aug 61. NOD.

Elmore, James; 9 Cav Co B, 9 Dec 63-2 Jun 65. HC death notice, 20 Jun 1907,: "James Elmore, age 61 years, died at his home near Willow Branch, Jun 14, service at the home, interment HC Hays Cemetery."

Elsbury, Frederick; 8 Reg Co B, 21 Aug 61-died 20 Dec 61. St. Louis, Missouri. HC newspaper, 25 Dec 1861: "Frederick Elsbury, a member of Capt. Walss company, died recently at St. Louis. He was the son of Richard Elsbury. His remains will likely be brought home."

Ely, James M.; 106 Reg Co D, 10 Jul 63-17 Jul 63. "James M. Ely was born 18 Sep 1821, Tennessee; married 17 Jun 1847 (no location given) Mary Adams. A physician, he died 13 Dec 1905, 84y 2m 25d . HC New Palestine Cemetery: J.M. Ely MD 18 Sep 1821-13 Dec 1905, Mary Adams Ely 26 Nov 1823-26 Oct 1897."

Endicott, Thomas H.; 12 Reg Co B, 15 May 61-19 May 62. NOD.

England, Henry A.; served in an Indiana Regiment, no unit numbers. HC Burris/Hendricks Cemetery: Henry A. England died 23 Jan 1865 27y 9m 18d, Jeffersonville, Indiana. A Henry A. England married 15 May 1862 Nancy Burris.

England, John; 106 Reg Co D, 10 Jul 63-17 Jul 63. A John England married 8 Sep 1853 Eliza Seward HC Bk 3-179; and a John England married 26 Mar 1874 Eliza Stutsman HC Bk 6-264. HC death notice 1 Oct 1903: " John England, age 69, died at his home, 1120 West North Street, September 24. Funeral at residence, interment Park Cemetery." HC Park Cemetery: a Jno England Co C 124 Ind Inf..1860 HC census records a John England and wife Eliza.

Hancock County Indiana Civil War Soldiers

England, William; A William England married 25 Apr 1866 Hannah Griffith HC Bk 5-55. HC Burris/Hendricks Cemetery: William England died 30 Nov 1866 29y 5m 5d, Co J 2nd Reg Ohio Vol.

Evans, Andrew; two units found for this man: 55 Reg Co F, 7 Jun 62-1 Sep 62; also 9 Cav Co F, 23 Dec 63-29 Jul 64/ An Andrew Evans married Maria Louisa Muth 27 Oct 1842 HC Bk 2-57. Maria is the d/o Ernst George Muth and Sara Weaver.

Evans, William; 75 Reg Co I, 20 Jul 62, residence or place of enlistment is Noblesville, Indiana. Andersonville Prison Profile Code #11279, Private William Evans, Company I, 75 Indiana Regiment, died 22 May 1864 of remittent fever grave #1279. NOD.

Evans, William; 105 Reg Co E, 11 Jul 63-18 Jul 63. A William Evans married 30 Sep 1863 Elizabeth Bennett HC Bk 4-403. HC newspaper 17 Dec 1891: "We are sorry to learn that Mr. W.H. Evans who moved from Cumberland to Greenfield recently is quite sick." HC Park Cemetery: William H. Evans 26 May 1811-17 Dec 1891, Elizabeth 13 Jun 1811-13 Dec 1898.

Everett, Charles; 9 Cav Co G, 9 Dec 63-died 9 Jun 65. HC newspaper 29 Jun 1865: " We regret to learn that Charles Everett, son of Harmon Everett, of this place, and a member of Co B, 9th Indiana Cavalry, died at Baton Rouge, Louisiana, on the 9th of June. The information comes from the Chaplain of that post, and is no doubt correct. Young Everett was a good boy, and an excellent soldier, and his friends at home as well as his companions in arms will learn of his death with much regret."

Everson, Amos; 8 Reg Co B, 21 Aug 61- 4 Sep 64. HC New Palestine Cemetery: Amos Everson died 1 Nov 1887 45y 2m 29d. NOD.

Everson, Jacob; 100 Reg Co K, 21 Aug 61-3 May 65. "Jacob Everson, born Ohio. father William Everson. Jacob was an

Hancock County Indiana Civil War Soldiers

invalid, cut his throat and died 31 Aug 1896, age 63. HC New Palestine Cemetery: Jacob Everson 1833-1896.

Everson, Joseph; 106 Reg Co D, 10 Jul 63-17 Jul 63. A Joseph Everson married 1 Jun 1862 Sarah Jane Allen HC Bk 4-332. HC New Palestine Cemetery: Everson, Joseph 1835-1922, Sarah Jane 1837-1913, William H. s/o Joseph died 11 Jun 1882 19y 8m 20d.

Everson, Wallace; HC Park Cemetery: Wallace Everson Co I 3rd N.Y. Light Artillery, 1840-1911. NOD.

Hancock County Indiana Civil War Soldiers

Joseph Roberds Eakes

Courtesy of Charles Murdoch, Jr.

Hancock County Indiana Civil War Soldiers

◄ F ►

Fair, Robert J. Sr.; 38 Reg Co G, 26 Sep 64-29 Jun 65. "He joined the ranks of the battle-scarred veterans, when they had driven Hood's army up to Franklin, falling in under the roar of cannon at the battle of Nashville to the final annihilation of Hood's command in Alabama. He marched in the Grand Review, June 1865 at Washington, D.C. Son of Robert C. and Nancy (Brown) Fair, Robert J. was born 3 Jun 1833, Shelby County, Indiana. He was twice married 1) 17 Jan 1856, Shelby County, Sarah A. Field, there were seven children from that union. Robert J. married 2) 3 Sep 1885 Laura E. Royer Reeves (HC Bk 7-629)."

HC obit 7 Jan 1909: "Robert Fair, Sr., age 78, died at his home in Green Township where he had been ill with lung fever. On 2 January he suffered a stroke of paralysis from which he never recovered. Mr. Fair was one of the well known and respected men of his township and a Civil War veteran. He is survived by the widow and children, George, David, Robert, Charles, Lincoln, John, Viola and Grace Fair, Margaret Liming and Dora Rensforth. Pall bearers were members of the Grand Army Post." HC Park Cemetery: Fair, Robert J. 30 Jun 1833-8 Jan 1909, Sarah w/o Robert died 13 Jun 1862? 47 y.

Fansler, Samuel O.; 33 Reg Co C, 31 Dec 63-21 Jul 65. HC obit 4 Jan 1917: "Samuel O. Fansler, aged 73 years, a Civil War veteran, died at his home in East Greenfield from infirmities of old age. The son of Henry Fansler, he was born 5 May 1844, Indiana, married Sarah (no maiden name nor location). Samuel died 1 Jan 1917 and buried HC Park Cemetery."

Farris, George W.; 51 Reg Co I, 8 Dec 61-14 Dec 64. NOD.

Faulkenburg, Caleb; 5 Cav Co G, 30 Oct 62, 22 Dec 62 transferred to Co D, out 27 Feb 63. NOD.

Faurot, Francis M.; 16 Reg Co E, 23 Apr 61-23 May 62. HC obit 13 May 1897: "The remains of (Francis) Marion Faurot , formerly a resident of this city, were brought here for

Hancock County Indiana Civil War Soldiers

interment. Mr. Faurot died at Bellvue, Kentucky, from paralysis. During Mr. Faurot's residence here, he was a large contractor and did work in this city and county and had always had a warm place in his heart for Greenfield and asked to be buried here. He is a brother of Thomas Faurot of this city. He is survived by a son and daughter. Interment (HC) Park Cemetery." His name, is listed on Park Cemetery Veteran's List, but no dates.

Faurot, Thomas, 139 Reg Co H, no dates given. HC obit 13 Aug 1925: "Thomas Faurot, for many years a widely known contractor died at his home, 416 North State Street, following an illness of several weeks. Son of John and Jane (Chanee) Faurot, widower of Anna, Mr. Faurot was born 18 May 1843, Indiana and a soldier in the Civil War. For many years he was engaged in road and street construction, having built West Main Street in Greenfield. There are no near relatives and Mr. and Mrs. Faurot had no children. Both buried HC Park Cemetery: Thomas J. Faurot 1843-1925 Co H 139 Ind Inf; Anna R. Faurot 1854-1925."

Fausett, Robert; 12 Reg Co B, 19 May 61, transferred to 79 Reg Co C, 19 May 62, out 7 Jun 65. A Robert Fausett married 10 Jun 1867 Elizabeth Lunsford HC Bk 5-110; also married 8 Mar 1871 Sarah Pool HC Bk 6-3. NOD.

Faussett, James H.; 12 Reg Co G, 16 Oct 62, transferred 8 Jun 65 to 48 Reg. A James Faussett married 30 Sep 1868 Margaret Brown HC Bk 5-249; also a James married 26 Apr 1882 Mary Faussett HC Bk 7-354. James H. Faussett buried HC Caudell/Simmons Cemetery, no dates, unit numbers only.

Ferrin, Jerry; 51 Reg Co D, 4 Dec 61-13 Dec 65. A Jerry Ferron married 27 Oct 1864 Sarah Jane Windsor HC Bk 4-483.

Fetron, Joseph; 148 Reg Co I, 10 Feb 65-5 Sep 65. NOD.

Fisk, Americus; 57 Reg Co A, 13 Dec 61-14 Dec 65. NOD.

Fisk, Granville; 57 Reg Co A, 13 Dec 61- Feb 65. Granville Fisk married 30 Apr 1857 Martha McKown HC Bk 4-18. "Granville Fisk was a soldier of the Civil War and now (1902) a farmer in Fayetteville, Arkansas."

Hancock County Indiana Civil War Soldiers

Fisk, Othneil; 9 Cav Co B, 2 Jan 64-21Jul 65. Othneil Fisk married 23 Jun 1868 H. Almira Archer HC Bk 5-226.

Fletcher, James M.; 57 Reg Co A, 13 Dec 61, lost on explosion of the steamboat, Sultana, 27 Apr 1865. NOD.

Fletcher, John W.; 57 Reg Co A, 13 Dec 61-5 Feb 65. John W. Fletcher married 12 Jan 1868 Arminda Humble HC Bk 5-191. "John W. Fletcher was born 21 Apr 1846, s/o Richard Fletcher, died 8 Jun 1905, buried HC Willow Branch Cemetery."

Fletcher, William; 99 Reg Co B, 13 Aug 62-died 13 Feb 63, La Grange, Tennessee. NOD.

Flowers, James; 99 Reg Co B, 13 Aug 62-5 Jun 65. A James Flowers married 20 May 1869 Elizabeth Lineback HC Bk 5-302; also James Flowers married 31 Jan 1878 Julia Davis HC Bk 6-576.

Flowers, John; 99 Reg Co B, 13 Aug 62-19 Jan 63. NOD.

Foley, Alexander; 38 Reg Co D, 11 Nov 64-5 Jun 65. "Alexander Foley was born 11 Feb 1833, Rush County, Indiana, s/o James and Eliza (Templeton) Foley. Alexander married 8 Jan 1852 Catherine Earl (HC Bk 3-75), she was the d/o Isaac and Sarah Earl. Mr. Foley's end was sad and tragic, as being kicked by a vicious horse and died 13 April 1889." HC Six Mile Cemetery: Foley, Alexander died 13 Apr 1889 56y 2m 2d; Catherine w/o Alexander died 23 Jan 1914 81y 3m 21d. "Catherine Foley w/o Alexander, had son, Oregon, daughters Mrs. James Keck and Mrs. Ellis Parrish."

Foley, William H.; 2 Cav Co B, 20 Sep 61-resigned 26 Apr 62. A William A. Foley married 18 Nov 1869 Sue Rouyer HC Bk 5-338. Old Fort Cemetery, Hamilton County, Indiana: Lt. W.H. Foley, Co B 2 Ind Cav.

Forbush, Walter; 10 Reg Co K, 18 Sep 61, 8 Sep 64 transferred to 58 Reg, out 25 Jul 65, Corp'l. HC obit 17 Apr 1913: "Walter Forbush, age 68, a veteran of the Civil war, died at his home in Greenfield, after having suffered a stroke of paralysis some months ago. He was born 3 March 1845, Grafton, Massachusetts, s/o Mr. and Mrs. Henry Forbush. When quite young he came to Indiana, locating in Lafayette where at age

Hancock County Indiana Civil War Soldiers

16, enlisted in the Civil War. On 17 April 1901, he was united in marriage with Rosina Riblet, of Londonville, Ohio. They since resided here. The body was taken to Londonville for burial."

Forgey, Andrew; 12 Reg Co G, 21 Jul 62-wounded 13 May 1863, Resaca, Georgia, died three days later, 16 May 63, age 24 years. He is not recorded as being buried at three National Cemeteries: Nashville, Chattanooga or Maritta (January 2002). He was the s/o John and Lucinda (Sprouce) Forgey. See page for his brother, Hugh Forgey.

Forgey, Hugh; 12 Reg Co G; 21 Jul 62 wounded 13 May 63, Resaca, Georgia, died of those wounds 9 Jun 1863, buried Nashville, Tennessee. His name is not on the index at Nashville National Cemetery, however, he may be in the long list of unknown burials Nor is he recorded as buried at National Cemeteries located In Marritta, Georgia or Chattanooga, Tennessee (January 2002). "Hugh and brother, Andrew, were wounded the same day, died within six weeks of each other, and buried in a strange land."

HC obit 11 Jun 1903: Hugh and Andrew's sister. Electa, died 4 Jun 1903, the following data is taken from her obit: "Electa J. Forgey, daughter of Jno. and Lucinda Forgey, was born 20 Dec 1842, died 4 Jun 1903, at the home of B.L. Barrett of blood poison. The deceased was one of eight children, namely, Benjamin, Andrew, Mary, Electa , Hugh, Anna, William and Eliza O., all having preceded her to the world beyond. Eliza O. was the only one of her brothers or sister to ever marry. Electa lived on the farm on which she was born all her life, except the last year. She has been known to send $10 to $20 several times to the famine victims in foreign countries. She was not perfect in her judgement, but strictly honest in all her dealings Let us imitate her good qualities and try to forget her mistakes. B.L.B."

HC obit 11 Jun 1903: "Electa Forgey was one of the oldest settlers and died of a complication of diseases. She was the last of a large family and leaves a very large estate." Eliza O.

Hancock County Indiana Civil War Soldiers

Forgey married 1 Sep 1875 Daniel F. Hays HC Bk 6-385; HC Hays Cemetery: Eliza O. Hays w/o Daniel died 6 Sep 1879 28y 3m 27d, Daniel F. Hays died 31 Oct 1878 33y 2m 27d. Many of the Forgeys are buried HC Cook Cemetery: John, Lucinda, Anne, Benjamin, Electa and Mary.

Forman, George W.; 18 Reg as Musician 16 Aug 61-20 Aug 62. A George W. Forman married 21 Mar 1860 Nancy Melton HC Bk 4-185.

Fort, Charles H.; 57 Reg Co A, 13 Dec 61-5 Feb 65. "The son of James and Malintha (Burch) Fort, Charles H. was born 11 October 1836, Hancock County. He married HC Bk 4-147, 1 Sep 1857 Delinda J. Addison, born 27 Dec 1840, Rush County, daughter of John Addison. Charles served three years during the Civil War, seeing action in many battles, Stone River, Missionary Ridge, Shiloh, Franklin, Nashville and others. He served two terms as Hancock County Treasurer."

Fort, Lorenzo D.; 57 Reg Co A, 13 Dec 61, died 1 Jan 63, from wounds received 31 Dec 62, at the battle of Stone's River, Tennessee. His body may or may not have been brought home for burial but in there is a grave marker in HC Simmons Cemetery: Lorenzo D. Fort died 31 Dec 1862, 17y 5m 2d, s/o James and Malintha Fort; also Malintha w/o James died 31 Mar 1855 41y 23d. The Charlottesville GAR Post was named for this young soldier who gave his life for his country.

Fort, M.; HC newspaper 11 Aug 1865: "Pvt. M. Fort was taken prisoner during the disastrous expedition commanded by General Stoneman." This must be Morris Fort who was a recruit in Company G, 5th Cav, 27 Feb 64-7 Jun 65. (A man named Moses C. Fort was a prominent and wealthy farmer in Hancock County (7 Jan 1842-30 Sep 1913) who was of the right age, however, no research was found to indicate that he was a soldier in the Civil War).

Fort, William; 2 Cav Co B, 20 Sep 61, Corp'l, promoted to Sgt, no out date. A William Fort married 19 Sep 1850 Mary Prickett HC Bk 3-8. HC Caudell/ Simmons Cemetery: William

Hancock County Indiana Civil War Soldiers

Fort, soldier, died 20 Jan 1891 60y. Mary w/o Will died 23 Apr 1902 71y.

Foster, John; 105 Reg Co E, 11 Jul 63-18 Jul 63. Greenfield Old Cemetery: John Foster died 11 Jul 63, 28y 9m, Volunteer Co E 105 Reg. If tombstone inscription is correct, he died during the Confederate raid into Indiana by Gen. John Morgan, but no John Foster is recorded on any roster during that time.

Foster, John F.; artificer, 1st. Missouri Engineers Co M, 19 Aug 61-14 Sep 64. " born Hancock County, age 28, 5' 9", fair complexion, gray eyes, light hair, farmer when enrolled." See data for William J. Foster.

Foster, Richard; 79 Reg Co C, 15 Aug 62-1 Sep 63. A Richard Foster married 15 Jul 1857 Sarah Burris HC Bk 4-25.

Foster, Thomas B.; 8 Reg, Musician, 5 Sep 61-28 Aug 65. See data for William J. Foster

Foster, William J.; 9 Reg Co B 9 Dec 63-died 14 Dec 64 of chronic diarrhea as prisoner of war at Castle Morgan Prison, Cahaba, Alabama, (captured at Sulphur Branch Trestle, Alabama, 25 Sep 1864). He was a veteran of Company D, 5th Indiana Infantry during the Mexican War, having enlisted 8 Oct 1847 and discharged 28 Jul 1828. He was the brother of Martha Bridges (Mrs. Andrew), and America Harris (Mrs. Lee) and all children of John and Abbyvilla Foster.

Fountain, Ira B.; 8 Reg Co B, 25 Aug 61-no out date. NOD.

Fouty, John H.; 79 Reg Co G, 21 Aug 62-7 Jun 65. John H. Fouty married 21 Sep 1870 Louisa Richey HC Bk 5-398. Buried HC Mt. Lebanon Cemetery: John H. Fouty Co G 79 Reg, no dates.

Fowler, Benjamin; 106 Reg Co D. 10 Jul 63-17 Jul 63. NOD.

Franklin, Columbus A.; HC obit 8 Jul 1926: "The funeral of Captain C.A. Franklin was held at his home in Shirley. He was 83 years old and resided in Shirley for thirty-six years. Captain Franklin was a member of Company G, Seventh Indiana Infantry during the Civil War." The son of Enos and Charlotte Franklin, he was born 14 Feb 1843, Virginia, married Rose

Hancock County Indiana Civil War Soldiers

___, Capt. C.A. died 30 Jun 1926, buried Crown Hill Cemetery (Marion County?).

Franklin, William; 79 Reg Co C, 22 Aug 62-26 May 63. Brothers, Allen and Edward also served in Civil War. They were the sons of Jasper and Sarah (Caldwell) Franklin; Jasper served in the War Of 1812 and is buried HC Eden Church Cemetery, old section.

Frazier, James; 79 reg Co C, 22 Aug 62-7 Jun 65. NOD.

Fred, Francis M.; 33 Reg Co G, 9 Mar 65 as substitute-21 Jul 65. Francis M. Fred married 7 Sep 1871 Sarah Dickerson HC Bk 6-42. The Fred brothers, Francis, Isaac and William served in the Civil War. See added data on page for William H. Fred and Isaac Newton Fred.

Fred, Isaac Newton; 70 Reg Co G, 28 Jul 62-8 Jun 65. " Isaac Newton Fred was born in Indiana, 7 October 1843, s/o Israel and Mary (Perkins) Fred who were married 28 May 1821. At time of enlistment, he was age 18, 5' 10" tall, light complexion, blue eyes, light hair and a farmer. His Regiment left the State 12 August 1862 and was engaged in several expeditions, including Russellville, Scottsville, Kentucky, and Gallatin, Tennessee...engaged in guard duty on the Louisville and Nashville Railroad ; took part in the Atlanta campaign and at Resaca (Georgia) captured a fort and four Napoleon guns; participated in Georgia and Carolina campaigns, marched to Richmond and was mustered out 8 June 1865 at Washington City.

Isaac received a pension of $12 per month but was refused an increase 5 April 1892, on the ground that the rate of pension (#335832) was fully commensurate with the existing degree of disability from pensioned cause, as shown by the evidence on file. Isaac was married 1) 3 Jan 1867 Mary E. Stoops, no location known; Isaac married 2) 26 Apr 1883, HC Bk 7-448, Rosa Belle Beagle (Bickle, Beeler) Rosa Belle w/o Isaac Newton Fred 31 Dec 1853-3 Sep 1901, buried HC McCordsville Cemetery.

Hancock County Indiana Civil War Soldiers

HC obit 15 Mar 1937: " Isaac Newton Fred, age 93, a highly respected citizen of near McCordsville died at the home of his daughter, Mrs. Crystal Teal of Mt.Comfort after a short illness. Mr. Fred spent practically all his life in that locality and was a Civil War veteran. He is survived by a son, Everett, Mrs. Teal and a sister, Mrs. Blanch Anderson, of San Francisco." Contributed by Elayne Stewart, Greenfield, Indiana.

Fred, William H.; 70 Reg Co G, 7 Nov 63-18 Mar 65. "He was wounded, 15 May 1864, at Resaca, Georgia, gunshot in the right arm resulting in resection and was in hospitals until November when he received a furlough to go home and vote at the Presidential election. (Did he vote for Abraham Lincoln?) The furlough was extended several times and he never did rejoin his company and was discharged 18 March 1865. William married 9Aug 1868, at Mendon, Indiana, to Sarah Elsbury who was born 28 October 1836, HC and died 27 August 1908.

In addition to the wound on his arm, he received a buckshot in his right thigh. On application for pension, he was first rated at $8.00 per month, and has been increased from time to time without his asking until he now (1900) receives $36.00 a month. He is unable to perform much manual labor, but still follows farming for a living. His brother, Isaac Newton and Francis M. served in the War; his wife's brother, Frederick Elsbury, served in an Indiana Regiment and died of measles while in the service."

Frederick, Henry; 9 Reg Co C, 14 Feb 64-28 Sep 65. NOD.

Frost, Richard; 134 Reg Co K, 24 May 64-term expired, no date. "The son of Richard and Elizabeth (Curry) Frost, Richard was born 19 Oct 1840. He married 19 Oct 1870 HC Bk 5-361, Sarah M. Elsbury, d/o Jackson Elsbury. Richard and Sarah buried HC Curry's Chapel Cemetery: Richard died 4 Feb 1907, Sarah M. 16 Aug 1850-21 Sep 1926."

Fry, John; no units. A John Fry married 3 Mar 1864 Melissa Roberds HC Bk 4-436; also a John Fry married 3 Oct 1869 Hettie Whitley HC Bk 5-324. HC obit 8 Nov 1917: "John Fry,

Hancock County Indiana Civil War Soldiers

a well known veteran of the Civil War died at the Soldiers' Home at Lafayette. The body was brought to Charlottesville for burial."

Fuller, Andrew J.; 8 Reg Co B, Aug 61-20 Aug 65. "Was color bearer for Regiment and proudly carried his flag in many of the fiercest battles: Rich Moutain, Virginia; Sugar Creek, Pea Ridge and Cotton Plant, Arkansas; Port Gibson, Jackson, Champion Hills and Vicksburg, Mississippi, and many others. On 23 May 1863, in a charge at Vicksburg, he received a gunshot wound in the ankle, after convalescing he returned to his command in November, 1863. His brother, Henry was in the 132 Ind. Reg. Son of Joseph and Jane (Wilson) Fuller, Andrew was born in Hancock County, 25 Sep 1837, and married 8 October 1863 (HC Bk 4-405) Barbara E. McCann (d/o Nelson and Maria (Jordan) McCann HC Sugar Creek Cemetery: Fuller, Andrew J. 1837-1925; Barbara E. w/o Andrew 1846-1919."

Fuller, Henry, 132 Reg Co F, 18 May 64-7 Sep 64. "Son of Joseph and Sarah Jane (Wilson) Fuller, he was born 30 Oct 1847, Hancock County and was only thirteen years old when his older brother, Andrew J. Fuller went to war in 1861, three years later 18 May 64 he enrolled in the 132. He went with the regiment into Tennessee and Alabama where war in all its hideous phases was in full blast in which Henry experienced his full share. He returned to marry Delphina Alexander on 4 Sep 1866 HC Bk 5-81. Henry lost his left arm in a threshing accident.

HC obit 4 Dec 1924: "Henry Fuller, 77 years of age, a veteran of the Civil War and retired farmer, who formerly lived at Mohawk, died at the Soldiers' Home at Dayton, Ohio. The body was brought to the home of his daughter, Mrs. Jesse Barnard in Greenfield. Survived by Mrs. Barnard and two sons, Sam; and Oliver. Funeral at the Nazarene Church in Mohawk, with interment in Sugar Creek Cemetery. HC Sugar Creek Cemetery: Fuller, Henry 1847-1924; Delphina w/o Henry 1848-1924."

Hancock County Indiana Civil War Soldiers

Furry, Francis; 106 Reg Co D, 10 Jul 63-17 Jul 63. NOD
Furry, James; 5 Cav Co G, 16 Aug 62-died 13 Dec 62, at Indianapolis, Q.M. Sgt. HC Little Sugar Creek/Low Cemetery: James Furry, s/o G. and M. died 13 Dec 1862 21y 8m 11d.
Furry, John; 5 Cav Co G, 16 Aug 62-20 May 63. NOD.

Hancock County Indiana Civil War Soldiers

Isaac Newton Fred

Courtesy of Hancock County Historical Society

Hancock County Indiana Civil War Soldiers

Civil War Pass

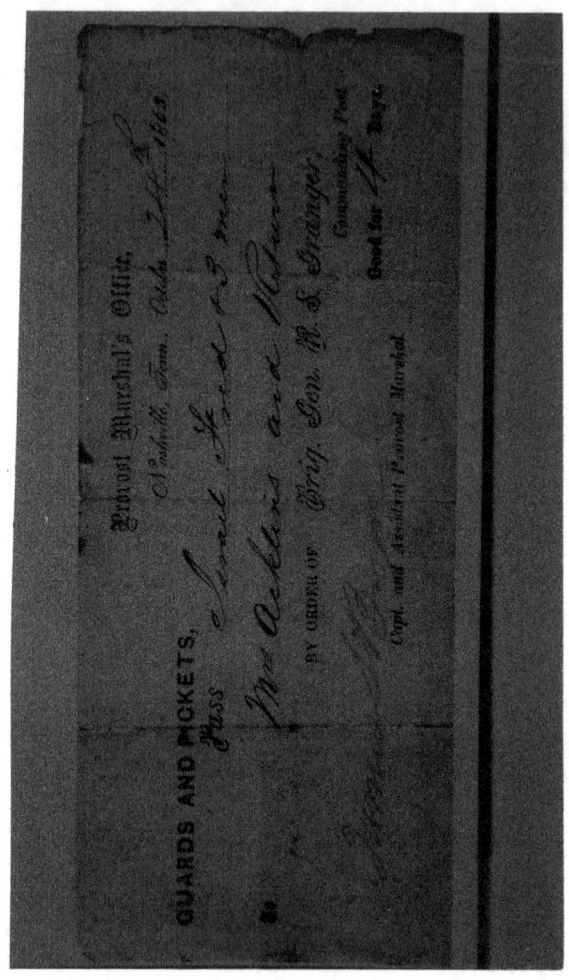

Courtesy of Hancock County Historical Society

Hancock County Indiana Civil War Soldiers

◄ G ►

Galligher, John; 5 Cav Co G, 16 Aug 62-died 11 May 64, Madison, Indiana. HC newspaper 25 Feb 1864: "We regret to learn that John Galligher, Company G, 5th Indiana Cavalry, departed this life, in the Hospital at Madison, Indiana, on 19 February 1864, of consumption. Mr. G. was every inch a man, and universally respected and esteemed by all having the pleasure of his acquaintance. The Chaplain of the Hospital, in a letter to Judge Gooding, says he was well nursed and cared for and died easy, and he would be carefully and decently buried." NOD.

Galloway, Jackson; 38 Reg Co A, 4 Nov 64- Jun 65. A Jackson Galloway married 31 May 1862 Alice Anne Siddell HC Bk 4-332. Ida May Galloway d/o Jackson and Ann died 27 Sep 1872, no location given. NOD.

Gant, Frank, (Benjamin Franklin Gant); 5 Cav Co G, 28 Dec 63-16 Sep 65. A Benjamin Franklin Gant married 20 Sep 1860 Lucinda Judkins HC Bk 4-209; also a Benjamin Franklin Gant married 17 Sep 1871 Mary McConnell HC Bk 6-47. HC newspaper, 22 Feb 1923: "Death of Frank Gant, M.T. Willett received a message stating that his father-in-law, Frank Gant died in Cherryvale, Kansas, on Monday last. Mrs. Willett was enroute to Kansas to be with her father but he died before she arrived."

Gant, Henry C.; 5 Cav Co G, 28 Dec 63-died 3 Dec 64. HC newspaper 11 Aug 1864: "Pvt. H.C. Gant, Company G, 5th Cavalry, was taken prisoner during the disastrous expedition commanded by General Stoneman." "Henry C. Gant, Company G., 5th Cavalry, died 3 Dec 1864, of diarrhea at Andersonville, Georgia, Prison, code#2216, grave #12216.

Gapen, (Gappen) Alfred; 8 Reg Co G, 22 Apr 61-6 Aug 61; also 57 Reg Co K, 22 Feb 62-died 26 Mar 62, Terre Haute, Indiana. He was born abt. 1838, probably Wayne County, Indiana, s/o Stephen and Sarah ___ Gapen. No record of marriage. Contributed by Mel Gapen, Lakeside, California.

Hancock County Indiana Civil War Soldiers

Gapen (Gappen), Charles; "Son of Otho and Amanda (McClure) Gapen, Charles was born about 1842, probably Hancock County, Indiana, died after 8 Dec 1863, married Mattie Sparks about 16 Jul 1861, Indianapolis, Indiana, according to a newspaper account near that date. He served in D Company, 8 Indiana Infantry Regiment, 5 Sep 1861; D Company, 5 Indiana Infantry Regiment, December 1861; G Company 39 Missouri Infantry Regiment in 1862.

He deserted at Missouri 7 Feb 1863; enlisted in 17 Battery, Indiana Light Artillery. Apparently, he had enough of this terrible conflict and probably was in the thick of it as stated by the four different regiments in which he served. I know it's not honorable to desert, but he did serve his country. What happened to him after he deserted on 7 Feb 1863? Was he prosecuted by the military—or did he return to his wife in Indiana?" Contributed by Mel Gapen, Lakeside, California.

Gapen (Gappen), James B.; 79 Reg Co B, 9 Aug 62-7 Jun 65. James B. Gapen, s/o Otho and Amanda (McClure), was born about 1848, probably Hancock County, Indiana, married 18 Apr 1872 Rosella Bidgood HC Bk 6-106. Contributed by Mel Gapen, Lakeside, California.

Gapen, (Gappen) Otho; 1 Cav Co K, saddler, 20 Jun 61-19 Jun 64. He was born about 1844, probably Hancock County, Indiana, s/o Otho and Amanda (McClure) Gapen. Apparently, he was also in Co B of the 1st Cavalry. Died after 19 Jun 1864. Contributed by Mel Gapen, Lakeside, California.

Gapen, (Gappen), Samuel Eli; 15 Reg Co E, 29 Dec 63-8 Jun 65. Son of Otho and Amanda (McClure) Gapen, Samuel Eli was born about 1840, married 1) Susan McNeal, 27 May 1858, Scioto, County, Ohio, known at marrige as "Eli Gapin." Verified marriage 2) Letitia Madaris, 31 May 1866 HC Bk 5-65. Samuel Eli died 19 Dec 1914, Hancock County. Contributed by Mel Gapen, Lakeside, California.

Gapen, (Gappen) Samuel G.; 13 Reg Co A, 20 Dec 62-8 Jun 65. Son of Stephen and Sarah Gapen, Samuel was born about 1843, probably Hancock County, Indiana, married 5 Apr

Hancock County Indiana Civil War Soldiers

64 Mat Smith HC Bk 4-445. A Samuel Gappen, Co A 13 Ind Inf died 4 Feb 1890, about age 50 years, buried Old Greenfield Cemetery. HC newspaper 9 Feb 1890: "Samuel Gapen, an old ex-soldier of Greenfield, who has been sick for some time past with consumption, passed peacefully away on Saturday last. A post mortem was held on his body Sunday by the attending physician to determine whether he died from consumption or from other disabilities with which he was effected."

Gapen (Gappen), William; 8 Reg Co G, 22 Apr 61-6 Aug 61; 8 Reg Co B, 25 Aug 61; 79 Reg Co B, 9 Aug 62; 79 Reg Co C, out 2 Sep 61. HC newspaper 14 Aug 1862: " William Gapen, Co B 8 Regiment is discharged." William Gapen, s/o Stephen and Sarah ___ Gapen, was born about 1833, probably Wayne County, Indiana. William married 17 Jan 1856, Sarah Ann Tharp HC Bk 3-317. William died 13 Apr 1896, age 65, buried HC Park Cemetery, stone says: Co C 79 Ind Inf." Contributed by Mel Gapen, Lakeside, California.

Gappen, (Gapen) Eli; 8 Reg Co B, 25 Aug 61-4 Sep 64. Took part in action at Blackwater Creek, Missouri; pea Ridge, Arkansas; Port Gibson, Vicksburg, and Jackson, Mississippi; and Sheridan's Shenandoah Valley Campaign plus others. He was born abt. 1835, probably in Wayne County, Indiana, the son of Stephen and Sarah ___ Gapen. Eli married 5 Feb 1868 HC Bk 5-198, Eliza Melton (born 11 Jan 1851, d/o Milton and Mildred Randall Gappen, died 14 Dec 1926 and buried HC Park Cemetery). This Eli died 25 Feb 1896 and was buried at the Old Greenfield Cemetery and later reinterred at HC Park Cemetery. "Eliza Gappen received $35.00 a month pension for Eli's Civil War service and treated her grandchildren with little gifts on pension-pay-day." Contributed by Dollie Whitaker, Greenfield, Indiana. And Mel Gapen, Lakeside, California.

Garberick, George; 75 Reg Co I, 20 Jul 62-8 Jun 65. NOD.

Gard, Samuel; 99 Reg Co B, 13 Aug 62-17 Jul 65. 99 Regiment History states, "Samuel Gard, Warrington, is dead in 1900.

Hancock County Indiana Civil War Soldiers

Gardner, Archibald; 12 Reg Co G, 19 Aug 62-15 Jul 64, killed at Atlanta. NOD.

Gardner, Hiram; 12 Reg Co G, 12 Feb 64-23 Feb 64 transferred to 48 Reg. NOD.

Gardner, Nicholas; 101 Reg Co D, 14 Aug 62-14 May 63. "The Regiment was sent into Kentucky, and immediately experienced the hardships of camp life, the constant exposure to all kinds of weather brought on a sickness, and he was stricken with spinal fever. In hospitals until he rejoined his command, March 1863, but after the battle of Perryville, he broke down and was sent to the hospital at Murfreesboro, where he was discharged 14 May 1863, for total disability.

His brother, Paul, served in the 5 Indiana Infantry and died of measles in three months at Louisville, Kentucky, his remains were brought home for burial. His brother, Adam, 74 Indiana Infantry, was killed at Jonesboro and buried where he fell.

Nicholas was born 14 May 1834, Germany, s/o Adam (survived cholera plague in 1812 Germany) and Susanna (Moppus) Gardner. Nicholas was three months old when the family left Germany and they were forty-eight days at sea, landing in New York. They went to Millersburg, Pennsylvania and in the spring of 1835 came to Hamilton County, Indiana. Nicholas learned the carpenter trade and 13 Mar 1856, married Mary A. Kinnaman (2 Oct 1834-20 Oct 1912).

He followed his trade until he was compelled to abandon it because of disability and total blindness." HC obit 3 Sep 1906; "Nicholas Gardner died at his home in Fortville, where he had lived for thirty-five years. He leaves a widow, four daughters and two sons. Mr. Gardner was age 72 and a veteran of the Civil War." Nicholas and Mary are buried Madison County, Indiana, Gravel Lawn Cemetery.

Garriott, Henry C.; 57 Reg Co A, 4 Nov 61-1 Mar 65. "..age 19, 5' 7", light complexion, blue eyes, light hair, farmer when enrolled." HC newspaper 14 Jul 1921: "Henry C. Garriott, of Wilkinson, had a paralytic stroke, the affliction affects his

Hancock County Indiana Civil War Soldiers

speech and at age 79 is in serious condition." HC obit 13 April 1922: "Henry C. Garriott, a merchant of this County, died at his home in Wilkinson, of uremic poisoning and bronchial pneumonia. He was born in Hancock County, 1 July 1842, the son of William L. and Margaret (Steel) Garriott. He went to the front line in the Civil War where he saw action at the battles of Stone River, Champion Hill, Missionary Ridge, Resaca and was wounded in the hip at Rock Face Mountain.

On 15 December 1864, he married Eliza Newman HC Bk 4-491. In 1874 Mr. Garriott opened a store in Warrington and in 1890 moved to Wilkinson where he opened a general store. He leaves a widow and nine sons, namely, William I.; Oliver N.; Charles O.; Allen; Korie; John W.; Homer C.; Herbert L.; and Frank E. A son, Walter, was killed accidentally in Wilkinson, 7 Aug 1882." Henry and Eliza are buried at Glen Cove Cemetery (Henry County, Indiana).

Gates, Henry; 106 Reg Co D, 10 Jul 63-17 Jul 63. HC obit 11 Mar 1909; "Henry Gates was born 14 April 1824, Chillicothe, Ohio, s/o John and Mary (Weaver) Gates who came to Rush County, Indiana, in 1826. Henry married 1) 22 Oct 1846 Nancy Ball, seven children, Nancy died 14 Dec 1862. Henry married 2) 1 Mar 1865 Mary Ann Lewis (5 Feb 1831-26 Mar 1905). Mr. Gates experience was varied but he was preeminently a farmer. In 1856 he built the flouring mill at New Palestine and remained in business there for eleven years, then returned to his farm.

In 1871 he formed a partnership with William T. Eaton for the general merchandise business at New Palestine. After eight years he again returned to farm life. In 1891 he retired from the farm and came to Greenfield. Nearly eighty-five years old, Mr. Gates died 4 March 1909, survived by three children, Mrs. John Gundrum and Mrs. John Huber of New Palestine and Miss Vania, Greenfield; three sisters, Mrs. Jacob Catt, Mrs. Elizabeth Hunt and Mrs. Margaret Newsom. Henry and Mary Ann Gates are buried (HC) New Palestine Cemetery."

Gates, Henry 8 Reg Co B, no dates. A Henry

Hancock County Indiana Civil War Soldiers

Gates is recorded at Andersonville, Georgia, Prison, survived and exchanged 19 Sep 1864 at Atlanta, code #52927. Most likely this is not the Henry Gates (above) who served a week when the Confederates invaded Indiana in 1863.

Gates, John Wesley; John W. Gates is listed as a member of Company G, 52 Regiment, 1 Feb 62-died 4 May 64. "John Wesley Gates died in the service of his country; while encamped he became violently ill with camp diarrhea and died 4 May 1864; buried Franklin Cemetery, Rush County, Indiana. He was one of thirteen children born to John and Mary (Weaver) Gates. Contributed by Mary Hoss, Greenfield, Indiana.

Geary, Enos; 124 Reg Co K, 26 Jan 64-31 Aug 65. "Enos Geary died 14 August 1900, age 72 or 80, buried HC Park Cemetery."

Gephart, John C.; 8 Reg Co B, 26 Aug 62-14 Jun 65. "..at enlistment, born Decatur County, Indiana, age 21, 5' 7", fair complexion, gray eyes, auburn hair, blacksmith." HC Slifer Cemetery, Mary Gephart, d/o John C. and Sarah H., only one date legible, 1863.

Gibbons, Jacob H.; 79 Reg Co G, 12 Aug 62-7 Jun 65, Sgt. A Jacob H. Gibbons married 11 Jan 1872 Mary E. Vest HC Bk 6-76. HC McCordsville Cemetery, Jacob H. Gibbons, 1836-1915, soldier Co B 11 Ind Reg 1861, Co G 79 Ind Reg.

Gibbs, Alonzo; 99 Reg Co B, 13 Aug 62-5 Jun 65. " at enlistment, born Rush County, Indiana, age 23, 5' 6", light complexion, black eyes, light hair, farmer." 99th Regiment History records: "Alonzo M. Gibbs died near Fort Scott, Kansas, 1899."

Gibbs, John D.(B); 57 Reg Co A, 18 Nov 61-5 Feb 65. " at enlistment, born Ohio, 5' 10", light complexion, brown eyes, dark hair." NOD.

Gibson, W.T.; 106 Reg Co D, 10 Jul 63-17 Jul 63. NOD.

Gilbert, Andrew J.; 8 Reg Co B, 25 Aug 61-no out date. NOD.

Gillian, Lewis; 5 Cav Co G, 30 Oct 62-transferred to Co D 22 Dec 62. NOD.

Hancock County Indiana Civil War Soldiers

Gilson, Archimedes; 4 Ind Cav, 7 Aug 62-29 Jun 65. An Archimedes Gilson married 11 Dec 1850 Amy Rynearson HC Bk 3-23. HC Philadelphia Cemetery: Gilson, Archimedes 11 Apr 1826-31 Jul 1897, Pvt 4 Ind Cav, Amy 12 Jul 1838-16 Jul 1918.

Gimason, Daniel C.; 51 Reg Co F, no dates. HC obit 20 July 1916: "Daniel C. Gimason, a Civil war veteran, died suddenly at his home in Greenfield, having suffered pains in his chest for a day or two. He was born in Clinton County, 10 August 1840, and married there to Mary Jane Cue on 9 March 1862. Mr. Gimason and his family came to Greenfield thirteen years ago from Hamilton County. He served as justice of the peace in Hamilton County and had been a justice since coming to Greenfield. He is survived by the widow and two daughters. Burial (HC) Park Cemetery."

Ginder, (Gruder) John; 12 Reg Co G, 12 Feb 64-8 Jun 65. NOD.

Gipe, Henry H.; 101 Reg Co E, 1862-no out date. "He was in the battles of, Atlanta, Resaca, Chickamaugua and Stone River. Henry, s/o George and Lydia (Blymire) Gipe, was born 12 Nov 1836, Pennsylvania, married 1854 Ruan Hines, and came to Hancock County in 1882, being a resident of Wilkinson in 1895. HC McCray Cemetery: Gipe, Henry 1836-1900, Sgt Co E 101 Ind Inf, Ruan 1837-1916."

Glass, Fleming; 79 Reg Co G, 15 Aug 62-7 Jun 65. NOD.

Glass, George; 105 Reg Co E, 11 Jul 63-18 Jul 63. A George Glass married 15 Jun 1865 Cinderella Thompson HC Bk 4-517.

Glass, Thomas; 79 Reg Co B, 9 Aug 62-7 Jun 65. NOD.

Goar, Henry; 8 Reg Co B, 9 May 64-deserted 6 Aug 65. NOD.

Goble, James M.; 8 Reg Co B, 6 May 64-28 Aug 65. A James M. Goble married 20 Sep 1868 Gretchen (Rachel) Chapman HC Bk 5-247.

Goble, Martin; 148 Reg Co C, 17 Feb 65 5 Sep 65. NOD.

Goble, Robert Jackson; 74 Reg no Co, 26 Jul 62-died 17 May 63 at Lavergne, Tennessee, and is buried at the National

Hancock County Indiana Civil War Soldiers

Cemetery, Nashville, Tennessee. Robert Jackson is the brother of David H. Goble, who established a printing business in Greenfield and they are sons of Isaac and Elizabeth (McBride) Goble.

Gooding. Lt. Clay; HC newspaper, 8 Sep 1862: " We are gratified to learn that our former young townsman, Lieut. H. Clay Gooding has been promoted to the Adjutancy of Col. Palmer's Illinois Regiment. We predict that our young friend will make an efficient and acceptable officer." Henry C. Gooding, s/o Asa and Matilda (Hunt) Gooding, married 22 Feb 1871 Mary Babcock, no location given.

Gooding, Judge David S.; 105 Reg Co E, 11 Jul 63-18 Jul 63; severely wounded during the accidental friendly-fire shooting at Lawrenceburg, Indiana, as his Regiment was in pursuit of the Confederates . "David, son of Asa and Matilda (Hunt) Gooding, was born 20 Jan 1824, Fleming County, Kentucky; married 12 Mar 1844 HC Bk 2-112 Frances Maria Sebastian (1825-1895). He was licensed to practice law in 1845 and was the first Democrat of Hancock County ever elected State Senator, County and Circuit Court Prosecuting Attorney, Common Pleas Judge and a United States Marshall for the District of Columbia. He died 20 Mar 1904 and with his wife, Frances M., is buried HC Park Cemetery."

Gooding, Lemuel W.; 105 Reg Co E, 11 Jul 63-18 Jul 63. HC obit 10 April 1913: "Lemuel W. Gooding, one of Greenfield's oldest and best citizens, died at his home on West Main Street of pneumonia. He was born at Moscow, Rush County, Indiana, 11 March 1833, coming to Hancock County with his parents, Asa and Matilda (Hunt) Gooding when three years of age. His parents erected the property known as the Gooding Corner on State and Main Streets, and for many years, when the only manner of travel was by stage coach, or on horseback, they kept what was then the best hotel between Columbus, Ohio and Indianapolis.

He studied law and was admitted to the bar when quite a young man. On 9 July 1856, he married Mary Melvina Foley

Hancock County Indiana Civil War Soldiers

(1828-1916), who survives him, and to them were born two sons, Charles (1 Nov 1857-23 Apr 1889), and Horace (21 Aug 61-14 Feb 65). Lemuel died 7 April 1913. Besides the widow, he leaves a sister, Elvira Gooding and a brother, Judge Henry Clay Gooding. Lemuel, Mary, Charles and Horace Gooding are all buried HC Park Cemetery."

Gooding, Oliver P. HC obit 23 Sep 1909: "General Oliver Paul Gooding, for many years one of the well known men of the city and county, died at the Government Hospital, Washington, D.C., where he had been a patient for a number of years. He was the only Hancock County man in the Civil War that attained the rank of general. He was highly educated and an interesting man in every way.

"In 1892 his mind began to fail and later during the last administration of Grover Cleveland, and while a visitor of the President, his actions were such that an investigation was held as to his sanity. It resulted in his being placed in the Government Hospital, where he remained until his death. He was born 29 January 1835, in the village of Moscow, Rush County, Indiana, and when two years old came to Greenfield with his parents, Asa and Matilda (Hunt) Gooding.

He was a graduate of the class of 1858 of the United States Military School at West Point and attached to the Fourth United States Infantry. He was attached to Tenth U.S. Infantry at Fort Bridger, Utah, and served against the Mormons in 1859 and 1860. On 13 March 1865 he was made a Major General by brevet, His commission says: 'For gallant conduct in the assaults on the enemy's works at Port Hudson, Louisiana, in 1863, and gallant and distinguished conduct throughout the Red River campaign in 1864.'

"He leaves two brothers, Henry Clay Gooding, of Los Angeles, California; Lemuel W. Gooding, Greenfield; and one sister, Miss Elvira Gooding, Greenfield. The pall bearers were J.M. Larimore, John A. Barr, J. Ward Walker, Charles Barr, William Barnard and U.S. Jackson. Burial HC Park Cemetery."

Hancock County Indiana Civil War Soldiers

Gooding, Willaim H.; 5 Cav Co G, 21 Oct 62-15 Sep 65. HC Park Cemetery: William H. Gooding, s/o Asa and Matilda, 11 Nov 1840-12 Jul 1895, Co G 5 Ind Cav 90 Vol Reg't.

Gordon, Eli; 147 Reg Co H, 15 Feb 65-4 Aug 65. Eli Gordon married 1 Sep 1865 Ellen Robinson (Robertson) HC Bk 4-531. HC Willow Branch Cemetery: Gordon, Eli 25 Dec 1836-15 Mar 1906, Agnes d/o Eli and Ellen 19 Sep 1872-_ Dec 1892.

Gorham, Perry T.; 86 Reg Co A, 1 Aug 62, enlisted as Sgt.; 4 Jan 63, promoted 2nd Lt.; 20 Oct 63 promoted 1st Lt.; 1 Mar 64, promoted Captain; out 6 Jun 65. There are four military-related documents in the Civil War collection of the Hancock County Historical Society.

Gray, David; 106 Reg Co D, 10 Jul 63-17 Jul 63, and 148 Reg Co C, 17 Feb 65-5 Sep 65. A David Gray married 12 Feb 1862 Mary Rittenhouse HC Bk 4-315; and a David Gray married 9 Jun 1867 Susanna Helms HC Bk 5-138.

Gray, George; 106 Reg Co D, 10 Jul 63-17 Jul 63. A George Gray married 16 Feb 1862 Eliza Jane Nichols HC Bk 4-310. A George Gray died 3 Apr 1874 34y 6m 24d and buried HC McNamee Cemetery.

Gray, John H.; 106 Reg Co D, 10 Jul 63-17 Jul 63. NOD.

Gray, John W.; HC Phildelphia Cemetery: John W. Gray 132 Reg Co K 1851-1924. There are two HC marriages for a John W. Gray: 9 Jul 1866 Isabelle Smith, also 2 Oct 1869 Mary A. Smith HC Bk 5-325.

Gray, John W.; 106 Reg Co D, 10 Jul 63-17 Jul 63. See two marriages (above) for John W. Gray. The 1860 Sugar Creek Township, Hancock County census records a John W. Gray, born 1843, and what appear to be brothers, George born 1833, Joseph H., born 1837 and David, born 1840 appear to be sons of Joseph H. born 1803 and Miriam Gray born 1806.

Gray, Joseph H.; 9 Cav Co B, 16 Dec 63-8 Jul 65. Joseph H. Gray was born 10 Jul 1836, s/o Joseph H. and Miriam Gray. He is listed as a survivor on the steamboat, Sultana, when it exploded and burned 27 April 1865, on the Mississippi River, near Memphis. Joseph H. Gray married 4 Jul 1876 Mary

Hancock County Indiana Civil War Soldiers

Mehaffey HC Bk 6-455. Joseph died 9 Apr 1904 of tuberculosis and buried HC Philadelphia Cemetery.

Green, John A.; HC Courthouse Soldier Burial List Book: 37 Reg Co H; died __ Oct 1892; 49 years; occupation, laborer; burial, Knightstown, Indiana. NOD

Griener, George W.; 11 Reg Co K, 31 Aug 61-died 7 Jul 63 at Memphis from wounds received at Vicksburg. NOD.

Griffith, Albert S.; 18 Reg, musician, 16 Aug 61-20 Aug 62. NOD.

Griffith, Benjamin, 34 Reg Co D, 21 Sep 61-died 27 Oct 62, Helena, Arkansas. NOD.

Griffith Hiram; 13 Dec 61-16 May 63. A Hiram Griffith married 16 Dec 1861 Leanah Sheets HC Bk 4-301. HC newspaper 14 Jul 1921: "Hiram Griffith, a former resident of Greenfield, died at the Soldiers' Home, Sawtelle, California. Mr. Griffith was soldier of the Civil War and had many friends and relatives in this county. Mrs. Henry Brown, Greenfield, was a sister. Mr. Griffith married Mrs. Jacob Andrews, formerly of this city, for his second wife. The body was taken to Kansas City for burial, where he formerly resided and where his children reside."

Griffith, Marquis D.; 34 Reg Co D 21 Sep 61, wagoner-3 Feb 66..NOD.

Griffith, Thomas H,; 57 Reg Co A, 13 Dec 61-14 Dec 65. HC Simmons Cemetery: a woman named Mary w/o Thomas Griffith, died 5 Oct 1869 22y 4m 15d.

Griffith, William; 34 Reg Co D, 7 May 64-3 Feb 66. NOD.

Grigsby, Daniel; 71 Reg Co A, 16 Aug 62-23 Feb 63 transferred into 6 Cav Co A, 9 Jul 63 discharged wounds. A Daniel Grigsby married Sarah Duncan 17 Sep 1868 HC Bk 5-245. HC Mt. Lebanon Cemetery: Daniel Grigsby Co A 6 Ind Cav.

Grigsby, Elzy; HC obit 18 Oct 1928: "Funeral services for Elzy Grigsby were held in Philadelphia, with interment in Mt. Lebanon Cemetery. Mr. Grigsby died at the home of his daughter, Mrs. Mabel Rodewald, with whom he made his home since the death of his wife. Mr. Grigsby was 81 years old and

Hancock County Indiana Civil War Soldiers

was a soldier in the Civil War, Co G. Thirtieth Infantry." HC Mt. Lebanon Cemetery, Grigsby, Elzy, 1 Apr 1847-13 Oct 1928 Pvt 30 Ind Inf, Emily w/o Elzy 15 Dec 1847-7 Dec 1922.

Grigsby, Isaac; 9 Cav Co B, 2 Jan 64-died 9 Jan 64, Indianapolis. HC Mt. Lebanon Cemetery: Isaac Grigsby s/o Levi and Rachel died 9 Jan 1864 17y 2m 0d.

Grigsby, John; 53 Reg Co A, 24 Feb 62, no out date, 9 Cav Co B, 13 Nov 63 wagoner-14 Jun 65. A John Grigsby married 9 Sep 1858 Louisa Jane Cartwright HC Bk 4-96.

Grigsby, Levi; HC Mt. Lebanon Cemetery, soldier. NOD.

Grigsby, Samuel; 36 Reg Co D, 23 Oct 61-21 Sep 64. "Samuel Grigsby, s/o Eli and Rachel (Klem) Grigsby, was born 17 Aug 1838, Virginia, wife Elizabeth Grigsby. Samuel died 18 Mar 1907 and buried HC Park Cemetery. See page for his comrade, Wiley W. Butts.

Grigsby, Sanford; 5 Cav Co G, 21 Oct 62-15 Sep 65. A Sanford Grigsby married 22 Jun 1855 Permilia Linder HC Bk 3-286.

Gross, John A.; 148 Reg Co C, 17 Feb 65-5 Sep 65. A Mary Grose, w/o John died 24 Feb 1864. NOD.

Groves, Robert; HC obit 26 Jan 1928: "Robert Groves, age 85 years, a Civil War veteran, was a member of Company B, 11 Ind Volunteers. He was born 19 Jan 1844, Illinois, died 19 Jan 1928 and is survived by a daughter, Mrs. Jane Craft. Interment in St. John's Cemetery. location not given."

Grundon, (Gumden), William; 3 Cav Co I, 5 Sep 61-27 Oct 64. "..he was born Hamilton County, Ohio, age 27, 5' 5", light complexion, hazel eyes, dark hair, occupation butcher when enrolled."

Gundrum, John; 106 Reg Co D, 10 Jul 63-17 Jul 63. A John Gundrum married 3 Dec 1866 Mary Jane Gates HC Bk 5-101. A John Gundrum 1843-1904 buried New Palestine Cemetery.

Gunn, Charles Scott; 8 Reg Co B, 8 Aug 62-14 Jun 65. "..born Hancock County, Indiana, age 23 years, 5' 9", dark complexion, black eyes, dark hair and farmer when enrolled.. During Charles' three years with the 8th Indiana Volunteer

Hancock County Indiana Civil War Soldiers

Infantry, the regiment marched many hundreds of miles from Indiana and participated in hard-fought battles at Pea Ridge, Arkansas; Port Gibson, Champion's Hill, Big Black River, Vicksburg and Jackson, Mississippi.

Also the regiment saw action at the Capture of Mustang Island, Texas, before being ordered to join Sheridan's Shenandoah Campaign, including the battles of Opequan, Winchester and Cedar Creek, Virginia. They were on duty at various points in South Carolina and Georgia until Charles was mustered out 14 Jun 1865 at Savannah.

"Charles married Mary Jane (Molly) Alyea in Hancock County, 19 Feb 1860. Duty to country was strong in his mind, therefore, he went to war leaving Molly and young son, John, not unlike many other men in Hancock County. On the day of his return, Molly said she had a feeling that Charles would return that very day.

" While digging potatoes, she saw a man trudging down the road with a pack on his back. She knew in an instant that it was Charles, dropped her hoe and raced to meet him, but in her excitement forgot about little son, John. The two cousins hoeing with Molly quickly grabbed John by a hand and whisked him between them over the potato patch, his little feet barely skimming the ground as they hurried him to his Daddy.

" Charles was only twenty-seven-years old upon his return from the War, but was exhausted and ill from the harshness of marching in the extreme heat and cold, rain and snow, sleeping on the ground and lack of nourishing food. After a thirty-mile march, he was overcome by extreme heat, caused by swimming many trips across a wide stream with comrades who could not swim on his back.

" Not only was Charles a kind man but talented with a fife and perhaps played it at Vicksburg when his regiment was engaged in the siege that ended 4 July 1863. The music giving the men a small measure of comfort. . Also, during his year-long convalescence from the harshness of military life, Charles built a bedroom chest for Molly, made from cherry timber grown on

Hancock County Indiana Civil War Soldiers

her father, James Alyea's, homestead. Charles Scott Gunn was born 8 October 1838, Brandywine Township, son of Robert and Sarah (Scott) Gunn. Charles applied for a pension 18 April 1888, #629088. On 6 July 1916 while hurrying to finish his work so he could attend the funeral of a friend, he fell from the haymow and died of injuries twenty-two days later. Molly survived him fourteen years, but never rallied from her sorrow and a fall, perhaps from a light stroke, eventually caused her death 21 June 1930. Charles and Molly are buried at (HC) Mt. Lebanon Cemetery." Contributed by Richard Andis, Greencastle, Indiana.

Gwinn, (Gunn) Joseph A.; 12 Reg Co B, 15 May 61-19 May 62. NOD.

Hancock County Indiana Civil War Soldiers

Eli Gappen

Courtesy of Dollie Holden Whitaker

Hancock County Indiana Civil War Soldiers

Charles Scott Gunn

Courtesy of Richard Andis

Hancock County Indiana Civil War Soldiers

◄ H ►

Hackleman, John F.; 9 Reg Co F, 4 Feb 65, didn't report. He married 13 Sep 1860 Mary E. Lineback HC Bk 4-206. HC death notice 2 Apr 1914: "The funeral of John Hackleman occurred at the home of Mrs. Cora Williams on East Main Street. The interment was at Park Cemetery." HC Park Cemetery: Hackleman, John F. 3 Aug 1838-30 Mar 1914; Mary E w/o John F. died 5 Mar 1870 36y 5m 7d.

Hafner, Ferdinand; 105 Reg Co E, 11 Jul 63-killed 15 Jul 63 at Lawrenceburg, Indiana, during the accidental firing disaster in pursuit of Confederate General John Morgan.

Hahn, John R.; HC Philadelphia Cemetery: John R. Hahn, Civil War soldier. NOD.

Haines, Cyrus; 8 Reg Co B, 25 Aug 61, captured Cedar Creek, Virginia, 19 Oct 64, out 8 Sep 65, Sgt. A Cyrus Hanes married 28 Sep 1887 Lula Ashcraft HC Bk 8-8.

Haines, Francis; 8 Reg Co B, 25 Aug 61-14 Jun 65, Corp'l. A Francis M. Haynes, born 27 Nov 1843, Marion County, Indiana, married 7 Jan 1868 Susan Everson HC Bk 5-190..

Hall, George; 79 Reg Co B, 9 Aug 62-7 Jun 65, Corp'l. NOD.

Hall, John; 8 Reg Co B, 21 Dec 63-26 Jul 65. A John Hall married 21 Apr 1864 Samantha Dobenspeck HC Bk 4-450.

Hall, Thomas; 19 Indiana Light Artillery; roster at Chickamauga National Battlefield, records his residence or place of enlistment as Fortville, Indiana. NOD.

Halley, John B. (V); 57 Reg Co A, 13 Dec 61-24 Sep 62. NOD.

Ham, George W.; 57 Reg Co F. HC obit 3 Feb 1916: "George W. Ham, aged 75 years, died, 28 January 1916, at his home in Shirley of Bright's disease. He was one of the well known men of the county having come from Tipton a number of years ago. George Washington Ham was born 16 Mar 1840, at Waterloo, Fayette County, Indiana, son of Vernon and Virginia (Sampson) Ham who were Virginians by birth.

He was a soldier in the Civil War, having seen active service in the engagements of Perryville, Shiloh, Murfreesboro,

Hancock County Indiana Civil War Soldiers

Chickamauga, Dalton, Resaca, Atlanta, Peach Tree Creek and Nashville. He was in the forefront of the memorable defense of the Rock of Chickamauga, Geneal Thomas' charge on Missionary Ridge and the disastrous charge on Kennesaw Mountain. He was never wounded, but was picked up from the battlefield of Shiloh in a helpless condition suffering from typhoid fever and taken to a hospital at Louisville, Kentucky, where he remained for nine months before he was able to return to duty.

On 17 March 1867 he married Adalaide Titus, at her father's home near Markleville. He is survived by the widow and eight children, Samuel Vinton Ham of the U.S. Army; Walter; Zora Reeves; Viola Gable; Thaddeus; Estella Cannon; Maybelle Kitterman and Georgia Guinevere Ham. Interment at Glen Cove Cemetery, Knightstown (Henry County, Indiana).

Hamilton, Charles G.; 99 Reg Co B, 13 Aug 62-5 Jun 65. " born Harrison County, Kentucky, sandy complexion, black eyes, sandy hair, 6' 1", age 29, farmer when enrolled.." married 18 Apr 1853 Rosanna Lineback HC Bk 3-159. HC newspaper 9 Jun 1864; "Private C.G. Hamilton was wounded in the hip during the battle of Dallas, Georgia, 28 May 1864." HC Gilboa Cemetery: C.G. Hamilton Co B 99 Ind Inf (no dates); Martha d/o Charles and Rosanna died 18 Sep 1854 4y 13d; Margaret d/o C. and R. died 27 Jul 1861 3y 7m 1d. 99 Regiment History states: "Charles G. Hamilton was wounded 28 May 1864 and dead in 1900."

Hamilton, John C.; Co B 7 Ohio Inf, no dates. "John C. Hamilton was born 10 May 1833, England, s/o John Hamilton, born England, married (HC Bk 4-524) 28 Jul 1865 Rosetta Seward, John C. died of heart disease 5 Aug 1905, buried HC Park Cemetery."

Hamilton, Mark; 9 Cav Co B; 13 Nov 63-military source, died 12 Jan 65, Nashville, Tennessee . HC newspaper source: 9 Jun 64: "Mark Hamiton died recently at Nashville." Buried Nashville National Cemetery 13 Jun 1865, private, Indiana, section G, grave #8682.

Hancock County Indiana Civil War Soldiers

Hamilton, Wilson; 9 Cav Co B, 9 Dec 63-12 Jul 65. HC Harlan Cemetery: Wilson Hamilton Co B 9 Cav no dates.

Hampton, Isaac; 28 USCT Co F, 31 Mar 64-13 Oct 64. HC obit 27 Mar 1913: "Isaac Hampton, aged 67 years, son of Reece Hampton and wife, and one of the best known colored men in the county, died at his home in Greenfield of heart failure. Mr. Hampton was a soldier in the Civil War, enlisted in the Co F of the United States Colored Troops at Hamilton County and was assigned to the company of Captain Snow, of this city. Isaac came to this city from Noblesville in 1869 and accepted a position in the George Knox barber shop. He was united in marriage with Sarah Hunt, d/o of the late Irvin and Jane Hunt. Isaac died 23 Mar 1913 and buried HC Park Cemetery."

Handy, Alexander; 53 Reg Co A, 28 Mar 64-21 Jul 65. NOD.

Hanes, no first name, HC Philadelphia Cemetery: Hanes 132 Reg Co F. NOD.

Hanley, Patrick, 9 Cav Co B, 13 Nov 63-27 May 65. NOD.

Hansing, Anthony; 148 Reg Co I, 8 Feb 65-5 Sep 65. NOD.

Hansing, Henry; 148 Reg Co C, 8 Feb 65-5 Sep 65. NOD.

Hardin, Charles Van; 12 Reg Co G, 12 Aug 62-8 Jun 65. "Charles V. Hardin was born 26 Sep 1838, Philadelphia, Pennsylvania, fifth in the family of Philip and Mary (Freeborn) Hardin. In 1840 Charles came to Indiana with his parents, settling on eighty acres near Alfont. He saw active service during the Civil War and was captured at the battle of Richmond, Kentucky but later exchanged.

He also participated in the battles of Vicksburg and Jackson, Mississippi; joined Sherman's army for the battles of Missionary Ridge, Resaca, Dallas, New Hope Church, Atlanta, Jonesboro and the march to the sea. His Regiment participated in the Grand Review at Washington, and was soon afterward discharged.

Before he enlisted he learned the blacksmith trade, married 17 Jan 1860 Susan Marsh (1841-1909), d/o David and Sarah (Jordan) Marsh, and cast his first vote for

Hancock County Indiana Civil War Soldiers

Abraham Lincoln. Charles and family moved to Fortville in 1874 where he died 22 Jan 1923 and is buried Madison County, Gravel Lawn Cemetery."

Hardin, Joshua; 13 Nov 63-died 1 May 65, Vicksburg. NOD.

Harlan, J. K.; 99 Reg Co B, 13 Aug 62-died 7 Aug 63. NOD.

Harris, Alexander B.; 9 Cav Co B, 9 Dec 63-promoted to 1st Sgt, then 2nd Lt. "Alexander Harris, brother of Lee O. Harris, was painter by trade who died before 1902 in Marion County."

Harris, G.W.; 106 Reg Co D, 10 Jul 63-17 Jul 63. NOD.

Harris, Henry; 5 Cav Co G, 15 Dec 63-15 Sep 65. NOD.

Harris, Lee O.; "Lee O. Harris was born 20 January 1839, Chester County, Pennsylvania, son of Samuel and Mary (Robinson) Harris. He enlisted as Orderly Sergeant in Co I, 8th Indiana Infantry, and received an early promotion to second lieutenant, at the battle of Rich Mountain, on recommendation of General Roscrans, serving in that capacity until expiration of enlistment. He reenlisted and commissioned First Lieutenant in Co G, 5th Cavalry, served one year and resigned due to serious illness.

He served respectively as Captain and Major of the Indiana Legion and in the spring of 1865 recruited a company at Greenfield for the 148th, Indiana Volunteer Infantry, was commissioned First Lieutenant, acting as Adjutant of the regiment. Thus Mr. Harris had a varied war experience, having also served in the 13th Indiana Infantry and the 9th Cavalry with honor and credit. His brother, A.B. Harris, and his sister's husband, W.D. Barwick, were in the 5th Cav., the latter was captured and confined in Andersonville Prison for one year.

His wife's brother, William J. Foster, died in the rebel prison, Castle Morgan, located at Cahaba, Alabama. Details for these three men are listed in alphabetical order.

Lee came to Hancock County about 1859, and kept in close touch with the educational interests, having taught all grades of school and has filled the position of Hancock County Superintendent of Schools. He married 14 March 1861, America, daughter of John and Aberilla (Tyner) Foster. HC

Hancock County Indiana Civil War Soldiers

obit 4 Aug 1921: "Mrs. America Harris, widow of Lee, passed away at her home, 111 West South Street. She was born in Kentucky, the daughter of John Foster, who came to Hancock County and became a member of the legislature. Mrs. Harris is survived by one child, Miss Lizzie Harris, a daughter, Anna, having died several years ago." Lee and America Harris are buried HC Park Cemetery; Lee 30 Jan 1839-23 Dec 1909; America 20 Aug 1839-1 Aug 1921."

Harris, William; HC obit, " William Harris, died at his home in Shirley, Indiana, at the age of 85 years. Mr. Harris was born in Virginia and a soldier in the Confederate Army and came to Indiana after the Civil War. He is survived by a son, Frank, of Shirley and two daughters at Martinsville, Indiana. Funeral at the home with burial at Martinsville."

Harris, William; 106 Reg Co D, 10 Jul 63-17 Jul 63. A William Harris married 27 Mar 1881 Letitia Gray HC Bk 7-256.

Harrison, David; 79 Reg Co G, 11 Aug 62-died 13 Mar 63, Nashville, Tennessee. NOD.

Harrison, George Washington; 186 Ohio Inf Co H, no dates. "HC obit 2 Feb 1932: "George Washington Harrison, a Civil War veteran, died at his home in Fountaintown, from influenza. He was a son of William and Rhoda Harrison, and was born 6 Jun 1845 at Grant's Lick, Kentucky, being at the time of his death, eighty-six years, Sixty years ago he moved to the Fountaintown community and was well thought of. On 4 Nov 1875 he married Martha Elizabeth Gunn of Hancock County and they were the parents of ten children."

Harrison, Jabez E.; 8 Reg Co G, 22 Apr 61-6 Aug 61. NOD.

Hart, John Edward; 27 Reg Co C, 12 Sep 61-1 Sep 64. HC obit 31 Aug 1933: "John Edward Hart, 91 years old, passed away at his home on South Street, (Greenfield). Mr. Hart is the last of the immediate family of James B. and Elizabeth (Foreland) Hart, one of the pioneer families and prominent in the development of this city. Mr. Hart's father came to Greenfield in the 1830s and purchased from Joseph Chapman

Hancock County Indiana Civil War Soldiers

the tavern known as the Gooding Corner which stood for so many years at the corner of State and Main Streets. This was the famous Joseph Chapman, the originator of the Democrat Rooster, the national emblem of the democratic party. Mr. Chapman entered the land from the Government and before the tavern was completed, sold it to Mr. Hart and later Mr. Hart sold it to the Gooding family. These were the only transfers that were made on the property until its sale to the Standard Oil Company.

John E. Hart was born in Greenfield, 22 January 1842, and when nineteen years of age enlisted and was assigned to Company C, 27th Regiment. He served throughout the War, participated in the battle of Antietam, wounded in action at Chancellorsville and was in the hospital when his regiment was nearly wiped out at Gettysburg (see his description of the battle in newspaper article chapter in this volume). He married Mary E. Dille of Knightstown who passed away in 1909. On 11 March 1911 he married Mary Warrick Gardner who survives him. Burial on the family lot at Knightstown." John Edward Hart was the brother of Andrew T. Hart.

Hart, William E.;18 Reg, Musician, 16 Aug 61-20 Aug 62; also a 1st. ..."born Hancock County, Indiana, 5' 8" tall, age 21, light complexion, blue eyes, light hair, clerk when enrolled, in the Band's 18 Reg..." Lieut. 105 Reg, Co E, 11 Jul 63, died of wounds 13 Jul 63. "He was the s/o Andrew T. Hart and his second wife, Gabriella Sebastian (d/o William and Elizabeth Sebastian). William E. Hart was a soldier in the 18th Indiana Volunteers; after his discharge, he joined and served in Capt. A.K. Branham's company of State troops in the pursuit of the celebrated Confederate General John Hunt Morgan, in his raid on southern Indiana and Ohio, and was killed in that unfortunate disaster at Lawrenceburg, Indiana, 13 July 1863."

HC Park Cemetery: William E. Hart 18 Ind Inf, Musician, no dates of birth or death; Andrew T. Hart 7 Jul 1811-11 Oct 1888; Gabriella A. Hart w/o A.T. 8 Feb 1816-4 Aug 1890. The Gem, Indiana, GAR Post was named for this soldier.

Hancock County Indiana Civil War Soldiers

Hartley, Joseph L.; 19 Reg Co F, 20 Sep 61-1 May 62, Sgt.; promoted to 2nd Lt. 1 Oct 62; promoted to Captain 13 Feb 63. HC newspaper 26 Feb 1863: "Lt. John C. Rardin of the 19th resigned his commission due to wounds received at the battle of South Mountain; Sgt. Hartley of his Company will be promoted to the Captaincy." A Joseph L. Hartley married 18 Oct 1856 Rachel Collins HC Bk 3-372.

Hartner, Charles; 8 Reg Co G, 22 Apr 61-6 Aug 61. NOD.

Harvey, David A.; HC Gillium Chapel Cemetery: David A. Harvey, soldier unit # illegible, died 20 Feb 1864 20y 9m 25d. NOD.

Harvey, Charles; 79 Reg Co C, 15 Aug 62, 22 Dec 62 transferred to U.S. Army 18th Infantry. A Charles Harvey married 22 Mar 1866 Nancy Emery HC Bk 5-45.

Harvey, William; 9 Cav Co B, 23 Dec 63, killed Sulphur Trestle 25 Sep 64. HC newspaper 20 Oct 1864: "Pvt. William Harvey was killed in action 25 Sep 1864 at Sulphur Trestle, Alabama."

Haskell, Ulysses; 12 Reg Co B, 15 May 61-19 May 62. A Ulysses Haskell married 29 Feb 1864 Sarah Jane (Elsbury) (Emery) HC Bk 4-435.

Haskett, Nathan H.; 5 Cav Co G, 18 Aug 62-15 Sep 65. " born Hancock County, Indiana, 5' 6" tall, light complexion, blue eyes, black hair, age 20, farmer when enrolled.."Nathan Haskett married 10 Aug 1867 Melissa Brock HC Bk 5-151.

Hasley, William; 12 Reg Co B, 4 Jun 61-19 May 62. NOD.

Hatfield, John Q.; 105 Reg Co E, 11 Jul 63-18 Jul 63. "John Q. Hatfield, age 60, died at his residence in Jackson Township of heart failure. HC Gilboa Cemetery, Hatfield, John Q. s/o Thomas and Hannah, died 12 Nov 1891; Hannah died 4 Sep 1860 74y 9m 9d."

Hatfield, T.W.; 132 Reg Co K, 18 May 64-7 Sep 64. Theodore W. Hatfield married HC Bk 5-428 14 Dec 1870 Anna Kinder (1840-22 Dec 1919). HC obit 30 Dec 1880: "Mr. T.W. Hatfield, late Principal of the Charlottesville Graded School, died at his residence 26 Dec 1880. Mr. Hatfield was born in

Hancock County Indiana Civil War Soldiers

Cleveland, Indiana, 22 Sep 1845; married Anna Kinder, who with three children are left to mourn the loss of a kind and loving father who died a devoted Christian. Cause of death was consumption. Interment HC Gilboa Cemetery"

Hawk, Adam C.; "106 Reg Co D, 10 Jul 63-17 Jul 63, the regiment was part of the offensive against the Confederate General John Morgan's raid into southern Indiana. Adam, s/o Henry and Susannah (Flaugher) Hawk, was born 16 Oct 1811, Ohio. In 1832 he married Mary Campbell (died 20 Apr 1896, 73y 7m 8d). Adam and Mary were the parents of nine children: Margaret; Allison; Sarah Jane; Martha J.; Mariander; Joshua M.; Caleb; Henry G.; and Tobitha. Adam and Mary are buried at the Philadelphia Cemetery on U. S. 40 in Philadelphia, Indiana." Contributed by Retta Arbuckle Livengood, Greenfield, Indiana.

HC Newspaper 20 Aug 1891: "Adam Hawk, probably one of the oldest settlers in this township, is slowly dying of dropsy. He is in his 80th years, and the attending physician, Dr. King, of Greenfield, is of the opinion that he will not last many days. Mr. Hawk is a good citizen. One of his many peculiarities was that he never rode to town; he invariably walked."

HC newspaper 4 Feb 1892: "Adam Hawk, a venerable old man, over eighty years of age, has crossed the Great River and his body was buried at the Philadelphia Cemetery. His funeral was probably the largest ever assembled at that place. It was a solemn occasion and but few dry eyes among his many kindred and old neighbors. He was an honest man, kind father, frank, truthful and a Christian. He was buried beside his good wife who had not long since preceded him His residence in this County dates back nearly sixty years; he resided on a farm on the banks of Sugar Creek for many years and later removed to a farm in Center Township. He told the writer that he had no uneasiness about his future, his peace had long been made and only awaited the Master's call. Farewell, old friend. Signed, A Friend of Fifty Years."

Hawkins, James; 8 Reg Co B, 25 Aug 61-no out date. NOD.

Hancock County Indiana Civil War Soldiers

Hawkins, Reason; 51 Reg Co K, 22 Feb 62-8 Dec 63 transferred to Veteran Reserve Corps (indicates an illness or wound). Reason Hawkins married 3 Jul 1870 Marie Wilson HC Bk 5-383. HC newspaper: "Reason Hawkins, a young married man, resident of Buck Creek Township (HC), was killed in a very curious manner He was cutting a tree, and as it began to fall stepped backward from it, and, it is supposed, slipped and fell backward striking the back of his neck dislocating it against a root. He was found dead sometime afterward by a small boy." HC Sugar Creek Cemetery: Hawkins, Reason 16 May 1837-31 Dec 1875; Maria 11 Apr 1831-15 Apr 1914; Marshall s/o R and M. 4 Apr 1871-24 Oct 1877.

Hays, Francis M.; 9 Reg Co D, 24 Feb 65-28 Sep 65. NOD.

Heath, Corydon; three Indiana regiment rosters record a Corydon Heath: 1)2 Cav Co B, 20 Sep 61, Commissary Sergeant;5 May 62, discharged; 2) 11 Reg Co B, residence or place of enlistment , Noblesville, Indiana, 10 Jul 63, 1st Lieut., mustered out 15 Jul 63; 3) 132 Reg Co I, 18 May 64, Capt., mustered out 7 Sep 64, residence or place of enlistment, Germantown, Indiana. Newspaper obit about 28 Jun 1916: "Corydon Heath was born near McCordsville, (HC) Indiana in 1841, and received his early education there. He left that neighborhood at the opening of the Civil War when he enlisted in the northern army. When he reenlisted later he became Captain of Company I, 132 Indiana Cavalry.

"At the close of the war he came to Indianapolis and began his work as a merchandise broker. Mr. and Mrs. Heath both took an active part not only in the work of the Roberts Park Church, but in starting other churches in the city. He organized a class of mixed adults as "Class No. 10" at the church, and was its teacher for thirty-two years. Through his efforts the class took an active interest in foreign missions and kept an average of seven native missionaries in India. The class still exists under the same title and carries on its work. The Heath Memorial M.E. Church, 1420 Arsenal Avenue, which formerly was the

Hancock County Indiana Civil War Soldiers

Howard Place Church, was renamed because of the work done by Mr. and Mrs. Heath in starting a mission at that place and later in helping to establish a church there. The East Park M.E. Church, 2226 East New York Street, was another church organized through the efforts of Mr. and Mrs. Heath. A Sunday school class of girls at the East Park Church has been named the Sarah C. Heath class, in memory of Mrs. Heath, who died seventeen years ago.
"The funeral of Corydon A. Heath, one of the prominent Methodist church workers in Indianapolis, who died 28 June 1916 was held at the family home, 721 East Eleventh Street. The Rev. Albert Hurlstone, pastor of Roberts Park Church, of which Mr. Heath had been a member since 1868, preached the funeral service. Burial will be in Crown Hill (Indianapolis). Mr. Heath was the oldest merchandise broker in Indianapolis when he retired two years ago, because of ill health. He was actively engaged in the canned goods business for forty years." Contribute by Irene Shireman, Greenfield, Indiana.

Heavenridge, Samuel; no units. Samuel Heavenridge married 5 Nov 1849 Emily Ogg HC Bk 2-353; also married 26 May 1853 Mary Myers HC Bk 3-166. HC Gilboa Cemetery: Emily Heavenridge w/o Samuel died –Oct 1852 21y 11m 1d. HC newspaper 5 Sep 1861: "The war fever now running over the land should not prevent husbands and wives, young men and young ladies, from dropping into the store of Samuel Haevenridge, and buying some of his substantial and cheap goods. Sam is going off to war, and wants to clean out his stock before his company takes up the line of march."

Hedges, Abram; 99 Reg Co B, 23 Mar 64-18 May 65 transferred to 48 Reg, out 15 Jul 65. NOD.

Hedrick, Peter; 99 Reg Co B, no dates. 99th Regiment History states: "Peter Hedrick, __ Nov 62, discharged, sick. HC death notice 11 Mar 1909: "Peter Hedrick, an old citizen, living north of Shirley, Indiana, died 2 Mar and was buried 4 Mar, in the Harlan cemetery. It was partially grief that took the old man away, as his wife died just nine days before, and they were

Hancock County Indiana Civil War Soldiers

much devoted to each other. He had purchased last summer the old house that he had courted his wife in, and moved it closer to their home, and fitted it up with two fire places, to summer in, but they did not live to enjoy it. He was seventy-nine years old and a Virginia Democrat." HC Harlan Cemetery: Peter Hedrick 1 Nov 1829-2 Mar 1909; Sophia Hedrick 28 Jan 1834-21 Feb 1909.

Heller, Henry; 132 Reg Co F, no dates. NOD.

Helms, Abram; 75 Reg Co I, 16 Jul 61, died 4 Dec 63 at Chattanooga, Tennessee, from wounds received at Missionary Ridge 25 Nov 63. NOD.

Helms, Eastly; 12 Reg 1st Lt., 16 Aug 62, discharged 4 Mar 64. Eastly Helms married 29 Dec 1851 Martha Ann Mingle HC Bk 3-262.

Henby, John K.; 51 Reg Co F, 27 Sep 61-25 Apr 65. "John K. Henby (8 Mar 1840-16 Oct 1919), Hancock County, s/o Elijah and Elizabeth (Haskett) Henby of Hancock County. His Regiment took part in the campaigns of Kentucky and Tennessee, the excessive marching, constant skirmishing and fighting in the battles of Crab Orchard, Perryville, Wild Cat Mountain, Pulaski, Lebanon and Stone River, Tennessee. He was captured at Stone River by Texas Rangers, held at various places forty-five days, ending up in Libby Prison.

"He was on special detail in 1864, taking up the dead from battlefields and reburying them at the National Cemetery, Chattanoonga. He received a gunshot wound at Dalton (Georgia) 15 Aug 1864, spent time in the hospital, on furlough and was discharged 25 April 1865. He returned home and on 22 March 1868 married Ruth Haskett (22 Feb 1844-1928);. children, Elijah, Nora, John, Silas and Abbie. John and Ruth buried HC Park Cem. " John's brother, Elijah Henby enlisted in the same company and regiment, but died in 1862 at Nashville, Tennessee.

Hendren John; "he was a brother to Lydia Hendren, wife of Charles Edward Chittenden, and brother to Jeremiah Hendren

Hancock County Indiana Civil War Soldiers

who served in the Mexican War." A John Hendren enlisted at Perkinsville, Indiana, served in Co C 101 Indiana Infantry

Hendricks, John; 8 Reg Co C; 5 Sep 61-21 Aug 65. A John Hendrix married 11 Jun 1848 Ann Cooper HC Bk 2-285. He is buried HC Park Cemetery, no dates, military units only.

Henner (Henon) Thomas; 9 Cav Co B, 23 Dec 63-28 Aug 65. NOD.

Henry, John T. 147 Reg Co F, 7 Feb 65-31 May 65. A John Henry married 19 Oct 1896 Louisa Piper HC Bk 5-330. HC newspaper 15 Nov 1917: "John T. Henry, 76 years of age, a Civil War veteran, died at his home in Maxwell of heart trouble. Mr. Henry was one of the well known men of his community. He leaves a daughter, Mrs. Mattie Pfeifer, of Jay County. Services were held at the home."

Henry, Major Samuel; 89 Reg Co B, 7 Aug 62 as 1st Lt; 29 Aug 62 promoted to Captain, 18 Jul 63 promoted to Major, 1 Nov 64 murdered by guerillas at Greenton, Missouri, ten miles south of Lexington. He was born at Eden (HC), 1838, s/o George Henry, who died 1853, and is buried at Pendleton, Indiana.

Herod, Lt. John B.; 9 Cav Co B, 13 Aug 62-promoted 8 Dec 63. HC newspaper 20 Oct 1864: "Lt. Herrod of Co B, 9th Cavalry, was wounded in action 25 Sep 1864 and taken prisoner at Sulphur Tressel (sic), Alabama." 99th Regiment History states, "In 1900 Lt. Herod residence is Red Oak, Iowa."

Herron, Ambrose J.; 52 Reg Co E, 1 Feb 62-26 May 64 transferred as Corp'l to Co I. HC obit 26 Jan 1928: "Ambrose J. Herron, age 85 years, died at the home of his son, George Herron. The funeral was held at the home yesterday and the body then brought to (HC) Park Cemetery for burial. Mr. Herron was a veteran of the Civil War and was Mayor of Greenfield for two terms, from 1885-1894.

"Mr. Herron was familiarly known to those of his day in Greenfield as "Jack" Herron. He had not resided in Greenfield for more than thirty years and a majority of those of the present generation were not aware that there was a surviving mayor of

Hancock County Indiana Civil War Soldiers

forty years ago. Mr. Herron is survived by four sons and three daughters." Ambrose Herron married 27 Jun 1873 Cinderella Gephart HC Bk 6-200.

Herron, John E.; HC obit 26 Dec 1912: "John E. Herron, well known in this city, and who resided here a number of years ago, died at his home southeast of Shelbyville. He was a veteran of the Civil War and had been a most excellent soldier. He was a bachelor and leaves a number of brothers and sisters to mourn his death. He was 68 years of age."

Hervey, Dr. Thomas P.; 17 Sep 62, received a commission from Gov. Morton as Assistant Surgeon of 50th Regiment; Jun 63 resigned commission; Jul 63 entered into a special contract to serve as Surgeon in Veteran Reserve Corps at Burnside Barracks, Indianapolis. "Thomas P. Hervey was born 26 Feb 1821 in Franklin County, Indiana, s/o Thomas and Hannah (Waylan) Hervey. Thomas Hervey, the father, died when his son was an infant and he moved eight years later to Butler County, Ohio, with his mother who died 28 Jun 1844.

After reaching his majority, he took up the study of medicine at the old Central Medical College in Indianapolis. He began the practice of medicine in 1848 and followed it successfully until 1899. In the first part of his service, he was constantly with his regiment in the field in the Army of the Cumberland, at Corinth, Jackson, Parkers Cross Road, City Mound and many smaller engagements.

He married 1) Mary McCord, one son, Frank; married 2) 29 Nov 1864 Anna M. Cory (not HC), children, Samuel,; John C.; Anna Caldwell; and Lyda Jane. Thomas Hervey was the brother of Dr. Thomas Hervey and James Walter Hervey, surgeon in the 50th Regiment; their uncle, William Hervey, was in the War of 1812; and Mrs. Hervey's grandfather Cory was in the War of 1812. HC McCordsville Cemetery: Hervey, Dr. Thomas P., soldier, 1821-1909; Annie Mary 1841-1931."

Hervey, Dr. James Walter; "he was born 5 Apr 1819, near Brookville, Indiana, but was raised and educated in Butler County, Ohio (see above for his brother, Dr. Thomas P.). After

Hancock County Indiana Civil War Soldiers

graduating from Asbury University, Dr. Hervey came to Hancock County, near the place where Mt. Comfort now stands, and close to the Madison and Hamilton County lines.

"He was commissioned as Surgeon of the 50th Indiana, and served with his regiment until disabled at Parker's Cross Roads, on the last day of 1862. He was discharged due to disability on 3 Feb 1863. After partial recovery, he was appointed Acting Assistant Surgeon at Burnside Barracks, Indianapolis, where he served until the end of the War. He then moved to Indianapolis where he entered upon the practice of medicine. He was the author of many papers on Public Hygiene, and was a member of many Marion County and State medical societies."

Hiday, Archibald; 11 Reg Co B; 31 Aug 61-30 Aug 64. "To All Whom It May Concern: Know ye that Archibald C. Hiday enlisted from Madison County, Indiana, 5 July 1861 and mustered into service at Indianapolis, Indiana, 18 July 1861, as a private of Company B, 11th Regiment Indiana Volunteer Infantry under Captain Charles W. Lynam to serve three years or during the War.

"The regiment was assigned to Colonel Lew Wallace's Division; later Harvey's Division, 13th Corps and participated in engagements at Ft. Henry, Tennessee, 6 February 1862; Fort Donelson; February 15-16, Shiloh; April 6-7 Corinth Siege; April 30-May 30 Port Gibson, Mississippi; May 1, 63 Champion Hills; May 16 siege of Vicksburg; May 22-Jul 4 expedition to Jackson; July 5-8 Opelansas; 1864, veteranized 1 February; furlough in March; returning assigned to 2nd Brigade, 2nd Division, 19th Corps.; skirimshed August and early September near Winchester and engaged at that place. Sep 19 Fisher's Hill; Sep 20 Cedar Creek; Oct 19 marching to Baltimore upon conclusion of Sheridan's Shenandoah Campaign.

"Said Archibald C. Hiday was wounded at Jackson, Mississippi, by gunshot in right hip breaking the bone and causing painful wound. Was confined in hospital at Jackson suffering with wound, then transferred by boat to Vicksburg

Hancock County Indiana Civil War Soldiers

then to Washington Hospital until discharged. Was captured at Memphis, Tennessee, by being surrounded. Honorably discharged at Indianapolis, Indiana, 30 Aug 1864 on expiration of term of service." Archibald Hiday was born Jan 1837, probably Madison County, Indiana, on the land where Gravel Lawn Cemetery is now located; married 24 Jan 1872 Elizabeth Clark (HC Bk 6-81). Archiblad died 13 Aug 1922, buried Madison County, Indiana, Gravel Lawn Cemetery. See page for his brother, Jacob Hiday.

Hiday, Jacob; "Henry and Mary (Winn) Hiday are the parents of five soldier sons, Jacob, Thomas and John, volunteers in the 39th Indiana, Archibald in the 11th Indiana and Joseph in the 32nd Iowa. Jacob Hiday was born 14 Jan 1823, Franklin County, Indiana,and settled in Hancock County as an infant. At age 39 in August, 1862 he joined Company G, 12th Indiana Volunteers, as a private. The regiment was engaged in the battles of Richmond, Kentucky (where Jacob was captured and held prisoner for twenty-four hours), Lookout Mountain, Missionary Ridge, Vicksburg, Jackson, Champion Hills, Chattanooga, the Atlanta campaign and hundreds of skirmishes, plus marches, exposure to cold, heat, rain and snow.

"He was promoted to Corporal and later to Sergeant. In the battle of Missionary Ridge, he received a gunshot wound in the right arm fracturing the bone; he received a furlough 26 Dec 1863, for sixty days to go home. At the expiration of which he joined his command at Bridgeport, Tennessee; and he received his final discharge Jun 1865 at Indianapolis. He was married 1) Marguretta Wallace; 2) Sarah Emery and 3) HC Bk 5-203 23 Feb 1868 Nancy Stanberry (3 Mar 1843-7 Apr 1933). Jacob died 21 Nov 1902; he and Nancy are buried at Madison County, Indiana, Gravel Lawn Cemetery."

Hiday, John Henry; 12 Reg Co G 8 Aug 62-8 Jun 65. He was born 25 Mar 1825, Madison County, Indiana, married 1) 21 Oct 1882 Mary Ellen Carroll (HC Bk 7-406); married 2) Mary Whelchel, no other data available. John Henry died 24 Jun

Hancock County Indiana Civil War Soldiers

1886 and buried HC Wynn Cemetery. See page for his brother, Jacob Hiday.

Hiday, Joseph; 32 Iowa Reg Co F, "residence, Union, Iowa, age 33, born Indiana, 15 Aug 62-24 Aug 65. A Joseph Hiday married 25 Oct 1873 Sarah Huston HC Bk 6-231. Madison County, Indiana, Gravel Lawn Cemetery: Joseph Hiday 9 Jan 1830-11 Dec 1902. See page for his brother, Jacob Hiday.

Hiday, Thomas; 12 Reg Co G. "A native of Madison County, Indiana, Thomas Hiday was born 29 Nov 1828, s/o John Henry and Mary (Winn) Hiday. After enlistment the regiment was hurried to the field and on 29 Aug 62, fought in the battle of Richmond, Kentucky, where he was captured, held prisoner for one day and released on parole. In Jul 1863 he was sent to the hospital at Corinth suffering with malarial fever. Among his battles are siege of Vicksburg, Jackson, Missionary Ridge, Resaca, Rome, Kennesaw Mountain, Peachtree Creek, Ezra Church, Dalton, siege and fall of Atlanta; at the battle of Ezra Church, he fired his musket so rapidly that the barrel became heated and blistered his hands.

"He was considered a dead shot and was detached on special duty when good shooting was to be done. He was discharged 8 Jun 1865. His four brothers all served in the War; his wife's two brothers also served, Thomas Doty in the 2nd Cav and John Doty in an Indiana Regiment. He married 17 Oct 1850 in Madison County, Sarah Jane Doty (22 Nov 1822-29 Aug 1902). Thomas Hiday died 18 Dec 1908 and with his wife, Sarah Jane is buried at Madison County Gravel Lawn Cemetery." See page for his brother, Jacob Hiday.

Higbee, William; 144 Reg Co A, 2 Feb 65-5 Aug 65. A William Higbee married 14 Feb 1869 Mary Blessinger HC Bk 5-279. William buried HC Simmons Cemetery, no dates, only units.

Higgenbotham, Thomas W.; 106 Reg Co D, 10 Jul 63-17 Jul 63. Married 30 Jun 1866 Sophia Ashcraft HC Bk 5-30.

Higgins, Joseph; 3 Cav Co I, enlisted 1861 and served three years. "Born in Jackson Township (HC), the s/o Joseph and

Hancock County Indiana Civil War Soldiers

Elizabeth Higgins. Joseph married Martha Cooper, d/o Benjamin and Nancy (Thomas) Cooper. Joseph returned home after the Civil War, resumed farming, was a successful thresher of grain, operated a saw-mill and took a lively interest in his community, especially the Pleasant Hill Methodist Church. In 1871, the family migrated to Kansas. He made the journey to the West by wagon and finding a favorable location in Crawford County, purchased a quarter section of land and lived there until his death in August, 1872. He was buried with military honors in the Fort Scott National Cemetery. His wife then returned to Hancock County with her son, Morris, where she died 7 Jul 1880 and is buried at Pleasant Hill Cemetery beside their five infants."

Higgins, Lawson (Jeremiah); 22 Illinois Infantry, 11 Jun 61, died 7 Nov 1861. "He was born about 1836, Hancock County, the s/o John and Lucinda (Alderman) Higgins. Lawson was age 22 and single at time of enlistment, private, 5' 9" tall, brown hair, hazel eyes, dark complexion, and a farmer." "On 11 Jul 1861 the Regiment moved to Bird's Point, Missouri; 7 Nov 61 seven companies engaged in the battle of Belmont where Lawson Higgins was killed in action; by the end of the day, the losses were 144 killed, missing and wounded. His brothers, John and Samuel were also killed in the War." Contributed by Patti Higgins, Minier, Illinois.

Hill, Lt William G.; 8 Reg Co G, 22 Apr 61-6 Aug 61; also 8 Reg Co B, 30 Dec 61 as 2nd Lt; 18 Jan 63 promoted 1st Lt. HC newspaper 11 Jun 1863: "Lt. W.G. Hill was painfully wounded in the right hand near Vicksburg, May 1863." HC newspaper 3 Dec 1863: " We were much surprised to receive a call from our old friend and fellow citizen, Lieut. William G. Hill, Company B, 8th Regiment. He is looking rather bad, from an attack of "camp diarrhea" and has come home to recuperate." HC newspaper 23 Jun 1864: "Our readers will be sorry to learn of the death of Lt. William G. Hill, a tried and gallant young soldier from this county, by accidental drowning at Vicksburg, Mississippi, while with his Company and Regiment en route to

Hancock County Indiana Civil War Soldiers

New Orleans. The deceased came to this county from his parental home at Albany New York, about the year of 1854 and being proficient with the pen, was employed as a Deputy County Auditor. He enlisted with Capt. R.A. Riley's 8th Regiment, in the three months campaign in Western Virginia as a private. On the reorganization of the Company, he was elected Orderly Sergeant and served in that capacity until he was promoted to 2nd Lieutenant on the resignation of S.T.Kauble.

"He was promoted to 1st Lieutenant upon the resignation of Capt. Wall. He was wounded in the hand in the celebrated charge of Vicksburg. He had a premonition that he would never be with us again, and so informed many of his friends on the eve of his departure." *Hancock Democrat*, 23 Jun 1864: "A letter from Capt. S.H. Dunbar details the death of Lt. Willliam Hill, At Vicksburg, in the night of 3d inst. Lieut. Wm. C. Hill walked off the upper deck on the steamer, Mississippi, on which we were being transported, and was drowned. The men were asleep. He had himself been in bed. He was not missed until next morning, when inquiry was made, and it was found that some of the crew had seen a man in the water, but was unable to save him."

Hinchman, Joseph Vincent; 105 Reg Co D 11 Jul 63-18 Jul 63; also 9 Cav Co B 13 Nov 63 Sgt., 18 May 64 promoted 2nd Lieut.; out 17 May 65 as 1st. Lieut. *Hancock Democrat*, 20 Apr 1865: "Lieut. J.V. Hinchman, Company B, 9th Indiana Cavalry, and son of John Hinchman, Esqr., of this county, arrived in town yesterday morning from Vicksburg, Mississippi. Lieut. H. was captured by the rebels at Sulphur Trestle, Alabama, sometime last fall, and was in prison until the 16th of March last. He gives the usual account of the hardships endured by our men, twenty-six-hundred of whom were confined on a piece of ground containing only three-quarters of an acre. We hope our young friend will soon gain his accustomed health and vigor." He was in prison at Cahaba, Alabama, along with the others captured 25 Sep 1864 at the battle of Sulphur Branch

Hancock County Indiana Civil War Soldiers

Trestle. "Joseph V. Hinchman, s/o John and Charlotte (Blackledge) Hinchman who was the daughter of Jacky Blackledge."
"Joseph Vincent Hinchman married 30 Nov 1867 Thursey I. Crane HC Bk 5-171. HC obit 13 Jul 1906: "John Hinchman died a the home of Dr. and Mrs. M.M. Adams on West Main Street, Greenfield. He was age 84 years and one of the prominent men of this part of the State. Mr. Hinchman spent last winter with his son, Dr. J. Vincent Hinchman, in Brock, Nebraska, and since his return to Greenfield had been with Dr. Adams, the condition of his health demanding almost constant medical attention.
"John Hinchman was born in Virginia 20 March 1822, came to Indiana in 1840 and four years later married Miss Charlotte Blackledge, daughter of Mr. and Mrs. John Blackledge, a prominent family of Rush County, who came from Kentucky. Mrs. Hinchman died in 1892. They had five children, all of whom are living: Dr. Joseph Vincent Hinchman of Brock, Nebraska; Mrs. Nancy Adams, w/o Dr.Adams; John M. of Greenfield; Mrs. Rebecca Goldsmith of Kinsley, Kansas; and Mrs. Rhoda Morris who lives on the farm in Rush County, Indiana, entered by her Grandfather Blackledge. The last two children are twins. Interment at East Hill Cemetery, Rushville."

Hinchman, Morris; 54 Reg Co I, no dates. HC obit 19 Oct 1922: "Morris Hinchman, for many years a resident of this county, passed away at his home, 746 North State Street, following an illness arising from a complication of diseases. Mr. Hinchman was 78 years of age, a Civil War veteran and a member of the local G.A.R. post. He is survived by two sons, Harry and John Hinchman and one daughter, Margaret Hinchman. Interment HC Park Cemetery."

Hind, W. E. 10 Ind Inf Co K. buried HC Mt. Lebanon Cemetery. NOD.

Hinds, James H.; 11 Reg Co K, 31 Aug 61-26 Jul 65, Corp'l. HC obit 10 Aug 1933: "James H. Hinds, age 89, died at his

Hancock County Indiana Civil War Soldiers

home in Fortville following a week's illness. A retired plasterer he was born 15 Mar 1844, (s/o James H. and Elizabeth (Apple) Hinds), served in the Civil War, participating in seventeen battles, including Shiloh, Vicksburg, Winchester and Cedar Creek and in the four years he marched 9,318 miles. He was body guard for Abraham Lincoln and was guard at the White House a short time. Surviving are Peter Hinds, and a sister, Mrs. Mary Cory." A James H. Hinds married 5 Dec 1867 Harriett Emery HC Bk 5-181.

Hobbs, Thomas J.; 106 Reg Co D, 10 Jul 63-17 Jul 63. NOD.

Hobbs, William; 10 Reg Co A; no dates. HC New Palestine Cemetery: William Hobbs, only military units on stone. "A J.W. Hobbs, carpenter, age 45, died 25 Dec 1887, New Palestine."

Hogle, Adam Poe; Ohio Reg Co H, no dates. HC obit 30 Aug 1917: "Adam P. Hogle, age 79 years, died at his home in New Palestine, son of Langdon and Catherine (Carr) Hogle. He was born 24 Jun 1838, Ohio, married (HC Bk 5-248) 24 Sep 1868 Ella Smith (1847-1929). Adam was engaged in the milling business in Greenfield and was a justice of the peace at the time of his death and member of G.A.R. His wife survives." Adam and Ella Hogle both buried HC Park Cemetery.

Holden, Caleb; 53 Reg Co A, 16 Mar 64-20 Oct 65. HC obit 19 Jan 1928: "Caleb Holden, age 82 years, died at the home of his sister, Mrs. Florida Wagner, on Cemetery Street. The son of Thomas and Sarah (Cannon) Holden, and widower of Luvina. Mr. Holden was born 21 Jun 1845, Shelby County, Indiana. He was a veteran of the Civil War and is survived by two daughters and two sons. Burial HC Mt. Lebanon Cemetery." His gravestone only says, Caleb Holden, soldier.

Holden, J.; 19 Reg Co F, no dates. HC newspaper 15 May 1864: "J. Holden of 19th Indiana was wounded slightly in the hand during recent battles across the Rapidan." A Joseph Holden married 21 Jan 1875 Susan Kidwell HC Bk 6-343.

Hancock County Indiana Civil War Soldiers

Holding, Leroy; 19 Reg Co F, no dates. HC newspaper 19 May 1864: "Leroy Holding of the 19th Indiana, Company F, was wounded in recent battles across the Rapidan." A Leroy Holding married 1 Jun 1868 Elizabeth Andrick HC Bk 5-188.

Holland, James; 99 Reg Co K, 30 Dec 62-6 Jul 63, residence/place of enlistment, :Liberty, Indiana. See data for his brothers, John and Thomas Holland.

Holland, John; 99 Reg Co K, 30 Dec 62-6 Jul 63, residence/place of enlistment, Connersville, Indiana. See data for his brothers, James and Thomas Holland.

Holland, Thomas Stevenson; 5 Cav Co G, 30 Aug 62-5 Jun 65, Sgt. "Thomas Holland was born 26 June 1824 in Fayette County, Indiana, son of Robert (born Ireland) and Margaret (Stevenson) Holland (born Pennsylvania) who came to Hancock County, in 1855. Thomas enlisted in the Civil War in 1862 and his regiment (99th) was at the siege of Vicksburg, Jackson, and later with Sherman in the Atlanta campaign and all engagements of that memorable march, winding up in the Grand Review at Washington City before being discharged. In November 1862 he was accidentally knocked off the deck of the steamboat, Mary Miller, in the Ohio River, between Louisville, Kentucky, and Cairo, Illinois, on the way to Memphis, but was rescued without serious injury.

"Thomas was 5'7' tall, dark complexion, black eyes, black hair and farmer when enrolled. On 30 Oct 1870 he married (HC Bk 5-411) Asbrene Curry, daughter of James Curry, a native of Hancock County. Thomas' two brothers, James and John shared the fortunes of war in Company K, 99th Regiment; Mrs. Holland's cousin or brother, Isaiah Curry was a Captain in the 99th Regiment.

"On 31 Jan 1891 Thomas Holland applied for a military pension #774214, and following is the document, written by him and quoted verbatim, that accompanied the application: 'As you wanted a history of my diseases and suffering, I will give it. In Camp Morton 1862 fever and ague; since that time up to now I have had the following diseases and treated by

Hancock County Indiana Civil War Soldiers

doctors, chronic camp diarrhea, pleurisy, mumps, enlargement of spleen. I am worse at times more so when I labor or move about tolerably fast. I have a hurting in my left side and have suffered a great deal of pain. I have had rheumatism and thought I would not get over it. Doctors Butterworth, Carter and Justice have treated me. I think I could not work more one fourth of the time at manual labor, sometimes I am so weak I can not hardly go at all.' Uncle Tommie, as he is familiarly known, attended his first school on 16 August 1842, in the little Robinson Chapel, in Fayette County." HC Curry's Chapel Church: Holland, Thomas died 15 Apr 1914 90y 9m 19d; Asbrien died 19 Oct 1895 57y 0m 18d. Contributed by Bob Holland, Greenfield, Indiana.

Holoway, Jesse; 9 Cav Co B, 9 Dec 63-28 Aug 65. NOD.

Holt, John G.; 9 Cav Co E, 19 Dec 63-28 Aug 65, residence/place of enlistment, New Castle, Indiana, promoted, Sgt. HC obit 22 Oct 1925: "John G. Holt, a widely known resident of Henry County for many years. Failing health and advanced age induced him to come to the home of his, son Howard Holt, in Greenfield, where he died. Mr. Holt was born 8 Oct 1843, son of Drury and Sarah (Kimbell) Holt, in Carthage (Rush County). He was a soldier in the Civil War, in the Ninth Cavalry, and for the last thirty years was secretary of the association formed by the regiment for annual reunions. Mr. Holt was a retired farmer. He is survived by three sons, Warren Holt of Ogden, Perrin Holt of Knightstown and Howard. The funeral was held at the Friends Church in Spiceland, burial at Spiceland."

Hoobler, John; 5 Cav Co G, 26 Aug 62, wagoner. NOD.

Hook, Charles; 105 Reg Co E, 11 Jul 63-18 Jul 63. a Charles Hook married 27 Jan 1863 Harriett Williams HC Bk 4-375.

Hook, George; HC Philadelphia Cemetery, George Hook Co B 14 Reg 1839-1903. NOD.

Hook, Jacob; 8 Reg Co G, 22 Apr 61-6 Aug 61; also 148 Reg Co C, 17 Feb 65-5 Sep 65. A Jacob Hook married 31 Dec 1873 Rachel Gray HC Bk 6-248; also a Jacob Hook married 24 Jan

Hancock County Indiana Civil War Soldiers

1889 Jane Hudson HC Bk 8-125. HC Philadelphia Cemetery: Hook, Jacob no dates; Rachel w/o Jacob 11 Nov 1833-2 Nov 1887.

Hook, James; 105 Reg Co D, 11 Jul 63-18 Jul 63; also 9 Cav Co B, 9 Dec 63-28 Aug 65. HC newspaper 20 Oct 1864: "Pvt. James Hook, Co B, 9th Cavalry, was wounded 25 Sep 1864 at Sulphur Trestle (Alabama) and will soon be home." A James Hook married 10 Jan 1866 Harriett Rittenhouse HC Bk 5-24.

Hook, John; 51 Reg Co D, 14 Dec 61-died 28 Mar 62 Jeffersonville, Indiana. A John Hook married 9 Jul 1853 Martha Ann Marks HC Bk 3-169.

Hook, Joseph; HC Philadelphia Cemetery: Joseph Hook Co B 9 Ind Inf. NOD.

Hook, Samuel; 11 Reg Co F, 16 Jul 61-16 Jun 65. HC obit 14 Jul 1921: "Samuel Hook, son of William and Elsie Hook, was born near Cumberland, Marion County, on 24 Oct 1841, and departed this life 4 Jul 1921, at his home in Greenfield, Indiana, aged 79 years. When nineteen years of age, he enlisted in what was known as the Zouave Regiment with Lew Wallace as its Colonel. Lee C. Thayer, of Greenfield was the drummer boy of this regiment and Edmund P. Thayer and William P. Denny were members of Company A.

"Mr. Hook fought in many battles, notably those of Fort Donelson, Shiloh, the siege and capture of Jackson, Mississippi. At the battle of Opequan, Winchester, Virginia, on 19 September 1864, he was severely wounded through the left leg which disabled him and he was discharged 16 Jun 1865. On 21 August 1865 he married Harriett Hook (HC Bk 4-530) and to this union were born eight children. He is survived by the widow, five children and one brother, James. Interment (HC) Park Cemetery."

Hook, Samuel T.; 79 Reg Co B, 9 Aug 62-discharged 7 May 63, wounds. A Samuel T. Hook married 13 Oct 1864 Sarah A. Burk HC Bk 4-479. Both buried HC Park Cemetery: Hook, Samuel T. 1842-1917; Sara A. 1844-1930.

Hooker, Jacob; 12 Reg Co H, 8 Aug 62-8 Jun 65, Sgt. NOD

Hancock County Indiana Civil War Soldiers

Hooker, Josiah; Co F N.C. Jr. Res. CSA; HC obit 19 Mar 1925. "Josiah Hooker, died 12 March 1925, after a brief illness at his home, 420 North Wood Street, Greenfield. He was 79 years old and lived with his widow and daughter, Miss Cora Hooker. He is also survived by daughters, Florence Alford, Minnie Windsor and son, Orlando. A retired well driller, he was born 16 May 1846, Randolph County, N.C., son of Robert and Martha (Bell) Hooker. Interment (HC) Park Cemetery."

Hoover, George W.; listed as George W. Hover on roster of 5 Cav Co G, 20 Oct 62; HC newspaper 11 Aug 1864: "George Hoover was taken prisoner during the disastrous expedition commanded by General Stoneman." Andersonville Prison Database, code #54155, George W. Hoover, Company G, 5th Indiana Cavalry, survived and exchanged Atlanta, Georgia, 19 Sep 1864 George died 14 Jan 65, Annapolis, Maryland.

Horton, Elijah; 12 Reg Co H, 8 Aug 62-8 Jun 65, Corp'l. An Elijah Horton married 2 Apr 1857 Elizabeth Brantlinger HC Bk 4-15.

Hover, George; see George W. Hoover.

Howard, John B.; 9 Cav Co B, 9 Dec 63 2nd Lt.; 1 Jan 65 1st Lt. A John Howard (HC) obit dated 19 Mar 1914 details his life but says nothing about being a Civil War soldier... "On 16 Jul 1838, there was born to Henry and Elizabeth Howard of Pendleton, Madison County, Indiana, a son, John. At the tender age of eighteen months, his father died, but he was taken into the home of an uncle, Daniel Snider of Pendleton. Those days spent with "Uncle Dan" served as cherished memories in later years. At the age of eighteen he came to Hancock County to live with his mother, who had remarried.

"After being with his mother a few years, he married Susan Henry, and settled on a farm near Maxwell, Indiana. Susan died 20 Apr 1879, and on 3 Sep 1882 John married Martha Graves. John suffered heart trouble for ten weeks before he died 3 March 1914 at age 75. He is survived by two sons, William T. and Samuel H.; one daughter, Bernice Barrett; a half brother Milton Henry; a half sister Martha Barnard,; three

Hancock County Indiana Civil War Soldiers

grandchildren and a devoted wife." HC Mt. Carmel Cemetery: Howard: John 1838-1914; Susan w/o John died 20 Apr 1879, 38y 7m 1d; and Martha A. 1850-1914

Howard, Dr. Noble P.; 1862, commissioned as assistant surgeon in 12 Indiana Regiment. HC newspaper 28 May 1862: "Dr. N.P. Howard, Assistant Surgeon of the 12th Indiana Regiment, recently discharged, arrived at home. The Doctor looks well, considering the hard service he has undergone since he entered the army. He brings with him quite a selection of interesting relics of the rebel army gathered from Bull Run, Manassas Junction, Winchester and other points, among them an armor for the face, which he kindly presented to us.

"The Doctor informs us that he intends to remain at home and continue the practice of his profession, in all its branches. The experience of the past year--attending the sick and wounded of our gallant army adds to previous medical knowledge. The Doctor may be found at his office, one door West of Edwards' Drug Store, or at his residence on Main Street, third house from the corner of Pennsylvania Street."

HC newspaper 8 Jan 1863: "Drs. Howard and Duncan, of Greenfield, are among the Physicians dispatched by Gov. Morton to look after the wounded at Murfreesboro."

HC obit: 29 Aug 1895: "Dr. N.P. Howard, Sr. died after a long and patient siege. He was born 11 Sep 1811 in Warren County, Ohio. His father was an early citizen of Cincinnati, and was a soldier in the War of 1812. In 1840 Dr. Howard began the study of medicine at Rushville, Indiana, three years later he moved to Greenfield and began the practice of surgery and medicine. He was active in many county and state medical societies; for eight years he was deputy collector of internal revenue.

"He was married 23 Apr 1844 (HC Bk 2-117) Cinderella Gooding, daughter of Asa and Matilda Gooding, and sister of Judge D.S. Gooding. Dr. Howard is a genial gentleman, and a man of firm convictions and uncompromising integrity, and stood well both in his profession and as a man." Dr. Howard

Hancock County Indiana Civil War Soldiers

applied for a military pension 17 Jun 1889, # 712534, stating, "near Winchester, Virginia, March, 1862, was disabled with diarrhea resulting in piles, disease of the rectum, bowels, stomach and lungs. For quite a spell was confined to bed under treatment for his piles trouble; that said trouble continues to afflict him, requiring that he follow a strict regimen and avoid horseback riding." (Being in the Cavalry increased his suffering, and he was afflicted with these diseases the remainder of his life.). HC Park Cemetery: Howard, Dr. N.P, Sr. Co F 12 Ind Inf, died 25 Aug 1895 72y 11m 4d; Cinderella, w/o N.P. Sr. died 15 May 1899 65y 1m 15d.

Hubbell, Joseph; 53 Reg Co A, 28 Mar 64-21 Jul 65. HC Gilboa Cemetery: Joseph Hubble, soldier, no dates. HC death notice 26 Dec 1901: "Joseph W. Hubbell, aged 55 years, died at his home in Frankfort, Indiana, 21 Dec. Mr. Hubbell lived in this county a number of years ago, leaving here going to the northern part of the State. He returned here some two years ago and while here had a stroke of paralysis, from which he never recovered. Some months ago, he returned to Frankfort where he remained until his death. His remains were brought here for burial at Gilboa Cemetery."

Hudson, Abijah; 4 Cav no dates. See page for his brother, Dudley D. Hudson.

Hudson, Amos; 148 Reg no dates. See page for his brother, Dudley D. Hudson.

Hudson, Benjamin; 51 Reg Co D, 14 Dec 61-discharged disability 1862. Certificate of Disability for Discharge states: "Benjamin Hudson, a Private in Company D, 51st Regiment of Ind. Vols, was enlisted in Captain Sylvester Brown at Indianapolis, Indiana, on the fourteenth day of October, 1861 to serve three years; he was born in Champaigne County in the state of Ohio, is thirty nine years of age, five feet five inches high, dark complexion, gray eyes, black hair, and by occupation when enrolled, a farmer.

"During the last two months said soldier has been unfit for duty fifty days. Since the loss of his wife in January last he has

Hancock County Indiana Civil War Soldiers

had frequent attacks of a mild insanity which has rendered him unable for duty. He was a sound and healthy man when enlisted done good duty until the date of the above disability. Signed Sylvester R. Brown, Capt., Moorsville, Alabama, 3 July 1862.

"I certify, that I have carefully examined the said Benjamin Hudson of Captain Brown's Company, and find him incapable of performing the duties of a soldier because of mental imbecility with frequent attacks of a mild form of insanity; probably the result of nostalgia, aggravated by the loss of his wife, by death, in January last. This disability is of about six months standing. I do not think he will recover in camp, or that he will again be fit for the service. Signed, Erasmus B. Collins, Surgeon. Discharged this fourteenth day of August, 1862, at Stevenson, Ala. Signed, A.L. Streight, Col. commanding the Reg't.

"Declaration For Invalid Pension, on 24 December 1879, appeared before Ephraim Marsh, Clerk of Circuit Court, Hancock County, Indiana, states in part: "Near Standiford, Lincoln County, Kentucky, on 3 Feb 1862, having heard of the death of his wife and the condition of his family, his health having been affected by the exposure and incidents of the service his nervous system gave way and became affected and his mind weakened and he became worse every day unable for duty or labor until his discharge for disability. He never was in the hospital but at times done light duty with the regiment. Since his discharge he has been unable to earn a subsistence by manual labor. When he entered the service he was a stout and able bodied man without any disease of mind or body.

"Benjamin Hudson received a pension #250856.

"On 12 Nov 1892, Benjamin Hudson was dropped from the Pension Roll, because of death, Diseased Brain, having been last paid at $24 to 4 Mar 1890. Contributed by Ruth Bundy, Greenfield, Indiana. *Hancock Democrat* obit 27 Mar 1890: "Benjamin F. Hudson was born 11 Feb 1821, in Champaigne County, Ohio, and about four years later came with his parents

Hancock County Indiana Civil War Soldiers

to Indiana, and when yet a boy, on Sugar Creek. He was married first 2 Apr 1846 (HC Bk 2-190) to Mary Roberts, the daughter of Benjamin Roberts. Mary died 19 Jan 1862, while Benjamin was in the service of his country. After his return home, he married 4 Dec 1862 (HC Bk 4-3) Mrs. Elizabeth Smith, who, with three sons still survive.

" 'Uncle Benny' as he was known before the War, was a very hard working man, a good neighbor and will be missed by many. He expressed repeatedly that he was ready and willing to die, and was called to cross the narrow stream just after midnight, 20 March 1890, at his home near Philadelphia (HC). Interment in Philadelphia Cemetery (no grave marker in 1988)." HC McNamee Cemetery: Mary A. Hudson w/o Benjamin died 19 Jan 1862. 1860 Hancock County Census, Sugar Creek Township records: Benjamin Hudson, age 39; Mary, age 38; Willis age 13; Mary age 9; Edward age 7; Dudley age 3; Benjamin age 1 and a female Hudson age 15, first name begins with Elic rest illegible.

Hudson, Benjamin; there are two Benjamin Hudsons recorded 1) "a brother to Dudley D. Hudson named, Benjamin served in the 7th Indiana Cavalry, promoted to Major" and the Benjamin Hudson who served in 51st Indiana? Are they the same soldier??

Hudson, David; 16 Reg no dates. See data for his brother, Dudley D. Hudson.

Hudson, Dudley Didget; 79 Reg Co B, 9 Aug 62-1 May 65. "Dudley D. Hudson bravely says, 'the proudest incident of my army life was the charge on Missionary Ridge.' He was 5' 9" tall, fair complexion, blue eyes, light hair and farmer when enrolled. The 'gallant 79th' was attached to the Army of Kentucky and Tennessee where the exposures of camp life, the fatigue of the march began to tell and on account of pain in the kidneys, resulting in lumbago. He was sent to hospitals at Nashville, Louisville and Gallipolis, Ohio before returning to his regiment in May 1863, at Murfreesboro.

Hancock County Indiana Civil War Soldiers

"At the battle of Chickamauga, he received a gunshot wound on the top of his head, knocking him down, but he got up and kept in the fight until the finish. At the battle of Atlanta, he received a gunshot in the right shoulder, landing him in the hospital. From the Jeffersonville Hospital, he was furloughed home to vote in the Fall of '64. He was then sent to Jefferson Barracks, Missouri, where he was discharged 1 May 65 due to disability: 'gunshot wound in the right shoulder fracturing the clavicle, received in action near Atlanta, Georgia, 3 Aug 1864, resulting in the entire loss of use of arm. He is unfit for the Veteran Reserve Corps. Disability total.' "

"The son of Thomas and Permelia (Cheney) Hudson, Dudley was born 6 Jan 1834, Hancock County,; married 29 Aug 1856 (HC Bk 3-355) Mary Ashcraft who was born 17 Mar 1838, Butler County, Ohio; they were the parents of Manora, Sarah and George. After Mary's death Dudley married Margaret McCormick (1842-1929), one child, Mattie (Hudson) Thomas. Dudley's six brothers served in the War: Edward and James were in the 9th Indiana Cavalry; David in the 16th Indiana Infantry; Benjamin in the 7th Indiana Cavalry and promoted to Major; Abjiah on General McCook's staff of the 4th Cavlary; and Amos in the 148th Indiana Infantry. Dudley died 10 Oct 1908; he and Margaret are buried HC Park Cemetery.

Hudson, Edward; 105 Reg Co D, 10 Jul 63-17 Jul 63; also 9 Cav Co B, 13 Nov 63-12 Jun 65. See page for his brother, Dudley D. Hudson. HC newspaper 14 Dec 1920: "Edward Hudson, of Route 6, will leave in a few days for his annual visit with B.F. Hudson and Mrs. F.D. Burk of Arkansas. This visit marks his thirtieth annual visit." See page for Dudley D. Hudson.

Hudson, Francis; 8 Reg Co B, 16 Jul 62-14 Jun 65. NOD.

Hudson, George; 99 Reg Co B, 13 Aug 62-5 Jun 65. A George Hudson married 17 Oct 1849 Sarah Kennedy HC Bk 2-35; also a George Hudson married 8 Mar 1851 Eleanor Carr HC Bk 3-35. 99 Regiment states, "George Hudson, Greenfield, is dead in 1900."

Hancock County Indiana Civil War Soldiers

Hudson, James; 5 Cav Co G, 15 Dec 63-15 Sep 65. NOD. See data for Dudley Hudson, he had a brother, James.

Hudson, Peter; 79 Reg Co C, 15 Aug 62-7 Jun 65. A Peter Hudson married 21 Nov 1867 Louisa Burns HC Bk 5-177; a Peter Hudson married 3 Oct 1869 Emily Johnson HC Bk 5-32.

Hudson, Willis; 9 Cav Co B, 9 Dec 63-12 Jul 65. The 1860 Hancock County census records a Willis Hudson, age 15, in household of Benjamin and Mary Hudson. NOD.

Hughes, Quinton D.; 105 Reg Co E, 11 Jul 63-18 Jul 63. "Quinton D. Hughes was born 1839, Christiansburg, Kentucky, son of John W. and Mary (Rogers) Hughes; married 2 Jul 1856 Mary Martin HC Bk 3-348; Quinton was a merchant and died 8 Jan 1855 at his residence in Greenfield, and buried HC Park Cemetery."

Huguneard, Claude; 12 Reg Co B, 4 Jun 61-19 May 62. NOD

Humbles, William H.; 75 Reg Co I, 16 Jul 62-9 Apr 64. A William H. Humbles married 20 Jul 1865 Jane Wood HC Bk 4-522.

Humphries, James; 12 Reg Co G, 8 Aug 62-8 Jun 65. A James Humphries married 31 Mar 1866 Ellen Maulsby HC Bk 5-49. NOD.

Hunt, Elijah; 148 Reg Co C, 17 Feb 65-5 Sep 65. HC obit 18 Apr 1912: "Elijah Hunt, son of Elijah and Hanna Hunt, was born 8 May 1844, in Miami County, Ohio. Departed this life at his home in Greenfield 11 Apr 1912, aged 67 years. He was married to Rachel Curry, 3 Oct 1864 (HC Bk 4-81). To this union were three daughters and three sons. This companion and three of the children have preceded him to the other world. Three children survive, Charles and Henry Hunt and Olive Cox. His second marriage was to Mary Finney, 9 Apr 1886, who died 29 Nov 1902; his last marriage was to Sarah Midlam, who still survives him. He was a soldier in the Civil War and served his country as a brave and faithful soldier during the term of enlistment. He had a birthright in the Friends Church, affiliated with this organization all his life and is buried at the Westland Friends Church Cemetery."

Hancock County Indiana Civil War Soldiers

Hunt, John; 148 Reg Co C, 17 Feb 65-5 Sep 65. A John Hunt, s/o Libni and Jane Hunt, born 13 Mar 1823, died 21 Jul 1910; a John Hunt married 16 Sep 1842 Nancy Lemay HC Bk 2-54.

Hunt, Junius; 28 U.S. Colored Troop, Co F. 31 Mar 64-died Aug 64 of wounds. NOD.

Hunt, Nelson; 28 U.S. Colored Troops Co F, 31 Mar 64-4 Jan 65. Died. NOD.

Hunt, William H.; 79 Reg Co C, 15 Aug 62-no out date. A William H. Hunt married 26 Feb 1863 Elizabeth Denney HC Bk 4-380. HC Maple Grove/Jackson/Olvey Cemetery: William H. Hunt died 20 Jan 1866 22y.

Hunter, John; 12 Reg Co G; 8 Aug 62-8 Jun 65. A John Hunter, born 1837, died 25 May 1902. NOD.

Hunter, Melville; 12 Reg Co G, 8 Aug 62-8 Jun 65. NOD.

Huntsinger, Captain John S. HC obit 11 May 1905: "Captain Huntsinger was born in Indiana, 25 Dec 1829, son of Joseph and Susanna (Schock) Huntsinger. He was raised in his native State, attended schools there and worked as clerk until 1862 when he enlisted in 22nd Indiana Battery and Light Artillery for six months. He then assisted in raising a unit of Illinois Light Artillery, was in turn second lieutenant, first lieutenant and captain. He went through the Southern States and participated in a number of engagements and raids. He escaped being wounded by the enemy, but was injured by a horse falling on him while engaged in battle and was disabled for six months. after the close of the War, Captain Huntsinger returned to Indiana, went to Iowa and after nine years returned to Greenfield and acted as cashier of a bank for six years. In 1882 he located in Park Rapids, Minnesota, where he died 22 Apr 1905."

Huston, David; 8 Reg Co K, 5 Sep 61-28 Aug 65. A David Huston married 2 Jan 1866 Seantha Cummins HC Bk 5-21. NOD.

Huston, Captain James; 12 Reg Co B, 23 Apr 61 as 2nd Lt, died 13 Oct 64 from disease as a P.O.W. NOD.

Hancock County Indiana Civil War Soldiers

Huston, John B.; 8 Reg Co B, 25 Aug 61-Jun 65. HC obit 13 Jun 1907: "John B. Huston, one of Greenfield's well known citizens is dead at his home on the corner of Pennsylvania and South Streets. Mr. Huston has been in poor health for several months, but not considered dangerously ill until a few weeks ago. He was born in Madison County, Indiana, 14 March 1846, the son of Thomas W. (died 7 Feb 1889, age 63) and Lucinda (Woodard) Huston (died 13 Jan 1902, age76). When sixteen years of age, he enlisted as a member of Company B, Eighth Indiana Regiment. His command was first sent to Helena, Arkansas, then participated in the siege of Vicksburg and was taken prisoner at Cedar Creek but escaped unharmed with a companion. John married Sarah Jane Roberts (1847-10 Feb 1916) daughter of Joshua and Catherine Roberts. After being discharged from the service, John engaged in the blacksmith business at Fortville, and in 1881 moved to Greenfield being in the blacksmith and livery business. Leaving the widow and two children, Lulu Wilson and Charles Huston, John died 13 Jun 1907 and with his wife, Sarah J. is buried HC Park Cemetery."

Huston, Thomas J.; 8 Reg Co B, 25 Aug 61, died 6 Feb 63 at Salem, Missouri. NOD.

Hutson, J.; 5 Cav Co G. HC newspaper 11 Aug 1864: "Pvt. J. Hutson was taken prisoner during the disastrous expedition commanded by General Stoneman." A James Hudson was in 5 Cav Co G, 15 Dec 63-15 Sep 65. See data for Dudley D. Hudson. Or is this man Pvt. J. Huston??

Hutton, A.; 5 Cav Co G, no dates. HC newspaper 11 Aug 1864, "Pvt. A. Hutton was taken prisoner during the disastrous expedition commanded by General Stoneman." Listed as Adam Hutton on roster on Co G, 5th Cavalry. See page on Adam Hutton. Additions or corrections?

Hutton, Aaron, 53 Reg Co A, 24 Feb 62, died 6 Oct 62. See letter section telling of his death.

Hutton, Adam; 5 Cav Co G, 18 Aug 62-15 Sep 65, Corp'l. HC obit 21 Jan 1926: "Friends here received word of the death of

Hancock County Indiana Civil War Soldiers

Adam Hutton, well known resident of this city and member of the Grand Army of the Republic, at the home of his son, John Hutton, in Eldorado, Illinois. Mr. Hutton, age 86, had been in poor health several months. Mr. Hutton was a resident of Hancock County and returned after the Civil War, but in 1866 moved to Illinois. He is survived by the wife, two sons, Elmer and John Hutton, and a daughter, Anna Starwalt. Mr. Hutton will be buried in Illinois. Caleb Moncrief, a life-long friend of Mr. Hutton, will leave for Eldorado this evening to attend the funeral." Is this the Pvt. A. Hutton who was taken prisoner?? See data for A. Hutton.

Hutton, James; 8 Reg, 2nd Lt. NOD

Hutton, Joseph; 9 Cav Co B, 9 Dec 63. HC newspaper 20 Oct 1864: "Private Joseph Hutton, Company B, 9th Cavalry, was killed in action at Sulphur Trestle, Alabama, 25 Sep 1864."

Hutton, William; 79 Reg Co B, 9 Aug 62-discharged 8 Jun 63, wounds. A William Hutton married 23 Sep 1859 Lydia Kirkman HC Bk 4-153; Also a William Hutton married 28 Aug 1881 Deborah Baker HC Bk 7-275. HC obit 5 Sep 1918, recorded the death of a William Hutton: "William Hutton, aged seventy-nine years, a veteran of the Civil War, died at his home in Phildelphia, Indiana, of cancer of the stomach. The funeral was in charge of Dunbar Post G.A.R. of Greenfield, of which the deceased was a member."

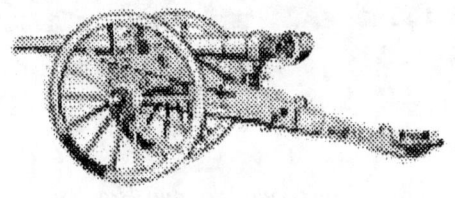

Hancock County Indiana Civil War Soldiers

Samuel Henry

Courtesy of Samuel Harden

Hancock County Indiana Civil War Soldiers

Thomas Holland

Courtesy of Bob Holland

Hancock County Indiana Civil War Soldiers

◄ I ►

Irish, William O. ; 12 Reg Co B, 15 May 61-19 May 62, Corp'l. NOD

◄ J ►

Jack, James M.; 63 Reg Co F, 30 Aug 62-10 Feb 63; also a James Jack 134 Reg Co K, 24 May 64-time expired. HC obit 13 Oct 1892: "Mr. James Jack, of Brandywine Township, in attempting to cross the track of the C.H.& I. railroad at Fountaintown in a buggy, was struck by the vestibule train on that road. Mr. Jack was thrown some distance to the side of the road and fatally hurt. His horse was killed instantly, and his buggy completely demolished. Mr. Jack was picked up and taken to a neighboring house where he lingered for two hours when he passed peacefully away. Mr. Jack was hard of hearing and at the point where he crossed the track the train could not be seen until one was upon the track. We understand a suit will be brought against the company for the killing of Mr. Jack at no distant day." A James M. Jack, blacksmith, died 6 Oct 1892, buried HC Mt. Lebanon Cemetery.

Jack, John; 8 Reg Co B, 25 Aug 61, no out date. HC newspaper 5 Feb 1862: "Otterville, Missouri, 22 Jan 1862, John Jack is discharged on account of physical disability induced by inclemencies (sic) of camp life, signed, Lt. Samuel Dunbar, commander of Co B."

Jackson, David E.; 39 Reg Co E, 21 Sep 63-Sep 65. "David E. Jackson became ill with a serious case of chronic diarrhea and was confined to a hospital for six months; he joined his regiment again the summer of 1864 at Point Lookout, Maryland, and the following winter was attached to the Veteran's reserve corps and finally discharged. He was the son of William and Phoebe (Nancy) Jackson, born in Bond County, Illinois, 26 Dec 1844, and departed this life 22 Aug 1923.

"He spent his boyhood days in and around Pendleton (Madison County, Indiana) and moved to Hancock County in

Hancock County Indiana Civil War Soldiers

1885. On 24 Jun 1866 he was united in marriage to Margaret J. Rench, and to this union were born eight children, of whom four and the wife preceded him in death. Those who remain to mourn their loss are: Joseph Jackson; Carrie Slifer; Maud Cross and Nannie Shinn, all of Greenfield. Mr. Jackson was a member of Dunbar Post GAR. Buried HC Park Cemetery."

Jackson, Francis Marion; 89 Reg Co B, 6 Aug 62-9 Jul 65. "The regiment was hurried to the field of conflict at the battle of Mumfordsville, Kentucky, where he was captured, 16 Sep 62, held a few hours and released on parole. His battles were: Fort DeRusie, Pleasant Hill, Bayou La Mour, Marksville Prairie, Yellow Bayou, Tupello, second battle of Nashville, Fort Blakely, and in the spring of 1864 in pursuit of Gen. Price, until he was driven out of Missouri. He married 8 Mar 1866, Lucinda, daughter of William and Barbara (Hines) Cook. Children: William, Frederick, Minnie, Jessie and Charles."

Jackson, George H.; 79 Reg Co C, 15 Aug 62-7 Jun 65 Corp'l. HC obit 18 Feb 1915: "George Henry Jackson, for many years one of the best known men in Fortville and Vernon Township, a cousin of the late Stokes Jackson, died at his home after a long illness. The son of John and Sarah (Denny) Jackson, George was born 18 Apr 1842; and married 11 Dec 1865 (HC BK 5-112) Telitha Ann Parks (9 Nov 1846-25 Feb 1920) and died 11 Feb 1915. Both buried Madison County, Indiana, Gravel Lawn Cemetery."

Jackson, Hughlander; 79 Reg Co C, 15 Aug 62-26 Jun 63. A Hughlander married 1 Oct 1863 (HC Bk 4-404) Samira C. Hunt. Samirah w/o Hughlander died 2 Oct 1864 18y 7m 27d, buried HC Maple Grove/Jackson/ Olvey Cemetery

Jackson, John; 8 Reg Co B, 25 Aug 61-died 23 Mar 63, Memphis, Tennessee; comments in a letter written by Andrew Fuller to Adam F. Wilson: "John Jackson died at Memphis, was poisoned and died in twenty-four hours after he took sick."

Jackson, Milton; 8 Reg Co G, 22 Apr 61-6 Aug 61; also 5 Cav Co G 18 Aug 62-15 Jan 63. NOD.

Hancock County Indiana Civil War Soldiers

Jackson, Stephen; 89 Reg Co B, 8 Aug 62-19 Jul 65. "He was promoted to Corp'l 26 Nov 62 and to Sergeant 1 Sep 64. He received a gunshot in the right hand in the Red River Expedition, 12 Apr 64, was put on a hospital boat above Shreveport. He was in the hospital at Vicksburg and Memphis and to a convalescent camp at Fort Pickering. After a thirty day furlough, he joined his comrades at Memphis. He was once captured and held prisoner about ten hours before being released at Mumfordsville, Kentucky. He was in the battles of Fort De Rusie, on hospital boat, Choctaw, on the Red River five days constant fighting, second battle of Nashville, Fort Blakely, Tupelo, Mississippi, besides many skirmishes and lesser battles."

HC obit 23 Oct 1930: "Stephen Jackson, soldier of the Civil War, and known as "Uncle Steve" to hundreds of friends in this city and county, died yesterday at his home, 226 Lincoln Street. The son of Levi and Elizabeth (Hardin) Jackson, he was born in Madison County, Indiana, 18 Nov 1842, at Greenfield, 27 Feb 1867, he married (HC Bk 5-119) Susan Fry (born 16 Dec 1842), d/o John and Sallie (Noel) Fry. Mrs. Jackson died 1925 and since that time Mr. Jackson has made his home with his son, Cassius. Stephen and Susan Jackson are buried HC Park Cemetery."

Jacobs, William K.; HC Courthouse, Soldier Burial List Book; 5 Reg Co D; died 15 Oct 1893; 64 years; occupation, farmer; burial, (HC) Simmons Cemetery. NOD.

James, Samuel; 123 Reg Co K, 3 Mar 64-25 Aug 65. "He shared with comrades the fortunes of war on a number of bloody fields, never wounded or being made a prisoner, but by reason of exposure while on the march and in the field, contracted rheumatism and heart trouble, from both he suffered greatly the remainder of his life. The son of Samuel and Kate (Larson) James, he was born 3 May 1837, in Rush County, Indiana; on 4 Nov 1857 he married Nancy Irvine, daughter of George and Lottie (Scott) Irvine. five children: Willard, Frank, Walter, Mary and Fred." " HC obit 21 Jun 1900: "Samuel

Hancock County Indiana Civil War Soldiers

James, aged about sixty, died at his home in Jackson Township. He leaves a wife and five children. Buried HC Simmons Cemetery."

Jarrett, Benjamin; 33 Reg Co H, no dates. "Benjamin Jarrett married 17 Feb 1870 Martha Walker, who died 9 Feb 1880 in fall from a wagon 35y 3m 6d. Benjamin 20 Sep 1846-31 Aug 1899. Both buried HC Mt. Carmel Cemetery."

Jarrett, Cornell; HC obit: " Cornnel Jarrett, 79 years old, died at his home in Fortville. Mr. Jarrett was a Civil War veteran and survived by his widow, one daughter, Mrs. Frank Crouch, and one son, Harry Jarrett." A Cornnell Jarrett married 28 Oct 1874 Theodosia Stuart HC Bk 6-312.

Jarrett, Harrison; 45 Reg Co H, 1 Feb 65-Sep 65. "The Regiment was attached to the Army of Tennessee that was closing in on the Confederate Army in all quarters. After the War was over, the Regiment was assigned to garrison duty along the railroad between Louisville and Pulaski, Tennessee. His brother Lambert was a volunteer in the 39th Mounted Infantry. The son of Robinson and Caroline (Brawley) Jarrett, Harrison was born 6 Mar 1847, near Eden (HC) and married (HC Bk 5-444) 22 Jan 1871 Abagill (Ominda)Walker Two daughters, Daisey and Grace. Harrison died 20 Aug 1903 and is buried HC Eden Cemetery."

Jarrett, James Mathers; 79 Reg Co C, 15 Aug 62-7 Jun 65. " born Hancock County, 5' 4' tall, light complexion, blue eyes, light hair, age 18, farmer when enrolled." "The son of Andrew and Elizabeth (Mathers) Jarrett, James was born 4 Jun 1844, married Nancy Frazier 24 Jun 1866 HC Bk 5-71. Eight children: Herman; Orville; Herbert, Dallas, Alva, Minnie, Una and Elsie." HC obit: 11 Dec 1930: "Funeral services were held in Mohawk for James M. Jarrett, who had lived all his lifetime in the community. Burial Gravel Lawn Cemetery (Madison County, Indiana). He died 4 Dec 1930 and is survived by the widow, Nancy Frazier Jarrett and seven children." Contributed by Eva B. George, Midlothian, Illinois.

Hancock County Indiana Civil War Soldiers

Jarrett, Lambert; 39 Mounted Infantry, no dates. Jarrett Lambert married 21 Sep 1865 Mary Ann Cox HC Bk 4-537. HC Eden Church Cemetery: Jarrett: Lambert 6 Jun 1844-11 Apr 1917; Mary Ann w/o Lambert 6 Jul 1845-3 Apr 1913. See page for his brother, Harrison Lambert.

Jeff, David; 5 Reg Co G, no dates. A David Jeff was in Andersonville, Georgia, Prison, code #54328; survived and exchanged 15 Apr 1865. NOD.

Jenkins, James; 36 Reg Co F; no dates. "His occupation was a mason when he died 17 Mar 1903 at age 81 and buried Hamilton County, Indiana, Old Fort Cemetery."

Jennings, John A.; 8 Reg Co B, 25 Aug 61-13 May 64, drowned at Saluria Bayou, Texas. NOD.

Johnson, Berry; 5 Cav Co G; 21 Oct 62-10 Jun 65. HC newspaper 11 Aug 1864: "B. Johnson was taken prisoner during the disastrous expedition commanded by General Stoneman" Andersonville, Georgia, Prison, code #54399, survived and sent to Millen 11 Nov 1864. A Berry N. Johnson married Fannie Pierson 14 Apr 1880 HC Bk 7-177. HC obit 2 Apr 1914: " Berry N. Johnson, age 65 years, died at the home of his sister, Margaret Wilson, in Green Township. He had been in poor health for some time, being a sufferer of dyspepsia and heart trouble. Mr. Johnson came to this county from Kentucky, his birthplace, when very young, and his parents William and Mary Johnson settled in Green Township. The old log house they occupied is still standing on the homestead and is still in use near the home of Mrs. Wilson, where Mr. Johnson died. He leaves two brothers, William N. and Benjamin Johnson, and two sisters, Mrs. Martha Wilson and Margaret Wilson. Interment HC Cooper Cemetery."

Johnson, Brazil; 12 Reg Co B, 15 May 61. NOD.

Johnson, George W.; 188 Ohio Inf Co D Sgt., no dates. HC obit 24 Jan 1924: "George W. Johnson, a well known and highly respected citizen of this city, passed away at his home. He served through the Civil War and also served in the cavalry on the plains after the Civil War was over. George was born 9

Hancock County Indiana Civil War Soldiers

May 1843, Ohio, the son of John and Nancy (Townsend) Johnson Mr. Johnson is a widower and is survived by six children: Otis, Elmer, Homer and George Johnson; Mrs. George Baker and Mrs. Emma Walton. Burial at HC Park Cemetery."

Johnson, George W.; 8 Reg Co G, 21 Apr 61-6 Aug 61. A George W. Johnson was also in 79 Reg Co G, 15 Aug 62-died 12 Apr 63, Nashville, Tenneesse.

Johnson, John; HC Courthouse, Soldier Burial List Book: 79 Reg Co G; died 3 Oct 1895: 54 years; occupation, farmer; burial, Greenfield. NOD.

Johnson, John; 106 Reg Co D, 10 Jul 63- 17 Jul 63. Too many men named John Johnson in sources for clarity.

Johnson, John F.; 5 Cav Co G; 21 Oct 62-Nov 62. NOD.

Johnson, Lewis; 5 Cav Co G, 21 Oct 62-15 Sep 65. "A Lewis Johnson was born 10 Aug 1815, laborer, who died 10 May 1904, Greenfield, widower, buried HC Philadelphia Cemetery. A Lou Johnson and w/o Lou, no other data, are buried at Philadelphia Cemetery. Also HC Cooper Cemetery, Lewis Johnson, no other data, stone broken.

Johnson, Peter; 33 Reg Co H, 16 Sep 61-no out date. A Peter Johnson married 10 Apr 1862 Mary Nibarger HC Bk 4-323. A Peter Johnson buried HC Park Cemetery but the Government marker has sunk into ground and cannot be read.

Johnson, Robert; 148 Reg Co C, 17 Feb 65-died 28 Feb 65, Pecksburg, Indiana. NOD.

Johnson, Thomas E.; 11 Ohio Reg Co G, age 23, 9 Jul 61-21 Jun 64. HC obit 5 Jan 1911: "Thomas E. Johnson, age 73 years, and a Civil War veteran, died at his home on South Pennsylvania Street. He leaves a widow, two brothers, George and Quinn Johnson and a sister, Mrs. Emma Stewart, all of Greenfield. He had no children. Mr. Johnson was born in Clinton, County, Ohio, 20 Oct 1838, and was one of a family of nine children. At the close of the War in 1865, he married at Washington City to Mary Ellen Smith, who survives him, although she is in critical condition. Mr. Johnson came to this

Hancock County Indiana Civil War Soldiers

County and located at Charlottesville in 1866, and came to Greenfield a year later. Thomas E. Johnson is buried at HC Park Cemetery."

Johnson, William; 9 Cav Co B, 13 Nov 63-18 Jul 65. NOD.

Jonas, L.; 5 Cav Co G, no dates. HC newspaper 11 Aug 1864: "L.H. Jonas was taken prisoner during disastrous expedition commanded by General Stoneman." Andersonville, Georgia, Prison, code #54506, survived and exchanged 15 April, no year given.

Jones, Francis M.; 79 Reg Co B, 9 Aug 62-7 Jun 65. A Francis M. Jones married 12 Oct 1870 Marie Calvin HC Bk 5-411.

Jones, Francis P.; 9 Cav Co B, no dates. NOD.

Jones, George E.; 19 reg Co C; died 21 Mar 1892; 60 years; burial, HC Philadelphia Cemetery. NOD.

Jones, Henry; 8 Reg Co G, 22 Apr 61-6 Aug 61. Also a Henry Jones; 9 Cav Co B, 13 Nov 63-28 Aug 65. NOD.

Jones, Isaac; 8 Reg Co G, 22 Apr 61- 6 Aug 61; 8 Reg Co B, 25 Aug 61-died 4 Oct 62, Sgt. NOD.

Jones, R.E.; buried HC Philadelphia Cemetery, stone reads, 19 Ind Inf Co C. NOD.

Jones, Samuel; 105 Reg Co E, 11 Jul 63-18 Jul 63. HC obit 1 Nov 1917: "Mary Jones, widow of Samuel Jones, died at the home of her daughter, Mrs. John Gardner, at Fortville.." a Samuel Jones married 18 May 1864 Margaret Edwards HC Bk 4-454.

Jones, Stephen A.; 8 Reg Co B, 14 Aug 61, promoted in succession Corporal, Sergeant, 1st Lt. and Captain; out 8 Aug 65. HC newspaper 14 Aug 1862: "Stephen A. Jones of Co B, 8th Regiment, is promoted to Corporal." A Stephen A. Jones married 26 May 1863 Alice Martindale HC Bk 4-457. HC Philadelphia Cemetery: Capt. Stephen A. Jones 1838-1890; three children, not named, of Capt. Stephen and Mary A. years of death: 1885; 1887; 1889.

Jones, Thomas S.; 8 Reg Co B, 22 Apr 61-6 Aug 61; also a Thomas S. Jones; 8 Reg Co B, 25 Aug 61-no out date. Too

Hancock County Indiana Civil War Soldiers

many men named Thomas Jones in sources for accurate identification.

Jones, William: 9 Cav Co B, 9 Dec 63-28 Aug 65. Too many men named William Jones in sources for accurate indentfication.

Jones, William H.; 57 Reg Co A, 13 Dec 61-21 Nov 62. NOD, same as above.

Jones, William I.; 118 Reg Co I, 9 Aug 63-1 Mar 64. Madison County, Indiana, Gravel Lawn Cemetery: William I. Jones 1842-1932 Co I, 118 Ind Vol Inf; on same stone is Susan 1845-1938.

Jones, William R.; enlisted 6 Aug 62, 19th Battery, Light Artillery. "Now I will give you a short sketch of my army life, beginning in 1862. At that time, I was living in a Quaker settlement, northeast of Knightstown, was thirty-two-years old with a wife and seven children, four boys and three girls, the oldest being age eleven years. After enlistment on 6 Aug 1862, the Nineteenth Battery was ordered to Mumfordsville, Kentucky, to guard a bridge; then to Perryville, Kentucky, where we were in the field till dark when our lines broke. We left four pieces on the field.

"The main engagements we were in during long marches were Chickamauga, Lookout Mountain, Missionary Ridge, Ringgold, Resaca, Kennesaw Mountain, Peach Tree Creek and Atlanta, besides numerous skirmishes and repeated shellings along the way. In a word about myself, I was Sergeant in the 19th Battery and was awarded the first prize as the best shot or gunner in the battery. I was born in 1829, and when about ten years old, my father sold his farm in Ashtabula County, Ohio, and started for Illinois, but stopped at Eaton, Ohio. This was 1840, the year of 'log cabins and hard cider' and we saw General Harrison as he made a speech.

"My father operated a cheese factory in connection with a dairy. In 1843 we moved to Henry County, Indiana, near Lewisville, where my mother, a sister and brother died. My father later married Mrs. Daniel Custard, putting together children ranging in age from six to fourteen. I married Miss Frances Custard and we lived together near forty-one years. I moved to Hancock County in 1872 and expect to end my days here."

HC newspaper 10 Sep 1908: "Captain William R. Jones of Greenfield, one of the best-known veterans of the Civil War, who has been ill for several months, will, with his wife, leave this week for the Soldiers' Home in La Fayette, Indiana, where they expect to spend the remainder of their days on earth." HC Park Cemetery: Captain William R. Jones 19 Ind L.A.; Frances C. w/o William R. died 11 Apr 1891 59y 5m 13d. It appears that William R. Jones married a second time as Frances died 1891 but a wife went with him to La Fayette, in 1908. A William R. Jones married 20 Nov 1892 Mrs. Lorinda Baker HC Bk 8-461.

Jordan, James C.; 12 Reg Co B, 15 May 61-4 Aug 61. A James Jordan married 30 Jul 1865 Sarah Van Zandt, no place given. Madison County, Indiana, Gravel Lawn Cemetery: James C. Jordan 16 Jan 1841-15 Sep 1921, Co B 12 Ind Inf.

◀ **K** ▶

Kappeler, Anthony; HC obit 15 Jan 1920: " Anthony E. Kappeler, of New Palestine, died at his home at the age of 74 years. He had a stroke of paralysis on Christmas Day. He enlisted in the 108th Ohio Volunteers in 1862 when he was 16 years old and campaigned in Kentucky, Tennessee and Georgia and was with Sherman on his march from Atlanta to the sea.

"At the close of the War, he came to this vicinity; was a charter member of the German Veteran's Association and its secretary for twenty-five years; and was a member of the firing squad which fired the cannon in the court house square here each year, on Washington's birthday. He is survived by three sons, Edward, William and Oscar; two daughters, Mrs. Henry Ames and Miss Agnes Kappeler." HC New Palestine Cemetery: Anthony Kappeler 7 Sep 1845-7 Jan 1920; M. Elizabeth 14 Nov 1851-1 Jan 1919.

Hancock County Indiana Civil War Soldiers

Kauble, Solomon T.; 8 Reg, 25 Aug 61; resigned 26 Dec 61; reentered as 1st Lt. in Co G 5 Cav, 2 Sep 62 ; resigned 3 May 63. Solomon Kauble married (HC Bk 3-14) 3 Nov 1850 Clarissa Elsbury (16 Oct 1827-15 Dec 1909). HC newspaper 16 Dec 1909: "Pierce Kauble went to visit his mother, Mrs. Solomon Kauble, age 81 years, at Hannibal Missouri." In 1930 Pierce Kauble's brother, Douglas, lived in Perry, Missouri.

Kearns, William; HC Westland Cemetery, William Kearns, soldier NOD.

Keeley, Alfred; 8 Reg Co G, 5 Sep 61-4 Sep 64. "born Shelby County, Indiana, 5' 8" tall, fair complexion, blue eyes, brown hair and bricklayer when enrolled.. "HC obit 25 Apr 1895: "Alfred Keeley was born in the State of Indiana in the year 1830. He enlisted in defense of the old flag in the late War, 5 Sep 1861, in Company G, Eighth Indiana Regiment, and was discharged therefrom on 4 Sep 1864, on account of disability incurred during his service as a soldier. He was a consistent member of the Samuel H. Dunbar Post G.A.R. until he died 20 April 1895. Laid to rest Sugar Creek Cemetery." Alfred Keeley married 4 Feb 1866 Elizabeth Lynam HC Bk 5-31. Mary E. Keeley, w/o Alfred, 1844-1910, also buried HC Sugar Creek Cemetery.

Keffer, Albert; 12 Reg Co B, 15 May 61-19 May 62. NOD.

Keifer, Almon; "Almon Keifer, son of Ferdinand and Margaret (Loehr) Keifer, was born In Greenfield, 15 Sep 1845. He learned the printer's trade which he was following when the nation was plunged into war. In August 1862, at Greenfield, he laid aside his printer's stick and enlisted in Company G, 5th Cavalry (90th Reg. Ind. Vols). The command was hurried to the front and saw the dread realities of war in camp, on the weary march, and gory battlefield.

"Mr. Keifer received a gunshot wound in the right fore-arm, at the battle of Altoona Hills, near Dallas, Georgia, fracturing the bone, landing him in the hospital at Nashville, and Totten, Field Hospital." HC newspaper 9 Jun 1864: "We regret to learn that our friend and fellow typo, Almon Keifer (better

Hancock County Indiana Civil War Soldiers

known as Buck) of the 5th Cavalry, was wounded in the right arm, in one of the recent battles in Georgia." HC newspaper 7 Jul 1864: "Our young friend, Almon Keifer, of the 5th Cavalry, is at home on a wounded furlough. His wound is getting better. "Buck" is a good soldier, and we hope he will soon recover the use of his arm."

"After a furlough he joined his regiment 10 Nov 1864, at Louisville, Kentucky. His battle list includes, Salina, Kentucky; Buffington Bar, Ohio; Atlanta campaign; Resaca; Buzzard's Roost; Peach Tree Creek and numerous small engagements. He was captured with a number of comrades, near Ringgold, Georgia, and they were held in a schoolhouse all night. Mr. Keifer raised two floor boards and crawled through the opening, under the building and remained in hiding until the other captives were taken away when he made his escape, joining the Union forces that had by this time come along. He was discharged July 1865, at Pulaski, Tennessee, enrolled on the disability roll.

"He is plying his trade in a printing office in Greenfield." HC obit 20 Jul 1916: "Almon (Buck) Keifer, a Civil War veteran, old time printer and personal friend of James Whitcomb Riley, was found dead at the home of his sister, Mrs. David Loehr, South East Street. Mr. Keifer was one of the best known men in Greenfield, having been a life long resident. He was the oldest printer in Greenfield, both in point of age and years of service. He was with the Mitchell Printing Company for about sixty years, starting work with them in 1860 and retired five or six years ago; spending some of the intervening time on his homestead in North Dakota. Mr. Keifer is unmarried and is survived by two sisters, Mrs. Loehr and Mrs. George Slifer. He was a member of the Dunbar Post G.A.R., and was a life pensioner of the printer's union, drawing $5.00 weekly for life. Burial HC Park Cemetery."

Keiser, Joseph H.; 34 Reg Co D, 21 Sep 61-3 Feb 66. NOD.
Kellenberger, Charles; 79 Reg Co B, 9 Sep 62-7 Jun 65. NOD.

Hancock County Indiana Civil War Soldiers

Keller, Jacob; 60 Reg Co A, 2 Nov 61, Sgt.-13 Apr 65. HC obit 30 Dec 1915: "Jacob Keller, aged 80 years, died at the home of his daughter and son-in-law, Mr. and Mrs. Jerry Meek, of 920 West North Street, of the infirmities of old age. Son of John (born Virginia) and Margaret (Embray, born Ohio), Joseph was born 22 Apr 1836, widower of Susan (Downing, married 11 Apr 1861 HC Bk 4-259). He died 27 Dec 1913, was a soldier in the Civil War and member of Dunbar Post G.A.R. Interment Philadelphia Cemetery: " Jacob Keller died 27 Dec 1915; Susan 8 Dec 1840-11 Sep 1910.

Keller, James; 12 Reg Co G. "died in the South 28 Jan 1864, brought home and buried near Fortville." Most likely Madison County, Indiana, Gravel Lawn Cemetery.

Keller, Jonathan; 57 Reg Co A, 13 Dec 61-4 Feb 62. A Jonathan Keller married 16 Feb 1865 Sarah Miller HC Bk 4-501.

Kellum, John; 5 Cav Co G, 18 Aug 62-died at home. HC Mt. Lebanon Cemetery: J.W. Kellum military units only on stone; Sarah w/o J.W. 2 Sep 1838-4 Apr 1870.

Kelly, Benjamin F.; 99 Reg Co B, 15 Aug 62-killed 28 May 64. HC newspaper 9 Jun 1864: "Pvt. B.F. Kelley was killed at battle of Dallas, Georgia, 28 May 1864." Benjamin, 22y 4m 4d, son of William and E., is buried at HC Shiloh Church Cemetery; also buried there are six other children of William and E., Lewis died 22 Sep 1861 3y; Andrew died 24 Sep 1861 6y; Sarah died 12 Mar 1865 11 y; John died 17 Mar 1865 21y; Mary died 9 Apr 1865 19y; Emily died 10 May 1865 13y. The father William died 20 Mar 1863 51y; the mother Elenor died 10 Apr 1876 56y. This family must have suffered intense heartache.

Kelley, George W. 12 Reg Co G, killed 25 Nov 186. NOD.

Kempton, Solomon D.; 12 Reg Co B, enlisted 23 Apr 61 as 1st documents referring to Lt. Col. Kempton's resignation which Lieutenant; mustered out 19 May 62; 17 Aug 62, appointed Major by Gov. O.P. Morton; 17 Nov 62 received and accepted commission as Lieut. Colonel; 19 Jun 63, resignation accepted.

Hancock County Indiana Civil War Soldiers

The 1860 Federal Census for Hancock County, Vernon Township records, Saul D. Kempton, age 30, Medical Dr., born Indiana, living in the household of William Foley, age 30, merchant, and Sara Foley, age 22.

The Indiana State Archives microfilm records 12th Regiment Correspondence where part of service seems clouded in mystery. HC obit 23 Oct 1863: Died at Indianapolis on Thursday, 15 Oct 1863, Lieut. Col. Sol. D. Kempton, of Walpole, Hancock County, aged 34 years. Only a few weeks ago, Col. K. was here (Greenfield) in apparent good health, elastic and buoyant, and with indications of a healthful life. He then vowed his intention of locating in this place and practicing his profession of medicine. We were gratified at the prospect of soon claiming him as a citizen.

"But truly, 'in the midst of life is death.' Col. K., in this life, was guided by a high principle which never shrunk from danger. He was a true friend, a kind neighbor, a genial companion. His body has returned to mother earth yet let not, "The good be interred with the bones." He sacrificed the comforts of home and a lucrative practice to fight for his country's honor and the unity of the States. During his last illness, he declared his faith in the Christian system, and received its consolations, and we may well trust that his disembodied spirit, though it has passed away from earth, has found a happy and eternal home amid brighter climes."

Kennedy, Levi; 100 Reg Co K, 15 Aug 62-29 Jun 65. NOD.

Kenyon, William; 13 Cav Co I, 29 Feb 64-18 Nov 65, blacksmith. HC obit 24 Apr 1924: "William Kenyon is dead at his home in Charlottesville, following a long illness. The son of Milton (born England) and Matilda (Hargrove, born Kentucky) Kenyon, William was born 15 Mar 1845 and died 21 Apr 1924, widow, Adeline. He was for many years a blacksmith near Cleveland and was a soldier in the Civil War. He was the father of Mrs. Walter Bridges of Greenfield."

Hancock County Indiana Civil War Soldiers

Kern, Hiram; 105 Reg Co E, 11 Jul 63-18 Jul 63. A Hiram Kern married 4 Nov 1869 Christina Jane Plummer HC Bk 5-335.

Kesner (Kessler), John; "Born about 1849, Germany, died 17 Jan 1911, about age 62, occupation, cooper, cause of death, lobar pneumonia." A John Kesner married 1 Nov 1870 Louisa Smith HC Bk 5-418. HC Simmons Cemetery: John Kesner 16 Oct 1849-17 Jan 1911; Louisa Kesner 19 Jan 1848-death date unknown Found no source that he was a soldier except the similarity to John Kessler?

Kessler, Herman; 12 Reg Co B; 15 May 61-19 May 62. NOD.

Kessler, Jacob; 53 Reg Co A, 7 Apr 64-21 Jul 65. NOD.

Kessler, John; Green Township Reflections: excerpt from a letter sent home during the Civil War: "The brass that I wore on my Cartridge Belt was shot through and the Ball lodged in my Cartridge Box at the Battle of Yellow Bayou in Louisiana on 18 May 1864 by some unthoughted Rebel that Didn't care Where he shot. You can see by the size of the hole How large their Bullets was.:

Kiger, John J.; 5 Cav Co G, 18 Aug 62-20 May 65. " born Rush County, Indiana, 5' 8" tall, fair complexion, black eyes, dark hair, age 24, farmer when enrolled.." Son of John Jr. and Sarah (Gwinnup) Kiger, John J. Kiger was born 24 Aug 1838, married 1 Aug 1861, Elizabeth Wiggins who was born 20 May 1842, Indiana, d/o Jonas and Dorcas (Munson) Wiggins; Elizabeth died at daughter, Grace's home 21 Nov 1924 in Indianapolis. John J. is buried HC Park Cemetery, only military units on stone. Contributed by Dick Andis, Greencastle, Indiana.

Kiger, Mathias; 9 Cav Co B, 13 Nov 63-5 Sep 65, Corp'l. NOD.

Kimberlin, James H.; HC obit 1 May 1924: "James H. Kimberlin, aged 80 years, an old citizen of Hancock County and Civil War veteran died 28 April 1924 at his home in McCordsville. The son of Lewis Kimberlin (born Virginia), James H. was born 8 Jul 1844, Kentucky. He enlisted in the

Hancock County Indiana Civil War Soldiers

Union army at the outbreak of the Civil War, when only seventeen years of age, and was a sergeant in Company C, 124 Indiana Volunteer Infantry. After active service through half the war, he was captured by the Confederate troops in the battle of Franklin, Tennessee.

"He was held in the famous Andersonville Prison, profile code #54958, Sgt. James Kimberlin, Company C, 124 Indiana Infantry, exchanged 15 April 1865, survived the Sultana tragedy. While on the way home after the War with a large number of war prisoners, the Sultana steamship went to the bottom, seventeen hundred soldiers lost their lives and Mr. Kimberlin was one saved. (See his first-person narrative in Sultana chapter of this book.) He married Lucy Maria Church, 9 Apr 1868. He is survived by six children: W.G.; Homer; George; and Lewis Kimberlin; Mrs. R.E. Blageon; and Mrs. Flora Young. Interment HC McCordsville Cemetery: James H. Kimberlin 8 Jul 1844-28 Apr 1924; Lucy w/o James H. 1 Jan 1849-10 Mar 1914.

Kinder, George; 57 Reg Co A, 13 Dec 61-5 Feb 65. HC obit 11 May 1905: "George Kinder, age 81, of Charlottesville, suffered a stroke of paralysis. He is the father of Mrs. W.R. White." HC Six Mile Cemetery: George Kinder 11 Jul 1824-11 May 1905; Eliza w/o George 28 Feb 1826-21 Jan 1914. George Kinder married 11 Aug 1846 Eliza Ann Probasco HC Bk 2-202.

Kinder, Jefferson; 19 Reg Co G, 1 Jan 64, Sgt.-12 Jul 65. HC obit 29 Oct 1903: "Jefferson Kinder, age 61 years, departed this life at his home on North Pennsylvania Street, of a complication of diseases. Mr. Kinder was the son of Joseph and Matilda (Matthews) Kinder, and was born 9 Feb 1842, Henry County, Indiana. Wife, Catherine, and seven children survive. Funeral under the auspices of Dunbar Post G. A. R. Interment HC Park Cemetery: Jeff Kinder Sgt Co G 19 Reg; Catherine 1851-1926.

Kinder, Wesley; 148 Reg Co C, 17 Feb 65-5 Sep 65. NOD.

Hancock County Indiana Civil War Soldiers

King, Warren R. "Warren Robinson King was born 6 Feb 1842, Hamilton County, Indiana, s/o Benson and Esther (Robinson) King. Left an orphan at age three, he was taken by an uncle, Daniel Shortridge, of Fayette County and lived with him until August of 1862 when he enlisted in the War. The regiment was sent into Kentucky taking part in the battle of Richmond, 30 Aug 62, where he received a gunshot wound in the thigh, was captured and sent to a hospital where he remained until 20 Sep 62 when he was exchanged.

"After being wounded and captured, he was stripped of his clothing and threatened with bayoneting by a rebel belonging to Texas Rangers, while another rebel, a fifteen-year-old lad, kindly tied a bandage above the wound on the right leg. He feared loss of the leg and it was saved but was partially paralyzed the rest of his life. He was discharged Dec 62; he returned to Fayette County and taught school that winter. In 1863 he entered the Medical School at Keokuk, Iowa, and took "courses at Iowa State University. In Aug 64 he enlisted in the U.S. Navy as a paymaster's clerk and served in that capacity until the end of the War. He was on the gunboat, Carondolet, serving at his desk during the battle of Nashville. Dr. King was twice married, in 1865 to Martha Haynes of Miami County, Indiana, who died in 1881, leaving one son, Frank. In 1883 he married Belle Reed who survives him. The son, Frank is connected with a bank in Piqua, Ohio. Dr. King came to Hancock County in 1876. HC Park Cemetery: Warren R. King 1842-1913 Co K 69 Ind Inf; Belle Reed w/o Warren R. 1837-1924."

Kingen, Riley; 99 Reg Co B, 19 Aug 62-5 Jun 65. " born Hancock County, 5' 7" tall, age 25, dark complexion, black eyes, dark hair and farmer when enrolled.." Riley Kingen was born 1837, s/o John Kingen and his first wife, Nancy Bowers. Riley married 25 Sep 1857 Elizabeth (1838-1921) Wiggins HC Bk 4-37; three known children, John Franklin born 7 Jan 1859; Marshall E. born abt 1869; and Mattie A. born abt. 1876. The last of six sons (only his sister, Martha J. was younger; she was

Hancock County Indiana Civil War Soldiers

the only daughter), Riley died 9 Feb 1895, Bond County, Illinois, buried there in Montrose Cemetery along side Elizabeth. Contributed by Sharon Kingen, McCordsville, Indiana. 99th Regiment History states, "Riley Kingen was wounded 11 Aug 64, Atlanta."

Kingery, John; 106 Reg Co D, 10 Jul 63-17 Jul 63. A John Kingery married 27 Jun 1875 Eliza Myer HC Bk 6-372.

Kinneman, John H.; 75 Reg Co I, 14 Jul 62-8 Jun 65. A John Kinneman married 4 Nov 1877 Mary Hall HC Bk 6-554.

Kirkhoff, Charles A.; 106 Reg Co D, 10 Jul 63-17 Jul 63; also 9 Cav Co B, 13 Nov 63, died 29 Sep 64 at Athens, Alabama, of wounds received at the battle of Sulphur Trestle, Alabama, 25 Sep 64. HC newspaper 20 Oct 1864: "Pvt. Charles A. Kirkhoff was killed in action at Sulphur Trestle, Alabama, 25 Sep 1864." Charles A. Kirkhoff was the son of Anthony Kirkhoff (26 Dec 1811- 29 Aug 1882) and Anna Marie Finck (11 Nov 1824-4 Sep 1892), sister of Henry Finck. The New Palestine GAR Post was named for this young soldier.

Kinsey, Henry; 9 Reg Co C, 14 Feb 64-28 Sep 65. NOD.

Kirkman, John D.; 12 Reg Co B, 15 May 61-19 May 62. NOD.

Kiser, J.H.; HC Simmons Cemetery, Co D 34 Ind Inf. NOD.

Kitchen, William N.; 106 Reg Co D, 10 Jul 63-17 Jul 63; also 51 Reg Co I, 31 Mar 65-13 Dec 65. William N. Kitchen was born 7 May 1842, and died 16 Oct 1907; s/o Andrew and Retta (White) Kitchen. HC Phildelphia Cemetery: William N. Kitchen Civil War Soldier 1842-1907; Mary C. w/o William N. 1847-1926.

Kite, Isaiah; 79 Reg Co K, 22 Aug 62-19 Aug 63 transferred to Veteran reserve Corps (indicates wound or illness). Isaiah died 14 Feb 1904, age 75, wood workman, buried HC Park Cemetery.

Klem, John Wesley; 94 Ohio Reg, Co K, Aug 62-Sep 65. "John W. Klem was born 24 Apr 1843, in Miami County, Ohio, and is the son of George and Margaret (Lambert) Klem. He enlisted in the Union army before coming to Indiana, and was engaged in the battles of Richmond, Kentucky, Stone River,

Hancock County Indiana Civil War Soldiers

Lookout Mountain, Missionary Ridge, Chickamauga, the siege of Atlanta and marched with Sherman to the sea. Upon discharge and returning home to Ohio, he married 19 May 1870 Miss Maggie (1844-1933), daughter of Joseph Jones of Covington, Ohio. John died 2 Dec 1917 and with his wife, Margaret is buried at HC Philadelphia Cemetery.

Knight, Joel; 53 Reg Co A, 24 Feb 62-21 Jul 65. HC obit 2 Aug 1905: "Joel Knight, died with dropsy and heart trouble. Funeral at his residence. Interment HC Park Cemetery: Joel H. Knight Cpl. Co A 53 Ind Inf died 29 Jul 1905, 62y 9m 10d. A Joel Knight married 21 Oct 1864 Sarah Rebecca Carmichael.

Knoop. Frederick; 79 Reg Co D, 16 Aug 62-7 Jun 65. Buried HC Zion Lutheran Cemetery. military units only on stone.

Knoop, William; 79 Reg Co D. "William Knoop was born 1841, Germany, s/o Christian and Christina Knoop; at age twenty-one, in 1862 he enlisted and served until the end of the War. He participated in battles of Lookout Mountain, Kennesaw Mountain, Atlanta, Stone's River, Franklin and Nashville. He was wounded in the leg and his health completely undermined by the exposure to which soldiers were exposed. He never fully recovered and hence his death in 1878 at the early age of thirty-seven. He was united in marriage 17 May 1866 Louisa Roesner. HC Zion Lutheran Cemetery: Wilhelm Knoop died 25 May 1878 37y 7m 17d; child of Wilhelm and Louisa 13 Sep 1878-7 Jan 1879.

Knotts, George W.; 12 Reg Co B, 15 May 61-19 May 62. NOD.

Knox, George L.; 28 Reg U.S. Colored Troop, no dates. "The s/o a free mulatto woman and a colored Baptist preacher, George was born 16 Sep 1841. He went to Wilson County, Tennessee, from where he entered the Union army as a teamster. By traveling at night, he reached Indianapolis in 1864. On 2 Oct 1865 Mr. K. married Arilla Harvey of Marion County, Indiana, and moved to Greenfield and opened a barber shop in the Gooding Corner."

Hancock County Indiana Civil War Soldiers

Kowan, Paul; 5 Cav Co G, 21 Oct 62-roster says, deserted 20 Apr 63. NOD.

Kraft (Kreft), Frederick C.; 148 Reg Co G, 17 Feb 65-5 Sep 65. "He was born 10 Dec 1824, Germany and when young came to the United States and located in Indianapolis. Being poor he was obliged to borrow money to pay his passage and after coming to Indiana, he worked at any honest employment he could find to earn sufficient means to settle the debt. Mr. Kraft married in Indiana, Mrs. Sophia (Eichman) Schmidt (widow of Ferdinand) after which they settled in New Palestine and opened a shoe shop.

"He worked at this trade until sometime during the Civil War, when he was induced to enter the army as a substitute for a man which had been drafted, receiving for such service, nine-hundred-dollars. When the War closed, he returned to Hancock County and invested his savings in forty acres of land, which he later sold and bought eighty acres, the land on which he lived until his death 10 Sep 1887. HC Schildmeier Cemetery: Frederick Kraft died 10 Sep 1887 63 y 9m 0d; Sophia died 1 Oct 1898.

Kreager, Christian; 8 Reg Co B, 16 Jul 62-28 Aug 65. He is buried HC New Palestine Cemetery, stone only has military units, no dates.

Kroening, John Henry; 132 Reg Co I, 18 May 64-7 Sep 65. He is buried HC New Palestine Cemetery: John Henry Kroening 1884-1915. A John Kroening married 22 Nov 1883 Ursela Kuhner HC Bk 7-492.

Kuntz, George; 79 Reg Co D, 24 Aug 62-22 Oct 63. NOD.

Kunz, Herman; 11 Reg Co F; no dates. HC obit 18 Nov 1915: "Herman Kunz, son of Rev. J.G. Kunz, formerly of Sugar Creek Township this county, died at his home in Philadelphia, Pennsylvania. Rev Kunz was pastor of the German Lutheran Church in Sugar Creek Township for more than thirty years."

Kurtz, Byron; 75 Reg Co I, 30 Jul 62-18 Jun 65. "Byron Kurtz was born in Van Buren County, Iowa, January 1843, came to Hamilton County, Indiana, at age eleven years where he grew

Hancock County Indiana Civil War Soldiers

to manhood. After enlisting for service in the War, his regiment was engaged in the Kentucky and Tennessee battles of Tullahoma, Huntsville, Hoover's Gap, Stone River and Chickamauga where he received a gunshot wound above the left knee and was captured. He was taken to Libby Prison (Richmond, Virginia) where he was held until the spring of 1864 and then transferred to Andersonville Prison (code #55084) where he experienced horrors of that death pen. On 28 Jul 1864, he with others in a squad were taken by the Confederates to Macon, Georgia, to nurse Union prisoners who had been captured during the Atlanta campaign and Stoneman's Raid.

"From Macon he was sent on hospital duty to care for Union prisoners at Savannah and then to Florence, North Carolina, to be exchanged. He was sent northward and at Wilmington, North Carolina, was taken sick with a fever and became a patient in a field hospital where, in a delirious condition, he wandered away in search of water and got lost in a thicket of underbrush. He remained there for two or three days all alone suffering with fever and at intervals would crawl to a ditch to drink its water. After recovery he was sent to Washington City where he was mustered out with his regiment. While in the prison stockade at Florence, he with a squad was detailed to go after some wood. They captured a dog, brought him in and killed him for their New Year's dinner, and Mr. Kurtz to this day has a piece of that canine's bone which he cherishes as the most memorable army relic in his possession. Upon his return home, he married 6 March 1866, Matilda Mc Kay, a native of Hamilton County, born 19 Nov 1844. His wife's two brothers, Lewis Mc Kay, in the 2nd Indiana Cavalry and Jonathan in an Indiana infantry regiment."

◀ L ▶

Lace, Edward; 79 Reg Co G, 1862-7 Dec 64. "He was plying his trade as a carpenter in Shelby County, Indiana, when he enlisted for service in the Civil War. He was a robust and

Hancock County Indiana Civil War Soldiers

healthy young man, marched shoulder to shoulder with his comrades, and while in the line of duty sustained an injury to the spinal cord. Weakened by continued service in the field, he was sent to hospitals in Kentucky and Tennessee, where he spent the winter and spring of '62 and '63. Unfit for service he was sent to Indianapolis, where he received a furlough and went home, at the expiration of which, he reported for further orders.

"His disability increased and he was discharged at Indianapolis. Edward was born 8 Jan 1841, HC, (s/o Henry and Jemima (Helms) Lace), he married 1) 27 Feb 1859 Nancy A. Wellman (HC Bk 4-125), and to them were born five children. Nancy died 17 Mar 1883 and Edward married 2) 21 Mar 1886 Mrs. Ellen (Davis) Thornton. In 1890 Edward had a paralytic stroke, resulting in hemiplagia, causing total disability, for which he is receiving a just pension." HC obit 3 Jun 1905: "Edward Lace, aged 65 years, died of stomach trouble and paralysis at his home on North School Street.

"Mr. Lace was a hero in the Civil War being a member of the 79th Regiment. He leaves a widow, four daughters, Letha; Amanda; Monnie; and Cora and one son, Albert." HC obit 22 Mar 1883: "In Greenfield on 17 Mar 1883, Mrs. Nancy Ann Lace, died, age 40, wife of Edward Lace Mrs. Lace was for years a citizen of Brandywine Township. She leaves a husband and several children, two of them nearly grown." Edward and Nancy both buried HC Mt. Lebanon Cemetery.

Lacey, William P.; 134 Reg Co K, 24 May 64-_ Sep 65. HC obit 4 May 1899: "Mr. W.P. Lacey of Jackson Township, died very suddenly of appendicitis. He was one of the best and most prosperous farmers in the county. He leaves a wife, ten daughters and one son, who is now in the Indian Territory in delicate health, having gone there to be benefited by the climate." William Preston, s/o Jordan, married 6 Jun 1865 (HC Bk 4-514) Barbara Reeves; HC Simmons Cemetery: William P. Lacey 9 Feb 1848-28 Apr 1899; Barbara w/o William P. 26 Oct 1848-14 Jul 1902; Jordan 10 May 1803-27 Aug 1862.

Hancock County Indiana Civil War Soldiers

Lacy, James A.; 38 Reg Co E, 4 Nov 64-26 Jun 65. A James A. Lacy married 31 Jan 1861 Catharine Hatton HC Bk 4-239.

Lacy, Nimrod; 38 Reg Co E; 4 Nov 64-26 Jun 65. A Nimrod Lacy married 8 Dec 1862 Cynthia Barrett HC Bk 4-366; also a Nimrod Lacy married 2 Oct 1871 Ann Hittle HC Bk 6-51.

Lain, Isaac; 13 Cav Co I, 23 Dec 63-18 Nov 65. "Isaac Lain was born 18 Nov 1846, Hancock County, Indiana, son of Jacob (born New York) and Sarah (Jones) Lain; Isaac's sister, Elizabeth, married Adam F. Wilson. They came to Hancock County in 1843 and located in Vernon Township on land her father, William Jones, owned.

Isaac enlisted in the Union army and experienced the battles of Murfreesboro, Tennessee; Mobile, Alabama; and Grierson's Raid in 1865, and in one of the engagements Isaac had a horse shot from under him and received a gunshot wound in the right leg. He married 9 Feb 1875 Louisa Dobbins, d/o John W. and Susanna Dobbins, a union resulting in the birth of the following children: Nellie; John; May; Hazel; Ruth; Ray; Willam died age two; Otto died age fifteen; and Grace died age eighteen. "

HC obit 6 May 1905: "Isaac Lain died at his home northwest of Mohawk of heart failure, the result of diabetes. Mr. Lain was 58 years old, a successful farmer and a good, honest citizen. He leaves a widow, two sons and four daughters. Mrs. Belle Reeves, Greenfield, is a sister. HC Mt. Gilead/Reeves Cemetery: Isaac Lain 18 Nov 1846-6 May 1905; Louisa 15 Aug 1855-10 Nov 1927." Contributed by Philip and Charlotte Slaughter, Greenfield, Indiana.

Laird, John P. 105 Reg Co E, 11 Jul 63-18 Jul 63. A John Laird married 19 Dec 1895 Elizabeth Rozzell HC Bk 9-176. NOD.

Lake, Albert H. 8 Reg Co B, 25 Aug 61-28 Aug 65. NOD.

Lakin, William F.; 57 Reg Co A, 13 Dec 61-7 Mar 63. William married 17 Nov 1864 Levina E. Addison HC Bk 4-487. HC Simmons Cemetery: W.F. Lakin died 5 Sep 1891 49y; Levina w/o W.F. 15 Jun 1842-30 Mar 1901 58y.

Hancock County Indiana Civil War Soldiers

Lamb, Isaac; 19 Reg. See newspaper article, dated 16 Oct 1861, about the 19th Regiment in this book.

Lamb, John A. 19 Reg, no date; transferred 1 Jan 64 into 20 Reg Co E, out 12 Jul 65. A John A. Lamb married 4 Oct 1866 Zerilda Wolf HC Bk 5-91.

Lamb, Peter; 8 Reg Co B, 25 Aug 61, 8 Mar 64 transferred to 19th Reg, no out date. HC newspaper 19 May 1864: "Peter Lamb of the 19th Indiana reported wounded in recent battles across the Rapidan." A Peter Lamb married 16 Jan 1868 Nancy Clayton HC Bk 5-191. HC Philadelphia Cemetery: Lamb, Peter Civil War Soldier died 18 Sep 1883 44y 7m 1d; Nancy 1842-1928.

Lamb, Richard; 8 Reg Co B, 25 Aug 61-killed 21 May 1863 at Vicksburg. HC newspaper 11 Jun 1863: "28 May 1863, near Vicksburg, ..while the Company was sharpshooting, Richard Lamb was killed by a minie ball striking him in the bowels.."

Lamb, William; 9 Cav Co B, 13 Nov 63 no out date. A William Lamb married 22 Oct 1868 Samantha Wilson HC Bk 5-256; a

Lamb, William; married 24 Dec 1889 Josephine Tolbert HC Bk 8-202.

Lambertson, John W.; 18 Reg, Musician 16 Aug 61-20 Aug 62. NOD

Landis, George W.; 57 Reg Co A, 13 Dec 61-5 Feb 65. "Served throughout the Great Rebellion, he was Justice of the Peace, taught in the public schools of Hancock County and eventually died from the effects of sickness contracted while in the Army. He was born 9 Feb 1840 in Hancock County, Indiana, s/o George W. and Mary (Higgins) Landis. HC Six Mile Cemetery: George W. Landis 9 Feb 1840-21 Mar 1884; George W. Landis, Sr. 8 Dec 1806-12 May 1870; Mary K. Landis, w/o George W. 17 Feb 1802-8 Jan 1882. The Charlottesville Post GAR Post was named for George W. Landis and most likely it was named for George, W. Jr.

Lane, Gilman; 148 Reg Co C, 17 Feb 65-5 Sep 65. NOD.

Hancock County Indiana Civil War Soldiers

Langenberger, George; 79 Reg Co D, 16 Aug 62-died 21 Nov 62. HC Langenberger Cemetery: George Langenberger s/o Wilhelm and Charlotte (Hespa) Langenberger Co D 79 Ind Inf, Died in camp hospital at Stone River, Tennessee (The battle of Stone River was fought at Murfreesboro, Tennessee.); Wilhelm 2 Mar 1800-10 Mar 1872; Charlotte w/o Wilhelm 21 Feb 1804-1 May 1899.

Langford, William; 79 Reg Co G, 15 Aug 62, transferred to Engineer Corps 20 Jul 64; no out date.

Lanham, Charles; 105 Reg Co K, 11 Jul 63-18 Jul 63. "Charles Lanham was born 5 May 1845, died 9 Feb 1917 at Shirley, HC. wife Sarah Lanham; George buried HC Harlan Cemetery."

Lankford, Thomas; 148 Reg Co I, 9 Feb 64-5 Sep 65.

Laporte, Miller J. 8 Reg Co G, 22 Apr 61-6 Aug 61. Miller J. Laporte married 9 Mar 1862 Nancy E. Crider HC Bk 4-318. HC Park Cemetery: Miller J. Laporte, died Indianapolis, Indiana, 17 Nov 1905 at age 65; Ellen w/o M.J. 1842-1908.

Larimore, Dr. James Madison; 7th Missouri Cavalry Troop E, 24 Aug 61-Jul 63. HC obit 21 Mar 1925: "James M. Larimore, a practicing physician in this county for many years and a soldier of the Civil War, died at his home in Greenfield. He was 82 years old. Dr. Larimore received his early education in Boone County and later attended Abington College in Illinois. When the War broke out he enlisted in Troop E, Seventh Missouri Cavalry, doing scouting and general guard duty in the campaign against the guerrillas. During the battle of Lone Jack, he was severely wounded in the arm and was taken to the hospital at Macon, Missouri. He presently recovered and joined his regiment and participated in the battle of Pea Ridge. He was honorably discharged in 1863 and returned to his home in Illinois. He attended the Physicians and Surgeons College in Keokuk, Iowa, graduating in 1867, and became a salesman to save sufficient money to see him through a post graduate course in the College at Keokuk, where he received his supplementary degree in 1877.

Hancock County Indiana Civil War Soldiers

"Dr. Larimore returned to Indiana and located at Carrollton, Brandywine Township, now known as Finly He moved to Greenfield and opened an office in July 1893 where he continued until his retirement in 1907. On 11 Jul 1878 (HC Bk 7-3) he married Florence C. Taylor, born 1 Apr 1860 and died 1925, the daughter of William and Carolyn (Martindale) Taylor. Dr. Larimore was born 12 Jun 1843, son of Joseph and Mary (McIntyre) Larimore. Dr. James and Florence are buried HC Park Cemetery."

Larkin, Michael; 12 Reg Co B, 15 Aug 61-19 May 62. NOD.

LaRue, Sidney; 111 Reg Co H, 12 Jul 63-15 Jul 63 residence/place of enlistment, Rush County, Indiana; also 134 Reg Co C, 24 May 64-2 Sep 64 residence/place of enlistment Decatur County, Indiana. HC obit 3 Apr 1884: "Mr. Sidney LaRue died 2 April 1884, of kidney trouble, in Greenfield. He was born 20 Apr 1853 in Andersonville, Franklin County, Indiana.

"In 1870 he engaged in the mercantile business at Raleigh, Rush County, with his brother, R.M. LaRue, where on the 17th of May 1870, he married Caroline V. Hall, daughter of Dr. J.A. Hall, a resident of the same village. Mr. LaRue leaves a wife, son and daughter to mourn his departure across the dark waters. Mr. L. was a member of the Dunbar Post G.A.R., whose members were unremitting in their care and attention, and by whom he will be interred with all honors. It is not decided when or where he will be buried."

Lawson, Hiram; 5 Cav Co G, 18 Aug 62-14 Jun 65. " born Keiver County, Ohio, 5' 9" tall, dark complexion, black eyes, dark hair, age 38, miller when enrolled.." HC newspaper 11 Aug 1864: "Hiram Lawson was taken prisoner during the disastrous expedition commanded by General Stoneman." Andersonville (Georgia) Prison profile, code #55283: Hiram Lawson of 5th Cav, Co G, survived and exchanged April 1865. He also survived the Sultana steamboat tragedy when it exploded and burned on the Mississippi River, 27 Apr 1865. NOD.

Hancock County Indiana Civil War Soldiers

Layman, Cornelius; 12 Reg Co B, 5 Aug 61-19 May 62. NOD
Layton, James Alexander; HC obit 22 Nov 1923: "James Alexander Layton, son of William and Catherine (Campbell) Layton, was born in Fayette County, Indiana, 16 Aug 1839, and departed this life, 12 Nov 1923, being 84 years of age. On 28 Aug 1873 (HC Bk 6-216) he was united in marriage to Mrs. Emily Bingham, (1848-1918) who preceded him in death five years ago. To this union were born ten children, three having died in infancy. Those who survive are Ida Walls; Emma Barrett; Daisy Martin; Mina Gates; Eldora Witte; Roland and John Layton; George Bingham and Etta Yoh, stepchildren who will also miss him.

"He enlisted in the Union army for his country's cause and later came to Hancock County and made his home with Mr. and Mrs. Samuel Stephens and Mr. and Mrs. Joseph T. Loehr. After his marriage he became interested in a revival at the Brown's Chapel Church, and while chopping wood at his home was happily converted and united with the church. James and Emily are buried HC Park Cemetery. HC Caldwell Cemetery: Julia A. Layton d/o J.A. and E. A. died 10 Mar 1877 5m 16d."

Leakey, Joseph R.; 2 Cav, Co M, 18 Nov 61-Oct 65. "Joseph R. Leakey was born 29 Nov 1826 in Henry County, Indiana, son of Levi and Rachel (Elliott) Leakey. He was following the carpenter trade when he the dark shadows of war gathered over the Union and after enlistment he participated in the battles of Shiloh, Corinth, Stone River, Chattanooga, Chickamauga, Missionary Ridge, Knoxville and numerous minor engagements. His trade secured the position of wagon repairer. In the fall of 1862, he was thrown out of an ambulance near Chattanooga, receiving injuries to his back, landing him in hospitals and also suffering from camp diarrhea. After a thirty day furlough, he rejoined his regiment at Nashville. His company was armed with Colt's seven shooter revolvers and revolving pistols, and when they let loose it rained leaden shot.

"Mr. Leakey married 1) 18 Feb 1849 Rebecca Stubblefield who died Aug 1850, buried Cadiz, Indiana; a marriage in 1853

Hancock County Indiana Civil War Soldiers

to a Rebecca Collier is also mentioned, who died Nov 1878. Joseph married Catherine Rose, 17 Jan 1880 (HC Bk 7-157). (Catherine was the widow of Bradley Rose who was in the 19th Indiana, a part of the famous Iron Brigade; he was wounded in the battle of the Wilderness and died at Nashville, Indiana, Dec 1878.). Joseph's three brothers were in the Civil War: Isaac in the Marine Corps (Mississippi Marines?); Amos in the 72 I.V.I.; and George in the 125th Illinois." HC Park Cemetery: J.R. Leakey died 26 Jan 1908; Catherine 1841-1912.

Leamon, John N.; 54 Reg Co E, 30 Oct 62, no out date. HC newspaper 17 Nov 1905: " The statement was made in these columns yesterday that the remains of Mr. John Nelson Leamon, father of Mrs. Walter Baldwin, of North State Street, would arrive in Greenfield from Marion this morning by way of Knightstown, and be interred here this forenoon. There seems to have been a failure of connections in some manner, the remains did not reach this city this forenoon, hence different arrangements for the interment will be made. The funeral escort arrived at Knightstown and the remains were brought to this city in a hearse and taken to the home of Walter Baldwin and will be kept in state until Saturday when they will be interred at (HC) Park Cemetery. John N. Leamon Co E 54 Ind Inf; Cynthia w/o J.N. died 4 Feb 1872 30y 4m 15d." A John N. Leamon married 12 Nov 1879 Laura Chambers HC Bk 7-134.

Leamon, Richard; 8 Reg Co B, 25 Aug 61-died 14 Mar 63, Greenfield, Indiana. HC newspaper 14 Aug 1863: "Richard Leamon, Co B 8th Indiana is promoted." Hc obit 19 Mar 1863: "Richard Leamon, aged about 27 years, died in Center Township, 14 Mar 1863, after a lingering and painful illness of chronic diarrhea. Deceased was a soldier of the Union army and a member of Company B, 8th Indiana Regiment.

"He entered the service as a private, but his worth and excellent qualities of head and heart, soon promoted him to the very responsible and honorable position of Orderly Sergeant, which he held when he died. He leaves many relatives and

Hancock County Indiana Civil War Soldiers

friends to mourn his untimely end, but none will sorrow more than his gallant comrades of his late company." Buried at the Old Greenfield Cemetery, military data only on stone. Quoted from a letter written by Alfred Wilson to his brother, Adam F. Wilson, dated 28 Oct 1862: "Richard Leamon is at Benton Barracks St. Louis, he is no better, his is getting worse all of the time and he said that if he did not git away from this in a short time hee would die."

Ledmore, John W.; 75 Reg Co I, 14 Jul 62-died 25 Jul 63, McMinnville, Tennessee.

Lee, Marion T. 134 Reg Co C, 24 May 64-2 Sep 64. Marion buried HC Harlan Cemetery, military units only. A daughter of Marion T. and Harriett was born 6 Feb 1877 and died 23 Jan 1898, no other data given.

Lemay, Charles; 57 Reg Co A, 13 Dec 61-2 Aug 62. NOD.

Leonard, Hiram; 79 Reg Co C, 15 Aug 62-died 25 Jul 63 McMinnville, Tennessee. NOD.

Leonard, Jacob; 79 Reg Co C, 9 Aug 62-discharged 23 Mar 63 wounds. "Jacob was born 23 Sep 1843 in Davidson County, North Carolina, son of Abraham and Elizabeth Leonard. Jacob married 28 Aug 1864 Martha J. Bales (HC Bk 4-468), nine children: Oscar; Delia; Carrie; Inez; Leslie; Guy; Rufus; Charles; and Edward. HC newspaper 16 Dec 1920: "The funeral of Jacob Leonard was held today at the home of his daughter, Mrs. Wilson at Beech Grove. He leaves five sons and three daughters. He formerly lived west of Philadelphia. HC Philadelphia Cemetery: Jacob Leonard 23 Sep 1843-14 Dec 1920; Martha J. 17 Aug 1847-26 Sep 1909. Contributed by Bob and Don Leonard, Greenfield, Indiana.

Lewis, Deane (Duane); 9 Cav Co B, 13 Nov 63-killed 17 Dec 64, Franklin, Tennessee. NOD

Lewis, James; 79 Reg Co G, 15 Aug 61-9 Apr 63. A James Lewis married 10 Apr 1859 Mary Creviston HC Bk 4-133.

Lincolnfelter, (Lingenfelter) Thomas J.; 13 Cav Co I, 11 Jan 64-25 May 65. NOD.

Hancock County Indiana Civil War Soldiers

Lineback, Albert B.;105 Reg Co E, 11 Jul 63-18 Jul 63. HC newspaper 15 Feb 1917: "A.B. Lineback, aged 70 years, son of the late Martin and Cornelia (Branham) Lineback, died at his own hands. "Uncle B." as he called himself, carried out his threat and had taken his own life, by shooting himself through the head. He having for many years taken the gloomy view of nearly all subjects had taken a great liking to Master James Eshelman, son of Hiram Eshelman, and during the day drew up his will, giving James his watch. He wrote a note, of which the following is a copy: 'A.B. Lineback, Feb 13, You will find my body on mother's grave.

"Please return the gun to A.A. Gappen (sporting goods store), and oblige Uncle B. also take my body to Eshelmann's, bury me in these clothes, just as I am, I don't want a coffin—a plain box. May God have mercy on my unhappy soul.' Mr. Lineback was a member of the Home Guards during the Civil War and went with them on their way to meet Morgan and his raiders. He was with the company in the unfortunate battle at Lawrenceburg. One sister survives, Mrs. Matha J. Brown, Crazeysburg, Ohio, who on account of old age and feebleness was unable to attend the funeral. Interment HC Park Cemetery."

Lineback, Benjamin; HC newspaper 9 Oct 1862: "Died in this place, Benjamin, eldest son of Martin and Cornelia (Branham) Lineback, 20y 10m 3d. Deceased was a Volunteer in the Union Army and was a member of Capt. Riley's cavalry Company at the time of his death. He was not a very stout young man and exposures of camp life, for the few weeks he was in the service, was more than he could endure. He returned home last week, quite unwell, and departed this life as above. The bereaved parents and mourning sisters and brother have our sympathies in this their hour of deepest affliction. Their son and brother sleeps in a soldier's grave, with name and fame untarnished, and though not killed in battle, with his face to the foe, the sympathies of all who love their country will

Hancock County Indiana Civil War Soldiers

cluster around the young soldier's last resting place. Peace to his remains." Buried HC Park Cemetery.

Lineback, Isaac; 8 Reg Co B, 25 Aug 61, no out date. An Isaac Lineback married 11 Aug 1854 Martha Wilson HC Bk 3-229.

Lipscomb, George ; 8 Reg Co G, 22 Apr 61-6 Aug 61.NOD

Lipscomb, Henry B.; 51 Reg Co I, 26 Sep 61-17 Dec 64. "..born Hancock County, 5' 7" tall, fair complexion, gray eyes, light hair, age 16, farmer when enrolled.." NOD

Lister, James M.; 12 Reg Co B, 15 May 61-19 May 62; 12 Reg Co B, 12 Sep 62, died 2 Oct 64, Marietta, Georgia.

Lister, Samuel; 12 Reg Co G, 21 Jul 62-8 Jun 65, wagoner. A Samuel Lister married 2 Jan 1862 Rhoda Wisehart HC Bk 4-303.

Lockwood, John; 9 Reg Co E, 14 Feb 65-28 Sep 65. NOD.

Loder, C.C.; 9 Cav Co C, 18 Dec 63-24 Jul 65. HC McCray Cemetery: C.C. Loder 19 Jul 1848-19 Aug 1895 Co C Ind Cav; Jennie w/o C.C. 1846-1916.

Loder, James W.; 7 Reg Co C, no dates. HC obit 14 Dec 1916: "Rev. James W. Loder, aged eighty-two years, died at the Methodist Hospital, Indianapolis, after an illness of several days of liver trouble. He was born in Green Township, near Eden and was a minister of the gospel in the Northwest Indiana Conference. He was a member of the Dunbar Post G.A.R. and is survived by the widow and a step-daughter, Mrs. Nellie Kroon, of Detroit. Interment HC Park Cemetery: Rev. James W. Loder, h/o Annie 1844-1916.

Loehr, John S.; 9 Cav Co B, 19 Dec 63-died 23 Jan 65, Madison, Indiana. HC newspaper 26 Jan 1865: "John S. Loehr, Co B 9th Cavalry died at Joe Holt Hospital, Madison, Indiana, and his remains will be brought here for interment." A John S. Loehr married 16 Jan 1840 Eliza Ann Dennis HC Bk 1-191. John S. Loehr was buried at the Old Greenfield Cemetery but his remains were moved 28 May 1901 to Park Cemetery. John S. Loehr died 23 Jan 1865 of typhoid pneumonia, 46y 10m 1d; Eliza w/o John S. stone broken, illegible.

Hancock County Indiana Civil War Soldiers

Long, Henry: HC obit 1 Apr 1915: "Henry Long, age 71 years, a Civil War veteran died at his home on North Swope Street, of pneumonia and heart trouble, after a week's illness. He was born in Cincinnati, Ohio, 8 July 1844. His father died when the son was five years old and he was reared by an uncle, Henry Hildebrant, at New Vienna, Ohio. At the beginning of the Civil War, he enlisted in Company G, 11th Ohio Infantry and served four years, or until the close of the war. He was wounded five times. The late Thomas E. Johnson, of Greenfield, was a member of his company. (At age 18 years, Henry Long enlisted 9 Jul 61 as a private into Company G, 11th Ohio Infantry; 21 Jun 64 transferred to Company H, 11 Battn Infantry; 11 Jun 65 transferred to Company C, 31st Ohio Infantry; mustered out 20 Jul 65. He was listed as POW 8 Mar 63, Middleton, Tennessee; exchanged, paroled and returned 9 Nov 63, place not stated.)

"At age 23 years he was married to Ann Moon and to them were born two sons; Henry and Leroy, both of whom, with the wife and mother are deceased. Later he married Rachel Moon, 5 Nov 1874, and to this union was born one daughter, Alvaretta, wife of William Hunt, who with the widow and five grandchildren survive. Mabel was at her grandfather's home when his death occurred. He was an honest, honorable citizen who had the complete confidence of everyone and not with standing his age, did considerable work as a carpenter. Burial at his former home at Martinsville, Ohio."

Long, John W.; 8 Reg Co G, 5 Sep 61-23 Aug 65. A John Long married 25 Sep 1865 Nancy Ashcraft HC Bk 4-539. Sheridan, s/o John W. and Nancy Long, 1871-4 Feb 1882. NOD.

Lonsberry, Andrew J.; 13 Reg Co D, 30 Oct 62, transferred to Co B 6 Dec 64, out 5 Sep 65. HC obit 14 Apr 1899; "Andrew J. Lonsberry was born in Franklin County, Indiana, 25 Mar 1843 and he obeyed the call of the Master from his home in Warrington, Hancock County, 11 Mar 1899, aged fifty-five years. He was united in marriage with Adaline Carroll, 4 Oct

Hancock County Indiana Civil War Soldiers

1870, born to them were three daughters and two sons, one daughter having passed away in infancy.

"At the age of ten, Andrew was left an orphan, when he was bound to William V. Armstrong, and was cared for as one of the family. He enlisted in the Union Army and served his country as a true and faithful soldier. It was the privilege of the writer to know Brother Lonsberry from the time he came to Hancock County. We can only say farewell, dear brother, till we shall meet again in the sweet by and by. Signed, W.R. Williams."

Loomis, (Lummis), Benjamin: 79 Reg Co C, 15 Aug 62, transferred 14 Jul 63 as artificer, to Co E 1st Reg US Engineers, out 24 Jun 65. " born Hancock County, 5' 10" tall, dark complexion, blue eyes, dark hair, age 22, farmer when enrolled.." "Benjamin was born 30 Jan 1842, Kentucky, s/o William and Julia (Gosney) Lummis. Benjamin died 11 Jun 1904, Maxwell, of heart disease, buried Eden Church Cemetery."

Loomis, (Lummis) John G. 79 Reg Co C, 15 Aug 62, 6 Jan 63, missing in action, Stone's River. NOD.

Low, Joseph; 51 Reg Co I, 8 Dec 61-3 Jan 62, disability. "Joseph Low was born 3 Mar 1841, Shelby County, Indiana, s/o Wood Beck and Malinda (Neal) Low, and died 29 Mar 1927. A Joseph Low married 17 May 1863 Mary Kirkly HC Bk 4-390. HC Park Cemetery: Joseph Low 3 Mar 1841-29 Jun 1927; Mary R. w/o Joseph 4 Nov 1847-23 Mar 1907." See data for his brother, William Eli.

Low, William Eli; 13 Cav Co I, 23 Dec 63, Corp'l-25 May 65. HC newspaper 6 Mar 1924: "It isn't often that we can celebrate the birthdays of two brothers each over eighty years of age and both Civil War veterans, as was the case on March 3rd, when relatives gathered in the home of William Eli Low on Howard Street, Greenfield, with prepared dinner and enjoyed the 83rd birthday of Joseph Low and the 81st birthday of William Eli Low. Both of these veterans come in for a certain amount of sympathy, Joseph on account of his helpless condition from

Hancock County Indiana Civil War Soldiers

blindness and William Eli is almost helpless because of the fact that his wife has been paralyzed and has neither walked or talked for over five years. 'It makes a person happier by trying to shed a ray of sunshine into these afflicted lives,' was remarked today by one who attended the birthday dinner."

HC obit 4 Mar 1926: "On 13 February 1926 William E. Low, died at his home on Howard Street, Greenfield, of pneumonia. He was the son of Wood Beck and Malinda Low, born 3 Mar 1843, Shelby County, Indiana. He married 6 Feb 1868 (HC Bk 5-199) Sarah Kirkley, who died in 1872; two children, Lenna Gilmore and Beck Low. On 3 Sep 1873 (HC Bk 6-217) William married Mary Jane Smith (1848-1926): ten children, seven of whom survive: Myrtle Ware; Gertrude Bussart; Alice Daniels; Maggie McMahan; Rosa Rienier; William E.; and Goldie Phillips; three children preceded him to the other shore: Robert, Flora and Sadie. He was a Civil War veteran, having been wounded in the battle of Murfreesboro, Tennessee, but served until the close of the War."

Lowder, Adam: 8 Reg Co B, 25 Aug 61-28 Aug 65. Adam married 17 Aug 1866 Mary Porter HC Bk 5-77. HC Philadelphia Cemetery, Adam Lowder Civil War Soldier 1829-1905; Mary A. 27 Mar 1830-29 May 1894. See data on page with brother, William A. Lowder.

Lowder, Alfred; 8 Reg Co B, 25 Aug 61-died 25 May 63 Vicksburg. HC newspaper 11 Jun 1863: "Alfred Lowder of Co B, 8th regiment, died from wounds; report of S.H. Dunbar of 8th Regiment." See data on page with brother, William A. Lowder.

Lowder, James V.; 8 Reg Co B, 25 Aug 61-25 Aug 65. HC newspaper 5 Feb 1862: "Otterville, Missouri, 22 Jan 1862, letter written by Lt. Samuel Dunbar, commanding Company B, 8th Reg. Lames Lowder is discharged on account of physical disability, induced by the inclemencies of camp life." James Lowder married 10 Sep 1864 Sarah Elizabeth Mower HC Bk 4-474. HC Arnett Cemetery: James V. Lowder 5 Mar 1837-3

Hancock County Indiana Civil War Soldiers

Aug 1904; Sarah E. 7 Feb 1847-13 Mar 1905. See data on page with brother, William A. Lowder.

Lowder, William A.; 8 Reg Co B, 20 Aug 61-20 Sep 64. "The hardships of army life and exposure to heat and inclement weather in the early part of his service, landed him in hospitals at Jefferson Barracks, Missouri, Madison, Indiana, and Indianapolis where he received a three month furlough. At the expiration of which he again joined his comrades at Helena, Arkansas, May, 1862. He was in the battles of Port Gibson, Champion Hills, Big Black River, siege and capture of Vicksburg, besides other numerous engagements.

"Three brothers, Adam, Alfred and James were in the same company and regiment; Alfred was killed at Vicksburg. William was transferred to Veteran reserve Corps, Feb 1864, where he remained until discharge, 20 Sep 64. The son of Elijah and Leah Deliah (Pox) Lowder, William was born 24 Oct 1829, Fayette County, Indiana, and came to Hancock County in his infancy. He has lived most of his life at Mohawk, Indiana, where he now (1899) lives a life of single blessedness."

Lowe, Nimrod; 79 Reg Co G, 22 Aug 62-15 Jun 63. A Nimrod Lowe married 10 Mar 1864 Mary E. Furry HC Bk 4-438. HC obit 15 Jun 1922: "Nimrod Lowe, born and reared in this county, and a resident near Charlottesville, died at the National Soldiers' Home, Hampton Roads, Virginia. Mr. Lowe was a soldier in the Civil war, enlisting from this county. He was 81 years old."

Loy, John; 147 Reg Co F, 7 Feb 65-4 Aug 65. HC obit 14 Jan 1892: "A few days ago, John Loy, deputy Marshall of Greenfield, had one of his fingers mashed off by a piece of gas pipe falling on it. He had his hand dressed, and from exposure caught cold in it and tetanus set in, and he died of this terrible disease. Mr. Loy was a large and powerful man. thought nothing would hurt him, and he did not take the proper care of himself. He was in the forty-third year of his age and leaves a wife and two children to mourn his death. He was well liked

Hancock County Indiana Civil War Soldiers

by everyone, and his death will be greatly regretted. He was buried in the new Cemetery (HC Park) by the G.A.R. Post." A John Loy married 4 Sep 1867 Catharine Miller HC Bk 5-161; also a John Loy married 5 Mar 1869 Rachel Coberly HC Bk 5-286.

Lucas, William H.; 79 Reg Co B, 9 Aug 62, died 18 Dec 62, Nashville, Tennessee. A William Lucas married 7 Jan 1860 Hannah Alyea HC Bk 4-171.

Lunsford, Elijah; 12 Reg Co G, 28 Jul 62-1 May 65. He was captured, a prisoner and released from Andersonville, Georgia, Prison, code #55472. An Elijah Lunsford married 6 Apr 1867 Julia Bolander HC Bk 5-129.

Luntsford, James; 12 Reg Co H, 12 Aug 62-15 Jun 65. A James Luntsford married 19 Jan 1859 Rena Dishman HC Bk 4-119. James is buried at the Old Fort Cemetery in Hamilton County, Indiana, only military data on stone.

Lutes, Irvin; 26 Reg Co I, 24 Sep 64-6 Sep 65. NOD.

Lymon, Thomas; 34 Reg Co E, 10 Oct 61, died 24 Nov 65; another source says: 10 Oct 61, discharged as commissary Sergeant, disability, 24 Nov 65. NOD.

Lynam, George; 3 Cav Co I, 5 Sep 61-27 Oct 64.. "..born Hancock County 5' 10" tall, light complexion, blue eyes, brown hair, age 24, farmer when enrolled.. "HC obit 26 Jul 1917: "George Lynam, in his 77th year, died at his home, 330 North Baldwin Street, Greenfield after an illness of several weeks of paralysis. Mr. Lynam was one of the well known men in the city. He was a retired farmer, born 1840, Henry County, Indiana, (another source says Hancock County) son of William Jr. and Lucy (Taylor) Lynam, but had resided in this county some twenty-five years. He was a veteran of the Civil War, He is survived by, a widow and four children, George, Frank, Mrs. W.B. Flowers and Mrs. Elmer Johnson." George Lynam married (HC Bk 4-512) 27 Apr 1865 Mary Miller 1844-1929. George and Mary buried HC Park Cemetery.

Lynam, Perry C. HC obit 7 Jul 1921: "Perry C. Lynam, son of William and Lucy Taylor Lynam, was born in Hamilton

Hancock County Indiana Civil War Soldiers

County, Ohio, 25 Apr 1838, and left his earthly home 23 Jun 1921, at the advanced age of 83 years. at an early age he came to Hancock County, where he spent the remainder of his life. On 24 Feb 1864 he answered his country's call and served in the 147th Regiment, Company H, Indiana Volunteers, until 4 Aug 1865, when he received an honorable discharge at Harper's Ferry, Virginia. On 4 Dec 1865, he was united in marriage to Mary Jane Binford (HC Bk 5-9). Three children, Charley who died in 1903, Oscar and Ethel who survive. On 19 Oct 1918, his companion for fifty-three years Mary Jane (1850-1918), was called to her heavenly home." Perry C. and Mary Jane are buried HC Park Cemetery.

Lynch, John L.; 79 Reg Co D, 13 Aug 62-7 Jun 65. NOD.

Lyon, Capt. Stephen D.; HC obit 18 Aug 1870: "Capt. Stephen D. Lyon, a citizen of Greenfield, died 16 Aug 1870, after a protracted general debility. He was buried in the new cemetery by the Masonic fraternity, attended by a large number of our citizens. Capt. L. came to this place in 1865, and in the practice of his profession as a pension solicitor acquired a band of competency, and made many warm friends. He was honored with the position of State Librarian, which position he filled with credit to himself and friends.

"During the Civil War, he was, for a time in Capt. Bracken's cavalry company, and later transferred to the 27th Indiana Infantry, in which regiment he was severely wounded in the leg in one of the Virginia battles, and which contributed in a large degree to the debility causing his death. He leaves a wife to mourn his demise." Stephen D. Lyon married 30 May 1867 Inez L. Gwin HC Bk 5-136. HC Park Cemetery: Stephen D. Lyon died 16 Aug 1870 Lt. Co H 27 Ind Inf; Inez L. 29 Mar 1849-9 Apr 1912.

Lyman, J.A.; HC Philadelphia Cemetery: J.A. Lyman 15 Ind Inf, no dates on stone; Hannah 1839-1876, c/o J.A. and Hannah no dates. A John A. Lyman married 19 Feb 1863 (HC Bk 4-379) Hannah West.

Hancock County Indiana Civil War Soldiers

Lynam, John; 8 Reg Co L, and 3 Cav Co I, he served from 13 Sep 62 to 8 Jun 65. ",,born Hancock County 5' 10" tall, light complexion, blue eyes, dark hair, age 24, farmer when enrolled..." HC Gilboa Cemetery: Jno. Lynam Co I 3 Ind Cav no dates on stone; A John Lynam died 24 Oct 1892, age 56 years, buried Gilboa Cemetery. A HC obit 15 Apr 1880: "Mary S., wife of John Lynam, in the 33rd year of her age, died 9 Apr 1880, at her residence in Jackson Township. The deceased was born in Scott County, Kentucky, 6 Jul 1847, and came to this State with her father, Harvey Reed, in 1863. On 3 Apr 1866 (HC Bk 5-52) she married John Lynam, and has resided in this county up to the time of death. Her husband and two children survive."

◄ M ►

Mack, Michael; 12 Reg Co H, 17 Aug 62-8 Jun 65. NOD

Mack, Thomas; 5 Cav Co G, 20 Jan 64. HC newspaper 11 Aug 1864: "T. Mack was captured." Andersonville Prison profile code #55703: T. Mack, Company G, 5th Cavalry was exchanged 1 April 1865; survived. NOD.

Madison, John; 57 Reg Co A, 13 Dec 61-14 Dec 65, Sgt. A John Madison married Elizabeth Sparks 13 Mar 1864 HC Bk 4-438. HC Harlan Cemetery: Elizabeth Madison died 17 Feb 1885; infant/o J. and E. died 3 Feb 1885. "Elizabeth Madison w/o John was born 15 May 1842, married 13 Mar 1864. She was the d/o John and Mary Sparks."

Madden, Riley; 148 Reg Co C, 17 Feb 65-5 Sep 65. NOD.

Magee, George; 6 Cav Co I, 26 Aug 62-15 Sep 65. "...born Fairhaven, Ohio, 5' 5" tall, light complexion, blue eyes, light hair, age 18, farmer when enrolled..." NOD. HC Mt.Gilead/Reeves Cemetery records a George Magee 10 Aug 1818-18 Apr 1877; Elizabeth w/o George died 3 Dec 1852; Elmira 2nd w/o George 17 May 1831-21 Nov 1890.

Manche, John; 106 Reg Co D, 10 Jul 63-17 Jul 63, commanded by 1st Lt. Conrad Shellhouse; also 9 Cav Co B, 9 Dec 63-28 Aug 65. HC obit 23 Jun 1927: " John Manche died suddenly at

Hancock County Indiana Civil War Soldiers

his home, six miles southwest of Greenfield. He fell dead while leaving the dining room after eating breakfast. Mr. Manche was one of the prominent and prosperous citizens of this county. The deceased was born on the old family homestead in Sugar Creek Township, 26 Jan 1845, the son of John and Catherine (Lang) Manche, both of whom were born in Germany. His father died when Mr. Manche was only eight years old.

"He enlisted as a private during the Civil War at age seventeen and served until the end of the War. At the close of the war, he assumed ownership of his part of his father's estate and on Christmas, 1865, he married (HC Bk 5-16) Miss Mary L. Ashcraft, who died in 1909. Four children survive Mr. Manche: Della; Charles; Morris; and Mrs. Carl Hardin. Interment New Palestine Cemetery: John Manche 26 Jan 1845-18 Jun 1927; Mary L. w/o John 14 Nov 1847-29 Jan 1909.

Mann, Henry J.; 8 Reg Co B, 25 Aug 61-28 Aug 65. NOD.

Manning, Joel: 8 Reg Co K, 10 Aug 62-24 May 65. "The son of Joseph and Catherine (Whisler) Manning, was born in Wayne County, Indiana, 21 Apr 1842. He settled in Hancock County in 1858 and learned the carpenter trade, which he was following when the Civil War came on. He was in the battles of Magnolia Hill, Champion Hills, Big Black River, siege of Vicksburg, Bayou Lafouche, Winchester, Cedar Creek and many others in between.

"He received a gunshot wound in the nose and right eye at Cedar Creek, Virginia, 19 Oct 1864. He was in several hospitals until 24 May 1865 when he received his final discharge. He was captured at Cedar Creek, with the entire command, all the horses being killed, and was a prisoner twelve hours before being released by Federal troops. At Vicksburg he was in the rifle pits for 47 days, and had comrades shot down by his side in that long siege. He stood shoulder to shoulder with his comrades until the War ended. He returned to Hancock County where he married 19 Dec 1867 (HC Bk 5-182) Nehusta Redmond, d/o McKay (Michael) and

Hancock County Indiana Civil War Soldiers

Susan (Troy) Redmond. Joel was the father of Charles and Clara. He is in the mercantile business and Postmaster at Milner's Corner, Indiana." HC Eden Church Cemetery: Joel Manning 1842-1921 Co K 8 Ind Inf; Nehusta 1849-1926.

Market, (Merket) Henry; 8 Reg Co G, 22 Apr 61-6 Aug 61. NOD

Marlin, John T.; 40 Ohio Reg Co G, age 24 yrs. 29 Oct 61 as Sgt.; 10 Dec 64 transferred to 115 Ohio Inf.; 11 Dec 64 out. HC obit 27 Aug 1927: "John Thomas Marlin, aged 78, died at his home on Brook Street, Greenfield. He was born 15 Sep 1836, Ohio, and died 23 Aug 1914. He was an old soldier, one of the well known veterans of the Civil War, and the Regular Army, having enlisted in Company C, 115th Ohio Volunteers, and at the end of his service enlisted in Company G of the 40th Ohio.

"In 1881 he enlisted in the regular army for a period of five years, at the close of this service, he enlisted for another five year term and at the end of three years, one of his arms was seriously injured. He was given an honorable discharge. He was a member of the G.A.R. and is survived by five sons and three daughters. Interment Park Cemetery (HC)."

Marsh, (Christopher) Columbus; Oct 61 in 19 Reg, veteran promoted to Captain and transferred to 20 Reg 1 Jan 64; died 4 Jan 65 as P.O.W., place not given.

Marsh, Elias; 5 Cav Co G, 16 Aug 62-15 Sep 65, Sgt. HC newspaper 11 Aug 1864: "Pvt. E. Marsh was taken prisoner during the disastrous expedition commanded by General Stoneman. (The following paragraph was at the end of the article) The name of Pvt. E. Marsh is probably very erroneously printed in the above list, as on the 2nd he was at Nashville, and had not had time to reach his company before it started with General Stoneman. Since the above was in type, we have received a letter from Lt. W.H. Pilkenton, corroborating the above account, except as to Elias Marsh, who was not with the company." See Seth Marsh.

Hancock County Indiana Civil War Soldiers

Marsh, Elihu; 53 Reg Co A, 29 Dec 63-21 Jul 65. An Elihu Marsh married 9 Aug 1860 Nancy Jackson HC Bk 4-201.

Marsh, Joseph; 5 Cav Co G.. HC newspaper 21 May 1863: "On the 19th inst., Joseph Marsh departed this life in the hospital in Glasgow (Kentucky) of lung fever. In him we lost a good soldier, a kind comrade, and we feel to sympathize with his companion and friends for his loss." A Joseph Marsh married 10 Mar 1861 Eliza Jane Whitaker HC Bk 4-250. A Joseph Marsh is buried HC Park Cemetery s/o Elias and Emeline 1 Mar 1848-1 Jan 1863. A Joseph Marsh was buried in the Old Greenfield Cemetery 1840-1863 and moved to HC Park Cemetery 25 Feb 1892.

Marsh, Samuel; 53 Reg Co B. HC newspaper 14 Jul 1864: "Lieut. Samuel Marsh was severely wounded 27 Jun 1864 by a ball through the upper thigh, badly breaking the bone at Kennesaw Mountain where the men of the 53rd Indiana met with disaster." HC newspaper 21 Jul 1864: "We are sorry to announce that Lieut. Samuel Marsh, of Company A, 53rd Indiana, died of his wounds on the 1st inst. He was a brave and gallant soldier, a true man and warm friend. Lieut. M. leaves a wife and four small children, and hosts of friends, to mourn his loss."

Marsh, Seth; 8 Reg Co B, 22 Apr 61-6 Aug 61; also 51 Reg Co D, 14 Dec 61, promoted to 2nd Lt. and Captain, out 17 Jun 65. HC newspaper: "Mr. Elias Marsh, of Greenfield, has just been notified of the death of his brother, Seth Marsh, and also that of his that, which occurred at their home in Missouri during the latter part of February. It will be remembered by the old settlers of this city and county that Seth Marsh was one of the most gallant soldiers who ever enlisted in the Union army. He was noted for his bravery, and enlisted at the beginning and served throughout the war in defense of his country."

Marshall, Caleb; HC Philadelphia Cemetery: Caleb Marshall Co K 117 Ind Inf, died 15 Nov 1930; Ruby Adeline w/o Caleb died 1928.

Hancock County Indiana Civil War Soldiers

Marshall, Elijah; 12 Reg Co G, 3 Aug 62-roster records 1 May 63, deserted. NOD.

Marshall, Eli; 148 Reg Co C, 17 Feb 65-9 Sep 65. NOD.

Martin, Albert; 5 Cav Co G, 16 Aug 62-10 Nov 65. NOD.

Martin, Alonzo; 53 Reg Co A, 24 Oct 62-21 Jul 65. "The son of Sampson and Rebecca (Lewis) Martin, Alonzo married 13 Jun 1867 (HC Bk 5-140) Sarah S. Miller, 1846-1925; he was a farmer and ran a planing mill at Pendleton, Madison County, Indiana, and died 1881. Alonzo and Sarah are buried HC Curry's Chapel Church Cemetery."

Martin, Edward; "..born Hancock County, 5' 3" tall, age 21 years, dark complexion gray eyes, light hair, farmer when enrolled.." "HC obit 5 April 1923: " Edward Martin, son of William and Charlotte (Chapman) Martin, was born 27 Jun 1841, and died 20 Mar 1923, aged 81 years. Joseph Martin of the immediate neighborhood is the surviving twin brother, they have lived within less than one and a half miles of each other all their lives. Their mother died when they were nine years old, and their father later married Eliza McClarnon, who was a true and loving mother to these boys, although other children were born. Mary S. Curtis was a half-sister.

"At school the teachers had considerable trouble to keep them identified. Many are their girls and sweethearts that were imposed upon by their pranks in relation to their identity. And. even in later years they delighted in seeing their friends confused as to which was which, and many times their acquaintances not being sure to whom they were talking would address them by the name of Joe-Ed, being sure that they were calling them by the right name.

"When the demon of war sounded a blast, the twin brothers both joined the same regiment, and company, Co A, 53rd Infantry. They were at the siege of Vicksburg and Atlanta, and were with General Sherman on his celebrated march to the sea. On one occasion at the siege of Atlanta, Ed and some of his comrades were hidden in a hollow stump with rebels on all sides, and although the stump bore evidence of the rebel

Hancock County Indiana Civil War Soldiers

marksmanship, they were uninjured and escaped in the cover of darkness.

"They were mustered out in May, 1865, but Ed came near losing his life at Washington. While a number of soldiers were bathing in the Potomac River, one called for help as he was drowning, and Ed went to his rescue, and succeeded in saving his life but came nearly losing his own in the struggle. Ed was married to Celestine Curry on 16 May 1867 (HC Bk 5-136) and to this union three children were Leora dying in infancy, Cora died 20 Apr 1902, and Mrs. Inez Radcliff with the widow survives. Interment Curry's Chapel Cemetery." See data on page of his twin brother, Joseph Martin.

Martin, Jacob; 8 Reg Co B, 25 Aug 61-28 Aug 65, promoted Corp'l, and Sgt. HC Muth Cemetery: Jacob Martin Co B 8 Ind Inf; Elizabeth w/o Jacob 1846-1919.

Martin, Joseph: HC obit 20 Sep 1923: "..born Hancock County, 5' 2" tall, age 20, dark complexion, gray eyes, dark hair, and farmer when enrolled.." "On 27 Jun 1841, Joseph, son of William and Charlotte Chapman, was born near Greenfield, and died 29 Aug 1923. Joseph was one of five children, and his early life was spent in this immediate neighborhood where he attended the district school and endured the hardships of early days.

"When the Nation was aroused from its "dream of Peace," Joseph enlisted in Company A, 53rd Indiana Regiment in February, 1862 and served until the close of the War when he was discharged 21 Jul 1865. His twin brother, Edward, served in the same unit. The twins were together throughout three long years of this bloody strife, and carried each others pack, shared their hardtack, and drank from the same canteen.

"In later life Joseph took great delight in relating to his children and grandchildren his experiences in the Civil War. One story he told more frequently than others was of the battle of Kennesaw Mountain. This battle occurred on 27 Jun which was also his birthday and he seldom failed to relate his experiences of this battle. Joseph was married 16 Dec 1867

Hancock County Indiana Civil War Soldiers

(HC Bk 5-184) Sarah Wagner. To this union were born nine children, one dying in infancy, Minnie in the bloom of young womanhood, and Mollie seven years ago.
"Surviving him are: Mrs. Riley Whitaker; Mrs. Will Alford; Arthur; William; Mrs. Ben Burk; and Mrs. Noble Beagle. His faithful companion preceded him seven years ago, and his daughter, Mrs. Will Alford came to his home to make his remaining days as pleasant and comfortable as possible. He enjoyed the family gatherings at his home on his birthday and on Christmas Eve, when a large Christmas tree and an oyster supper were enjoyed." Joseph and Sarah (1832-1916) both buried HC Curry's Chapel Cemetery.

Martin, Lot W.; 8 Reg Co G, 22 Apr 61-6 Aug 61; also 77 Reg Co A, 3 Aug 62-29 Jun 65. "..born Hancock County 6' tall, age 24, light complexion, blue eyes, black hair, farmer when enrolled. A Lot Martin married 14 Apr 1867 Matilda Tice, no place given; Matilda Martin was born 28 Feb 1849, died 13 Dec 1915, w/o Lot W. Martin and d/o Daniel and Susan Tice. NOD.

Martin, Matthias; 105 Reg Co E, 11 Jul 63-18 Jul 63. NOD.

Martin, Oliver; 4 Cav Co A, 3 Aug 62-8 May 64 transferred to Veteran Reserve Corps, indicates wound or illness. An Oliver Martin married 20 May 1866 Mary E. Hawkins HC Bk 5-62. Oliver was a shoemaker, died at age 49 of cancer, married but no name given. HC Philadelphia Cemetery: Oliver P. Martin 4 Ind Cav, 20 Jan 1845-5 Nov 1890; Mary E. died 2 Mar 18__.

Martin, Dr. Samuel M.; No units given. "He was born 7 Mar 1842, in Rush County, Indiana, the son of Dr. William H. Martin. Began the study of medicine that was interrupted by the Civil War but was discharged due to a gunshot wound through the left side of his body at the battle of Pea Ridge, Arkansas, Mar 1862. He graduated in 1865 from the Cincinnati College of Physicians and Surgeons. On 3 May 1866 he married Florence Howard, only daughter of Dr. N.P. Howard. Dr. Samuel Martin died 13 Jun 1897."

Hancock County Indiana Civil War Soldiers

Martin, Samuel; 18 Reg, Musician, 16 Aug 61-20 Aug 62. NOD

Martin, Thomas M.; 8 Reg Co G, 22 Apr 61-6 Aug 61; also 25 Aug 61-25 Aug 65. "..born Ireland, 5' 5" tall, age 30, dark complexion, blue eyes, dark hair, laborer when enrolled..." HC newspaper 11 Jun 1863: "Private Thomas M. Martin, arm amputated from wound near Vicksburg." Transferred from Co B 8th Indiana Infantry to 2nd Battalion Veteran Reserve Corps, 6 Apr 1864." A Thomas Martin married 20 Jul 1873 Winnaford Southard HC Bk 6-210.

Martin, William B.; 8 Reg Co B, 20 Aug 61-21 Dec 63. "..born Jefferson County, Indiana, 5' 4" tall, age 19, dark complexion, dark eyes, dark hair, harness maker when enrolled. Participated in battles of Pea Ridge, Cotton Plane, Champion Hill, Black River Ridge, Vicksburg and Jackson.

Martin, William B.; 8 Reg Co B, 25 Aug 61-killed 5 Sep 64, Perryville/Berryville, Virginia. NOD.

Martin, William H.; 87 Reg Co A, 11 Aug 62-17 Jun 63. HC Park Cemetery William H. Martin 87 Reg Co A 17 Feb 1845-18 Jun 1902. NOD.

Mavity, Uriah; 68 Reg Co B, 19 Aug 62-19 Nov 62, discharged disability. NOD.

Mayer, John; 53 Reg Co A, 22 May 64-21 Jul 65. NOD.

Mays, Frank; 8 Reg Co B, 25 Aug 61. HC newspaper 14 Aug 1862: "B. Frank Mays was promoted to Corporal." HC newspaper 11 Jun 1863: "1st Sgt Frank Mays was killed at Vicksburg, 22 May 1863." NOD.

McBane, Isaac; 13 Cav Co I, 23 Dec 63-18 Nov 65. HC Little Sugar Creek/Low Cemetery: Isaac McBane military data only on stone, NOD.

McBane, John S.; 79 Reg Co G, 15 Aug 62-7 Jun 65. "...born Bourbon County, Kentucky, 5' 10" tall, dark complexion, blue eyes, dark hair, age 39, carpenter when enrolled..." John S. Mc Bane married 1844 Hepatia Harter, no place given. HC Little Sugar Creek/Low Cemetery: John S. McBane died 9 Aug 1867 44y 3m 5d.

Hancock County Indiana Civil War Soldiers

McCole, Neal; 79 Reg Co C, 15 Aug 62-7 Jun 65. NOD.

McCollum, Ira; 12 Reg Co B, 15 May 61-19 May 62. NOD.

McConnell, John W.; 12 Reg Co B, Musician, 15 May 61-19 May 62. A John McConnell married 21 Sep 1869 Angie Staats HC Bk 5-320.

McConnell, William; 8 Reg Co B, 25 Aug 61-no out date. The son of Hiram and Allie (Plummer) McConnell, William died 23 Feb 1906 of cancer of the stomach, wife, Marian. HC Mt.Gilead/Reeves Cemetery: William McConnell 6 Nov 1845-23 Feb 1906; Marian 9 Feb 1845-2 Nov 1907.

McCord, Cyrus ; 79 Reg Co D, 17 Aug 62-died 24 Jan 1864, Nashville, Tennessee. Cyrus was the s/o Elias and Eliza (Newkirk) McCord.

McCord, Green; "The son of William and Hannah (Warren) McCord, Green was born 28 Dec 1826, married Aug 1849 Susan Noakes of Decatur County, Indiana. Green was a member of the Fall Creek Guards (not HC) and served during Confederate General John Hunt Morgan's raid into southern Indiana in July 1863. Green died 2 Jan 1913."

McCorkhill, Henry: 8 Reg Co B, 25 Aug 61-28 Aug 65. NOD.

McCorkhill, John; Newspaper 18 Jun 1831: "John McCorkle, born 8 Dec 1850, s/o James and Sarah (Dillie) McCorkel, died, 13 Jun 1931, at his home in Charlottesville, leaving a widow, and five children. Burial at Walnut Ridge Cemetery." Nothing is said about him being a Civil War veteran.

McCorkhill, John; 57 Reg Co A, 13 Dec 61-1 Jan 62; also 9 Cav Co B, 7 Jan 64-6 Jun 65. 9th Cavalry History states: "The last dispatch sent out of the fort at 7: AM on the day of surrender was carried by John McCorkhill, and accomplished the feat by coolness and bold riding (The battle of Sulphur Branch Trestle, Alabama, 25 Sep 1864)." A John McCorkhill married 10 Apr 1873 Sara Jane Binford HC Bk 6-193. HC death notice 10 Jan 1907: John McCorkhill died at his home in Maple Valley 2 Jan of uremic poisoning, aged 62 years and nine months. Funeral at the Friends Church in Wilkinson; pallbearers were members of the G.A.R. Interment McCray

Hancock County Indiana Civil War Soldiers

Cemetery." HC McCray Cemetery: John McCorkhill Co B 9 Cav no dates; Sarah 1846-1927

McCorkhill, R.B.; HC Allford Cemetery: R.B. McCorkell Co G 147 Ind Inf, military stone only, no dates.

McCorkhill, Richard; 147 Reg Co F, 7 Feb 65-4 Aug 65. An R.J. McCorkhill, age 60, died 4 May 1892, in (HC) Brown Township, HC obit 12 May 1892: "Jackson McCorkhill died at his residence, east of Wilkinson, aged 60 years. He was born 9 Oct 1834; married Annie Dent 12 Aug 1874 HC Bk 6-297. To them were born four children; the oldest and the youngest preceded him to that land beyond. One boy and one girl are still living. He leaves a wife, two children and one brother. Interment (HC) Simmons Cemetery (there is no listing of him as having a stone in 1993). There is an R. B. McCorkell, Co K 147 Ind Inf recorded in HC Allford Cemetery; only a military stone, no dates.

McCorkhill, William; 9 Reg Co E, 14 Feb 65-28 Feb 65. NOD.

McCray, Edwin; 18 Reg, Musician. NOD.

McDaniel, Jesse; 12 Reg Co A, 12 Sep 64-8 Jun 65. A Jesse McDaniel married 22 Nov 1857 Minerva Snodgrass HC Bk 4-52.

McDonald, Clark; 8 Reg Co B, 25 Aug 61-28 Aug 65. HC newspaper 11 Jun 1863: "Corp'l Clark McDonald was wounded slightly in the hip at the siege of Vicksburg, Mississippi." NOD.

McDuffey; Samuel 79 Reg Co D, 8 Aug 62-7 Jun 65. NOD.

McFadden, William H. "The son of Jefferson and Sophia (Ramsey) McFadden, William was born in Indianapolis, 17 Feb 1838 and at age eight moved with his family to Hancock County, where he has lived most of his life. He was living in Greenfield when he answered the call to arms, 3 Feb 1865, enlisting in Company G, 148 Indiana Regiment. The regiment was sent to the field on the Tennessee and Cumberland Rivers, where all the armies were on constant move, winding up the greatest war on earth. After the cessation of hostilities, the regiment performed garrison duty at Pulaski, Tennessee,

Hancock County Indiana Civil War Soldiers

Franklin and other points. He was discharged 5 Sep 1865 at Indianapolis. He has in his possession three "hard tacks," kept out of the last rations issued to him. On 3 Feb 1896 he married Mary J., born 7 May 1841 in Hendricks County d/o John and Ann (Vestal) Atkinson." HC Maple Grove/Jackson/Olvey Cemetery: W.H. McFadden died 9 Sep 1908 69y 6m 17d.

McFall, Daniel; 9 Cav Co B, 13 Nov 63 died 27 Feb 64, Indianapolis. NOD.

McFarland. Henderson; 5 Cav Co G, 28 Dec 63-15 Sep 65. NOD.

McGahey, Andrew S.; 106 Reg Co D, 10 Jul 63-17 Jul 63; also 9 Cav Co B, 9 Dec 63-died 26 Oct 64, of wounds, Nashville, Tennessee. HC New Palestine Cemetery: Andrew McGahey Jr. died 26 Oct 1864, 18y 9m 18 d, s/o Andrew Sr.

McGee, George; 5 Cav Co G, 16 Aug 62-15 Oct 65. HC Simmons Cemetery George McGee 1846-1909 Co G 5 Ind Cav. NOD

McGee, Ike; 8 Reg Co B, 25 Aug 61-4 Sep 64. HC newspaper 28 May 1863: "Ike McGee of Company B, 8th Regiment had his nose skinned by a shell and a finger amputated." NOD.

McGuire, Amos; 12 Reg Co B, 15 May 61-19 May 62. NOD.

McGuire, Harrison; 12 Reg Co B, 15 May 61-19 May 62, wagoner. NOD.

McGuire, Dr. Isaac W.; HC obit 28 Jul 1927: "Dr. Isaac W. McGuire, a citizen of Greenfield until about two years ago, died at the State Hospital at Madison, Indiana, where he had been taken only a few days before. The body was brought here where the funeral was held and interment at Eden Cemetery. Dr. McGuire was 88 years of age and a Civil War veteran (Co F 93 Ohio Inf) and also a member of the G.A.R. Dr. McGuire came to the county about forty years ago from Ohio and practiced his profession as a veterinarian until age made it necessary for him to retire a few years ago. Mr. McGuire moved from Greenfield to the southern part of the state. He is survived by the widow and an adopted son, Wilson McGuire of this city."

Hancock County Indiana Civil War Soldiers

McGuire, Joseph; 12 Reg Co G, 7 Aug 62-8 Jun 65

McGuire, Patrick; Co C 1st Batt. 11 U.S. Infantry, 15 Jan 62, served three years. "..born Ireland 5' 3" tall age 23, dark complexion, blue eyes, black hair, laborer when enrolled,, character very good..." NOD

McGuire, Thomas; 99 Reg Co B, 13 Aug 62-5 Jun 65. 99th regiment History states he is a "resident of Lebanon in 1900."

McKelvy, Jasper C.; 8 Reg Co B, 22 Apr 61-6 Aug 61. HC obit 25 Jul 1918: "Jasper C. McKelvey, formerly of Philadelphia, Indiana, died at his home near Irvington (Marion County, Indiana). His death was due to paralysis. He leaves a wife, two sons and one daughter. He was a Civil War veteran and his remains will be laid to rest at the Philadelphia Cemetery." Jasper C. McKelvey married Rebecca Galloway 5 Jun 1862 HC Bk 4-333. HC Philadelphia Cemetery: J.C. McKelvey 1841-1918, Soldier; Rebecca 1843-1905; Rosa d/o J.C. 1862-1897; Jessie s/o J.C. 1865-1921.

McKenzie, David H.; 6 Cav Co A, Jul 62-18 Jun 65. " His regiment participated in battles of Richmond, Kentucky, siege and capture of Knoxville, then joined Sherman's forces in Macon, Georgia where the command was cut to pieces and General Stoneman was captured. At the battle of Richmond he received a gunshot wound in the right leg, captured but paroled the next day and then sent to Indianapolis. Mr. McKenzie was born Perry County, Pennsylvania, 13 Apr 1838, the s/o Daniel and Mary (McClintock) McKenzie and he married December 1865 Miss Isabelle Altland. They moved from Vermillion County, Indiana, to Hancock County about 1877. HC Park Cemetery: David H. McKenzie 1838-1921; Isabelle 1843-1923."

McKinley, William; 9 Reg Co D, 24 Feb 65-died 16 Apr 65 Shield's Mill, Tennessee. NOD.

McKinne, Jesse; 5 Cav Co G, 16 Aug 62-6 Jun 65, disability. "...born Highland County, Ohio, 6' 2" tall, age 45, dark complexion, hazel eyes, black hair, farmer when enrolled..."

Hancock County Indiana Civil War Soldiers

A Jesse McKinne married 10 Jul 1845 Harriett Duncan HC Bk 2-163.

McMillen, William; 9 Cav Co B, 9 Dec 63-missing 12 Sep 1864, Florence, Alabama. NOD.

McNamee, George F.; 8 Reg Co G, 22 Apr 61-6 Aug 61; also 106 Reg Co D, 10 Jul 63-17 Jul 63. George McNamee married 21 Aug 1864 (HC Bk 4-466) Agnes Ashcraft. HC McNamee Cemetery: Agnes, died 19 Feb 1865, 19y 8m 7d, w/o George F., d/o J.and S. Ashcraft,

McQuerry, Perry; 99 Reg Co B, 13 Aug 62-died 30 Jul 64 of wounds received 28 Jul 1864. Perry McQuerry married 20 Sep 1849 Charlotte Reeves HC Bk 2-347.

McRoberts, H.M.; 106 Reg Co D, 10 Jul 63-17 Jul 63. A Henry McRoberts married 29 Sep 1886 Maggie Boyce HC Bk 7-725. HC obit 22 Sep 1892: "The dead body of Henry McRoberts, of New Palestine, was found at the residence of Henry J. Hilligoss in Brandywine Township. Mr. McRoberts was a carpenter by trade and was at work on the new residence of Mr. Hilligoss. The last seen of Mr. McRoberts was by a hired girl at the residence who gave him a drink of water. Sometime afterwards the body of Mr. McRoberts was found where he had been engaged in putting weather boarding on the new building. From the position of his body it is thought he died without a struggle. His death is attributed to heart disease, as he has been afflicted with this disease for some time past."

Meek, Anton; HC Philadelphia Cemetery: Anton Meek Corp 79 Ind Inf. NOD.

Meek, Cornwell Preston; family tradition says he was a soldier in the Civil War and there is discussion about whether it was for the North or the South; he was born 17 Jul 1834 in Indiana; died 7 Apr 1876. Contributed by Ruth Bundy, Greenfield, Indiana. *Hancock County History*, published 1916, states: "There are no dates or markers but Cornwall Meek; wife of Cornwall Meek; and Jeremiah Meek are all buried in Greenfield's Old Cemetery on South Street." Cornwell Preston Meek married 1)Mary Aminta Elizabeth . America Willett 31

Hancock County Indiana Civil War Soldiers

Jan 1858 (HC Bk 4-64); Cornwell married 2) Latica Scotten 5 Dec 1875 HC Bk 6-407.

Meek, Jared; 5 Cav Co G. HC obit 20 May 1915: "Jared C. Meek, aged 87 years, son of Jeremiah and Catherine (Williams) Meek, died at his home on West Fifth Street, Greenfield, following a stroke of paralysis. He was the first white child (as opposed to Indian) born in Greenfield. and lived to see its growth from a few cabins in a wilderness and swamp to its present beautiful proportions. His father, Jeremiah, kept a tavern in a two-story log cabin which stood on the site of the present Goble printing plant. It was in this cabin that Mr. Meek was born, 15 Jun 1828.

"At the time the National Road had not been built and the cabin faced south where the old State Road passed over the ground occupied by the county jail. The National Road work was begun about two years after Mr. Meek was born. His uncle, Cornwell Meek, John Wingfield and Benjamin Spillman donated 60 acres of land in order that Greenfield might be the permanent county seat. In 1848 Mr. Meek learned the blacksmith trade under the instruction of George Plummer, who at that time was a master of the trade, and whose shop was located where Dr. C.K. Bruner's office now stands (Southest corner of Riley Avenue and West Main Street). For fifty-five years, Mr. Meek continued as a blacksmith until his eyesight failed.

"He served in the Civil War, Company G, 5th Cavalry, and his regiment was in twenty-one battles of record and Mr. Meek was in the siege of Knoxville. He was honorably discharged and has been drawing a well deserved pension from the Government. Mr. Meek was intimately acquainted with all the early history of Greenfield and her people of the early days. His father was one of the prominent citizens of his day and served as judge of the probate court of this county for seven years and of Wayne County for fourteen years, having been appointed by William Henry Harrison, territorial governor of Indiana. Jeremiah kept the first tavern at a time when

Hancock County Indiana Civil War Soldiers

immigration was mostly on horseback. He laid out the first plat of Greenfield and donated the ground for the courthouse in Meek's Reserve and also donated the ground for the first M.E. church south of the railroad.

"Jared Meek enjoyed to talk on matters of early history of this community. In talking recently, he said he remembered the first tailor shop in town was started in his father's tavern by Jonathan Dunbar and that the first blacksmith shop was run by Noah Perry in the southeast corner of the old Gooding block. Mr. Meek was a member of the Dunbar Post G.A.R. and of the Methodist Church. He is survived by the widow who was third wife; one son, William Meek; one daughter, Mrs. Nancy Barr; one brother, Fielding Meek, who is now 90 years of age,; and one sister, Mrs. Laurinda Eastes. Interment Park Cemetery." Jared C. Meek married 1) Martha Crockett, 23 Sep 1852 HC Bk 3-116; married 2) Mrs. Rebecca West, 1 Jan 1885 HC Bk 7-574; married 3) Margaret Curtis 17 Nov 1904 HC Bk 11-56.

Meek, Marshall M.; 5 Cav Co G, 20 Jan 64-15 Sep 65. HC newspaper 11 Aug 1864: "M.M. Meek has been captured, signed Lt. W.H. Pilkenton" Andersonville, Georgia Prison Profile, code #55705; M.M. Meek, private in Co G, 5 Cav, survived and was exchanged 1 Apr 1865." Marshall M. Meek married 29 Jul 1887 Angeline McConnell HC Bk 7-785.

Meek, Nathan Crawford; 53 Reg Co A, 24 Feb 62-21 Jul 65. "Nathan Crawford Meek was born 14 Sep 1837, Greenfield, Indiana and died 20 Aug 1920, Indianapolis; married 29 Nov 1865 (HC Bk 5-8) Mary C. Hughes who was born 21 Feb 1838, Missouri, died 10 Mar 1912, Indianapolis." Contributed by William Jenkins, Pendleton, Indiana.

HC obit 23 Mar 1923: "The body of Nathan Meek was brought from the home of his daughter, Mrs. Charles Furry, Indianapolis, to the home of his son, Harry Meek in Greenfield, where the funeral services were held under the auspices of Dunbar Post Grand Army of the Republic. Mr. Meek served two enlistments in Company A, 53rd Indiana Volunteers. He played second E flat clarinet in the old Greenfield Band, as told

Hancock County Indiana Civil War Soldiers

in James Whitcomb Riley's poem. He is survived by three sons, John; Walter and Harry." Nathan and Mary Meek both buried HC Park Cemetery.

Meek, Noah; 4 Cav Co A, 3 Aug 62-23 May 65. "..born Hancock County, 5' 11" tall, age 25 years, light complexion, blue eyes, brown hair, farmer when enrolled..."

Meek, Ranson Monroe; 5 Cav Co G, 20 Jan 64-15 Sep 65. HC newspaper 11 Aug 1864: "R.M. Meek was taken prisoner during the disastrous expedition commanded by General Stoneman." Andersonville Georgia Prison Profile #49484: Ransom M. Meek, Company G 5th Indiana Cavalry was captured 31 Jul 1864, at Macon, Georgia, survived and was paroled 25 Apr 1865 at Jacksonville, Florida." He was born 11 Dec 1842, and died 11 May 1905, s/o Joshua and Anna (Russell) Meek. He married 1 Jun 1870 HC Bk 5-379, Loretta Dorsh (1 Jun 1850-2 Nov 1900).

HC obit 18 May 1905: "Monroe Meek, Postmaster, died at his home in Philadelphia (Indiana) of fatty degeneration of the heart. Mr. Meek was one of the old settlers of the county, having been born and raised in Sugar Creek Township. He was a member of the 5th Indiana Cavalry and was captured during the siege of Atlanta and placed in Andersonville Prison where he remained some three months. After his release from prison he joined his command and remained with it until he was mustered out at the end of the War. On his return home, he, with his brother, Oscar Meek, went into the mercantile business, the partnership continuing until his death. Ransom and Loretta both buried Philadelphia Cemetery."

Meek, Richard: 26 Reg Co I, 24 Sep 64-5 Nov 65 transferred from 89 Reg. NOD.

Meek, Stephen R.; It appears he served in 8th Reg, Co B; and 8th Reg Co G, dates unclear; and 105 Reg: Co E, 11 Jul 63-18 Jul 63. " Born Henry County, Kentucky, 5' 6" tall, age 39, dark complexion, hazel eyes, auburn hair, laborer when enrolled." NOD.

Hancock County Indiana Civil War Soldiers

Melton, Francis M.G.; 130 Reg Co B, Oct 63-2 Dec 65. "At the age of twenty-eight years, he hung up his saw, laid aside his plane and shouldered his musket in defense of his country as a private and soon promoted to Duty Sergeant. He fought in all the battles from Dalton to Atlanta where he was wounded, by the concussion of a shell, injuring his head. The command was in the battle of Nashville before being sent to Charlotte, North Carolina.

"Francis M.G. Melton was born 20 Nov 1837, Rush County, Indiana,; his parents (father Mylon) coming to Hancock County shortly after his birth. He learned the carpenter's trade and was married September 1856, in Madison County, to Cynthia Compton. They were blessed with six children: John; Aheba; Francis; Ephraim; Julius; and George." Buried HC Park Cemetery.

Mendenhall, James P.; 8 Reg Co H, 5 Sep 61-28 Aug 65. James P. Mendenhall married 5 May 1874 Helen Harrison HC Bk 6-272.

Mesler, William; 26 Reg Co H, 24 Sep 64-5 Sep 65. A William Mesler married 17 Mar 1853 Jane Ginder HC Bk 3-151; also a William Mesler married 27 Sep 1864 Lydia Thomas HC Bk 4-477.

Messler, John A.; 12 Reg Co B, 15 May 61-19 May 62. "HC newspaper December 1870: John A. Messler, a well-to-do bachelor farmer in the Fortville neighborhood, was found in his barn with a bullett hole in his head, entering over the left eye, and leaving the head from just behind the right ear. A stake was then used to beat his brains out after which the house was ransacked. Who did the deed is not known and suspicions point to no one."

Meyer, Charles; 99 Reg Co B, 13 Aug 62, missing in action 4 Dec 64. NOD.

Meyer, Christian; 53 Reg Co A, 31 Oct 64-21 Jul 65. A Christian Meyer married 1 Apr 64 Sophia Reasoner HC Bk 4-442.

Hancock County Indiana Civil War Soldiers

Meyer, Christian F.; 79 Reg Co D, 16 Aug 62-7 Jun 65. A Christian F. Meyer married 1 Mar 1857 Eliza Bennett HC Bk 4-19.

Michael, Henry; 8 Reg Co G, 22 Apr 61-6 Aug 61. Buried New Palestine Cemetery, military data only on stone, no dates. NOD.

Miller, Abraham; 38 Reg Co A, 4 Nov 64-15 Jun 65. An Abraham Miller married 8 Feb 1847 Charlotte Tyner HC Bk 2-224. Abraham buried HC Gilboa Cemetery, military data only on stone, no dates.

Miller, Ambrose; 9 Cav Co B, 9 Dec 63-11 May 65. An Ambers Miller married 11 Jul 1844 Elizabeth New HC Bk 2-127.

Miller, Benjamin; 57 Reg Co A, 13 Dec 61-4 Feb 62, buried HC Gilboa Cemetery, military data only on stone. Following is additional data found on Benjamin Miller but none may detail the soldier: married 19 Oct 1856 Angeline Hazlett HC Bk 3-364; married 4 May 1861 Catherine Ashley HC Bk 4-263; married 29 Dec 1864 Susannah Stuart HC Bk 4-494. Other Miller burials at HC Gilboa Cemetery: Benjamin h/o Susanna no other data; Susannah w/o Benjamin died 6 Aug 1854 52y 2m 12d; Lydia d/o B. and Susannah died 28 Oct 1830 4y 1m; Deborah d/o B. and Susannah died 27 Feb 1838 2y 14 d. Lydia is recorded as the first burial in Gilboa Cemetery.

Miller, F.M.; 8 Reg Co B, 25 Aug 61. HC newspaper 11 Jun 1863: "Pvt. F.M. Miller reported wounded slightly in chin during the siege of Vicksburg, May 1863." 13 Mar 64, Corp'l. F.M. Miller drowned at Saluria Bayou, Texas.

Miller, G.W.; 5 Cav Co G, 16 Aug 62-15 Jun 65. HC newspaper 11 Aug 1864: "Corp. G.W. Miller was taken prisoner during the disastrous expedition commanded by General Stoneman." (not listed on Andersonville Prison Profile) .A G.W Miller married 15 Sep 1866 Hettie Ann Lewis HC Bk 5-85. A George Miller is listed as having died 22 Nov 1892, but found no obit.

Hancock County Indiana Civil War Soldiers

Miller, Henry; 99 Reg Co B, 2 Feb 62, promoted 2nd Lt. 24 Mar 64, resigned 13 Feb 65. Three marriages for a Henry Miller: 19 Aug 1854 Mary Richman HC Bk 3-229; 7 Sep 1854 Margaret Jane Curry HC Bk 3-233; 27 Apr 1873 Cynthia Toler HC Bk 6-198. 99th Regiment history states: "Henry Miller's 1900 address is Jennings, Kansas."

Miller, Isaac; 148 Reg Co C, 17 Feb 65, died 13 Mar 65, Indianapolis. NOD

Miller, Jacob; 148 Reg Co I, 17 Feb 65-5 Sep 65. A Jacob Miller married 28 May 1865 Miranda Hawk HC Bk 4-513.

Miller, John; 15 New York Cav Co E, 20 Jul 63-17 Jun 65. HC obit 16 Jul 1908: "John Miller, aged 62 years, and a Civil War veteran, died in his room in the Gates block on East Main Street of chronic diarrhea, liver and heart trouble. His nurse, William Davis called quickly for Dr. Milo Gibbs, who placed him in bed but the Silent Messenger had called and he passed into the great beyond.

"Mr. Miller, during the Civil War, enlisted in Company H. 27th New York and when honorably discharged reenlisted in the 15th New York Cavalry, serving until the close of the war. He came here afterward where he worked his trade, that of a boot and shoemaker. He was united in marriage with Miss Lucretia Alice Chittenden 19 Oct 1871 (HC Bk 6-57) who preceded him in death some years ago. His funeral service was conducted jointly by the Odd Fellows and Grand Army of the Republic." HC Park Cemetery: "John Miller Co E 15 NY Cav, 8 Jun 1844-13 Jul 1908; Alice w/o John Miller 4 Jan 1852-29 Nov 1892.

Miller, John G.; 5 Reg Invalid Corps, Co G, 4 Jul 62, discharged 18 Jan 64, disability. "..born Marion County, Kentucky, 6' 1" tall, age 33, dark complexion, gray eyes, dark hair, farmer when enrolled.."

Miller, Joseph; 17 West Virginia Inf, Co F, no dates. HC Park Cemetery, age 84, died 16 May 1921. NOD.

Hancock County Indiana Civil War Soldiers

Miller, Michael; "..Michael Miller served in the army in much of the Civil War...he was the s/o John and Susan (Keffer) Miller...and sister of Nancy who married Azzel Shull." NOD.

Miller, Nicholas; 8 Reg Co B, 25 Aug 61-28 Aug 65. Promoted Sergeant then 2nd Lt 17 Sep 65. NOD.

Miller, Reuben R.; 8 Reg Co H, 29 Aug 61-4 Sep 64. "..born Fayette County, Indiana, 5' 6" tall, age 23, fair complexion, blue eyes, dark hair, farmer when enrolled.." A Reuben R. Miller married 27 Oct 1859 Sarah Lineback HC Bk 4-158. Mrs. Reuben Miller died Jul 1889.

Miller, Thomas J.; 99 Reg Co B, 15 Aug 62-5 Jun 65. "..born Hancock County, Indiana, 5' 9" tall, age 19, fair complexion, blue eyes, red hair, farmer when enrolled..." A Thomas Miller married 8 Aug 1867 Mary C. Brooks HC Bk 5-150. 99th Regiment History states, "Thomas J. Miller's 1900 address is Marion, Indiana."

Miller, William; 13 Reg Co I, 10 Mar 65-29 Jul 65. Too many William Millers in sources to differentiate.

Miller William H.; HC obit 29 Mar 1923: "Funeral services were held in Morristown for William H. Miller, age eighty-three years and a Civil war veteran. For thirty-five years, Mr. Miller was a leading merchant of Martinsville and moved to Morristown when his health failed. Mr. Miller was born near Marietta, Shelby County, Indiana. when the Civil War began he organized a company which was assigned to the 33rd Indiana Regiment. He was made 1st Lieutenant and later promoted to Captain. He is survived by the widow and the following children: Albert; Edward; Mrs. Alice Carville; and Bernice and Laura Miller. Mr. Miller was a brother of Jap Miller, of Morristown, formerly of Brooklyn and who was made famous by one of Riley's poems."

Miller, William T.; 79 Reg Co G, 13 Aug 62, died 17 Apr 63, Murfreesboro, Tennessee.

Millikan, E. P.; HC Park Cemetery: Edmond P. Millikan 54 Ohio Inf Reg Co C, died 26 Apr 1929, Kokomo, Indiana, age 87. "He was a shoemaker and soldier, married 29 Dec 1864

Hancock County Indiana Civil War Soldiers

Florence Belle Gwinn (HC Bk 4-493). HC Park Cemetery: Chester Millikan s/o E.P. and F.B. 1868-1870; c/o E.P. and F.B. 1870-1871.

Milner, Amos; 99 Reg Co B; 13 Aug 62-5 Jun 65. "..born Fayette County, Indiana, 5' 8" tall, age 26,light complexion, blue eyes, light hair, farmer when enrolled..." 99th Regiment History: " Amos Milner, was born 9 Sep 1834, Fayette County, Indiana. was engaged in farming when he enlisted in 1862 and served throughout the war, a faithful and true soldier. In 1868 he moved to Kansas, and has lived in or near Madison, Greenwood County, ever since, living on his farm up to 1893, and since has lived a retired life in the city of Madison.

"Comrade Milner has been twice married: 1) Martha Franks 28 Oct 1857 (HC Bk 4-45) dying 1861; married 2) Phebe Ann Blakely 24 Dec 1865 HC Bk 5-16. He has two sons living. Comrade Milner says: "Company B suffered more because they were charged twice while on picket line and nearly all were killed or wounded. Address in 1900, Madison, Kansas." His brother, William, died Feb 1885, in Lyon County, Kansas, leaving a wife and seven children."

Milner, Job; 99 Reg Co B, 14 Aug 62-5 Jun 65. "...born Fayette County, Indiana, 6' tall age 24, dark complexion, blue eyes, black hair, farmer when enrolled..." Job was sick in camp hospitals and General Hospitals with illnesses of intermittent fever, malaria, diarrhea and a flesh wound during his enlistment. Job married 20 May 1866 HC Bk 5-61, Elizabeth Nichols, d/o Josiah and Margaret (Bray) Nichols, born 28 Jun 1844. 99th Regiment History states: "Job Milner's 1900 address is Cleveland (HC), Indiana."

"By Act of Congress, 11 May 1912, Job was eligible and applied for a pension as a veteran of the Civil War; on 18 May 1912; he states the following: born 12 Feb 1837; since leaving the service, his residences have been Hancock County, Indiana till about 1912; and since then in Ingalls, Madison County, Indiana, Pension Certificate #241397. Job died 3 Aug 1912 and Elizabeth (Nichols) Milner applied and received a Widow's

Hancock County Indiana Civil War Soldiers

Pension from 21 Aug 1912 until her death 10 Jan 1937. HC Hays Cemetery: Job Milner Co B 99 Ind Inf; Elizabeth (Nichols) Milner is buried Hays Cemetery but her stone was gone or illegible when the inscriptions were transcribed in 1980. Contributed by Sherry Rigney, Wilkinson, Indiana.

Milner Joseph T.; 99 Reg Co B,13 Aug 62-5 Jun 65. "...born Grant County, Kentucky, 5' 10" tall age 35, dark complexion, black eyes, black hair, farmer when enrolled..." A Joseph Thomas Milner married 22 Nov 1849 Margaret Reeves, no place given; a Joseph Milner married 14 Feb 1874 Eliza Roseberry HC Bk 6-256. 99th Regiment History states: "Joseph T. Milner's 1900 address is Mt. Moriah, Missouri." Fayette County, Indiana, 5' 10" tall, age 23, fair complexion, blue eyes, dark hair, farmer when enrolled..." A William

Milner, William; 99 Reg Co B, 13 Aug 62-5 Jun 65. "...born Milner married 25 Oct 1860 Sarah Ann Humble HC Bk 4-217. 99th regiment History states: "William Milner died in Kansas in 1885."

Milroy, Albertus; 5 Cav Co G, 16 Aug 62-10 Nov 65. NOD.

Mingle, Cornelius; 79 Reg Co C, 15 Aug 62-7 Jun 65. Cornelius Mingle married 28 Dec 1865 Malinda Umbenbrower HC Bk 5-17.

Mintz, William P.; 5 Cav Co G, 13 Jan 64, died 10 May 64, Louisville, Kentucky. NOD.

Mitchell, James L.; 19 Reg Co A, 29 Jul 61, 6 May 64 wounded at Wilderness, Virginia, out 28 Jul 64. HC obit 14 Jun 1917: "James L. Mitchell, in his 78th year, died at his home on East Main Street, Greenfield, after an illness of more than a year. He was born 31 Aug 1839, and was one of the well known and well liked veterans of the Civil War, having served four years as a member of Company A in the Iron Brigade, 19th regiment.

"He was a former auditor of Hancock County, member and elder of the Christian Church and member of the Dunbar Post G.A.R. Mr. Mitchell was thrice married. (4 Jul 1865 Elizabeth Blake no place given; 6 Aug 1890 Emma Lineback HC Bk 8-248; 1 Jun 1912 Almira Sample HC Bk 12-167). He is

Hancock County Indiana Civil War Soldiers

survived by the widow and three children, a son and two daughters, Ida Mitchell and Mrs. Minnie Dorsey." HC Park Cemetery: James L. Mitchell 1839-1917 Co A 19 Ind Inf; Elizabeth S. w/o James L. died 22 Aug 1889 41y 8m 19d; Emma A. w/o J.L. 1851-1910.

Mitchell, John; 53 Reg Co A, 24 Feb 62-24 Jun 65. A John Mitchell married 28 Sep 1841 Elizabeth Smith HC Bk 2-25; also married 16 May 1889 Amanda Crider HC Bk 8-151.

Mitchell, Robert S.; 13 Reg Co H, 19 Jun 61-1 Jul 64, wagoner. "...born Harrison County, Kentucky, 5' 4" tall, age 38, dark complexion, hazel eyes, black hair, carpenter when enrolled..." A Robert Mitchell married 30 Dec 1856 Catharine Scotten HC Bk 3-383.

Mitchell, Rufus; Corp'l. 18 U.S. Regular Infantry. "...born Cornwall, England, 5' 10" tall, age 23, light complexion, gray eyes, auburn hair, farmer when enrolled...Under my hand at Lookout Mountain, Tennessee, this 17 May 1865, character, good, signed Henry Mizney, Captain commanding, 18th U.S. Infantry. Oath of idenity: same as above, residence, town of Eden, Indiana." A Rufus Mitchell married 15 May 1866 Eunis Walker HC Bk 5-58.

Mitchell, William; 105 Reg Co E, 11 Jul 63-18 Jul 63, "served against Confederate General John Hunt Morgan in his raid in southeastern Indiana and was under fire at Harrison, Ohio. William was born 15 Aug 1823, in Montgomery County, Kentucky, the second child of John Fowler and Charlotte (Ralls) Mitchell. On 23 May 1852 he married Calasty Long in Cincinnati, Ohio; she was born 1836 in St. Louis, Missouri, and died 25 Sep 1892. They were the parents of thirteen children, eight of whom attained maturity: John F.; Thomas; Fannie; William; Eliza; George; Nellie; and Mattie. William learned the printing business in an old-fashioned country printing office and traveled extensively; in 1849 he was the foreman of the largest printing plant of the West.

"He came to Hancock County in 1856, taking charge of the Greenfield Sentinel and in 1859 founded the *Hancock*

Hancock County Indiana Civil War Soldiers

Democrat. In 1886 he had the great misfortune of losing his eyesight. He died 7 Apr 1899. He and Calasty are buried HC Park Cemetery." *Hancock Democrat* 13 April 1899, page 4: IN MEMORIAM William Mitchell, Sr. Answers Final Call after A Busy, Honorable and Successful Life William Mitchell, Sr., the veteran editor and publisher of the *Hancock Democrat* and one of the best known men and honored citizens of this section of the State, died at his home on South State Street in this city at five o'clock, Friday, 7 April 1899, at the age of seventy-five years, seven months and twenty-two days. He had been in his usual good health until about four weeks prior to his demise when he was taken ill and among his ailments was a bad case of erysipelas of the foot. This , however, his physicians were unable to relieve, but the trouble was found to be of a more serious character and the vital forces which had been so marked and vigorous in former years were seen to be gradually failing and the honored and courageous old man, surrounded by his children and friends, sank into the deep sleep that knows no waking.

"William Mitchell was born in Kentucky, 15 Aug 1823. His father John F. Mitchell, was a native Kentuckian, his birth occurring in 1791, in a fort built by Daniel Boone. William Mitchell received a partial education at Maysville, Kentucky, and while there learned the printing business. He traveled extensively for several years and engaged in his chosen business in a number of cities. In 1849 he located at Cincinnati and was foreman of the old *Dollar Times* which in those days was the largest printing offices in the West.

"For a time he managed the New York office of Dye's *American Bank Note Detector*, which was considered authority on banking. In 1855 he removed to Lafayette, but in 1856 he came to this city and took charge of the Greenfield *Sentinel*, owned by the late Thomas D. Walpole, which he managed until 1859 when he founded the *Hancock Democrat*, which under his management grew as the city and county developed and has been a great force in the education of the people and in upbuilding and bettering the community. In connection with the paper he established a job printing office, which has few equals and no superiors in point of efficiency and quality of work produced. There is not a better equipped office outside of the large cities anywhere in the State.

"Mr. Mitchell filled many positions during his long and eventful life with credit to himself and to the advantage of those who trusted him with places of preferment. He was an earnest advocate of the public schools, with which he was connected in an official capacity for years. He served as postmaster, County Recorder, as Deputy Provost Marshall of this District, as a member of the Democratic Central Committee, as Sergeant of the Home Guards, and filled several municipal offices. He served with the Indianians during the Morgan raid and was under fire at Harrison, Ohio.

"In politics Mr. Mitchell was originally a Whig, but with the demise of that party became a Democrat, to which party he adhered until his death during the Civil War he was a strong Unionman, and his pen was vigorous, used for the support of the Union and the suppression of the rebellion. As an editorial writer he was terse and vigorous, driving to the point without any evasion or obscurity. His opponents long ago learned to respect the courage of his convictions, while his political friends admired the vigorous and pointed sentences which he penned.

"He united with the Christian Church at an early date, and was a prominent Odd Fellow until some thirteen years ago, when he had the misfortune to lose his eyesight. In 1852 Mr. Mitchell married Calasta Long, an orphan girl without a living relative. They lived as husband and wife until 25 Sep 1892, when Mrs. Mitchell died at their home in this city. This bereavement with the loss of his eyesight, weighed upon him heavily, but he continued to live at the old home where he was cared for by his daughters, and daily he was led to his office where he sat in his arm chair and listened to the reading of the current events of the day in which he retained a lively interest and upon which

Hancock County Indiana Civil War Soldiers

he still continued to express his views through the columns of the *Democrat* until the close of his life. After the loss of his eyesight the business of his establishment was managed by his eldest son, John F. Mitchell, who has shown rare good judgement and business ability, and added largely to the fortune of his father. For several years past a partnership has existed between William Sr. and John F. Mitchell.

"The deceased was indulgent to a fault, and even when in great need of money would not ask those who owed him to pay. Another characteristic of the man was kindness to the poor, which in turn caused them to look upon him as friend and adviser. To William and Calasty Mitchell were born thirteen children; of whom eight are still living, viz: John F.; George; Thomas; William Jr.; Mrs. Nellie Kinder, Mattie; Eliza; and Fannie Mitchell. The funeral occurred at the Christian Church on Sunday, the 9th inst., and was attended by a large crowd of relatives and friends both in and out of the city.

"The Grand Army and the city officials marched to the residence and from the house to the church and thence to the cemetery after the services. The old veterans, though becoming somewhat aged, are loyal to their comrades and never fail to show respect and love for their comrades and friends. The final sermon was preached by the Rev. T.H. Kuhn, and was an able and inspiring discourse. Numerous beautiful and costly floral tributes were presented, among them a number from the different members of the family, one from each of the printing houses of the city, the city officers, the Helping Hand Society of the Christian Church, the Bimetallic Club of Hancock County and the employees of the *Democrat* office.

"The remains were laid to rest in a beautiful vault in Park Cemetery and the earthly career of one of Hancock County's best and most influential citizens is at an end. While this is true the influence of his life will live for years and is interwoven in the business, social and intellectual life of the county. While he, like all mortals, may have made mistakes, the influence of his life and his motives were right, and the world is better by the influence he exerted."

Millard, Mordecai; " He was a son of Matilda and Mordecai Millard. At age 21, he enrolled 25 Dec 63 in Indianapolis and was mustered in 2 Jan 64, to serve three years in Company B, 9 Cav. He died 1 May 64 in Indianapolis of typhoid pneumonia. He was married 4 Mar 1861 to Amanda Plummer (born 1842) at Oaklandon, Marion County, Indiana, a child, Mary Eliza Millard born Feb 1862. His widow applied for pension 21 May 1864 with a post office address of Mt.Comfort." Contributed by Jane Ross, Indianapolis, Indiana.

Moncrief, John Thomas; 11 Ill Inf Reg Co G, 25 Jul 61-30 Jul 64, discharged disability. "He was born about 1824 in Jennings County, Indiana, the son of Caleb and Jane (Blackburn) Moncrief. He was reared in his native County and followed the pursuit of farming until the Mexican War was declared in 1846. at age twenty-four John Thomas Moncrief enlisted in theUnited Sates military as a member of the Teaming and Ambulance Corps. In 1848 after eighteen months service, he returned to his home in Jennings County where he resumed farming. In 1854 he, his parents, Caleb and Jane, and perhaps some of their other children migrated from Indiana to Effingham County, Illinois, where they purchased a farm and cultivated one-hundred-twenty acres of land.

"The Moncriefs may have been neighbors, or at least acquainted with Milo and Elizabeth (Crider) Gibbs family in Effingham County. Milo Gibbs died leaving a twenty-nine-year-old Elizabeth with four children. Women rarely remained a widow very long in those days because both women and men were needed to keep a farm and family together. John Thomas and Elizabeth (Crider) Gibbs were married 17 Sep 1857 in Effingham County, Illinois. Their first child, Caleb, was born 24 Jun 1858 in Effingham County, and later a daughter, Mary Jane, was born. At age thirty-seven, John Thomas heard the howling winds of war again and on 23 Jul 1861 enlisted in Company G, 11th Illinois Infantry. At the battle of Memphis,

Hancock County Indiana Civil War Soldiers

Tennessee, he was "struck in the head by a bullett, so seriously injured with a fractured skull that he never regained his reason." Brought home from the War and in hopes of a cure, he was sent to a hospital in Jacksonville, Illinois, where he remained for two years. His condition did not improve and sometime before 1865, he was sent to a hospital in Washington, D.C. In 1865 John Thomas' wife, Elizabeth, and children migrated to Hancock County to be near her Crider family who had been residents since the 1830s.

"John Thomas remained in the Washington, D.C., hospital for twenty-four years before he was sent to a hospital in Logansport, Indiana, where he remained for two years. He was in hospitals for twenty-seven years before he was finally taken to Indianapolis where he died 3 October 1893, at age sixty-nine years. At age sixty-five, Elizabeth (Crider) Moncrief was once again a widow and living in Hancock County with her daughter, Mary Jane Sipe, who married John Sipe, 21 August 1881. Elizabeth Moncrief died 12 October 1922, and is buried beside John Thomas in (HC) Park Cemetery."

Mooney, John; 9 Cav Co B, 9 Dec 63-17 Jul 65. He survived the explosion and burning of the steamboat, Sultana, on the Mississippi River, 27 Apr 1865, as it was returning Union soldiers to their northern homes." NOD.

Moore, John O.; 38 Reg Co D, 4 Nov 64-Jun 65. HC obit 20 Mar 1919: "John Oliver Moore, a prominent farmer in Hancock County for many years, died at his home in Jackson Township. Mr. Moore was born in Kanawha County, Virginia, 11 Mar 1842, and with his parents, John W. and Julia (Hazlett) Moore, moved to this county some years later.

"After John Oliver's marriage 18 Feb 1862 (HC Bk 4-315) to (Isepena) Margaret Catt (1842-1933), he began farming on his father's place, and soon was farming 120 acres of land in Center Township. He died 15 Mar 1919 and is survived by the widow and four children, George; William; Howard; and Mrs. Roxey Bussell." John O. and Isaphena M. are buried (HC) Simmons Cemetery."

Hancock County Indiana Civil War Soldiers

Moore, Lester, 8 Reg Co B, 5 Apr 63-28 Aug 65. "...born Washington County, Iowa, 5' 4" tall, age 18, fair complexion, blue eyes, auburn hair, farmer when enrolled..."

Moore, Sidney; 79 Reg Co C, 15 Aug 62-7 Jun 65, Sgt. HC Eden Church Cemetery: Sidney Moore died 16 May 1886 48y 16 d; Nancy J. Moore 12 Oct 1839-8 Jan 1931. Sidney Moore s/o Paul and Eunice (Bacon) Moore married 22 May 1859 Nancy Alford HC Bk 4-137. HC obit 15 Jan 1931: "Funeral services were held for Mrs. Nancy J. Moore, pioneer settler of Hancock County whose ninety-two years exceeds that of most people. She spent nearly her entire life in the Eden community where her death occurred. She is survived by one daughter, Nora Frank and one son, Marion. Burial Eden Cemetery."

Moore, William; 106 Reg Co D, 10 Jul 63-17 Jul 63. A William Moore married 10 May 1860 Matilda Newhouse HC Bk 4-192. HC Shiloh Church Cemetery: William Moore died 1 May 1885 60y 4m 28d; Matilda w/o William died 3 May 1864 28y 4m 16d.

Morford, Elisha; 99 Reg Co B, 13 Aug 62, killed in action 28 May 1864. HC newspaper 9 Jun 1864: "E. Morford reported killed in battle at Dallas, Georgia, 28 May 1864." 99th Regiment History states: "Elisha Morford was killed near Dallas, Georgia." HC 1860 census records a Daniel (age48) and Julia (age 38) and Elisha (age 14) Morford.

Morford, John A.; 8 Reg Co G, 22 Apr 61-6 Aug 61; also 99 Reg Co B, 13 Aug 62-27 Oct 64. HC newspaper 6 Jun 1864: "Pvt. J.A. Morford was wounded in the thigh and abdomen in battle at Dallas, Georgia, 25 May 1864." 99th Regiment History states: "John A. Morford was discharged for wounds received 28 May 1864, Dallas, Georgia. His residence in 1900 is Marion, Indiana." A John A. Morford married 13 Dec 1868 Ellen Price HC Bk 5-267.

Morford, Joseph B.; 99 Reg Co B, 13 Aug 62-5 Jun 65. HC newspaper 9 Jun 1864: "Pvt. J.B. Morford, Company B, 99th Regiment, was wounded in the leg at the battle of Dallas, Georgia, 28 May 1864." 99th Regiment History states: "Corp'l

Hancock County Indiana Civil War Soldiers

Joseph B. Morford was wounded 28 May 1864, Dallas, Georgia. His residence in 1900 is Edwardsport." 1860 Hancock County census records Joseph (age 51), Margaret (age 46) and Joseph (age18) Morford.

Morford, (Zachary) Taylor; HC obit 31 Mar 1932: "Taylor Morford, Hancock County's foremost Civil war veteran and one of the few remaining residents who participated in the war, died at his home, 230 West North Street (Greenfield), following an illness of little more than three days. Mr. Morford, who was eighty-four years old, enjoyed unusually good health until stricken with cerebral hemorrhage a few days before his death. From the time he was stricken until his death, he did not regain consciousness . In the death of Mr. Morford, Greenfield and Hancock County loses one of its finest citizens. From many lips have come high praises of the life with which this venerable war veteran and substantial citizen has led.

"Mr. Morford retired from business a number of years ago but has always been very active in county and city affairs despite his advanced years. He was commander of the Greenfield G.A.R. post and when that organization disbanded a few years ago he continued to serve as the leader of the group. It was only last spring, a week or two before Decoration Day, that he spent considerable time in getting data on the living Civil War veterans in this county. At that time there about twelve veterans, but the ranks of these warriors have been reduced to about one-fourth that number with the death of Mr. Morford.

"Enlisting in the Union army at the age of sixteen, Mr. Morford served almost a year before the war ended. He enlisted in Company A, 184th regiment, Ohio Infantry Volunteers, which was composed of Butler County, Ohio, men. It was in that county that Mr. Morford had two brothers who served in the Union army during the Civil War, one of them dying in service, Elisha Morford died of typhoid fever aboard a river steamer en route to the siege of Vicksburg. The second brother, Daniel B. Morford, died at Memphis, Tennessee, about eleven years ago. After being discharged at Edgefield,

Hancock County Indiana Civil War Soldiers

Tennessee, in October of 1865, Taylor returned to Butler County, Ohio, where he lived until about nineteen years old. He then came to Greenfield where he entered the blacksmith business. A long and successful career was written by Mr. Morford in the blacksmith and wagon building business. He was associated with John A. Barr, Allen F. Cooper and others in the wagon building business. The company gained the reputation of producing one of the finest lines of wagons.

"Retiring from the blacksmith business a few years ago, he was succeeded by his son, Edward, who now operates the business at the corner of South and Pennsylvania Streets. Mr. Morford was born in Butler County, Ohio, 25 January 1848, and while a very young child his father died (mother, Mary Ward). Mr. Morford was married to Miss Kate Walsh (1849-1926) in this city, 25 Dec 1871 (HC Bk 6-73). To this union four children were born: Charles; Edward; Paul; and Miss Clara. Mrs. Morford's death occurred five years ago. Funeral services were conducted at the Bradley M.E. Church. The flag-draped casket was borne by A.H. Rottmam; Percy Ellis; Wood L. Walker; Riley White; Roy Roudebush and L.H. Wolfe. HC Park Cemetery. Z. Taylor and Kate are buried HC Park Cemetery. (A Mary Morford 1813-1889 is buried there also, could be his mother?).

Morgan, William; 79 Reg Co B, 9 Aug 62, 6 Apr 64 transferred to Veteran Reserve Corps, indicates wound or illness. HC newspaper 11 Jun 1863: "Pvt. William H. Morgan of Company B, 8th Regiment, had his collar bone broken near Vicksburg, May 1863."

Morical, Robert; 148 Reg Co C, 17 Feb 65, died 10 Mar 65, Amo, Indiana. NOD.

Morris, Emanuel; 8 Reg Co B, 25 Aug 61, died 1862 Hancock County. NOD.

Morris, George S.; 99th Regiment History states: "George S. Morris was born 7 Sep 1843, Hancock County, Indiana, enlisted April 1861 in 8th Regiment Co E; discharged fall of 1862 due to small pox. Enlisted March 1864 as a recruit in Co

Hancock County Indiana Civil War Soldiers

B, 99th Regiment and served to end of war, a faithful soldier. He has been a great sufferer for years from the exposure of army life. His address in 1900 is Jonesboro, Grant County, Indiana."

Morris, Milton T.; 5 Cav Co G, 16 Aug 62-5 Sep 65. HC death notice 15 May 1920: "Word was received here of the death of Milton T. Morris, which occurred at the Soldiers' Home in Dayton, Ohio, where he was taken three weeks ago after he had been ill for some time. He was an active member of the G.A.R. Post and faithful in visiting his old comrades who were sick and feeble and was always cheerful and optimistic. He lived in Hancock County all his life and is survived by two sons and two daughters. Interment (HC) Park Cemetery." A Milton Morris married 15 Jun 1870 Nancy J. Foley HC Bk 5-381.

Morrison, John; HC newsaper death notice: "John Morrison, aged 86, a Civil War veteran, died at the home of his daughter, Mrs. John Cooper, Wilkinson. He had lived in Mt. Comfort for many years until the death of his wife about a year ago. Burial Oaklandon Cemetery." John Morrison was born 15 Feb 1853 in Kentucky, died _Feb 1924, s/o Squire and Susan (Pitts) Morrison.

Moulden, James W.; 12 Reg Co G, 3 Aug 62, killed Atlanta 22 Jul 1864. NOD.

Mosier, Theodore; 12 Reg Co B, 15 May 61-19 May 62. NOD.

Mullen, Ephraim; 7th Indiana Light Artillery, 7 Mar 63-20 Jul 65. "...born Hamilton County, Ohio, 5' 9" tall, age 54, dark complexion, blue eyes, gray hair, cooper when enrolled..."

Mullen, Jacob; 8 Reg Co G, 22 Apr 61-6 Aug 61, Musician; 8 Reg Co B, 25 Aug 61, wagoner, NOD.

Munden, Augustus; 53 Reg Co A, no dates. HC obit 15 Aug 1929: "Augustus Munden, one of the few Civil War veterans of Hancock County, passed away at his home in Charlottesville following an illness of three weeks. He was born in North Carolina but came to Greenfield from Rensselaer, Indiana, a number of years ago. He is survived by the widow and a son, Don, of Illinois. Short funeral services were held at his home

Hancock County Indiana Civil War Soldiers

and the body was taken to Rensselaer for burial. Mr. Munden was well known to a large number of Greenfield people, and not withstanding his age, he was interested in all public matters and kept well informed on current events and was known as one of the best informed of the old soldiers on matters of Civil War days." He was born 25 Feb 1846, wife, Demaris; and died 9 Aug 1929 of chronic cystitis, s/o Isaiah and Mabel (Bidgood) Munden.

Munden, Thomas; 9 Reg Co C, 14 Feb 65-no out date. HC newspaper 19 Nov 1914; " Thomas Munden died at his home near Savannah, Missouri, 9 Nov 1914, aged 83 years. He was a native of Indiana, having gone to Missouri, 1 Mar 1881 and spent the rest of his life on his farm. He leaves to mourn his death a sister, Mrs. Pharaba Bentley, of Greenfield, two sons, John and Chris who lived with him, and two daughters, Mrs. Aaron Bowman and Mrs. William Breet, of Savannah."

Murphy, Amos David; 57 Reg Co K, 3 Sep 62-14 Dec 65. Amos D. Murphy was born 1844, died 6 Oct 1906, aged 62 years, s/o James and Sarah (Evans) Murphy; Amos' occupation was laborer; widow, Addie Murphy. Amos David Murphy married Melissa A. Shaffer 28 Dec 1882 HC Bk 7-427. HC newspaper obit 17 Oct 1906: Amos David Murphy died at his home in Cleveland (HC) of inflammation of the stomach following an illness of about five hours. He leaves a widow and eight children: Chester; Albert: Arthur: Melton; Ross; Russell, Dora and Hester. Funeral at Cleveland Methodist Church, interment Gilboa Cemetery."

Murphy, James; 99 Reg Co B, 13 Aug 62-10 May 63. Three HC marriages for a James Murphy: 25 Mar 1847 Mahala Wilson Bk 2-231; 9 Sep 1870 Sarah Jackson Bk 5-396; and 3 May 1883 Martha Wilson Bk 7-449. 99th Regiment History states: "James Murphy, discharged 10 May Moscow; 1900 address is unknown."

Murphy, John P.; 79 Reg Co D, Aug 62-16 Jun 65. " John P. Murphy was farming in Buck Creek Township, Hancock County, when the shrill music of the fife and drum was

Hancock County Indiana Civil War Soldiers

marshalling the boys in blue to march to Dixie. He enlisted as a private and was promoted to Corporal. The regiment experienced the fierce and stormy battles of Stone River, Chickamauga and Missionary Ridge where they were so near the enemy that their stars and stripes touched the stars and bars while climbing over fortifications.

"Next came the Atlanta campaign of New Hope Church, Resaca, Peach Tree Creek and at Kennesaw Mountain where on 23 June 1864, . John was wounded in the left ankle by a musket ball. He reached Jeffersonville, Indiana, where he received a furlough to go home until after the Presidential election , then joined his regiment at Nashville, 13 Dec 1864 and was mustered out 16 Jun 1865.

"John was born 17 Jul 1843 in Marion County, Indiana, s/o James H. and Elizabeth (Evans) Murphy; married 23 Oct 1865 (HC Bk 4-551) Clara Wilson, d/o Isaac and Ann (Griffith) Wilson. They have six children: Ella; Etta; James; Benjamin; Alva; and John. Clara (Wilson) Murphy had two brothers who died in the Civil War, Alfred Wilson of the 8th Indiana was killed at Vicksburg; Samuel Wilson died while in an Indiana unit. The Murphys address is Mohawk, Indiana." HC Park Cemetery: John P. Murphy 17 Jul 1843-6 Sep 1912, Union soldier 1861-1865, Co D 79 Ind Vol Inf, GAR; Clara w/o John P. 17 Apr 1838-16 May 1918.

Murphy, Lewis B.; 106 Reg Co D, 10 Jul 63-17 Jul 63. NOD.

Murrer, Freeborn G.; HC obit 9 Jun 1932: "Freeborn G. Murrer, age 87, resident of Fortville for many years died at his residence following an attack of heart trouble. Mr. Murrer enlisted in the 11th Indiana Cavalry when he was sixteen years old, serving throughout the Civil War. He was a member of the Sol D. Kempton Post G.A.R. at Fortville in the 80s and was well known. He is survived by the widow, Isabelle, two sons, Arden and Claude; and two daughters, Mrs. Albert Brown and Mrs. Ward Alford. Mr. Murrer lost the sight in both eyes three years ago." A retired liveryman, he was born 11 Aug 1845; died 4 Jun 1932, s/o Benjamin and Maria (Fausett) Murrer.

Hancock County Indiana Civil War Soldiers

Muth, Augustus (Gus) W.;enlisted at post office, (New) Palestine, Indiana, 9 August 1862 Company B, 79th Infantry Regiment, to serve three years. ...blue eyes, dark hair, dark complexion, farmer and excellent carpenter when enrolled...The 79th was engaged at the battle of Stone's River (late Dec 1862 and early Jan 1863); spelling and punctuation of the following is transcribed as written on Affidavit for Pension: "at the Battle of Stone River, Gus was detailed to hall amunition to Regt. and Batery got his back hert lifting amunition; after Battle took Measels was exposed cought cold settled in his eyes and lungs also something rong with his Heart."

"On 7 Dec 1863 Gus was transferred to the Invalid Corps, later known as the Veteran Reserve Corps, at Madison, Indiana, and was assigned to 110th Company of the 2nd Battlion, due to " him being incapable of performing the duties of a soldier because of hypertrophy of heart with slight aolvular (sic) disease, spinal irritaion and chronic bronchitis, contracted in service and has done no duty for nine months, not able for duty in the Invalid Corps and not physically able to reenlist in same. Disability, total. Honorably discharged 26 December 1863. He was granted a pension, #42863.

"Gus Muth married Elizabeth Conner, 27 Oct 1859 (HC Bk 4-159), they divorced 1894 and Gus never remarried. His several places of residences since leaving the service are: Indiana until 1869; Missouri February 1871; Kansas February 1871; Missouri March 1894; Georgia to present (1912). Gus Muth, s/o Ernst George Muth and Sara Weaver, was born 2 May 1838, in Hancock County, Indiana, died 17 Jun 1924 and is buried at Sparks Cemetery, Sparks, Georgia." Contributed by Laura Tuttle, Miami, Florida.

Muth, David Maguachua; enrolled with his brother, Augustus (Gus) W. Muth, 9 Aug 1862 in Company B, 79th Regiment for three years. When enrolled David M. Muth states "born Hancock County, Indiana, 5' 8" tall, dark complexion, blue eyes, light hair, age 21, farmer. Muster Roll, dates April, May,

Hancock County Indiana Civil War Soldiers

1863, David was absent as he was "sick in Hospital." Mustered out and honorably discharged 7 Jun 1865, at Nashville, Tennessee: age, 21 years; rank, private; last paid to 31 Aug 64; clothing account last settled, 31 Aug 1863; amount for clothing in kind or money adv'd $70.93; bounty paid, $25; due $15. Remarks: mustered out in accordance with instructions from War Department.

"David M. Muth was born 4 May 1841, Carrollton, Hancock County, Indiana, s/o Ernst George Christian Muth and Sara Weaver; David married Anna Belle Wilkinson 2 Feb 1862 (HC Bk 4-309) Anna Belle was born 4 Aug 1845, Napoleon, Ripley County, Indiana, d/o Charles L. and Ruth Ogden. On 23 Jun 1880, David M. Muth applied for a pension, witness, Hannah Ridant who states "I have been well personally acquainted with David Muth since June 1865and he complained of having neuralgia and of the loss of the right eye and the vision of the left impaired."

"On 9 Jul 1890 David filed a Declaration for Invalid Pension stating: He is 49 years of age, living in the city of Republic, Kansas, and that he is entirely unable to earn support by reason of entire loss of right eye and defect in left eye and neuralgia. Pension certificate #199946. On 20 May 1912 David filed Declaration For Pension and states he is 71 years of age, a resident of Republic, Kansas, and that his several places of residence since leaving the service have been as follows: Carrollton, (HC) Indiana, until Fall of 1868; Newton, Iowa to 1871; Republic, Kansas to the present date.

"David died 11 Jul 1925 in Big Bend, Republic, Kansas, at the age of 84 yers, 2 months and 6 days, death certificate #79-2074. On 8 Aug 1925, Anna B. Muth filed for Widow's Pension and states that she is 80 years of age, born 4 Aug 1845; $72 monthly pension payment dropped effective 4 Jul 1925 due to his death on 11 Jul 1925; his widow to be paid a monthly pension of $50 until her death; she died 7 Feb 1929. David (aka D.M. and Doc) and Anna Belle (Wilkinson) Muth are buried in Washington Cemetery, town of Republic, Republic

Hancock County Indiana Civil War Soldiers

County, Kansas. A Bureau of Pension document, completed by David M. Muth, dated 3 April 1915, states the names and birth dates of his children as follows: Ina Belle born 25 Jul 1866; Charles Alvah born 15 Nov 1867; William Edward born 27 Aug 1870; David Clinton born 12 Apr 1872; Cora May born 23 Oct 1873; George Clarence born 17 Mar 1877; and Iva Myrtle 20 Jul 1879; all living,.

"The following was received from Marcia Wilberg-Smith who states that the article's dates/places are unknown: "Brothers Meet After 33 Years The writer and family enjoyed a visit from his parents, Mr. and Mrs. D.M. Muth, of Republic, and his father's brother, A.W. Muth, of Sparks, Georgia, and they went to Fairbury to visit relatives for a few days. These two brothers, Gus and Doc, were both born and raised in Indiana, and not long after they were married responded to their country's call for volunteers, and the 9th day of August, 1862, enlisted in Co. B, 79th Indiana Volunteers at Indianapolis, and on the 27th day of the same month they left for the front with a regiment of brave Hoosier boys that saw almost constant service until the close of the war.

"Of the 116 officers and men that enlisted in Co. B, only thirteen officers and thirty-two privates remained when the company was mustered out at Nashville, Tennessee, in the latter part of July 1865. At the close of the war, they farmed in Indiana and Iowa until the Spring of 1871, when they came to Republic County and homesteaded the east half of Sec 14, Township 1, Range 4 in Washington Township, sixteen miles due west of Narka. After filing on their claims they rented farms near Haddam. During the summer they did some breaking on their homesteads and the next spring they moved onto them. Gus left his homestead a short time later and returned to Nadoway County, Missouri, where he remained until March 1895, when he went to Georgia, where he has since made his home.

"D.M. Muth remained on his homestead until 1882, when he moved to Republic City. A.W. came out for a short visit in

Hancock County Indiana Civil War Soldiers

1884 and after that these two brothers lost track of each other, and for the past fifteen years or more we supposed Uncle Gus was dead. And we found him a pretty lively corpse, and sure enjoyed the short visit he made us. We took them and Mother over to Haddam to note the changes in that vicinity since they tilled the virgin soil of Old Mill Creek and one day shot a buffalo that had evidently been separated from a herd and was wandering across the plains." Contributed by Laura Tuttle, Miami, Florida; and Marcia Wilberg-Smith,

Muth, Rev. Ernst George; "The following is a sworn statement given by George Muth, dated 26 October 1874: George Muth of Carrollton P.O., Hancock County, Indiana, late a Captain in Co, I 131st Regiment of 13th Indiana Cavalry Volunteers, being duly sworn deposes and says that the only military or naval service he ever performed for the United States was as follows, Went into camp at Indianapolis with his men of Co I, 131st Ind Vols (13th Cav) on 9 Dec 1863.

"His commission was dated 1 March 1864 and he served until 29 Oct 1864 in said organization. He was not in any service, military or naval, prior to said service, except was first commissioned as 1st Lieut. of the 9th Ind. Cavalry on 23 Dec 1863 but not mustered in said service but was assigned to Co. I, 13th Ind. Cavalry Vols together with his recruits. Was Captain of "Eagle Cavalry" of Indiana Legion from 14 July 1863 up to time of commission in said 9th Indiana Cavalry Vols. Signed, George Muth."

HC newspaper 12 Nov 1863: "Captain George Muth, of the Eagle Cavalry, has received an appointment as recruiting officer for one of the new cavalry regiments. A good many of his company, we understand, have signified the intention to go with him into active service. Captain Muth is a gentleman, a scholar and a Christian and will make an excellent and fatherly officer. We commend him to all who intend to enter the service."

"At age 64, he obtained a release from his pulpit and enlisted to serve in the Civil War for a term of three years, residence,

Hancock County Indiana Civil War Soldiers

Brandywine Township, Hancock County, Indiana, and was described in his military records as: German soldier, served at Waterloo, is robust and has good health; 5 feet, 11 inches, fair complexion; gray eyes; dark hair; born Europe, Hanover.

"Officer's Certificate of Disability, Personal knowledge of Sam. H. Moore, Adjutant, 131st Regiment of 13th Indiana Cavalry Volunteers states, " George Muth, on the 10th day of August 1864 near Huntsville, Alabama, while he was acting field officer of the day and by reason of over exertion examining the pickets and being exposed to the hot sun, he was attacked with what is known as "Sun Stroke" while he was riding on his horse-he fell from the horse, which materially disabled him from active duty afterward. He was treated by Dr. R.H. Buck from that time for four or five days almost continuously. (Treated by Regimental Surgeon in quarters and in regimental hospital from 10 August 1864 to about 20 October 1864.)

"When he was able to be up and being a man of unusual nerve and ambition, he went on duty and did all he could when he was able to do so. And that the said George Muth was a sound, able bodied man up to 10th August 1864 and when he entered the service. Signed Sam H. Moore, Late Adjutant.

"Resignation of George Muth, 8 October 1864, Huntsville, Alabama: "I have the honor to tender my resignation as Captain of Co. I, 13th Indiana Cavalry Volunteers on account of my advanced age (being in my 67th year). Service on foot, which we had to render ever since our Regiment left Indianapolis, doth not agree with me, find a great portion of my resting time to be very painful producing very much cramping of my legs and feet.

"Having known and well considered my age and physical abilities before I entered service, I preferred Cavalry at the same time being willing to do as much for my country as possible, I was ready at all times without a murmur, to render service on foot required of me, but find it more and more burdensome and incompatible with my physical abilities.

Hancock County Indiana Civil War Soldiers

"I certify on honor, that I am not indebted to the United States on any account whatever, and that I am not responsible for any government property, except what I am prepared (according to properly kept books) to turn over to the proper officer on the acceptance of my resignation, and that I was last paid by Major Griffin up to the 30th of June 1864. I am, Sir, very respectfully, Your Obedient Servant, George Muth, Captain, Co I, 13th Indiana Cavalry Volunteers.

"William T. Pepper, late Liuet. Col 13th Ind. Cav. testifies: Against my remonstrance he tendered his resignation and it was 'for the good of the service,' the language was not intended nor should it be contrued as reflecting in the least upon his character, as officer, soldier or citizen, his misfortune impaired his health, for the conmmand of a military company, but being well assisted I urged him to remain the service. Filed May 25, _7" Quoted from *History of Hancock County*, J.H. Binford, 1882, and speaking of George Muth: "A few remaining members of his company made him an agreeable surprise in the presentation of a gold-headed cane as a token of their high regard for his faithful services."

"The following obituary was written by Ernst H. Faut, a friend of George Muth's, and published in *Hancock Democrat* 13 Sep 1883: "Dear Editor, You and your readers will excuse me for writing at this late date an obituary on Captain George Muth, the reason that I have not written sooner being that he did not live in this immediate neighborhood, and I supposed that someone living in Brandywine Township, where the deceased had lived for over forty years an interesting life, would have sent a communication to our county papers in regard to this old soldier, teacher, missionary, pioneer and philanthropist.

"But up to this time I failed to see anything of the kind, and therefore, I step out of my range and hope to say something in regard to the deceased which may be of interest to your readers, as I think that Capt. Geo. Muth had lived a remarkable life, from what I knew of him in my acquaintance with him, as

Hancock County Indiana Civil War Soldiers

he told me in different conversations, and some of my personal knowledge.

"Captain Geo. Muth was born 26 September 1798, on the river Weser, in the principality of Hesse-Kassel, Germany (son of G. Wilhelm Muth and Maria Christiane Friederike Henrici). When christened he received the name of George Ernst Christian Muth. He was the oldest of a family of nine children. His father was a husbandsman or farmer. He had his son, George, as he called him, educated for a merchant and gave him in those days in the vicinity where he lived what was then called a first-class classical education. As he was the master of seven different languages.

"After he quit school, he went to England to obtain employment as a salesman in the mercantile business, but the opportunities were not as he expected them to be. He, therefore, changed his intention, and enlisted in the British army, wherein the course of time he became a commissioned officer in a regiment of mounted grenadiers.

"He participated while in this regiment at the hard fought battle of Waterloo, under General Wellington, the British Commander, "who wished to God that night or Blucher would come." Night did not come, but Blucher arrived and there ended the first Napoleon Dynasty. It was interesting to hear Capt. Muth talk about this historic battle. After serving his time in the British army he went back to his state, Hesse-Kassel. Being a young man, for which nature had done much, together with his experience in the army, the Duke gave him a very lucrative position in his army at the capital of the State. This position he held a few years.

"While in England he informed himself in regard to the United States of America, which impressed him as being very favorable, and while everything was not satisfactory in the position he held, in 1819, he resigned and emigrated for America. He landed at Baltimore where he adopted his first calling as a salesman in the mercantile business. There he remained a few years and went to Adams County,

Hancock County Indiana Civil War Soldiers

Pennsylvania, where he became acquainted with an orphan girl, Sarah Weber, by name. On 9 June 1822, they became man and wife. While at this place he became religiously impressed, and joined the united Brethren Church.

"They also lived in York and Cumberland Counties, Pennsylvania, where he was engaged with other parties in the manufacture of cloth, but failed in this enterprise. In 1827 he, with his family, came West, and settled in Madison Township, Butler County, Ohio. He adopted school teaching for a living until 1837, when he came and settled near Morristown, Shelby County, Indiana, and in 1840 came to Brandywine Township, Hancock County, Indiana, settled on a farm where he lived until one year of his death.

"From the time of his conversion in Pennsylvania until his death, he preached the word of God to his fellow men, and was a regularly ordained minister in the United Brethren Church for 52 years. He was the first German minister that for three years preached to the first German settlers of Sugar Creek Township in this vicinity, and one year ago they heard him preach in his mother-country's tongue in the town of New Palestine.

"In his union of married life, he and his wife were blessed with thirteen children, some of whom are dead and where the living ones are is impossible for me to mention. His wife died 17 November 1880, after a union of 58 years. He married the second time to Joseph Hawkins' widow, Mary J. (Gray) Hawkins (14 Sep 1882, HC Bk 7-391), who survives him.

"When the Civil war broke out, he at first thought himself too old for the front but he organized a cavalry company of Home Guards, of which he was the Captain. During the Morgan Raid (July 1863), he, with his company, took to the field, returned without losing a man and exhibited some of their military tactics by going through a drill and parade on the streets of (New) Palestine.

"In the winter of 1863-1864, he raised Company I, 13th Regiment Indiana Cavalry for active duty. This regiment was on active duty when Captain Muth was "sun struck" and about

Hancock County Indiana Civil War Soldiers

eighteen months ago, he received back pension to the amount of $3,000. Out of this he gave each one of his children $100. with the balance he built a house of worship in Carrollton, which was dedicated about a year ago. Once before he built a church on his farm near his residence, which is there to this day.

"In politics he never took much interest, although a Radical Republican. Before the organization of the Republican Party, he was an Abolitionist and for a number of years he cast the only Abolition vote in that Democrat stronghold, Brandywine Township, this county. Captain Muth made a very fine appearance on horseback, and his erect soldier-like air and military bearing always impressed one with the idea of some grand old hero of history. Always popular with his men, yet he preserved order and discipline. The members of his church also appreciated him and his labors and deeply regret the loss of a pastor and friend.

"He was admitted to full citizenship of the United States in 1836, Hamilton County, Ohio. Only one brother remains of a family of nine brothers and sisters. Mr. Augustus Muth, the youngest of the nine, is a prominent and wealthy citizen of Cincinnati, Ohio. Captain Muth's health was always good, complaining only a few days before he died at the advanced age of 85 years, ending a life full of usefulness and honor.

"The funeral was attended by a large number of his friends and citizens of the surrounding country. HC Eden Chapel/Muth Cemetery: George Muth 26 Sep 1798-29 Aug 1883, born in Europe on the river Weser, Co I, 13 Ind Cav; Sara (Weaver) Muth w/o George died 17 Nov 1880, 76y 6m 0d, born Adams County, Pennsylvania, this couple lived together 58y 5m 8d. George Muth was born on the river Wese, Lippoldsberg, Hesse, Kessel, Germany. Contributed by his 3rd great-granddaughter, Laura, Armstrong, Miami, Florida.

Myer, Charles: 99 Reg Co B, 15 Aug 62-missing in action 4 Dec 64, place not given. NOD.

Myers, Erasmus; 12 Reg Co G, 3 Aug 62-1 Mar 63. NOD.

Hancock County Indiana Civil War Soldiers

Myers, William; 148 Reg Co C, 17 Feb 65-15 Jul 65. HC Park Cemetery: a William J. Myers 27 Nov 1849-20 Aug 1894; and Mary L. w/o William J. 2 Dec 1853-30 Mar 1921. a William Myers married 19 Aug 1873 Mary L. New HC BK 6-213.

Hancock County Indiana Civil War Soldiers

John Manche Document

Courtesy of Lewis Strahl

Hancock County Indiana Civil War Soldiers

Job Milner

Courtesy of Sherry Rigney

Hancock County Indiana Civil War Soldiers

Mess Kit Utensil Belonging to Job Milner

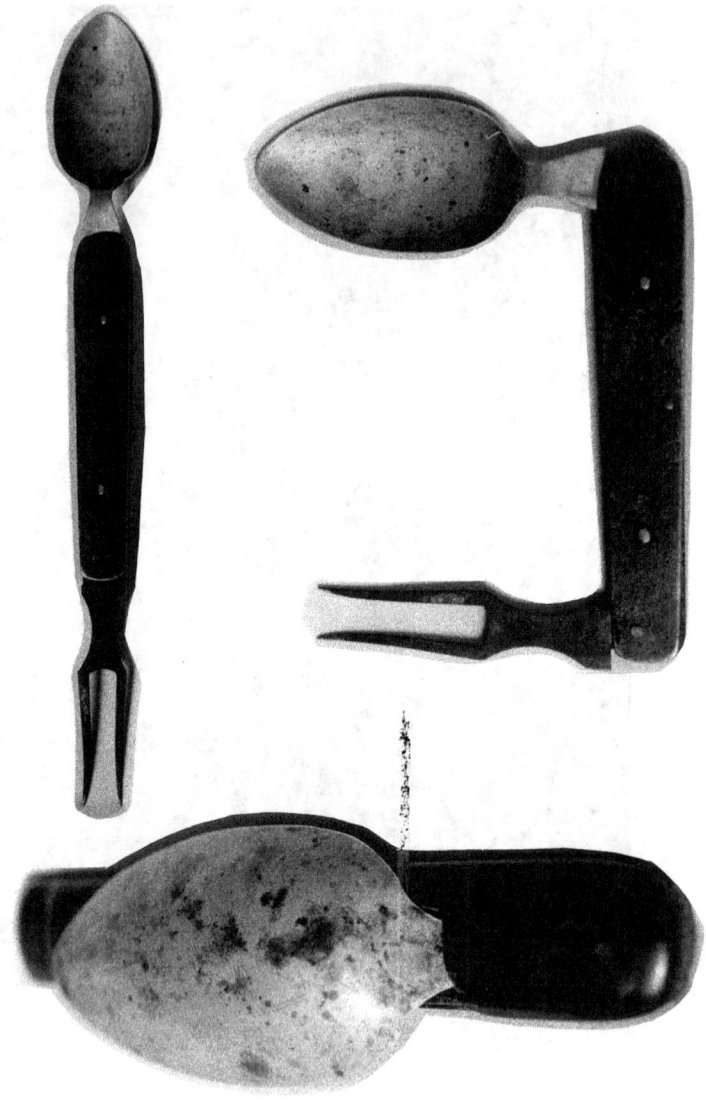

Hancock County Indiana Civil War Soldiers

Gus Muth

Courtesy of Laura Armstrong

Hancock County Indiana Civil War Soldiers

◄ N ►

Nagley, James W.; HC McCordsville Cemetery: James W. Nagley, soldier, 25 Jul 1830-20 May 1903, no military data. He was the s/o Henry and Naoma (Taylor) Nagley, born West Virginia, died McCordsville, occupation cooper, married, wife Emily.

Neal, Asbury; 53 Reg Co A, 2 Feb 64-21 Jul 65. NOD.

Nealis, Thomas; 99 Reg Co B, 13 Aug 62-16 Sep 63, wagoner. 99th Regiment History states: "Thomas Nealis was discharged 16 Sep 1863, his residence in 1900 is Anderson, Indiana." A Thomas Nealis married 21 Nov 1854 Elizabeth Sidall HC Bk 3-251.

Neff, Allen; 9 Cav Co B, 13 Nov 63-17 Jul 65, Commissary Sergeant. NOD

Nelson, J.N.; HC Hays Cemetery: J.N. Nelson 1 Reg Co K, no dates. A John Nelson married 15 Apr 1852 Margaret Eakin HC Bk 3-92. HC newspaper death notice 19 Jan 1893: John Nelson died at his son's home near Warrington on the 16th inst. of dropsy, aged 68 years. Interment Hays Cemetery."

Nibarger, Harrison J.; 99 Reg Co B, 14 Aug 62-5 Jun 65. "...born Hancock County, Indiana, 5' 9" tall, age 18, fair complexion, blue eyes, light hair, farmer when enrolled..." 99th Regiment History states: "Harrison J. Nibarger was born 13 Dec 1843, Hancock County, Indiana, served throughout the war and was wounded 26 Aug 1864, near Atlanta, recovered. Married 28 Sep 1865, Margaret Murphy (HC Bk 4-540), three children and has lived in Hancock and Henry Counties since the war. Current address (1900) in Knightstown, Indiana."

1860 Hancock County Census, Brown Township: Abram Nibarger age 53; Sarah age 40; Thomas age 23; Lemuel age 19; Harrison J. age 16. This family had three sons who enlisted in the Civil War on the same day in the same company and regiment and after battles in Tennessee--only one returned.

Nibarger, John; 99 Reg Co B, 14 Aug 62-5 Jun 65. 99th Regiment History states: "John Nibarger was born 24 Jun 1843,

Hancock County Indiana Civil War Soldiers

Hancock County, Indiana, served faithfully during the war, and afterward settled in Jay County, Indiana where he was married 1 Mar 1866 to Mary L. McKinney. They live on their farm and their current (1900) address is Red Key, Indiana."

Nibarger, Lemuel; 99 Reg Co B, 14 Aug 62, died 15 Mar 1863. 99th regiment History states: "Lemuel Nibarger died 18 Mar 1863, LaGrange, Tennessee." For family data see page for his brother, Harrison Nibarger.

Nibarger, Thomas J.; 99 Reg Co B, 14 Aug 62, died 30 Mar 63. 99th Regiment History states, "Thomas J. Nibarger died 30 Mar 1863, Moscow, Tennessee. For family data see page for his brother, Harrison Nibarger.

Nichols, James; 12 Reg Co G, transferred to Co I, 48 Reg, out 17 Jul 65. NOD.

Nichols, Stewart; 106 Reg Co D, 10 Jul 63-17 Jul 63; also 132 Reg Co K, 18 May 64-7 Sep 64. HC New Palestine Cemetery: Stewart Nichols Co K 132 Ind Inf. NOD.

Nichols, William; Co H Indiana Light Artillery, 8 Mar 62-9 Mar 65. "...born Wayne County, Indiana, 5' 4" tall, age 21, dark complexion, blue eyes, brown hair, farmer when enrolled..." HC obit 28 Jun 1905: "William Nichols died at his home in Willow Branch of paralysis, at the age of 64 years. Interment Hayes Cemetery." There was no stone in 1980 when the cemetery was transcribed.

Nigh, John; HC obit 26 Dec 1912: "John Nigh, one of the well known Civil War veterans, who was badly injured by a fall at the home of his son, Charles Nigh, on South State Street, died at an early hour. In the fall he suffered a broken hip bone. His age and poor health were against his recovery. His wife preceded him in death some years ago. A retired carpenter, Mr. Nigh was a well known resident of this city and county for many years, having been born 1 Mar 1837 in Shelby County, coming to Hancock from that place. In politics he was a Republican and a member of Dunbar Post G.A.R. who will have charge of the funeral services."

Hancock County Indiana Civil War Soldiers

Niles, Reuben; 9 Cav Co B, 9 Dec 63, died 1 Aug 64, Pulaski, Tennessee. NOD.

Niles, Thomas E.; HC obit 1 Feb 1923: "Thomas Niles, son of Reuben and Susan (Harris) Niles, was born at Charlottesville, Hancock County, Indiana, 23 March 1844, and passed away 22 December 1922, aged 78 years. In his young manhood, when the war clouds hung heavy over the land, he answered his country's call and enlisted 4 November 1861, in the 57th Indiana Infantry, later received an honorable discharge and reenlisted in the 10th Battery Indiana Light Artillery and served faithfully and well until he received his final discharge at Chattanooga, Tennessee, 10 Jul 1865.

"On 27 February 1868 (HC Bk5-200) he was united in marriage with Miss Irene Stewart, who was born 24 Aug 1844, and called home 13 February 1899. To this union were born six children: Ora; Elsie Peters; Gertrude Fort; G.B.; Harry; and Verle. On 1 January 1904 (HC Bk 10-524) Thomas married 2) Miss Maude Stevens, who survives him." Thomas and Irene buried HC Six Mile Cemetery.

Nixon, Aaron B.; 9 Cav Co B, 9 Dec 63-28 Jul 65. NOD.

Nixon, Azor M.; 8 Reg Co B, 25 Aug 61, no out date. HC newspaper 14 Aug 1862: "Azor M. Nixon, Company B, 8th Regiment, promoted to Corporal."

Noble, John; 18 Reg, Musician, 16 Aug 61-20 Aug 62. NOD.

Noel, Thomas Rutherford; 12 Reg Co B, 15 May 61-19 May 62. HC newspaper 28 Aug 62: "We understand that the friends of Capt. Thomas R. Noel, of this county are making an effort to secure a position for him in some of the new regiments now being organized. This is a good move. Capt. Noel has been in the service for one year, and is therefore well qualified for such position. We fully endorse him. we hope Gov. Morton will favorably receive the recommendations of Capt. Noel. He can appoint no better or truer man or soldier." Thomas R. Noel, age 74, died 6 Dec 1889 at Fortville, s/o Milwood and Anna (Vance) Noel.

Hancock County Indiana Civil War Soldiers

Nogle, John A.; 13 Maryland Inf. Co I, no dates. HC obit 30 Jan 1930: "Another of the Hancock County Civil War veterans answered the last call, John A. Nogle, age 81 years, passed away at his home at 517 Mount Street, Greenfield, following an illness of several weeks. Mr. Nogle is survived by the widow, Josephine and two sons, Walter and Charles, two daughters, Glenna Nogle and Mrs. Charles Dunn. Mr. N. was a member of Dunbar Post G.A.R who will be assisted in the funeral by the American Legion." John A. Nogle, a veterinarian, was born 15 Dec 1848, Maryland, s/o John and Sephia Nogle, died 23 Jan 1930, cause interstitial nephritis.

Hancock County Indiana Civil War Soldiers

Thomas E. Niles

Courtesy of Hancock Democrat

Hancock County Indiana Civil War Soldiers

◄ O ►

O'Donnell, Thomas; HC obit 15 Sep 1898: "Mr. Thomas O' Donnell, an old and honorable citizen of Greenfield, has passed peacefully away. His death was caused by heart failure and rheumatism. He has been a citizen of this city for many years and has raised a large and respectful family of children who are an honor to his memory. He was born in County Clair, Ireland, and came to this country some fifty years ago. He was 66 years of age (another source said he was age 69).

"He was a member of Company A, 53rd Indiana Regiment and served through the war as a brave and fearless soldier. He was also a member of the Catholic Church and his funeral was conducted accordingly." HC newspaper 15 Sep 1898: "William O'Donnell, of Toledo, Ohio, arrived in Greenfield to attend the funeral of his father, Thomas O' Donnell." HC Park Cemetery: Thomas O'Donnell Co A 53 Ind Inf. military stone with no dates.

Offutt, Charles G.; 105 Reg Co E, 11 Jul 63-18 Jul 63. HC obit 3 Sep 1903: "Judge Charles G. Offutt passed into eternity at his home on North Street. The news of his sudden death shocked the community and cast a great gloom over the entire city. Judge Offutt, son of Lloyd and Elizabeth Offutt, was born in Georgetown, Kentucky, 4 Oct 1845 and departed this life in the city of Greenfield, Indiana, on 28 August 1903. When about one-year-old, his parents removed from Georgetown to Greenfield, which has ever since been his home.

"At the age of seventeen, he became a clerk in the general store of Carr and Ryan where he remained two years; afterwards while clerking in a dry goods house in Indianapolis, he decided to make the legal profession his life's work. He studied for three years in the office of Hon. James L. Mason, at the end of which he was admitted to the Hancock County Bar. On 15 July 1874 he married Miss Anna Hammel, eldest daughter of the late Frederick Hammel, and to them were born three children: Clara; Samuel J; and Charles G. who survive

Hancock County Indiana Civil War Soldiers

him, his wife having died in Greenfield 21 July 1899." Judge Offutt and Anna are buried HC Park Cemetery.

Offutt, Lloyd; HC obit 24 May 1894: "Lloyd Offutt was born 4 Mar 1813, in Baltimore, Maryland. At the age of seven years, he removed to Scott County, Kentucky with his parents, where he resided until October, 1846, when he removed to Greenfield, at which place he resided until his death, which occurred 20 May 1894. On 18 December 1833 he was married to Elizabeth Offutt (28 Aug 1812-29 Nov 1902) with whom he continued to live until his death.

"In his younger days he learned the carpenter's trade and followed this vocation in Kentucky and Greenfield for many years and later was engaged in various occupations. Shortly after the breaking out of the War, Mr. Offutt (age 49) enlisted in Company G, Fifth Indiana Cavalry, with which command he served for nearly a year, when he was discharged on account of disabilities from the hardships of a soldier's life. He was the father of ten children, six survive: Mariah Barnett; Thomas H.; Margaret Price; Louisa Taylor; Charles G.; and California Beecher." Lloyd and Elizabeth are buried HC Park Cemetery.

Ogg, Adams Lee; "Adams Lee Ogg was one of the gallant men who not only served as a soldier during the Civil War but also served his country from 1846-1848 in the Mexican War. On 20 August 1846, three months after the beginning of the War, he, born 27 February 1828, 7th of the 13 children of John S. and Catherine (Hall) Ogg, enlisted in the Company K, First Regiment of the Mounted Rifles of the regular army of the United States.

"His enlistment was for five years but he was honorably discharged, 28 Aug 1848, shortly after the end of the War. While serving his country with the Mounted Rifles, he lost the ring finger of his right hand at Cerro Gordo, one of the important battles of the War. It took place on 17 and 18 April 1847, at the Cerro Gordo mountain pass, 60 miles northwest of Vera Cruz, near the city of Jalapa..

Hancock County Indiana Civil War Soldiers

"When word was received of gold discovery in California in 1849, Adams Lee, same as many other young men of the day, contracted "gold fever" and hurried west. He spent ten years on the Pacific coast near the town of Placerville, Eldorado County, California. On his way back to Indiana, he tarried for awhile in Iowa where he bought a farm near the town Indianola, Iowa, where he fully intended to settle. Ten days after the attack on Fort Sumter started the Civil War, he volunteered for service in the Iowa Militia He was appointed Captain of Company G, Third Regiment of the Militia of the State of Iowa which he served as company commander until the end of his military service.

"While on a short leave of absence from military duties, Adams Lee Ogg and Mary Elizabeth Longnaker were married 4 December 1861 at Greenfield, Hancock County, Indiana. Mary went with her new husband to Jefferson Barracks, Missouri, where he and his unit trained, and waited for the call to battle. It came in March 1862. Mary Elizabeth returned to Greenfield and Adams was bound for the battle of Shiloh, where he was wounded the first day. He spent the next five months convalescing, first at home in Greenfield and then in an army camp near Indianapolis where he trained recruits and performed other light duty.

"He returned to his regiment and spent the winter of 1862-1863 trying to survive the rigors of winter engagements in Mississippi and Tennessee. In the early spring the regiment moved to a camp near the Mississippi River to join the siege of Vicksburg. During the forty-two days from arrival to surrender on 4 July 1863, Adams Lee's Company G of the Third Iowa was attacked almost every day and night." Letters he wrote to his wife during the War are included in this book.

"Several years after the Civil War he sold his Iowa property and he and Mary Elizabeth purchased a farm in Hancock County where they lived until he died in 1904. They are both buried HC Park Cemetery. Mary Elizabeth was born 7 Jan 1842 and died 27 Mar 1908 in Woodburn, Oregon. "

Hancock County Indiana Civil War Soldiers

The carving on Adams Lee's tombstone proudly declares: "Adams Lee Ogg 1828-1904, Mexican War Soldier, severely wounded in Battle of Cerro Gordo April 18 1847; Union Soldier in Civil War and wounded nigh unto death April 6 1862.; a man of decided convictions which he fearlessly followed throughout his life in religious as well as in political matters." Contributed by Robert Ogg, Missouri City, Texas.

Ogg, William Lucas; 18 Reg Musician, 16 Aug 61-20 Aug 62. William was born 1843. One of his letters is in a chapter of this book. He was a brother of Adams Lee Ogg.

Oldham, Jeremiah; 134 Reg Co K, 24 May 64-term expired. A J. J. Oldham who died 6 Oct 1872, 28y 4m 5d, is buried HC Six Mile Cemetery.

Oliphant, Robert G.; HC Courthouse, Soldier Burial List Book: 2 Cav Co L; died 5 Jan 1900; 87 years; occupation, farmer; burial, (HC) Simons Cemetery. NOD.

Oliver, Jas. B. HC McCray Cemetery: Jas. B. Oliver Co B 32 Ind Inf. NOD.

Oliver, Joseph B.; HC obit 19 Apr 1923: "Funeral services were held at Shirley (HC) for Joseph B. Oliver, age 80 years, who died at the home of his daughter, Mrs. James Brummett, after a long illness. He suffered a stroke of paralysis last week from which he never regained consciousness. Mr. Oliver was born in Sommereld, Ohio, and while living there, enlisted and served in the Civil War from 1861-1863.

"He, with his wife, Elizabeth, moved to Shirley a few years ago. She and four daughters and one son survive: Arline Steen; Nora Wadkins; Mrs. Jessie Thomas; Mrs. Brummet; and Edgar Oliver; and two brothers." " Joseph was born 23 Jan 1843, and died 12 Apr 1923, s/o Henry and Hester (Burton) Oliver. Jas. B., and Elizabeth are buried at HC McCray Cemetery.

Olvey, Levi D.; 12 Reg Co B, 15 Aug 61-28 Aug 65. "About the time of his reaching manhood, the Civil War engulfed the nation and young Levi enlisted for service and gave two years to the defense of his country. At the end of his military service, he returned home somewhat broken in health and went west

Hancock County Indiana Civil War Soldiers

where he saw the golden spike being driven to complete the first transcontinental railroad. He pitched camp on the plains in the dead of winter and the cold was so terrific that his feet were so badly frozen that the doctors wanted to amputate them, but he refused and eventually recovered."

HC obit 27 Nov 1913: "The funeral of Lee. D. Olvey, Civil War veteran and wealthy farmer, who died 22 Nov 1913, at his country home, was held at Maple Grove. He was born 20 Aug 1840, in Green Township, Hancock County, the son of Enoch and Martha (Denny) Olvey. He married 24 Nov 1872 (HC Bk 6-157) Elizabeth Cauldwell (8 Jan 1844-24 Jun 1931). The deceased was a member of the Friends Church for thirty-two years, a life-long Democrat and attended the first National Convention at Baltimore. The widow and a daughter, Mrs. Fannie Lee Andis, survive" Levi and Elizabeth both buried HC Park Cemetery. See page for his brother, Ransom Olvey.

Olvey, Ransom R.; 12 Reg Co B, May 61-Jun 62; also 79 Reg Co C, 15 Aug 62-7 Jun 65. "...born Hancock County, 5' 7" tall, age 28, dark complexion, blue eyes, brown hair, farmer when enrolled..." "His regiment participated in the battles of Crab Orchard, Winchester, Manassas, Harper's Ferry, Stone River, Missionary Ridge, Chickamauga, Atlanta campaign, Resaca, Kennesaw Mountain and others. At the battle of Atlanta, a bullett grazed the back of his neck, passing through the collar of his blouse; in the summer of 63, he was confined in the hospital at Chattanooga due to chronic diarrhea; at the battle of Knoxville, his left eye was injured, totally destroying it.

"While at Harper's Ferry, he had the pleasure of visiting the Engine House known as John Brown's Fort. Upon returning home, Ransom (3 Feb 1833-20 Jul 1908) married 4 May 1868 (HC Bk 5-220) Martha Fuqua (26 Feb 1848-27 Aug 1932). They were the parents of Dora and Rosetta. Ransom and Martha are buried HC Maple Grove/Jackson/Olvey Cemetery. See page for his brother, Levi D. Olvey.

Hancock County Indiana Civil War Soldiers

Olvey, William; 12 Reg Co H, 15 Aug 61, died 9 Feb 63, Grand Junction, Tennessee. A William Olvey married 22 Aug 1850 Susan Clark HC Bk 3-3.

O'Maley, Martin; "Martin was an apprentice at the blacksmith's trade in Connersville, Indiana, when he enlisted 27 Sep 64, in Company A, 16th Indiana Regiment of Mounted infantry, at the tender age of fifteen years, when he shouldered his musket and followed the flag, sharing all the hardships on the march, in camp and on the battlefield until he was discharged 30 Jun 1865."

HC obit 2 Jul 1931:"Martin O'Maley was born in Ireland, 9 Nov 1848, and died at his home in Eden, 25 Jun 1931. His parents emigrated to the United States when he was about one year old and settled near Connersville, Indiana; he had three brothers, Thomas, Matthew and Michael, and one sister, Agnes. Martin came to Hancock County about 1872 where he married 4 Jun 1876, Clara Osborn who died 2 Sep 1890. They had one daughter who married a Mr. Kassens. When the daughter died in January 1903, he made his home with the O'Neals in Eden. Martin is buried at Eden Church Cemetery.

Orear, Daniel; 9 Cav Co B, 2 Jan 64-9 Sep 65. NOD.

O'Reilly, Thomas; 17 Reg Co I, 25 Aug 64-28 Jun 65. NOD.

Ormsten, Andrew; 147 Reg Co H, 14 Feb 65, term expired. An Andrew Ormsten married 1 Jan 1863 Barbara Blessinger HC Bk 4-361.

Orr, Thomas; 57 Reg Co A, 13 Dec 61-14 Dec 65. HC obit 4 Sep 1902: "Thomas J. Orr, an old citizen of Greenfield and a veteran of the late war, died at his home, of liver trouble of which he had been afflicted for the past two years. He leaves a wife and one daughter." "Thomas Orr, s/o Jacob Orr, was born 9 Sep 1844, occupation, merchant, died 2 Sep 1902, buried HC Simmons Cemetery."

Oertel, Christian; HC newspaper 4 Feb 1864: "Christian Oertle, 99 Reg Co B, was carried from the battlefield severely wounded in the thigh. He was a noble young man, and has the love and esteem of all who knew him. His wounds proved fatal

Hancock County Indiana Civil War Soldiers

and he died 17 Dec 1863 and now rests in the cemetery at Chatanooga, Tennessee." 99th Regiment History states: "Christian Oertle died 16 Dec 1863 of wounds received at Missionary Ridge, 25 Nov 1863."

Osbon (Osborn) George W.; 8 Reg Co D, 5 Sep 61, no out date. "George W. Osborn, a retired farmer, was born 19 May 1836, s/o Jack Osborn, and died 14 Dec 1908, cause, suicide by drinking carbolic acid, burial HC Mt.Gilead/Reeves Cemetery." HC obit 17 Dec 1908: "George Washington Osborn, a veteran of the Civil War, died at his home in Maxwell. from a dose of carbolic acid self administered with suicidal intent. Mr. Osborn was a well known citizen of Center Township and his death was a shock to his many friends. His home life had not been a bower of roses for years past, discord growing between him and his wife.

"He went upstairs where he is supposed to have taken the poison. Mr. Osborn was found on the bed the next morning cold in death. He leaves a widow, two sons and a daughter."

Osborn, Alexander; 8 Reg Co D, 5 Sep 61-28 Aug 65. HC obit 28 Apr 1921: "Alexander Osborn died at the home of his sister, Mrs. Margaret Johnson, 304 West Fourth Street. Mr. Osborn was a Civil War veteran; his wife died about one year ago and he is survived by two sisters, Mrs. Johnson and Mrs. Chandler. Burial Mt. Lebanon Cemetery: Alexander 1844-1921, Co D. 8 Ind Inf; Margaret E. 1847-1920." An Alexander Osborn married 11 Sep 1871 Margaret Andis HC Bk 6-43.

Osborn, Benjamin; 53 Reg Co A, 24 Feb 62-21 Jul 65. HC obit 23 Jul 1903: "Benjamin Osborn, formerly of Greenfield, died at his late home in Florence, Kentucky. Mr. Osborn has been a sufferer of cancer of the stomach for many years. He is the brother of Thomas Osborn of this city. During the Civil War, Mr. Osborn was in the 53rd Indiana Regiment" A Benjamin Osborn married 17 Aug 1847 Agatha Curtinhour HC Bk 2-249; a Benjamin Franklin Osborn married 24 Sep 1861 Rebecca Smith HC Bk 4-286.

Hancock County Indiana Civil War Soldiers

Osborn, Jasper; 53 Reg Co A, 24 Oct 62-21 Jul 65. A Jasper Osborn died 19 Feb 1916 in Florida; a Jasper Osborn married 24 Jun 1868 Levica Wilson HC Bk 5-228.

Owens (Owings), George; 38 Reg Co D, 16 Jan 65-15 Jul 65. George Owings, Civil war Soldier 1845-1876, buried HC Philadelphia Cemetery.

Owens, George W.; 51 Reg Co I, 31 Mar 64-13 Dec 65.

Owens (Owings) Marion: 38 Reg Co D, 31 Oct 64-16 Jul 65. The Owens/Owings Cemetery in Sugar Creek Township has evidence of five graves plus fragments of broken markers on the ground. One stone has the death date broken off but the name and age are legible: Marion Owings, 28y 3m 7d. Original will and guardian records at the Hancock County courthouse detail that Marion Owings is the son of Nathaniel Owings and the father of Francis, Wiley and Clara Owings.

Owens, Thomas J.; HC obit 5 Jun 1913: "Thomas J. Owens died at his home in Charlottesville after a lingering illness of several weeks, with cancer. The funeral will be at the Christian Church, Charlottesville, where he was a member. The deceased was a Mason and a member of the G.A.R. Post at Charlottesville, where he resided for more than 45 years. He leaves a widow and many relatives and friends who mourn his death."

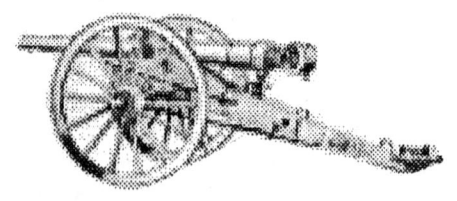

Hancock County Indiana Civil War Soldiers

Adams Lee Ogg

Courtesy of Robert Ogg

Hancock County Indiana Civil War Soldiers

◄ P ►

Palmer, Joseph; 1st Missouri Light Artillery Co H; no dates. HC obit 24 Nov 1933: "Joseph Palmer, age 87 years, died at his home, 424 North Noble Street (Greenfield). Mr. Palmer was one of the last Civil War veterans, and had been blind and helpless for several years. He is survived by the wife, one daughter, Mrs. Mattie Myers and one son, John Palmer." Joseph was born 2 Jan 1846, was retired when he died 23 Nov 1933 of chronic myocarditis, wife is Sarah J. Palmer, Joseph is buried (HC) Park Cemetery. Military data only on stone, no dates. A Joseph Palmer married 11 Nov 1920 Sarah Jane Wilson HC BK 13-453.

Pardee, Reuben; 148 Reg Co I, 2 Feb 65-5 Sep 65. NOD.

Pardue, Francis M.; 79 Reg Co C, 15 Aug 62-7 Jun 65. HC Eden Church Cemetery: Francis M. Pardue 10 Jun 1833-11 Jul 1875.

Parker, George W.; 9 Cav Co B, 3 Dec 63-28 Aug 65. HC obit 25 Dec 1924: "George W. Parker, second son of John and Isabella (Forsythe) Parker, was born 13 Nov 1842, in Hancock County, near the present site of his late home; and departed this life 12 Dec 1924. His entire life was spent in this county. His parents, Mr. and Mrs. John Parker, were pioneers of this community having migrated to this county in 1834 from southern Ohio.

"Of the ten children born to them, all have now passed beyond, but one daughter, Mrs. Angie Howard, wife of Dr. E. B. Howard, of Greenfield. Mr. Parker was married to Mary C. Coleman 7 Jan 1866 (HC Bk 5-22). He taught school in this county for thirteen years before enlisting in the Civil War and serving with the Army of the Cumberland in the battles of Nashville, Franklin, Columbia and Pulaski.

"His life was saddened more than one year ago by the death of his faithful wife, Mary. Of the nine children born to them, five survive, four having died in infancy; those yet living are Clint, William, George, Mary Pratt and Dora Dill." HC Philadelpia

Hancock County Indiana Civil War Soldiers

Cemetery: George W. Parker 1842-1924 Co B 9 Cav; Mary C. 1844-1923.

Parkhurst, Adam; 38 Reg Co A, 4 Nov 64-5 Jun 65. NOD.

Parks, James; 18 Reg, Musician, 16 Aug 61-20 Aug 62. A James W. Parks married 27 Jan 1846 Mary Jane Hunt HC Bk 2-184.

Paris, Lewis B.; 57 Reg Co A, 13 Dec 61-5 Feb 65. HC newspaper 2 Nov 1865: "The body of Lewis Paris, a plasterer and citizen of Cleveland, in this county, was found on the track of the railroad about fifty yards west of the Grist Mill, shockingly mangled and bruised. His brains and pieces of skull bone were scattered along the track for some distance. His right thigh was broken, his left knee dislocated, and the flesh very much lacerated, and his left forearm was broken. The sight was horrible to behold.

"A Coroner's inquest was held over the body, but it failed to elicit any satisfactory evidence as to the manner of death, whether he was killed by the cars, or murdered and placed on the track to keep down suspicions. There are circumstances to indicate he was murdered for his money as he was seen on the day of his death with money in the amount of $100 to $300, this money and his pocketbook were missing, only $1.15 being found on his person. Dr. Howard, Dr. Cooper and Dr. Adams were of the opinion that life was extinct when the cars passed over the body.

"The deceased was intoxicated and was last seen near the railroad about 6:00 PM, lying in the old house, formerly occupied by Madam McCarty. He leaves several small children upon the cold charities of the world." HC Simmons Cemetery: Lucy A. w/o L.B. Paris died 1 Sep 1854 40y 5m 9d. Lewis B. Paris married 25 Nov 1854 Lucy Ann Jacobs HC Bk 3-253.

Parrish, Joseph; "Joseph Parrish, cousin of John Davis, served in the Civil War. See page for John Davis."

Parsons, George; 9 Cav Co B, 13 Nov 63-15 Jun 65. NOD.

Hancock County Indiana Civil War Soldiers

Patterson, Jefferson C.; 64 Illinois Co I, 10 Feb 64-11 Jul 65, wagoner. HC obit 17 Oct 1929: "Jeff C. Patterson, a Civil War soldier, has joined the grand army of the Great Beyond. He died 11 Oct 1929, at the home of his son-in-law, Irvin Teal. Son of John Patterson, Jeff Patterson was born 29 Nov 1842, and had lived in Greenfield for many years and for a long period conducted a sporting goods store during the popularity of the bicycle for pleasure riding and back into the period of the high-wheel machine. He was interested in the many bicycle tours and races of the period.
"Mr. Patterson was born and reared in Wayne County, Indiana, but served in an Illinois infantry company during the Civil War. His wife, Ellen is deceased, five children, one brother, William Patterson, and sister, Mrs. Laura Brant survive." HC Park Cemetery: Jefferson C. Patterson 1842-1929 Co I 64 Ill Inf, GAR; Ellen C. 1853-1921, Charter member of W.R.C.

Patterson, Samuel F.; 148 Reg Co C, 17 Feb 65-5 Sep 65. HC Park Cemetery: S.F. Patterson military data only on stone, no dates; Mary E. Patterson 1841-1918. Married 15 Nov 1861 (HC Bk 4-295) Mary Elizabeth Morris, d/o Hiram Morris, brothers, Milton, Clinton, and sister, Mrs. Lafayete Slifer.

Pauley, Andrew; 147 Reg Co F, Musician, 26 Feb 65-22 Jul 65. The following data was found but may or may not be the soldier, Andrew Pauley. An Andrew Pauley died 1 Mar 1881, wife, Amanda; four marriages for Andrew Pauley, 15 May 1840 Rebecca Higgins HC Bk 1-209; 23 Mar 1847 Elvira Paris HC Bk 3-231; 29 Aug 1849 Mary Ann Francis HC Bk 2-343; and 9 May 1868 Amanda Lacey HC Bk 5-222. HC Simmons Cemetery: Andrew Pauley died Jun 1867, no other data.

Pauley, Edward; 12 Reg Co G, 11 Aug 62, killed 30 Aug 62, Richmond, Kentucky. Edward, son of J. and M, died 14 Apr 1863, 27y 5m 16d and buried HC Gilboa Cemetery.

Pauley, James; 9 Reg Co E, 24 Feb 65-28 Aug 65. A James Pauley married 8 Feb 1863 Naomi Babcock HC Bk 5-32.

Hancock County Indiana Civil War Soldiers

Pauley, Joseph; 9 Cav Co B, wagoner, 9 Dec 63-28 Aug 65. HC Park Cemetery: Joseph Pauley military data only on stone, no dates. A Joseph Pauley, s/o Edward, married 15 Jun 1866 Mary E. Morris HC Bk 5-68. A Joseph Pauley died 5 Sep 1908, no place given.

Pauley, Robert 38 Reg Co A, 10 Nov 64-5 Jun 65. A Robert Pauley married 5 Aug 1862 Nancy L. Chapman HC Bk 4-341.

Paullus, Matthew L.; at age 38, enlisted in 93 Ohio Volunteer Infantry Co G, chosen Captain. Took part in battles of Richmond, Perryville, Crab Orchard, Nashville and Stone's River, where he was wounded in the shoulder. He was discharged in Feb 1864 and soon after moved to Hancock County, Indiana, and opened a blacksmith shop. Also enlisted in "Apr 1847 at Newark, Ohio, in a mounted company to serve in the Mexican War; went to New Orleans and Point Isabella on the Rio Grande River under General Zachary Taylor; discharged 4 Aug 1848 as Corporal.

"Went to the California gold rush in 1849; returned to Ohio in 1851 and 1 Sep 1852 married Mary Danner of Preble County, Ohio. Matthew Paullus was born 1 Oct 1824, Fairfield County, Ohio, s/o John and Elizabeth Laney. HC Park Cemetery: Matthew L. Paullus 1824-1905; Mary 1834-1920.

Pennock, Alexander; 26 Reg Co H, 22 Sep 62-6 Sep 65. NOD.

Perigo, Henry; HC Courthouse, Soldier Burial List Book: 115 Reg co F; died 20 Jun 1891; 78 years; occupation, farmer; burial, Knightstown, Indiana.

Perkins, Henry C.; 58 Reg Co A, 24 Feb 62-no out date. NOD.

Perkins, Newton; 5 Cav Co G, 28 Aug 62, Commissary Sgt, Intra Regiment transfer from Co G to Field and Staff, NOD.

Perman, Ephraim; 9 Cav Co B, 2 Jan 64, missing and presumed dead when the steamer, Sultana, exploded and burned near Memphis, on the Mississippi River 27 Apr 65. Listed as a victim of the disaster.

Perry, Elijah; "19 April 1861, enrolled as a volunteer 6th regiment, Company G, at North Vernon, Jennings County, Indiana; 22 April 1861, mustered in at Indianapolis, Indiana.

Hancock County Indiana Civil War Soldiers

30 May 1861, Regiment left Indianapolis, via Cincinnati and Parkersburg, for the scene of conflict in western Virginia, first being fully armed, equipped and clothed. 2 Jun 1861, arrived at Webster and marched with other troops the same night for fourteen miles, through a drenching rain, and on the morning of June 3rd took part in the first battle of the war at Phillippi. Returning to Grafton, the regiment was made a part of General Thomas A. Morris' Brigade.

"12 Jul 1861, regiment participated in the march to Laurel Hill and the engagement with Garnett's rebel command at Carrick's Ford. The latter part of the month was spent returning to Indianapolis, where the regiment was honorably discharged on 31 July 1861. Participated in battles of Laurel Hill, Cheat Nut, Garrett's Ford and Hawk's Nest, West Virginia. Mustered out 2 August 1861, at Indianapolis, term expired. Note on Company muster out roll: for clothing furnished by state, 1 uniform $7.75; 2 flannel shirts 2.80; 2 pr. drawers 80 cents; 3 pr socks 60 cents; 1 pr shoes 1.15; 1 hat 1.25, for transportation from place of organization to place of rendezvous 1.26; 5.00 advanced by state; 1 shirt 1.40; 2 pr drawers 80 cents.

"Elijah served a total of three months, fourteen days in Companies D and G of the 6th Indiana Infantry. As stated in pension records, "was an engineer on Madison, Jeffersonville and Indianapolis Railroad, during the War. Elijah J. Perry was born 14 May 1833 in Shelby County, Indiana; died 22 Oct 1914, Eureka Springs, Carroll County, Arkansas; married 22 Nov 1863, Hancock County, Indiana, Elizabeth "Lizzie" Ann Muth who was born 13 Sep 1846, Hancock County and died 19 Feb 1919, Hancock County. Elijah and Elizabeth "Lizzie" were divorced 14 Mar 1878 in Cassville, Barry County, Missouri. Contributed by Laura Tuttle, Miami, Florida.

Perry, James W.; 11 Reg Co K, 31 Aug 61-26 Jul 65. NOD.

Perry, John; 8 Reg Co B, 24 Apr 61-29 Jul 61. He is buried HC Low Cemetery, military data only on stone, no dates. NOD.

Personett, James M. 53 Reg Co A, 12 Apr 65-21 Jul 65. NOD.

Hancock County Indiana Civil War Soldiers

Personett, Joseph; HC obit 1 Apr 1915: "Joseph Personett, age 77 years, died at the home of his daughter and son-in-law, Mr. and Mrs. Elza Richey, of South Mount Street. Mr. Personett was born in Wayne County, Indiana, 11 December 1838, son of William and Julia (Fulton) Personett. He had been a resident of Greenfield for seventy years and was well posted in the early as well as the later history of the county. He was a carpenter by trade; three daughters survive, Mrs. Richey; Mrs. Riley Andrick; and Mrs. William Dildine; and brother, William Personett. Interment (HC) Park Cemetery." Joseph Personett may or may not have been a Civil War soldier; his brother, William, served in 9 Reg Co D.

Personett, William; 9 Reg Co D, 24 Feb 65-28 Aug 65. HC obit 12 Aug 1926: "William Personett, one of the old and widely known residents of Hancock County, died at the home of his daughter, Mrs. A.S. Kirkpatrick, Greenfield, after a week's acute illness. At the time of his death, Mr. Personett was bailiff of the circuit court, having been appointed by Judge Arthur VanDuyn. A meeting of the Hancock County bar was held to take observance of Mr. Personett's death. He is survived by two daughters, Mrs. Kirkpatrick and Mrs. Ed Hays. Funeral at the Kirkpatrick home with burial at Park Cemetery." William Personett was born 24 Jul 1847, Wayne County, Indiana, s/o William and Julia (Fulton) Personett. HC Park Cemetery: William H. Personett h/o Hulda 1847-1926; Hulda H. 1849-1902. See page for his brother, Joseph.

Philpot, Henry; 79 Reg Co D, 12 Aug 62-7 Jun 65. NOD.

Philpot, Marion; 8 Reg Co B, 25 Aug 61-28 Aug 65, Sgt. HC obit 8 Sep 1921: "Marion Philpot, son of Harris and Dicie Philpot, was born near Mt.Comfort, Indiana, 20 July 1844, and died at Charlottesville, Indiana, 27 Aug 1921. He was married 27 Nov 1867 (HC Bk 5-180) to Miss Mary J. Martin (1846-1930). He enlisted at the beginning of the Civil war in Company B, 8th Indiana Regiment, and served during the entire war. He was employed by the Pennsylvania Railroad for forty-two years and retired on a pension in 1912. He is survived by

Hancock County Indiana Civil War Soldiers

his wife, and two sisters, Mrs. Emma Ferguson and Mrs. Dicie Satter, three brothers, John, Johnty and Harris Philpot." Marion and Mary J. both buried (HC) Philadelphia Cemetery.

Pickard, Albert; Certificate of Disability for Discharge states: " Albert Pickard, a private of Captain Smith's Company G, 86th Indiana Volunteers, was enlisted by N. R. Smith of the same regiment at Frankfort, Indiana, on the 8th day of August 1862 to serve three (?) years; he was born Chatauqua County, New York is 37 years of age, 5 feet, 10 ½ inches high, dark complexion, gray eyes, black hair, and by occupation when enlisted a farmer. I certify, that I have carefully examined the said Albert Pickard and find him incapable of performing the duties of a soldier because of chronic periostitis, disease of covering of bones. Signed, 11 April 1863, William W. Goldsmith, act. asst. Surgeon-in-charge, Hospital No. 7. Discharged 11 April 1863. The soldier desires to be addressed at Pickard's Mill, Clinton County, Indiana."

"He applied for invalid pension 21 July 1888 stating: "…in the line of his duty near Nashville, Tennessee, about 20 December 1862, he was taken with jaundice and sent to the convalescent camp where he remained five or six days and was then sent to a temporary hospital and remained three or four days and then sent to General Hospital No. 6, Ward No. 6. There his back and legs gave way so he had to use a crutch and cain (sic) that they have not recovered , remaining weakened and painful, his kidneys and bladder are also diseased and have been from the same date.

"Since leaving the service this applicant has resided in Pickard's Mill, Indiana, occupation, carpenter, when enrolled, a farmer. That he is totally disabled from obtaining his subsistence by manual labor by reason of his injuries, above described, received in the service of the United States; and he therefore makes this declaration for the purpose of being placed on the invalid pension-roll of the United States. Signed, Albert his mark Pickard. Attest: Wilson T. Cooper, William J. Barnett." Declaration For Pension "dated 21 February 1907 for

Hancock County Indiana Civil War Soldiers

the purpose of being placed on the pension roll of the United States under the provisions of the act of 6 February 1907; That his several places of residence since leaving the service have been as follows: Clinton County, Indiana; Vernon County, Missouri; Randolph County, Arkansas; Shelby and Hancock Counties, Indiana; that he has heretofore applied for a pension Certificate # 867788, Indianapolis Agency; signed, Albert (X) Pickard.

"Albert Pickard s/o James I. and Nancy Matilda (Boyer) Pickard, was born 5 Jun 1825, Ellery, Chautauqua County, New York; Albert married Mary Ann Reveal 25 Sep 1845, Tipton County, Indiana; Albert married Mary Jane (Alexander, Boggs) Williams, 12 Feb 1895 HC Bk 9-94. Albert's death certificate states "he died of chronic bronchitis, contributory La Grippe, buried HC Sugar Creek Cemetery, however, there was no stone, or one that was illegible, when the cemetery was transcribed in 1993. Contributed by Donnie Pickard, Kokomo, Indiana.

Pickle, Daniel; HC obit 18 Jul 1929: "Daniel Pickle, age 90, a Civil War veteran died at the home of his daughter, Mrs. Edward Day, south of McCordsville. Death followed a stroke of paralysis. Mr. Pickle was born near the Hancock-Marion County border, had lived in the house of his father-in-law all his married life. He was a man of influence in his community, always standing for the better things in life, He enlisted in the Civil War and after serving three years, he reenlisted and served until the close of the War. He was a member of Company K, 44th Indiana Volunteer Infantry. Mr. Pickle belonged to a family of thirteen children, his sister, Eliza Jane (Pickle) Apple, w/o Andrew Jackson Apple was the youngest and last to die, 7 Nov 1929.

"The funeral will be military, in charge of the soldiers from Fort Benjamin Harrison. Surviving Mr. Pickle are three daughters, Mrs. Lettie Day; Mrs. Anna Cory; w/o John; Mrs. Carrie Olvey w/o Ray; and two sons, Leroy and Andrew Jackson Pickle. Mrs. Pickle preceded her husband in death 24

Hancock County Indiana Civil War Soldiers

Feb 1899. Interment Mock Cemetery, Oaklandon, Indiana." Daniel Pickle was born 29 Jul 1839, died 16 Jul 1929, s/o George Sr. and Mary Elizabeth (Apple) Pickle." Contributed by Bonnie Andrews, Greenfield, Indiana.

Pierce, B.H.; 105 Reg Co E, 11 Jul 63-18 Jul 63. NOD.

Pierson, Martin E.; 18 Reg, Musician, 16 Aug 61-20 Aug 62. Martin E. Pierson married 17 May 1859 Caroline Hawkins HC Bk 4-137. HC newspaper 12 Aug 1897: "Martin E. Pierson, of Indianapolis and well known in our city, mysteriously disappeared from his home after drawing his quarterly pension. He adjusted several little bills he was owing to merchants at the Capitol and disappeared. No tidings of him have been received.

"His disappearance is a mystery, as his domestic relations have always been very pleasant. He is a brother of Dr. Pierson, of Fountaintown, and Mrs. Capt. Snow of Greenfield." HC Newspaper 19 Aug 1897: "Martin E. Pierson, of Indianapolis, whom we mentioned had mysteriously disappeared from his home at Indianapolis without any apparent cause, was found in St. Louis last week and returned to his home. He was in a very critical condition as his mind was unbalanced and he was a very sick man. His friends are in hopes that he will shortly be restored to good health." HC Philadelphia Cemetery: Martin E. Pierson, Civil War Soldier 1834-1911; Caroline 1842-1921.

Pilkington, James W.; 9 Cav Co B, 18 Aug 61-1 Aug 65. A James W. Pilkington married 27 Oct 1859 Margaret Jones HC Bk 4-159.

Pilkington, William H.; 5 Cav Co G, 30 Apr 64 as 2nd Lt., 14 Mar 65 commissioned 1st Lt., out 27 Jun 65. married 14 Dec 1857 Isabell Shafer HC Bk 4-53. A William H. Pilkinton was born 1832 and died 15 Jul 1892, no places given.

Piper, George W.; 12 Reg Co G, 22 Jul 62-8 Jun 65. "...born Hancock County, Indiana, 5' 7" tall, age 20, dark complexion, blue eyes, light hair, farmer when enrolled..."

Hancock County Indiana Civil War Soldiers

Poole, Franklin R.; 9 Cav Co B, 13 Nov 63-28 Aug 65. A man named Frank R. Poole married 15 Jun 1872 (HC Bk 6-113) Sarah Mollie Troy d/o Dr. S.A. Troy.

Pope, Elijah; 5 Cav Co G, 16 Aug 62-15 Sep 65. An Elijah Pope married 8 Jan 1861 Elizabeth Linder HC Bk 4-235.

Pope, Jasper N.; 9 Cav Co G, 16 Aug 62, died 25 Sep 64. HC newspaper 11 Aug 1864: "Jasper N. Pope of Company G, 5th Cavalry, was taken prisoner during the disastrous expedition commanded by General Stoneman." Andersonville Prison profile #19705: Jasper N. Pope, Co G 5th Cav, died 24 Sep 1864 of scorbutus and buried grave #9705. A Jasper N. Pope married 18 Oct 1855 Mary Richardson HC Bk 3-305.

Pope, John; 8 Reg Co B, 22 Apr 61-6 Aug 61; also 79 Reg Co B, 9 Aug 62-7 Jun 65. A John Pope married 26 Mar 1879 Almeda Moore HC Bk 7-86.

Pope, Newton; HC death notice 23 Nov 1899: "Information was received in Greenfield by William Webb of the heart failure death of Newton Pope of Dodge City, Kansas, but formerly a resident of Brandywine Township. Mr. Pope was a most excellent citizen and has many friends here who will be grieved to learn of his sudden death. Mr. Pope was born in Brandywine Township 15 Jul 1834. He first entered the army in the three months service in Company I, 8th Indiana Infantry. After his discharge, he enlisted in Company G, 5th Indiana Cavalry and served until 31 Jul 1864, when he was captured and sent to Andersonville Prison, where he was confined until the close of the war."

Pope, Peter, 99 Reg Co G, 16 Aug 62, died 15 Dec 62, Indianapolis. HC newspaper 18 Dec 1862: "The remains of Peter Pope, Jr. of Brandywine Township were brought to Greenfield from Indianapolis, where he departed this life on the same day. He belonged to Capt. Riley's cavalry company. Mr. Pope was a worthy and industrious young man, and his place at home, and in his compnay, will not be easily filled. He was aged about 26 years and leaves a wife and five children." The

Hancock County Indiana Civil War Soldiers

1860 Hancock County census records Peter Pope age 27; Sarah age 27; America age 5; William age 3; and Cassius age 1.

Pope, William; 5 Cav Co G, 16 Aug 62-16 Sep 65, as Q.M. Sgt. A William Pope married 19 Apr 1869 Mary Weber HC Bk 5-297.

Porter, Benjamin; 105 Reg Co E, 11 Jul 63-18 Jul 63. "Benjamin Porter was born 10 Mar 1840, s/o Franklin and Hannah (Sebastian) Porter, and died 21 Mar 1908 of heart failure. Mr. Porter was one of the old settlers of Greenfield and for many years was section foreman of the Pan Handle Railroad, and later was in charge of the saws that were used in sawing wood for the engines by the railroad company. Later he was elected city marshal for two terms and of late was superintendent of the street cleaning department. Funeral services were held at his home on the corner of Wood and Lincoln Streets." A Benjamin F. Porter, married 28 Sep 1872 Elizabeth Sylvester HC Bk 6-137; he is buried HC Park Cemetery.

Porter, John; 105 Reg Co E, 11 Jul 63, killed in action at Lawrenceburg, Indiana, at the lamentable disaster of friendly fire during the pursuit of Confederate General John Morgan as he raided into Indiana..

Porter, Melvin; HC Courthouse, Soldier Burial List Book: 25 Illinois Co D; died 1 Dec 1900; 59 years; occupation, clerk; burial, Indianola, Indiana. NOD.

Porter, William; 105 Reg Co E, 11 Jul 63-18 Jul 63. "William Porter died 31 Oct 1910 and was born 28 Sep 1831, Kentucky, s/o Benjamin F. and Hannah (Sebastian) Porter, buried HC Philadelphia Cemetery: William L. Porter 28 Sep 1811-31 Oct 1910.

Potts, Larkin; 99 Reg Co B, 13 Aug 62-5 Jun 65, Sgt. 99th Regiment History states: "Larkin Potts was a Sergeant and in 1900 resides in Rensselaer, Indiana."

Powell, Elihu; 19 Indiana Light Artillery as recorded at Chickamauga National Battlefield (January 2002), residence or

Hancock County Indiana Civil War Soldiers

place of enlistment, Greenfield, Indiana, 20 Aug 62-10 Jun 65. NOD.

Power, William Hendershot; 99 Reg Co B, 22 Mar 64, transferred to 48 Reg 18 May 65, out 15 Jul 65, Corp'l. "...age 18, 5' 6" tall, light complexion, gray eyes, dark hair, farmer when enrolled..." 99th Regiment History states: "He was a recruit in the winter of 1864 to Company B, and being only 15 years old, was soon called 'Company B's baby.' He was one of the forty men of Company B detailed for the picket line at Dallas, 28 May 1864, and passed through that terrific fight where all but seventeen of the forty were killed, wounded or captured. He escaped but was slightly wounded by a gunshot the next day, the 29th. (That bullet became a prized relic and was passed from generation to generation.)

"Billy, as he was often called, was in every battle of the company, health always good, never missed a detail for duty and marched every foot of the way, via Savannah to Washington, and was not 17 years old when mustered out at the close of the war. He was of German-Irish stock and a true soldier."

HC obit 1 Sep 1932: "Taps sounded for one of Hancock County's Civil War veterans when funeral services were held for William H. Powers. Mr. Powers died at his home in Wilkinson, and he was the last Civil War veteran of Brown Township. He was born in Pottsville, Pennsylvania, 25 June 1848, two years later, in 1850, he came to Henry County, Indiana, with his parents. Seven years later the family moved to Brown Township in Hancock County and since that date Brown Township has been Mr. Power's home.

"When only fifteen years old the youth joined the Union army, becoming a member of Company B, 99th Infantry. He served until the close of the Civil War. Probably one of his most trying experiences during the War occurred at Dallas, Georgia, 28 May 1864, when he, along with thirty-nine other men were detailed for picket line duty. During the terrific fighting which followed, more than half of the men were killed or wounded. He escaped but was slightly wounded the following day. He marched with his comrades to Savannah and then to Washington, D.C., where he was mustered out of service.

"On returning to this county following the War, he was engaged in construction work. He built many residences and other buildings in this county. Survivors, one daughter, Mrs. Freeman Smith; one sister, Mrs. James Clark; and one brother, George Power." William Power married 19 Sep 1869 (HC Bk 5-320) Sarah Mariah Garriott, 4th child of William L. and Margaret Garriott. Sarah (Garriott) Power was born 29 May 1849 and died 3 Aug 1928. See autobiography of William Hendershott Power in this volume. Contributed by William Smith, Indianapolis, Indiana.

Powers, Isaac; 5 Cav Co G, 16 Aug 62-15 Sep 65. An Isaac Powers married 27 Oct 1865 Synthia Richey HC Bk 4-553.

Prather, Nathan; 8 Reg Co E, no dates. HC newspaper 17 Nov 1892: "Mr. Nathan Prather, of Vernon Township, was in Greenfield to help the democracy jollify. He is a Democratic soldier of ye olden times. he served five years in the service of his country. He was in the first battle and was in the last battle of the war. We would like to hear of any soldier who can beat this record." A Nathan Prather married 21 Aug 1870 Esther Beaver HC Bk 7-10.

Pratt, James C.; 147 Reg Co H, 14 Feb 65-4 Aug 65. A James C. Pratt married 10 Nov 1868 Mrs. Mary Ellen Mattox HC Bk 5-261.

Price, James; 53 Reg Co A, 29 Dec 63, transferred 20 Mar 65 to Veteran Reserve Corps, indicates wound or illness; out 25 Jul 65. "...dark complexion, black eyes, black hair, farmer when enrolled..." HC newspaper 11 Jun 1903: "James Price, a well-known old soldier of Greenfield, received official notice that he has been granted a pension, and that there is now due him back pay in the sum of $240. "Now the next step is to apply for an increase," said Mr. Price humorously, when a friend congratulated him on his good fortune."

Hancock County Indiana Civil War Soldiers

HC obit 16 Feb 1911: "James M. Price, age 65 years, died at the Marion Soldiers' Home of disease contracted during the Civil War. Mr. Price's home was in Greenfield many years until he went to the Home to live. He was a Civil War veteran and member of Samuel Dunbar Post G.A.R. He has a half sister, Mrs. Ed Brokaw. Funeral service and burial (HC) Park Cemetery in charge of the G.A.R.

Price, John; 9 Reg Co E, 24 Feb 65-28 Aug 65. A John Price married 25 Dec 1863 Nancy Jane Deshong HC Bk 4-420.

Price, Lewis; 79 Reg Co C, 15 Aug 62, transferred 14 Jul 63 to Engineer Corps. A Lewis Price married 3 Oct 1866 Lucinda Bell HC Bk 5-90.

Price, Reese; HC Courthouse, Soldier Burial List: 21 New York Reg Co A; died 13 Nov 1893; 48 years; occupation, nailer; burial, Park Cemetery, Greenfield, Indiana. NOD.

Price, William W.; 5 Cav Co G, 16 Aug 62-15 Sep 65. HC newspaper 11 Aug 1864: "Corp. W.W. Price was taken prisoner during the disastrous expedition commanded by General Stoneman." William Price not recorded on Andersonville Prison profile. A William Price married 22 Mar 1866 Nancy Brizendine HC Bk 5-47.

Prickett, Eli; 9 Reg Co D, 24 Feb 65-28 Aug 65. HC newspaper 1 Nov 1866: "We are informed that a man named Prickett was killed by another young man named Copper, in Fortville, last week. Copper knocked Prickett down and kicked him twice, from the effects of which Prickett died in about half an hour. Prickett was in delicate health and had been since his return from the army. Copper was not arrested at last accounts."

HC newspaper 8 Nov 1866: "We announced in our last that a murder had been committed at Fortville, in this County. The victim was Eli Prickett, the murderer Benjamin Copper. The fight grew out of an old grudge. As Copper is under bonds for $4,000 for his appearance at the February term of the Circuit Court, we think it just that the facts in the case should reach the public at the trial. Let the law take its course." Buried HC Caudell/Simmons Cemetery: Eli Prickett died 1866.

Hancock County Indiana Civil War Soldiers

Prickett, Jasper, 79 Reg Co D, 12 Aug 62-2 May 63. HC Gillium Chapel Cemetery: Jasper Prickett Co D 79 Ind Inf, no dates.

Priddy, John; 34 Reg Co D, 21 Sep 61-3 Feb 66, Sgt. NOD.

Prince, Jno.; HC Park Cemetery: Jno. Prince Co F 3 W Va Cav, died 6 Apr 1906, age 66. NOD.

Pritchard, Joseph; 7 Ohio Cav Co E, 1 Sep 62-8 Jun 65. Recorded as P.O.W. 6 Nov 63, Rogersville, Tennessee. "...born England, 5' 7" tall, age 28, light complexion, hazel eyes, dark hair..."

Probasco, John; 57 Reg Co A, 13 Dec 61-5 Feb 65. A John Probasco married 15 Jul 1849 Sarah E. Ramsey HC Bk 2-338. NOD.

Pugh, James; 5 Cav Co G, 16 Aug 62-roster records him as deserted 23 Nov 1862. NOD.

Purdue, Thomas L. 148 Reg Co G, 2 Feb 65-11 Sep 65. NOD.

Pyeatte, Thomas; 57 Reg Co A, Musician, 13 Dec 61-4 Mar 62. NOD.

Pyle, Absalom; 12 Reg Co G, 19 Jul 62-8 Jun 65. Old Fort Cemetery, Hamilton County, Indiana, Absalom Pyle Co G 12 Ind Inf, military stone, no dates. An Absalom Pyle married 1 Jan 1853 Sarah Richards HC Bk 3-135.

Pyles, Thomas; HC Philadelphia Cemetery: Thomas R. Pyles, Soldier, 1847-1896. NOD. He died 21 Mar 1896, age 40.

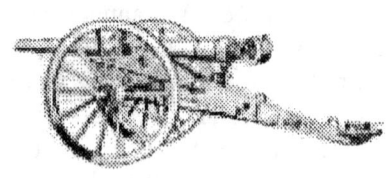

Hancock County Indiana Civil War Soldiers

William Hendershot Power

Courtesy of 99th Regiment History

Hancock County Indiana Civil War Soldiers

◄ Q ►
No entries.

◄ R ►

Rabe, Anton Frederick.; 79 Reg Co D, 16 Aug 61-7 Jun 65. HC History, published 1916: "He participated in the battles of Lookout Mountain, Stone River and was with Sherman on his march to the sea but before arriving at Savannah was transferred to another unit. Anton Rabe was born 22 Nov 1841, Indianapolis, Indiana, and lived there until he was three years old, then moved with his father to the Rabe homestead in Sugar Creek Township, Hancock County.

"Anton married 31 Oct 1872 HC Bk 6-150 Anna Marie Kuhner. Children of this union, Anton H.; Anne; Mary; Louise; Bertha; and August." HC obit 11 Jul 1914: Agrees with above details with the following additions: "At the age of 21 years, he enlisted in Company D, 79th Indiana Regiment, saw service in a number of hard-fought battles. Henry Eikman of Sugar Creek Township was a messmate in the army. He started with General Sherman on his celebrated march to the sea but did not complete the march for the reason that his company received different orders.

"Mr. Rabe was married when he was 31 years old, and to the marriage were born 13 children, six of whom with their mother survive; Anton H.; Mrs. Chris Kleiman; Mrs. Louisa Wooten; August; Miss Bertha; and Mrs. Mary Kipler. One brother, Charles Rabe, Florida; two sisters, Mrs. Wm. Rusharp and Mrs. Solomon Mattox, of Texas, also survive." HC Philadelphia Cemetery: A.F. Rabe 22 Nov 1841-4 Jul 1914, as a family tradition, an American flag always flies in the G.A.R. holder placed in the ground next to his grave marker; Anna M. Rabe 22 May 1852-13 Nov 1926. Government military grave markers are unmistakable and Mr. and Mrs. Rabe both have one. A strange occurrence with no explanation until a metal plaque was found near their grave sites bearing the following

Hancock County Indiana Civil War Soldiers

statement: Wife of a Soldier, 1861-1865, W.R.C. Mr. Rabe was an active member of the Kirkhof Post Grand Army of the Republic in Sugar Creek Township and without a doubt Mrs. Rabe was a member of the group of women who assisted the post, known as the Women's Relief Corps (WRC).

After conversation with a family member, it is the opinion of the author that Mrs. Rabe became eligible for the Government marker due to her charity work for the Women's Relief Corps, thus the plaque that was found, somehow came loose from Mrs. Rabe's stone, fell to the ground, was lost in the soil for decades until January, 2002, when it was discovered by the caretaker of the Cemetery. Sometime after the Civil War, a friend, who worked as a glass-blower at a factory on the west edge of Greenfield, made a bugle of glass and presented it as a gift to Mr. Rabe. Today, it is a prized possession of his granddaughter, Ruthanna Fenter.

Ragan (Reagan), James; 53 Reg Co A, 24 Feb 62-20 Jun 65. HC newspaper 4 August 1864: "We are sorry to learn that Co A, 53rd Regiment has met another loss, James Reagan of Hancock County is wounded and in the hands of the enemy." Andersonville Prison Profile #58423, Cpl. James Reagan, Company A 53rd Indiana, survived."

Ragan (Reagan) Wallace; 53 Reg Co A, 24 Feb 62, promoted 30 Jan 65, 1st Lt. NOD.

Rains, Benjamin F.; 105 Reg Co E, 11 Jul 63-18 Jul 63. Benjamin F. Rains died 3 Mar 1900 of pneumonia, s/o Walter and Levina (Loyd) Rains. HC obit 8 Mar 1900: "Benjamin F. Rains, a time honored citizen of Greenfield, passed peacefully away. Mr. Rains was a gunsmith and one of our oldest citizens having come to this city from Scott County, Kentucky, over fifty years ago. He was born 8 Oct 1819 and served in the defense of his country with honor. The gray haired veterans of Samuel Dunbar Post G.A.R. attended his funeral in a body. Mr. Rains leaves a wife; three children; four brothers; and one sister to mourn his demise" Buried HC Park Cemetery." HC

Hancock County Indiana Civil War Soldiers

Park Cemetery: Benjamin F. Rains 9 Oct 1819-3 Mar 1900 Co E 105 Ind Vols; Rosanna w/o B.F. 21 Jan 1835-21 Jan 1920.

Ramsdell (Ransdell), Cornelius; 148 Reg Co C, 17 Feb 65-5 Sep 65. NOD.

Raridan, Captain John C.; HC newspaper 9 Oct 1861: "The readers of the *Democrat* will be glad to learn that our fellow-townsman, Mr. John C. Raridan, who left a private in Capt. Lindley's Company, 19th Indiana, has been promoted to a Lieutenancy. A soldier in the Mexican War, and seeing active service in that country, he is deserving of promotion in this war."

HC newspaper 22 Jan 1862: " Lieut. John C. Raridan of Company F, 19th Indiana regiment, stationed at Fort Craig, near Washington City, arrived at home on furlough, to recruit his health. He reports the boys from this county in good health and well satisfied." HC newspaper 26 Feb 1863: "Lieut. John C. Raridan on account of his wound, received at the battle of South Mountain, has resigned his commission, and returned to his home. The command of the company now devolves upon Sergeant Hartley, of this county, who has been, or will be promoted to the Captaincy."

"John C. Raridan enlisted in Co B, 9th Cavalry, 10 Dec 1863-28 Aug 65. ...born Decatur County, Indiana, 5' 10" tall, age 39, fair complexion, blue eyes, dark hair, mechanic/carriage maker when enrolled..." HC newspaper 3 Aug 1865: "Capt. Raridan arrived home and will return to his company in a few days."

HC newspaper obit 21 Jul 1898: "Captain John C. Raridan, an old soldier, passed from time to eternity. He was as brave a soldier as ever enlisted in the war of the rebellion. For a few years past he has been suffering from epileptic fits, and it is surmised he died in one of these, as he was dead when found. The son of John Raridan, Captain Raridan was 71 years of age and an old resident here. He leaves two daughters and three sons to mourn his death. He was buried with all honors due an old soldier by the Samuel Dunbar Post G.A.R. Thus the old

Hancock County Indiana Civil War Soldiers

soldiers who have brought much good to our land are one by one meeting the last roll call." John C. Raridan married 17 Jan 1850 Abigail Mead HC Bk 2-367. HC Park Cemetery: Capt. J.C. Raridan Co B 9 Cav, military data only, no dates; Abigail w/o J.C. died 8 Sep 1889 63y 7m 7d.

Rardin, Thomas C.; 105 Reg Co E, 11Jul 63-18 Jul 63. HC newspaper 5 Nov 1863: "Thomas C. Rardin, aged about 34 years, died in this place on 5 November 1863, after a short but painful illness of billious vomiting. Mary Jane Rardin, aged 35 years, wife of Thomas C. died of the same disease on 3 November 1863. Thus in a few short days, a family of small children are left without father or mother, with only relatives to watch over and give them counsel and advice in years of infancy and childhood. But the Lord has promised to be a father to the fatherless. May those who keep them in the right path for the ultimate fulfillment of this blessed promise. Mr. R. was a member of the Hancock Guards, by whom he was buried with honors of war."

Rash, Amos; 12 Reg Co G, 21 Jul 62-8 Jun 65. "...born Hancock County, Indiana, 5' 7" tall, age 21, dark complexion, dark eyes, dark hair, farmer when enrolled..." An Amos Rash married 25 Aug 1865 Sarah C. Apple HC Bk 4-467.

Rash, Daniel; 12 Reg Co G, 5 Aug 62-8 Jun 65. "...born Hancock County, 5' 9" tall, age 22, light complexion, gray eyes, light hair, farmer when enrolled..."A Daniel Rash married 20 Sep 1858 Rose Ann Apple HC Bk 4-99.

Rash, John T.; 12 Reg Co G, 19 Jul 62-8 Jun 65. John T. Rash, born 9 Sep 1839, s/o John K. and Margaret (Fuqua) Rash, died of chronic diarrhea, Fortville, 14 Apr 1906, wife Sarah. HC Wynn Cemetery: John T. Rash 8 Sep 1839-14 Apr 1906; Verlinda w/o John T. Rash 13 Jan 1842-21 April 1867; Sarah w/o John T. Rash 26 Oct 1839-13 Jan 1914.

HC newspaper 19 April 1906: "John T. Rash, age 66 years, a veteran of the Civil War and well known resident of Vernon Township died at his home in Fortville after an illness of two

Hancock County Indiana Civil War Soldiers

months duration. He leaves a widow and two sons, John and Alexander Rash. Funeral and burial at Fortville."

Rash, Lawson; 9 Reg Co C, 14 Feb 64-28 Sep 65. A Lawson Rash married 14 Aug 1869 Angeline Fort HC Bk 5-290.

Rash, Thomas M.; 12 Reg Co G, 5 Aug 62-8 Jun 65. '...born Hancock County, 5' 10" tall, age 21, dark complexion, blue eyes, dark hair, farmer when enrolled..." Thomas M. Rash, s/o Levi Rash; died 26 Mar 1927; married Eliza Fry 29 Oct 1867 HC Bk 5-171. HC newspaper 31 Mar 1927: "Thomas M. Rash, age 86 years, a pioneer resident of this county, died at his home three miles southeast of Eden. Mr. Rash leaves three sons, E.J.; S.B.; and Charles. Mr. Rash was a volunteer soldier during the Civil War." HC Cooper Cemetery: Thomas M. Rash 2 Jul 1840-25 Mar 1927; Eliza J. Rash 5 Jul 1846-21 Apr 1905.

Rawlings, Aaron J.; 9 Cav Co B, 13 Nov 63-28 Aug 65. An Aaron J. Rawlings married 13 Oct 1861 Jennie Stewart HC Bk 4-289.

Rawlings, Jasper; 8 Reg Co G, 22 Apr 61-6 Aug 61. See above Aaron J. Rawlings, may be same man?

Ray, George W.; 79 Reg Co D, 8 Aug 62, died 12 Dec 62, Nashville, Tennessee. A George W. Ray married Sarah J.M. Eastes 6 May 1860 HC Bk 4-190.

Ray, William; 79Reg Co D;8 Aug 62, died 9 Nov 62, Somerset, Kentucky. NOD

Reams, William; 45 Ohio Inf Co I, 19 years old, 25 Jun 62, transferred to Veteran Reserve Corps 15 Dec 65, indicating light duty due to wound or illness. "William Reams, died 7 Dec 1922, of chronic interstitial nephritis, occupation, retired mechanic, married, wife, Josephine Reams, William born 13 Jan 1844, s/o Vinton and Mary (Vasser) Reams." HC obit 7 Dec 1922: "William Reams, age 78 years, and Civil War veteran, passed away at his home, 615 North Spring Street, due to a complication of diseases and followed an illness of one month. Mr. and Mrs. Reams moved to Greenfield two months ago from Ohio. Mr. Reams is survived by the widow and three sons. Burial Park Cemetery."

Reamsheart, Nicholas; 8 Reg Co B, 25 Aug 61-4 Sep 64. NOD.

Redman, Michael; 99 Reg Co B, 13 Aug 62-5 Jun 65. "...born Brown County, Ohio, 5' 5" tall, age 37, dark complexion, black eyes, black hair, farmer when enrolled..." 99 Regiment History states, "Michael Redman, dead 1900, residence, Willow Branch, Indiana." NOD.

Redmire, Christian; 8 Reg Co B, 25 Aug 61-15 Dec 62. NOD.

Reed, George W.; HC newspaper obit 24 Jul 1924: "George joined as a recruit to Company K, 16th Indiana Infantry and did service in Virginia at Harper's Ferry, Winchester and battle of Bull Run, after which the regiment was mustered out of service 14 May 1862. Young Reed again heard the call and on 17 June 1862 joined Company K, 54th Indiana Volunteers for three months service. He was appointed 1st Sergeant in this company and was discharged 15 September 1862 at Indianapolis. On 6 May 1864, he entered service by joining Company C, 134th Indiana Volunteers as 1st Sergeant to serve 100 days and was discharged 2 September 1864. In early spring of 1865, George, in company with Thomas Spellman, of Greensburg, raised a company of volunteers, and this company was the first to report to Governor Morton for the 146th Indiana Infantry, consequently, George was commissioned as captain and was discharged 31 August 1865 at Baltimore, Maryland, by reason of the war having ended.

"George W. Reed, son of James A. and Mary M. Reed, was born 19 February 1843, at St. Omer, Decatur County, Indiana, and died 16 July 1924, at his home at 515 North State Street, Greenfield, age 81 years. His mother died when George was nine years old and he was taken to live with relatives until he was about fourteen years of age, at which time he was taken to live with his father and step-mother at St. Paul, Indiana, where he was apprenticed to learn the cabinet trade, in consideration

Hancock County Indiana Civil War Soldiers

of his board, and washing and the sum of $5.00 per year and became a proficient wood work man.

"George was married three times, 1) 12 Dec 1872, Rhoda Amsden, of Shelby County, Indiana, four children: Charles; Grace; Esther; and Harry; Mrs. Reed died 31 Oct 1882, at Shelbyville, Indiana. George married 2) 29 Oct 1889 Ettie Searight of Fredericksburg, Ohio, after which he took up residence in Greenfield where he built the beautiful home in which he lived until his death. He married 3) 17 Aug 1922, Mrs. Virginia Hoover, Indianapolis. He is survived by the widow, Virginia, and two daughters, Grace Savage, Esther Davis and son, Charles. John Stevens, a member of Dunbar Post G.A.R., was detailed to fire the salute at the funeral of his deceased Captain." HC Park Cemetery: George W. Reed 1843-1924; Marietta B. 1861-1915.

Reed, James T.; 18 Reg musician, 16 Aug 61-20 Aug 62. NOD.

Reedy, Jeremiah; 5 Cav Co G, 16 Aug 62-10 Mar 63. HC obit 22 Mar 1883: "At the residence of his son in the northern part of Center Township, 17 March 1883, Jeremiah Reedy died of consumption, aged 67 years. Mr. Reedy was born in Pennsylvania, and at an early day went to Kentucky. About thirty years ago, he came to Hancock County, and remained here until January, 1877, when he was sent to the State Prison at Jeffersonville, for a period of ten years for the killing of his son, James, a short time previous.

"Although he was kindly treated by the officers of the prison, the life was too hard for him and sometime in the forepart of the winter was sent to the hospital with no prospect of recovery. His case was reported to Gov. Porter, and he kindly granted him a pardon to come home and die in the midst of his friends and relatives. He was out only a few short weeks when he paid the debt that all must pay. He was the father of five children, only one of whom survives him."

According to the statement of Mrs. James Reedy, the only witness of the terrible tragedy on 30 Aug 1876, " the parties had returned from town and both declined to partake supper prepared for them. The father and son drank four glasses of whiskey each in town and began a quarrel about "bossing the household" when the elder Reedy first used a buggy whip and then an axe on his son. Young Reedy died in a few hours leaving a wife and unborn child." A James D. Reedy married 4 Jul 1875 (HC Bk 6-375) Sarah Eaks. HC Cooper Cemetery Jeremiah Reedy, Civil War soldier; Emily, w/o Jeremiah 1 Jan 1829-16 Dec 1874.

Reese, George; 138 Ohio Reg Co H, no dates. HC obit 26 Mar 1925: "George Reese, son of Williamson and Eliza Reese, was born in Hamilton County, Ohio, 22 February 1846, and died 14 Mar 1925, at his home in Brandywine Township. His boyhood days were spent in Ohio and at the age of 18 years answered his country's call and enlisted in Company H., 138th Ohio Regiment. While still a young man, he came to Hancock County, Indiana, and on 25 December 1878 (HC Bk 7-57), was united in marriage to Laura J. Scott who departed this life 17 August 1891. To this union were born four children, one of them dying in infancy.

"He spent several years in Alabama, returning to Indiana in 1900 and made his home with his son, William E. Reese and wife, where he spent the remainder of his life. He leaves two sons, William and James, and one daughter, Edna Piles; two sisters, Mrs. Marshall Smith and Mrs. Emma Mattox." HC Brandywine Cemetery: George Reese died 14 Mar 1925; Laura J. w/o George W. died 17 Aug 1891 30y 4m 0d.

Reeves, James S.; 8 Reg Co G, 22 Apr 61-6 Aug 61. A James S. Reeves married 2 Sep 1866 Mary McCorkhill HC Bk 5-79; also married 24 Dec 1875 Laura Rouyer HC Bk 6-329.

Reeves, Nevil; 99 Reg Co B, 13 Aug 62-5 Jun 65. "...born Brown County, Ohio, 5' 9' tall, age 26, sandy complexion, black eyes, black hair, farmer when enrolled..." "Nevil Reeves, son of Benjamin and Elizabeth (Crawford) Reeves, was born 17 Aug 1835 in Brown County, Ohio. and came to Hancock County at the age of five years with his parents. At

Hancock County Indiana Civil War Soldiers

the age of twenty he married Virginia Pace, and to this union were born three children, Jane, Mary and Martha.

"When the Civil war came Nevil answered his country's call and he joined Company B, 99th Regiment, and was in the ranks at the siege of Vicksburg, Jackson and the entire Atlanta campaign. He was promoted to corporal and was detailed as special sharpshooter, and another time was to assist in the exchange of prisoners, after the fall of Atlanta. His brother, Oliver, was in the same company, and Newton C. served in an Indiana Regiment. Nevil marched in the Grand Review at Washington City and received his discharge 5 Jun 1865. Five more children were born, Alva, Dallas, Leonard, Rosa and Frank. Nevil Reeves is a brick mason and comrade of Dunbar G.A.R." HC obit 6 Mar 1919, "Nevil Reeves, an old Civil War veteran, died at his home on Third Street, at age 84 years, and had only been ill a week from a paralytic stroke. Interment (HC) Park Cemetery."

Reeves, Newton; 134 Reg Co K, 24 May 64-30 Sep 65. A Newton Reeves married 12 Jan 1881 Mary J. Chandler HC Bk 6-236. See page for his brother, Nevil Reeves.

Reeves, Oliver; 99 Reg Co B, 13 Aug 62-5 Jun 65. HC newspaper 9 June 1864: "Private Oliver Reeves, Company B, 99th Regiment, was wounded in the face at Dallas, Georgia, 28 May 1864." 99th Regiment History states, "Oliver Reeves wounded Dallas, Georgia, 28 May 1864; 1900 residence is Ravena, Misouri." See page for his brother Nevil Reeves.

Reeves, Riley; 99 Reg, Co B, 23 Mar 64-5 Jun 65. HC obit, 6 Jul 1922: "Riley A. Reeves, aged 74 years, died at the family home in Vancouver, Washington, where he had lived for the past eight years. He was born in Hancock County, Indiana, and during the Civil War was a member of Company B, 99th Indiana Infantry. Survivors include his wife, Sarah Reeves, and six children: Mrs. Dell Dillon; Mrs. Gertrude Neal; Mrs. Pearl Waldrep; Mrs. Hazel Smith; Mrs. Anne August; and W.R. Reeves; and sister Mrs. Rebecca Rock of Hancock County, Indiana."

Hancock County Indiana Civil War Soldiers

99th Regiment History states: "Riley A. Reeves was born 8 October 1847, Hancock County, Indiana, enlisted as recruit in March 1864, age 16 years; wounded in Dallas, Georgia, 28 May 1864; mustered out July 1865 and returned home; married Sarah Crane 24 Feb 1876 (HC Bk 6-436); in 1882 the family moved to Trinidad, Colorado, where he now resides."

Reeves, William; 99 Reg Co B, 13 Aug 62-5 Jun 65. HC newspaper 9 Jun 1864:" Pvt. William Reeves, Company B, 99th Regiment, was wounded in both legs 28 May 1864, Dallas, Georgia." A William Reeves married 5 Nov 1865 Sarah Brown HC Bk 4-555. 99th regiment History states: "In 1900 William Reeves resides in Revena, Missouri."

Reeves. William W.; 99 Reg Co B, 13 Aug 62-5 Jun 65. "...born Hancock County, Indiana, 5' 11" tall, age 19, fair complexion, blue eyes, fair hair, farmer when enrolled..."

Reitsell, Aaron; 148 Reg Co C, 17 Feb 65-5 Sep 65. NOD.

Renan, William R.; 66 Reg Co H, 10 Aug 62-3 Jun 65. NOD.

Renforth, Thomas Shepherd; HC obit 16 Aug 1906: "Thomas Shepherd Renforth, son of James and Ellen (Shepherd) Renforth, was born near Wheeling, Virginia, 22 Mar 1827, departed this life, 31 July 1906. He lived in the fertile bottoms of Wheeling Creek, near the Ohio River, until the Civil War when he enlisted in the 15th Virginia Union Volunteer Regiment.

"After the War he returned to his native home which he found wrecked, ruined and laid waste. He brought his family to Hancock County, settling in Vernon Township, near Fortville, where he died at the home of his son, Edward Renforth. He leaves a widow, Ellen, five sons, William; Edward; Thomas; Harvey; and Dillon; and daughter, Mrs. Mary Schrader. "Dad" as he was known, never was sick, worked all of his days and sowed a patch of turnips the day before he passed away. He was laid to rest beside his daughter, Mrs. Maggie Reynolds, at Mt.Comfort Cemetery." HC Mt.Comfort Cemetery: Thomas S. Renforth 1827-1906; Ellen w/o Thomas S. 1826-1910.

Hancock County Indiana Civil War Soldiers

Rensford, Henry; HC newspaper 19 Dec 1906: "Henry Rensford, age 84 years, of Sullivan County, is spending the winter at Charlottesville with his sister, Mrs. Susan Pherigo. This visit is the second during a period of thirty years. Mr. Rensford served in two wars, having enlisted 7 Jun 1846 in the Mexican War, and honorably discharged, and having also served in the rebellion."

Reynolds, James E.; 148 Reg Co I, 17 Feb 65-5 Sep 65. Two HC marriages for a James E. Reynolds: 1) 5 Feb 1848 Lydia Hiatt Bk 2-272; 2) 17 Jun 1874 Nancy Radcliff Bk 6-280.

Reynolds, James F.; 13 Cav Co I, 23 Dec 63-30 Sep 65. HC Mt.Gilead/Reeves Cemetery: J.F. Reynolds 1846-1925, 13 Ind Cav Co I, 1863-1865; Nancy J. 1st wife of J.F. Reynolds 1853-1880; Sadie P. 2nd wife J.F. 1866-1917. A James F. Reynolds married 23 Jan 1881 Sarah Ware HC Bk 7-240. The following contributed by Jean Hughes Demegret about her great-grandfather, Rev. Frank Reynolds:"he was shot in the elbow during service in the Civil War, leaving his arm somewhat maimed; owned a farm across the road from 'Sugar Hills' area in Hancock County; was a minister at the United Brethren Church, Mohawk, Indiana; taught school in McCordsville/Woodbury; and taught theology at Indiana Central College (now University of Indianapolis).

Reynolds, John W.; 12 Reg Co G, 3 Aug 62-discharged 19 Jun 63, wounds., no date nor place given. a John W. Reynolds married 29 Nov 1871 Maria Bower HC Bk 6-66.

Reynolds, Joseph; 57 Reg Co A, 13 Dec 61-died 15 Jun 63, no place given. A Joseph Reynolds married 10 Jun 1858 Margaret Goddard HC Bk 4-84.

Reynolds, Robert; 132 Reg Co I, 18 May 64-no out date, term expired. See page for his brother, William Reynolds.

Reynolds, William; "William Reynolds was born In Hamilton County, Indiana, 4 Oct 1839, and came to Hancock County at the age of thirteen years. His father, Lewis Reynolds enlisted in Company K, 2nd Indiana Cavalry, and died in the service at

Hancock County Indiana Civil War Soldiers

Louisville, Kentucky. His mother, Matilda (Wallace) Reynolds, is living at the ripe age of 91 years (in 1899).

"William enlisted in Company C, 79th Indiana Infantry, 15 Aug 1862, and served in the battles of Stone River, Chickamauga, Missionary Ridge, with Sherman at Buzzard Roost, Rockyface Ridge, Kennesaw, Rome, Ringgold, siege and fall of Atlanta, Jonesboro, and the final engagements of Franklin and Nashville. At Stone River the explosion of a shell nearby knocked him down, where he lay unconscious between the firing lines until rescued by Union men. The effect of the explosion is permanent damage to his hearing.

"He was discharged 15 June 1865, at Indianapolis. His brother, Robert, served in the 133rd Indiana Regiment. William was married 27 Mar 1862 (HC Bk 4-19) to Nancy Roberts, d/o of Jessie and Martha (Frazier) Roberts. To William and Nancy were born four children: Jesse; Saphronia; Walter; and Julia." HC obit 21 Jul 1917: "William Reynolds died at his home in Maxwell after an illness of some length.

"He was mustered into Company C, 79th Regiment 19 August 1862 and was honorably discharged 3 June 1865 as a sergeant. He is survived by the widow, two sons, Walter and A.C.; two daughters: Mrs. John Plummer; and Mrs. Orville McConnell. Interment Reeves Cemetery." HC Mt.Gilead/Reeves Cemetery: William Reynolds 4 Oct 1839-22 Jul 1917; Nancy A. w/o William 1 Mar 1836-21 Jun 1906. "...William Reynolds, born Hancock County, 6' tall, age 22, light complexion, blue eyes, dark hair. farmer when enrolled..."

Rhue, Perry Jackson; HC obit 2 June 1898: "Perry Jackson Rhue, son of Hiram J. and Margaret Rhue, was born in Hancock County, Indiana, five and one-half miles north of Greenfield, on 28 November 1843. His parents moved to Marshall County in his youth, where he grew to manhood. He volunteered in the service of the late rebellion, enlisting in Company K, 29th Indiana Regiment. 15 July 1861 and served faithfully for four years, four months and seventeen days. He was engaged in the campaigns of Kentucky, Tennessee,

Hancock County Indiana Civil War Soldiers

Tullahoma, including the battles of Shiloh, siege of Corinth, Stone River, Chickamauga, Atlanta and many minor engagements.

"He was married to Sarah C. Fry 20 January 1875 (HC Bk 6-341); to them were born six children, four sons and two daughters; two sons and one daughter preceded him to the spirit land. There survives him a wife, two sons and one daughter, namely: Harvey aged sixteen years; Bertha, nine years; and Ward, five years; an aged father, Hiram J. Rhue of Brandywine Township; one sister, Mrs. Robert Glascock; one brother, A.N. Rhue." HC newspaper 2 Jun 1898: "The funeral of the late Perry Rhue took place at the Cooper graveyard, and was largely attended. The following brethren and comrades served as pall bearers: George W. Duncan; John T. Henry; William P. Denney; David H. Baity; John Kessler; and Martin O. Maley."

Rice, James T.; 106 Reg Co D, 10 Jul 63-17 Jul 63. NOD.

Rice, Perry; 106 Reg Co D, 10 Jul 63-17 Jul 63. NOD.

Richards, David R.; "David R. Richards, s/o John and Rebecca (Moore) Richards, was born in Lawrence County, Pennsylvania, 3 Nov 1840, the day that General William Henry Harrison was elected President of the United States. The Richards family came to Madison County, Indiana, in 1842, where David spent most of his life. He enlisted July 1861, in Company B, 11th Indiana Infantry; was discharged January 1862; and reenlisted July 1862 in Company G, 12th Regiment and was promoted to Orderly Sergeant; he was in the battles of Jackson, Missionary Ridge, Dalton, Resaca, Big Shanty (Marrietta, Georgia), Kennesaw, Buzzards Roost, Peach Tree Creek, the siege and fall of Atlanta, plus other smaller battles.

"At the battle of Resaca, fourteen of his comrades were shot, some of them killed. He was discharged 6 Jun 1865, at Indianapolis. He has been twice married: 1) Emily Davis 1 May 1865, in Hamilton County; 2) Lottie Davis 9 May 1885, no place given. He receives his mail (1899) in Fortville."

Hancock County Indiana Civil War Soldiers

Richardson, Edward; 106 Reg Co D, 10 Jul 63-17 Jul 63. NOD.

Richardson, Henry; 106 Reg Co D, 10 Jul 63-17 Jul 63. NOD

Richardson, Richard; 148 Reg Co F, 9 Feb 65-5 Sep 65. HC Gilboa Cemetery: Richard Richardson, soldier 17 Mar 1835-23 Oct 1906, another source states he died 23 Oct 1900. age 65 years; Jane Richardson w/o Richard, died 22/ 25 Sep 1867, 36y 8m 11d; infant of Richard and Jane, dates illegible.

Richardson, Solomon; 79 Reg Co G, 11 Aug 62, Sgt.-7 Jun 65. A Solomon Richardson married 2 Mar 1858 Matilda Newby HC Bk 4-67.

Richardson, Thomas; 18 Reg, Musician, 16 Aug 61-20 Aug 62. A Thomas Richardson married 1 Jan 1883 Margaret Pope HC Bk 4-370.

Richey, John; HC Mt.Lebanon Cemetery: John Richey died 20 Dec 1888, 65y 7m 2d. No military data.

Richey, John W.; 79 Reg Co G, 13 Aug 62-7 Jun 65. "John W. Richey, died of vascular heart disease, 5 Apr 1912, age 72y 0m 20d; born 16 Mar 1840, s/o Peter and Sarah (Wortman) Richey, John W. Richey's wife is recorded as Barbara; John W. buried HC Mt. Lebanon Cemetery." HC obit 11 Apr 1911: "John Richey, aged 72 years, a veteran of the Civil War, died at his home in east Greenfield. He leaves a widow and several children. Funeral in charge of G.A.R." John W. Richey married 7 Nov 1879 Barbara Grigsby HC Bk 7-132.

Richey, Joseph; 79 Reg Co B, 9 Aug 62-7 Jun 65. NOD.

Richey, Samuel; 79 Reg Co G, 13 Aug 61-2 Dec 62. NOD.

Richie, William G.; 5 Cav Co G, 10 Aug 62-16 Sep 65, Sgt. "...born Tyrone, Ireland, 5' 9" tall, age 31, dark complexion, blue eyes, dark hair, farmer when enrolled..." A William G. Richie married 31 Oct 1867 Lunett Keiffer HC Bk 5-172. HC Park Cemetery: William G. Richie Cpl Co G 5 Ind Cav died 10 Sep 1887, 56y 8m 9d; Lounettie w/o W.G. Richie died 29 Jan 1877 25y 8m 4d.

Richman, Lewis, 99 Reg Co B, 10 Aug 1862-13 Jun 65. "He was in some of the important engagements of the war, among them being the siege of Jackson, Mississippi; Big Black River;, New Hope Church; Dalton; Marietta; Kennesaw Mountain; and the siege of Atlanta. On 22 Jul 1864 he was wounded in the arm at Atlanta and lay in the hospital at Marietta for three weeks, after which he received a thirty day furlough to return home. He rejoined his regiment six miles from Atlanta and from this point was with Sherman on his famous march to the sea.

"His regiment was transferred by boat to Beaufort, and were within a few days march of Raleigh when Lee surrendered. They went on to Washington and took part in the Grand Review before President Johnson. Lewis Richman, s/o Anton and Louisa Richman, was born 15 Feb 1844 on his parents farm in Sugar Creek Township (HC). Lewis was united in marriage 27 Dec 1853 HC Bk 1-82) Sophia Steinmeier (died 10 Nov 1910); eight children: Louisa; Louis; Benjamin; Emma; Annie; Mary; Maggie; and Clara." Contributed by Janet Cox, Shelbyville, Indiana.

Richmond, William; 79 Reg Co D. "The 79th regiment was among the first to arrive on the bloody field of action and took part in the engagements of Richmond, Kentucky; Perryville; Crab Orchard; Stone River; Chickamauga; Missionary Ridge; siege of Atlanta; Dalton; Kennesaw Mountain; Peach Tree Creek; Buzzard's Roost; Lovejoy Station; Ringgold; Wild Cat; Utoy Creek; and the pursuit of Hood to Franklin and Nashville. He stood shoulder to shoulder with his comrades on the march and on the battlefield, and for meritorious conduct was promoted to Corporal and then to Sergeant.

"The early exposure to camp life landed him in the hospital at Nashville where he remained from 25 Dec 1862, until 21 Sep 1863 when he was sent to a convalescent camp near Nashville. In the spring of 1864 he joined his regiment near Resaca and continued with it through the siege of Atlanta, mustered out 7 Jun 1865. Returning to civil life he married Mary Robertson, 20 Aug 1865 His wife's brothers, George and Ralph were

Hancock County Indiana Civil War Soldiers

comrades in Company B, 79th Indiana Regiment, serving until the final muster at Nashville, "

Ridlen, Herman; 5 Cav Co G, bugler, 16 Aug 62-15 Sep 65. "...born Hancock County, 5' 10" tall, age 29, fair complexion, black eyes, dark hair, farmer when enrolled..." HC Mt. Lebanon Cemetery: Herman Ridlen Co G 5 Ind Cav, no dates on stone. Two marriages for a Herman Ridlen: 1) 5 Jan 1854 Maria Duncan HC Bk 3-198; 2) 5 Jul 1881 Sarah McCormick HC Bk 7-268. HC obit 4 May 1905: "Mrs. Sarah Ridlen, age 63 years, wife of Herman Ridlen, died 28 April at her home, 231 West Osage Street, Greenfield. Funeral and interment Mt. Lebanon Church and Cemetery. (There was no stone for Sarah when the cemetery markers were transcribed in 1965.).

Rigney, Willis Griffin; 1st Heavy Artillery/21st Indiana Infantry Co L, roster states, "enlisted 22 Jul 63, deserted 27 Jul 65." During the time Willis Rigney was a member of the 21st Indiana Infantry (1st. Indiana Heavy Artillery), the unit was engaged at Sabine Pass, the Red River campaign and participated in the investment of Mobile (Alabama), and the reduction of Forts, Morgan, Gaines and Spanish on April 1865. At the close of active operations the battery was assigned to duty in Forts, Morgan, Pickens and Barrancas (Florida)...and at other points of river defense, until mustered out 13 Jan 1866.

"The unit rosters described Willis Rigney as age 27; occupation, farmer; gray eyes; dark hair; florid complexion; 5' 8 ½ " tall; enlisted 22 Jul 63, Indianapolis. He was present in Company L, 1st. Heavy Artillery, from 22 Jul 63, until 28 Sep 63 when he was in the hospital with diarrhea at Indianapolis until 11 Oct 63 when he returned to duty. The 1st Heavy Artillery roster report continues, Willis G. Rigney was present in company L for a year from Oct 63 to Oct 64, (but came upon distressing misfortune) and he was confined in Barrune Barrowne (sic) St. prison, New Orleans, Louisiana on 20 Nov 1864; and confined at Police Jail, New Orleans in Dec 1864.

"He was again reported as present in ranks from Jan 65 until Jul 1865. The war was officially over in April of 1865 but "at

Hancock County Indiana Civil War Soldiers

the close of active operations the batteries were assigned to duty in Forts, Morgan, Pickens and Barrancas…and other points of river defense until mustered out 13 Jan 1866." The Descriptive List of Deserters recorded at Fort Gaines, 6 Sep 65 states: Willis G. Rigney deserted 27 Jul 65 at Barrancas, Florida, age 27 years; 5' 8 ½" tall; gray eyes; dark hair; florid complexion; born Pittsylvania, Virginia; due the Government for 1 knapsack/haversack; 1 canteen; 1 half shelter tent; 1 bed sack, single; total $13.15.

A document from the War Department, "dated 20 Jul 1887, states: by Act of Congress, 5 Jul 1887: all charges of desertion and absent without leave subsequent to 1 Jul 65 against Willis G. Rigney, of Company L, 1st Indiana Heavy Artillery, have been removed from his record in this office and he has been discharged 2 Jul 1865.

"Willis Griffin Rigney, s/o William and Mary (Polly) Gibson Rigney, was born in Pittsylvania County, Virginia, 16 Feb 1836. Willis married Elizabeth Hedrick (d/o John and Susan (Midkiff) Hedrick), in Pittsylvania County, Virginia, 26 Oct 1855. A son was born to them 29 Oct 1856. Shortly after his birth Willis and Elizabeth started to Hancock County, Indiana, to an area north of Shirley on the Henry-Hancock line, to be near her brother, Peter Hedrick and his wife, Sophie. Elizabeth died on the trip, place unknown, but Willis continued the trip to Hancock County, with his son, Raleigh Francis, and lived with the brother-in-law, Peter Hedrick. Willis then married 25 May 1860, Elizabeth Stone and their son, Charles was born 1 Jul 1861.

"Willis enlisted in the Union army (as described above), wrote to Elizabeth, but the letters soon stopped, she never heard from him again and assumed that he was dead. In July of 1893, she applied for a Widow's Pension and got the shock of her life. Her husband, Willis G. Rigney, who had not returned to her and his children after the War, was not dead, but living with a third wife, Elizabeth Lane and eleven children in Wayne County, Mississippi. This couple also had two sons, named

Hancock County Indiana Civil War Soldiers

Raleigh and Charles and it was quite convenient for him as all three wives were named Elizabeth and he was never tripped up. "The Widow's Pension application contained affidavits from the father of Willis and from the brother of Willis, also named, Charles, stating they had not heard from Willis since 1868 or 1869 when he wrote to ask for travel money to come home; Willis received the money but did not come home. Willis died in Mississippi on 30 May 1906; Elizabeth (Stone) Rigney died 1928 in Hancock County, Indiana. Elizabeth (Lane) Rigney died in Mississippi 22 Nov 1917. So ends the saga of Willis Griffin Rigney. Two of Willis' brothers fought for the Confederacy, Charles, who survived, and Eli, who died at White Sulphur Springs, now in West Virginia. Contributed by Sherry Rigney, Wilkinson, Indiana.

Riley, George W.; 8 Reg Co I, 8 Aug 61, resigned 4 Mar 63. HC newspaper 10 Jul 1861: We have been informed that Ensign Geo. W. Riley, Company I, 8th Regiment, has been promoted to the Captaincy of a Delaware County company, signed, W.R. Walls, Adjutant of the Regiment, and Orderly L.O. Harris, 2nd Lieutenant." NOD.

Riley, James A.; 5 Cav Co G, no dates. HC newspaper 11 Aug 1864: "Sgt. James A. Riley was taken prisoner during the disastrous expedition commanded by General Stoneman." Andersonville Prison profile, Code #58682, survived, exchanged 1 Apr 1865.

Riley, Mart. W.; 5 Cav. HC newspaper 30 Apr 1863: "Sgt. Mart. W. Riley, 5th Indiana Cavalry, captured a horse thief in Columbus, Indiana, last night, by the name of Hudson Guman. He had in his possession, furloughs from the 12th and 17th regiments. He has been sneaking around the country stealing horses for the last six months. The Sergeant deserves great credit for his energy. During the last four months he has arrested one-hundred-seventy-two deserters. He is well worthy of a promotion."

HC newspaper 19 Jul 1863: "Sergeant M. W. Riley, of Capt. Riley's Cavalry Company, is one of the most successful of

Hancock County Indiana Civil War Soldiers

Capt. Braden's police force. On yesterday he handed over his two-hundredth man, the same being Charles Gapen lately of this place, and often reported as dead. "Mart" has proved himself an efficient soldier and is honestly entitled to promotion, which we understand is in store for him on a suitable vacancy opening."

Riley, Reuben; organized and Captain of first unit in HC, 22 Apr 16-6 Aug 61; 30 Oct 62 commissioned into Company G, 5th Cavalry, resigned 25 Dec 63. HC obit 7 Dec 1893: "Reuben Alexander Riley, father of James Whitcomb Riley, died at his home in Greenfield of la Grippe, complicated with pneumonia, after an illness of ten days. His daughters, Mr. Henry Eitel and Mrs. Frank C. Payne, of Indianapolis, were with him at his death, but his son, James Whitcomb, did not arrive from Chicago until thirty minutes after his father died. His eldest son, John A. Riley, is at Albuquerque, New Mexico. Short funeral services will be held at the residence, and public services at the First M. E. Church.

"For nearly fifty years Reuben Riley has been a conspicuous and widely known figure in Indiana. His numberless friends scattered throughout the State, who knew him in the days when he wont to set political audiences on fire with character stories dramatically told and always with a point at the end to clinch and argument or embarrass an opponent by setting the audience roaring. He was presumably Irish on his father's side and German on his mother's side, her maiden name was Margaret Schleich.

"Capt. Riley was born in Bedford County, Pennsylvania, 7 June 1819, and soon afterward came to Randolph County, Indiana. After reading law with Hon. Andrew Kennedy of Muncie, Mr. Riley was admitted to the bar, went West where he practiced law for two years in Iowa and then returned of Indiana. He married 20 February 1844, Miss Elizabeth, daughter of Rev. John Marine, at Union Port, Randolph County. He and his bride then came to Greenfield, which has been his home ever since.

Hancock County Indiana Civil War Soldiers

"On the breaking out of the war of the rebellion, he forsook his law practice and all his personal interests and enlisted and organized the first company of soldiers that went into the service from this county. He was elected captain of same, and joined the Eighth Indiana Regiment, participating in the West Virginia campaign. During the engagement at Rich Mountain a shell burst in a few paces of where Capt. Riley was discussing the situation with a lieutenant. The captain fell stunned, being left for dead. The lieutenant was pierced with a piece of the shell and also fell, but leaped to his feet and ran down the hill, crying: "Charge! charge! charge!" falling dead before he had covered sixty yards. Throughout the remaining years of his life, Capt. Riley suffered from the shock of the explosion. His left side was partially paralyzed thereby for a time and the hearing in his left ear almost wholly destroyed. At the close of three months service he organized Company G of the Fifth Cavalry for three years service, and was commissioned captain thereof, and with the same he was assigned to the Ninetieth Regiment.

"His health became so impaired that he resigned 25 December 1863, and was honorably discharged 14 Oct 1864. He served for a short time as judge advocate general, being appointed by General Hovey, and had charge of a number of cases against those suspected of disloyalty to the Union cause, known in history as "Sons of Liberty" or "Knights of the Golden Circle"

"After the war he returned to his home at Greenfield and continued the practice of law, but in a desultory manner, never having the strength or the heart to put in his work that he had before his injuries in the war. His first wife, who was ever delicate but of courageous as well as poetic and sweet temperament, died suddenly in 1870. She was a graceful, poetic writer, and the honored mother of all of his children, the surviving four of whom are above mentioned. Of the other two, Martha, the eldest daughter, died in infancy, and Alexander Humboldt, the youngest son, of brilliant genius, died soon after attaining his majority. The death of his wife was an

Hancock County Indiana Civil War Soldiers

irreparable loss to Capt. Riley, spreading a somber cloud over all his ambitions, and he dwelt within its shadow until he was called to join her in another and better sphere/. After remaining a widower a number of years, he married Miss Martha Lukens, of near Pendleton, who survives him. From the time of his second marriage he did but little work in the line of his profession. He continued, however, to take a good deal of interest in politics and at one time received the nomination for Congress on the Greenback ticket and made the race but unsuccessfully. He also interested himself in literary work. In addition to being a prose writer, he was endowed to a considerable extent with poetic talent. His sincerity and honesty of purpose were so apparent that he always commanded the respect and enjoyed the confidence of all who knew him, even those with whom he differed the most widely.

"He was a member of the Masonic Fraternity, but had not for a number of years been in affiliation or actively in the work of the order. Capt. Riley was instinctively a gentleman, always polite and courteous to those whom he came in contact without regard to their circumstances or condition in life. He was generous to a fault, and his memory will be held sacred by those whose privilege it has been to meet and know him as a friend." HC Park Cemetery: Reuben A. Riley 1819-18931 Capt. Co G 8 Reg Ind Vol; Co G 5 Cav Ind Vol; Elizabeth M. Riley w/o Reuben 1823-1870; Martha Lukens Riley 1836-1918.

Riley, S.P.; HC McCordsville Cemetery: S.P. Riley 41 Ind Cav, no other data; Lizzie w/o S.P. Riley 11 Aug 1847-17 May 1894. NOD.

Ringwalt, Isaac; 12 Reg Co B, Sgt, 15 May 61-19 May 62. NOD.

Rittenhouse, John; 51 Reg Co D, 14 Dec 61, discharged, no date. NOD.

Robb, Thomas; 9 Reg Co C, 14 Feb 64-28 Sep 65. NOD.

Roberts, Albert Thomas; 9 Reg Co G, 8 Mar 65-28 Sep 65. HC obit 20 Jan 1921: " Sorrow has come to us through the

Hancock County Indiana Civil War Soldiers

death of our dear companion, father and friend, Albert Thomas Roberts, who departed this life 8 Jan 1921. He was born in Hancock County, Indiana, 10 April 1835, and was the son of Michael G. and Susan Roberts. He was married to Rachel Addington 14 August 1862 (HC Bk 4-344), to this union were born four sons and two daughters.

"On 13 February 1877, he was married to Amy Addington (HC Bk 6-502) and to this union were born two sons, now deceased. On 18 September 1880, he was married to Sarah Ellen Sears (HC Bk 7-204) and to this union were born three sons and one daughter who is deceased.

"He gave service to his country being a member of Company G, 9th Indiana Regiment, drafted 8 March 1865, and received an honorable discharge 28 September 1865. "Uncle Abbie," as he was familiarly known, had been a sufferer from cancer for a long time, but always had a cheerful word. He was a member of the Greenfield Friends Church from which funeral services were conducted. Interment Wilson (Cook) Cemetery." HC Cook Cemetery: Albert T. Roberts Co G. 9 Ind Inf, no dates; Rachel Roberts w/o Albert T. died 13 Aug 1874 28y 3m 3d; Jesse Roberts s/o Albert T. died 22 Aug 1874.

Roberts, James; 26 Reg Co I, 13 Aug 62. NOD.

Roberts, Samuel; HC Philadelphia Cemetery: Samuel Roberts Civil War Soldier, no unit nor dates. HC obit 18 Mar 1880: "Samuel Roberts died at his residence in Philadelphia (HC), 14 March. He leaves a wife and three children to mourn his loss. His remains were followed to the cemetery by the Philadelphia Brass Band." A Samuel Roberts married 28 Jan 1878 Clarissa Scott HC Bk 6-576.

Roberts, Sebastian; 9 Cav Co B, 2 Jan 64, died Vicksburg, 15 May 1865, Corp'l. A Sebastian Roberts married 3 Apr 1861 Mary Heathcock HC Bk 4-256.

Roberts, William H.; 79 Reg Co C, 15 Aug 62-7 Jun 65. "...born Marion County, Indiana, 5' 5" tall, age 27, light complexion, blue eyes, dark hair, farmer when enrolled..." A

Hancock County Indiana Civil War Soldiers

William H. Roberts married 19 Sep 1861 Rebecca Reper HC Bk 4-284.

Robertson, George; 79 Reg Co B, 9 Aug 62-7 Jun 65. NOD.

Robertson, Ralph; 79 Reg Co B, 9 Aug 62-7 Jun 65. "...born Hancock County, 5' 6" tall, age 18, dark complexion, blue eyes, light hair, farmer when enrolled..." NOD.

Robinson, Benjamin; 13 Cav Co I, 23 Dec 63-30 Sep 65. NOD.

Robinson, Peter; 9 Reg Co D, 24 Feb 65-28 Sep 65. "Peter Robinson, widowed, age 65 years, died 17 Jun 1909, Wilkinson, Hancock County, Indiana, s/o Peter and Katherine (Sheets) Robinson; buried (HC) Harlan Cemetery." No data when grave markers were transcribed in 1989.

Robinson, Samuel; 8 Reg Co B, 25 Aug 61, died Vicksburg Jul 63. NOD.

Robinson, William; 9 Cav Co B, 13 Nov 63-10 Jul 65. NOD.

Rock, William Henry Harrison; 139 Reg Co E, 5 Jun 64-29 Sep 64; also 147 Reg Co H, 11 Mar 65-4 Aug 65. "Washington 21 Mar 1865, Special Order No. 137:The following named enlisted men are hereby discharged the service of the United States, to date 10 Mar 1865 to enable them to accept promotion as commissioned officers. They having been mustered in a as such 11 Mar 1865 pursuant to instructions from this office. They will refund all Bounties which they may have received as enlisted men:
"Private William H.H. Rock, Company G 147th Indiana Volunteers, mustered in as 2nd Lieutenant, same regiment. Signed, By order of Secretary of War, E.D. Townsend, Assistant Adjutant General." Son of Charles (1816-1888) and Lucinda (Stratton, 1825-1912) Rock, William H.H. Rock was born 1844, married 1) Mary E. Stewart 26 Nov 1867 HC Bk 5-179; married 2) Rebecca Ann Reeves 8 Aug 1862 HC Bk 6-119. HC Park Cemetery: William H.H. Rock 1844-25 Mar 1910, Lt. Co H 147 Ind Inf; Rebecca Ann Rock w/o Lt. William H. 1851-25 Jan 1930. Contributed by Rebecca Pernice, Augusta, Michigan.

Hancock County Indiana Civil War Soldiers

Rockey, Isaac; 79 Reg Co B, 9 Aug 62, roster states: "deserted 9 Nov 62." NOD.

Rockey, John; 5 Cav Co G, 18 Aug 62, no other dates. HC Philadelphia Cemetery: John Rockey Civil War Soldier. NOD.

Roland, George; 99 Reg Co B, 23 Mar 64-5 Jun 65. "George Roland, Jackson Township, Hancock County, Indiana, died 20 Sep 1910, wife Minerva Roland, George born 6 Sep 1847, s/o Chapman and Elsa (Kiser) Roland." 99 Regiment History states: "George Roland, recruit; 1900 residence, Charlottesville, Indiana." HC Simmons Cemetery: George Roland 1847-1910; Minerva Roland 1850-1921.

Roland, Jefferson; 34 Reg Co D, 21 Sep 61-3 Feb 66. HC obit 13 Jul 1899: "Jefferson C. Roland, a citizen of Greenfield and an old soldier, died very suddenly of heart failure. He was a gallant soldier and served through the War in the 34th Indiana Volunteers. He was 58 years of age and leaves a wife and several brothers and sisters to mourn his sudden death. He was buried by the G.A.R. boys of Greenfield at Simmons Cemetery." HC Simmons Cemetery: Jefferson Roland 8 Apr 1842-8 Jul 1899.

Rollins, Jasper; HC New Palestine Cemetery: Jasper Rollins Co B 8 Ind Inf. NOD.

Romack, George; 12 Reg Co B, 15 Mar 61-19 May 62. HC obit 26 Feb 1885: "George Romack, age 54, died 20 Feb 1885, of lung fever at the residence of Wilson Johns in Blue River Township. Years ago George and his wife separated as man and wife, on account of his using too much intoxicants. Living in a lonely hut, his life was a sorrowful one, but he bore his fate without complaint, and worked and drank as the desire or appetite demanded. His wife has always been kind to him, and in his last sickness she gave her undivided attention to his comfort. But all to no purpose for owing to his habits he was an easy victim for the great destroyer." A George Romack married 10 Sep 1854 Mary A. John HC Bk 3-234.

Roney, _ T; "died in Civil War." NOD

Hancock County Indiana Civil War Soldiers

Roney, Ben A.; 8 Reg Co B, 25 Aug 61-28 Aug 65, wagoner. Benjamin Roney married 15 Mar 1869 Isabella Arnett HC Bk 5-288. " Benjamin A. Roney, Sr., age 72, died 21 Jan 1915, Buck Creek Township, Hancock County, Indiana, wife Isabelle, occupation farmer, born 2 May 1842, Marion County, Indiana, s/o John and Pattie (Plummer) Roney." HC obit 28 Jan 1915: "Ben Roney, for years one of the best known farmers and stockmen in Buck Creek Township, died at his home, resulting from a fall some weeks ago, when he suffered a broken hip, and a complication of troubles arising from old age.

"He was a Civil War veteran and badly wounded in the neck at the battle of Cedar Creek. He leaves a widow and four children: Porter and Benjamin; Mrs. Jesse Keller; and Mrs. W.E. Stookey." HC Arnett Cemetery: Benjamin A. Roney 1842-1915; Isabella Arnett Roney 1847-1932; children of Benjamin and Isabella: Ella died 11 Feb 1888, 18y 10m 26d; Laura Belle died 28 Oct 1889, 2y 3m 6d; and Walter died 7 Apr 1875, 9y 17m 0d.

Roney, Edward; 8 Reg Co B, 25 Jul 61, died Syracuse, Missouri 15 Dec 1861. NOD.

Roney, Samuel; 79 Reg Co D, 8 Aug 62, 20 Jul 64, transferred to Pioneer Corps which is a unit used with the Engineer Corps to clear rough terrain, build roads and bridges making a route on which the Army could travel easily and quickly. A Samuel Roney married 17 Mar 1867 Sarah Dilman HC Bk 5-123.

Rowland, Joseph; 57 Reg Co A, 13 Dec 61-17 Aug 63. NOD

Rozel, (Rosel) William; 148 Reg Co A, 2 Feb 65-5 Sep 65. A William Rozzell married 28 Apr 1889 Gertrude Hawkins HC Bk 8-149.

Rumler, Anthony Vantley; residence, Alfont, 12 Reg Co G, 14 Aug 62-8 Jun 65. Participated in the battles of Shenandoah, Leesburg and Winchester, West Virginia; Richmond; Holly Springs; Missionary Ridge; the Atlanta campaign; battles of Resaca; Kennesaw; Jonesboro; "Sherman's March to the Sea;" Savannah; Columbia and Goldsboro. HC obit 15 Aug 1910:

Hancock County Indiana Civil War Soldiers

"Again we are reminded that the place we now occupy is not our home, but one by one we are called to enter the realms of the undiscovered country of the soul, the bourne from which no traveler ever returns.

"This time the remembrance comes from the death of Anthony V. Rumler, who was born 1 September 1838, in Hancock County, Indiana, died 25 July 1910, age 71years, 10 months and twenty-four days. At the tender age of seven he was thrown upon his own resources and had to battle with the stern realities of life, but being of that strong character, which marked his every step in later life he was able to successfully overcome his early environments and make such a success in life that few ever do.

"At the age of 23, he was married to Nancy Jane Eakes 25 June 1861 (HC Bk 4-270). About fourteen months after entering the blessed ties of matrimony, he heard the call of our nation, and on 14 August 1862, he bade the companion and first-born son goodbye and served until the end of the war. The sacrifice, the heartaches, the ordeal through which he passed no one knows but those who have had the experience. But we would not leave him struggle thus alone. The faithful wife had a share in this ordeal and followed him through the papers and letters. At night when her babe was fast asleep she would kneel and pray that God would send him back..

"That prayer was answered. He did return. They later learned from each other that at the same time each had had a dream that he would not return. But the wife prayed the more ardent and he that night promised God if he would let him come home, he would serve him. He kept his vow and upon returning joined the United Brethren Church and was converted and followed the Lord faithfully. Nine children were born to this union, two died in infancy, one Mrs. Jane Tuttle died in early married life. There remain to mourn their loss: George M. Rumler; Mary E. Rumler; Luzene Price; Ella Wilson; Viola Bell; Maggie Swartz; and eleven grandchildren, with a host of friends and comrades. He fought for the Lord and the church and when

Hancock County Indiana Civil War Soldiers

nearing the crossing he told his children at different times all was well. He was ready to meet the Master and his Lord. His constant theme was his family, the church and the boys in blue. "He was a member of the G.A.R. post at Fortville and attended as often as possible. He was never too tired to tell the children and grandchildren the stories of the army which he served so faithfully. We lay him to rest and say sleep faithful one until the trumpet shall sound and God shall call the faithful to reward." The obit states "buried Mt. Gilead Cemetery," however, according to cemetery records he is buried (HC) Park Cemetery: Anthony V. Rumler 1 Sep 1838-25 Jul 1910; Nancy J. Rumler w/o Anthony V. 8 Oct 1843-3 Jul 1926; Mary E. Rumler d/o Anthony and Nancy 17 Sep 1866-22 Nov 1932. Contributed by Diana True, McCordsville, Indiana.

Ruddick, (Rudrick) William; 11 Reg Co I, 28 Feb 65-26 Jul 65. NOD.

Rush, James; HC Caudell/Simmons Cemetery, James Rush 15 Ind Inf. NOD.

Russell, James; 9 Reg Co D, 24 Feb 65-28 Sep 65. A James Russell married 14 Oct 1858 Elizabeth Humphries HC Bk 4-102. NOD.

Russell, John; 106 Reg Co D, 10 Jul 63-17 Jul 63. HC soldier burial record: John Russell, 61 years, farmer, died 17 Aug 1902, buried Mt. Comfort Cemetery." No data on him when the grave markers were transcribed in the 1960s.

Russell, Joseph M.; 9 Cav Co B. "Joseph M. Russell, s/o James T. and Nancy (Carter) Russell was born in Madison County, Indiana, 3 Aug 1845. Joseph was living at Fortville (HC), Indiana, when he enlisted 15 Oct 1861, and later was promoted to farrier. He was with his command in pursuit of Hood and was in numerous engagements before the final stand at Franklin and Nashville. At the battle of Franklin his command was cut off from the main force and cut their way through enemy lines, nine men in his company were killed. At Sugar Creek, Alabama, a bullet just grazed his leg saving a wound.

Hancock County Indiana Civil War Soldiers

"He was discharged at Vicksburg 20 Aug 1865. His father, James T. Russell and three brothers served in Indiana regiments. Upon returning he resumed farming and 5 Sep 1870, married (HC Bk 5-399) Sarah Farrell, who was born 1 Jul 1848, Green Township, Hancock County, Indiana. Their children: Minnie; Maud; Nora; and Mattie. Joseph is a comrade of the Kempton G.A.R. Post at Fortville. HC obit 7 Jun 1923: "Joseph Russell, who was a Civil War veteran and had long resided in Hancock County, died at his home near Eden, age 77 years. Four daughters survive: Nora; Minnie Murphy; Maud Manifold; and Mattie Bradley. Interment Cook Cemetery." HC Cook Cemetery: Joseph M. Russell 3 Aug 1845-5 Jun 1923; Sara J. Russell w/o Joseph M. 1 Jul 1848-10 Sep 1909.

Russell, William; 9 Reg Co D, 24 Feb 65-28 Sep 65. NOD.

Rynearson, George; 8 Reg Co G, 22 Apr 61-6 Aug 61. NOD.

Rynearson, William; 38 Reg Co D, 3 Oct 64-24 Jun 65. HC obit 9 Sep 1909: "William Rynearson, an old soldier, 82 years of age, died at the home of his daughter, Mrs. C.M. Jackson, Mechanic Street. He was stricken with paralysis. Funeral services at Phildelphia M.E. Church." HC Phildelphia Cemetery: William Rynearson died 1909, 38 Ind Inf Co D.

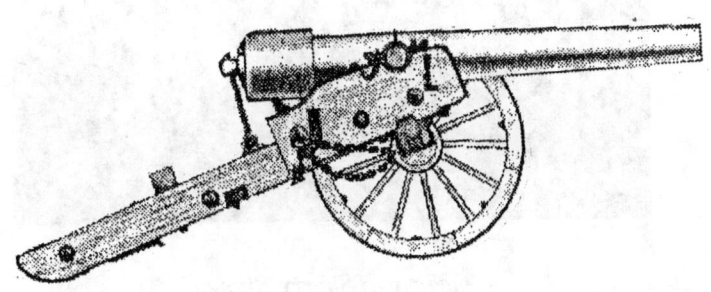

Hancock County Indiana Civil War Soldiers

Willis Rigney

Courtesy of Sherry Rigney

Hancock County Indiana Civil War Soldiers
William H.H. Rock

Courtesy of Rebecca Strickland Pernice

Hancock County Indiana Civil War Soldiers

Anthony V. Rumler

Courtesy of Louise Boyd

Hancock County Indiana Civil War Soldiers

◄ S ►

Sample, James Q.; 99 Reg Co B, 13 Aug 62, died of wounds 7 Jul 64. A James Quincy Sample married 29 Sep 1853 Elizabeth McQuarry HC Bk 3-180.

Sample, John S.; 12 Reg Co G, 22 Feb 64-29 May 65, Sgt. A John Sample married 17 Jan 1845 Elizabeth Drake HC Bk 2-145. HC McCordsville Cemetery: John S. Sample 1829-1894; J. S. Sample Sgt Co G 12 Ind Inf; Ellen Sample w/o John S. 1832-1915.

Samuels, John A.; 5 Cav Co G, 18 Aug 62-15 Sep 65. HC newspaper 11 Aug 1864: "John A. Samuels was taken prisoner during the disastrous expedition commanded by General Stoneman." Andersonville Prison profile code #59082: John Samuel, Company G, 5 Indiana Cavalry, survived. "John A. Samuels, age 69, died 6 Feb 1909; born 9 Nov 1839 s/o Addison and Nancy (Tharp) Samuels; wife Phebe A. Samuels."
HC obit 11 Feb 1909: "John A. Samuels, 69 years of age, veteran of the Civil War, died at his home on South East Street (Greenfield) from the effects of a stroke of paralysis.
"He was taken prisoner at Macon, Georgia, in 1864, and taken to Andersonville Prison, where he was confined for nine months. He leaves a widow and four children. The funeral was in charge of the G.A.R. of which the deceased was a member " HC Park Cemetery: Jno. Samuels Co G 5 Ind Cav.

Samuels, Thomas; 105 Reg Co E, 11 Jul 63-18 Jul 63. HC newspaper 18 Jun 1903: "Thomas Samuels, of Kansas City, Kansas, is in the city (Greenfield). He formerly resided here and will be remembered by the many old citizens. He recently suffered the loss of all his belongings in the recent flood in and around Kansas City."

Sanders, William H.; 75 Reg Co I, 15 Jul 62-8 Jun 65, Corp'l. A William H. Sanders married 2 Jan 1887 Clara Brier HC Bk 7-747.

Sandy, John A.; 148 Reg Co F, 17 Feb 65-5 Sep 65. NOD.

Hancock County Indiana Civil War Soldiers

Sanford, Francis Marion; 8 Reg Co B, 8 Aug 62-14 Jun 65. "...born Hancock County, Indiana, 5' 7" tall, age 26, dark complexion, gray eyes, dark hair..." "He was in engagements of Grand Bluff, Magnolia Springs, Winchester, Black River, was wounded in battle and had his feet frozen from exposure." "Francis Marion Sanford, widowed, age 94 years, died 30 Jun 1931, of gangrene of the feet, he was born 7 Aug 1836, s/o Moses and Jane (Hill) Sanford."
HC obit 2 Jul 1931: " Francis Marion Sanford, a Civil War veteran, answered the call at his home two miles north of Philadelphia (HC), after an illness of some duration. Mr. Sanford was born in Greenfield (Indiana), 7 August 1836, and was the second white child born in this city. For a number of years he resided in Green Township on a farm. He was a member of Company B, 8th Indiana Infantry during the Civil War and was the second oldest veteran in the county. He was the father of Isaac; Jasper; Noble; and Lewis Sanford; and a daughter Mrs. Lula Lamb, who with a brother, Joseph, survive. Services were conducted at Otterbein Church where he had been a member nearly all his life. Interment Philadelphia Cemetery." Francis Sanford married 20 Mar 1858 Rebecca Adams HC Bk 4-129. HC Philadelphia Cemetery: Francis M. Sanford 1836-1931; Rebecca J. Sanford 1840-1921.

Sapp, William; 26 Reg Co I, 24 Sep 64-6 Sep 65. NOD.

Sargent, James; HC Courthouse, Soldier Burial List: no unit given; died 16 Jan 1904; 71 years; occupation, cooper; burial, Simmons Cemetery, Fortville, Indiana. NOD.

Sargent, Thomas; 34 Reg Co D, 21 Sep 61, no out date. A Thomas Sargent married 23 Feb 1850 Julia Ann Snider HC Bk 2-374.

Savage, John; 12 Reg Co B, 15 May 61-19 May 62. NOD.

Schaub, Phillip; 116 Ohio Inf Co C, 12 Dec 63, wounded 5 Jun65, Piedmont, Virginia, out 14 Jun 65. "Phillip Schaub, age 89, died 20 Aug 1926, born 24 Sep 1836, Ohio, s/o Phillip Schaub, born Germany and Cathrin Schaub, born Germany. HC obit 26 Aug 1926: "Phillip Schaub, a veteran of the Civil

Hancock County Indiana Civil War Soldiers

War and one of the county's oldest residents, died at his home in Charlottesville. He was ninety years old and a bachelor. He was a member of the G.A.R. and had been wounded during his three years' service in the War. Funeral conducted at the McCarty Funeral Home in Fortville."

There is also another Phillip Schaub "who died at age 88 years, 11 Dec 1891, residence Fortville, born Germany, s/o of Christopher Schaub, (father of above Phillip?) reported by J.H. Alford."

Schleter, Christian; HC New Palestine Cemetery: Christian Schleter Company B 25 Ind Inf. NOD.

Schrieber, Henry A.; 106 Reg Co D, 10 Jul 63-17 Jul 63. HC newspaper 13 Oct 1881: "Another of our businessmen died 5 October, Henry A. Schrieber, at the age of 41 years. He had been sick for about five months, during which medical aid was employed but to no purpose. During his life he taught several schools in this township (Sugar Creek) and for four years was Justice of the Peace, and in business in New Palestine fifteen years. He may also have been a member of the Hancock bar. Mr. Schrieber leaves a wife and one daughter, twelve years of age. He was buried at the New Palestine Cemetery." HC New Palestine Cemetery: Henry A. Schrieber died 5 Oct 1881, 40y 10m 12d; Alice E. w/o Henry died 9 Mar 1918, 88y 8m 27d.

Schultz, Henry; HC McCordsville Cemetery: Henry Schultz, soldier, 9 Jul 1833-20 Jan 1914. NOD.

Scott, Aaron; 8 Reg Co B, 25 Aug 61-4 Sep 64. "...born Hancock County, Indiana, 5' 10" tall, age 29, fair complexion, gray eyes, fair hair, farmer when enrolled..." HC newspaper 25 Sep 1861: "While in line awaiting orders, Aaron Scott was quoted as saying 'wherever Capt. Walls wants Aaron Scott to go, he will go or die.' " HC newspaper 18 Aug 1862: "Corp'l. A. Scott of Company B, 8th Regiment, has been promoted to Sergeant" HC newspaper 25 May 1863: "Sgt. Aaron Scott, Company B, 8th Regiment, was wounded in the finger." HC obit 6 Mar 1919: "Aaron Scott, aged 83 years, formerly of Greenfield, and a well-known Civil War veteran, died at the

Hancock County Indiana Civil War Soldiers

home of his daughter, Mrs. Daisy Daugherty, of Elwood, Indiana.

"Mr. Scott served through the entire duration of the war, in the 8th and 18th Indiana Regiments. He participated in twenty-six battles. For many years he was an active member of the G.A.R. post having attended all the reunions of the veterans. Mr. Scott was born in Hancock County, near Greenfield, 5 June 1835, and was married to Matilda Elsbury. They moved to the vicinity of Elwood in 1866, where they have since resided. eight out of twelve children survive: Nannie Robertson; Daisy Daugherty; Carrie Quinn;Oma Miles; Cora Nuding; Lodina Pontius; and Ed Scott. His wife died twenty-four years ago."

Scott, Burt; 53 Reg. Co A, 24 Oct 62, killed 22 Jul 64, Atlanta, Georgia. HC newspaper 4 Aug 1864: "We are sorry to learn that Company A, 53rd Indiana, has met with another severe loss, Burt Scott of Hancock County has been killed."

Scott, Charles W.; 99 Reg Co B, 13 Aug 62-23 Aug 64, 18 May 65, transferred to 48 Reg. A Charles W. Scott married 23 May 1866 Adaline Brown HC Bk 5-63. HC Simmons Cemetery: Charles W. Scott s/o E. and M., 1 Jul 1846-13 Oct 1868. 99 Regiment History states: "Charles W. Scott was wounded at Dallas, Georgia 28 May 1864; he is dead in 1900."

Scott, David; HC newspaper 1 May 1864: "We paid a visit to Capt. Riley's command. We found the boys well, and full of hope and spirit and anxious for the active duties of a soldier. The company ranks with any on the ground. We return our thanks to David S. Scott, cook of the Captain's mess, for a good and wholesome dinner. Though physically disabled from bearing arms, Davy is determined to do what he can for his country."

Scott, George W,; 4 Cav Co A, no dates. "A George W. Scott, widowed, 73 years, occupation: ex-soldier, died 24 Mar 1909, Hancock County, Indiana, of cerebral hemorrhage, born 15 Jun 1835, Ohio, s/o Arthur Scott." HC Philadelphia Cemetery: George W. Scott Co A 4 Ind Cav no dates.

Hancock County Indiana Civil War Soldiers

Scott, James; 53 Reg Co A, 24 Oct 64-31 May 65. HC newspaper 4 Aug 1864: " Company A, 53rd Regiment, has met another severe loss. James Scott has been wounded and is in the hands of the enemy." Andersonville Prison Profile, code #59257: Private J. Scott, Company A, 53rd Indiana, survived, exchanged Atlanta, 17 Sep 1864."

Scott, James; "A James Scott, Greenfield (HC), age 62 years, died 1 Feb 1885, born Coshocton, County, Ohio, s/o David and Lisha (Lord) Scott, reported by William Scott, Greenfield." A James Scott married 3 Apr 1845 Jane Plummer HC Bk 2-156. HC Curry's Chapel Cemetery: James Scott 1 Feb 1823-1 Feb 1885; Jane died 26 Jul 1892.

Scott, James P.; 8 Reg Co B, 27 Aug 62, died 30 Oct 62, St. Louis, Missouri. NOD.

Scott, John; He was born 26 June 1830 in Hancock County, Indiana, to Noble Felix Scott and Elizabeth (Gunn) Scott. John married Eliza Ann Alyea 15 Sep 1850 (HC Bk 3-8) and was a school teacher in the Scott School, #5, on land given by his father, Noble Scott, in Brandywine Township before entering the Civil War. On 8 August 1862 John Scott enlisted at Indianapolis for three years service, and was a Private Company B, 8th Regiment Volunteers. He died of disease 12 Sep 1863 in a hospital in New Orleans, Louisiana, and is buried at Monument National Cemetery situated at Chalmette, Louisiana, in the parish of St. Bernard, six miles below the city of New Orleans, #3322

"Although his body was never brought home to Hancock County, there is a monument in Mt. Lebanon Cemetery, on State Road 9 south of Greenfield, Indiana, stating these facts. John's widow, Eliza, received a pension, certificate #41483, for soldier John Scott service: P.B. 8th Indiana Infantry. It was reported by the Commissioner of Pensions: Eliza A. Scott was last paid at $12.00 to 4 May 1900 and has been dropped because of death, date unknown. HC Mt. Lebanon Cemetery: Eliza A. Scott 23 Oct 1829-26 May 1900. See letter written during the Civil War by John Scott to his wife, Eliza, and the

Hancock County Indiana Civil War Soldiers

letter Eliza received at John's death, in the letter chapter of this volume. Contributed by Doris Scott Badgley, Greenwood, Indiana.

Scott, John; HC Courthouse, Soldier Burial List Book: 155 Reg Co E; died 25 May 1901; 73 years; occupation, farmer; burial, Kinnamon Cemetery, location not given. NOD.

Scott, John H.; 79 Reg Co G, 22 Aug 62-7 Jun 65, Sgt. HC obit 13 Jan 1916: "Death invaded the home of Mr. and Mrs. John H. Scott, husband and wife passing to the great beyond within hours of each other at their home on Douglas Street, Greenfield. John H. Scott was 86 years old and his death occurred at an early hour. Mrs. Emma Munden Scott was 78 years old and her death occurred twenty-four hours later. Mr. Scott was born in Rush County, Indiana, and came to this county, Jackson Township, with his parents in 1834. He was a soldier in Company C, 79th Indiana Volunteers.

"He was twice married, his first wife has been dead a number of years. Seven years ago he married Mrs. Emma Munden. They were members of the Bradley M.E. Church, where the double funeral was held. Mr. Scott is survived by four children from his first marriage: John and Benjamin Scott, Mary Tarbott and Mrs. Cross. "John Harding Scott, age 85, occupation, teacher, died 10 Jan 1916, s/o John and Margaret (Harding) Scott, burial (HC) Park Cemetery, reported by John Scott." HC Park Cemetery: John H. Scott 1830-1916.

Scott, John N.; 16 Ind Mounted Infantry, Co H, 12 Aug 62-30 Jun 65. "...born Fayette County, Indiana, 5' 10" tall, age 35, dark complexion, blue eyes, light hair, farmer when enrolled..." NOD.

Scott, Newton; HC Curry's Chapel Cemetery: Newton Scott Civil War Soldier 2 Feb 1829-31 Aug 1905, no units given. " Newton Scott, age 76 , occupation: farmer, died 31 Aug 1905, cause: chronic diarrhea, s/o David (born Delaware) and Lesha (born Maryland) (Lord) Scott, wife: Rose Scott. An Isaac Newton Scott married 15 Mar 1864 Rozella Graham HC Bk 4-439.

Hancock County Indiana Civil War Soldiers

Scott, Rufus; 9 Reg Co D, 14 Feb 65, no out date. A Rufus Scott married 11 Jul 1859 Elvira Plummer, no place given. HC Park Cemetery: Rufus J. Scott 1831-1897; Elvira C. Scott 1841-1922.

Scott, William J. 54 Reg, no Co; reenlisted into 1st Indiana Heavy Artilley at New Orleans.

Scott, William H.; 12 Reg Co G, 5 Aug 61, transferred to Veteran Reserve Corps, for light duty indicating wound or illness. "A W. H. Scott, age 68, married (no name given), died 1 Feb 1888, Hancock County, Indiana, cause: concussion of brain, born: Ohio, s/o David and Lesha (Lord) Scott, reported by Rufus J. Scott, Greenfield." HC Curry's Chapel Cemetery: A William H. Scott died 1 Feb 1888, 67 years.

Scott, William J.; 8 Reg Co G, 22 Apr 61-6 Aug 61; also 12 Reg Co G, 5 Aug 62, transferred to Veteran Reserve Corps for light duty due to wound or illness. HC obit 31 Jan 1884: "On 24 January 1884, William J. Scott, a soldier of the late war, died at his home in Greenfield (HC) after a short illness. During the War a bombshell burst over his head and since that time he has been an invalid. Some months ago he received a pension from the government amounting to nearly $800.

"A few days before his death he was stricken with paralysis and his condition was too weak to recuperate. He leaves a wife and two children to mourn his sudden death." A William J. Scott married 20 Oct 1861 Susan Atkinson HC Bk 4-292.

Scotten, Ebenezer; 8 Reg Co B, 27 Aug 62, died 29 Mar 63, Helena, Arkansas. See page for his brother, William W. Scotten. Comments in a letter written in a letter from Andrew Fuller to his cousin, Adam F. Wilson, 11 Apr 1863 "E.C. Scotton had been sick or poorly for some time."

Scotten, John B.; 8 Reg, Co B, 26 Aug 61, killed 22 May 63, Vicksburg. HC newspaper 11 Jun 1863: "Private John Scotten, 8th Regiment, killed, signed, S.H. Dunbar, 8th Regiment."

Scotten, William W.; 8 Reg Co B 8 Aug 62-5 Jul 65. HC newspaper 11 Jun 1863: "Private William Scotten of Company B, 8th Regiment, was wounded, left ear amputated." He was in

Hancock County Indiana Civil War Soldiers

the engagements of Thompson's Hill, Big Black River, siege of Vicksburg, wounded 22 May 1863, lost an eye and ear. William was born 6 Jan 1836, in Ohio, s/o Ebenezer and Ann (Welling) Scotten; William married 12 May 1857 Rebecca Hawkins (not HC). HC Philadelphia Cemetery: William W. Scotten 6 Jan 1836-13 Jul 1904; Rebecca Scotten w/o William W. 24 Feb 1833-28 Dec 1908. William W. had two brothers in the War: John B. was killed at Vicksburg 22 May 1863; and Ebenezer C. died Helena Arkansas, 3 Feb 1863.

Sears, Christopher Hugh (Kip); 9 Cav Co B, 9 Dec 63-22 Jun 65. HC obit: " Private Christopher Hugh Sears, late of Company B, 9th Ind. Vol Cav, aged 19 years, seven months and fifteen days, died 7 July 1865, at the residence of his father, one mile northwest of Greenfield. The writer knew him personally from childhood. His life was short and eventful. He was a brave, energetic, industrious boy--restless and uneasy when unemployed, always prompt and confident of success in his undertakings.

"His ardent patriotism only waited the acceptable age--eighteen--the next day he was a volunteer in the glorious army of patriots, so many of whom have fallen, but who have swept armed treason and rebellion from the United States, and purified, vindicated and restored to the suffering down-trodden millions of earth, freedom's hopes and heritage in the United States of America. He was prompt, brave and obedient as a soldier, and was in that unequal and bloody battle at Sulphur Tressel, Alabama, 25 September 1864, where a part of the 9th Ind. Cav. and 4th Tenn. Cav. fought Forrest's entire division of rebels. The entire Union forces there, were captured, but not until the rebel losses were greater than the entire Union forces there.

"He, with the other prisoners, was taken to Cahawba, Alabama, where he remained a prisoner five months and twenty-two days, when he was exchanged and sent to Vicksburg, and after waiting some time for transportation, was crowded onto the ill-fated steamer, Sultana, and started up the

Hancock County Indiana Civil War Soldiers

Mississippi. At 2 A.M., the steamer blew up; the scene that followed defies description; over 1,000 Union soldiers perished. Being unable to swim, he had become insensible; when he came to, he found himself clinging to a floating trough. He floated down 7 miles, and was rescued at daylight, chilled, exhausted and almost perished.

"He arrived at home in feeble health, about the 1st of May. He was honorably discharged by special Order War Dept., on 22 June 1865. He lingered in feeble health, and on 24 June was taken with fever, followed by acute inflammation of the bowels, and as before stated, expired on 7 July. His young and hopeful life, with thousands of others, was patriotically given, that his country with its free institutions might live. He has gone to report to an ever just and merciful God--friend of the young, the approver of the right--and whose only begotten son declared freedom to the world. While patriotism shall endure, memory of her martyrs will ever be sacred. Signed, R.A.R."
HC Park Cemetery: Christopher Sears died 7 Jul 1865 19y 7m 16d.

1860 Hancock County Federal Census, Greenfield, Center Township: William Sears, age 35; Lauretta Sears, age 20; Francis O. Sears, age 18; Christopher Sears, age 14; Serepta Sears, age 12; Mary E. Sears, age 10, Sarah E. Sears, age 8; King A. Sears, age 6; Eliza J. Sears, age 5; William H.H. Sears, age 4; and Washington Sears, age 8/12

Sears, Francis O.; 9 Cav Co B, 9 Dec 63-27 May 65, Sgt. "...born Hancock County, Indiana, 5' 4" tall, age 19, light complexion, hazel eyes, dark hair, farmer when enrolled..." A Francis O. Sears married 4 Sep 1867 Sarah E. Taylor HC Bk 5-160. HC Park Cemetery: Francis Sears died 9 May 1874, 29y. See page for his brother, Christopher Hugh Sears.

Seely, William; 9 Cav Co B,13 Nov 63, died 25 Feb 65, Gallatin, Tennessee. NOD.

Seely, William H.H.; 25 Aug 61, no out date. HC newspaper 6 Nov 1862: "**Deserter** KNOW ALL MEN BY THIS THAT William H. H. SEELY, a private in Captain William R. Walls

Hancock County Indiana Civil War Soldiers

company B, 8th Indiana Foot Volunteers, deserted the service of the United States, on the 8th day of October, 1862. Said soldier was enlisted 20 August 1861, was mustered into service 25 August 1861. He is 19 years of age, 5 feet 4 ¾ inches high, fair complexion, fair hair, blue eyes, born in Gallatin County, Illinois, and by occupation when enlisted a farm laborer. Signed, William R. Walls, Capt. Co B, 9th Ind Inf. "

Sellery, Peter; 8 Reg Co B, 25 Aug 61, died 8 Apr 62, Lebanon, Missouri. NOD.

Sellery, Thomas J.; 26 Reg Co I, 18 Feb 65-15 Jan 66; also listed on roster as Thomas J. Siberry. NOD

Sellery, William; 26 Reg Co I, 17 Feb 65-15 Jan 66; also listed on roster as William Siberry. NOD.

Seward, William H. HC Philadelphia Cemetery: William H. Seward 15 Ind Light Artillery, no dates; Annie 1849-1894. A William H. Seward married 10 Sep 1865 Maria Ann Cly HC Bk 4-533. "William H. H. Seward, died 30 Nov 1903, age 75, cause: apoplexy, married: name not given, born 5 Feb 1828, Indiana, s/o Samuel P. and Eliza (Smith) Seward, buried (HC) Philadelphia Cemetery."

Sewell, Jacob; 79 Reg Co D, 14 Aug 62-7 Jun 65. A Jacob Sewell s/o Fielding married 19 Sep 1866 Mary Barnard, no place given.

Shafer, Hiram Robert; 12 Reg Co G, 16 Oct 62-14 Jun 65. "He was first sent to Memphis, then to Vicksburg which was evacuated on the third day he was there. He was in the engagement of Chattanooga, Tennessee, 25 Nov 1863, served in and around Knoxville, Tennessee, Scotsboro, Alabama, took part in the severe engagement at Resaca, Georgia, where he was wounded in the left arm above the elbow by a musket ball, 13 May 1864, a wound which confined him to a hospital until the close of the war, when he was honorably discharged.

"Hiram Robert Shafer was born in Lawrence County, Pennsylvania, 21 Sep 1845, s/o John and Mary Ann (Joseph) Shafer, another source states his mother was Eliza Snodgrass; and married 1) Mary C. Hood 24 Oct 1869 (HC Bk 5-333), two

Hancock County Indiana Civil War Soldiers

children, Mary and Annie; married 2) Minerva Allen 11 Mar 1875 (HC Bk 6-352), three children: James, Minnie and Ida." HC Simmons, Caudell Cemetery: Hiram R. Shafer Soldier 21 Sep 1845-28 Jul 1911; Mary C. Shafer w/o Hiram 24 Oct 1849-2 Mar 1874; Minerva Shafer w/o Hiram 25 Jul 1848-6 Jun 19_4.

Shafer, Isaac; 9 Cav Co B, 13 Nov 63-7 Jul 65. NOD.

Shafer, Ira; 57 Reg Co A, 13 Dec 61-10 Mar 63. Three marriages for an Ira Shafer: 1) Mary Harris 31 Mar 1867 HC Bk 5-126; 2) Maria Lummis 17 Mar 1870 HC Bk 5-364; and 3) Minerva Anderson 1 May 1879 HC Bk 7-94.

Shafer, Jacob; 5 Cav Co G, 18 Aug 62-8 Jun 65. HC newspaper 11 Aug 1864: "Private J. Shafer, Company G, 5th Cavalry, was taken prisoner during the disastrous expedition commanded by General Stoneman." Andersonville Prison Profile Code # 59405: Private Jacob Shafer Company G, 5th Regiment, survived and sent to Millen, 11 Nov 1864. Jacob Shafer married Katherine Shaffer (?) 24 Nov 1859 HC Bk 4-164. "Jacob Shaffer, age 68 years, died 31 Aug 1903, cause Bright's disease, born 1 Dec 1834, Pennsylvania, s/o Samuel and Betty (Basor) Shaffer, wife Katie Shaffer, burial, Fortville, Indiana."

Shaffer, James; 9 Cav, Co B, 13 Nov 63-7 Jul 65, saddler. Hamilton County, Indiana, Old Fort Cemetery: James Shafer Co B 9 Ind Cav, no dates.

Shaffer, Joseph; 12 Reg Co G, 21 Jul 62-8 Jun 65, absent at muster out, sick. Three marriages for a Joseph Shafer: 1) Margaret Atkinson 22 Feb 1857 HC Bk 4-5; 2) Sara Fort 12 Mar 1866 HC Bk 5-41; 3) Kate Reynolds 27 Nov 1872 HC Bk 6-159.

Shaffer, Milo; 12 Reg Co G, 21 Jul 62-8 Jun 65, Corp'l. NOD. 1860 Census, Hancock County records a Milo, age 17 and William, age 19, in household of John Shaffer, age 58, no female recorded as possible mother.

Shaffer, Peter; 12 Reg Co G, 21 Jul 62-8 Jun 65. A Peter Shaffer married 4 Jan 1866 Mary Beaver HC Bk 5-106.

Hancock County Indiana Civil War Soldiers

Shaffer, William; 12 Reg Co G, 8 Aug 62, killed 17 Aug 64, Atlanta. A William Shaffer married 19 Nov 1862 Sarah Springsteal HC Bk 4-361. See data for Milo Shafer.

Shaw, George; 79 Reg Co B, 9 Aug 62-7 Jun 65. NOD.

Shaw, Isaac; 99 Reg Co B, 13 Aug 62, died 30 Mar 64, at Andersonville Prison, wounds. 99th Regiment History states: "Isaac Shaw died 18 August 1864, in service." He is not on the database at Andersonville Prison.

Shaw, William R.; 99 Reg Co B, 13 Aug 62, died 5 Nov 1864, Andersonville Prison. HC newspaper 9 June 1864: "W.R. Shaw, Company B, 99th Regiment, missing in action, 28 May 1864." Andersonville Prison Profile Code #21842: Private William R. Shaw Company B, 99th Indiana Infantry died of wounds, 5 Nov 1864, grave #11842.

Sheets, Benjamin; 79 Reg Co B, 9 Aug 62-7 Jun 65. NOD.

Shelby, Calvin; 38 Reg Co C, 31 Oct 64, no out date. A Calvin Shelby married 28 May 1864 Sarah Eastes HC Bk 4-457. "Calvin Shelby, retired farmer, age 71 years, died 7 Apr 1914, Tague Street, Greenfield, Indiana, wife Sara A. Shelby; Calvin was born 5 Mar 1841, s/o Joshua and Nancy (Dunn) Shelby." HC Philadelphia Cemetery: Calvin F. Shelby 1841-1914 Co C 38 Ind Inf; Sara A. Shelby 1844-1922. See data on his brother Samuel Newton Shelby.

Shelby, Samuel Newton; 8 Reg Co B, 28 Feb 62, 20 Nov 62, discharged disability. ..."discharge certificate states: Samuel N. Shelby was born in Hancock County, Indiana, is 18 years of age, 5 feet 8 ½ inches high, dark complexion, dark eyes, dark hair, and by occupation when enlisted a farmer. dated, 20 November 1862." He told of being a member of the Mississippi Marines (see chapter telling of this unit). Samuel told of an encounter about firing from the boat on a town near Vicksburg, and of being in a camp where he saw and heard President Lincoln give a speech.

HC newspaper 16 Feb 1933: "Samuel Shelby, aged Greenfield resident and Civil War veteran, was the object of two youths who attempted to extort fifty dollars from him. Mr. Shelby was

Hancock County Indiana Civil War Soldiers

accosted by the two youths, who were riding in a Ford roadster, as he was walking down town. They represented themselves as being federal employees of the pension department. After producing several papers pertaining to Mr. Shelby's pension, the youth's informed Mr. Shelby that a fifty dollar fee was required by the government. Refusal of Mr. Shelby to pay led the youths to reduce this amount to twenty-five dollars.

"Mr. Shelby informed the youths that he was on his way to the bank, and it was arranged for them to meet him at the same place later in the morning. Mr. Shelby continued to the bank and informed Freeman Wilson, an employee of the bank, what had taken place. City police were called and Mr. Shelby returned to North Street, where he had encountered the youths. Although Mr. Shelby waited for them to reappear and city police made an extended search in that vicinity, no trace of the two men could be found."

"In Memory of Samuel N. Shelby, 2 Feb 1936: Samuel N. Shelby, son of Joshua W. and Nancy Dunn Shelby (married 26 Dec 1839 HC Bk 1-190) was born in Buck Creek Township, Hancock County, Indiana, 1 September 1843. Here he resided with his parents on the farm. Rural life in those days was not easy. We can recall many interesting descriptions given by him, of life on the farm at that time. The home was a log cabin. Crops were raised on plots cleared of trees and undergrowth which they formerly bore. In later years he derived much pleasure by telling of experiences and acquaintances of those earlier days. On 8 August 1862, at the age of 18, he was enlisted in Company B of the Eighth Regiment of Indiana Volunteers. Here he served his country in the war for preservation of the union.

"At the time of his discharge from the army he returned to the home of his parents in Buck Creek Township. Here he resided until 14 September 1874, when at age 31, he was married to Miss Nancy Grist (HC Bk 6-302), a young woman of that neighborhood. To this union were born three children, one daughter and two sons. The family lived together on a farm in

Hancock County Indiana Civil War Soldiers

their home neighborhood until 12 July 1880 when Nancy Shelby, the beloved wife and mother, passed away (at age 26y 10m 11d, buried HC Park Cemetery).

"He and the children remained together on the farm and in July 1884, he was united in marriage with Sarah J. Handy. To this union were born five children, two sons and three daughters. In 1888 the family moved to a farm in Jackson Township. In 1928 the home was destroyed by fire and the old couple moved to Greenfield. Here they lived together until 27 April 1931, when again his beloved companion was taken.

"After her death he remained at his home in Greenfield until last September when he took up his residence with his daughter, Mrs. Bertha Kirkpatrick, who lives five miles east of Greenfield. Here on 30 January 1936, he quietly passed away at the age of 92 years and five months. He is survived by three sons, Edgar, Harry and Raymond Shelby; four daughters, Stella Johnson; Bertha Kirkpatrick; Helen Hull; and Mary Sullivan. He has been a Mason for sixty-five years, being the oldest Mason in Hancock County and was the last surviving member of Dunbar Post G.A.R. He leaves three comrades of the Union army in Hancock County." Interment HC Park Cemetery. Contributed by Jim Shelby, Greenfield, Indiana.

Shell, Louis; HC New Palestine Cemetery: Louis Shell Co B. 8Ind Inf. NOD

Shellhouse, Chandler 106 Reg Co D 10 Jul 63-17 Jul 63. NOD.

Shellhouse, Conrad H.; 8 Reg Co G, 22 Apr 61-6 Aug 61; 106 Reg Co D, 1st. Lieut:10 Jul 63-17 Jul 63; and 26 Reg Co I, 24 Sep 64-6 Sep 65. A Conrad Shellhouse married Netta Anderson 22 Oct 1862 (HC Bk 4-355) he was buried 6 Mar 1918 Crown Hill Cemetery, Marion County, Indiana. An Esther R. Shellhouse was buried 21 Sep 1896 at Crown hill Cemetery. Conrad's son, Frank, was born in New Palestine 4 Sep 1863, and was Commander-in-Chief of Sons of Union Veterans of the Civil War; died 16 Oct 1942, buried Crown Hill Cemetery.

Hancock County Indiana Civil War Soldiers

Shellhouse, Edward S.; 144 Ohio Inf Co D, 2 May 64, 13 Aug 64, wounded at Berryville, Virginia, out 31 Aug 64. HC Park Cemetery: Edward S. Shellhouse Co D 144 Ohio Inf died 17 Apr 1910, age 75.

Shelton, James T.; 29 Reg Co K, 5 Oct 64-21 Oct 65, enlisted as substitute. HC death notice: "James T. Shelton died at his home on Wood Street (Greenfield). He was seventy-nine years old and one of the youngest men who served in the Union army during the Civil War." HC obit 13 Oct 1927: James T. Shelton was born in Brown County, Ohio, 31 March 1848, son of Martin A. and Cornelia (Pitcher) Shelton.. When a small boy, the family came to Clay County, Indiana, and later to Sugar Creek Township, Hancock County, Indiana, and sixteen years ago moved to Greenfield where he continued to live until his death 4 October 1927.

"Mr. Shelton was a Civil War veteran, having volunteered and served his country in Company K, 29th Indiana Infantry. He was honorably discharged 27 October 1865. On 5 April 1874, he married Sirmilda (Sirilda) Stafford (HC Bk 6-268). To this union were born two children: William N., Spring Lake; and Myrtle who died in 1893 at age 12 years (buried Park Cemetery). He is survived by the wife, one son, William, and one brother, Asbury Shelton. Interment (HC) Park Cemetery." HC Park Cemetery: James T. Shelton died 6 Oct 1927, age 79 years, Co K 29 Ind Inf, 1848-1927.

Shelton, Martin; 8 Reg Co B, 28 Feb 62, died 28 Feb 65, Savannah, Georgia. A Martin Shelton married 22 Dec 1844 Cornelia Pitcher HC Bk 2-139.

Shepherd, Thomas; HC Courthouse, Soldier Burial List Book, 9 Cav Co M; died 23 Mar 1906; 63 years; occupation, mail carrier; burial, Rushville, Indiana. NOD.

Sherf, Felix; 12 Reg Co B, 23 Oct 61, recorded as "1 Dec 1861, sent to insane asylum, Washington, D.C."

Sherman, Jeremiah; 75 Reg Co I, 15 Jul 62-8 Jun 65. NOD.

Sherman, John; 75 Reg Co I, 15 Jul 62-8 Jun 65. Pension papers state "slightly wounded in the left arm at the battle of

Hancock County Indiana Civil War Soldiers

Chickamauga, 20 Sep 1863; slightly wounded in the head at a battle near Atlanta, July 1864; was in Sherman's 'march to the sea' and became ill in December 1864 with rheumatism, yellow jaundice, and a rupture of the stomach."

"John Sherman was born 4 Dec 1838, Hamilton County, Indiana, married Mary Hiday 7 Dec 1867 HC Bk 5-181. Mary Hiday was born 22 Jul 1842, Fortville, Hancock County, Indiana, d/o John Henry and Mary (Wynne) Hiday. John and Mary (Hiday) Sherman were the parents of Cora, Oscho, Jasper, Clinton and Perry; Cora and Oscho died just a few days apart in August 1877, family tradition says they died in a diphtheria or typhoid epidemic.

"According to pension records, John Sherman moved his family to Missouri in autumn of 1878, possibly to Bates County as reference was made by a neighbor. John Sherman stated in pension record: "In Indiana 'till 1879; in Missouri 'till 1883; in Oregon 'till 1885 0r 1886 (recorded on 1885 Oregon territorial census) and since then in Washington." He applied for a Declaration of Homestead in Lewis County, Washington, 7 February 1897. John Sherman died 9 March 1927, Lewis County, Washington.

Obit 11 Mar 1927, Lewis County, Washington: "John Sherman, a resident of Harmony for the past 46 years, died at the family home at age 89 years. Mr. Sherman was a veteran of the Civil War, and always a respected citizen of his community. He ;eaves one son, Perry Sherman, a well known farmer of Harmony, and three grandchildren. Funeral service at the home and interment at Harmony Cemetery." Contributed by Harriett Miller, Salem Oregon.

Sherman, Thomas; 12 Reg Co B, 15 May 61, record states, "deserted 19 May 61." NOD.

Sherrett, Isaac; HC death notice 8 Nov 1928: "Isaac Sherrett, who was a soldier in the Civil War, died at his home three miles east of Fortville. Funeral at Menden Church with interment in the church cemetery. Mr. Sherrett was 88 years

Hancock County Indiana Civil War Soldiers

old and is survived by three sons: Charles and Howard of Fortville and Lon of Eden."

Sherrill, John W.; 9 Cav Co B, bugler, 13 Nov 63-28 Aug 65. Hamilton County, Indiana, (Old) Fort Cemetery: John W. Sherrill, bugler Co B 9 Cav. NOD.

Shipley, Francis, 5 Apr 64-26 Dec 64. A Francis Shipley married 9 Mar 1868 HC Bk 5-210 Menora Brizendine. 99 Regiment History states: "Francis Shipley, recruit, discharged 26 Dec 1864; dead in 1900." HC Mt. Gilead/ Reeves Cemetery: Francis M. Shipley died 1 Jan 1873 30y 4m 0d; James C. s/o Francis M. died 6 Feb 1871 3m 7d.

Shipley, Reason; 99 Reg Co B, 14 Apr 64-26 May 65. A Reason Shipley married 12 Feb 1867 HC Bk 5-116 Ann Bright. 99 Regiment History states: "Reason Shipley, recruit, residence, Greenfield; dead in 1900."

Shipman. James J.; 99 Reg Co B, 13 Aug 62-5 Jun 65. 99 Regiment History states: "James J. Shipman, residence in 1900, North Branch, Kansas."

Shipman, William; HC newspaper 9 June 1864: "Corp'l. William Shipman, Co B, 99 Cavalry, wounded badly in the face in battle at Dallas, Georgia, 28 May 1864." 99 Regiment History states: "Corporal William Shipman, Cleveland (HC) died 30 May 1864 of wounds received 28 May 1864. A William Shipman married 30 Dec 1859 Sarah Kingen HC Bk 4-114.

Shirley, Doctor J.; 30 Ind Co G, 26 Sep 64-15 Aug 65. HC obit: "Doctor Jackson Shirley, age 78 years and a Civil War veteran, died at his home on Spring Street, following an illness of more than a year of heart trouble. Mr. Shirley fought through the Civil War as a member of Company G, 30th Indiana Infantry. He was a member of the Grand Army and the United Brethren Church. Mr. Shirley is survived by the widow and five children: Mrs. William Andis; Mrs. Thomas Cohee; Mrs. George Gleaner; Roy and Alvah Shirley. HC Mt. Lebanon Cemetery: Doctor J. Shirley Co G 30 Ind Inf 1843-1921; Margareta w/o Doctor J. 1849-1929.

Hancock County Indiana Civil War Soldiers

Shirley, William R.; 148 Reg Co C; 17 Feb 65-5 Sep 65. NOD.

Shirm, Jacob; "died from effects of wounds sustained in the Civil War," his widow, Elizabeth, was the daughter of John K. and Margaret (Fuqua) Rash.

Shorn, Sylvester; 8 Reg Co G, Musician, 22 Apr 61, discharged 6 Jun 61, disability. NOD.

Short, Hugh; 105 Reg Co E, 11 Jul 63-18 Jul 63; 9 Cav Co B, 9 Dec 63, died 12 Sep 64, Pulaski, Tennessee. NOD.

Short, Joseph; 8 Reg Co G, Band, 5 Sep 61-28 Aug 65. HC Philadelphia Cemetery: Joseph F. Short Co A 41 Ind Inf 1839-____. A Joseph Short married 4 May 1871 Jennie Burk HC Bk 6-17.

Short Joseph T. 77 Reg Co A 4 Aug 62-3 Jun 65. "...born Hamilton County, Ohio, 5' 1 ½" tall, age 21, light complexion, gray eyes, light hair, painter when enrolled..." NOD.

Short, William; 8 Reg Co G, 22 Apr 61-6 Aug 61; 8 Reg Co B, Sgt. 25 Aug 61-no out date. NOD.

Shroy, Dezra; 12 Reg Co G, 16 Aug 62-8 Jun 65. NOD.

Shull, Freeman; 12 Reg Co G, 18 Aug 62-8 Jun 65. A Freeman Shull married 10 Dec 1865 Emeline Gwin HC Bk 5-11.

Shull, John; 12 Reg Co G, 18 Aug 62-8 Jun 65. HC Caudell/Simmons Cemetery: John Shull 1842-1911 Soldier. Two marriages for a John Shull: 1)27 Apr 1856 Sarah Robbins HC Bk 5-53; 2) 6 Jul 1860 Elizabeth Morris HC Bk 4-191.

Shull, Joseph; 77 Illinois Inf Co G, 12 Aug 62-10 Jul 65. "...born Ohio, 5' 8" tall, age 34, light complexion, gray eyes, brown hair, farmer when enrolled; battles: Yazoo Swamp; Port Gibson; Black River Bridge; Hansfield, Spanish Fort; Arkansas Post; Champion Hills; Vicksburg; and capture of Mobile." A Joseph Shull married 4 Nov 1868 Mary Ann Kingen HC Bk 5-259.

Shull, William J.; 26 Reg Co H, 24 Sep 64-6 Sep 65. HC obit 8 May 1924: "William J. Shull, age 87, Civil War veteran and pioneer of this community died at the home of his son, Willis, south of Fortville, after a two weeks' illness occasioned by a stroke of paralysis. Mr. Shull, s/o M___ and Mary (Caudell)

Hancock County Indiana Civil War Soldiers

Shull, was born near the scene of his death and lived his entire life in this community.

"He was a retired farmer and since the death of his wife five years ago, he made his home with his son. He is survived by two sons, Edward and Willis; a brother Jackson; and a half sister, Miss Nettie Shull." William J. Shull married 1 Oct 1862 Nancy M. Smith HC Bk 4-350. HC Caudell/Simmons Cemetery: William J. Shull Soldier 15 Dec 1836-3 May 1924; Nancy M. Shull 1 Sep 1842-18 Jan 1918.

Shultz, Joseph F.; 57 Reg Co A, 17 Oct 61-27 Dec 65. "In 1862 he was promoted to First Sergeant and his command almost constantly engaged with the enemy. He participated in the battle of Shiloh, Stone River, Chattanooga, Lookout Mountain, Missionary Ridge, Bull's Gap, then to Atlanta where his regiment joined Sherman and engaged in battle of Kennesaw Mountain where on 23 June 1864, he received a gunshot wound in the left side. He was taken to a hospital in Big Shanty (Marrietta, Georgia) where he recuperated enough to be sent home to Charlottesville (HC) and was mustered out 27 Dec 1865, Indianapolis.

"Joseph F. Shull was born 25 Dec 1835 in York County, Pennsylvania, s/o Jacob and Mary (Feree) Shull. He learned the shoemaker's trade early in life and followed it until the spring of 1857, when he came to Hancock County. He located at Charlottesville with Peter Case in his boot and shoe shop until he joined the union army in 1861." Joseph F. Shull, age 76, died 5 Aug 1912 at Charlottesville, cause septicemia, gunshot wound with fistula resulting, duration 50 years; retired shoe maker, wife, Margaret; Joseph buried Henry County, Knightstown, Indiana. Joseph F. Shull married 1) 3 Nov 1859 Margaret Dungan HC Bk 4-160 who died 21 Jan 1871, 30y 8m and is buried HC Six Mile Cemetery: married 2) Margaret Brown 14 Mar 1878 (no place given) who died 7 Jul 1897."

Shumway, Salem O.; 123 Reg Co K, 18 Jul 64-21 Aug 65. "The regiment was moving on with Sherman into the Atlanta campaign when Salem fell into line with his comrades at

Hancock County Indiana Civil War Soldiers

Resaca, Kennesaw Mountain, Buzzard's Roost, Peach Tree Creek, Atlanta and numerous minor engagements. At the battle of Kennesaw Mountain, he was one of six who volunteered to make a hazardous advance on the enemy's picket and skirmish line, resulting in the loss of three of his comrades. The next day while erecting a fort, a log rolled on him causing permanent damage to his back and he was sent to the hospital at Marietta, Georgia.

"He was granted a thirty day furlough in time to go home and vote. He was honorably discharged 21 Aug 1865. He married 1) 25 Jan 1866 Harriett Bowling, a native of Rush County, Indiana; married 2) 13 Mar 1893 Clara Coffin. Greenfield has been his home his 1872. Salem O. Shumway's father, Salem M. Shumway, served as Lieutenant in Company F, 52 Indiana Infantry."

HC obit 15 Mar 1917: "Salem O. Shumway, aged 76, died suddenly at his home on Pennsylvania and Pierson Streets, Greenfield, from the effects of a stroke of paralysis. He was a son of Rev. and Mrs. Salem M. Shumway, born in Vermont, coming to Greenfield many years ago from Franklin County, Indiana. The younger Salem was a well-known citizen, a contracting carpenter and constructed a number of the best residences and other buildings in this community, among them the Methodist Protestant Church in 1887. He is survived by the widow and four children, Mrs. Sam Knight; Mr. F. Shumway; Tadd Shumway and Miss Grace Shumway." HC Park Cemetery; Salem O. Shumway Co K 123 Ind Inf 31 May 1841-14 Mar 1917' Harriett Shumway w/o Salem O. 11 Nov 1846-4 Mar 1892.

Shutes, Joseph (David); 51 Reg Co K, 23 Feb 63, missing in action Stone's River, Murfreesboro, Tennessee.

Siberry, Thomas J.; 26 Reg Co I, 18 Feb 65-15 Jan 66. Also listed on roster as Thomas J. Sellery. NOD.

Siberry, William; 26 Reg Co I, 17 Feb 65-15 Jan 66. Also listed on roster as William Sellery. NOD.

Hancock County Indiana Civil War Soldiers

Siddell, William; 99 Reg Co B, 13 Aug 62-5 Jun 65. HC Simmons Cemetery: William Siddell Co B 99 Ind Inf. 99 Regiment History states: William Siddell, residence, Cleveland (HC), dead in 1900.

Siders, William; "enlisted 1864 to serve in Civil War; he died from eating poisonous food after having gone for days on scant rations during the Nashville campaign and is buried in Nashville National Cemetery; wife Hester (Unrue) Siders, two children, George and Amanda."

Simcox, John W.; 9 Reg Co D, 14 Feb 65-28 Sep 65. NOD.

Simmons, John A.; 57 Reg Co A; 13 Dec 61-24 Dec 62. HC obit 2 Feb 1911: "John A. Simmons, an old soldier of Company A, 57th Indiana Volunteers, died Saturday evening. His funeral was preached at the Friends Church with interment in McCray Cemetery (military data only on stone)." "John A. Simmons, widower (wife not named), died 28 Jan 1911, Brown Township (HC), cause: desire to die and failure to take medicine and nourishment, age about 68 years, born Ohio, s/o Matthias and Mary Simmons."

Simmons, William; 9 Reg Co C, 14 Feb 65-28 Aug 65. This soldier may or may not be the following William H. Simmons, as his obit says nothing about having served in the Civil War.

Simmons, William H.; HC obit 3 Apr 1919: "William Simmons died at his home south of Wilkinson, after an illness of several years. He was 77 years of age and was one of the oldest and wealthiest pioneer residents of the county, having come here as a baby with his father from Virginia. He is survived by the widow, formerly Miss Charity Williams (married 4 Oct 1866 HC Bk 5-89), and several children. Funeral at Wilkinson and interment at Simmons Cemetery, which many years ago was located on his father's farm." HC Simmons Cemetery: William H. Simmons h/o Charity 1841-1919. See above William Simmons.

Simpson, Absalom; 84 Reg Co F, 10 Aug 62-14 Jun 65. "..born Butler County, Ohio, 5' 7 ½ " tall, age 20 years, light

Hancock County Indiana Civil War Soldiers

complexion, gray eyes, dark hair, clerk when enrolled..." NOD.

Siplinger, William H.; 8 Reg Co B, 25 Aug 61-28 Aug 65. HC newspaper 11 Jun 1863: "Pvt. William H. Siplinger reported wounded slightly in foot near Vicksburg, Mississippi." William H. Siplinger married 24 Jan 1859 Destimony Adkins no place given; also married 20 Nov 1877 Barbara Shirrell HC Bk 6- 559.

Sisson, Marquis Lafayette; 139 Reg Co E, 5 Jun 64-29 Sep 64, residence or place of enlistment, Henry County, Indiana. "HC newspaper 22 Aug 1907: "I find that Marquis Lafayette Sisson, age 61 years, 11 months and 2 days, came to his death at the home of his son, Dr. Ernest Sisson, 103 Grant Street, in the city of Greenfield, Hancock County, Indiana, on the 19th day of August 1907, from natural causes. signed Joseph L. Allen, Coroner Hancock County." "Marquis Lafayette Sisson died 19 Aug 1907, age 61 years, wife Nancy (Harold) Sisson, occupation, farmer, cause, valvular heart disease since Civil War, born 17 Sep 1845 in New York, s/o Nelson (born New York) and Jane (Thompson born Pennsylvania) Sisson, burial, Shiloh, Rush County, informant, Dr. Ernest Sisson, Greenfield."

Sitton, Raleigh; no units given. "Raleigh Sitton died 19 Apr 1915, Maxwell (HC), cause: injuries received from falling brick wall due to gas explosion, wife Nancy J. Sitton, Occupation, farmer, born 11 Aug 1841 in North Carolina, s/o William and Massey (Pendergraft) Sisson, burial Park Cem." Raleigh Sitton married 5 Mar 1863 Mary Jane Chappell HC Bk 4-381.

HC newspaper 22 Apr 1915: "A gas explosion caused by hunting a leak with a match happened at Maxwell. For some days past a gas leak at the barber shop of Jacob Sutton was quite noticeable. Jesse Anderson, a plumber was called to find and repair the leak. Like in all small towns there is generally a good number around and about a barber shop. This was the case at Maxwell. Among those at the building while the leak

Hancock County Indiana Civil War Soldiers

was looked for and repairs made were Jesse Anderson, Jake Sutton, Raleigh Sitton, Fred Fort, Walter Roberts, Sam Roberts and John Hudson.

"The leak was found on the outside of the building at a connection some inches from the south wall. It took only a few minutes to make repairs and stop the leak. None of the above named was in the shop, all being on the outside watching the progress of the work, with the exception of the two who were sitting on the west side of the building. After the work had been completed, Mr. Raleigh Sitton, a soldier of the Civil War, with the half of one leg long since gone, said, "Strike a match and see if the leak is stopped." No sooner had the match been lighted than the long escaping gas under the building was ignited, this followed by a second explosion.

"The east and south walls of the building were blown entirely out and Raleigh Sitton, Civil War veteran and ex-recorder of Hancock County, was caught under the falling debris, being entirely covered by the brick of the south wall. His cries were heard from beneath the brick and debris and willing hands were soon at work locating the place where he was. He was taken to his home, just back of the wrecked building, where death soon followed from injuries received. Mr. Sitton was one of the best known men of the county, and for many years was in the huckster business. He was 73 years of age and leaves a widow and ten children: Mrs. Volney White; Mrs. Bruce Alford; William Sitton; Mrs. William Hudson; Mrs. Riley Jacobs; Fred Sitton; Marion Sitton; Mrs. Ira Dobbins; Mrs. Worth Crossley; and Mrs. James Garrett." HC Park Cemetery: Raleigh Sitton 11 Aug 1841-19 Apr 1915; Nancy J. Sitton w/o Raleigh 20 Jan 1846-____.

Sivey, Dewitt; 5 Cav Co C, 14 Aug 62, Corp'l,-15 Jul 65. HC newspaper 26 Jan 1899: "Dewitt Sivey, Greenfield, was a member of Company C, Fifth Cavalry, during the Civil War." Dewitt Sivey married 19 Nov 1868 Anna Snider HC Bk 5-264; also married 16 Oct 1888 Mary Davis HC Bk 7-30. HC Park

Hancock County Indiana Civil War Soldiers

Cemetery: Dewitt C.Sivey 1840-1929; Mary D. Sivey w/o Dewitt 1853-1913.

Skinner, Alfred; 105 Reg Co E, 11 Jul 63-18 Jul 63. HC obit 5 May 1898: "Alfred Skinner died at the East North Street (Greenfield) residence of his daughter, Mrs. Jesse Millikan after a long illness. "Uncle Alfred" as he was familiarly called, came to Greenfield in the forties and was eighty-two years of age at the time of his death. He was the father of three children, all who survive him, Mrs. Millikan; John Skinner; and a son who lives in Kentucky. He leaves one sister, Mrs. Martha A. Osborn. Interment (HC) Park Cemetery." Three marriages for an Alfred Skinner, 1) 13 May 1849 Mary D. Godding (Gooding?) HC Bk 2-326; 2) 22 Feb 1852 Mary Jane Reed HC Bk 3-84; 3)7 Feb 1860 Mary Jane Skinner (?) HC Bk 4-177. HC Park Cemetery Mary J. Skinner w/o A. died 12 Mar 1865 36y 10m 14d.

Sleeth, Aaron A.; 8 Reg Co G, 22 Apr 61-6 Aug 61; also 53 Reg Co A 24 Feb, no out date. An Alexander Sleeth died 2 Feb 1863, Civil War. NOD.

Sleeth, M. A.; 105 Reg Co E, 11 Jul 63-18 Jul 63. HC death notice 16 Mar 1893: "Morris A. Sleeth, age 72 years, died at Morristown of cancer. Funeral at Morristown, interment Asbury Cemetery."

Sleeth, William M.; 8 Reg Co G, 22 Apr 61-6 Aug 61; also 5 Cav Co G, 18 Aug 62-15 Sep 65. HC newspaper 11 Aug 1864: "Orderly William M. Sleeth was with the company but made his escape with Col. Adams of the 1st Kentucky, signed, Lieut. W.H. Pilkenton, 5 Cav." A William M. Sleeth married 9 Nov 1865 Nancy A. Windsor HC Bk 5-4.

Slifer, George, #1; 51 Reg Co D, 14 Dec 61-25 Jun 65. "George Slifer, age 85 years, widower of Julia, occupation, farmer, died 23 Dec 1928, of organic heart disease, born 19 Dec 1843, Hancock County, Indiana, s/o Jacob and Jane (Lewis) Slifer,." HC Park Cemetery George Slifer 1843-1928; Julia Slifer 1843-1926.

Hancock County Indiana Civil War Soldiers

Slifer, George, #2; transcription of Furlough Document: "The bearer hereof, George Slifer, Private of Captain John Greelish's Company F of the 15th Regiment of the Veteran's reserve Corps, aged 37 years; 5 feet 6 ½ inches high; light complexion; grey eyes; black hair, and by profession a farmer; born in the State of Ohio, and enlisted at Indianapolis, Indiana, on 12 August 1862, to serve three years, is hereby permitted to go to Greenfield, Hancock County, Indiana, he having received a FURLOUGH from the second day of February, to the third of March, at which period he will rejoin his Company or Regiment at Camp Douglas, Illinois or wherever it then may be, OR BE CONSIDERED A DESERTER. Signed Major Cornelius, 3 Feb 1865.

"Claim For Widow's Pension, With Minor Children: Brief in the case of Fanny Slifer, widow of George Slifer, Private Company F, 15th Vet Res Corps, Resident of Hancock County, Indiana, Post Office, Greenfield; Medical Certificate on which furlough was granted shows that soldier was (10 Jan 1865) suffering from chronic diarrhea; Army physician testifies that he was at home on furlough in Feb 1865, was physically unfit to return on account of chronic diarrhea and that he died of said disease at Greenfield 30 Apr 1865; the marriage of George Slifer and Friday Andrake solemnized, 1 Oct 1846, Wayne County, Indiana; Names and Dates of Birth of Children: Mary Ann born 8 Mar 1852; Catharine O. born 14 Mar 1854; Amanda M. born 10 Apr 1862; Issue Certificate for $8.00 dollars per month, commencing 1 May 1865, and two (?) dollars per month additional for each of the above-named children, commencing 25 Jul 1866.

"Declaration For Widow's Army Pension: 5 Apr 1866; Fanny Slifer, age 35 years, widow of George Slifer, deceased, applied for pension on George Slifer's army service (all above facts included); witnesses to the document are John Andrake, brother and sister, Mary Wortz, of the applicant. Widow's Claim For Increase Of Pension: 15 Jan 1867 Fanny Slifer, age 38 years,

Hancock County Indiana Civil War Soldiers

applied for an increase of pension #124744." Contributed by Sandra Day, Greenfield, Indiana.

Slifer, Lafayette; 8 Reg Co G, 22 Apr 61-6 Aug 61. HC obit 7 Jul 1927: "Lafayette Slifer, an old soldier, was born in Knightstown, Indiana, 24 December 1839, s/o Jacob and Jane Slifer and departed this life 22 Jun 1927, at age 87 years, at the home of his daughter, Mrs. Walter Christy, Indianapolis. He is survived by his wife, Arabella Morris Slifer, to whom he was united in marriage 2 Oct 1862. Survivors, Mrs. Christy; Mrs. W.G. Evans; grandson Harry Seger Slifer; two brothers, Washington and George; three sisters, Mrs. Sarah Stephens; Pauline Rumwell; and Emma Pruice. His son, Harry Otis Slifer, preceded him to the Better Land some ten years ago." Lafayette Slifer married 5 Oct 1862 Arabella Morris HC Bk 4-350. HC Park Cemetery: Lafayette Slifer, Co I 8 Ind Inf 1839-1927; Arabella Morris Slifer 1845-1931.

Slifer, Levi; 8 Reg Co G, 22 Apr 61-6 Aug 61; 99 Reg Co B 13 Aug 62-5 Jun 65. "...born Burkes County, Pennsylvania, 5' 3" tall, age 29 years, dark complexion, blue eyes, dark hair, farmer when enrolled..." HC Caldwell Cemetery: Levi Slifer Co B 99 Ind Inf no dates.

Slifer, Wilson; 8 Reg Co B, 28 Feb 62-18 Dec 62. HC newspaper 6 Dec 1917: "Wilson S. Slifer, of Shelbyville, Illinois, arrived in Greenfield on Friday last. He is now 80 years of age and very active for one of his years. He reads without the use of glasses. He is the last of his father's family which consisted of twelve children. Wilson is the father of thirteen children, eleven of whom are alive today. He has one son and five grandchildren in the present war and he is an old soldier himself, having passed through the War of the Rebellion. Some fifty years ago he was a resident of this county."

HC obit 18 Nov 1920: from Shelbyville, Illinois newspaper: "Mr. W.S. Slifer was born in Wayne County, Ohio, on 22 Nov 1837, and died at his home near Beecher City, on 13 Nov 1920, age 82y 11m and 21 d. He was united in marriage to Amanda

Hancock County Indiana Civil War Soldiers

Gephart of Hancock County, Indiana, on 26 Feb 1857, at the home of John Craft. To this union were born thirteen children, eight sons and five daughters, all living except two, Mary, who died in infancy, and Mrs. Charles Bartscht, who passed away about nine years ago. His loving helpmate preceded him to the better world 5 Aug 1905."

Smail, John; "In 1863 he enlisted for the Civil War, subject to call, belonging to the National guards, but was never called out. John Smail for many years was the favorite boot and shoe maker and dealer in Fortville (HC) and a resident of the village since 2 January 1866. He was born in Berks County, Pennsylvania, 20 April 1844, son of Beneville and Hannah (Ulrich) Smail. John married Josephine Stuart (20 Jan 1867 HC Bk 5-113), five children: Clara May; John Charles; Mary Melvina; Horace Beneville; and Oma Eliza."

Smith, Andrew; 5 Cav Co G, 18 Aug 62-15 Sep 65. The following data detailing a man, who was born in 1817, making him age about 44 years old at the outset of the War, may or may not concern the Civil War soldier, An Andrew Smith married Sarah Fitzpatrick 3 May 1840 HC Bk 1-207. An Andrew Smith is recorded in HC obit 26 Dec 1889: "Andrew Smith died at his home north of Cleveland (HC) 22 Dec 1889, aged 72 years. Funeral services at the M. E. Church in Cleveland, interment Caldwell graveyard." HC Caldwell Cemetery: Andrew Smith 16 Sep 1817-22 Dec 1889; Sarah Smith 19 Aug 1818-8 Aug 1897.

Smith, Asa; 148 Reg Co C, 17 Feb 65-5 Sep 65, Corp'l. An Asa Smith married 12 Jun 1867 Elizabeth Arnold HC Bk 5-139. NOD.

Smith, August; 9 Cav Co B; 9 Dec 63-28 Aug 65, bugler. An Augustus Smith married 10 Dec 1869 Mary Jane Leachman HC Bk 5-340.

Smith, Bright ; also recorded on roster as Smith as first name and Bright as last name; 99 Reg Co B, 13 Aug 62, 2 Jun 64, killed at battle of New Hope Church. NOD

Hancock County Indiana Civil War Soldiers

Smith, Charles; 34 Reg Co D, 21 Sep 61, discharged disability 17 Mar 63. HC soldier burial: a C.C. Smith, age 68, died 19 May 1901, Greenfield. NOD.

Smith, C.W.; Andersonville Prison Profile Code #59912: Private C.W. Smith, Company G, 5th Indiana Cavalry, survived and released." NOD

Smith, Edward; 12 Reg Co B, 15 May 61-19 May 62; 99 Reg Co B, 13 Aug 62-5 Jun 65. "...born Hancock County, Indiana, 5' 7" tall, age 20 years, light complexion, blue eyes, light hair, farmer when enrolled..." An Edward Smith married 14 Sep 1865 Josephine McCray HC Bk 4-536. 99 Regiment History states; "Edward C. Smith, in 1900 resides Centralia; Kansas."

Smith, George W.; 8 Reg Co G, 22 Apr 61-6 Aug 62; 8 Reg Co B 25 Aug 61-18 Feb 63. Two marriages for a George Smith: 1) 25 May 1848 Martha Plummer HC Bk 2-284; 2) 5 Feb 1876 Elizabeth Rosebury HC Bk 6-438.

Smith, Henry; HC Courthouse, Soldier Burial List Book: 11 Cav Co B; died 26 Dec 1899; 57 years; occupation, butcher; burial, (HC) New Palestine Cemetery. NOD.

Smith, Henry; HC McCordsville Cemetery: Henry N. Smith Ind Cav, no company number, died 28 Dec 1866. NOD.

Smith, John; 5 Cav Co G, 18 Aug 62-15 Sep 65. Andersonville Prison Profile, code #60015: Private John Smith, Company G, 5 Indiana Cav, prisoner, survived; released, no date."

Smith John H.; 6 Cav Co I, 16 Aug 62-15 Sep 65. "...born Rush County, Indiana, 5' 10" tall, age 30 years, fair complexion, blue eyes light hair, farmer when enrolled..."

Smith John P.; 94 Reg Co F, no dates. "A John P. Smith, age 74, occupation, farmer, died 9 Sep 1917, at his home, 118 Wood Street, Greenfield, born 1 Jun 1844, s/o John and Jane (McCollins) Smith." HC Park Cemetery: John P. Smith Co F 94 Ind Vol 1843-1917.

Smith, John W.; 79 Reg Co B, 9 Aug 62-7 Jun 65. "...born Berhead, Scotland, 5' 5" tall, age 23 years, fair complexion, blue eyes, light hair, teacher when enrolled..."

Hancock County Indiana Civil War Soldiers

Smith, Oliver; 5 Cav Co G, 18 Aug 62-15 Sep 65. An Oliver Smith married 30 Apr 1870 Amanda Snider HC Bk 5-374. "Oliver Smith, age 77 years, widower of Amanda, died 7 Apr 1926, of cancer of the lower lip, born 2 Apr 1848, s/o Monroe Smith." HC Philadelphia Cemetery: Oliver Smith 1849-1926; Amanda Smith 1853-1917.

Smith, Philander; 8 Reg Co B, 25 Aug 61, Sergeant; 18 Jan 63, 2nd Lieut.; 1 Jul 65 1st Lieut.; 30 Sep 65, Captain, never mustered. NOD.

Smith, Robert; 57 Reg Co A, 13 Dec 61-1 Mar 65. NOD.

Smith, Robert J.; 8 Reg Co G, 25 Aug 61-31 Dec 61, discharged wounds. A Robert J. Smith married 15 May 1862 Easter Burris HC Bk 4-329. HC Burris/Hendricks Cemetery: R.J. Smith Co G 8 Ind Inf. NOD.

Smith, William; 148 Reg Co I, 17 Feb 65-5 Sep 65. NOD.

Smith, William; 9 Cav Co B, 13 Nov 63, transferred to 13 Reg, out 28 Aug 65, Sgt. NOD.

Smith, William G.; 51 Illinois Reg Co C, 1861-22 Jun 65. " William G. Smith joined the great Rebellion and soon after enlistment his regiment assisted in the opening of Ft. Pillow, participated in the battles of Farmington, siege of Corinth, Stone River, Chickamauga, Chattanooga, Resaca, Kennesaw Mountain and the Atlanta campaign. He was wounded first in the battle of Stone River, when he was struck by a grape shot as to inflict a severe but not dangerous injury.

"At New Hope Church, in the Atlanta campaign, he received a gunshot wound in the left shoulder and hand; at Kennesaw Mountain, on 27 Jun 1864, while attacking the enemy's breastworks his right eye was shot out and a slight wound in the right shoulder. He was honorably discharged 22 Jun 1865. Mr. Smith was born 9 Nov 1840, Coschocton County, Ohio, s/o Martin (Marcellus) and Rebecca (Welling) Smith, and they came to Hancock County about 1850. William G. Smith married 22 Mar 1866 Kezziah Price, no place given. Mr. Smith served as Treasurer of Greenfield from 1894 to 1898."

Hancock County Indiana Civil War Soldiers

HC Park Cemetery: William G. Smith died 22 Jan 1912 Co C 51 Ill Inf; Kezziah Smith 1845-1900.

Smith, William J.; HC obit 24 Jan 1929: "William J. Smith, a veteran of the Civil War, died at age 85 years, at the home of his daughter, Mrs. Charles Davis, Fortville, after an illness of several weeks. Survivors: Mrs. Davis; son, Harley Smith; stepson Herman McDonald. Interment Fort Cemetery, Hamilton County, Indiana." "William J. Smith, age 84 years, widower of Lela, retired farmer, born 12 Apr 1844 in Ohio, s/o James and Eliza (Dill) Smith."

Snell, Lewis; 8 Reg Co B, 25 Aug 61, discharged disability 10 Apr 63. A Lewis Snell married 12 Jul 1855 Mary Grine. HC Bk 3-290

Snell, Zachariah; 5 Cav Co G, 9 Feb 64-15 Sep 65. NOD.

Snider, Joseph; 79 Reg Co D, 8 Aug 62, 15 Feb 63, transferred to Marine Corps; could this be the unit called the Mississippi Marines??

Snider, Oregon; 9 Cav Co A, 6 Feb 64-no out date. An Oregon Snider married 24 Mar 1867 Nancy England HC Bk 5-124. HC Burris/Hendricks Cemetery: Oregon Snider Co A 9 Ind Cav, no dates; George s/o Oregon and Nancy 6 May 1883-2 Feb 1898.

Snider, William T.; 8 Reg Co B 25 Aug 61, promoted to 1st Sergeant. .Two marriages for a William T. Snider 1) 15 Aug 1867 Martha Boyd HC Bk 5-153; 2) 14 Feb 1873 Anna Tague HC Bk 6-178. Newspaper death notice 21 Jul 1917: "Word was received here of the death of William T. Snider at the soldiers' home, Marion, Indiana. He was a former well-known businessman of this city, having been in the furniture business for several years, going from here to Chicago and then to the soldier's home at Marion. He was a brother of Walter Snider, Greenfield; burial at the cemetery at the Marion home."

Snodgrass, David; "Cousin of John Davis, served in the Civil War." See page for John Davis.

Snodgrass, John; "Cousin of John Davis, served in the Civil War." See page for John Davis.

Hancock County Indiana Civil War Soldiers

Snow, David; 51 Reg Co K, 23 Feb 62-13 Dec 65. A David Snow married 17 Mar 1864 Elizabeth Jane Wynn HC Bk 4-439. HC Wynn Cemetery: Elizabeth Snow w/o David died 28 May 1870, 27y 4m 20d; Joseph s/o D and E. died 30 Sep 1867, 8m.

Snow, Capt. Henry; "He was teaching school before enlisting, 18 Apr 61, in Company I, 8th Ind for three months and was mustered out with the regiment 6 Aug 61. He reenlisted the same day in the band of the 18th Indiana Regiment and served until the fall of 1863. He recruited for the 28th U.S. Colored Troops and was promoted and commissioned captain 10 May 1864. He was wounded in the head and hand in the Charge of Petersburg, 30 Jul 1864; he was in several hospitals before he was assigned to light duty at Springfield, Illinois, serving as Assistant Adjutant, Provost Marshall, until he was mustered out November 1865.

"He participated in the battles of Rich Mountain; Pea Ridge, Arkansas; White House Landing, Virginia; and several minor engagements. He was born 4 Dec 1838 in Shelby County, Indiana, (another source says Shelbyville, Kentucky) s/o Thomas and Ann (Monks) Snow, and settled in Hancock County in 1847. Henry Snow married Francis (Fannie) Pierson 8 Oct 1877 (HC Bk 6-543); two children, Lena and Thad. Henry Snow had two brothers who served in the 18th Regiment during the War: Nathaniel and William; and his wife had two brothers who served in the War: Edward, Captain of Indiana Regiment; and Martin Pierson, Private in Indiana Regiment."

HC obit 29 Dec 1921: " Henry Snow, one of the best-known citizens of this county and city, prominent in business, politics, social and Masonic circles, died at the home of his son, Thad Snow, in Charleston, Missouri, where he and Mrs. Snow had been for several months. Captain Snow was born Shelbyville, Kentucky, 4 December 1837. His father, Thomas P. Snow and his mother were born in London, England, and sailed for America in 1828, first settling in Shelbyville, Kentucky, and then to Freeport, Shelby County, Indiana, and came to Greenfield in 1850, and died here in 1870.

"Captain Henry Snow was always fond of fishing and was never happier than when engaged in this sport whether it was along the banks of Brandywine, Sugar Creek or some imposing stream. The funeral will be in charge of the Grand Army, assisted by the Greenfield Commandery, Knight Templar and the Blue Lodge of Masons. Interment (HC) Park Cemetery."

Snow, Jonathan; 5 Cav Co G, 9 Oct 62, died 24 Jun 64. Andersonville Prison Profile Code # 12420: Private Jonathan Snow, Company G, 5th Indiana Cavalry died 24 Jun 1864, cause diarrhea, grave # 2420. 1860 U.S. census, Hancock County, Indiana, records a Jonathan Snow age 14, in the household of Thomas Snow age 52, and Ann age 48, brothers, Charles age 23 and Nathaniel age 19.

Snow, Nathaniel; 18 Reg, musician, 16 Aug 61-20 Aug 62; 105 Reg Co E, 11 Jul 63-18 Jul 63. He was a teacher and died just after his discharge.

Snow, William. 18 Reg, Musician, 16 Aug 61-18 Aug 64. Deceased by 1902; brother of Capt. Henry Snow and Nathaniel Snow.

Snyder, Thomas C.; 5 Cav Co G, 16 Oct 62-15 Sep 65. HC newspaper 11 Aug 1864: "Pvt. T. Snyder, Company G, 5th Cavalry, was taken prisoner during the disastrous expedition commanded by General Stoneman." He is not recorded as having been at Andersonville Prison as other soldiers were after this event. Two marriages recorded for Thomas C. Snyder: 1) 5 Mar 1868 Lusetta Ray HC Bk 5-208; 2) 8 Aug 1873 Cinderella Young HC Bk 6-212.

Soots, Addison; 148 Reg Co C, 17 Feb 65-5 Sep 65. NOD.

Spangler, William; 9 Cav Co B, 9 Dec 63-26 Sep 64. NOD.

Sparks, William; HC Park Cemetery William Max Sparks Co C _ Ind Cav, age 83, died 26 Sep 1926, Vermillion County, Illinois, cause, myocarditis.

Hancock County Indiana Civil War Soldiers

Spilker, Christian; 79 Reg Co D, 16 Aug 62, no out date. A Christian Spilker married 13 Mar 1873 Henrietta Burger HC Bk 6-187.

Spurry, Samuel W.; 87 Reg Co I, 15 Oct 64, substitute, 10 Jun 65 transferred to 42 Infantry. A Samuel Spurry married 28 Oct 1868 HC Bk 5-258, Mary A. Roberts. HC Park Cemetery: Samuel W. Spurry Co I 87 Ind Inf, died 10 Mar 1923, age 76.

Squire, Oliver; 148 Reg Co I, 8 Feb 65, died 14 May 65, Columbia, Tennessee.

Staats, John W.; 12 Reg Co B, 15 May 61-19 May 62. NOD

Staats, Peter; 12 Reg Co B, 15 May 61-19 May 62. A Peter Staats married 24 Aug 1857 Mary Edwards HC Bk 4-30.

Stanbrough, Solomon; 148 Reg Co F, 17 Feb 65-5 Sep 65, 1st Lieut. NOD.

Stanley, John; 79 Reg Co D, 16 Aug 62, no out date. A John Stanley married 31 Dec 1857 Rhoda Ann ____ HC Bk 1-58. "John Stanley, age 73 years, widowed, farmer, died 14 Feb 1910, cause, paralysis, born 20 Nov 1836 (?), s/o Louis and Ann (Johnson) Stanley, burial Steele graveyard." HC Steele Cemetery: John Stanley 27 Sep 1837 (?)-____; Roda A. 27 Jan 1843-13 Nov 1904.

Stanley, Martin; 79 Reg Co D, 10 Aug 62, killed 2 Jan 63, Stone's River, Tennessee. NOD.

Stanridge, George; 9 Cav Co B, 2 Jan 64-31 May 65. NOD.

Stanridge, Henry; 9 Cav Co B, 2 Jan 64-18 May 65, promoted, farrier, NOD.

Steele, Samuel; 79 Reg Co C, 15 Aug 62-7 Jun 65. NOD.

Steele, William; 79 Reg Co D, 8 Aug 62, age 27. HC Steele Cemetery: William Steele died 21 Dec 1862, Civil War, Nashville, Tennessee. HC newspaper 25 Dec 1862: We learn with sincere regret that our old friend and fellow citizen, William Steele, of Buck Creek Township, is no more. A few months since, he entered the service of his country under Capt. Buchanan, of the 79th Regiment and went to Kentucky with it. The hard marches and exposed life of the soldier was too much for him. His remains were brought home for interment. We

Hancock County Indiana Civil War Soldiers

are, also informed that two members of the same company by the name of Ray, also from this county, have recently died, at some hospital in the South." William Steele married Olive McCord __ Sep 1859 HC Bk 4-149. See highlights of letters in this volume.

Steffey, Joseph; 147 Reg Co H, 24 May 64-__Aug 65. A Joseph Steffey married 25 Oct 1865 Martha Weaver HC Bk 4-552.

Steller, Frederick, 75 Reg Co I, 5 Aug 62, 27 Jul 63, transferred to Veteran Reserve Corps for light duty indicating illness or wound; out 1 Jul 65. "...born Bavaria, Germany, 5' 9" tall, age 40, dark complexion, blue eyes, dark hair, cooper when enrolled"

Stephens, Eli; 8 Reg Co B, 25 Aug 61-28 Aug 65. An Eli Stephens married Sarah Evans 10 Jul 1867 HC Bk 5-144. HC Park Cemetery: Eli Stephens Co B 8 Ind Inf 29 Aug 1843-10 Jun 1909; Sarah Stephens w/o Eli, 30 Jun 1844-15 Mar 1928.

Stephenson, George; 8 Reg Co G, 22 Apr 61-6 Aug 61, Musician. NOD.

Stephenson, John; 8 Reg Co G, 22 Apr 61 Sgt., 2 Jul 61 promoted to 2nd Lieut.; out 6 Aug 61.

Stephenson, Marion; 8 Reg Co G, Sgt, 22 Apr 61, died 20 Jul 61 of wounds, Rich Mountain, Virginia.

Sterling, E.W.; 148 Reg, Co B, no dates. HC obit 18 Apr 1912: "Prof. E. W. Sterling and his companion moved to Greenfield five years ago where they lived happily together up to the time of his death. He taught mathematics in the Greenfield schools. He enlisted in Company B, 148 Regiment Indiana Volunteers, and served his country as a faithful soldier. He had a birthright in the Friends Church where his funeral discourse was preached and was laid to rest in Westland Cemetery, with ritualistic services by Dunbar Post G.A.R. Survived by the widow, and three children by his first wife, one brother, Abram Hunt; and one sister, Susan Beard."

Stevens, (Stephens) Eli; 8 Reg Co B, 25 Aug 61-28 Aug 65. HC Newspaper 28 May 1863: Eli Stevens, Company B, 8 Regiment, was shot through the oil cloth wrapped 'round him,

Hancock County Indiana Civil War Soldiers

narrowly escaped wound." An Eli Stephens married 10 Jun 1867 Sara Evans HC Bk 5-144. HC Park Cemetery: Eli Stephens Co B 8 Ind Inf, 29 Aug 1843-10 Jun 1909; Sarah Stephens w/o Eli 30 Jun 1844-19 Mar 1928. See data on his brother, Reuel Stephens.

Stevens (Stephens) Reuel John; 8 Reg Co B, 9 May 64-28 Aug 65. HC obit 22 April 1926: "Reuel John Stephens, s/o John and Phoeba (Manlove) Stephens, was born 11 October 1845, on the family homestead in Jackson Township, Hancock County, Indiana. He is the last member of his father's family, of which there were eleven children, namely, Prudence; William; Cynthia; Washington; Harriet; Eli; Nancy; Samuel; Lafayette; Mary and John, whose death marks the passing of a generation. When less than 19 years of age, he enlisted in the military service of the United States.

"It was during the Civil War and his brother, Eli, was at home on a furlough, and being inspired by his example of patriotic service, accompanied him upon his return to the front, leaving Greenfield 20 May 1863, as a member of Company B, 8th Indiana Volunteer Infantry, where he served with honor until the close of the war. He was mustered out 28 August 1865, and returned to his father's home in Jackson Township.

"He was united in marriage to Mary E. Miller 28 July 1869 (HC Bk 5-308). To this union were born eight children, five of whom survive: Ira; Maggie Hamilton; Luther; Oscar; and Ada Schuh; Lillie; Ethel; and Oakley have preceded the father in passing. About 1879, upon the advice of physicians, Mr. Stephens left the farm and with his family came to Greenfield to live, and ever since resided on Wood Street. He served as Center Township constable for years and was a member of the Grand Army of the Republic." HC Park Cemetery: Ruel J. Stephens Co B 8 Ind Inf, died 12 Apr 1926, age 80.

Stewart, Henry; HC Park Cemetery: Henry Stewart Co A 139 Ind Inf, died 1883. NOD.

Stewart, James F.; 18 Reg, Musician, 16 Aug 61-20 Aug 62. NOD.

Hancock County Indiana Civil War Soldiers

Stewart, John; 106 Co D, 10 Jul 63-17 Jul 63; 8 Reg Co E, 29 Aug 61-20 Jul 65. Three marriages for John Stewart: 1) Eliza Jane Caldwell 20 Jan 1848 HC Bk 2-269; 2) Eliza Ann Bartlow 26 Mar 1863 HC Bk 5-30; 3) Nancy Patterson 10 Mar 1870 HC Bk 5-422. HC Wynn Cemetery: John Stewart Co E 8 Ind Cav.

Stewart, John F.; HC obit 15 Nov 1928: "John F. Stewart, died at his home on West Fourth Street, Greenfield, at the advanced age of 86 years. Mr. Stewart was born 19 Aug 1842, in North Carolina and was a soldier in the Confederate army during the Civil War. He is survived by the widow, Albora Stewart, and two daughters, Mrs. Butler and Mrs. Kirchner. Interment HC Park Cemetery." No marker found during transcribing in 1992.

Stineback, G.W.; 106 Reg Co D, 10 Jul 63-17 Jul 63, 2nd Lt. NOD.

Stirk, Pressley; 106 Reg Co D, 10 Jul 63-17 Jul 63. NOD.

Stockdale, William; 48 Reg Co D, 1 Jan 62-15 Jul 65. "Living in Marshall County, Indiana, age 25 years, farming when he enlisted; he followed his flag, endured the hardships of camp life and fought in the battles of Iuka, first and second battles of Corinth, Port Gibson and Jackson. At the battle of Jackson, Mississippi, 14 May 1863, he was wounded by a gunshot in the right leg, and in that condition fell into the hands of the enemy, and his leg was amputated by Confederate surgeons.

"He was sent to the hospital at Jackson and Brandon, Mississippi, where he remained nine months in the hands of the Confederates, thence to Military Prison at Cahaba, Alabama, for two months, then to Andersonville Prison, arriving in the Spring of 1864 and held until November 1864, when he was exchanged and taken with others to Savannah, Georgia, turned over to the Union and sent to Annapolis, Maryland. He received a furlough to go home and was discharged 1 January 1865 at Indianapolis. He served on a detail of ammunition trains for the regiment. William was born 4 September 1836 In England, s/o William and Esther (Levesey) Stockdale. On 14 September 1898, at Indianapolis, the soldier, William, married

Hancock County Indiana Civil War Soldiers

Margaret (Nolen) Gashbach; one child, Marietta." HC Park Cemetery: William Stockdale Co D 48 Ind Inf, no dates.

Stokes, William; 34 Reg Co E, 10 Oct 61, no out date. A William Stokes married 9 Oct 1857 Malinda Leonard HC Bk 4-46. HC McCordsville Cemetery: William Stokes Soldier died 27 Nov 1922.

Stout, Eli; 26 Reg Co I, 21 Sep 64-6 Sep 65. HC Philadelphia Cemetery: E.M. Stout 4 Aug 1840-28 Nov 1924; Rachel 7 Feb 1842-31 Aug 1907; children of Eli and Rachel: Laura Bell died 18 Jul 1875, 1y 2m 22d; Mary Ruth died 3 Apr 1876, 19y 1m 12d; William 22 May 1864-8 Oct 1864; and Zella 23 Apr 1876-21 Jul 1877. HC obit 5 Sep 1907: "Mrs. Rachel Stout died at her home in New Palestine Saturday evening. She was sixty years of age and leaves a husband and four children."

Stowder, Stephen; 53 Reg Co A, 24 Feb 1862-21 Jul 65. A Stephen Stouder married 30 Dec 1869 HC Bk 5-344 Malinda Perky. NOD.

Strahl, Oliver; 148 Reg Co C, 17 Feb 65-5 Sep 65. Two marriages for an Oliver Strahl: 1) Martha Snodgrass 27 Jun 1858 HC Bk 4-87; 2) Hannah Thompson 31 Jan 1865 HC Bk 4-449. HC obit 23 Oct 1913: "Oliver Strahl, age 77 years, died at his home in Brandywine Township. He had been in poor health for some time suffering from leakage of the heart and dropsy, his death was sudden. He was in his usual condition during the evening when neighbors called. On retiring the family found Mr. Strahl dead.

"He was a native of Ohio, coming to this county when 6 years of age and resided here ever since. He was a veteran of the Civil War, having served in Company C, 148 Regiment Indiana Volunteers. He is survived by the widow and one son, Ruckle." Another HC obit 23 Oct 1913, The same details as above with the following additions: "Mr. Strahl was born in Gurnsey County, Ohio, but cam to this county when six years old. He has lived in the same community ever since, except a year during the Civil War, when he served in Company C, 148th Indiana Regiment. The deceased leaves a widow, one

Hancock County Indiana Civil War Soldiers

son, Ruckle Strahl and one brother, Brewer Strahl." HC Park Cemetery: Oliver Strahl Co C 148 Ind Inf 1836-1913; Hannah Strahl 1835-1916.

Strickland, Richard J.; 78 Reg Co F, 7 Aug 62-3 Oct 62; also 105 Reg Co F, 10 Jul 63-17 Jul 63. "Governor of the State of Indiana and Commander-in-chief of the Militia thereof, Greetings, Know Ye, that in the name and by the authority of said State, I, Oliver P. Morton, Governor as aforesaid do hereby appoint and commission Richard J. Strickland to the office of Captain in and for 78t^h Regiment of the Indiana Volunteer Militia.. In testimony whereof I have hereunto set my hand, and caused to be affixed the seal of the above State at Indianapolis the 7th day of Aug in the year of our Lord, 1862, signed O.P. Morton, Governor of Indiana."

Richard J. Strickland was born 28 Sep 1830 at Richland County, Ohio, and came to Indiana in the early fifties, locating at Centerville where he edited a newspaper and came to Greenfield in 1878 and published the *Hancock Jeffersonian* until 1889. He married Ann E. Hamlyn, born 4 October 1830, Widdicomb-on-the-Moor, Devonshire, England, daughter of Richard and Jane (Coker) Hamlyn. R.J. Strickland was a portly man with a booming voice and garrulous disposition and a familiar character around Greenfield."

HC obit 2 Jun 1898: "Word was received in this city of the death of R.J. Strickland of Centerville. Mr. Strickland was well and favorably known in this city and county having lived here for a number of years, and at one time was editor of the Greenfield *Jeffersonian*. He was about seventy years of age and leaves a wife and three sons, H.L.; Harry ; and Ben of Greenfield and one daughter, Mrs. Grace Carter of Indianapolis. His remains will be interred at Centerville under the auspices of Odd Fellow and G.A.R." Ann (Hamlyn) Strickland died 16 May 1910 in Greenfield and is buried at Centerville.

Stuart, Andrew T.; HC Gilboa Cemetery: Andrew T. Stuart Soldier died 2 Oct 1896, 60y 7m 25d. HC obit 8 Oct 1896:

Hancock County Indiana Civil War Soldiers

"Andrew T. Stewart, aged 60 years, son of Absalom and Elizabeth Stuart, died 2 Oct 1896, at his home 47 North East Street, Greenfield, of dropsy. Funeral from the house, service and interment Gilboa Cemetery." An A. T. Stuart married 4 Dec 1862 Margaret Grunden HC Bk 4-364.

Stump, Jesse; 51 Reg Co D, 14 Dec 61-13 Dec 65. A Jesse Stump married 13 Jun 1866 Margaret Smith HC Bk 5-67.

Sturges, John T.; 9 Cav Co B, 13 Nov 63-28 Aug 65, bugler. NOD.

Stutsman, Andrew; served in three different regiments as follows: 8 Reg Co G, 22 Apr 61-6 Aug 61, wounded 11 Jul 61, Rich Mountain, Virginia; 105 Reg Co D 10 Jul 63-17 Jul 63 serving in the forces against Confederate General John Hunt Morgan as he and his cavalrymen raided into southern Indiana; 38 Reg Co D, 24 Sep 64-6 Sep 65, as listed on roster of the 38th who participated in the battle of Chickamauga. Andrew Stutsman married Mary Griffith 22 Sep 1878, HC Bk 7-19.

"Andrew Stutsman, age 46 years, died 21 Sep 1885 Center Township; cause, gangrenous inflammation of the mouth; occupation, merchant; married, no name given; parents, Nicholas and Catherine (Travis) Stutsman (married 8 Feb 1838 HC Bk 1-135). (Nicholas Stutsman was killed by a train as he attempted to cross the tracks, as reported in *Hancock Democrat*, 3 Jul 1884.) HC Philadelphia Cemetery: Andrew Stutsman 17 Apr 1840-2 Sep 1885; Mary Stutsman 1848-1907.

Stutsman, Henry; 106 Reg Co D, 10 Jul 63-17 Jul 63. A Henry Stutsman married Victoria Dommanget 23 Dec 1869 HC Bk 5-345.

Stutsman, Isaac; 79 Reg Co B, 9 Aug 62-7 Jun 65, Corp'l. An Isaac Stutsman married Edith Loehr 5 Sep 1865 HC Bk 4-533. "Isaac Stutsman died 31 Oct 1912, age 70 years, cause, colitis; occupation, retired blacksmith, born 17 Mar 1842 s/o Nicholas (killed by a train as he attempted to cross the tracks about 3 Jul 1884) and Kate Travse (Travis?)." HC obit 7 Nov 1912: "Isaac Stutsman, aged 72 years, one of the well known veterans of the

Hancock County Indiana Civil War Soldiers

Civil War, died at his home, 216 Broadway (Greenfield) after a long illness of kidney and bladder trouble.

"Mr. Stutsman served throughout the war as a member of Company B, 79 Regiment Indiana Volunteers. He was a member of Dunbar Post, Grand Army of the Republic, and of the Bradley M.E. Church. He leaves a widow and several children, all grown. Funeral services were held at the Church."

HC Philadelphia Cemetery: Isaac Stutsman 1842-1912; Edith Stutsman 1843-1929.

HC obit 28 Nov 1912: "Isaac N. Stutsman was the son of Nicholas and Catherine Stutsman and was born in Randolph County, Indiana 27 Mar 1842. He departed this life in Greenfield, Indiana, 31 Oct 1912. At an early period of his life he became a resident of Hancock County and for many years lived in and about Gem, Indiana. He was married to Miss Edith Loehr on 6 Sep 1865, by Rev. George Bowers. To this union three daughters and one son were born and all are living, Mrs. Clara Haine; Mrs. Theresa Harbaugh; Mrs. Nora Leonard; and Noble P. Stutsman of Des Moines, Iowa.

"During the dark days of the sixties, he heard the call of his country for those who were willing to place their lives upon its altar and he responded, joining Company B, of the 79th Indiana Volunteers. He was in the service for about three years, and was in some of the bloodiest battles of the war, being in all but one in which his regiment engaged. He also leaves nineteen grandchildren and a sister, Mrs. Mary Shepherd and three brothers who live so far away they were not able to attend the funeral. For the past eight years he has resided in Greenfield and has been a member of the Bradley Methodist Episcopal Church and even when his dullness of hearing made it impossible for him to get much of the service, he was found in his place, for as he said, "I like to be in the atmosphere of the religious service."

Sullivan, Calvin; 8 Reg Co G, 22 Apr 61-6 Aug 61; 9 Cav Co B, 13 Nov 63-17 Jun 65. HC Old Greenfield Cemetery: Calvin Sullivan Co B 9 Ind Cav died Dec 1865. 1860 Federal Census,

Hancock County Indiana Civil War Soldiers

Hancock County, Indiana, Center Township records a Calvin Sullivan, as head of household, age 30, born N.C.; Eliza, age 25, born New Jersey; John R., age 5, born Indiana; Phoebe A., age 3, born Indiana.

Sutherland, Ashley; 50 Reg Co I, 9 Dec 61-Jun 65. Ashley was the s/o Jacob (born Tennessee) and Martha (Selgrove) Sutherland. I am sure that as a lawyer and farmer in Hancock and Marion Counties, Ashley Sutherland had no idea that his service to his country would bring him to be a prisoner of war in Richmond, Virginia. Ashley was born in Orange County, Indiana, 1 October 1827 and married Elizabeth C. Richardson 8 December 1852 in Indianapolis, Indiana. The Sutherlands were a large pioneer family in Franklin Township, Marion County, Indiana. Elizabeth's parents, George B. and Sarah (?) Richardson migrated from Kentucky with Ashley's parents in the early part of the nineteenth century.

Ashley and Elizabeth were the parents of twelve children: William H.; George B.; Sara A. Davis; Joel F.; Salathiel Lincoln; Louisa K. (died at age 22 months); Fannie Baas; Anna Benjamin; Edward H.; Laura; Harri H. (Bud); and Mattie Hamlyn. Ashley Sutherland enrolled as a Private on 9 December 1861 into Company I, 50th Regiment of Indiana Volunteer Infantry at Bedford, Indiana, by Colonel Heffren and was mustered in 13 December 1861 for a term of three years in Silverville, Indiana, by Captain Miller.

Ashley served in Company I, 50th Regiment from December 1861 until December 1862; was taken prisoner at Pilot's Knob, Sumner County, Tennessee, 20 August 1862. He appears on the muster roll of Company A, 2 Regiment Paroled Prisoners of the United States Army from 30 April to 31 August 1862. Ashley was left sick in camp at Jackson, Tennessee 27 December 1862 by order of Sergeant Hervey. He rejoined Company I, 50 Regiment January 1863. He is shown on the roll of Company D, 106 Regiment from 10 Jul 1863 until 17 Jul 1863, serving in the forces against Confederate General John Hunt Morgan as he and cavalrymen raided into southern

Hancock County Indiana Civil War Soldiers

Indiana. On 26 November 1863, Ashley was detailed to guard a wagon train and continued as a teamster until 25 March 1864, when he was again taken prisoner at Mark's Mill, Arkansas.

He is listed as missing in action on 25 April 1864 at the Saline River. It is unclear what happened next but he is also listed as a Prisoner of War taken at the Battle of Jenkins Ferry, Arkansas, 30 April 1864; also National Archives records Ashley Sutherland was taken prisoner 29 May 1864. He was transferred from the 50th to the 52nd Regiment, Company A, of the Indiana Infantry, 26 May 1865, which was a consolidation of the two regiments and was mustered out June 1865 in Indianapolis, Indiana.

At the time of his enlistment, Ashley was described as being 29 years old, 5 feet, 11 inches with a light complexion, blue eyes and light hair. Ashley died 28 July 1900 in Indianapolis; his wife, Elizabeth died 28 April 1928 and they are buried in Founders Cemetery, New Bethel Baptist Church Cemetery, Wanamaker, Indiana. Contributed by Retta Arbuckle Livengood, Greenfield, Indiana.

Sutherland, David; HC McCray Cemetery: David Sutherland Co B 75 Ohio Inf. NOD.

Swift, Oliver P.; 106 Reg Co D, 10 Jul 63-17 Jul 63. An Oliver Swift married 5 Jan 1862 Malinda Daugherty HC Bk 4-308.

Swope, Henry A.; 105 Reg Co E, 11 Jul 63-18 Jul 63. HC obit 21 Jun 1877: "On 18 June 1877, Henry A. Swope, an old and respected citizen of Greenfield, breathed his last, after an illness of several months duration due to a disease known as ulceration of the stomach. In 1857 Mordecai Millard, of Buck Creek Township, was elected Sheriff of the County, and Mr. Swope became his principal deputy. During the early stages of the War, Mr. Swope secured the position of sutler at Camp Morton (in Indianapolis), in which many thousand prisoners were confined. Soon after surrendering this position, he was appointed Deputy Provost Marshall, under Captain Braden.

"In 1865 Mr. Swope was elected Clerk of the Hancock Circuit Court for four years, by the Union party. After retiring from the Clerk's office, he commenced the practice of law, and zealously followed that pursuit until his sickness some months ago. Mr. Swope was issued at the time of his death in the New Jersey Mutual for $7,500; in the Northwestern Mutual for $5,000; and in the Masonic Mutual for $4,100, making in all thereabouts $16,600. The policies are all, as we understand, payable to his wife." HC Park Cemetery : Henry A. Swope 25 Aug 1832-18 Jun 1877; Mary E. Hart Swope died 5 Jun 1900, w/o Henry A.; d/o Andrew T. Hart; Sarah Swope mother of Henry, born 1790 Montgomery County, Kentucky, died 2 Aug 1873; Elmer T. Swope 6 Jul 1859-18 Feb 1919, unmarried, s/o Henry and Mary.

Hancock County Indiana Civil War Soldiers

John Sherman

Courtesy of Harriett Miller

Hancock County Indiana Civil War Soldiers

Richard J. Strickland

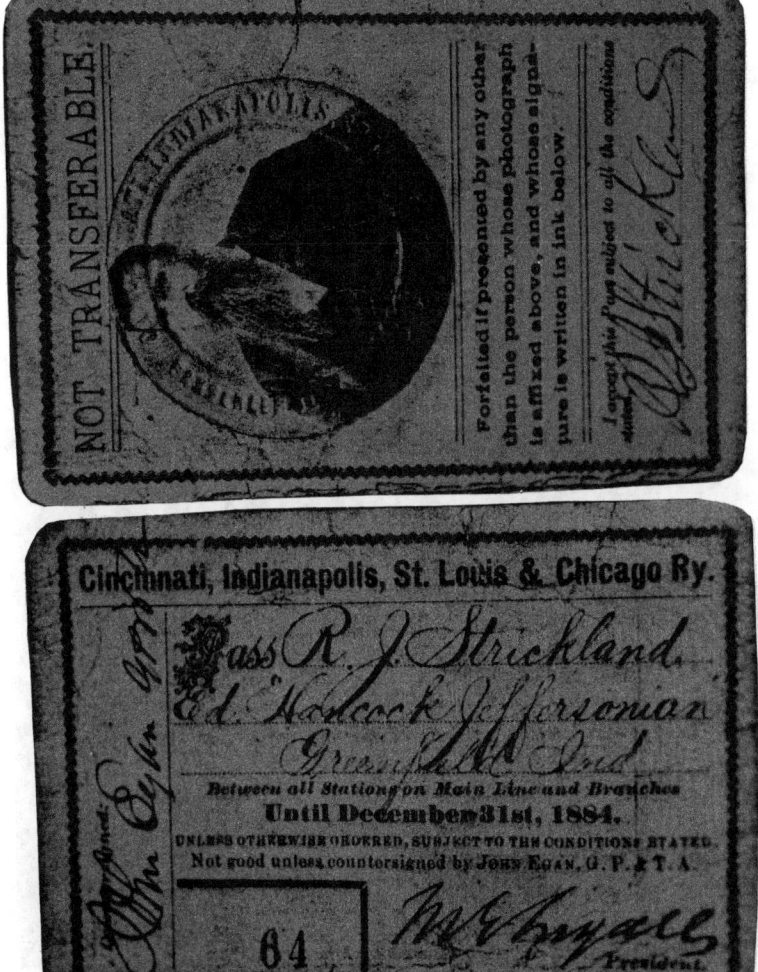

Courtesy of Rebecca Strickland Pernice

Hancock County Indiana Civil War Soldiers

Isaac Stutsman

Courtesy of Don Leonard

Hancock County Indiana Civil War Soldiers

◄ **T** ►

Tague, George; 99 Reg Co B, 13 Aug 62, 1st. Lieut.; 22 Jan 63, Captain; 5 Jan 64 (65) honorably discharged. 99 Regiment History states: "George Tague, entered as 1st Lieutenant , Company B; succeeded Captain Carr in April 1863; served until ill health compelled him to resign 5 January 1864 (65); physician by profession died about 1896 at his home in Greenfield. " George Tague, age 64 years, died of pneumonia 28 Mar 1896, at his residence in Greenfield."
HC obit 2 Apr 1896: "We regret to announce the death of a worthy citizen, Captain George C. Tague, of Greenfield, one of our oldest pioneers and a highly esteemed citizen, died after a long protracted siege of sickness from Bright's disease. He was a good soldier of the late war and veteranized during the progress of the rebellion. He was a devoted christian and member of the M.E. Church." HC Park Cemetery: George Tague died 28 Mar 1896, 64y 7m 26d; Emily w/o George 1831-1912.

Tague, William; 79 Reg Co B, 9 Aug 62-no out date. Two marriages for a William Tague, 1) Elvira Pauley 14 Oct 1877 HC Bk 6-547; 2) Nancy Pauley 6 Jul 1877 HC Bk 6-285.

Tattman, Francis M.; 106 Reg Co D, Sgt., 10 Jul 63-17 Jul 63. A Francis M. Tatman married 5 Feb 1865 Cinthia Westlake HC Bk 4-500. HC New Palestine Cemetery: Frank M. Tattman 7 May 1836-31 Jan 1899; Cynthia Tattman no dates.

Taylor, John H.; 5 Cav Co G, 27 Feb 64-20 May 65. A John Taylor married 29 May 1885 Eliza Ford HC Bk 7-610.

Teush, Ambrose H.; HC Courthouse, Soldier Burial List: 2 NJ Cav Co B; died 8 Feb 1897; 49 years; occupation, nail cutter; burial, Highland Cemetery, Vigo County, Indiana. NOD.

Thayer, Edmund P.; 11 Reg Co A (Zouaves), 22 Apr 61 enlisted as private; 31 Aug 61 promoted to Sergeant; 1 May 64 promoted to 2nd Lt.; 13 Dec 64 promoted to 1st Lt.; 14 Dec 64, promoted Capt.; 8 May 65 transferred to Company B. HC obit 9 Apr 1925: "Captain Edmund P. Thayer, for several years a

Hancock County Indiana Civil War Soldiers

resident of Greenfield, and who engaged in the meat business, and of late years moved to California, died at the American Soldiers Home Hospital in Sautenn, California. We regret to learn of the death of our old friend and neighbor. He was highly respected by all of our citizens and held in high esteem by every one." See data on his brother, Levi Thayer.

Thayer, Levi C.; 11 Reg (Zouaves) Co A, drummer, Jun 1861- May 62. "When the exciting times of the Civil War dawned upon our nation, Levi C. Thayer was 16 years old, and the bugle's wild and war-like blast was mustering in brave boys. In June 1861 he enrolled his name as a drummer boy in Company A, 11th Indiana Zouaves, leaving his classmates at school to join the defenders and beat the drum to the music of the Union as they took up their march for Dixie's land. The regiment was organized by Lew Wallace, who became its Colonel, and was immediately sent to the field of action where engaged in the battles of Fort Henry, Fort Donelson and Pittsburg Landing plus minor engagements.

"Levi was wounded at Shiloh and Fort Donelson. In January 1862 the War Department issued an order asking dismissal and discharge of all musicians under eighteen years of age, therefore Levi was discharged May 1862 at Pittsburg Landing. His brother E.P. Thayer also served in the 11th Indiana Zouaves. Levi was born 10 Mar 1845, at Chicopee Falls, Massachusetts, s/o Carelton and Louisiana Thayer. The family came to Indiana when Levi was ten years old and a year later moved to Hancock County.

"He was thrice married: 1) Mary Oakes 26 Jun 1869 HC Bk 5-306; 2) 1880 but name not given; 3) Iona Williams 10 Apr 1893 HC Bk 8-498. HC obit 28 Jun 1923: "Lee C. Thayer, one of the oldest merchants in Greenfield, passed away at his home on West Main Street, 26 June 1923, age 78 years, following a lingering illness. Mr. Thayer was the son of Carlton and Louisiana Thayer, born in Chicoppee, Massachusetts, 10 March 1845. As a young man Mr. Thayer came to Greenfield and for two years was a clerk in the store of Hart and Thayer,

Hancock County Indiana Civil War Soldiers

and in 1879 started in the dry goods business for himself. He conducted the Long Branch Store until 1890, when he built the Lee C. Thayer block on Main Street, moving his store there from south State Street.

"In 1901 he sold his store to his brother, Hollis B. Thayer, who combined the two stores under the name of the Spot Cash Department Store. In 1906 after the death of his brother, Mr. Thayer bought back the Spot Cash Store, and continued it until 1911, when he retired from business. In his young manhood Mr. Thayer was a railroad locomotive engineer and followed this calling for several years. Mr. Thayer was a soldier during the Civil War and was a member of the Grand Army of the Republic. Surviving Mr. Thayer are four children: Mrs. Harry Hume; Mrs. Frank Lineback; Lee C. Thayer; and Mrs. Ross Roberts." HC Park Cemetery:Levi Thayer Co A 11 Ind Inf Musician; Iona V. Thayer 10 May 1857-23 Nov 1921; Mary Oakes Thayer no other data; Carlton Thayer 27 Jan 1802-22 May 1859; born New Hampshire; Louisiana Thayer 22 Feb 1804-29 May 1861, born New Hampshire.

Theobald, Daniel; HC Courthouse, Soldier Burial List: 106 Ohio Reg, no Co given; died 6 Jan 1902; 56 years; occupation, merchant; burial, Sabina, Ohio. NLD.

Thomas, Amzi; 12 Reg Co B, 15 May 61-19 May 62. NOD.

Thomas, Ezekiel; 105 Reg Co E, 11 Jul 63-18 Jul 63. HC Park Cemetery: Ezekiel Thomas died 28 Jan 1890, 81y 18d; Jamima w/o E. died 13 Mar 1890.

Thomas, Henry; 8 Reg Co B, 5 Feb 64-28 Aug 65. NOD.

Thomas, James; 57 Reg Co A; 10 Sep 62, discharged 10 Dec 64, arm amputated. James Thomas was born 6 May 1845, the son of Elias and Leeanna (Messmore) Thomas, and at the age of eighteen was five-feet, nine-inches high, fair complexion, gray eyes, dark hair and by occupation a farmer when enrolled into Company A, 57th Indiana Infantry Regiment, 10 September 1862, at Charlottesville, Indiana.

"Under the command of Colonel Wagoner in the Army of the Cumberland, James Thomas was in the historic battle of

Hancock County Indiana Civil War Soldiers

Stone's River, Murfreesboro, Tennessee, in December of 1862 and January 1863, and was in the storming of Missionary Ridge, Tennessee, "and behaved most gallantly at both engagements." By the Spring of 1864, the Confederacy was weakening and the mighty power of the Union was being employed. General Ulysses Grant ordered a concerted offensive and General William T. Sherman was to attack the Confederate army in Georgia, "go into the interior of the enemy's country as far as you can, inflicting all the damage you can upon their war reserves."

This was the beginning of the Atlanta campaign and the course of action that the 57th Indiana Regiment followed. James Thomas was wounded seriously on 23 April 1864 while on the skirmish line at the battle of Kennesaw Mountain,. "In the assault of US forces under General Sherman upon the enemy entrenched, received at the hands of the rebels a gunshot wound on the right arm breaking the Humerous bone and causing amputation the same day about midway between the elbow and shoulder." Mr. Thomas was discharged 'by reason of Surgeon's Certificate of Disability on 10 December 1864." On 30 Nov 1865, Mr. Thomas and Susan Orr were united in marriage and to them were born seven children, of whom only three lived to adulthood, namely, Elmer and Harry Thomas and Nellie Zimmerman.

"Mr. Thomas was a past commander of Samuel Dunbar Post, G.A.R., was a prominent hardware store owner in Greenfield and served eight years as Hancock County Recorder before his death 7 March 1914, at age 68. Mr. Thomas had been sick for several weeks, and his death was expected and he was surrounded by all members of his family when the final summons came. Interment Park Cemetery."

Thomas James; 5 Cav Co G, 18 Aug 62-15 Sep 65. " born Hancock County, 5' 6 ½" tall, age 27 years, dark complexion, black eyes, dark hair, farmer when enrolled..." NOD.

Thomas, James Sr.; "Died 9 Jul 1907, age 80y 3m 13d, farmer, born 26 Mar 1827, s/o William and Naoma (McCray) Thomas, wife named Margaret Thomas, buried Glen Cove Cemetery, Knightstown, Indiana." This may or may not be the above soldier.

Thomas, Lewis; 34 Reg Co D, 21 Sep 61-3 Feb 66. A Lewis Thomas married Matilda Wood, 14 Apr 1864 HC Bk 4-447.

Thomas, Summerfield; 70 Reg Co G, 14 Jul 62, no out date. He was a Sergeant; promoted to 2nd. Lt and then to 1st Lt. He participated in the Atlanta campaign, received a head wound at the battle of Resaca and was on Sherman's "march to the sea." Upon the healing of the wound, he rejoined his unit somewhere in the Carolinas and mustered out of service near Washington 8 Jun 1865 (and most likely marched in the Grand Review passed the White House). Summerfield Thomas married Cinderella Smith 14 Nov 1872 at her father's home near McCordsville and were the parents of four children: John Worthington; Harriett Narcissus (Morehead); Myrtis (Sweezy); and Edgar Morton; all born in Rest, Kansas. Summerfield was the brother of John S. Thomas who settled in Vernon Township in 1871. Contributed by Caroline Agoes, Helen, Georgia.

Thomas, Taylor; 53 Reg Co A, 12 Jan 62, commissioned 1st Lt.; resigned 4 May 63. HC newspaper 28 Aug 1862: "We announce the return of Lieut. T.W. Thomas, who is at home on a furlough to recruit his health. We are glad to announce that he is rapidly recovering his usual good health. Lieut. T. will recruit a few men for the 53rd. Those wanting to enter the army can do no better than to call on Lieut. Thomas." Taylor W. Thomas married Zurilda Gibbs 9 Jul 1843 HC Bk 2-86. HC Park Cemetery: Taylor Thomas Lt Col Co H 53 Ind Inf. "Taylor Thomas, born 9 Mar 1823, the youngest of eleven children born to Phineas and Hannah (McComas) Thomas."

Thomas, William; 12 Reg Co G, killed Atlanta 15 Aug 1864. NOD.

Thomas, William; 8 Reg Co B, 23 Jan 64, 19 May 65 transferred to Veteran Reserve Corps indicating light duty due to illness or wound, out 10 Oct 65. NOD. Too many named William Thomas in sources to differentiate.

Hancock County Indiana Civil War Soldiers

Thomas, William Howell; "born 1840, served in Civil War and married Mary Adams." NOD. Too many named William Thomas in sources to differentiate.

Thomas, Wellington; 51 Reg Co D, 13 Sep 63-13 Dec 65. A Wellington Thomas married Matilda Marsh 3 Apr 1856 HC Bk 3-336.

Thompson, Andrew; 106 Reg Co D, 10 Jul 63-17 Jul 63. NOD.

Thompson, Isaac; 8 Reg Co B, 25 Aug 61, no out date. NOD.

Thompson, Mark; 26 Reg Co H, 24 Sep 64-6 Sep 65. NOD.

Thompson, Mark, 132 Reg Co I, 18 May 64, term expired. NOD.

Thompson, Ralph; 51 Reg Co D, 14 Dec 61, 25 Jun 62; also 5 Cav Co G, 18 Aug 62, died 15 Sep 64, Andersonville Prison. He is not recorded on database or website as a prisoner?

Thompson, Robert F.; 9 Cav Co B, 9 Dec 63-28 Aug 65. A Robert F. Thompson married Sarah E. Hudson 22 Aug 1867, no place given.

Thompson, Samuel C.; 51 Reg Co D, 14 Dec 61-25 Jun 62; also 5 Cav Co G, 18 Aug 62-15 Sep 65. HC newspaper 11 Aug 1864: "Pvt. S.C. Thompson was taken prisoner during the disastrous expedition commanded by General Stoneman." Many of the soldiers captured during this expedition were sent to Andersonville, but S. C. Thompson is not on their database nor website?

Thompson, Thomas C.; HC obit 26 Jul 1934: "Thomas C. Thompson, age 85 years died at the home of his son Noble Thompson, three miles northwest of Charlottesville, due to a cerebral hemorrhage. Four children survive: Noble; Mrs. Burgess Tuttle; Samuel; and William. Funeral and interment at Mt. Lebanon Church and Cemetery." There was no grave marker when the cemetery was transcribed in May 1965. The obit does not mention that he was a Civil War veteran, however, two men named Thomas Thompson are recorded on two Civil War soldier rosters: 16 Reg Co A, 23 Apr 61-23 May 62; and 70 Reg Co B, 1 Aug 62-8 Jun 65; and may or may not be the Thomas Thompson who died in 1934.

Hancock County Indiana Civil War Soldiers

Thompson, William H.; HC obit: 20 Dec 1928: Former sheriff, William H. Thompson, age 86, died at the home of his son, Bert Thompson on South East Street, Greenfield, of the infirmities of old age. Mr. Thompson was elected sheriff of Hancock County in 1877 and served four years. He was also deputy sheriff during the two terms of the late Mack Warrum. Mr. Thompson is survived by two children, Bert; and Miss Iduna Thompson; one son, Robert, is deceased. Burial Park Cemetery." "William H. Thompson, age 86, died 20 Dec 1928, wife named Malenda Thompson, born Ohio, William was born 10 Apr 1838, s/o William Thompson, mother not named." HC Park Cemetery: William H. Thompson 1842-1928. None of this data mentions that he was a Civil War soldier?

Thornburgh, Alfred M.; 18 Reg, Musician, 16 Aug 61-20 Aug 62. NOD.

Thornburgh, Jonathan W.; 18 Reg, Musician, 16 Aug 61-20 Aug 62. NOD.

Thornton, Daniel; 9 Cav Co B, 9 Dec 63-28 Aug 65. NOD.

Thornton, Henry W.; 5 Cav Co G, 18 Aug 62, died 11 Dec 62. HC obit 18 Dec 1862: "Henry W. Thornton, aged 21 years, died 11 December 1862, at Indianapolis, after a brief illness produced by camp life. He was a member of Capt. Riley's Company G, 5th Cavalry. He was an excellent young man, quiet, civil and unobtrusive in his habits and manners, and held in high esteem by all who made his acquaintance. He came to Philadelphia (HC) with his father, Dr. Thornton, only a few years since. Though not destroyed in battle's fierce array, he died a Soldier of the Union Army, and all who love their country, and its institutions, will drop a tear over the grave of the youthful soldier."

Tibbetts, Alvin B.; 51 Reg Co K, 7 Apr 64, died 22 Aug 64, Chattanooga, Tennessee. HC Alford Cemetery: Alvin B. Tibbetts Co K 51 Reg Ind Vol died 22 Aug 1864, 32y 7m 14d. An Alvin B. Tibbetts married Louisa McCorkill 29 Mar 1855 HC Bk 3-270.

Hancock County Indiana Civil War Soldiers

Tibbetts, Henry C.; "...born Hancock County, Indiana, 5' 9" tall, light complexion, blue eyes white hair." Three marriages for Henry C. Tibbetts: 1) Martha McPherson 9 Oct 1861 HC Bk 4-290; 2) Mary McCorkhill 20 Aug 1876 HC Bk 6-464; 3) Amanda Duncan 9 Aug 1908 HC Bk 11-422. 99 Regiment History states: "In 1900 Henry C. Tibbetts resides at Soldiers' Home, Marion, Indiana." HC obit 15 Feb 1917: "Henry Tibbetts, aged 80 years, one of the well-known veterans of the Civil War, and for nearly a life time a resident of Hancock County, died at the home of W.S. Alford near Ingalls.

"Mr. Tibbetts was a member of Company B, 99th Indiana Volunteers, mustered in 16 Aug 1862, mustered out 13 Aug 1865. He served under Capt. Robert P. Andis and Capt. Isaiah Curry. Funeral services at the G.A.R. room at the court house conducted by members and officers." "Henry C. Tibbetts,, age 80 years, widower of Amanda Tibbetts, died 9 Feb 1917 of influenza, born 21 Aug 1836, parents not given." HC Park Cemetery: children of H. C. Tibbetts: infant died 17 Jul 1876; Elmer died 17 Mar 1876; and Martha died 17 Mar 1876; no grave marker for Henry C.

Toon, Eben; 106 Reg Co D, 10 Jul 63-17 Jul 63. NOD.

Toon, John; 106 Reg Co D, 10 Jul 63-17 Jul 63. A John Toon married Fannie B. Anderson 22 May 1866 HC Bk 5-63.

Torrence, Samuel; 79 Reg Co C, 15 Aug 62-7 Jun 65. Three marriages for a Samuel Torrence: 1) Amanda Lunsford 9 Nov 1864 HC Bk 4-468; 2) Mary Shepherd 16 Jan 1868 HC Bk 5-192; 3) Sarah Ireton 28 Sep 1887 HC Bk 8-9. Samuel Torrence, soldier, died 23 Sep 1901, age 64 years, laborer, buried Caudell/Simmons Cemetery. No marker when the cemetery markers were trancsribed in 1976.

Torrence, William; 79 Reg Co C, 15 Aug 62, 14 Jan 64 transferred to Veteran Reserve Corps indicating light duty due to illness or wound. NOD.

Travis, George W.; 8 Reg Co G, 22 Apr 61-6 Aug 61. A George W. Travis married Elizabeth Banks 14 Jan 1857 HC Bk 3-386.

Hancock County Indiana Civil War Soldiers

Troy, Christohper; 99 Reg Co B, 13 Aug 62-5 Oct 63. Three marriages for Christopher Troy: 1) Letta Watson 29 May 1856 HC Bk 3-342; 2) Caroline Piper 7 Sep 1871 HC Bk 6-41; 3) Sarah Nibarger 27 Jun 1883 HC Bk 7-458. HC Cook Cemetery: Caroline Troy w/o C.C. died 2 Dec 1882 51y 8m 10d; HC Harlan Cemetery Sarah Troy w/o Christopher died 13 Jun 1897 71y 2m 8d.

True, Dr. Benjamin; 148 Reg Co I, no dates. "...went to War as a physician and soldier..." The son of Whitfield and Catherine True, Dr Benjamin married Mary Gift 1 Jan 1860 HC Bk 4-170. HC Sugar Creek Cemetery: Dr. B.F. True 19 Oct 1828-8 Sep 1896, Co I 148 Reg Ind Vol Inf; Mary C. w/o Dr. B.F. 11 Feb 1834-15 Dec 1900. See pages for his brothers, David Nelson True and Harvey True.

True, David Nelson; "at the time of his enlistment David is described as being 27 years old, 5 feet, 7 ½ inches tall, dark complexion, gray eyes, and black hair. Served in three units as follows: 8 Reg Co G, organized by Captain Reuben Riley to serve three months, 22 Apr 61-6 Aug 61 and participated in the battle of Rich Mountain, Virginia; 106 Reg Co D, served 10 Jul 63-17 Jul 63 to serve against Confederate General John Hunt Morgan and his cavalrymen who raided into southern Indiana; and 38 Reg Co D, 4 Sep 64-24 Jun 65, saw action at Perryville, Kentucky; Stone's River, Chickamauga, Siege of Chattanooga; Resaca; Jonesboro; Siege of Atlanta; Siege of Savannah; and Bentonville among others.

"While on a march in Decatur, Alabama, about the first of January 1865, David contracted a deep cold from severe exposure which settled in his throat and eyes causing permanent laryngitis and disease of the eyes from which made him unable to perform manual labor. He received hospital treatment in Chattanooga, Tennessee. He was honorably discharged 24 Jun 1865 in Louisville, Kentucky, by telegram from the War Department to W.T. Sherman, dated 18 May 1865 In 1912 the Secretary of the Interior awarded David a pension rate of $24 per month.

Hancock County Indiana Civil War Soldiers

"David Nelson True, son of Whitfield and Catharine Elizabeth (Hawk) True, was born 1 April 1837 in New Palestine, Hancock County, Indiana and married 28 January 1864 (HC Bk 4-429) Nancy Ann Ashcraft, daughter of John M. and Sophia (Bennett) Ashcraft. David and Nancy were the parents of eight children: Luemma, died at age 2 months; Catherine (Kate) Breese; Frank H. True; William H. True; James Francis True; Susanna May Niccum Eaks; John Calvin True and Anna Rosella (Rosie) Wulf Coffin. David lived most of his life in the Fortville area and died from paralysis and acute bronchitis." Contributed by Retta Arbuckle Livengood, Greenfield, Indiana.

HC obit 12 June 1920: "David N. True, son of Whitfield and Catharine True, was born 1 April 1837, near New Palestine, Indiana, where he grew to manhood helping to clear and drain the land and cultivate it until he answered the call of fife and drum. He enlisted on the 18th day of April 1861, for three months service, being assigned to Company G, 8th Regiment of Infantry, serving until mustered out 6 August 1861, when he returned home to civil life. He was united in marriage to Nancy A. Ashcraft 28 January 1864 (HC BK 4-429). But the great conflict was still raging so he left his young wife of a few months in the care of others who were not able to go and went forth again to battlefields, having enlisted in Company D, 38th Volunteers, where he went through to the end of the war, enduring hardships and privations without murmur until 24 June 1865, when he was mustered out and returned home, where he engaged in farming in Sugar Creek Township (known as the Milt Pitcher farm). The family moved to Buck Creek Township near what is known as the Old Union U.B. Church until 1885 when they moved to Madison County, Indiana, at which place the wife and mother passed away 10 April 1885. He remained there for a few years, his children having grown up and went to different places of employment.

"He then moved to Fortville where he lived until moving to Eden in 1897. He carried mail between Eden and Maxwell for four years. He then lived with his children, having spent the last few years with his youngest daughter, Mrs. Carl Coffin, at which place he passed away 12 June 1920, at the ripe old age of 83y 2m 12d. He is survived by six children: Kate Breece; Frank True; James True; Susan Eakes; John True; and Mrs. Coffin." Contributed by Ada Headlee, Greenfield, Indiana. HC Park Cemetery: David N. True Co D 38 Ind Inf; Nancy A. True died 10 April 1885, 43y 7m 5d. See pages for his brothers, Dr. Benjamin True and Harvey True.

True, Harvey: 99 Reg Co B, 13 Aug 62-7 Dec 64. HC newspaper 9 June 1864: "Harvey True, Company B, 99 Regiment was wounded in the leg at Dallas, Georgia, 28 May 1864." 99 Regiment History states: "Harvey True was wounded 28 May 1864, Dallas, Georgia, discharged for wounds 7 Dec 1864." "Harvey True was born 28 February 1834, in Brown County, Ohio, s/o Whitfield True and Catherine Hawk. Harvey came with parents to Hancock County, Indiana, when he was six months old; his siblings were Susanna; Melissa; Alonzo; David Nelson; Benjamin; Francis; and Elizabeth. The family settled first in Sugar Creek Township and then moved to Buck Creek Township.

"Harvey married Phoebe Ashcraft 15 Oct 1856 (HC Bk 3-364) and they were the parents of seven children; John A. Amos Nelson; Ottilie Jane; Suemma; and three deceased unnamed infants. Harvey enlisted in the Civil War 13 August 1862 as a private in Company B, 99th Regiment of Indiana Volunteers at Greenfield, Indiana. He was shot in the foot on the 3rd day of battle at Picketts Mill, near Dallas, Georgia, 28 May 1864, near the time of the siege of Atlanta. He spent time in a field hospital and his Certificate of Disability is dated 25 November 1864, for which he received a pension. It is interesting to note that Harvey True married Phebe Ashcraft and his brother, David Nelson True, married Phebe's sister, Nancy Ashcraft. Harvey died 2 February 1916; Phoebe Ashcraft died 11 August 1890. Both buried (HC) Steele Cemetery." Contributed by Judy Martin, Knightstown, Indiana.

Hancock County Indiana Civil War Soldiers

"Harvey True was born 28 February 1834, Brown County, Ohio to parents, Whitfield and Catherine Elizabeth Hawk. His maternal grandparents were Henry and Susannah (Flaugher) Hawk. Henry was a veteran of the War of 1812. Harvey married Phoebe Ashcraft 15 October 1856 (HC Bk 3-364), daughter of John M. and Sophia (Bennett) Ashcraft. They were the parents of seven children: John A.; infant; Amos Nelson; infant; Ottilie Jane; Sarah Catherine; and Suemma (Emma). Harvey enrolled in Company B, 99th Regiment of Indiana Volunteers on 13 August 1862 and was mustered in 22 August 1862; he was wounded in the heel in Georgia and was discharged December 1864 on surgical certification of disability. When enrolled in the Union Army, Harvey is listed as being 28 years old, and 5' 8" tall. Harvey died 2 February 1916 and is buried with Phoebe in (HC) Steele Cemetery." Contributed by Retta Arbuckle Livengood.

HC obit 3 February 1916: "Harvey True, aged 82 years, died at his home in Buck Creek Township, northwest of Mohawk, of apoplexy. He had been in his usual state of health during the day, retiring about 9:30 p.m. Funeral service will be at the home."

True, Whitfield; family tradition says he was a Civil War soldier; he married Catherine Hawk, d/o Henry and Susan Hawk; HC McNamee Cemetery: Whitfield True died 31 May 1863, 59y 7m 15d; Catherine w/o Whitfield 25 Nov 1809-1875. Contributed by Cyndi True, McCordsville, Indiana.

Trueblood, Albert; HC obit 24 Jan 1895: "Albert H. Trueblood, of Eden, probably one of the oldest citizens of Green Township, died of kidney trouble of several years standing. During the War he was one of the few men in this county that were drafted. His remains were laid to rest amid a large circle of friends and neighbors and relatives. Funeral services were conducted by the former pastor of the Eden M.E. Church according to the rites of the order Masonic." There was no grave marker when they were transcribed in 1985.

Hancock County Indiana Civil War Soldiers

Turner, William M.; 8 Ohio Inf, Co B, 12 Aug 61-9 Nov 64. "...born Vinton County, Ohio, 6' tall, age 22 years, dark complexion, black eyes. black hair, blacksmith when enrolled..."

Tuttle, Elijah; 8 Reg Co G 22 Apr 61-6 Aug 61; 8 Reg Co B, Sgt., 25 Aug 61-28 Aug 65. NOD.

Tuttle, Oliver H.; 106 Reg Co D, 10 Jul 63-17 Jul 63. HC obit 7 Dec 1905: "Oliver H. Tuttle, rural route mail carrier out of Greenfield died of paralysis. Mr. Tuttle attended a meeting of the G.A.R. Post after which he went to his home, 127 South East Street, where he suffered strokes, the third of which caused his death. Mr. Tuttle was born in Hamilton County, Ohio, 23 Jul 1846. On 2 December 1867, he was united in marriage with Eliza Toon. To them were born nine children, all of whom are living. He enlisted in the Civil War 29 February 1864 (Yes, it was Leap Year.), being assigned to Company I, 17th Regiment Indiana Volunteers, and was honorably discharged at Macon, Georgia, 17 Aug 1865. Eliza (Toon) Tuttle died 10 Oct 1903. On 18 October 1904 he was united in marriage with Marie Jeffries, who survives him. Funeral services conducted at Bradley M.E. Church. Burial Park Cemetery." HC Park Cemetery: Oliver H. Tuttle 1846-1905 Co I 17 Ind Inf; Eliza A. Tuttle 1850-1903.

Tuttle, Thomas C.; 105 Reg Co D, 10 Jul 63-17 Jul 63, Capt. HC obit 9 Oct 1873: "It is our painful duty to announce the death of our old friend. Capt. Thos. C. Tuttle, of Sugar Creek Township. He had been to Indianapolis with his team, and on his way home, either fell or was thrown from his wagon, and received such injuries on his head as to cause his death in a few hours after he was found. when found the horses had stopped and he was lying on the double trees with his head severely injured. Whether he was kicked by one of his horses or was otherwise injured, is not known, as he was alone.

"Since the above was in type, we have learned that Capt. T. came to his death in the following manner: he stepped on the double trees for the purpose of righting the lines when the

Hancock County Indiana Civil War Soldiers

horses started to run. He fell from his position and two wheels of the wagon passed over his head and face, crushing the same so as to cause his death." A Thomas Tuttle, Jr. married Emily Eaton 7 Mar 1867 HC Bk 5-122.

Tuttle, William .H.; 26 Reg Co H, 30 Aug 61-15 Jan 66. A William Tuttle, age 45 years, and two nephews, Joseph Tuttle, age 25 years, and Washington Kirby, age 25 years, were killed in a railroad accident, reported in *Hancock Democrat*, 28 Oct 1897.

Tygart, John M.; 57 Reg Co A, 9 Sep 64, transferred to Veteran Reserve Corps 3 Mar 65, indicating light duty due to illness or wound. A John McClure Tygart married Jane Reed 3 Jun 1852 HC Bk 3-100.

Tygart, Thomas N.; 57 Reg Co A, 13 Dec 61-14 Dec 65. NOD.

Tyner, Elbert Shirk; 148 Reg Co C, 17 Feb 65-5 Sep 65. He was born 7 Dec 1843 at the Tyner homestead in Blue River Townsip (HC), s/o Elijah and Sarah Halberstatt. Elbert Tyner married 23 Oct 1872 at Shelbyville, Indiana, to Pearl Updegraff and they moved to Greenfield in 1882. HC Park Cemetery: Elbert Shirk Tyner 1843-1902, Co C 148 Ind Inf; Pearle E. Tyner 1851-1921.

Tyner, Elijah H.; 8 Reg Co B, 25 Aug 61-12 Jun 65, listed as Prisoner of War but date and place not given. HC obit 23 Mar 1905: "Elijah H. Tyner, aged sixty-one years, died at his home in Morristown, 22 March 1905. Funeral under the auspices of G.A.R. at Christian Church, interment Asbury Cemetery."

Tyner, Oliver; 3rd Indiana Battery, Co A, 1864 killed in battle at Camden, Arkansas, Son of Elijah and third wife, Sarah Halbertsatt, brother of Elbert Shirk Tyner.

Hancock County Indiana Civil War Soldiers

James Thomas

Courtesy of Max Zimmerman

Hancock County Indiana Civil War Soldiers

James Thomas Certificate

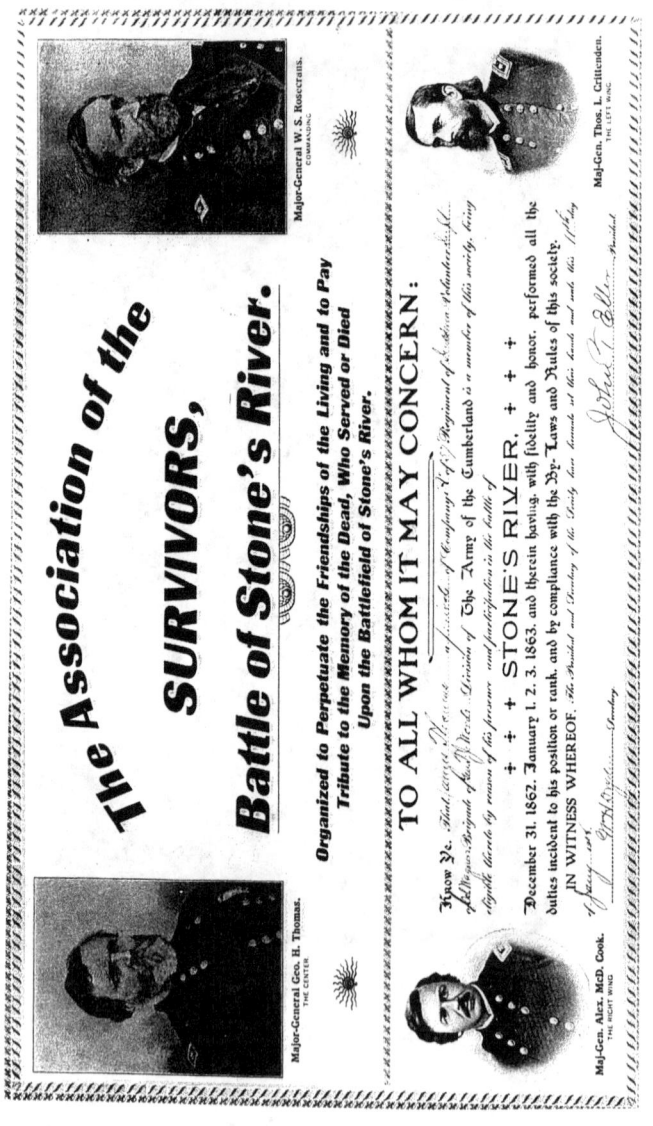

David N. True and Wife Nancy
Harvey True and Wife Phoebe

Courtesy of Judy Martin

Hancock County Indiana Civil War Soldiers

◄ U ►

Ulrey, David; 8 Reg Co G, 22 Apr 61-6 Aug 61. A David Ulrey married Tabitha Lipscomb 24 Mar 1864 HC Bk 4-442. David went to Tennessee in 1882 and died at Athens, Tennessee 21 Feb 1920.

Ulrey, Jefferson; 106 Reg Co D, 10 Jul 63-17 Jul 63. 26 Reg Co I, 24 Sep 64-6 Sep 65. A Jefferson Ulrey married Mary Catherine Kingery 18 Oct 1860 HC Bk 4-215. "Jefferson Ulrey died 23 Jun 1883, age 46, at Sugar Creek Township, cause, consumption, s/o John and Jane Ulrey." HC New Palestine Cemetery: Jefferson Ulrey 7 Jun 1838-22 Jun 1883; Mary C. Ulrey 8 Nov 1841-8 Oct 1912.

Ulrey, John; HC newspaper 13 Nov 1862: " DESERTER KNOW ALL MEN BY THIS THAT JOHN ULREY, a musician of Captain William R. Walls' company B, 8th Indiana Foot Volunteers, deserted the service of the United States, on 24 January 1862. Said soldier enlisted on 20 August 1861, was mustered into the service 25 August 1861. He is 34 years of age, 5 feet, 7 inches high, dark complexion, dark hair, blue eyes, born in Warren County, Ohio and by occupation when enlisted, a cooper. signed, William R. Walls, Capt. Co B, 8th Ind. Inf."

Underwood, James N.; 8 Reg Co B, 25 Aug 61, no out date. HC newspaper 11 June 1863: Private James N. Underwood, arm amputated from wound received near Vicksburg, Mississippi." A James N. Underwood married Margaret Dickson 26 Aug 1869 HC Bk 5-313.

Underwood, John; 8 Reg Co B, 5 Aug 61; A John Underwood married Mary Jane Kennedy 15 Jan 1847 HC Bk 2-221. HC newspaper 28 May 1863:"Pvt. John Underwood, Company B, 8th Regiment, had a hole shot in his cap box." He died 15 Oct 1863, New Orleans. A John Underwood married Mary Jane Kennedy 15 Jan 1847 HC Bk 2-221.

◄ V ►

Hancock County Indiana Civil War Soldiers

Vail, John; 5 Cav Co G, 14 Dec 63-15 Sep 65. See newspaper article, dated 20 October 1921, telling of comrades reunion.

Valentine, Henry; 54 Kentucky Mounted Infantry, Co H, 1 Sep 64-1 Sep 65. A Henry Valentine married Delia Humble 8 Jun 1873 HC Bk 6-203. HC Eden Church Cemetery: Henry Valentine Co H 54 Ky MTD Inf.

Valentine, William; 79 Reg Co C, 15 Aug 62, roster for Company C, 79 Regiment states: "Deserted in face of the enemy." NOD.

Vandyke, Marshall; 57 Reg Co A, 13 Dec 61, discharged wounds, 24 Nov 64. A Marshall Vandyke married 15 Mar 1864 Eliza Ann Carlton HC Bk 4-438.

Vandyke, Seward; 99 Reg Co B, 15 Aug 62-5 Jun 65. "He enlisted for three years in Company B, 99th Indiana Volunteers, Captain Carr's Company, and was a good soldier and in several hard-fought battles. ...born Rush County, Indiana, 5' 7" tall, age 18 years, light complexion, dark eyes, dark hair, farmer when enrolled...He was born 9 Jun 1845, s/o John and Mahala (Seward) Vandyke, and came to Brown Township, Hancock County in 1853, where he worked on the farm and in his father's blacksmith shop. Shortly after his return from the War, he was married to Miss Mary A. Hays, of Madison County and in the spring of 1880 moved to Anderson."

Vanlangingham, Leroy; 79 Reg Co D, 4 Aug 62-7 Jun 65. NOD

Vanzant, Francis, 12 Reg Co H, 17 Aug 62-8 Jun 65, absent, sick. A Francis Vanzant married Martha Shull 11 Jun 1874 HC Bk 6-279. "Francis Vanzant died 28 Feb 1907, age 71 years, s/o Gilbert and Mary (McVay) Vanzant." HC McCordsville Cemetery: Francis M. Vanzant Soldier 1836-1907; Martha 1851-1930.

Vanzant Jesse; 12 Reg Co H, 17 Aug 62, captured 14 Feb 65, died in Rebel Prison. Not on Andersonville Prison database, March 2001; nor on roster of prisoners at Cahaba, Alabama on file at Andersonville Prison Library, March 2001.

Hancock County Indiana Civil War Soldiers

Vanzant, Joseph; 12 Reg Co H, 17 Aug 62-8 Jun 65. A Joseph Vanzant is buried HC Gillium Chapel Cemetery: died 25 Dec 1869, 36 years.

Varner, John; 34 Reg Co D, 21 Sep 61, 30 Dec 63 transferred to Mounted Artillery. "He was disabled in army and draws a pension. Son of Samuel and Mary Slifer, John was born about 1842 in Hancock County, married (no place given) Malintha McDaniel, (d/o Levi McDaniel).

Vernon, John A.; 9 Cav Co B, 23 Dec 63-28 Aug 65. NOD.

Vernon, Robert H.; 99 Reg Co B, 15 Aug 62, died 9 May 65. HC newspaper 9 Jun 1864: "Pvt. Robert H. Vernon, Company B, 99 Regiment, was wounded in hip at Dallas, Georgia, 28 May 1864." 99 Regiment History states: "Robert H. Vernon, Company B, was wounded 28 May 1864, Dallas, Georgia; died 9 May 1865, Laurel Hill, North Carolina."

Vest, Roland; 106 Reg Co D, 10 Jul 63-17 Jul 63. NOD.

Vest, William; 116 Reg Co K, 17 Aug 63-1 Mar 64. HC McCordsville Cemetery: William Vest Co K 116 Ind Inf.

Vestal, W.L. Capt.; 53 Reg Co A, no dates.

Virgin, Various (Vanes); 12 Reg Co B, 15 May 61-19 May 62; 134 Reg Co K, 24 May 64, term expired. The names, Various Virgin and Vanes Virgin have been interchanged on rosters?

Volmer, Jacob, 148 Reg Co I, 8 Feb 65-5 Sep 65. NOD.

Voorhees, Frank; 17 Michigan Inf. Co G, 5 Aug 62-3 Jun 65; residence listed as Jackson, Michigan; age 22 years; after the War he lived in Brainard, Minnesota.

◀ W ▶

Wagoner, Leroy; 51 Reg Co I, 8 Dec 61-14 Dec 64. he is buried HC New Palestine Cemetery, military data only on stone. NOD.

Walker, Bernard; HC Park Cemetery: military data only on stone: Co I 54 Ind Inf. NOD

Walker, George; 105 Reg Co E, 11 Jul 63-18 Jul 63; also 12 Reg Co G, 17 Mar 64, died 19 Apr 65, Davis Island, N.Y.

Hancock County Indiana Civil War Soldiers

Harbor. A George Walker married 8 Apr 1847 Jane Olvey HC Bk 2-235.

Walker, James; 79 Reg Co C, 15 Aug 62-28 Aug 65. A James J. Walker, occupation carpenter, died 14 Nov 1899, age 76, s/o Isaac and Mary (Sanders) Walker. A James Walker married 29 Jul 1865 Mary Heck HC Bk 4-525. HC Park Cemetery: James R. Walker 29 Mar 1848-19 Feb 1919; h/o Mary.

Walker John W.; 105 Reg Co E, 11 Jul 63-18 Jul 63. HC obit 25 Feb 1915: " J. Ward Walker, aged 79 years, for more than a half century one of the well known men of this county in civic welfare, church and politics, died at his home on North State Street, death due to a stroke of paralysis suffered days ago. He was a man of lovable character, a man that looked on the bright side of all questions. Like many others, he was strong in his beliefs and disbeliefs, his likes and dislikes. He was the son of John Wood Walker, Monroe County, West Virginia. He was born at Pendleton (Madison) County, Indiana, 11 Mar 1836 and came to Greenfield in 1858 where he opened the G.H. and J. Ward Walker store.

"Mr. Walker's career as a business man was a busy, successful one. The original capital of $4,000 has grown until the time of his death it amounted to fifty or more thousand dollars. For years he was connected with the Hancock County Agricultural Association as an officer when the fair was held a mile and a half southeast of town. The track was one-third of a mile, or three times around for a mile, this made the horses pass you three times during the mile and was liked by the public. He was president of the Fair Association when the fairs were held on North State Street (where Hancock Memorial Hospital is located). He was united in marriage with Miss Mary J. Todd, who preceded him in death in 1892. To them were born: Luella, Arthur; Mrs. Allie Cook; Wood L. Walker; and Mrs. Ed Wilson. John Ward and Mary Walker are buried HC Park Cemetery."

Walker, Marcellus; "When the Civil War called to arms, Marcellus Walker was eighteen years old, enlisted in Company

Hancock County Indiana Civil War Soldiers

G, 12th Indiana Infantry and took part in many engagements. He was wounded at Richmond, Kentucky, 30 Aug 1862, and taken prisoner but was paroled and returned to his home. After recovering from a life threatening hemorrhage, Marcellus reenlisted 20 Jul 63, in Company B, 9th Indiana Cavalry, of which he was elected third duty sergeant. He was again wounded in August, 1864 at McMinnville, Tennessee. He saw action at Sulphur Trestle, Alabama; Franklin, Tennessee; Vicksburg and the fall of Mobile.

"In July 1865, Sgt. Walker was aboard a hospital boat that collided with another boat on the Mississippi River, knocking a hole in the hull causing the deaths of one-hundred-fifty souls on board. The survivors were picked up by a passing steamer and taken to Jefferson Barracks just below St. Louis, Missouri. He arrived home 28 August 1865. The son of Miles and Rachel Walker, Marcellus was born in Hancock County, Indiana, 1 Dec 1843, married 31 Dec 1865, Miss Mary Gray." Marcellus died 4 Feb 1920." HC newspaper 20 Oct 1864: "Sgt. Marcellus B. Walker, Company B, 9 Cavalry, was wounded in action at Sulphur Trestle (Alabama) 25 Sep 1864."

Walker, Samuel; "When the Civil War broke out in all its fury, Samuel Walker enlisted 8 Sep 1861 in Company D, 34th Indiana Infantry Regiment, age 22, 5' 8" tall, dark complexion, gray eyes, dark hair. The command proceeded to Port Gibson, Mississippi, taking part in that battle and later participated in the bloody engagement at Champion Hill and the long siege of Vicksburg. It fell to the command to meet the enemy in the last engagement of the War, which was fought 13 May 1865, at Palo Alto Prairie, Texas. He was never wounded nor fell into the hands of the enemy. He was discharged 4 Feb 1866, at Brownsville, Texas.

"Samuel was born 1 Dec 1841, Hancock County, son of Meredith and Verlinda (Wales) Walker; married (HC Bk 7-78) 6 Mar 1879 Matilda Margaret Barrett, born 16 Mar 1845, died 26 Mar 1886, daughter of Isaac and Sarah Barrett. HC obit 7 Aug 1919: Samuel Walker, a soldier of the Civil War, and an

Hancock County Indiana Civil War Soldiers

old resident of this county, died at his home in Charlottesville. He leaves a widow and three half brothers, Linza; George; and John of Jackson Township." Samuel and Matilda are buried HC Simmons Cemetery.

Wallace, George W.; 75 Reg Co I, 15 Jul 62-8 Jun 65. A George W. Wallace married 16 Sep 1879 Bettie Piersall HC Bk 7-118. NOD.

Wallace, William; HC Willow Branch Cemetery: William Wallace 20 Btry Ind Lt Arty. Military stone only, no dates.

Waller, Benjamin; 9 Cav Co B, 9 Dec 63-28 Aug 65. Benjamin Waller survived the explosion and burning of the steamboat, Sultana, on the Mississippi River, near Memphis, 27 Apr 1865.

Waller, Isaac; 105 Reg Co E, 11 Jul 63-18 Jul 63; also 134 Reg Co K, 24 May 64, term expired. NOD. Walls, John H.; 9 Cav Co B, 13 Nov 63, private; - 8 Jun 65, quarter-master. A John H. Walls married Maryander Hawk 25 Oct 1863 HC Bk 4-356. HC New Palestine Cemetery: John H. Walls died 18 Jun 1870, 27y 7m 27d Co B 9 Ind Cav. 1860 Federal Census Hancock County, Indiana, page 697 records: John H. Walls, age 26, born Tennessee; Jane Abicht, age 54, born Tennessee (mother of John H. Walls); and Isorah Walls , age 11, female, born Indiana.

Waller, William H.; 9 Cav Co B, 9 Dec 63-28 Aug 65, Sgt. A William H. Waller married 11 Aug 1867 Elizabeth Derry HC Bk 5-152.

Walls, John H.; 9 Cav Co B, 13 Nov 63, private; - 8 Jun 65, quarter-master. A John H. Walls married Maryander Hawk 25 Oct 1863 HC Bk 4-356. HC New Palestine Cemetery: John H. Walls died 18 Jun 1870, 27y 7m 27d Co B 9 Ind Cav. 1860 Federal Census Hancock County, Indiana, page 697 records: John H. Walls, age 26, born Tennessee; Jane Abicht, age 54, born Tennessee (mother of John H. Walls); and Isorah Walls , age 11, female, born Indiana.

Walls, William R.; 8 Reg Co B, 19 Aug 61, commissioned, Captain, resigned 17 Jan 63; reentered 9 Cav, 9 Dec 63 as

Hancock County Indiana Civil War Soldiers

Captain; promoted to Major 9 Dec 64, to Field and Staff; out 28 Aug 65. HC newspaper article 1 May 1861: "William R. Walls, of Palestine, has been elected to the first Lieutenancy of Captain Riley's company (Co B, 8 Reg). This was occasioned by the absence of Lieut. Rardin, at the time of mustering into the service of Uncle Sam."

HC newspaper notice 10 Dec 1863: "Died in Palestine, on Friday, 30 Oct 1863, of typhoid fever, Ida, daughter of Col. Wm. R. and Elvira J. Walls, aged 3 years." The 1860 Federal Census for New Palestine, Hancock County, Indiana, page 718 records: William R. Walls, age 32, attorney at law, born Tennessee; Elvira J. Walls, age 29, born Indiana; and the following four children, born Indiana, Mary age 9; Florence age 7; Elizabeth age 4; and William E., age 2.

Wallsmith, William; 79 Reg Co C, 15 Aug 62-7 Jun 65. A William Wallsmith married 11 Mar 1866 Hannah Apple HC Bk 3-40.

Walters, Samuel; HC Philadelphia Cemetery: Samuel Walters Co B 96 Ind Inf, military stone only, no dates. NOD

Ward, Hiram; 106 Reg Co D, 10 Jul 63-17 Jul 63. NOD

Ward, Michael; 57 Reg Co A, 13 Dec 61-23 Apr 62. A Michael Ward married 7 Oct 1869 Mary J. Ray HC Bk 5-237.

Ward, Theodore; 19 Reg Co F, 8 Mar 64, transferred to 20th Reg. NOD.

Warner, William; 9 Cav Co B, 13 Nov 63-27 Jun 65. William Warner survived the explosion and burning of the steamboat, Sultana, on the Mississippi River, near Memphis, 27 Apr 1865.

Waterman, John; 12 Reg Co G, 21 Jul 62, wagoner. "Enlisted at Fortville, Indiana, and with his regiment was hurried to the field of war. On 29 August 1862 he received a gunshot wound in the right shoulder at the battle of Richmond, Kentucky. As the battle raged around him, he laid on the field nearly thirty-six hours without food when he fell into the hands of the enemy whose surgeons dressed and treated the wound. On 6 July 1863, he was sent to the hospital at Camp Dennison, Ohio, where he remained until discharged 22 Jul 63.

Hancock County Indiana Civil War Soldiers

"He was captured at the battle of Richmond, after receiving the wound and was paroled the next day. John's two brothers, Isaac and William served in Indiana regiments; his brothers-in-law all served in Indiana regiments: Joseph, William, James, Francis, and Thomas Lakens. John Waterman was born 30 Jul 1829 in Hamilton County, Indiana, s/o Abraham and Nancy (Whelchel) Waterman; married 1) Barbara Cattleon 19 Jun 1855 who died 10 Sep 1867; married 2) Mary A. (Lakens) Lunsford who was born 2 May 1821."

Walters, Samuel; 99 Reg Co B, 13 Aug 62-12 Jul 63. A Samuel Walters married 22 Dec 1864 Catherine Seachrist HC Bk 4-492. 99th Regiment History states: "Samuel Walters, Philadelphia, Indiana, dead in 1900." HC Philadelphia Cemetery: Samuel Walters; wife; and child; no dates given.

Watson, James A.; 12 Reg Co B, 15 May 61-19 May 62; also 53 Reg Co A, 24 Feb 64-21 Jul 65. HC newspaper 14 July 1864: "J.A. Watson was wounded in the hip at Kennesaw Mountain but not severely." A James Absolom Watson married 25 Nov 1855 Mary Elizabeth Samuels. HC Park Cemetery: James A. Watson died 6 Mar 1886 57y 10m 14d; Mary E. w/o J.A. died 18 Mar 1900 63y 1m 4d.

Watson, William C.; 147 Reg Co H, 14 Feb 65-4 Aug 65. NOD.

Watts, George W.; 99 Reg Co B, 13 Aug 62. "...born Hancock County, Indiana, 5' 11" tall, age 27, light complexion, hazel eyes, light hair, farmer when enrolled..." Discharged, disability, 25 May 65, due to wounds received in battle. HC newspaper 9 Jun 1864: "Orderly G.W. Watts was wounded in the leg in battle at Dallas, Georgia, 28 May 1864." 99th Regiment History states: "1st. Sgt George W. Watts was severely wounded 28 May 1864, Dallas, Georgia; his 1900 residence is Indianapolis."

Watts. Winfield Scott; HC obit 20 Jul 1932: "The thin ranks of living Hancock County Civil War veterans were further depleted by the death of Winfield Scott Watts, at his home, 437 Fifth Street (Greenfield). Mr. Watts was the last of the

Hancock County Indiana Civil War Soldiers

members of Dunbar Post, Grand Army of the Republic. For several years he and Taylor Morford, whose death occurred recently, were the only G.A.R. men able to participate in public events of a patriotic nature. Mr. Watts is survived by the widow, Sally Watts, a grandson, Paul, a step-son, Marion Worland and a sister, Susan Ducus. Interment Lebanon." "Winfield Scott Watts, age 83 years, died 19 Jul 1932, occupation, carpenter, wife, Sallie E. Watts, Winfield was born 10 Aug 1848, parents not given."

Weaver, Charles; 57 Reg Co A, 13 Dec 61-14 Dec 65. NOD.

Webb, John K.; HC Cooper Cemetery: John K. Webb Co A 8 Ind Inf, died 14 Jan 1904; Lydia w/o John 28 Feb 1828-24 Jun 1896. NOD,

Welling, Hamilton; 148 Reg Co C, 17 Feb 65-5 Sep 65. NOD.

Welling, John S.; 8 Reg Co B, 30 May 64-28 Aug 65. A John Welling married 21 Dec 1870 Emma Snider HC Bk 5-435.

Welling, William W.; 8 Reg Co B, 25 Aug 61, no out date. HC newspaper 11 June 1863: "Corp'l. William W. Welling was wounded severely in the side and arm near Vicksburg." A William Welling married 21 Jan 1867 Margaret Black. HC Bk 5-114.

Wellington, Thomas; 105 Reg Co E, 11 Jul 63-18 Jul 63. NOD.

Welsby, John; 148 Reg Co F, 3 Feb 65-5 Sep 65. NOD.

Welsh, John S.; 40 Reg Co C, 6 Dec 61-16 Jun 65. A John Welsh married 13 May 1878 Lizzie Copper HC Bk 6-593.

Welsh, Thomas; 40 Reg Co C, 6 Dec 61, discharged, wounds, 4 Feb 62. NOD.

Welt, Daniel; 9 Reg Co C, no dates. NOD.

Werts, (Wort) John J., 5 Cav Co G, 16 Aug 62-7 Jun 65. "John Werts, farmer, born 25 Dec 1839, Ohio, died 13 Jun 1902, Hancock County, Indiana, s/o John (born Germany) and Mary (Andrick, born Germany) Werts. HC Hinchman Cemetery: John J. Wirts 25 Dec 1839-13 Jun 1902; John died 26 Mar 1872 62y 7m 28d; Mary w/o John died 29 Jul 1887 71y 7m 8d. HC death notice 25 Mar 1872: "John Werts, an old and

Hancock County Indiana Civil War Soldiers

respectable citizen of Center township, died of dropsy. He had been a citizen of the county for twenty-eight years, and all that time was a very good citizen and never known to harm anyone."

West, David W.; 105 Co E, 11 Jul 63-18 Jul 63. A David W. West married 24 Aug 1859 Elizabeth Nichols HC Bk 4-145.

West, Jno.; 11 Reg Co F, no dates. "John West, age 63, died 7 (another source states he died 10TH) Dec 1893, Buck Creek Township, widow, parents not given." Buried HC Burris/Hendricks Cemetery.

Whelchel, Abraham; 12 Reg Co G, 15 Aug 62-8 Jun 65. NOD.

Whelchel, Francis M.; 155 Reg Co E, 23 Mar 65-21 Jul 65. HC Caudell/ Simmons Cemetery: Francis M. Whelchel Co E, 155 Ind Inf, military data only on stone, no dates.

Whelchel, John; 12 Reg Co G, 21 Jul 62-8 Jun 65. NOD.

Whetsel, Isaac, 9 Reg Co D, 24 Feb 65-3 Oct 65. NOD.

Whitaker, James M.; 53 Reg Co A, no dates. "James M. Whitaker, (widowed, Harriett, deceased), age 93, born 20 Aug 1836, died 27 Jan 1930, s/o Mark and Mary (Prickett) Whitaker." HC obit 28 Jan 1930: "The rapidly thinning ranks of the veterans of the Civil War lost another when James M. Whitaker, age 93, passed away at the home of his daughter, Mrs. Inez Sloan, at the corner of Fifth and Indiana Streets. Mr. Whitaker is survived only by the daughter, one grandson, Ralph Sloan, and a sister, Mrs. Eliza Marsh. He had been in ill health for some time, and is the third veteran of the War of the Rebellion to pass away in this community within a few days.

"Mr. Whitaker was a member of Company A, 53rd Indiana Volunteers, and served for over two years with that regiment. During the past several years, Mr. Whitaker had become a familiar figure on the streets of Greenfield, using a wheel chair to get about after his age and disabilities rendered him unable to walk much." HC Mt. Lebanon Cemetery: James M. Whitaker 20 Aug 1836-27 Jan 1930; Harriett w/o James M. 4 Nov 1843-14 Mar 1909. James Whitaker and Harriett

Hancock County Indiana Civil War Soldiers

Chappell were married 29 Jan 1857 HC Bk 5-115. His brother, William also served in 53 Reg Co A.

Whitaker, Morris; 148 Reg Co C, 17 Feb 65-5 Sep 65. NOD.

Whitaker, William; 53 Reg Co A, 20 Sep 64-13 Jul 65. "William Whitaker, born 3 Jan 1832, died 7 Sep 1909, cause billiary dysentery, s/o Mark and Mary (Prickett) Whitaker." HC obit 2 Sep 1909: "William Whitaker, well-known veteran of the Civil War, died at his home on Swope Street. He was a son of the late Mark Whitaker, and was 77 years of age, and was the father of Joseph Whittaker, of Greenfield, The funeral and interment, Mt. Lebanon Church." A William Whitaker married 1) 28 Mar 1850 Josephine Moss HC Bk 2-381; married 2) 31 Dec 1867 Amanda Jackson HC Bk 5-187.

White, Elijah; 148 Reg Co I, 17 Feb 65-5 Sep 65. NOD.

White, James; 148 Reg Co C, 14 Feb 65-4 Aug 65. NOD.

White, John; 9 Reg Co C, 14 Feb 65-3 Oct 65. HC Mt. Lebanon Cemetery: John H. White 3 Dec 1824-28 Aug 1921; HC Simmons Cemetery: John W. White 18 Jul 1827-11 Nov 1911. NOD.

White, William; 105 Reg Co E, 11 Jul 63-18 Jul 63. Too many men named William White in sources to differentiate.

Whitecotton, John; 53 Reg Co A, no dates. NOD.

Whitehurst, Vinton; 99 Reg Co B, 23 Mar 64-29 May 65. 99th Regiment History states: "Vinton Whitehurst was wounded 28 May 1864 at Dallas, Georgia; his 1900 residence is Beloit, Kansas."

Whiteside, Obediah; 10 Oct 64, mustered into 38 Reg Co D, as substitute for Thomas Hamilton; out 15 Jul 65. Son of Benjamin, born Marion County, Indiana, 5' 11" tall, age 19 years, light complexion, Blue eyes, light hair. Obediah married Mary E.C. Eastes 10 Oct 1868. Contributed by Ruth Bundy, Greenfield, Indiana. *Hancock Democrat*, 24 Nov 1870: "We regret to learn that Obediah Whitesides, a citizen of Buck Creek Township, in this county, died on Friday, 11November 1870. He leaves a young wife and one child. They have lost a good husband and kind father, and the people a good citizen

Hancock County Indiana Civil War Soldiers

and warm friend." HC Eastes/Harvey Cemetery: Obediah Whitesides died 11 Nov 1870 25y 7m 8d. The widow, Mary Elizabeth Charlotta Whitesides married John Samuel Bell 22 Mar 1876 HC Bk 6-442. Brother of Oliver.

Whitesides, Oliver, 38 Reg Co D, 10 Oct 64-15 Jul 65 as substitute. Married Susan Lancaster, born Marion County, Indiana. HC Mt. Comfort Cemetery: Oliver Whitesides 3 May 1846-12 Jan 1911; Susan L. Whitesides 15 Dec 1852-23 Feb 1929. Brother of Obediah.

Whorton, Elisha; 51 Reg Co D, 14 Dec 61, died 5 Mar 64, Nashville, Tennessee. NOD.

Wiggins, George; 53 Reg Co A, 24 Feb 62, no out date. "Never heard from after the War, he was the son of Garrett and Harriett (Toadvine) Wiggins, who came to Hancock County in 1842. George's brothers, Lawson (Loss) and John F. served in the Union army; and brother, Phillip served in the Confederate army.

Wiggins, John F.; 8 Reg Co B 25 Aug 61, three months; reenlisted in 14th Reg Co K, served until 26 Aug 64. "...born Rush County, Indiana, 6' tall, age 21, dark complexion, hazel eyes, dark hair, farmer when enrolled..." HC newspaper 14 Aug 1862: "John Wiggins, Co B, 8th Regiment, was sick and left in a hospital boat several days ago." HC obit 25 Oct 1923; "John Wiggins, one of the old residents of Hancock County, died suddenly on the street in Fortville on the way to the home of his daughter, Mrs. George Sherman. Mr. Wiggins was 83 years old, a retired farmer who lived with his daughter, Mrs. Jesse Brown, eight miles northeast of this city and was going to spend Sunday with another daughter when he suffered the fatal attack. His wife was Miss Martha Clayton, who died in 1913.

"Mr. Wiggins was a soldier in the Civil War, serving three years and ten months in Company B, 8th Indiana Regiment. He was a member of the Grand Army of the Republic and is survived by eight children." Gravel Lawn Cemetery, Madison County, Indiana: John F. Wiggins 31 Aug 1840-20 Oct 1923

Hancock County Indiana Civil War Soldiers

Co B 8 Ind Inf; Martha M. w/o John F. 4 Dec 1847-30 Jun 1913. See data for his brother, George Wiggins.

Wiggins, Lawson (Loss); HC newspaper 14 Aug 1862: "Lawson Wiggins, Co B, 8th Regiment, was sick and left on a hospital boat a few days ago." HC obit 6 Jan 1916: "Lawson Wiggins, aged 77 years, a veteran of the Civil war, died at his home in Blue River Township, near Westland. He was born in Rush County, Indiana, 16 June 1838, the son of Garrett and Harriett (Toadvine) Wiggins. On 20 August 1861, he enlisted in Company B, 8th Indiana Volunteers, and served until the close of the War.

"On 27 February 1863, he was married to Margaret Cobble (1845-1931), to whom were born nine children, three of whom are deceased. Those surviving are: John; Mrs. C.R. Hill; Arthur; George; Marshall; and Mrs. L.O. Andrews. The deceased was a member of the Grand Army of the Republic and the Westland Friends Church. Lawson and Margaret are buried HC Park Cemetery. HC Curry's Chapel Church Cemetery: Garrett Wiggins died 11 Jun 1864 62y 6m 1d.

Wilborn, Martin V.; 9 Cav Co B, 16 Dec 63-8 Jun 65. NOD.

Wilcoxen, Edwin H.; 8 Reg Co B, 14 Jan 64, died 3 Aug 64, Washington, D.C.

Wilkins, Harrison; 13 Ohio Inf Co E, 20 yrs. old, 11 Jun 61-26 Jun 64. " Harrison Wilkins, died 11 Aug 1926, cause cerebral apoplexy, born 5 Mar 1841, s/o Ozias and Matilda (Hines) Wilkins, wife, Mary deceased." Shelby County newspaper obit 19 Aug 1926: "Harrison Wilkins, 85 years old, Civil war veteran, died at his home in New Palestine from a complication of diseases. He is survived by three sons, Harvey, Eugene and Charles; and two daughters, Flora Streng and Leoti Wilkins." HC New Palestine Cemetery: Harrison Wilkins 1841-1926 Co E 13 Ohio Inf.; Mary 1841-1916.

Willett, Charles; 5 Cav Co G, 5 Jun 64-7 Jun 65. HC newspaper 11 Aug 1864: "C.J. Willett was taken prisoner during the disastrous expedition commanded by General Stoneman." Andersonville Prison Profile #62025: Charles

Hancock County Indiana Civil War Soldiers

Willett, Company G, 5th Indiana Cavalry, survived and exchanged 1 April 1865." HC obit 17 Oct 1929: "Charles J. Willett, son of Matthew and Elizabeth Willett, was born in Hancock County, Indiana, 20 March 1845, and departed this life 10 October 1929, at the home of his son, Jesse, in Indianapolis.

"As a young man he heard the call of his country and enlisted in her service and was assigned to Company G, 5th Indiana Cavalry. It was his trying lot to be among his fellow soldiers as a prisoner in Andersonville Prison for nine months where thousands of Union prisoners perished from cruel treatment, starvation and exposure. He was united in marriage to Mary Jones (29 Sep 1867 HC Bk 5-165). To this union was born a son, Jesse, who survives, also a brother, Matthew. Interment (HC) Park Cemetery."

Willett, Clay; 79 Reg Co B, 9 Aug 62-23 Dec 62. NOD.

Williams, Charles J.; 11 Reg Co I, 24 Feb 65-3 Oct 65. NOD.

Williams, John M.; 53 Reg Co A, 24 Feb 62, no out date; also 105 Reg Co E 11 Jul 63-18 Jul 63. HC newspaper 16 April 1862: "John M. Williams, of Company A, 53rd Regiment, arrived in town yesterday morning. He reports the regiment at Savannah, eight miles from Pittsburg Landing where it was at the time of the battle. Mr. Williams says the boys from this county are in good health except Benajmin Osborn. Mr. W. is on sick furlough."

Williams, T.W.; 5 Cav Co G, no dates. HC newspaper 11 Aug 1864: T.W. Williams, Company G, 5th Cavalry, was taken prisoner during the disastrous expedition commanded by General Stoneman." Andersonville Prison Profile #62104: "T.W. Williams, Company G, 5th Indiana Cavalry, survived."

Williams, Thomas; "On 11 September 1842, there came to the home of Wesley and Catherine Williams a baby boy, who received the name of Thomas. When the Civil War broke out, though only a lad of eighteen, Thomas responded to the call of his country, and on 1 September 1861, enlisted in Company I, 7th Indiana Regiment at Indianapolis. Immediately, he was sent

Hancock County Indiana Civil War Soldiers

to the front and served in the eastern division of the army. His army life was very strenuous, engaging in twenty-seven battles, of which eighteen were the severest of the whole war, including Vicksburg, Mine Run, Gettysburg and Antietam. In the battle of the Wilderness, near Spottsylvania Court House, on 12 May 1864, he was wounded in the hand, and lingered for three months in the hospital. This wound caused him much trouble in his later life.

"While in the service, his father remembered his boy at the family altar, and on 12 August 1864, he saw his prayers answered in the return of his soldier boy. Indeed, it was a happy reunion they had on that day. Thomas Williams married 1) 22 June 1865, Eustatcia Moore who was born 24 October 1848, and died 30 July 1879 (buried HC Simmons Cemetery); he married 2) Cora D. Hackleman 11 April 1880, which union was blessed with two sons, John and Virgil. Virgil died 10 March 1910. Thomas Williams united with the Brown's Chapel Church in 1866 when a revival was held in the old school house and to this church he has made his allegiance ever since.

"One characteristic of his life is that of a tenacious persistency. In the struggle of the Rebellion, he displayed a dogged disposition that made of him a good soldier. In 1902 this same spirit was displayed when a storm made havoc of his home church. With a grim determination, he entered upon the task of rebuilding the church, and his work was well accomplished. He has served his three score and ten, almost. His faults may have been glaring. Who is faultless? His spirit, into the hands of the Good Father, we commend, trusting to Him, our every anxiety. Thomas leaves a wife, one son, John; one brother, Sanford; two sisters, Charity Simmons and Deborah Bever, and a host of relatives and friends. He passed from this life on 13 July 1912 at his late home in Greenfield, where he had lived since 1902. Written by his son, John Wesley Williams.

Hancock County Indiana Civil War Soldiers

"The Adjutant General's Office returned to the Commissioner of Pensions, Bureau of Pensions, Dept. of the Interior, 13 June 1908: "Thomas Williams, Co I, 7th Indiana Volunteer Regiment, age 19, was enrolled 7 Aug 1861 and mustered out 20 Sep 1864. From being mustered in to the time he was mustered out he held the rank of Pvt. and the rolls on file for that period do not show him absent except as follows: 3 April 1863 detailed as guard at Bde (?) Headquarters, and from 30 June to 31 August 1864 absent wounded.

"Medical records show him treated as follows: 12-15 May 1864, wound metacarpus. 16 May to 10 August 1864, gunshot wound 3rd and little finger right hand was wounded on 13 May 1864 at Spottsylvania by a Minie ball entering on the dorsal surface and passing out on the palmar aspect fracturing in its course the metacarpal bone of ring finger and very much lacerating the soft parts. 22 May 1864 erysipelas set in, the hand became enormously swollen , it is now reduced to normal size but the fingers remain somewhat stiffened. Furloughed 10 August 1864. No additional record of disability found." Thomas Williams pension #76399. Contributed by Omer S.J. Williams and Thomas E.Q. Williams.

Willis, Samuel; 13 Cav Co I, 11 Jan 64-7 Mar 65. A Samuel Willis married 16 Feb 1859 Nancy Blackford HC Bk 4-124.

Wills (Willis), A.D.; 105 Reg Co E, 11 Jul 63-18 Jul 63. An Alfred D. Wills died 5 Jan 1879, no place given.

Wills, Jacob; 105 Co E, 11 Jul 63-18 Jul 63. A Jacob Wills married 2 Sep 1863 Sara Winn HC Bk 4-396.

Wilson, Adam F.; "When the Civil War broke out he was farming in Hancock County, and the loyal blood of his ancestors who participated in the Revolutionary War and War of 1812 asserted itself, he vowed to assist in putting down the spirit of treason rising in the South, and on 4 July 1861, he celebrated the eighty-fifth anniversary of his country by enrolling his name as private in Company B, 8th Indiana Volunteer Infantry. The excessive hardships of camp life and the weary marches soon brought on sickness and in November,

Hancock County Indiana Civil War Soldiers

1861, he found himself in the hospital at Otterville, Missouri, with measles, where he spent three months, and in February 1862, received a sixty day furlough to go home, this was extended on account of disability until August 1862, when he joined his comrades at Helena, Arkansas.

"The most of his service was in pursuit of Price in Missouri, who they gave a lively chase and routed from place to place until he finally fled from the state into Arkansas, with his pursuers in hot chase after him. Adam was discharged 29 April 1863 at Indianapolis; his wife's brother, Isaac Lain, was in the 13th Indiana Cavalry. Adam F. Wilson (11 Dec 1836-31 Mar 1920) was born in Brown County, Ohio, the son of James and Catherine (Flaugher) Wilson. Adam was married 17 Jan 1864, near (HC) Mohawk, to Elizabeth Lain, (15 May 1845-31 Mar 1907) who was born in Bartholomew County, Indiana, 15 May 1843, daughter of Jacob and Sarah (Jones) Lain. There address in 1899 was Mohawk, Indiana." Adam and Elizabeth are buried HC Mt.Gilead/Reeves Cemetery. See Wilson family letters for details during the Civil War.

Wilson, Alfred; 8 Reg Co B, 25 Aug 61, killed 23 May 1863, Vicksburg. HC newspaper 11 June 1863: "On 20 May 1863, while advancing, Alfred Wilson was hit by a grape shot striking him on the head and would not be removed from the field to a hospital until he laid hold of his gun which he persisted in carrying with him. He died from the wound. Signed Samuel H. Dunbar." Alfred was the son of Isaac and Ann (Griffith) Wilson and brother of Jane Wilson who married John Cahill.

Wilson, Amos; 12 Reg Co G, killed Atlanta 3 Aug 1864. NOD.

Wilson, Charles C.; 26 Reg Co I, 14 Oct 64, no out date. Two marriages for a Charles C. Wilson: 24 Jun 1857 Clarissa Brooks HC Bk 4-23; and 21 Oct 1864 Martha Sewell HC Bk 4-482.

Wilson, George P. 9 Cav Co B, 9 Dec 63-10 Jul 65. George P. Wilson is listed as a survivor of the explosion and burning of

Hancock County Indiana Civil War Soldiers

the steamboat, Sultana, on the Mississippi River, near Memphis, 27 Apr 1865.

Wilson, Henry; 79 Reg   "Son of James and Catherine (Flaugher) Wilson and brother of Adam F., Henry died at Nashville, Tennessee, while serving in the Civil War."

Wilson, James; 8 Cav Co M, trumpeter, 26 Jan 64-20 Jul 65. "...born Delaware County, Indiana, 5' 7" tall, age 18, light complexion, hazel eyes, dark hair, saddler when enrolled..."NOD.

Wilson, James; 84 Reg Co E, 25 Aug 62-20 Aug 63. "...born Delaware County, Indiana, 5' 5" tall, age 18, fair complexion, blue eyes, auburn hair, mail carrier when enrolled..." NOD.

Wilson, John; HC Courthouse, Soldier Burial List: 68 reg Co D; died 16 Aug 1894; 51 years; occupation, buggy maker; burial, Knightstwon, Indiana. NOD.

Wilson, Samuel; 8 Reg Co G, 5 Sep 61, died of disease, Nov 61, at St. Louis, Missouri. He was the son of Isaac and Ann (Griffith) Wilson, sister of Jane Wilson who married John Cahill; Samuel's brother, Alfred, was killed at Vicksburg.

Wilson, William; 99 Reg Co B, 13 Aug 62-5 Jun 65. Too many William Wilsons in sources to differentiate.

Wilson, William; 99 Reg Co B, 13 Aug 62, listed on roster as deserted 1Mar 1863. NOD.

Windler (Windell), William R.; 12 Reg CoB, 15 May 61-19 May 62. A William R. Windell married 30 Sep 1865 Mary Morris HC Bk 4-545.

Windsor, George; 51 Reg Co D, 14 Dec 61-died 26 Aug 63, Indianapolis. A George Windsor married 18 Aug 1861 Nancy Chowning HC Bk 4-279. HC Old Greenfield Cemetery: George Windsor Co D 51 Ind Inf, NOD.

Wingfield, Jasper N.; 53 Reg Co A, 24 Feb 62-21 Jul 65. HC obit 27 Mar 1930: "Jasper N. Wingfield, born 1841 in Hancock County and a resident here most of his life, died at the home of his daughter, Mrs. L. R. Tabor, Indianapolis. Mr. Wingfield was 88 years old, a Civil War veteran having served in Company A, 53rd Indiana Volunteers more than three years.

Hancock County Indiana Civil War Soldiers

He married Miss Margaret Bridges 13 Sep 1866 HC Bk 5-83. He was a member of the Grand Army of the Republic and was highly respected in the community. He is survived by three children Cornell and Oscar Wingfield; and Mrs. Tabor. Interment HC Park Cemetery."

Winn, David; 12 Reg Co B, 15 May 61-1 Aug 61. A David T. Winn married 24 Dec 1876 Flora Piersall HC Bk 6-331.

Winn (Wynn), John J.; 9 Cav Co B, 13 Nov 63-28 Aug 65. HC newspaper 20 Oct 1864: "Pvt. J. Winn, Company B, 9th Cavalry, was wounded 25 Sep 1864 at Sulphur Trestle (Alabama) and will soon be home." A John Winn married 29 Jan 1879 Mary Roberts HC Bk 7-68; a John Wynn, born 2 Dec 1844 at Fortville, Indiana, s/o Abe Wynn; John served in 9 Cav Co B, married 25 Nov 1872 Lucinda Foster.

Winn, Joshua; 12 Reg Co B, 15 May 61-19 May 62. NOD.

Winn, Madison; 99 Reg Co B, 13 Aug 62, died 23 Feb 63. 99th Regiment History states: "Madison Winn died 22 Feb 1863, Moscow, Tennessee."

Winslow, Patrick Henry; HC obit 27 Oct 1921: "Patrick Henry Winslow, a soldier of the Civil War and a well-known resident of Greenfield, passed away following an extended illness. Mr. Winslow was born in Guilford, North Carolina, the son of Ezra and Martha (Ballard) Winslow. His father died when (Patrick) Henry was two years old and he came with his mother to Henry County, Indiana, one year later. The mother died when he was 12 years old.

"He enlisted for the Civil War from Henry County when a little over fifteen years old, and served thirty-one months in the 22nd Battery Light Artillery. Funeral services at the residence, 520 Wood Street and interment Park Cemetery." Henry Winslow married 8 Feb 1872 Sarah Clayton HC Bk 6-84. HC Park Cemetery: Patrick Henry Winslow 1847-1921; Sarah Margaret w/o Patrick Henry 1851-1918.

Wiseman, Levi; 12 Reg Co B, 15 May 61-19 May 62. NOD.

Wishmeier, Anton; 79 Reg Co D, 13 Aug 62-7 Jun 65. NOD.

Hancock County Indiana Civil War Soldiers

Wishmeier, Christian; 148 Reg Co C, 17 Feb 65-5 Sep 65. HC newspaper 15 Sep 1898: "New Palestine News: Please allow me to refer to an incident that has occurred. In February, 1865, I took Calvin Bennett and Christian Wishmeier to Indianapolis where they both mustered into Company C, 148th Regiment. They served together until the close of the war and I have received word that Calvin Bennett died 1 Sep 1898 in Hancock County and Christian Wishmeier died 1 Sep 1898 in Indianapolis. I think both of them serving in the same unit and dying the same day is a little remarkable, signed Ernest Faut."

Witham, Ephraim; 5 Cav Co G, 14 Dec 63-20 Dec 64. NOD.

Wolf, John; 8 Reg Co G, 22 Apr 61-6 Aug 61. NOD.

Wolf, Jonathan; 57 Reg Co A, 13 Dec 61-25 Feb 63, wagoner. A Jonathan Wolf married 3 Feb 1852 Catherine Wilson HC Bk 3-77.

Wolf, Joseph; 9 Reg Co C, 14 Feb 65-3 Oct 65. A Joseph Wolf married 19 May 1860 Jane Gordon HC Bk 4-194.

Wood, Jeremiah; 99 Reg Co B, 13 Aug 62-5 Jun 65. 99th Regiment History: photo of Jeremiah, "Have no sketch of Comrade Woods, but he served in all the campaigns of the regiment, and his address in 1900 is Knightstown, Indiana. Two marriages for a Jeremiah Wood: 30 Mar 1845 Phoebe Shipman HC Bk 2-155; 12 Oct 1870 Sarah Sample HC Bk 5-408.

Wood, Robert; 134 Reg Co K, 24 May 64-term expired. NOD.

Wood, Robert T.; 9 Reg Co C, 14 Feb 65-28 Sep 65. NOD.

Woodall (Woodhall), William; 148 Reg Co I, 8 Feb 65. NOD.

Woods, G.W.; see newspaper article on page for Columbus C. Marsh.

Woods, Joel; 75 Reg Co I, 20 Jun 62, died of disease, 20 Nov 62 at Frankfort, Kentucky. NOD.

Wray, Samuel William; HC obit 4 Nov 1912: "Samuel William Wray, age 87 years, a Civil War veteran and pioneer citizen of Greenfield, died at his home 403 West Main Street. He had been in poor health for some time. Mr. Wray was born in Ireland, 25 April 1825. He came to this country, landing in

Hancock County Indiana Civil War Soldiers

Quebec, Canada, in 1843; from there he went to Orville, Ohio, in 1844, where he learned his trade as a wagon and carriage maker. From there he moved to Pittsburg, Pennsylvania, and returned again to Ronsburg, Ohio.

"He came to Greenfield 5 April 1865, and has lived here ever since. He established a shop and manufactured wagons and carriages here for many years. In fact, he worked at his trade, which he loved, until recent years, when his health began to fail. Mr. Wray fought throughout the Civil War as a member of the 163rd Ohio Infantry and had many thrilling experiences. He was of a quiet and contented nature and an excellent citizen, who had the respect of all. His wife (Mary Jane born 15 Jul 1823) passed away 9 September, 1907. The deceased leaves four children, Samuel A.; William J.; Mrs. Margaret Hughes and Tillie Wray. Interment Park Cemetery."

HC obit 21 Mar 1928 of their son, Samuel Archiball Wray 21 Mar 1928: gives the following family details: He was born 24 August 1849, the son of Samuel William Wray, who was born in Coldrain County, Derby, Ireland, in 1825...at Pittsburg he married Miss Mary Jane McIlreavy, who was born in Balaymoney, Scotland, in 1823. She came to America when a little girl, making the passage alone, to the home of a relative. She acquired a good education and graduated from Wooster College in Ohio.

"Samuel Archiball Wray possessed a large property, including more than 400 acres of land in Hancock County. He was never married and is survived by the brother, William John Wray; two nephews, William A. Hughes; Samuel Hughes; and a sister, Mrs. Minnie Kingsbury." HC newspaper 20 Jul 1922: After the death of Samuel William Wray, his son, Samuel Archiball Wray, a Greenfield attorney, came across a Confederate $20 bill that the late Mr. Wray had put away shortly after the close of the war, fifty-seven years ago. Copies of the old Confederate money are common, but the genuine has now come to be numbered among the rare articles. The bill is

Hancock County Indiana Civil War Soldiers

in as good condition as when it was printed and bears the date of 1863."

Wright, Aaron C.; 12 Reg Co G, 10 Jul 62, killed 13 May 64, Resaca, Georgia. NOD.

Wright, Clark; 99 Reg Co B, 13 Aug 62, transferred to Veteran Reserve Corps, 14 Jan 64, out 30 Jun 65. ..."born Green County, Ohio, 5' 8" tall, age 38, dark complexion, blue eyes, dark hair, farmer when enrolled..." A Clark Wright married 16 Feb 1856 Mary Polk HC Bk 3-325.

Wright, George; 106 Reg Co D, 10 Jul 63-17 Jul 63. NOD.

Wright, Henry; 99 Reg Co B, 5 Apr 64, died 12 Aug 64. HC newspaper 9 Jun 1864: "Pvt. H.W.Wright, Company B, 99th Regiment, was wounded in the breast at Dallas, Georgia, 25 May 64."

Wright, James W.; 99 Reg Co B, 23 Mar 64, died 12 Jul 64 of wounds. A James W. Wright married 15 Sep 1861 Mary Jane Welling HC Bk 4-284. 99th Regiment History states: "James W. Wright, resident of Warrington (HC) died 12 Jun 1864 of wounds received 28 May 64, Dallas, Georgia."

Wright, William; 12 Reg Co G, 18 Aug 62, died 8 Sep 63, Camp Sherman, Mississippi. NOD.

Wright, William C.; 79 Reg Co D, 10 Aug 62, died 23 Oct 63. A William C. Wright married 23 Mar 1848 Anna West HC Bk 2-276.

Wyant, Isaac; 134 Reg Co K, 24 May 64-4 Aug 65. NOD.

◄ X ►
No entries

◄ Y ►

Yancey, Simeon T. 70 Reg Co A, 22 Jul 62-8 Jun 65. "Simeon T. Yancey was born near Frankfort, Kentucky, 2 Sep 1835, s/o Charles and Jane (Hancock) Yancey. Enlisted in Civil War, 22 Jul 1862, Company A, 70th Indiana Volunteers and served until the close of the War. He married 1) March 1867 Rachel Flanders, (daughter of James Flanders), but the lady was

Hancock County Indiana Civil War Soldiers

untimely called away the next August. Simeon married 2) Miss Harriett Willes of New York." HC obit 11 Jan 1905: "Simeon T. Yancey died at his home in Fortville (HC) on the morning of 4 January 1906. He was a veteran of the Civil War. He practiced medicine and was one of the well-known men of the county. In 1880 he was elected State Senator from the counties of Marion, Hancock and Shelby. Funeral at M.E. Church."

York, William H.; 79 Reg Co B, 9 Aug 62-17 Apr 63. NOD

Young, Leven; 148 Reg Co C, 17 Feb 65-5 Sep 65. NOD.

Youse, M.G.; 99 Reg Co B, 13 Aug 64-16 Feb 65. A Mickle George Youse married 16 Nov 1857 Louvena Davis HC Bk 4-49. 99th Regiment History states: Michael G. Youse, was wounded 22 July 1864, Atlanta, Georgia; recorded as died 1899 at home, Cleveland (HC)." HC death notice 19 Jan 1899: "M.G. Youse, aged 65 years, died of grippe, at his late home in Cleveland. Funeral at M.E. Church, Cleveland. Interment Gilboa Cemetery (military data only on stone, no dates)"

Youst, David, 18 Reg, Musician, 16 Aug 61-20 Aug 62. NOD.

◄ Z ►

Zumwalt, Henry; 79 Reg Co D, 18 Aug 62- 7 Jun 65, Sgt. NOD.

Hancock County Indiana Civil War Soldiers

5th Indiana Cavalry
90th Indiana Regiment

Reuben Riley was Captain of the first regiment organized in Hancock County on 22 April 1861, to serve for three months and was known as Company G, 8th Regiment. This unit was discharged on 6 August 1861, at the end of their three months duty. With about 90 Hancock County volunteers, Captain Riley reorganized his company G with it being attached to the Fifth Cavalry and assigned to the 90th Regiment Indiana Volunteer

The 5th Cavalry was officially organized in August and September of 1862, at Indianapolis. In December Company G was ordered to Newburg, (Indiana), located on the Ohio River near Evansville, where they remained until February, 1863, when the entire regiment came together at Glasgow, Kentucky. They scouted the countryside around the Cumberland River during the months of April, May and June of 1863, engaged in skirmishes with the enemy and they captured many rebel prisoners.

On 4 July 1863 the regiment went in pursuit of Confederate John Morgan's cavalry, reported to have crossed the Cumberland River and was raiding into southern and central Kentucky. At Louisville the 5th was put on steamers for the trip up the Ohio River to Pomeroy, Ohio. There was an engagement with Morgan's unit at Buffington Island, near Pomeroy, on 19 Jul 1863, when the 5th drove them from the river in every direction, killing and capturing many rebels, plus five pieces of artillery. A Hancock County soldier named Jonas Davidson was killed that day.

During the fall and early winter of 1864, the 5th saw heavy action northeast of Knoxville, Tennessee, with countless engagements and skirmishes, sometimes the fighting continued all day and did not end until it was too dark to see the enemy. At

Hancock County Indiana Civil War Soldiers

the end of January 1864, the regiment had to march, march, march on foot from Sieverville to Knoxville to Cumberland Gap, having been ordered to turn their horses over to the 14th Illinois Cavalry. Still without mounts, they left Cumberland Gap on 17 February 1864 and in nine days arrived at Mt. Sterling, Kentucky, a distance of roughly 140 miles. Cavalrymen being made into an infantry regiment must have brought loud protests and severe injuries to pride, not to mention muscles.

The companies of the 5th Regiment remained near Lexington, at Mt. Sterling, Paris and Nicholasville, until the first of May while being remounted and refitted for the long trek into Georgia for the Atlanta campaign. The regiment was constantly engaged in all cavalry operations from Dalton to Decatur, Georgia.

This is where Union General George Stoneman enters the drama. Stoneman was a graduate of West Point, ranked 33 in a class of 55, in the star-studded class of 1846, when he shared the parade ground and barracks with the likes of George Pickett, George B. McClellan and roommate Tom "Stonewall" Jackson While serving in the Indian Wars of the 1850s, George Stoneman was considered not only one of the best company commanders, but one of high achievement with strict discipline.

After cavalry reorganization in February of 1863, he was placed in command of the entire mounted Union force. There was a chain of command dilemma at the Union defeat at Chancellorsville in May of 1863, when, led by Stoneman, the planned raid behind enemy lines went awry. He became a partial scapegoat for the defeat and was relieved of his command, thought by many to be an unjust action. Stoneman was given a second chance in the Atlanta campaign of May and June of 1864. Capable leadership could be the giant step forward he so craved to restore his tarnished reputation, but on 27 Jul 1864 he was in command of a "disastrous expedition" near Macon, Georgia, where, by necessity, he surrendered himself and 700 of his command. The General was frustrated and disappointed that he did not attain the glory he desired, but after the war he became a politician. He was a native of New York but lived in California

Hancock County Indiana Civil War Soldiers

where ultimately he was elected Democratic governor from 1883 until 1887 and is reported that his administration was as troubled as his military career

Nearly ninety soldiers from Hancock County in Company G of the 5th Cavalry, were under the command of General George Stoneman near Macon, Georgia, on that fateful day of 27 Jul 1864. Thirty-one of those men were either captured, wounded or killed. The following was printed in the *Hancock Democrat*, 11 August 1864:"The recent disastrous expedition commanded by General Stoneman, has thrown sorrow into many families in our county. The 5th Indiana Cavalry was a part of the expedition, and lost 383 officers and enlisted men, in killed, wounded, or prisoners, most of them being captives (in Andersonville, Georgia).

"The following is the loss of Company G, (and found on their respective pages in this volume): W.D. Barwick; D.or E. Belville; A. Blakely; Francis M. Brizendine; Charles W. Campbell; John S. Chittenden; Reason Collins; George W. Duncan; Morris Fort; Henry C. Gant; George W. Hoover; James Hudson (Hutson); Adam Hutton; L.H. Jonas; Berry Johnson; Hiram Lawson; E. Marsh; Marshall M. Meek; Ransom Monroe Meek; Thomas Mack; George W. Miller; Newton Pope; Jasper N. Pope; William W. Price; James A. Riley; John Samuels; Jacob Shaffer; Thomas Snyder; Samuel C. Thompson; Charles J. Willett; and T.W. Williams. The name of E. Marsh is very probably erroneously printed in the above list, as on the 2nd inst. he was at Nashville, and had not had time to reach his company before it started with Gen. Stoneman.

"Since the above was in type, we have received a letter from Lieut. W.H. Pilkinton, corroborating the above account, except as to Elias Marsh, who was not with the Company. Orderly Wm. M. Sleeth was with the company, but made his escape with Col. Adams of the 1st Kentucky. Lieut. Chittenden was instantly killed by the explosion of a shell, a piece hitting him in the head. The boys of the company not captured, are at the dismounted camp at Marietta."

Hancock County Indiana Civil War Soldiers

Shortly after the surrender, the men of the regiment who had seen hard service remained in the rear near Decatur, Georgia, and by order from General Sherman they exchanged their carbines for muskets and remained on guard duty until 13 Sep 1864. They were remounted, armed and equipped early in January of 1865 when they were sent to the vicinity of Pulaski, Kentucky, scouting the countryside, capturing bushwhackers and outlaws until 16 Jun 1865. What remained of Company G was transferred to the 6th Indiana Cavalry and mustered out 15 Sep 1865, at Murfreesboro, Tennessee.

9th Indiana Cavalry
121st Infantry Regiment

The 9th Indiana Cavalry/121st Infantry Volunteer Regiment began to recruit in the fall and winter of 1863, during that time about 120 Hancock County men "jined the calvry" after reading the following Democrat newspaper article, dated 15 Oct 1863: "Col. Wm. R. Walls, of Palestine, Sergeant Mart W. Riley, of Greenfield, and J.B. Herrod, of Buck Creek, have been commissioned by order of Governor Morton, are duly authorized to recruit a Cavalry company for the 9th Indiana Cavalry. Col. Walls, our readers are aware, has had much experience in the service, and is well qualified for the position assigned him, and having recovered his health, he is resolved not to remain idle, while men are wanted to relieve those of our citizens already in the field. We hope that this company will be speedily recruited. Soldiers are needed--if they do not volunteer, a draft will surely come. Let all young men who love their country, come forward at once, and give their names to Col. Walls, Sergeant Riley, or Mr. Herrod, Remember that all who volunteer receive a bounty of $302, if new, or $402, if veterans. All those wishing to enlist can do so by applying at the Guymon House."

The recruits were not organized into a regiment until 1 March 1864, at Indianapolis, with George W. Jackson as Colonel. The regiment remained in Indiana to drill and learn to be soldiers,

Hancock County Indiana Civil War Soldiers

until 3 May 1864, when they were armed with Enfield rifles and traveled by rail to Tennessee, where they were kept on post duty at Pulaski all summer.

About the 20th of September, rumors circulated that the rebel cavalry led by the ingenious general, Nathan Bedford Forrest, was ready to cross the Tennessee River. On 21 Sep 1864 he, did indeed, cross the river, at Florence, Alabama, (located in the northwest part of the State, due west of Athens) with 4,500 men and eight pieces of artillery to destroy the railroads at Athens and Sulphur Branch Trestle, Alabama. Using his riders to advantage at Athens, the uncanny Forrest conveyed a much larger force causing the fort to surrender.

Before news of the surrender reached Pulaski, the mounted men of the 9th Cavalry Regiment, under the command of Major Lilly, were sent to fortify Athens against Forrest's rebel horde. Upon reaching the town, Major Lilly found it surrounded, rode the six miles to Sulphur Branch Trestle, where at 4:00 AM on the 25 Sep 1864, he reported "to make a desperate resistance." The engagement lasted five hours. John T. Sturges was a bugler for Company B.

The following remarks were made in an official military report concerning the battle at Sulphur Branch Trestle, by Col. George Spalding, Commander, Fourth Cavalry Division: "A stand was made worthy of the highest praise with a fort badly constructed, not fully completed, two guns worked by infantrymen, not artillerymen, a greatly superior force attacking them with much artillery, fought a battle worth its niche among well-contested battles of the war; but all to no avail. The brave Col. Lilly fell, killed by the first shot, ammunition became short and surrender stared them in the face. As brave men suffering heavy loss, they were compelled finally to surrender to a vastly superior force, after inflicting a much more severe loss upon the enemy. The trestle, railroad and blockhouse were destroyed and consumed by fire."

There were 196 men of Indiana's 9th Cavalry at Sulphur Branch Trestle, Alabama, with 37 killed and 159 captured. The

Hancock County Indiana Civil War Soldiers

following Hancock County soldiers from Company B were reported as being at the battle of Sulphur Branch Trestle, Alabama, 25 Sep 1864, the captured being taken to Castle Morgan Prison, located at Cahaba, Alabama: Frederick Blessinger, captured, lost on Sultana disaster; Charles E. Church, captured, lost on Sultana disaster; William J. Foster (also a Mexican War veteran) captured, died, chronic diarrhea, 15 Dec 1864, Castle Morgan Prison at Cahaba, Alabama, grave K3713; William Harvey, killed in action; John B. Herod, captured, survived; James Hook, wounded, survived; Joseph Hutton, killed in action; Charles A. Kirkhoff, killed in action; Ephraim Perman, captured, lost on Sultana disaster; Christopher Hugh (Kip) Sears, captured, Cahaba, Alabama, Prison, survived Sultana disaster; John Steward, captured, lost on Sultana disaster; Marcellus Walker, wounded in action, survived; and John J. Winn, wounded, survived.

The 9th Cavalry History states: "The last dispatch sent out of the fort the day of surrender was carried by John McCorkle of Company B, left the fort at 7:00 AM and accomplished the feat by coolness and bold riding." A Union cavalryman's weapons included a pistol on a belt, seven-shot carbine suspended from a broad strap across his chest, and a saber.

HC newspaper article, 14 April 1865: "We are sorry to learn that John S. Loehr, Company B, 9th Indiana Cavalry, died at Joe Holt Hospital. His remains will brought home for interment; Mark Hamilton, of the same unit, died recently at Nashville."

HC newspaper article, 3 August 1865: "Capt. Rardin, J.T. Barrett and Thomas Cady, of the 9th Indiana Cavalry, arrived home. The two latter have been honorably discharged from the service. Capt. Rardin will return to his Company in a few days."

The remainder of the regiment left at Pulaski, Tennessee, went into action in December at Franklin, Tennessee, with Forrest's Cavalry, and lost 26 soldiers, killed, wounded and prisoners. Under orders on 6 Feb 1865, the regiment went to New Orleans, where it embarked on transport boats, and on 25 March 1865, arrived at Vicksburg. Here it remained on post

Hancock County Indiana Civil War Soldiers

duty until May when it was remounted and sent to garrison posts in Mississippi, until being mustered out 28 August 1865, at Vicksburg. Hancock County soldier, Michael Chancery, died 4 Mar 65 at Vicksburg.

On leaving Indiana in 1864, the regiment numbered 1,150 strong and returned in September, 1865, with 386 men and officers. The 9th lost 55 war-weary prisoners of war when the Sultana exploded 27 April 1865, on the Mississippi River.

13th Indiana Cavalry Regiment

The 13th Cavalry Regiment, organized during the fall and winter of 1863 and 1864, was the last cavalry unit formed in Indiana and was attached to the 131st Indiana Infantry Regiment. On 11 March 1864, George Muth of Brandywine Township, Hancock County, was commissioned a Captain and mustered Company I, 13th Cavalry Regiment.

The 113 men mustered into Company I were from Hancock, Rush, Shelby and Delaware Counties and went off to war with Captain Muth, an experienced soldier who was on the field of battle at Waterloo when Napoleon was defeated (for details see page for George Muth).

Captain Muth and his Company I left Indiana 30 Apr 1864 with the 13th Cavalry for Nashville, Tennessee, where they remained until 30 May 64 when the unit was dismounted, armed with Enfield rifles, infantry equipment and ordered to Huntsville, Alabama. (For a cavalryman being dismounted, and to march nearly 200 miles, must have caused not only bruised egos but bruised feet.)

The regiment had garrison duty at Huntsville where they were engaged in several skirmishes with rebel cavalry from May until October when six companies, including I, were ordered to Louisville. At this place the regiment was remounted and sent for the defense of Paducah, Kentucky, from rebel forces commanded by General Nathan Forrest, after routing the enemy they returned to Nashville just before Christmas.

Hancock County Indiana Civil War Soldiers

The twelve companies of the 13th Cavalry reunited and were sent down the Mississippi River stopping at Vicksburg before moving to Mobile where they assisted in its capture. After the capture the regiment was engaged on raids through Alabama, Georgia and was garrisoned at Macon, Mississippi, patrolling a railroad line for sixty miles, taking possession of large amounts of captured stores and ordnance.

In November 1865, the regiment was ordered to Vicksburg to be mustered out and returned to Indiana.

The ten Hancock County soldiers of Company I, 13th Cavalry are as follows: Martin Akeman; Albert Alyea; Samuel Anderson; Samuel Collins; Isaac Lain, gunshot in right leg and horse shot from under him; Thomas Lincolnfelter; Isaac McBane; James F. Reynolds; Benjamin Robison; and Samuel Willis.

8th Indiana Regiment

The 8th Regiment Indiana Infantry Volunteers was organized 22 Apr 1861. Reuben Riley, a Greenfield attorney, enlisted about 75 Hancock County men into Company G, with Riley elected Captain (see pages on Union Guard of Hancock County). During their three months tour of duty, the regiment left Indiana on 19 June 1861, to join General Rosecrans Brigade in western Virginia, where he was ordered to secure the counties loyal to the Union.

The Confederates were entrenched at Rich Mountain, near the western Virginia towns of Clarksburg and Buckhannon. In the early morning of 11 July 1861 and led by a native of the area, 2,000 soldiers set out for a flank attack on the enemy occupying the mountain. They struggled through underbrush and thick woods, delayed by missed directions and drenched by rain but managed to surprise the Confederate outposts. The battle began about 2:30 PM with the enemy hiding behind rocks and trees and, with the help of their one cannon, held off the Union forces for two hours before being subdued. Andrew J. Fuller was color

Hancock County Indiana Civil War Soldiers

bearer for Company B, 8th Regiment and planted the colors in the enemy's fortification.

Four Hancock County soldiers became casualties on 11 Jul 1861: James Buchanan, wounded; Samuel Dye, died of wounds at Indianapolis; Marion Stephenson, killed; and Andrew Stutsman, wounded.

The three-months regiment returned to Hancock County and on 5 August 1861 the citizens of the county gave a reception at Pierson's Grove, adjoining Greenfield on the southwest, which was located west of Pennsylvania Street and south of the railroad (Pennsy Trail).

The regiment returned to Indianapolis where it was mustered out 6 August 1861, but was at once reorganized into a three year unit and left 10 Sep 1861 for St. Louis, Missouri. The 8th had 200-plus men from Hancock County in its ranks with most of that number in Company B, and a few sprinkled in Companies C, D, G and H. Samuel H. Dunbar, Lieutenant, Company B of the 8th wrote many Letters to the Editor of the *Hancock Democrat* that were printed as they overflowed with details that were of interest to readers. The following letters reveal happenings of Company B, 8th Regiment as they fought for their country.

Camp Jefferson, Jefferson City, Missouri, 18 Sep 1861: "Dear Mitchell, My promise to you would have been fulfilled sooner, had not the hurry of events, since we left Indianapolis, made it impossible. But now, that we have arrived in the country of the enemy, and have assumed a position of watchfulness over, and defense of. the institutions we all love, with arms in our hands, and determination in our hearts, and while a few lines right now be interesting to the friends at home, I take pleasure in contributing a short note of what we have done. I would not hesitate to tell you what we are going to do, if I knew; but Col. Benton's admirable qualifications for the position he holds, and for any position to which he may aspire, keeps these things to himself. Soldiers and inferior officers only know what is necessary, and that is to do strictly, promptly, and to the letter, what they are commanded.

As you know, we left Indianapolis on Tuesday morning the 10th (Sep, 1861). We arrived at St. Louis the next morning by daylight. Our passage thru' Illinois, and our march through St. Louis were marked by demonstrations of congratulation and welcome. In the city, the children, the ladies, and the men, from housetops, windows, and sidewalks, were waving flags, little flags, big ones, fine and coarse ones, and the cry was 'Hurrah for Indiana! Hurrah for the Hoosiers!' Hurrah for the bloody Eighth!' Everybody seemed to have heard about Col. Benton and his 'bloody Eighth.'

"We marched from the river to Camp Benton, five miles in the country, of which, if I ever return to it, I will give you a description where we remained until Friday night, when we received orders to march, whither we did not know, but to get ready and be off, was what we were told, and we did it cheerfully, for when the column commenced moving, leaving behind us comfortable and commodious buildings in which we had quartered, the boys began to cheer, and the enthusiasm among them was very great.

"The march back to the city was accomplished after dark, through the mud and rain, but in good time and excellent order. Arriving at the depot we were placed in box cars, where in consequence of an accident happening to the baggage wagons, which was unavoidable, we had to lay there until 7 o'clock the next morning, when we started for this point, which we reached about sundown, and disembarked in one of the heaviest and most drenching rains I ever saw. But nobody grumbles, nobody tho't it a bad time. Weary, sleepy and hungry as the men were, good cheer continued to reign. In the depot, engine house, in the seminary, and out of doors, the boys went to sleep in their wet clothes, waking up in the morning, ready for the next duty, which was to march to this camp.

"Jefferson City is a small place, situated upon a hill overlooking the Missouri River, and surrounded by a chain of

Hancock County Indiana Civil War Soldiers

hills which are being fortified rapidly. There are some eight to ten thousand troops here, and from what I know, and hear, and believe to be true, there are five or six thousand more forty miles above Boonville, at which point the enemy, very strong, attacked on Saturday last, when but a few hundred home guards were there, but who held them in check until reinforcements arrived, when "Secesh" left for parts unknown. The boys turned out like men. Many were the expressions I heard, which convinced me, as they would you, that we had the metal with us. One, whose name I give, said while in line waiting further orders, "Wherever Captain Walls wants Aaron Scott to go, he will go or die."

"Several who were sick, were among the first in the ranks: John Chittenden; George M. Davidson; David Dove; and Peter Lamb. And my old friend, Uncle Jimmy Norman, as we call him, bounced out of bed, and was out hunting a gun, eager for the fight, and though rejected on account of age, would have done as good fighting as the youngest, and best. Billy Snyder had lost his ramrod, but was in the ranks anyhow, borrowing one from his next companion, both using one. We have had but few cases of illness in the Company, but does not amount to much. My health is good. I am yours truly, Samuel H. Dunbar. (Adjutant General Terrell of Indiana, reports that William T. Askins, Company B, 8th Regiment, died 13 Oct 1861 at Georgetown, Missouri.)".

Otterville, Missouri, 22 January 1862: "Dear Mitchell, I have waited sometime, hoping to able after while to communicate something of importance happening out here in Missouri and in which the 'Bloody Eighth' had participated. But since Christmas we have remained here, banked up in our tents by accumulation of ice and snow, exerting almost superhuman efforts to keep up circulation. Your imagination can easily conceive of the drought of news and interest emanating from a military camp when there is no enemy nor prospect of any. Rumor has lost its power, to a considerable extent and you can find few among us who believe that the Eighth Regiment is going to Indiana for winter quarters

Hancock County Indiana Civil War Soldiers

or that we are going to St. Louis, or that the war will be over in thirty days.

"For the past two days we have been under orders to be ready to march at the shortest notice. I hear it said that the Paymaster has arrived, and the probabilities are that we will be paid before our march. Messrs. Hart and Eastman called upon us this morning bringing late news from home. Since last writing you, Jacob Bowers has died. He was sick since coming from Springfield. His death is another, among hundreds of cases, testimony of the folly, or at least destructive effects, of that ever to be remembered march. We have discharged on account of physical disability, induced by the inclemencies of camp life: Abijah Bales; Samuel H. Dillman; John Jack; and James Lowder. Since I began writing, we have been ordered to be in readiness to march tomorrow morning, with two day's rations cooked and in the men's haversacks. I presume, therefore, we will leave here, for what point, I have little idea. I must quit writing, and proceed to preparation. I will write when we stop. Yours respectfully, Samuel H. Dunbar, Lt. Com'd'g Co B, 8th Ind.

Helena, Arkansas, 14 July 1862: "Dear Editor Mitchell, Having had no opportunity for a long time to write to you, or any body else, and supposing that our friends are anxious to hear from us, I hasten to write you. After a march of eighteen miles, we arrived at Augusta, Arkansas, (on White River, northeast of Little Rock) from where companies A and B of the 8th joined a battalion of cavalry and went in search of a regiment of rebels, mostly conscripts. After a march of ten miles we came upon their camp, freshly evacuated. The infantry deployed as skirmishers in the cane brake which is hottest and hardest work ever the lot of man to perform. We remained thus for two miles, rallying at a point on the (White) river, three miles above a ferry where the "butternuts" (rebs) were crossing. We took their camp, equipage and provisions.

"We heard of a (military wagon) train concealed four miles above our position in the cane brake, and of course, we made for

Hancock County Indiana Civil War Soldiers

it. We found five wagons richly laden with the good things fixed up by special friends for palates of the traitors. They didn't get it. We ate our suppers, saved our breakfast and turned the balance over. This was on the 4th of July. On the 6th of July we left camp and marched sixteen miles to the banks of the Cache River. The road on each side of the stream having been blockaded by the rebels cutting timber across it, a game they have played until it is played out.

"Lieut. Hill, who commands the pioneers of the Brigade, went to work on the blockade and in two hours had a road cut through and the troops passing over. We encamped at Cotton Plant, on a bayou, and the next day marched to Clarendon, thirty-five miles under the hot sun of this climate, and through the deepest sand and the thickest and most suffocating dust. For miles we had to march without water, and when we did get any it was swamp water, the filthiest you ever saw in any swamp. This march beats everything in our military history, and had we not been iron-clad, we never could have stood it.

"By some management not in army regulations, our wagons, provisions and camp equipage were started upon one road and we upon another. We marched 41 miles to Helena, Arkansas, on the scant rations of four crackers per man. We are now encamped on the bank of the Mississippi. Helena is a beautiful little town and clean and neat. Shortly after our arrival, a trading boat came down, and you should have seen the effect it had upon the men. So long shut up in the darkness of Arkansas hills and swamps, cut off from all correspondence with friends and the world, exposed to danger and disease, almost naked, and but a few days rations of crackers left, you can imagine how exhilarating the sight of a boat would be.

"We are below Memphis about one hundred miles. Last night was a moon light one and Lieut. Hill and myself, after the camp had become still, seated ourselves upon the bank of the river and looked upon a scene beautiful as I ever saw. At this point the river is one and a half miles wide, Mississippi forming the other shore. This morning the camp is all gayety and life, the

Hancock County Indiana Civil War Soldiers

boys are in the highest spirits. Besides the prospects for bread, meat and clothes, we have a faint hope of being ordered out of Arkansas. The health of our company continues excellent, much to our surprise. Our friends can rest assured that for the present we are all doing well. Yours Respectfully, S.H. Dunbar, 8th Indiana Regiment."

Headquarters 8th Ind. Infantry, Helena, Arkansas, 21 Jul 1862: "Dear Mitchell, I wrote you from this point a hurried history of our wanderings. I did not say all that I wished to, contemplating nothing much beyond simply informing our friends that we were still alive. We have been here now eight days, but it is too hot to rest. Besides, our Regiment was detailed to furnish Provost Guards to protect the property of absent rebels. Was every man in the army discriminating and humane, this species of duty would be unnecessary, but I am sorry to say that we have men who would not hesitate to steal a bible, the gift of a mother to her son; the marble slab from the head of its grave; the last dress from the body of a sleeping infant to make a sweat rag; or the last dust of flour from a starving family.

"The following from Company B were sick and left in a hospital boat: John Dorman, John and Lawson Wiggins. The road we have traveled is now but a track of desolation. Fine, stately residences, habitations of wealth, and too often of treason, have been burned to the ground. Horses, mules and provisions for man and beast, have all fallen into our hands and been appropriated. I don't think you could find one in a brigade, no matter what is the length of his service or how intense have been his sufferings, who would accept peace upon any other terms than those of free, full acquiescence of rebellion. The country divided would be ruined, for ages the scene of strife and misery. Then why murmur at a few years of suffering, toil and danger, that generations yet unborn may reap the rewards. Your newspapers have all come in a bunch since our stay here. I see that you have not neglected me which is very pleasant. Refresh me with a letter when convenient. Yours respectfully, Samuel H. Dunbar, 8th Reg. In. Vols."

Hancock County Indiana Civil War Soldiers

Hancock Democrat. 18 Dec 1862: " Capt. Walls of Co. B, 8th Regiment Indiana Volunteers, informs us that the 8th has traveled 1,600 miles on foot, 400 by rail and 600 miles by water, since it entered service, and met the enemy twice, at Pea Ridge and Cotton Plant (Arkansas). at both of which places the rebels were soundly drubbed." (The Confederate 1st Cherokee Mounted Rifle Regiment, commanded by General Stand Waites (Wayt-ee) and attached to General Kirby Smith's Trans-Mississippi Department , forged his reputation at the battle of Pea Ridge, Arkansas, when his men captured a Union battery after a dramatic charge.)

Black River, Mississippi, 8 May 1863: "Dear Mitchell, I take pleasure, at this my earliest convenience, in informing our friends of the part taken and loss sustained by Company B in the fight near Port Gibson on the 1st inst. The battle field, and indeed the country, is a succession of hills and ravines. The enemy was concealed in the timber when our regiment began the musket fire. We fought there for some time, when we were ordered to charge down into the ravine and up the hill from which the enemy was firing…

"Company B fought gloriously. Five men were wounded in less than five minutes: Henry Bush, in shoulder, slight; Levi Collins, in shoulder, very slight; Isaac McGee, nose skinned and finger amputated; Ben A. Roney, in neck; Aaron Scott, in finger. Many narrowly escaped: Wallace Alexander, shot through haversack; Marion Philpott, shot through haversack; Eli Stevens, shot through oil cloth; and John Underwood, cap "box shot through. At sunset the battle closed and we sank to sleep on the field. In the morning the bird had flown leaving most of their dead and wounded. We are in nearly three miles of Black River where the enemy is strongly posted. I presume we are awaiting the "auspicious moment" to pounce upon them. Everything is cheerful here. The prospect seems bright and we are ready and anxious to make the grand trial. Yours Respectfully, S.H. Dunbar, 8th Ind. Infantry."

Hancock County Indiana Civil War Soldiers

Near Vicksburg, Mississippi, 28 May 1863: "Dear Mitchell, On the 19th inst. our artillery opened on the fortifications protecting Vicksburg. On the 20th, while advancing from a hollow to one nearer the enemy, Alfred Wilson was killed by a grape shot striking him on the head. He did not die immediately, and when removed to the hospital, he would not be removed from the field, until he laid hold of his gun which he persisted in carrying with him. On the 22 May, orders were for the whole line to charge. Upon this announcement to the men, all were fully convinced that it was a mad move, and that we would meet slaughter and defeat. Nevertheless, at the appointed hour, we fell into line and moved forward. The column had not been in motion but a few minutes when the enemy opened up from rifle pits and forts with musketry, grape, shell and shrapnel.

Confusion at once began. Men fell dead and wounded at every step. Many being wounded were afterward killed and the slaughter was terrible. Company B started into the charge with 43 men, officers included; its loss was as follows: W.W. Alexander, wound, severely in arm; George H. Black, wounded in shoulder, did not leave the field, though in too much pain to load and shoot, but carried water from the spring to the boys while they fought; Chas. Clapper, wound, slightly in arm; Andrew J. Fuller, wound painfully in ankle; Lieut. W.G. Hill, wound painfully right hand; Richard Lamb, killed by minie striking him in the bowels; Alfred Lowder, died from wounds; Thos. M. Martin, arm amputated; Frank Mays, killed; Clark McDonald, wound slightly in hip; F.M. Miller, wound, slightly in chin; Wm. H. Morgan, collar bone broken; Wm. Scotton, left ear amputated; James N. Underwood, arm amputated; and Wm. W. Welling, wound, severely in arm and side. I understand the wounded will be sent North as soon as possible. Our company is sadly in need of recruits and must be filled up. Will not some of our young men come to our assistance? I will write again. Respectfully, S.H. Dunbar. 8th Ind. Infantry."

Verm_ionville, Louisiana, 12 Nov 1863: "Dear Mitchell, I write merely that you may present to their friends of Company B

Hancock County Indiana Civil War Soldiers

the following: left in hospital in New Orleans, Geo. M. Davidson; Amos Everson; Francis Hodson; Albert W. Lake; Henry McCorkhill; Elijah Tyner, nurse; and John Underwood. I did not feel apprehensive of the death of any of them, ague and diarrhea being the principal diseases. John Scott, a good citizen of Brandywine Township, who had many friends throughout his neighborhood, died, Hospital in New Orleans, 11 Sep 1863.

Sgt. Cyrus Hanes and Elijah Tuttle, of Company B, with four others, left on a critical mission. They pressed an oyster boat, sailed out into the Gulf, and from thence though bayous, lakes and bogs far into the interior of Louisiana, passing themselves among the enemy as smugglers and accomplished their mission, (which was not given) returning safely. Let the names of all such gallant actors stand out in bold relief, high on the scroll of honor. How about the election, or is it over yet? Yours respectfully, S.H. Dunbar, 8th Indiana Infantry."

On the same day Lt. Dunbar wrote the above letter, 12 Nov 1863, the regiment embarked for Texas where, on 17 Nov, they took part in the attack and capture of a fort on Mustang Island and, on the 27 Nov, the capture of Fort Esperanza. The regiment reenlisted on 1 Jan 1864 and later received a month's veteran furlough; arriving in Indianapolis on 22 April 1864.

The regiment returned to New Orleans. They encountered the rebels several times during the summer before traveling by steamer to Washington City, arriving 12 Aug 1864. Then on to the Shenandoah Valley campaign under General Sheridan, and the battle of Cedar Creek, Virginia, where Cyrus Hanes (Haines), was captured 19 Oct 1864; Aaron Alyea died 15 Apr 1865 at Vicksburg, Mississippi; both men of Company B, 8th Regiment.

The regiment remained on duty in Georgia until being mustered out 28 Aug 1865, arriving in Indianapolis 17 Sep 1865 and being greeted by Governor Morton on the Capitol grounds.

The 8th Indiana Infantry Regiment continues today as a part of the 152 National Guard Regiment.

Hancock County Indiana Civil War Soldiers

11th Indiana Regiment
Colonel Lew Wallace's Zouaves

The 11th Indiana Infantry was mustered in April of 1861, at Indianapolis for three months service with Lewis Wallace as Colonel. They were sent 8 May 1861 to Evansville, Indiana, for blockade duty along the Ohio River. On 7 Jun 1861 it was ordered to Virginia where a week later, 13 Jun 1861, Col. Wallace wrote a letter to Governor Morton that was printed in the *Hancock Democrat* newspaper: "Cumberland, Virginia, 13 June 1861: To Gov. O.P. Morton: Yesterday after a sharp fight I took the town of Romney, forty miles from here, in Hampshire County, Virginia, dispersing four-hundred secession troops, two killed, one wounded of the enemy. One slightly wounded on my side. Capt. Quick took some prisoners, first class camp, equipment, provisions, surgeons, stock, arms, &c. The rout of the secessionists was quite complete. Returned with my regiment to Cumberland the same day. Signed, Lew Wallace, Col. 11th Regiment.

The three-month regiment moved to Martinsburg in western Virginia, Bunker Hill and Harper's Ferry before returning to Indianapolis to be mustered out 2 Aug 1861 and reorganized into a three year unit. Col. Lewis Wallace was appointed Brigadier General.

The 11th Indiana Regiment was known as Wallace's Zouaves who wore distinctly colorful uniforms patterned from French military fashion of the 1850s: a short, dark blue collarless jacket with red trim worn over a sleeveless vest, baggy red trousers tucked into the top of white canvas leggings, a long woolen sash wrapped at the waist and a tasseled red fez. Many said the officers who adopted such attire for their men would expect a daredevil bravado befitting their military finery. True or false, who knows if that happened? Picture in your mind's eye, the fourteen Hancock County soldiers proudly going to war dressed in gaudy but picturesque uniforms, including sixteen-year-old Lee Thayer as drummer boy.

Hancock County Indiana Civil War Soldiers

By 14 Feb 1863, the 11th Regiment joined General Grant's command and had been engaged in the battle and surrender of Fort Henry on the Tennessee River. Wallace then marched his troops to Fort Donelson on the Cumberland River where they were conspicuous in turning the battle into a Union victory and by way of reward was promoted to Major General. General Grant gave a memorable answer to the question of surrender terms at Fort Donelson: "No terms except unconditional and immediate surrender. I propose to move immediately on your works." The two forts were the first conspicuous Union victories and opened Tennessee to invasion. About fifteen-thousand Confederates were taken prisoner with many of them being sent to Camp Morton in Indianapolis.

Wallace's Zouaves then boarded a steamer for the trip down the Tennessee River and arrived in time to participate in the battle of Shiloh Church, on 7 April 1862. Built about 1850 for use as a Methodist Church, it was a small unpretentious building of hewn logs with two doors and one window, located on the brow of a hill. It was a plain country church for plain country people. The pulpit and seats had been removed for use at the Confederate camp, the floor boards were used to build coffins for Union soldiers and after the battle, the building was used as a hospital.

Grant's army was surprised by an assault of rebels at Shiloh on 6 April 1862, where the field was covered with the wounded and dead from both sides after desperate fighting all day. Due to muddled orders sent to Wallace at Crump's Landing, the Zouaves, did not arrive until the second day of the battle when the desperate fighting began again. The battle-hardened veterans of the 11th helped to break through the lines causing the Confederates to fall back. Thus the battle of Shiloh Church ended with 1,754 Union deaths and 1,728 Confederate deaths.

The 11th Regiment's engagements included the siege and capture of Corinth, Mississippi; joining Grant's army at Milliken's Bend, Louisiana, in April 1863, the 11th participated in operations at Port Gibson and Champion Hills, Mississippi; and

Hancock County Indiana Civil War Soldiers

was in the trenches in front of Vicksburg until the surrender of the city; and many skirmishes in Louisiana and Virginia, before marching to Baltimore where the regiment was mustered out, 26 Jul 1865.

The following Hancock County men are recorded as members of Wallace's 11th Regiment Zouaves: Stephen Bedgood; Joseph L. Crosley, died of injuries at New Orleans 16 May 64; Henry S. Davidson; William P. Denny; John J. Earl; George W. Grenier, died 7 Jul 63 at Memphis from injuries received at Vicksburg; James H. Hinds; Samuel Hook wounded 19 Sep 64; Herman Kunz; David R. Richards; William Ruddick (Rudrick); Edmond P. Thayer; Lee Thayer, drummer boy, wounded at Shiloh (Pittsburg Landing); and Charles J. Williams. See data on their respective pages.

The 11th Indiana Infantry Regiment that was in the Civil War continues today as a part of the 151st Indiana National Guard Infantry Regiment.

12th Indiana Regiment

The 12th Indiana Infantry Regiment, mustered at Indianapolis 11 May 1861 for one year service. Their first assignment was at Evansville (Indiana) for blockade duty where they remained until 23 Jul 1861 then departed for Sandy Hook, Maryland. From there the one year regiment participated in picket and outpost duty with frequent skirmishes near Winchester, Virginia and Martinsburg in western Virginia.

Hancock Democrat, 19 Mar 1862: "Martinsburg, Virginia, 3 March 1862: Dear Editor, Trusting the readers of your paper would not object to perusing a few lines from a soldier in the 12th Indiana Regiment, who will endeavor to give you a brief synopsis of our late Regimental Experiences, commencing with our departure from Sharpsburg, Maryland, for Virginia. Our Colonel ordered us to be ready to march at 8:00 AM, the news went from tent to tent throughout the whole Regiment, apprising us of the welcome order. The boys gave 'three cheers and a

Hancock County Indiana Civil War Soldiers

tiger,' and commenced packing up and preparing breakfast and halooing for joy with bright anticipation of marching into Dixie.

The orders were to march to the canal, and go on board some boats that lay in readiness for transportation to Williamsport (Maryland). The suffering coming to Williamsport was somewhat severe, owing to the inclemency of the weather. The quarters we occupied while there were also very uncomfortable, and in fact they were everything but pleasant. Several of the boys were afflicted with bad colds and other diseases caused by their exposure. We remained at Williamsport three or four days, before crossing the river (Potomac) on Saturday, the 1st of March. We crossed by means of a ferry boat, one company at a time with the boat making a trip every twenty minutes. We arrived at Martinsburg early on Sunday morning, and our three cheers were greeted with great applause by the loyal citizens, who were aroused by the soul-stirring national airs performed by the Regimental Bands in front of the court-house.

The day of our arrival here several prominent 'rebel' citizens were arrested and marched off to the guard-house. After going through the preliminaries necessary they were set at liberty on taking the oath of allegiance. That same morning, Dr. Noble Howard, our Assistant Surgeon, planted the old Stars and Stripes on the court-house steeple, exhibiting his patriotism to the surprise of the 12th Indiana Volunteers. The sanitary condition of the 12th Indiana Regiment is No. 1, very few sick and none dangerously ill. The soldiers are all in good spirits, and anxious to participate in bringing this rebellious war to a close. The weather has been changeable, not cold, but damp and disagreeable. Yours, respectfully, N. W. Holt, 12th Reg." The one-year 12th Regiment was mustered out at Washington, 14 May 1862."

The regiment was reorganized into a three year unit, mustered 17 Aug 1862, including about 150 Hancock County men, and was engaged in numerous battles, including Richmond, Kentucky, where most of the regiment was taken prisoner but later paroled. By June 1863 it reached the Union lines in the rear

Hancock County Indiana Civil War Soldiers

of Vicksburg where they went into the trenches and remained during the siege and surrender.

The 12th participated in General Sherman's arduous march from Memphis to Chattanooga, where the Union forces joined in the fight on Missionary Ridge, 25 Nov 1863. Union forces were ordered to attack Confederate forces at the base of the 800 feet high ridge and hold that position. Instead, the Union crushed the rebel line and stormed up Missionary Ridge to the crest where Confederate troops were in disorder, scattered and retreated, marking a Union victory.

They wintered at Scottsboro, Alabama, and in mid-May, 1864, on orders from General Sherman, it marched to participate in the Atlanta campaign that would be the beginning of the end for the Confederacy. The 12th saw action at Dalton, Resaca, New Hope Church, Kennesaw Mountain, Jonesboro, marched with Sherman on 14 Nov 1864 from Atlanta to the sea and was present at the official surrender of the Confederate Army at Savannah, 22 Dec 1864.

The 12th was active in South and North Carolina, and Virginia; was mustered out at Washington, 8 Jun 1865, and returned to Indianapolis on 14 June when it was publicly received by Governor Morton.

Following are the soldiers from Hancock County who were wounded or killed during the regiment's service (see their respective pages for details): William Alexander; Abraham Bannon; John H. Bannon; Benjamin F. Barnard; Benjamin Brown; Davis Catlin; Ezekiel Copper; Milton Curry; David Davidson; Henry Edwards; brothers, Andrew Forgey and Hugh Forgey; Archibald Gardner; Charles V. Hardin; James Huston; James Lister; Ransom Olvey; James W. Olvey; Edward Pauley; John W. Reynolds; Hiram Shaffer; William Shaffer; Jesse Vanzant; George Walker; John Waterman; James A. Watson; Aaron Wright; and William Wright.

Hancock County Indiana Civil War Soldiers

18th Indiana Regiment
Regimental Band

Members of the Greenfield Sax Horn Band joined the 18th Regiment, was mustered into service at Indianapolis on 16 Aug 1861, and became the Regimental Band. The entire regiment proceeded to St. Louis then on to the interior of Missouri where they participated in the grueling march to Springfield, and took part in the capture of a large number of prisoners at Black Water. In May 1862 the Regiment was on the battlefield at Pea Ridge, Arkansas, and in July were engaged with the enemy at Cotton Plant, Arkansas.

Members of the band quickly exchanged their instruments for guns when duty called on the field of battle. The Band was honorably discharged 20 Aug 1861, and on their return home were given a hearty welcome at the Dunbar corner (northeast corner of Main and State Streets) by the citizens.

Hancock Democrat, August 1861: "Gone To The Wars, Our Greenfield Sax Horn Band has played its last tune for the people of this vicinity. They are now discoursing the sweet strains of brass to the soldiers of Camp Morton. Health and good living attend them wherever Uncle Sam may order them."

Following are the names of band members: Omer Arnold; Samuel W. Barnett; James E. Cravens; F.M. Crawford; James H. Crowder; William Elliott; Albert G. Griffith; William E. Hart; John W. Lambertson; Edwin M. McCrarey; Samuel E. Martin; John H. Noble; William L. Ogg; Martin E. Pierson; Thomas E. Richardson; James T. Reed; Henry Snow; Nathan Snow; James F. Stewart; Alfred M. Thornburgh; and David Youst. See data on their respective pages.

19th Indiana Regiment

The 19th Indiana Infantry Regiment, one of the five regiments forming the Iron Brigade, was mustered in at Indianapolis, 29 July 1861, and joined the Army of the Potomac at Washington, 9

Hancock County Indiana Civil War Soldiers

Aug 1861. Its first engagement was at Lewinsville, Virginia; then Falls Church, Virginia, and into quarters at Fort Craig, near Washington, where the following was written by Lieut. John C. Rardin, *Hancock Democrat*, 16 Oct 1861: "We learned of the 19th Regiment Indiana Volunteers now at Washington City by letter dated 8 Oct 1861, that Columbus C. Marsh; Zachariah Coffin, G.W. Woods and Isaac Lamb all of this county may be expected home in a few days.

"He also informs us that C. Collins (painter), B.M. Clifford and A.T. Stuart, also of this county are in the hospital sick. He thinks they will recover and be fit for duty in a short time. About 300 of the regiment are unfit for duty from sickness. The regiment is now at Fort Craig, Fairfax County, Virginia." In March 1862 the regiment began moving toward Fredericksburg, Virginia, and the Shenandoah Valley; a reconnaissance toward Spottsylvania Court House, and joined in the fight at Cedar Mountain. On 30 August, 1862, it was engaged at Manassas Junction where Hancock County's John Cly was mortally wounded. Hancock County's Capt. John Raridan was wounded at the battle at South Mountain in Maryland, 14 Sep 1862, three days before the 19th was at Antietam, Virginia, where the battle claimed more than 23,000 men killed, wounded and missing.

This bloody fight led President Lincoln to issue the Emancipation Proclamation. The 19th was attached to the First Brigade, First Division, First Corps, which was first of the infantry to be on the field at Gettysburg on 1 Jul 1863, and were in a charge that assisted in capturing a rebel brigade, before occupying a position on Cemetery Hill. Moving with Grant's army across the Rapidan River during May 1864, the regiment was engaged, among others, at Wilderness, Laurel Hill and Cold Harbor.

The following tells of four Hancock County soldiers involved: *Hancock Democrat*, 19 May 1864: "We are sorry to learn that our boys in the 19th Indiana have suffered in the recent battles across the Rapidan (River). Peter Lamb, Leroy Holding, A.M. Cly and J. Holden are reported wounded. Cly and Holden

Hancock County Indiana Civil War Soldiers

slightly, the first in the hand, and the latter in the shoulder; the condition of the other two are not reported." Hancock County's James L. Mitchell and Elisha Burris were wounded 6 May 1864 at Wilderness, Virginia. Of the eleven men from Hancock County who served in the 19th Regiment, nine are listed above as wounded or killed, the other two are Joseph Hartley and Theodore Ward. See data on their respective pages for all the above mentioned soldiers.

On 23 Sep 1864, a portion of the 7th Indiana was transferred to the 19th after which they were on duty in a strong defensive position near Petersburg, Virginia, and on 18 Oct 1864, it was consolidated with the 20th and served until final muster, 12 Jul 1865, at Louisville. Kentucky. The Iron Brigade suffered 15% killed or mortally wounded.

Hancock Democrat, 15 Dec 1892, "Ex-auditor James L. Mitchell received last week a silver badge inscribed as follows: : Seargt. J.L. Mitchell, Co A 19 Reg't Ind. Vol., Iron Brigade, War of 1861, which he had lost in December 1862, thirty years ago. The badge was lost in a hickory woods in Stafford County, Virginia, four miles north of Falmouth, when Mr. Mitchell was serving under Gen. Burnside after the battle of Fredericksburg and the army was stuck in the mud. The badge was found by a man while digging potatoes last fall. A Mr. J.M. Wallace there wrote to the Quartermaster General of the G.A.R. of this State at Indianapolis, who in turn sent the letter to Captain A.I. Makepeace at Anderson and he forwarded it to Mr. Mitchell who very gladly forwarded the finder of the badge a dollar and in return received his badge. Mr. Wallace says he himself was a boy of thirteen at the time of the battle of Fredericksburg and that the Union Generals had their headquarters at his father's who lived in a large brick house in an open field there. Mr. Wallace himself now occupies the same house. This is much the style in the south, the sons live where their fathers did and property remains in the same family for generations."

Hancock County Indiana Civil War Soldiers
51st Indiana Regiment

The 51st Regiment was mustered at Indianapolis, Indiana, 14 Dec 1861. Twenty-two Hancock County men were enlisted on varying dates, and all under the command of 33 year-old Indianapolis publisher, Colonel Abel D. Streight.

The regiment moved at once to Bardstown, Kentucky, where Hancock County's John L. Duncan, Company K, died 3 Jan 1862 (no cause given). In Feb 1862, the command reached the Tennessee River, too late for the battle at Shiloh Church but took an active part in the siege of Corinth. Ebenezer Cross, Company D, is recorded as having died 20 Mar 1862, Nashville, Tennessee.

Streight's regiment moved on to Murfreesboro, Tennessee, where it was engaged in the three day battle of Stone's River, 31 Dec 1862, 1 and 2 Jan 1863. Joseph (David) Shutes, Company K, was listed as missing in action at Stone's River. John K. Henby was captured and confined in Libby Prison. The command remained in camp near Murfreesboro until spring, 1863.

Being a restless, impatient man, Col Streight disliked the inactivity of camp life and began to formulate a plan. He received permission from the Chief of Staff for a command sufficient to invade the interior of the South on a raid to cut the Western and Atlantic Railroad that supplied the Confederate army in Middle Tennessee.

Colonel Streight's infantry regiment would become a Mounted Infantry regiment to raid into northern Alabama. Mounts were requisitioned for the 1,700 man unit, horses and mules arrived but the number of horses was insufficient, therefore, the decision was made for Streight's brigade to have the mules. This move would have offended a cavalryman but most likely was accepted with pleasure from an infantryman, after all riding in any fashion was preferable to marching.

To soften the blow of using mules the logic was that the terrain of the Alabama raid would be better suited to them as they are tougher and would tolerate the long marches better than horses. And besides, it was the plan that they would travel through friendly territory of Alabama and could get horses from Union sympathizers. Not only did they not find many horses but the mules lived up to their reputation and caused no end of trouble for the inexperienced troopers who had to contend with the poor, unbroken colts, many were sick and died along the way.

Imagine a Union mule brigade raiding across Alabama into Georgia and trying to gallop ahead of the Confederate cavalry commanded by the legendary Gen. Nathan Bedford Forrest. On 30 Apr 1863 in Cullman, County, Alabama, the rebels attacked the rear guard of Streight's command at Day's Gap on Sand Mountain. The rebels were routed but running skirmishes continued until 2 May when Forrest finally surrounded the fatigued mule brigade near Rome, Georgia, where he forced their surrender. The entire Union force of enlisted men was committed to rebel prisons where they were held until parole was granted then they were sent to camp in Indianapolis until exchanged in November.

Thus ended the saga of Colonel Streight's raid and the Mule Brigade. And by the way, Col. Streight was imprisoned at Libby Prison in Richmond, Virginia, and in Feb 1864 he was one of 109 prisoners who escaped through a tunnel.

The 51st regiment joined the army at Nashville in November and was assigned to duty in Tennessee and Alabama until mustered out.

The following three men died during the above skirmishes: Alvin B. Tibbetts, died 22 Aug 1864, Chattanooga, Tennessee; Elisha Whorton. died 5 Mar 1864, Nashville, Tennessee; and George Windsor, died 26 Aug 1863, Indianapolis.

53rd Indiana Regiment

The 53rd Regiment was partially organized at New Albany, Indiana, in January 1862 and came to include men from

Hancock County Indiana Civil War Soldiers

Rockport before the regiment moved to Camp Morton, Indianapolis, guarding prisoners. On 15 Mar 1862 the command left for the field and was transported to St. Louis, Missouri, then to Savannah, Tennessee, for a month when it joined the army then moving toward Corinth, Mississippi.

In October of 1862, it participated in the Tennessee battle of Hatchie, where it crossed the bridge while it was on fire, and charged the rebel lines. There were two Hancock county casualties, Lt. Joseph Atkison was wounded here on 5 Oct 1862 and lived until 17 Nov.; Aaron Hutton was killed on 5 Oct 1862.

The 53rd was in action at Vicksburg and Jackson, Mississippi; joined Sherman's army to participate in the Atlanta campaign. In the assault on the rebel works on Kennesaw Mountain, 27 Jun 64; the battle of Nickajack Creek, 5 Jul 64; battle of Peach Tree Creek, 20 Jul 64; and in the engagements before Atlanta, 22 Jul 64. Also joined in Sherman's celebrated march to the sea in Nov 64, continued into the Carolinas and was present when the Confederates surrendered to General Grant in 1865.

The 53rd Regiment was mustered out 21 Jul 1865 at Louisville, Kentucky. On to Indianapolis to a public reception on the Capitol grounds on 25 Jul 1865 when they were welcomed by Governor Morton and General Sherman addressed the soldiers.

Hancock Democrat 27 July 1862, Camp near Memphis, Tenn.: 'Dear Mitchell, Your correspondent had the pleasure of a reunion with his friends in the bloodless 53rd on the 22d inst. On the last named day, General Hurlbut's Division arrived in this place, dirty, ragged and weary. His troops have endured great hardship in coming across the country from Corinth (Miss.) during the hot weather that for some time has prevailed in this part of the much-famed "sunny South."

"General Veatch's Brigade (who served valiantly at the battle of Shiloh), to which my attention was particularly directed, were literally half naked. Some were barefooted, and a considerable number were so destitute of that very useful article of clothing in very modest circles called "unmentionables," that hardly enough

Hancock County Indiana Civil War Soldiers

remained to attach their suspenders to. They have since drawn new clothing, which much improves their appearance as well as their comfort. The probability is that both Sherman's and Hurlbut's Divisions will be stationed at this point for some considerable time. It is also hoped that they will be allowed a day of rest and recreation.

"General Hurlbut is becoming odious in the opinion of his entire command. He time and again compelled his men on long marches during the heat of June and July when his men fell down with sun-stroke and exhaustion. Hurlbut is probably a good General in a fight; but being a drunkard I can not consider him reliable. It is said of him all over the Brigade, and by men whose character for truth is unimpeachable, that he is hardly ever sober. A man in Co. L, of the 53rd Indiana, who was on guard at Headquarters, says that he saw Gen. Hurlbut ride up to his quarters so drunk that he could not alight from his horse and that the General threw himself at full length upon the ground and was carried in by his attendants. When will the Government set about ridding all such men from the service? It is currently rumored in camp that Hurlbut has tendered his resignation. It is the wish and prayer of thousands of his command that the rumor may prove true and that the Department may accept his resignation.

"The health of the 53rd is good. They have done more and endured more during the marching and counter-marching between here and Corinth than any other regiment in the Division. They are now inured to the hardships incident to soldier life. Our Col. Gresham, always popular with his command, has more nearly endeared himself to the men by the care he has shown for their comfort and great care taken in their welfare. He has shown himself to be possessed of a heart as well as a commission; and on one or two occasions had warm altercations with both our Brigade and Division Generals, rather than that his men should lie for long hours in a land where there is no shade, or march through the broiling sun when they could just as well wait until evening.

Hancock County Indiana Civil War Soldiers

"The present camping-ground of the 53rd is, perhaps the best we have had. The water here is excellent, in deed, as good as any I ever tasted in Indiana. The boys here from Hancock are well, with the exception of one or two cases of slight indisposition. Hoping that you and the loyal men in the County will vigorously fight the traitors at home while we engage the rebels abroad, I am yours, &c, Signed, Jo. B. Atkison, 53rd Reg. Ind. Vols."

Hancock Democrat, "The following letter to Mr. Thomas Hutton, of this county, fully explains itself. Headquarters Co A, 53rd Ind. Vol. Inf., Collierville, Tenn., 3 Mar 1863: Dear Sir: Your letter of February 23rd is received, and I hasten to reply. In the first place, I wish to state that immediately after the battle in which your son, Aaron, was killed, I addressed a letter to you, in which I gave all the particulars of his death, and such other information as I thought would be of comfort and satisfaction to you in your great affliction. I should consider that I would have been remiss in my duty as an officer had I not also told you in that letter that I had certain articles which belonged to Aaron, and which were subject to your order. But it seems that you did not receive the letter.

"Your son was killed at the battle of "Hatchie," on the 5th day of October, 1862. One of the enemy's minie balls struck him on top of the head, which terminated his life at 9 o'clock that evening. He was insensible from the moment he received his wound until death ended his sufferings. I was with him a portion of the time, but could do nothing to alleviate his pain or keep death from claiming him as his own. He was wounded about 3 o'clock, and died at 9, as I have before stated. He died heroically and gloriously, died in defense of the best Government that God has ever vouchsafed to man, died amid the din and roar of battle, died as the brave desires to die, died while foremost among the brave, and his comrades will remember him and avenge his death.

"Aaron was a most excellent soldier, generous, kind, dutiful, prompt in the discharge of every duty, brave and heroic in battle.

Hancock County Indiana Civil War Soldiers

Aaron was buried on the battlefield, on the 6th day of October, 1862. I directed his comrades to dig his grave near where he died. He was buried as decently as it is possible to do upon the field of battle. A board was placed at the head of the grave, giving his name, company, regiment and when he died. He "sleeps the sleep that knows no waking," but his memory will live in the hearts of his comrades as long as life shall last. Let me repeat that he was a good soldier. Very Respectfully, W.L. Vestal"

Hancock Democrat, 28 May 1863: "By General Order No. 58 of General S.A. Hurlbut, issued at Memphis on the 22nd of May 1863, Thomas McGrain, Major 53rd Indiana, and Seth Daily, Captain Company D 53rd Indiana, are dishonorably dismissed from the service of the United States, under provisions of Adjutant General Thomas' Special Order No. 28. Major McGrain tendered his resignation on the ground of his disapproval of the policy of arming the negroes. Daily was dismissed for the same reason." *Hancock Democrat*, 7 Jul 1864: "We are sorry to learn that Lieut. Samuel Marsh has been severely wounded by a ball through the upper thigh, badly breaking the bone. J.A. Watson was wounded in the hip in the fight, but not severely. George W. and Harrison Berry were taken prisoners."

Hancock Democrat, 14 Jul 1864: "A correspondent from the *Cincinnati Gazette*, writing from before Kennesaw Mountain, 29 Jun 1864 gives the following account of the affair in which George Carr was killed, and Lieut. Sam Marsh and James A. Watson, of this county, were wounded. The occurrence took place on 27 Jun 1864: Further to the left, and nearly at the northeastern point of Kennesaw was where the brave men of the 53rd Indiana met with disaster. At eight o'clock that morning their skirmish line was formed four hundred yards from the rebel rifle pits at the base of the mountain, and with an open field three hundred and fifty yards in width between them. Five line officers and ninety-seven men stood strong and hopeful there.

Hancock County Indiana Civil War Soldiers

"When the sun went down and the torn and bleeding line returned to camp, it was composed of one line officer and forty-nine men, the rest were among the killed, wounded and missing. The men composing the advancing line were from Companies A, I and D; Company B, Captain A.H. Fabrique, and a portion of Company D being held in reserve. The whole being under the command of Major Vestal. The rebels securely covered in their rifle pits in the woods at the base of the mountain, or ensconced behind the great rocks on its rugged side, were in position to see every movement of the fated line, while the brave men composing it could see nothing of the danger before them. With these great disadvantages the officers and men gallantly advanced 'into the jaws of death,' at the command 'forward.'

"Blindly firing at the hidden foe, whose galling fire was fearfully thinning their lines, these men of iron continued to advance until a portion of their line had crossed the open field and reached the rebel works only to find themselves overpowered. The remainder of the lines was forced to fall back across the field, some of the men were so near the rebel line that they did not attempt to withdraw in daylight, but hid themselves until dark and crawled away."

Hancock Democrat 4 Aug 1864: "We are sorry to learn that Company A, 53rd Indiana, has met with another severe loss. The only Commissioned officer of the company, Lieut. Smith, has been killed, as has been Burt Scott, of this county, James Scott and James Ragan both of this county are wounded and in the hands of the enemy."

As a note of interest, twin brothers, Joseph and Edward Martin, of Hancock County, celebrated their twenty-third birthday at the battle of Kennesaw Mountain, 27 Jun 1864. Included in the obit for Edward Martin are the following two stories: at the siege of Atlanta. Ed Martin and some of his comrades, which surely included his twin brother, Joe, were hidden in a hollow stump, the rebels were on all sides, and although the stump bore evidence of the rebel marksmanship, they failed to injure the occupants and they escaped under the cover of darkness.

The 53rd was mustered out in May 1865, at Washington, where Ed came very near losing his life. While a number of soldiers were bathing in the Potomac River, one of them called for help as he was drowning, and Ed went to his rescue, and succeeded in saving his life but came nearly losing his own in the struggle. Another note of interest, General Stephen A. Hurlbut was promoted to major general in 1862, commanded troops at Shiloh, Vicksburg and participated in Sherman's raid toward Mobile. During his war and post-war career, he came under fire for his conduct. Charges of corruption were leveled at him for activities while assigned to the Gulf South and Louisiana, after the war, he was accused, apparently with good reason, of drunkenness and corruption. It seems the letter written by Lt. Joseph Atkison of the 53rd Regiment was on target for the General.

57th Indiana Regiment

The 57th Indiana Infantry Regiment was mustered in 18 Nov 1861 at Richmond, Indiana. It moved to Indianapolis early in December and on 13 Dec of 1861, the regiment enlisted Hancock County men from the communities of Cleveland Charlottesville, Warrington, Willow Branch and Greenfield, totaling 42 patriotic citizens in Company A, plus several who were recruited from 1862 to 1864.

The regiment marched to Louisville, Bardstown, Lebanon and Munfordsville, all in Kentucky, then marched to Nashville, Tennessee, arriving in March, 1862. The 57th was not engaged in any battles but the winter campaign had been very severe, and the regiment suffered a depletion. They arrived at Shiloh Church, Tennessee, on 7 Apr 1862, in time for the second day of battle, then on to Corinth, Mississippi, taking part in the siege, remained in middle Tennessee, frequently in skirmishes as they guarded foraging trains.

Hancock County Indiana Civil War Soldiers

In the battle of Stone's River, Murfreesboro, Tennessee, the regiment had an active part as it opposed the rebel assaults on the first day of the battle, 31 Dec 1862. The battle continued on the 1st and 2nd of Jan 1863, suffering a total of 13,249 Union casualties, and 10,266 Confederate casualties. Despite the Northern losses, the battle was a Union victory that boosted morale, especially after the message to the commander (Rosecrans) from President Lincoln, "I can never forget…you gave us a hard-earned victory, which had there been a defeat instead, the nation could scarcely have lived over."

The 57th was also at Missionary Ridge, near Chattanooga, Tennessee, on 25 Nov 1863. The rebels misplaced their artillery, allowing the advance Union forces to storm the ridge and quickly overran the rebels who began a quick retreat. Now almost 140 years after the battle, Missionary Ridge, on the outskirts of Chattanooga, is not easy to identify as it has been veiled by society with only stone markers sprinkled in between houses and streets to tell the grim tale of that bloody day long ago.

The 57th participated with General Sherman in the Atlanta campaign beginning in May 1864 with Rocky Face Ridge, suffered severe losses between 25 and 27 May at New Hope Church in northwest Georgia. Also, there was heavy fighting on those days at nearby Pickett's Mill and skirmishing all around Kennesaw Mountain where on 27 Jun 1864 the 57th was in the fierce battle in the woods at Cheatham Hill.

The artillery had set fire to the tinder-dry trees and the flames surrounded Union casualties, some of whom were wounded too badly to move and were being burned alive. The Confederate commander, General Benjamin Cheatham, ordered his men to cease fire, climbed to the top of the entrenchments and called to the Union soldiers, "Come get your wounded, they are burning to death." For a brief, time the two enemy armies worked together to remove the injured. Union leaders presented Cheatham matching Colt .45 pistols the next day. This incident was known

Hancock County Indiana Civil War Soldiers

in the Kennesaw Mountain battle as the "truce on Cheatham Hill."

"The scene at Kennesaw Mountain was enchanting; too beautiful to be disturbed by the harsh clamor or war, but the Chattahoochee lay beyond, and I had to reach it," were the words of General William T. Sherman, U.S.A.

The 57th saw action near Atlanta at Peach Tree Creek and Jonesboro before going into Tennessee at the battles of Nashville and Franklin where it sustained heavy losses, and prisoners taken. In Apr 1865, it was transferred to Port Lavaca, Texas, and was mustered out there on 14 Dec 1865.

The following Hancock County soldiers were wounded or killed in some of the above battles: Joseph Brooks, killed 31 Dec 1861, Stone's River; Daniel Burke, flesh wound at Kennesaw Mountain, 18 Jun 1864; William T. Byers, died 28 Jul 1864 from wounds received at Kennesaw Mountain; Lorenzo D. Fort, age 17, died 1 Jan 1863, Stone's River; Joseph N. Reynolds, died 15 Jun 1863, no place given; Joseph F. Shultz, wounded, 23 Jun 1864, Kennesaw Mountain; James Thomas, wounded, arm amputated, 23 Apr 1864, near Kennesaw Mountain. See data on their respective pages.

79th Indiana Infantry Regiment

The 79th Indiana Infantry Regiment was organized at Indianapolis and mustered on 2 Sep 1862. There were about 130 Hancock County men enlisted, when it left to support Louisville who was being threatened by the rebels nearing Perryville and Lexington. In pursuit of Confederate General Bragg in early October at Perryville, the 79th was held in the reserve force (whose mission in any attack is to clinch the victory or to exert success). They were engaged in a skirmish with the enemy's rear guard at Crab Orchard, Kentucky, before moving into Tennessee.

History of the 79th Regiment states: 22 Oct 1862: "Ordered to be ready to march, company drills, rations are scarce, crackers

Hancock County Indiana Civil War Soldiers

are wormy and water very hard to find. The worst experience up to date. 27 Nov 1862: Thanksgiving Day is a day of rest for the soldier; the battalion attended divine worship services in the afternoon. 25 Dec 1862: Christmas. No difference between this and other days for soldiers. Cannonading heard on the right."

The Regiment must have been near Murfreesboro, Tennessee, where it aided in the repulse of the rebels at the battle of Stone's River which began 29 Dec 1862, and continued until 2 Jan 1863, with 12,000-plus official Union casualties. Two Hancock County soldiers are recorded as casualties, one killed in action and one missing in action at Stone's River: John J. Loomis, missing; and Martin Stanley, killed.

The 79th Regiment History states: "The Stone's River battlefield indicates a great loss of life, will probably reach nine or ten thousand on Union side in killed, wounded and missing. Trees twelve inches in diameter are cut off in places where fighting was hot. Horses are laying around killed in every possible manner. Details are busy burying the dead."

The battle was a victory that boosted Union morale. President Lincoln sent the following message to the commander (Rosecrans): "I can never forget you…you gave us a hard-earned victory, which had there been a defeat instead, the nation could scarcely have lived over."

79th Regiment History: "16 Jan 1863: …stationed at an elegant house, formerly occupied by a man now in the rebel army. The house was at one time luxuriously furnished. It is now stripped of everything, books, furniture, pictures, etc.; nothing is left but the bare walls." 26 Apr 1863: An order published for a private in Company A, sentenced to carry a 24-pound ball and chain ten days for leaving post while on camp guard and getting drunk."

The 79th Regiment History tells of the punishment of a soldier in the 9th Kentucky who had deserted several times and apprehended several times and finally sentenced to be shot: "22 Jun 1863, The Battalion formed and marched one-and-one-half miles from Murfreesboro, halted on the left side of the Lebanon

Hancock County Indiana Civil War Soldiers

Pike in a clover field. Took position in the Brigade and the Division was formed into a three-sided square. A detail was made of a certain number of men from the Division and given guns, some loaded and some not. The deserter was blindfolded and seated on his coffin. At the command given, "Fire!" he fell over backward dead, and as he lay in this position, the whole division marched past the body and was given an opportunity to see the doom of the deserter."

The Regiment left Murfreesboro on 24 Jun 1863 when an almost steady rain began and continued for seventeen consecutive days. Slowed by muddy quagmires but undeterred, the soggy army marched to Tullahoma but on 1 Jul they found the enemy works empty. On the march to Chattanooga the 79th was engaged in heavy skirmishing and in the battle Of Chickamauga on 19 and 20 Sep, they charged and captured the first Virginia Battery.

The 86th was temporarily combined with the 79th and on 25 Nov 1863 the merged unit led the column that charged the invincible, Missionary Ridge. Up the cliff-like ridge and into the rebel works, they were the first unit to plant its flag on the enemy's works, captured eleven pieces of artillery and several hundred prisoners.

Now almost 140 years after the battle on Missionary Ridge, near the outskirts of Chattanooga, the site is not easy to identify, as it has been veiled by society with houses and streets and only the stone markers sprinkled here and there to tell the grim tale of that long ago battle.

The 79th remained in east Tennessee during the winter of 1863 and 1864, almost constantly engaged in skirmishes and marches at Strawberry Plains, New Market and Clinch Valley, suffering from exposure, short rations and no warm clothing. In April 1864 the 79th returned to Chattanooga where for the first time in months, rested in camp ten days.

The 79 Regiment History states, "10 May 1864, There is rain, thunder, lightning and the sound of shrill rebel yells as they call to the pickets." In May the regiment joined Sherman's Atlanta

Hancock County Indiana Civil War Soldiers

campaign and was engaged in heavy skirmishing at Tunnell Hill and Rocky Face Ridge not far from Dalton, Georgia.

Rocky Face Ridge was the first battle of Sherman's Atlanta campaign. The Confederates were to keep the Yankees from going any deeper into Georgia and at all costs defend Atlanta. The battle at Rocky Face Ridge was fierce from the 8th to the 11th of May 1864, Union casualties were high but Sherman's outflanking movement forced the rebels from the mountain on south to defend Resaca.

79th Regiment History states: "13 May 1864, ...struck Dalton, halted, captured some of the rebel knapsacks that are very nice, made in England and better than ours."

Despite the addition of cadets from the nearby Georgia Military Institute, the battle at Resaca on 14 May 1865, was a Union victory and the Yankees marched deeper into Georgia. The 79th was in the fight at New Hope Church, Pickett's Mill and Lost Mountain before engaging in the battle at Kennesaw Mountain, 27 Jun 1864.

79th Regiment History states: "30 Jun 1864, Regiment allowed to rest and sleep in the rear of the reserve force. Men are talking with rebels and are permitted to trade coffee for tobacco, the rebs have a large supply and are willing to trade; detail sent under flag of truce to bury the dead killed on 23 Jun."

Continuing southward the 79th was the first to cross Peach Tree Creek, three miles north of Atlanta. It was on active duty during the siege of Atlanta, from 22 Jul until 24 Aug 1864, when it again moved south to the Macon Railroad and was in action at Jonesboro and Lovejoy Station. After the surrender of Atlanta on 2 Sep 1864, the regiment remained in camp there for a month.

79th Regiment History states: "2 Sep 1864, Captain Dunbar (John G.) went too far in posting pickets and was captured. 6 Sep 1864, Six thousand bales of cotton are burning along the railroad. 29 Sep 1864, Captain Dunbar exchanged and returned to regiment."

On 1 Dec 1864 the 79th arrived at Nashville and took position where they stormed up Overton's Hill, captured the position and nine pieces of artillery. They pursued the rebel army through Tennessee into Alabama and were moved by train back to Tennessee in readiness for the possible advance to Richmond, Virginia, which was unnecessary after the Confederate surrender.

The 79th Regiment was mustered out 11 Jun 1865 at Indianapolis, they were present at a reception on the Capital grounds and listened to a welcome speech made by Governor Morton.

Following is a list of Hancock County soldiers who were casualties in the 79th Regiment, see their respective pages for details: John Allen, died 3 Apr 1863; Sylvester Barrett, died 2 Feb 1863; Amos Beeson, wounded 23 Jun 1864; Nelson Boyce, died 3 Dec 1862; Thomas Brinegar, died 29 Jan 1865; Thomas J. Carr, wounded, Sep 1863; Nathan Catt, died Feb 1863, disease; Philander Cox, died 19 Jul 1863; James F. Dillman, died 30 Nov 1863; Andrew J. Eakes, died 25 Mar 1863; Joseph R. Eakes, wounded 25 Oct 1863; James Elliott, 7 Sep 1863, transferred to V.R.C. indicating illness or wound; David Harrison, died 13 Mar 1863; George Langenberger, died 21 Feb 1862; Jacob Leonard, wounded 23 Nov 1863; William Lucas, died 18 Dec 1862; Cyrus McCord, died 24 Jan 1864; John Murphy, wounded 23 Jun 1864; William Steele died 27 Dec 1862; and William C. Wright, died 23 Oct 1863.

99th Indiana Regiment

The 99th Indiana Infantry Regiment; The 99th Regiment History states: "mustered into service 21 Oct 1862 at Camp Joe Reynolds, Indianapolis, on the west bank of the canal, between the canal and the river, where we were issued Enfield rifles, about the best guns available at the time." Company B came from Hancock County under the command of Captain James H. Carr. In November, 1862, the soldiers were busy breaking 72 mules to harness and the surgeons were vaccinating against small pox.

Hancock County Indiana Civil War Soldiers

After leaving Indianapolis on the train, 19 Oct 62, the regiment crossed the Ohio River at Jeffersonville on a pontoon bridge, and went aboard transports to travel down the Ohio River to Memphis. The regiment participated in battles at LaGrange and Moscow, Tennessee; Jackson and Vicksburg, Mississippi; and was with General Sherman when he began his Atlanta campaign early in May, 1864. And those of the regiment who were not sick from camp life, wounded or killed, went on the infamous March to Sea from Atlanta to Savannah; plus the little known, but equally important to ending the war, the march through the Carolinas.

The regiment was at Fort Fowler, five miles west of LaGrange, Tennessee, during the winter of November 1862 to March 1863, when "the eyes of some brave soldiers were closed in death:" the following seven deaths were recorded from Company B: Nathaniel Blakely; Andrew Curry; Thomas J. Collins; William Fletcher; brothers, Lemuel Nibarger (died 18 Mar) and Thomas Nibarger (died 30 Mar); and Madison Winn. Captain James H. Carr resigned 21 Jan 1863 due to failing health.

Recorded from New History of the 99th Regiment, Fort Fowler, 25 Feb 1863: "A hundred men went out on a foraging expedition yesterday, and they managed to pick up considerable plunder, so we had fried chicken for breakfast, and were told, 'Eat what is set before you, asking no questions for conscience sake.' We are to have one of our evening concerts at headquarters tonight; violin, flute, banjo and many fine singers. It helps us greatly in passing the weary evening hours.

27 Nov 1863: "We left our camp on the north side of the Tennessee River and crossed in boats to the south side and advanced at once to Missionary Ridge. Fifty men were thrown forward to the skirmish line and they were for a time in the thick of the fight. Christian Ortle (sometimes written as Whortle) was wounded and died 15 Dec after the battle."

The winter of 1864 at Scottsboro, Alabama: Jacob H. Davis discharged as unfit for further service; Nimrod Davis and Clark

Hancock County Indiana Civil War Soldiers

W. Wright were transferred to the Veteran Reserve Corps where they rendered efficient service as guards of posts until the war closed.

The regiment was engaged in battle on 28 May 1864 near Dallas, Georgia, "a small town on Pumpkinvine Creek, about thirteen miles west of Marietta, (or Big Shanty) on the Western and Atlantic Railroad, heading to Atlanta." The fierce fighting, with heavy Union and Confederate losses, extended from Dallas to New Hope Church and to Pickett's Mill, which are only a few miles apart.

Forty men of Company B were detailed for the picket line at the battle of Dallas, and passed through that terrific fight, with only seventeen of the forty returning. Doing the math, that leaves twenty-three men, the exact number reported from Hancock County as being wounded, killed or captured at the battle of Dallas, Georgia, 28 May 1864: George H. Alley, wounded in arm, survived; Samuel D. Alley, wounded in leg, died of wounds, 3 Sep 64, at Rome, Georgia; Jonathan Baldwin, wounded, survived; Joseph Bowman, wounded, survived; James R. Brown, wounded badly in body, survived; James W. Cass, captured, sent to Andersonville Prison, released, died 27 Apr 65 on the Sultana; Charles G. Hamilton, wounded in hip, survived.

Benjamin F. Kelly, killed; Elisha Morford, killed; John A. Morford, wounded in thigh and abdomen, survived; Joseph Morford, wounded in leg, survived; William H. Power, slightly wounded the next day, 29 May 1864, survived; Oliver Reeves, wounded in face, survived; Riley Reeves, wounded in arm, survived; William W. Reeves, wounded in both legs; survived; Charles W. Scott, wounded, survived; William R. Shaw, missing in action, captured, died Andersonville Prison, 5 Nov 64; William Shipman, wounded badly in face, died two days later; Harvey True, wounded in foot, on the third day of the battle of Pickett's Mill, survived; Robert H. Vernon, wounded in hip, died 9 May 65, Laurel Hill, NC; George W. Watts, wounded in leg, survived; Vinton Whitehurst, wounded, survived; James W. Wright, wounded, died 12 Jun 64.

Hancock County Indiana Civil War Soldiers

During the Atlanta campaign in July and August of 1864, the 99th was engaged at Marietta/Big Shanty; Kennesaw Mountain; Peach Tree Creek; Ezra Church and others. The following soldiers of Company B were reported as wounded or killed: Captain R.P. Andis, seriously wounded in the head; Corporal Lewis Richman, wounded; Michael G. Youse, wounded; Perry McQuery, killed; Riley Kingen, wounded; Harrison Nibarger, wounded (his two brothers were killed in 1863).

"On the 15th of November 1864, the Ninety-Ninth marched from its camp, and with colors pointing to the South, moved with Sherman on his great march to the sea. After having marched over three-hundred miles in twenty-four days, the regiment reached the front of Savannah. On 22 Dec 1864, General Sherman sent a dispatch to President Lincoln: 'I beg to present to you as a Christmas gift, the city of Savannah.' "

In January of 1865, the 99th Regiment began its march through the Carolinas. On 12 April 1865 the official announcement was made of the surrender of Lee to Grant at Appomattox and on 17 April 1865, General Sherman announced the assassination of President Lincoln. The next day a truce was called between the armies of Sherman and Johnston. There was much heated controversy between the Secretary of War and General Sherman over the terms of surrender. It was not until 26 April 1865, that the Confederate Army of North Carolina surrendered at Bennett's house, near Durham Station, North Carolina. The terms were the same given to Lee by Grant.

The regiment then made its way to Washington, marching 124 miles in six days, to take part in the Grand Review on 24 May 1865. The 99th did not get new flags but seemed proud to march with their old, battled-scarred ones of a few tattered strips on broken and splintered staffs. (See pages about Grand Review in Call To Arms section of this volume.)

The regiment was mustered out 5 June 1865. Leaving Washington, they traveled by train, and by the river-steamer, Nashville, to Lawrenceburg, Indiana, from there by train to Indianapolis, where they arrived 11 Jun 1865. The next day the

Hancock County Indiana Civil War Soldiers

regiment received a welcome from Governor Morton on the grounds of the old state house. Final payment was made on 15 June 1865, when all the regiment departed for home with the echoing words of a Company B veteran, "We are once more in God's country."

William H. Power, a member of Company B, 99th Regiment, wrote about his experiences and the following incidents are edited from his pages: "Sherman's army was called 'Shermans Bummers' because of the clothes they wore. When our uniforms were worn out we had to grab anything to wear. I have seen soldiers wearing plug hats, prince albert coats, and black trousers, foraged from houses along the way. I found my suit in a barrel in an old house. A pair of gray trousers, a roundabout coat with red cuffs and collar, red up in front and a red belt; gray cap trimmed in red. It was a rebel artillery uniform. I voted for Abraham Lincoln in 1864, at the age of sixteen years and four months. We were allowed to vote in the field; I was always very proud of that vote and think he was the greatest man America ever produced.

"While we were laying in the siege around Atlanta, we drew rations and cooked on the banks of the trenches to conceal us from the sharpshooters. We had a food called pressed vegetables which made a fairly good soup with crackers broken up in it. When we opened our cracker box, it was found to be full of worms. We picked out we could see, made our soup and was eating it, when a weak stomached boy found a worm in the soup, he turned sick and threw up all he had eaten. The cook said never mind Jake, they are just as good as the soup."

Our Regiment records tell that we marched 4,000 miles and carried forty to fifty pounds, sometimes going 27 miles in a day. On the fourth of July 1864, we were after Joe Johnstons army from Kennesaw Mountain towards Atlanta. It was an awful hot day, soldiers were laying all along the road sick from the excessive heat and many sun strokes; when we went into camp that evening, there only five men reached camp. I was one of the five, being 16 years and nine days old on that day."

Hancock County Indiana Civil War Soldiers

Civil War Prisons

Andersonville seems to receive the most attention of the prison pens of the Civil War era, however, there were many others just as unfit for human habitation. No matter if they housed Union or Confederate prisoners of war, all soldiers were at risk for death from exposure, starvation and disease.

Prisoners were not given serious thought in the early days of the war when both the North and the South thought the fighting would not last more than a few months. But as the few months stretched into a year and then billowed into two and then three years, commanders of both armies began to have very serious questions about prisoners.

For awhile parole and exchange seemed to be the answer with each prisoner being paroled and exchanged within ten days of capture. The captured soldiers were taken to a neutral site where their names were recorded and to pledge their word not to take up arms against the enemy until after the exchange when the men would then be sent back to their regiments for reassignment. The rate of exchange was based on the rank of a private: one private for one private, one Lieutenant for four privates, one Major for eight privates and so on up rank to a General for forty-six privates.

But by the summer of 1863 agreements were suspended because complications arose when former slaves, serving as Union soldiers, were captured and the Confederacy refused to recognize them as prisoners of war. They were reduced to slave circumstance once again and their white commanders were charged with insurrection under the penalty of death.

Therefore, the process unraveled. General Grant is quoted as saying, "Every man we hold, when released on parole or otherwise, becomes an active soldier against us at once either directly or indirectly . If we commence a system of exchanges

Hancock County Indiana Civil War Soldiers

which liberates all prisoners taken, we will have to fight on until the whole South is exterminated."

At first glance, prisons seemed to be a simple answer but there were difficult questions about location, commandants, guards, food and discipline. Soon the process of caring for prisoners of war became very complicated, especially when both North and South captured hundreds of soldiers at one time after victorious battles. Apparently, those prisoners were herded to an area where they remained under guard until arrangements were made to move them to a prison.

There were several prisoner of war camps in many of the states and among others were: Elmira but called "Helmira;" in New York; Florence and the Lunatic Asylum in South Carolina; Fort McHenry and Point Lookout in Maryland; Castle Thunder and Libby in Virginia; Rock Island in Illinois; Camp Chase in Ohio; Camp Morton in Indiana; Cahaba in Alabama; Salisbury in North Carolina; and Fort Jefferson in Florida. No matter if the soldiers were housed in North or South prisons, they all became known as "infernal death pens and Hell-holes."

The prisons ran the gamut from open stockades like Andersonville and Florence, South Carolina for Union prisoners; and for Confederate prisoners were the Ohio State Penitentiary and Fort Jefferson in the Gulf of Mexico, which had the reputation as "America's Devil's Island." . Not all soldiers in the prisons were captured on battlefields, some soldiers, both North and South, were criminals in the army same as they were in civilian life. These law breakers were arrested, tried and served their sentences in the military prisons.

An interesting tidbit, Dr. Samuel Mudd, the man who treated John Wilkes Booth's broken leg, was sentenced to life imprisonment at Fort Jefferson.

Food was so scarce and bad that rats were regular fare and high on the barter scale. Byron Kurtz, a soldier from Hancock County, was found during research for this volume, and the following is recorded about his capture and imprisonment : "While on the skirmish line during the second day's fight at

Hancock County Indiana Civil War Soldiers

Chickamauga, he was shot in the left leg above the knee and remained on the field where he was captured. Taken to Libby Prison (Richmond, Virginia), he was held until the spring of 1864, thence to Andersonville, where he experienced the horrors of that institution with thousands of others confined in that death pen.

"After the Atlanta campaign, he, with others in a squad, were taken by the Confederates to Macon, (Fort Oglethorpe) Georgia, to nurse a number of sick Union prisoners, captured by the rebels in the Atlanta campaign, and Stoneman's raid (see pages for 5th Indiana Cavalry). From Macon, they were sent to Savannah, another prison hospital filled with privates and officers, which they nursed for a time and were then sent to Florence, South Carolina. While in the prison there, Mr. Kurtz, with a squad of others, were detailed to go after some wood, they captured a dog, brought him in, killed him for their New Year's dinner, and Mr. Kurtz to this day (1899) has a piece of that canine's bone, which he cherishes as the most memorable army relic in his possession." Edited from a 1899 publication, *Statesmen, Patriots and Soldiers*.

A different version of that dog meal was found in Mr. Kurtz's obituary in 1925, "On one occasion when the prisoners were supplied with sweet potatoes, a dog followed the guards who brought the potatoes and was enticed to remain and the prisoners killed it and cooked its meat with the sweet potatoes." Two versions and the same end for the unwary dog, but the story proves the soldiers were not only hungry, they were, indeed, starving.

Nearly 26,000 Confederates died in Northern prison camps and 30,000 Federals died in Southern prison camps.

Andersonville Prison

Andersonville, located in Sumter County, Georgia, also known as Fort Sumter, is perhaps the most well-known Civil War prison, where captured Union soldiers were forced to

Hancock County Indiana Civil War Soldiers

endure food that ranged from worm-infested and spoiled to none at all, very little medical treatment, exposure of heat in summer and cold of winter--in fact the prison pens were truly where survival of the fittest was a day to day struggle, if not an hour to hour struggle.

A large number of Northern captives were held in Richmond, Virginia, at Belle Isle and Libby prisons, causing a city food shortage and guarding them kept able-bodied Confederates from the much needed troops at the front. Therefore the search for a new prison site began and in December, 1863, a remote area of Georgia was selected. Construction was not completed when the first 500 prisoners from Belle Isle arrived on 27 Feb 1864. By late June 26,000 prisoners were crammed into the stockade built for 10,000, and by August there were 32,000, the highest number at any one time of its existence.

Soldiers who had been POWs for a long time before being transferred to Andersonville were in rags when they arrived, others brought directly from the battlefields wore uniforms of that were nearly worn out and some prisoners had no clothes at all. The prisoners who had money could add to their scanty meals, of meal, bacon or beef and on occasion peas, rice vinegar and molasses, by buying food from the prison sutler. But the diet caused severe shortcomings and diseases that some prisoners endured the rest of their lives.

Even the slightest bite from a flea or scratch on the skin could mean death from infection. The mortality rate was high and most prisoners died from diarrhea, dysentery, gangrene, scurvy, not to mention typhoid and pneumonia. Of the 45,000 Union prisoners confined altogether during the prison's 13 month existence, nearly 13,000 died and are buried in the Andersonville Cemetery.

Violence by the "Andersonville Raiders," an organized group of thieves and murderers, was a daily occurrence for several months until, with help of prison officials, the six ringleaders were captured and after a speedy trial by inmates were hanged from a hastily built gallows. There was a bit of thievery

Hancock County Indiana Civil War Soldiers

afterward but the widespread murder upon inmates was at its end. Although, death was still a daily occurrence.

Escape from Andersonville was difficult but not impossible. During the prison's existence only 329 escaped with most being caught, due to the remote area and distance to the Union lines. Successful escapes were usually when the soldiers slipped away from the guards while on work details outside the stockade. Tunnels were tried but not to any degree of success.

When General Sherman captured Atlanta 2 Sep 1864, most of the able-bodied prisoners were moved to Charleston and Florence, South Carolina, and Savannah, Georgia, to prevent release by Union cavalry sent for that purpose. The prison continued to operate through the winter of 1865. In April 1865 the Union forces captured Columbus, Georgia, and within three weeks the last of the Andersonville prisoners were released.

There are forty-two Hancock County soldiers recorded as prisoners at Andersonville, Georgia. Of that number more than half belonged to Company G, 5th Indiana Cavalry who were taken prisoner during "the disastrous expedition commanded by General George Stoneman," on 31 July 1864, northeast of Macon, Georgia, at Clinton, but now near the town known as Gray, Georgia. Follwing are the Hancock County soldiers recorded as prisoners of war:

George H. Alford; W. Barton; W.D. Barwick; E. Belville; George Berry; Harrison Berry; Francis M. Brizendine; Erastus Brunson; Charles W. Campbell; James W. Cass; Charles Edward Chittenden; Reason Collins; George W. Duncan; William Evans; Henry C. Gant; Henry Gates; George W. Hoover; David Jeff; Berry Johnson; L. Jonas; James Kimberlin; Byron Kurtz; Elijah Lunsford; Thomas Mack; Marshall Meek; Ranson Meek; Newton Pope; Jasper N. Pope; James Reagan; James A. Riley; John Samuels; James Scott; Jacob Shaffer; Isaac Shaw; William R. Shaw; C.W. Smith; John Smith; Jonathan Snow; Ralph L. Thompson; Charles Willett; and T.W. Williams.

There are eight other Hancock County soldiers who were members of Company G, 5th Cavalry, who were taken prisoner in

Hancock County Indiana Civil War Soldiers

"the disastrous expedition led by General George Stoneman, on 31 Jul 1864, however, are not recorded on the Andersonville Prison Profile; and, according to the war experiences at different prisons related by Byron Kurtz, they may have been taken to Macon:

A. Blakely; Morris Fort; J. Hudson/Hutson; Adam Hutton; George W. Miller; William W. Price; Thomas Snider; and Samuel Thompson. See details on their respective pages.

Cahaba, Alabama, Prison

Cahaba Prison was located near Selma, Alabama, on the banks of the Alabama and Cahaba Rivers, fifty miles southwest of Montgomery. A cotton warehouse, was the prison home for 5,000 Union soldiers from late 1863 until the close of the war in April of 1865.

The prison was fenced-in by a tall brick wall with the enclosure being about 16,000 square feet where the prisoners cooked their own meals. Extending from the brick wall was a leaky roof under which were rough bunks, without bedding of any kind, where only 432 soldiers could sleep. There was one fireplace, therefore, the men built fires on the ground if there was wood, the green pine and decayed oak made welcome heat.

The water supply for drinking, cooking, laundry and bathing was an artesian well that flowed in an open gutter for two hundred yards into the prison. The water was badly polluted by townspeople who used the well as an open sewer for dumping slops, spitoons and all other filth, whether liquid or solid.

Starvation and disease at Cahaba were enemies worse than the horrors of the battlefield. After heavy rains, the Alabama and Cahaba Rivers flooded into the enclosure to a depth of one to four feet and, after the water receded, prisoners had to endure the mud.

Such was the daily living at Cahaba. Finally it was announced that all prisoners would be sent to an exchange camp at Vicksburg, Mississippi. One prisoner expressed the joy of all,

Hancock County Indiana Civil War Soldiers

"We are to leave this horrible hole. Hearts full of gratitude and thanksgiving to the great Almighty beat riotously in the bosom of every prisoner and the tears coursed down every cheek when the glad news was made known."

Eight Hancock County soldiers were prisoners at Cahaba and five were on the ill-fated Sultana when it exploded 27 April 1865. They were members of Company B of the 9th Indiana Cavalry who were captured at the bloody battle of Sulphur Trestle, Alabama, 25 Sep 1864. See the pages for the 9th Cavalry and respective pages for the soldiers:

Frederick Blessinger; Charles E. Church; John B. Herod; Ephraim Perman; John Steward; Marcellus Walker; William J. Foster; and Christopher Hugh (Kip) Sears.

Camp Oglethorpe, Macon, Georgia

Camp Oglethorpe, located near the Ocmulgee River on the site of the old fair grounds, was used as a militia camp in the days before it was used as a prison for Union POWs. The camp consisted of fifteen to twenty acres with a one-story building, used as a hospital, and other sheds clustered about, all surrounded by a high-board fence.

Upon arrival, prisoners were thoroughly searched to find any money that might be hidden, and were led into the compound one at a time. The gate was bridged on the top by an archway that spelled out the camp name in huge black letters and when it swung open, "there appeared a sea of ghostly, grizzled, dirty and haggard faces staring this way and that."

The prisoners varied in number from about 600 in 1862 and swelled to 1,900 in 1864, but rations rarely varied, unsifted corn meal, bacon twice a week and enough peas for two soup meals per week. Camp Oglethorpe was torn down after it served as a parole depot at the close of the war.

Hancock County's Byron Kurtz served as a nurse at the hospital to care for prisoners who were captured in the Atlanta campaign and Stoneman's "disastrous raid" in Georgia.

Hancock County Indiana Civil War Soldiers

Libby Prison

Libby was another of the dreaded prisons, however, only officers passed through its doors until May of 1864 when enlisted men were brought in. Formerly the Libby and Son Ship Chandlers (retail dealer in supplies or equipment of a specified kind) and Grocers, the three-story, 45,000 square foot brick building was situated on an isolated spot in Richmond, Virgina, bordered by the James River.

By 1863 men were sleeping in units on their sides to preserve space, only allowed to turn over on the order of an elected leader. There were short rations, lice and exposure to cold even for officers who bought extra food and received packages from home. There were captured black Northerners who served as servants to the white officers, plus running water and primitive flush toilets. A far cry from the unsanitary latrines and sinks at other prisons.

Reports were made in letters written by the officers about the ruthless living conditions, especially after a mass escape in early 1864, when sentries were ordered to shoot anyone looking out windows and hundreds of pounds of gunpowder were dangerously stored in the cellar. To quiet the ugly reports, the Confederate authorities invited impartial observers to make an opinion of the complaints, but not before the rebels made a hasty and contrived transformation in the cleanliness and fragrance of the building, and added in visible places were books, games, hams, bacon and other foodstuffs. Observers commented that "a picture of profusion met the eye and scrupulously clean and well ventilated."

Libby's notoriety outlived the War and in 1889 the building was dismantled and taken to Chicago where it was rebuilt as a tourist attraction.

There were five Hancock County soldiers who spent some months at Libby Prison: George H. Alford; Charles Edward Chittenden; Cyrus Ellingwood; John K. Henby; and Byron Kurtz. See details on their respective pages.

Hancock County Indiana Civil War Soldiers

The Sultana Explosion

At 2:00 A.M. on 27 April 1865, boilers of the steamboat, Sultana, suddenly, and without warning, exploded on the Mississippi River, near Memphis, Tennessee, with 2,100 Union soldiers and 200 civilians crammed on board. The northern homebound soldiers were hardened veterans of bloody battles and tough survivors of Confederate prison pens, such as Andersonville in Georgia, and Castle Morgan located at Cahaba, Alabama. The explosion, fire and cold, icy water claimed 1,800 lives. More lives were lost on the Mississippi River that night in 1865 than were lost in 1912 on the ill-fated Titanic.

The Sultana disaster is not widely known today-nor was it widely known in April of 1865. The newspapers were full of news about the surrender of the Confederacy ending the Civil War, the death of President Lincoln and the capture and death of assassin, John Wilkes Booth. These dramatic events clamored for attention and shoved the Sultana tragedy into the background.

Picture in your mind's eye the side-wheel Sultana churning the muddy Mississippi upriver from Vicksburg. The six-feet tall white letters spelling, Sultana, painted on the wheel housing, were obscured by the rainy, cloud-covered night. Built for a legal capacity to carry 376 people, its cabins and decks were overloaded six times capacity. Plus she carried 70-100 mules and horses on the rear section of the deck, 300,000 pounds of sugar and 90 cases of wine in the hold--and one large alligator kept in a wooden crate by the crew as a mascot.

During the War the Union and Confederate parole and prisoner exchange process was, at best, chaotic and the close of the War didn't seem to improve it. The Union soldiers being released from POW camps began pouring into Camp Fisk, Vicksburg, Mississippi, to be processed for transportation to Camp Chase, Ohio, located near Columbus, for mustering out.

Hancock County Indiana Civil War Soldiers

When the word spread that money was to be made transporting soldiers North, steamboats raced to the Mississippi River port of Vicksburg, hoping to receive Government contracts. Some of the boats had intriguing names, Belle Memphis, Henry Ames, Arthur, Lady Gay, Pauline Carroll, and the Luminary, sister-ship of the Sultana.

The Civil War was in full swing in 1863 when the Sultana was built at the Ohio River town of Cincinnati and it wasn't long until she was requisitioned by the Government for the shipment of troops and military cargo. Being requisitioned was a command performance for the boat owners, the order could not/should not be refused, and any protests, of overcrowding and loading beyond the legal capacity, were useless as the military always had its way.

Greed reared its ugly head resulting in heated profit making schemes, competition and bribes, involving military and civilians, to collect the Government fee of $10 per officer and $5 per enlisted man. Due to some fancy foot work of those in charge, political favors for personal gain, and the statement "all men could be put on one boat," resulted in most of the soldiers being steered to the Sultana. It seems too many Union army officers were involved to make an accurate count of the ex-prisoners arriving by train in Vicksburg daily, all clamoring to get home. One steamboat, the Lady Gay, left the Vicksburg wharf without a single soldier.

Despite being plagued with boiler trouble, the Sultana chugged away from the Vicksburg wharf on the 25th of April 1865. Her decks swarmed with blue uniforms, each jockeying for a comfortable position for the trip to Cairo, Illinois, where they would transfer to the train that would complete their journey to Camp Chase, Ohio. It seemed unimportant to the owner, who was on board, or to the captain of the Sultana, or to the military, that there were only 76 life preservers and two life boats for an emergency.

Through the evening hours, the soldiers on the main deck poked and taunted the mascot alligator, regaling in its hissing and snapping jaws until the crew moved its crate to a safe place. Also the men were entertained with songs and dancing by the Chicago Opera Troupe.

At 7:00 A.M. on the 26th the overloaded steamer neared Helena, Arkansas, where residents were in boats floating down the town's flooded streets. The soldiers all shifted to one side of the Sultana to see the spectacle, as they did so its decks began to tilt, and an officer vaulted to the top of the pilothouse shouting a caution not to change places when the boat was stopped.

By 7:00 P.M. the boat landed at the Memphis wharf where 200 or so hogsheads of sugar, the ninety-seven boxes of wine and all the hogs were unloaded and consigned to the Quartermaster Department. Passengers got on and several got off, including the Chicago Opera Troupe, to the disappointment of the soldiers. The unloading of freight was finished about 11:00 P.M. and just before midnight the Sultana backed away from Memphis and crossed the flood-swollen river to the Arkansas side to buy coal at the barges anchored above the city landing. About 1:00 A.M. on 27 April 1865 the steamship began its ill-fated journey north against the current.

The Mississippi River was far out of its banks and stretched for several miles covering the Arkansas landscape, only the high branches of the trees along the bank could be seen above the swirling brown water. The officers of the side-wheeler settled into the night's routine of navigating the river's islands, "running at her usual speed of nine or ten miles per hour." About 2:00 A..M., suddenly and without warning, the Sultana's boilers exploded! In an instant fire was raging, soldiers, many of them scalded by steam, and burning debris were catapulted into the air, landing not only in the water but into the gaping hole above the furnaces.

The following is a first-person account of "The Destruction Of The Sultana," by Sergeant James H. Kimberlin, Company C, 124th Regiment Indiana Volunteers. James H. Kimberlin was a citizen of McCordsville, Hancock County, Indiana, and a Civil

Hancock County Indiana Civil War Soldiers

War veteran. See page in this volume for data on James H. Kimberlin.

"From time to time, we see some article in our papers pertaining to the loss of the Steamer Sultana, but most of the articles are short and give but a part of the facts. Being one of the Survivors and having made great efforts to ascertain all the facts and circumstances, I am inclined to offer the following as being the fullest and truest account that it is possible to obtain at this late date, being 54 years after the occurrence. James Harvey Kimberlin, 1919.

"The loss of the Sultana was attended with a greater loss of life than ever occurred on American or adjacent waters. The Sultana was a large side-wheel Mississippi River packet, plying between St. Louis and New Orleans. She was built at Cincinnati, Ohio, and placed in commission 1 January 1863. She registered 719 tons and carried 1300 tons. On 21 April 1865 she left her wharf at New Orleans on her north bound trip. On 25 April 1865, she arrived at Vicksburg, Mississippi, near which place a parole camp had been established for the care of Union soldiers who had been confined in Confederate prisons at Andersonville, Georgia and Cahaba, Alabama.

"On the evening of the 25th, soldiers, non-commissioned officers and sixty-five commissioned officers, making a total of 2001 ex-prisoners, together with an officer and twelve men detailed as guards from some command stationed at Vicksburg took passage for "God's Country" with the happy thought of soon mingling with loved ones at home, having escaped the pangs of hunger and witnessing the death of thousands of their comrades from starvation, brutalities and disease. Sultana's passenger list and boat crew numbered about 300, making a total of a little over 2,300 aboard at the time of her destruction.

"The vessel landed at Memphis, Tennessee, about 4 p.m. on the 26th. When night came, every available nook and corner was occupied by some weary soldier, so much so it was with great difficulty the men could find room to lie down. The commissioned officers had found state rooms and bunks in the

Hancock County Indiana Civil War Soldiers

cabin, and the common soldier piled down where ever he could find room.

"A little after midnight on the morning of the 27th the Sultana left her landing at Memphis and moved up to the coaling wharf two miles above where she took on coal sufficient to run her to St. Louis. After re-coaling, the vessel again started on her northern journey and when about seven miles above the city of Memphis and at the upper end and on the east side of what was known as Hen and Chicken Islands, and at 3 A.M., 27 April 1865, one or more of her boilers (there being four in number) let go or exploded with terrific force and destruction. The force of the explosion was so great that the boilers were thrown to the east and partially from off the furnace, leaving a great mass of burning coal exposed. All that portion of the vessel over the boilers and furnace was torn asunder, and hundreds of human beings who were sound asleep, were scattered in every direction, many of them far out into the water; much of the wreckage with its human freight, mangled and torn, many of them killed out-right. dropping into the open, uncovered furnace. Many who were not killed out-right or badly injured were buried in the wreckage, where they soon burned to death.

"All that part of the vessel to the rear of the boilers was uninjured, the rubbish or parts of the wreckage falling on to the open furnace with its roaring blaze instantly took fire, and in a very few moments the whole vessel was a seething, burning mass. Those who were badly injured, with their comrades who were killed out-right, and others who had become entangled or covered up in the wreckage, though uninjured, but unable to extricate themselves, were soon burned to death. Others who became suddenly crazed by reason of the appalling disaster, lost all sense of reason and power to act; some crying, some singing, some praying, while others were cursing. Everything one could think of, or man was capable of, one could see or hear in a very few minutes, for in twenty minutes after the explosion the boat had burned to the water line

Hancock County Indiana Civil War Soldiers

The hull drifted down and lodged against the upper end of one of the small islands, where it was soon covered up with the drifting sand and silt of the Mississippi River, where it remained hidden from the eyes of man until eight or ten years ago)1910-1912), when some wrecking company with a dredging machine removed the sand and silt from off and about the old hull, raised and floated it ashore, broke it up for the material and machinery.

"When the explosion occurred everybody except a few of the vessel's officers and crew was sound asleep. Instantly all of those who were not killed or badly injured sprang to their feet, knowing that something awful had happened, but not knowing what. As soon as they realized that the boat's boilers had blown up and the vessel had taken fire, the great mass of the living became crazed with fright and made one mad rush for the sides of the vessel nearest to where he happened to be sleeping.

"Those who on the upper decks plunged into the water below; those on top, or the hurricane deck, were twenty-two to twenty-five feet above the water. The poor, crazed fellows never paused to look, but plunged as far from the vessel as possible, alighting in the midst of the dozens who had preceded them. Some had wrenched a door or a window shutter from its fastenings from some part of the cabin, others had secured sticks of wood, a plank, a scantling, in fact anything that might act as a float and with this they made one mad plunge for the water below, landing in the midst of dozens who had preceded them, and thus many poor fellows were killed through the mad frenzy of some comrade.

"Of the command to which I belonged, Company C, 124th Indiana, there was one commissioned officer, Joseph T. Elliott, of Indianapolis, fourteen non-commissioned officers and enlisted men and two enlisted men belonging to Company K, same regiment who were aboard the vessel at the time of the explosion, making seventeen in all. Of those, Lieut. Elliott, J.W. Thompson, Charles Bryant, Thomas White, Sidney Shinneyfield and myself succeeded in making our escape. The other eleven were lost.

Hancock County Indiana Civil War Soldiers

"When I first sprang to my feet, I rushed to the west side of the vessel and looked down from the hurricane deck upon which I was sleeping. The water around the vessel for a distance of twenty to forty feet was a solid, seething mass of humanity, clinging one to another. The best or luckiest man was on top. I, then after partially dressing, went forward, climbing down on the wreckage to the lower deck on the west side, and when I looked out over the water where but a few minutes before there were hundreds of men struggling for supremacy, now there were but few to be seen. The great mass of them had gone down, clinging to each other. Of those who went into the water with the first mad rush not more than one in ten escaped drowning; but of those who went into the water later, first taking off all their clothing, including shoes and boots, and securing some sort of float, about half escaped and lived to return home.

"At the time of the disaster, the river was very high, and the lands on the Arkansas side are very low, and at this time were covered with water in may places to the depth of eight or ten feet. Where the disaster occurred, the boat channel was between the islands and the Tennessee shore and about three hundred yards from the shore. Those who went into the water on the east had but a short distance to swim. Not so with those who went off on the west side, for they had from fifteen to eighteen hundred yards to go before reaching shore; by reason of the high water, a man never knew when he was on land. Scores of men after reaching shore could find no bottom and would climb some bush and cling to its branches until some one of the many row boats would take him off.

The steamer, Bostona, another large river packet, had passed the Sultana on her downward trip and was not more than one and a half or two miles below when the explosion occurred. She turned about and started back upstream in order to render what assistance possible to those less fortunate who might need it, but seeing the rapid progress of the fire and knowing who had escaped death in the explosion would be compelled to take to the water and realizing that they would drown more by the action of

Hancock County Indiana Civil War Soldiers

their wheels than they could save, they stopped their engines and let the vessel drift with the current, lowered all her small boats and sent them out over the river picking up men, here, there and everywhere. Never did men work more heroic than did the crew of the Bostona in charge of her small boats.

"Many an unfortunate owes the saving of his life to the heroic work of the Bostona's officers and crew. Fully 200 men were picked up by them, many of whom would have lost their lives had it not been for them. Those who went off on the Tennessee side had but a short distance to go, yet at home we think three to four hundred yards to swim would be an impossible feat for us. Scores of men, however, swam to shore and thought nothing of it when they considered the fate of the unfortunates who went into the water on the Arkansas side and had five or six times as far to go.

"I was one of the latter. I prepared my self for a desperate effort to save my life my removing my shoes and all my heavy clothing; securing some small pieces of plank, securely fastening them together to serve me as a float or life preserver. I remained on the guard (rail) of the vessel until I could stand the heat no longer. It must be remembered that on the 27th of April the water was still very cold, and the atmosphere very chilly. The night was very dark, none of us knew where we were. with a broad expanse of water in front, a raging fire behind us, with pitiful cries and pleadings of the poor unfortunates who were pinned down by parts of the wreckage, certain death if you tarry or remain where you are, a chance to save yourself if you but take it;

I, with many others took that chance in the great lottery of life. Many of them drew blanks and were never afterwards heard of. I remained on the boat as long as possible, for the heat was intense. The great mass of humanity who from frenzied fright had plunged into the water, most of them drowned. The few who had escaped were out away from the boat, consequently, I had plenty of room and no one to interfere for some time at least. The burning boat was drifting with the current, while the same current was carrying those in the water down also. Most of those at this time had secured some kind of float. The weak, timid and crazed, with the badly injured, were either burned up with the vessel or drowned.

"The row boats from the Sultana, Bostona, and a few from the shores of the river were out in the water rowing for dear life. No life saving crew ever surpassed them, picking up men here, and another there, until they would get a load of from two to eight, when they would pull for the Bostona, unload and return up the river to gather another load. We could hear the click of their oars in the oarlocks for more than a mile. Then it was one could hear anything and everything--cursing, praying, crying, halooing, begging for the boats to come to them. The boatmen would respond. "Here we come," and would soon load up again. And thus the work went on down to the city, and a few were carried down the river ten miles before being rescued. To these brave boatmen was accredited the saving of over 400 lives, at least half of whom would have otherwise been lost.

"Of the 2,300 human beings aboard the Sultana at the time of the explosion, something like 800 escaped with their lives, thus making the loss a little more than 1,500. (Two ardent researchers later revealed that 300 of the 800 survivors died in hospitals, making a total death count of nearly 1,800.)

"Mr. Kimberlin continues: I have the report of the Secretary of War, also the report of the committee appointed by Congress to investigate the loss of the vessel and so many innocent lives, but the blame was never fastened upon anyone. It was said at the time that the blame should be charged to the Quartermaster at Vicksburg; that he forced too many soldiers on the vessel over the protest of Capt. Mason, who was in charge. He and all the principal officers were lost with the vessel, and for that reason the Government was unable to fix the responsibility for the disaster.

"The survivors of that disaster have an organization known as The Sultana Survivors Association, which we have maintained

Hancock County Indiana Civil War Soldiers

for thirty years and the roster of 1918 showed the names and addresses of seventy known survivors living at that time.

"Our association, twenty-five years ago, appointed a monument committee to go before Congress and ask that an appropriation be made for the erection of a suitable monument to those dead martyrs, and every Congress has been appealed to, but the committee has as often met with the same cold indifference.

"Those who have endured the torments of hell on earth, starved, famished from thirst, eaten with vermin, having endured all the indignities, insults and abuses possible for an armed bully to bestow upon them, to be so soon forgotten does not speak well for our Government or the American people.

Signed, J.H. Kimberlin, Sgt. Co C, 124th Reg. Ind. Vol., Sgt. 409th Division, and Andersonville Prisoner. Contributed by Gary Kimberlin, Columbus, Indiana.

There were 407 Hoosier soldiers from various units on board the Sultana. As well as can be determined, there were 16 soldiers from Hancock County during that fateful journey; nine survived and seven perished. Blessinger, Frederick, died; Chappel, Isaac, died; Church, Charles E., died; Fletcher, James, died; Gray, Joseph H., rescued, taken to Memphis Soldiers' Home; Kimberlin, James H., rescued, taken to Memphis Soldiers' Home; Lawson, Hiram, rescued, taken to Washington Hospital, Memphis; Mooney, John, rescued, taken to Memphis Soldiers' Home; Perman, Ephraim, died; Read, William, rescued, taken to Memphis Soldiers' Home; Scott, Robert S., rescued, taken to Memphis Soldiers' Home; Slifer, George, died; Steward, John, died; Waller, Benjamin F., rescued, taken to Memphis Soldiers' Home; Warner, William C., rescued, slight contusion, taken to Washington Hospital, Memphis; Wilson, George P., rescued, chilled, taken to Adams Hospital, Memphis.

Hancock County Indiana Civil War Soldiers

Letters

No effort was made to correct spelling or syntax.

14 Dec 1861, Otterville, Missouri; from Adam F. Wilson to his parents: Dear Father and Mother, I take pen in hand to inform you that I am in good health considering I have never got entirely of the measles yet. I am still here at Otterville in the hospital but hope I shall soon be able to go to camp. Alfred is also here he has had a very sever spell of fever but is still able to be up and about again.
 We received our first two months pay last week. We got thirty two dollars a piece so if you particularly need any I can send you some as I have not much need of money here so if you want any write and tell me how much you want and I want you to write. I haven't had a letter from you for nearly two months.
 The boys are getting tolerably well in camp but there is a great deal of sickness here. I suppose you have not yet heard that Edward Roney was dead he died yesterday morning with the mumps and fever he caught cold and it settled in his jaws which caused his death we are expecting to hear of them fighting at Oceola there was about ten thousand troops left here yesterday our regiment has gone with them.
 General Price is there with about fifteen thousand rebel troops hundreds of Union men are leaving crops and all their property and following our troops for protection things looks kind a bilious (sic) here I am beginning to make calculations for a three years trip William McConnell is at Jefferson City and has been sick but was getting better the last time I heard from him that was about two weeks ago as I have not had time to write any more I shall close my letter nothing more but remain yours Respectfully, Adam F. Wilson. Contributed by Flaugher Wilson, McCordsville, Indiana.

Hancock County Indiana Civil War Soldiers

20 Jan 1862, Munfordsville Ky Co B 4/ Regiment 2 Cavalry Ind Vol Militia; Mr and Mrs Heath, as this is a nice day I will write you a few lines to inform you of my where abouts we have got so far south as ____ Co three miles from green river the boys are in good spirits thinking that they will have the oportunity of using their fire arms to some advantage and ___ of some service to their country we all load our revolvers well and rubed our sabers with sweet oil

Frank and Mark are taking it as it comes Mark just came from the hospital he has not bin well since he had the measles but he is getting along pretty well now we are encamped on a very nice place until further orders

Corydon and Fletcher are enjoying them silves well in fact none of the boys are down in the mouth It is thought that there is sufficient force here to whip old Buckner decently ther is some sixty or seventy thousand at Munfordville and some forty thousand here and some 50,000 at the rowling forks of blue river

this is fine weather for the time of year that ever saw in fact it has bin as open winters very much so there has bin no snow worth naming there was so little.

Hoping that you are well I will close Sylvester Day Contributed by Irene Shireman, Greenfield, Indiana.

10 Aug 1862, Camp at Helena, to Adam F. Wilson from Samuel S. Brooks: Dear Sir, I now take the present apportion of writing you a few lines to inform you that I am well at this present and hope these few lines may find you the same.

Andrew and Alfred are well and so is the rest of the boys. it is pretty warm here today but I reckon you know how warm the weather is here it is warm enough (to) roast a person. The orders is getting pretty strict now in camp. If one misses roll call then he is court martialed. Elijah Tuttle was reduced to the ranks for missing roll call and Thomas Martin was to, there is no orders for us to march yet. I wish we could leave this place for I am getting tired of it.

Peaches are getting ripe now there is plenty of them back in the country. if you was here now you could get as many ripe

Hancock County Indiana Civil War Soldiers

peaches as you want. I reckon most all the boys around the neighborhood of Philadelphia has gone in the army. when you write I want you to let me know how things going on around there.

That fleet has come up from vicksburg is here yet. this regiment does not have to stand provost guard now we have nothing to do but drill one half hour of evenings and go on dress parade in the morning.

On the eighteenth of this month there is going to be general inspection of arms and every man that don't have a clean gun he had better I think. my gun is clean enough it is the cleanest gun in the company.

I have not much more to write at this present time. I want you to write an answer to this letter as soon as you get it and let me know how all the folks are getting along and whether you arrived safely at home or not. So no more at present, write soon, Samuel S. Brooks to Adam Wilson Contributed by Flaugher Wilson, McCordsville, Indiana.

29 May 1862, from Taylor Thomas to his brother, Ephraim of Mt. Comfort; published 10 Oct 1929 in the *Greenfield Reporter* with the following comments, "The letter was contained in a yellow envelope upon which was printed in red a picture of a sailor in the garb of the time, labeled, 'Our Brave Gunboat Boys.' The letter had been mailed at the post office at Cairo, Illinois. It is likely that it was entrusted to the care of a sailor who transported it up the river and mailed there. The contents of the letter are in part as follows: Dear Brother: Your lines came to hand this morning and let me just say to you that a line from home to a man here is a great comfort. I want you to write as often as you can. I have but little time or room. Something is constantly going on.

"I was very sick with jaundice and camp fever but am feeling better and think I shall do some fighting at the proper time. Have done a little picket duty and have fired four times. I don't know what I did to them, but balls passed around us close and thick, killing several of our men, but none of our company.

Hancock County Indiana Civil War Soldiers

"We have had skirmish fighting for two weeks, almost every day. We are about three miles from Corinth (Mississippi) and have a breastwork a mile and a quarter further out, thrown up last night after dark, within half a mile of the works of the enemy and it seems to me that the ball is open and the ring clear, but it seems to be taking the form of a siege fight.

"We have hot days and cold or cool at night, bad water and considerable sickness. The land is high and rolling, solid yellow clay, most of it, and dense forest. Turkeys and some deer. This morning about daylight the butternut brethren scared up a deer and it ran and jumped the breastwork. Our men captured it by hand.

"We drove the Rebel pickets off their ground yesterday morning. Their officers heard the firing and came dashing up to their men but fortunately one of them rode into our men, so we politely invited them up and up he came. He was a lieutenant, keen and sharp. A large number of their men are deserting and coming to our camps. The letter was accompanied by a pencil diagram of the position of the armies."

4 September 1862, To William Steele, Corporal, Company D, 79th Indiana Regiment from Mollie McCord: family members ill with ague, one of Green McCord's children died last week of scarlet fever.

28 Aug 1862, Helena, Arkansas; letter from Samuel Brooks to Adam F. Wilson, Dear Friend is with great pleser that I set my self down to let you now how I am getting along at the present time I am well and hopen when these few lines comes to hand that it may find you injoying the same stat of helth.

We re still camped at Helena but I don't now how long we will stay some talk of marchin prety soon bit I don't beleve that we will Cap Walls has come back agine he has 12 new recruits but all sick nerly Cap has bine sick to Andrew Fuller has bine very sick Alfred Wilson is sick to

We hav drill twist a day and hell Wane hill makes yous ill ? I hant much to rit this time so I will bring leter to a close, I remane, Your frend fer ever so good by. To Adam F. Wilson

Hancock County Indiana Civil War Soldiers

from Samuel Brooks. Contributed by Flaugher Wilson, McCordsville, Indiana.

25 Sep 1862. to James Wilson, Mount Comfort, Hancock County, Indiana, from Henry Wilson: Dear Father and Mother I take this opportunity of informing you that I am well at this time and hope that this letter may find you all enjoying the same blessings our regiment is a lying in the rifle pits around Louisville and the people are in great panic almost all of the women and children that can leave has left

we are waiting for the Reble General Bragg his a marching on this place we intend to give him a bloody welcome I am out five or six miles in advance on picket and I thought that I would keep a good lookout and write you a few lines as I do not get any letters I would like to hear from all of the folks

it is a poor place here for to get any thing to eat I went in a house to get my breakfast and the woman was a crying and almost scared to death she had two or three little children and could not get away from the rebles and she thought that they was just at hand she got my breakfast and I paid for it I could not have the heart to not pay for it tho some of the boys do not pay for any thing that they get.

I want you to see that them apple trees are planted out and if Agnes has not got the money to pay for them you see to that and when I get the chance I will send you the money good bye write soon your obedient son, H. Wilson To James Wilson Contributed by Flaugher Wilson, McCordsville, Indiana.

11 Oct 1862 from Henry Wilson 79th Reg of Indiana Volunteers, 5 Division, 11 Brigade of the Army of Ohio, to Adam F. Wilson, Mount Comfort, Hancock County, Indiana: Dear Brother after a long while I take my pen in hand to let you know that I am well at this time we are encamped in the mountains on rock castle River in Rock Castle County Kentucky we started from Louisville on the second day of the present month and after the fourth day our advance have been a skirmishing on the 8 there was a tolerable heavy battle was fought at the town of Perryville in which our forces was

Hancock County Indiana Civil War Soldiers

victorious I saw a part of the battlefield and it was a fearful looking sight such as I never want to witness again then on the fifteenth I was in a tolerable heavy skirmish at the Crab Orchard in which shot and shell was freely used on both sides we have been a picking up prisoners every day since we have been on the road last night our boys picked up thirty and nine horses

I want you and Bill to manage things the best that you can I don't know how long this war will last but it is my impression that it cant last verry much longer you must forgive me for not writing to you before this time but thought that I would wait untill I had something of importance to write I am in as good health as ever I enjoyed but cant tell how long that will last we have not saw a tent since we left Louisville

I don't know where we are a going but from the course I think Cumberland Gap we get no news only a little rumor we don't hear from the army in the east no more than if there was no army in the east you and Bill get together and write all day and send it to me tell Father and Mother that I send them my best respects and you and all of my friends. H. Wilson to James Wilson Contributed by Flaugher Wilson, McCordsville, Indiana.

15 Mar 1863, Camp Genevieve, from Johnson Burris to Miss Rettie L. Snider: Dear Rettie I seat myself on the sabbath evening to write you a few lines to let you know that I am well and where I am I left Indianapolis on Friday night at 10 o clock in company with Mr. Scotton and we arrived in St. Louis on Saturday at 11 o clock and got aboard a steamer and started for St Genevieve and arrived here just at dark we found the 8 Regiment camped a quarter of a mile from where we landed the boys were all well and glad to see me

Rettie I would like to be at home to night if I could get to see you a while and talk to you a while not because I am dissatisfied at all for I am determined to see how the soldiers life the army here consists of two division of several regiment each I expect the division that Henry's Regiment belongs to will leave here tomorrow evening or next morning for Memphis Tennessee and

Hancock County Indiana Civil War Soldiers

I expect that I shall go along with them the boys here are quite lively and seem to enjoy them selves very well

St Louis is 275 miles from Indianapolis and St Genevieve is 70 miles below St Louis and Memphis is near 300 miles from here it will take about three days to go there and they have to land there and perhaps stay there a few days and then go down to Vicksburg

wel, Ret you never give your self any uneasiness about me Volunteering for I think and hope that I will be so fortunate as to get back to see you and all the rest of the folks I think if I keep well and stay with the army a month or two I can come home and stay satisfied to stay there Ret I will write an answer to your letter in a few days I am writing on Wm Wellings tent and he told me to tell you that he was well and hearty and would like to be at home and see you

wel Ret I want you to write just as soon as you get this letter and direct them to Memphis and to the 8 Reg Ind Vol Co G in care of Cap Riley it is a getting so dark that I cant see to follow the line and I will quit for the present you must excuse poor writing and spelling as I have a bad place to write I still remain your true lover with respects of highest regards for your Granma Signed Johnson Burris A note of interest, Johnson Burris died thirty eight days later, 23 Apr 1863. Indiana Historical Society Library, Indianapolis, Indiana.

26 Mar 1863 Home, from William Lucas Ogg to his brother Adams Lee Ogg: Dear Bro Lizzie has kindly offered that I should add a note to her letter. I am not in receipt of and answer to my last to you but as I left the army a week ago the letters in answer may possible be on hand at the command-so I shan't "scold."

Before quitting the army I sold out my stock-think I shall not do business immediately with the army-(i.e.) not follow anymore. I have a prospect of an arrangement at Memphis which if I succeed in shaping as I now hope to. I promise myself a good thing I shall go to Memphis in about ten day-look after

Hancock County Indiana Civil War Soldiers

this matter and spend a short time with the com'd when paid for purpose of collecting &c.

Let me hear from you at once Bro.-will you be at home before my leave? or will you meet me at Memphis? Greenfield's no place for "contrabands." Yours &c. W.L. Oge P.S. I left the command with orders for Memphis—It will probably join Rosecrans Corps otherwise Grants. Contributed by Bob Ogg, Missouri City, Texas Mr. Ogg comments that no one has, or had, a clue to why he changed the spelling of his name to Oge from Ogg.

18 May 1863 on board steamer, Crescent City; My Dear wife Your sweet interesting favor of the 10th inst reached me one hour ago, under romantic circumstances. We embarked yesterday morning and left Memphis about noon—Came along smoothly until 2 or 3 oclock this afternoon, when "bang, bang" went the cannon, and a hundred holes were made through our boat before I knew what it was. At the time, I was sitting in the main saloon reading, "Romola," much absorbed in the story. I heard the noise & saw a couple of women and a score of men tumbling on the floor around me but did not realize for a minute or two what was up till a charge of grape shot passed through the stateroom by my side.

Then I knew "what was the matter." I ran to my stateroom got my pistol and up on deck where most of my men were. By this time the rebs were running & firing about over. The rebels had placed two pieces of artillery on the bank at a point where the boats have to pass close in. They and their artillery were concealed in low growth of cane. As our boat came within 30 yards, they raised up and fired. Besides the artillery, there were about a hundred with rifles.

After firing 3 or 4 rounds & just as we were getting a good scaring they broke and run for the woods in the rear. It was all over in less than three minutes. They have wounded fourteen of our men—one I think will die in the night. Two of my best boys are wounded (Mosher and Barstow). I hope neither dangerously. Surprising we escaped so well. We had 500 men aboard, and the

Hancock County Indiana Civil War Soldiers

boat is litterly riddled, splinters lying all around. 3 horses that we had with us a year & a half were killed.

As soon as possible the boat was brought to shore and we landed, but the Rebs were gone and we did not pursue far. Other boats having troops aboard, came up and some cavalry got ashore, went out and captured a few.

A mail boat came up & we got our mail,--brought to us while we were out on land scouring the woods. So I sat down at the foot of a big cypress tree and read your affectionate letter. It did me much good. I was afraid you would think my former letter unkind. It was churlish I know, but I felt so bad. But, I am sure my wife is as good a little wife as any body has.

I will not perhaps get your present. Am sorry, but the to know that you sent it is quite a satisfaction. I haven't heard from Will. I have sent Mr. A. the pic. Wish I could see your big "Johnny Jump Up." Love to your Mom.

If you can read this letter, I will think you are the Same (sic).

Truly, your husband, ALO

Contributed by Bob Ogg, Missouri City, Texas.

1 Jun 1863, Camp 3rd Iowa Infy, near Vicksburg My dearest Wife, I closed a letter to you on the 29th of May. We were just starting out on a reconaisense –returned to camp about 4 oclock PM, when I found a mail bringing me two letters from you, one dated May 15th, the other (from Indianapolis)-the 20th. I was very, very glad to hear from you again, but your letter of the 15th was painfully dispondent. You ought not, my love, to write me anything to discourage. You would not, I am sure, have your husband act cowardly, but you have written me so much knowing that you will never see me anymore etc, that if I should alow my self to think of your expressions, it would unnerve me in the hour of trial.

No, my dear wife; though I wish very much to live, to see & be with you again yet for a thousand lives would I let my men see me flinch from any danger that duty may demand....But to return. When our Reg't was out on the ....., we drove in the

Hancock County Indiana Civil War Soldiers

pickets of the enemy, exchanging as we advanced. a few shots, but none of our Reg't was hurt.

After coming in, I had just completed reading my letters and drinking some coffee when we was ordered out again,--and moved a couple miles to the left, on picket and that night we captured eleven rebs trying to pass into Vicksburgh. They were carrying with them 200,000 gun caps. That night, a friend of mine, Capt Bradly of the 15th Ills was killed close to where I was. The enemy had been firing from the woods in our front all evening, but had done no harm till this fatal shot passed through Capt B's heart.

There has not been much hard fighting for several days. Our lines extend around the city, from 2 to 3 miles distant. Don't know what Grant's plans are. We watch & wait. Are blessed with splendid weather—Not very warm and dry. we left all our baggage at Youngs Point, and are getting dirty and ragged. Our boys continue in good health. I suppose Will (Adam Lee's brother) is at Greenfield by this time. On the other leaf of this sheet, I write a few lines to him. I also inclose letter from him which you will please take care of. Get what money you want from him. I have lost so much rest lately that I feel somewhat unwell and dull.

Give my love to all the folks, your Mother in particular.

We are in the 4th Div—General Lauman—16th Army Corps.

I am affectionately Your husband, Lee

P.S. Tell your Mother to call on Will for any counsel or assistance she may need. Contributed by Bob Ogg, Missouri City, Texas.

4 June 1863, Camp in the rear of Vicksburg; from John Scott to his wife, Eliza Alyea Scott: Having a little leasure time I shal write you another short letter however it has not been more than four days since I wrote you. My health is good as usual the health generally is not good as it was there is a great deal of diarrhea and the boys are tired and worried very much the fight is still going on we are trying to annoy them rebs all we can we

Hancock County Indiana Civil War Soldiers

are diging rifle pits within talking distance of them but they dar not show the tip end of their nose

from the best information that we can get some of which is very reliable they can hold out but a few days longer we captured two dispatches sent out for assistance rations stating that they must have help and something to eat or they could not stand it but a few days longer and there is deserters coming over every day and a great many more would come over if they were not afrade of being killed before they can get to our lines and they all tell the same tale they say that they are now on one fourth rations and that will last but a few days at most.

And we have heard that Jeff Davis is in town if so he is our pork he could not get out if he would convert himself into a ground mole we have seen it stated in the Rebs paper that he made a speech here about the time we took Jackson General Cars devision to which our Regiment belongs has won the title of first division in the Corps bully for us

The weather is tolerable warm through the day and cool through the night the water that use is not very good it being spring water and warm and as for grub we have a bountiful supply and variety, we have free access to the river now. It is reported that our troops had a brush with old Price a day or two ago he came to the river with the intention of crossing into Vicksburg but the Gunboats soon shelled them out of the neighborhood.

I am relieved at the hospital for the present our wounded have all been moved to the River on Hospital Boats and will be sent up the river to a cooler climate and perhaps home. John Alyea has not come to the Regiment yet we heard from him a few days since he is still unwell Levi Collins is not well but able to go about.

Now Ann see here I want you to save all the letters I write especially about the battles and if you can I want you to send for the Weekly Commercial take the money if you have it, to Ezra Fountain and get him to send for it. And tell him to send for back numbers to the first of May in order that it may contain all

Hancock County Indiana Civil War Soldiers

our operations then Anny I want you to save them all have them come to Fountaintown as it is the nearest place to send for it and don't forget to save them for it will be interesting to us when I come home.

I sent a tolerable nice book home the other day that I captured on the Battle Field if it gets home let me know I might have sent many valuable things home if I could have been on the River or railroad when I could have sent them I might have sent a thousand dollars worth

Tell squire to let me know if his hair is any longer and I would like to know if Robert goes to sleep while plowing any more tell Friday not to let his eyes get any whiter if he can help it. tell Dad and Gigles to keep the eggs well hunted up and I would like to know what that Lol is doing and be careful of your own nose, I scratched mine awfully in a blackberry patch the other day well I must close

I am now helping to cook for the company but as soon as there is any more wounded in the Regiment I will have to return to the Hospital I have been acting as Ward Master at the General Hospital of Cors Division

write me a darn good smooching letter once a week and few between times in wet weather and don't forget to put something in them, tell R Grimm and James Alyea and everybody else to write. No more, John Scott to E.A. Scott Contributed by Doris Scott Badgley, Greenwood, Indiana.

26 Sep 1863, John Scott's wife, Eliza Ann (Alyea) Scott received the following letter from Berwick, Louisiana: Mrs. Scott, Madame, It becomes my painful duty to inform you of the death of your husband on the 11th day of September 1863, at U.S. Marine Hospital at New Orleans, Louisiana. His disease was chronic diarrhea. Your miniature never reached him and is hereby returned to you. He had some clothing and $21.00 in money with him which is the hands of Surgeon in Charge of Hospital and will be duly reported to proper Headquarters from whence in due course of time you will get all the value of all in his possession.

Hancock County Indiana Civil War Soldiers

Thus another good man and soldier, husband and father has fallen victim to rebellion. May the horrors of war soon cease and the country saved is my soul's desire. In your bereavement accept my sympathy.

Your friend, Samuel H. Dunbar

P.S. Should you wish to communicate further with me concerning this business of John direct to 8th Indiana Infantry, 1st Brig. 1st Division, 13th Army Corps, New Orleans. Contributed by Doris Scott Badgley, Greenwood, Indiana

26 Jul 1864, Madison County, Alabama, from Isaac Lain to his sister Elizabeth Wilson, Walpool, Indiana,: I received your letter 16 and was glad to hear that you was well it found me well and on picket so I did not git to read your letter till this morning. I am to write once a week but sometimes I don't this is four letters I have wrote since the first of July tell Maron Wilson I seen Cap about an hour and a half or two hours ago and if she is in a hurry she will find him a mile ahead I sent sixty one dollars with Samuel we expressed ____ dollars south together.

Frank and Sam is well and able to make their hand at the table Benjamin Robertson has got well and hearty Captain Muth fell off his horse about a week ago and come very near killing him he is getting right smart better I think in the corse of a week or two he will be all right I tell you the price of a few things flour is 16 dollars a barrel eggs 50 cents a doze one chicken 75 cents butter 75 cents a pound that is the truth.

there is three negroes to one white person and five dogs to one negro in Alabama when we hunt on picket we drill two hours a day

If Samuel Fuller would tell a lie on me I about upset his apple house and spill his bag of potatoes I am glad to hear that was so nigh done harvesting I want to no if james jarrett ever paid for that mair yet Eli that day me and you went to Fortville and missed the train and i had to stay till night train i went up to james jarrett and I got my supper i got all the apples i could eat i had a very good supper

Hancock County Indiana Civil War Soldiers

there is right smart of talk of us leaving this place I think that it is camp nervs not much truth in it I have not got a letter from john jones for a week or two I don't write to anybody only john jones and home I have wrote john two letters I have got ten dollars yet I think that will be me till next pay day you no I am a grate han for money I will have money if any body else have any some boys gits ther money and hant satisfied till it is gon. I spen it as I need it

Mother if that money gits home you may take enough to git you a new dress I wont tell pap what to do with the rest for he knoes best he can buy a farm with it if he wants to.

Isaac Lain to E.J. Wilson Contributed by Flaugher Wilson, McCordsville, Indiana.

Brother vs Brother The following letters concern three Andis brothers, Robert and John in the Union army and Earl Carson in the Confederate army: **3 May 1864,** Dear Brother, I am sending you $3.00 I want you to write this to Robert—he pretends to be so right.

"When I am in need you gave me not,
When I am hungry, you gave me no food,
When I am sick you visited me not,
When I am thirsty, you gave me no drink."

If you want to write to sister Jane and Aunt Ellen, direct your letters to Johnson County, Bluff Creek. Signed, John Andis

23 May 1865, Scottsboro, Alabama, Dear Brother, I have received your second letter since you have been a prisoner. I am glad to know that you are well and hope that you will never again go into the Confederate Army.

You stated that you would write but you was short of means to buy paper. I will enclose a sheet of paper in each letter that I send to you so you can answer, if you like.

I acknowledge Allegiance to the Government of the United States, believing I am in just cause and expect to be there. We don't now nor ever intend to recognize a Confederacy.

Signed: Your Brother
  Robert Andis, Capt. Co B, 99 Reg Ind

Hancock County Indiana Civil War Soldiers

5 July 1864, Fort Delaware on the Delaware River, To Robert Andis, Esquire, Greenfield, Indiana, Hancock County: Dear Brother, You can imagine my condition—a prisoner of war and sick. I have made requests before but you did not comply. I now ask you again as a brother, to send me some money to sustain life and health. I know your political views are different from mine, but why should that rule out the feeling of humanity?
Signed; Earl Carson Andis

22 August 1865, Carrolton, Indiana, Dear Brother, I was seriously wounded in the Battle of Atlanta (summer of 1864). A soon as I was able to read and write, I sent you $5.00.
Signed: Your Brother
   Robert Andis

The above letters contributed by Dick Andis, Greencastle, Indiana.

Hancock County Indiana Civil War Soldiers

Grand Army of the Republic

The Grand Army of the Republic was born in the minds of Civil War veterans who had been drawn into close fraternal relations by the hardships and dangers they had encountered and suffered together. They talked of an organization that would continue the feeling of comradeship the Civil War had thrust upon them when they lived and fought and died together, creating a bond that could not be broken. The passing of years wore off the sharp edges of war, eventually the gaping wounds healed and veterans wanted to relive the comradeship forged in battle.

The Grand Army of the Republic was organized at Decatur, Illinois, 6 April 1866, by two tent-mates of the Fourteenth Illinois Infantry, Rev. William J. Rutledge and Dr. Benjamin F. Stephenson. Membership was limited to honorably discharged veterans of the Union Army, Navy, Marine Corps or the Revenue Cutter Service who had served between 12 April 1861 and 9 April 1865. One document states: "Membership limited strictly to veterans of the late unpleasantness."

The community level organization was called a Post which was included in a Department at the State and National levels. The naming of a Post required that the honored person be deceased and that no two Posts within the same Department could have the same name. Post Commanders, Senior and Junior Vice Commanders and the members of Council were elected. Each prospective member was voted into membership by casting black or white balls, more than one black ball was required to reject a candidate.

Indianapolis was chosen three times to host the National Encampments, 1866, 1881 and 1893, an honor no other city can claim. At the 1893 Encampment "accommodations were ample, free quarters were everywhere offered, Camps Lew Wallace,

Hancock County Indiana Civil War Soldiers

McGinnis, and Camp Wilder, the latter in Military Park, where many of the boys remember old Camp Sullivan. The camps were crowded with ex-soldiers, while schoolhouses and other public buildings held their full quota

The Grand Parade of 5 September 1893, dropped to scarcely a fourth of the number who stood in line the year before. Relentless time had made fearful in roads in the ranks with the aid of its faithful ally, Death, and the weight of advancing years reduced by thousands the number able to stand the fatigue of the march. Of the grizzled heroes present in the city, it was sad to see that the great majority stood among the lines of spectators instead of the few yet strong and sturdy who marched in the ranks. At this meeting for the first time was discussed the advisability of abandoning the parade altogether, in view of the veterans' increasing years.

The Commander-in-Chief paid a graceful tribute to the Women's Relief Corps, for the noble and self-sacrificing way in which they have aided the work of the G.A.R. Many Posts, indeed, owe their continued existence to the untiring efforts of those loyal women.

The Women's Relief Corps was organized in 1871. Any loyal woman was eligible to membership, whether related to an ex-soldier or not. The objects of the association were to aid the Grand Army in all its undertakings; to perpetuate the memory of the patriot dead; to aid Union soldiers, their widows and orphans and inculcate love of country in the children of each generation. The Ladies of the G.A.R. have the same purpose as the Relief Corps but only admits to its membership those who were mothers, wives, daughters and sisters of soldiers, sailors or marines, living or dead, who served in the Rebellion."

The first Grand Army of the Republic Post in Hancock County was chartered 9 August 1882, named Samuel H. Dunbar Post, situated in Greenfield, and held their meetings at the G.A.R. room in the courthouse. This Post was active until 1936 when the last of old veterans "answered the last Roll Call."

Hancock County Indiana Civil War Soldiers

Through the years there were six Posts in Hancock County communities and named in honor of deceased veterans. Charlottesvill Post #545, active from 1889 to 1898; Fortville, Sol D. Kempton Post #228, active from 1883 to 1930; Gem, William E. Hart Post #454, chartered 1886, no disband date given; Greenfield, Dunbar Post as named above; New Palestine, Charles A. Kirkhoff Post #534, active 1888-1907; and Willow Branch, Lorenzo Fort Post #438, active from 1886-1893. Charter members of the six Posts are listed below:

Women's Relief Corps Grave Marker

Courtesy of Joyce Morris

Hancock County Indiana Civil War Soldiers

Charlottesville George Landis Post #545

Mustered 5 February 1889 and they have selected the name of George W. Landis. The regular meetings will be on the 1st and 3rd Tuesday night each month with the following officers elected and installed:

Thomas C. Niles, P.C.; James C. Pratt, S.V.C.; Daniel Burk, J.V.C.; Marion Philpot, O.D.; Lafayette Griffith, O.G.; George Kinder, Chaplain; J.E. Wright, Surgeon; W.H.H. Rock, Q.M.; Thomas J. Owens, Adj't. The outlook for this new Post is very promising. The comrades all seem to be alive and wide awake to the best interest of the organization. The Corps of officers are all men who stand high in the community and noted for their integrity and honesty of purpose and will use their best endeavors in disseminating the grand principles of Fraternity, Charity and Loyalty. Signed, George P. Gra_, Mustering Officer.

We, the undersigned Ex-Soldiers and Sailors, who served under the United States Flag during the rebellion of 1861-1865, and were honorably discharged from the service of the United States of America, most respectfully ask that a charter be granted for the establishment of a Post at Charlottesville, County of Hancock, Indiana:

Allison, T.G., carpenter, age 46, born Indiana
Bell, Samuel, farmer, age 50, born Indiana
Bennett, Samuel H., shoemaker, age 42, born Ohio
Burk, Daniel, shoemaker, age 45, born Indiana
Conger, Mose, age 58, NOD.
Cross, Joe, laborer, age 44, born Ohio
Cross, William, laborer, age 49, born Indiana
Dailey, George W., physician, age 52, born Indiana
Davis, John, laborer, age 46, born Indiana
Green, John, no data given
Griffith, M.D., merchant, age 44, born Virginia
James, Samuel, farmer, age 52, born Indiana
Kinder, George, farmer, age 64, born Virginia

Hancock County Indiana Civil War Soldiers

Niles, Tom plasterer, age 44 born Indiana
Ormston, A., farmer, age 45, born Indiana
Owens, Thomas J., carpenter, age 46, born North Carolina
Patterson, A.M., no other data
Perigo, Henry, laborer, age 75, born Kentucky
Powers, James A., farmer, age 42, born Ohio
Philpott, Marion, R.R. agent, opr., age 44, born Indiana
Pratt, James C., carpenter, age 55, born Ohio
Rock, W.H.H., lumber, age 45, born Indiana
Roland, George, farmer, age 41, born Indiana
Scott, John H., carpenter, age 58, born Ohio
Shipman, Charles, farmer, age 37, born Indiana
Shipman, John, farmer, age 46, born Indiana
Shultz, J.F., shoemaker, age 57, born Indiana
Wilson, John L., D.V.S., age 47, born Kentucky
Wright, J.E., physician, age 49, born Indiana

The name of this Post was a posthumous honor for George W. Landis who died in 1884 from the effects of sickness contracted in the War.

Fortville Solomon D. Kempton Post No. 228

A Charter is granted 20 August 1883. Officers elected and installed:S.T. Yancey, P.C.; Josephus Bills, S.V.C.; David T. Wynn, J.V.C.; J.L. York, O.D.; Ruben Patterson, O.G.; M.B. Walker, Chaplain; A.J. Reynolds, Surgeon; Elmore West, Q.M.; and J. W. Richardson, Adj't.

We, the undersigned, Ex-Soldiers and Sailors, who were honorably discharged from the service of the United States of America, and who served under the Union flag during the rebellion, respectively ask that a Charter be granted for the establishment of a Post:

Samuel Allison, 12 Reg.; Charles Bargoner, 7 Cav; Josephus Bills, 12 Reg.; Milton Cobler, 25 Reg; Gershom W.Conger, 19 Reg.; Ralph Copper, 12 Reg; Thomas Cummins, 8 Reg; John C. Edmonds, 79 Reg; James H. Fausett, 12 Reg; James Hook, 9

Hancock County Indiana Civil War Soldiers

Cav; John A. Huston, 153 Reg; James Jordan, 12 Reg; William, Nicholas 16 Batt.

John S. Packard, 79 Ohio; Reg; Joseph Palmer, 1 Missouri; Reuben Patterson, 101 Reg; A.J. Reynolds, 2 Cav; J.W. Richardson, 75 Reg; Daniel Roberts, 8 Reg; John Scott, 155 Reg; John Stuart, 8 Cav; Ambrose Taylor, 11 Reg; Samuel Torrence, 79 Reg; William Torrence, 79 Reg; Ezra Watts, 10 Reg; M.B. Walker, 9 Cav; Elmore West, 6 Batt; D.T. Wynn, 12 Reg; Simeon T. Yancey, 70 Reg; and J.L. York, 2 Cav.

The name of this Post was a posthumous honor for Solomon D. Kempton, a Lt. Colonel in the 12th Regiment, who died suddenly 23 October 1863, at age 34 years.

Gem William E. Hart Post G.A.R. No. 454

Applied for Charter 17 April 1886, named William E. Hart Post, following officers were elected and installed: Milton T. Morris, P.C.; Isaac N. Stutsman, V.C.; Francis M. Sanford, V.C.; Peter Franzman, O.D.; Benjamin Elliott, O. G.; John H. Apple, Chaplain; Warren R. King, Surgeon; Calvin F. Shelby, Q.M.; and John Klem, Adj't.

We, the undersigned, Ex-Soldiers and Sailors, who were honorably discharged from the service of the United States of America, and who served under the Union flag during the rebellion, respectively ask that a Charter be granted for the establishment of a Post at Gem, Indiana:

John H. Apple, 17 Ohio Batt; William H.H. Brown, 99 Ill Reg; Benjamin Elliott, 8 Reg; Peter Franzman 13 Reg; John R. Hanes, 132 Reg; Hook, Jacob, 148 Reg; Warren R. King, 69 Reg; William N. Kitchen, 51 Reg; John Klem, 94 Ohio Reg; Milton T. Morris, 5 Cav; Stephen Ross, 16 Batt; Francis M. Sanford, 8 Reg; Oregon M. Snider, 9 Cav; Calvin F. Shelby, 38 Reg; and Isaac Stutsman 79 Reg.

The name of this Post was a posthumous honor for William E. Hart who died of wounds received in the unfortunate disaster at Lawrencebug, Indiana, 13 Jul 1863.

Hancock County Indiana Civil War Soldiers

Greenfield Samuel Dunbar G.A.R. Post No. 92

Application for Charter for Samuel H. Dunbar Post was granted 9 Aug 1882, with the following officers elected and installed; Henry Snow, P.C.; Joseph Baldwin, S.V.C.; Lee O. Harris, J.V.C.; Richard A. Black, O.D.; Almon Keefer, O.G.; George W. Duncan, Chaplain; Thomas J. Carr, Surgeon; I.A. Curry, Q.M.; and Enos George, Adj't.

We, the undersigned, Ex-Soldiers and Sailors, who were honorably discharged from the service of the United states of America, and who served under the Union flag during the rebellion, respectfully ask that a Charter be granted for the establishment of a Post at Greenfield, Hancock County, Indiana: Joseph Baldwin, 99 Reg; R.A. Black, 118 Reg; Noah W. Carr, 53 Reg; Thomas J. Carr, 79 Reg; Isaiah A. Curry, 99 Reg; G.W. Duncan, 5 Cav; Theodore Eskew 3 Cav; Jerry Ferren, 51 Reg; Enos Gery, 124 Reg; William H. Gooding, 5 Cav.

John B. Huston, 8 Reg; Lee O. Harris, 148 Reg; George W. Johnson, 4 Cav; Almon Kiefer, 5 Cav; Jno. A. Lynam, 15 Batt; N.C. Meek, 53 Reg; Francis M. G. Melton, 130 Reg; John Miller. NY Reg; Henry Snow, 8 Reg; John Wirts, 5 Cav.

The name of this Post was a posthumous honor for Samuel H. Dunbar, a Captain of Company B, 8th Regiment, who died of disease 9 July 1864, at age 24 years.

New Palestine Charles Kirkhoff Post No. 534

Applied for and granted a Charter 6 June 1888; the Post was mustered 9 June 1888, selected the name of Charles A. Kirkhoff; the following men were elected and installed as officers: David M. Dove, P.C.; Eli Stout, S.V.C.; James G. Boyce, J.V.C.; Harrison Wilkins, O.D.; James Burns, O.G.; A.P. Hogle, Chaplain; Jacob Buchel, Surgeon; Stewart Nichols. Q.M.; Albert Helms, Adj't.

We, the undersigned, Ex-Soldiers and Sailors, who served under the Union flag during the rebellion of 1861 to 1865, and were honorably discharged from the service of the United States of America, respectfully ask that a Charter be granted for the

Hancock County Indiana Civil War Soldiers

establishment of a Post at New Palestine, Hancock County, Indiana:

Armstrong, John P., plasterer, age 53, born Ohio
Boyce, James G., lumber dealer, age 56 born Indiana
Branson, John O., merchant, age 39, born Indiana
Buchel, Jacob, physician, age 61, born Germany
Burns, James, farmer, age 45, born Ohio
Cloud, F. M., tinsmith, age 47, born Indiana
Cummins, John, NOD
Dove, D. M., NOD.
Frankenstine, George, barber, age 62, born Germany
Groves, Robert, farmer, age 43, born Indiana
Helms, Albert, miller, age 50, born Indiana
Hogle, A.P., miller, NOD.
Holden, Ben, teamster, age 55, born Ohio
Johnson, George W., farmer, age 45, born Indiana
Johnson, J.E., salesman, age 42, born Indiana
Nichols, Stewart, farmer, age 42, born, illegible
Smith, Henry, butcher, age 46, born Europe
Stout, Eli, painter, age 48, born Kentucky
Tuttle, O. H., NOD.
Wilkins, Harrison, farmer, age 47, born Ohio

The name of this Post was posthumous honor for Charles A. Kirkhoff, who was wounded in action at the battle of Sulphur Trestle, Alabama, 25 Sep 1864, and died 29 Sep 1864.

Willow Branch Lorenzo Fort Post No. 438

Application for Charter, granted 10 February 1886; the following officers were elected and installed: Nevil Reeves, P.C.; George W. Ham, S.V.C.; John Miller, F.V.C.; Francis M. Vanhorn, O.D.; Angus Calder, O. G.; John C. Buckley, Chaplain; William B. Ryan, Surgeon; Henry C. Garriott, Q.M.; Henry Valentine, Adj't.

We, the undersigned, Ex-Soldiers and Sailors, who were honorably discharged from the service of the United States of America, and who served under the Union flag during the

Hancock County Indiana Civil War Soldiers

rebellion, respectively ask that a Charter be granted for the establishment of a Post at Willow Branch, Indiana:

William Boyer, 57 Reg; Isaac Brown, 132 Reg; John C. Buckley, 4 W. Virginia Reg; Angus Calder, 27 Ohio Reg; Adamson(?) Combs, 152 Illinois Reg; William E. Crane, 5 Cav; Richard S. Elliott, 140 Reg; John W. Fletcher, 57 Reg; Henry C. Garriott, 57 Reg; William H.H. Gipe, 101 Reg; Eli Gordon, 147 Reg; George W. Ham, 57 Reg; George W. Hunt?, 147 Reg; William Kenyon, 13 Cav.; Joel Knight, 53 Reg; George McGee, 5 Cav; Jared C. Meek, 5 Cav; John Miller, 27 N.Y Reg and 15 N.Y. Reg; Job Milner, 99 Rag; Joseph O'Neal, 51 Reg; William H. Power, 99 Reg and 48 Reg; Thomas Rash, 12 Reg; Nevil Reeves, 99 Reg; William B. Ryan, 13 Cav; Henry Valentine, 54 Kentucky Reg; and Frank Vanhorn 5 Ohio Batt.

The name of this Post was a posthumous honor for Lorenzo Fort, who was wounded 31 Dec 1862, at battle of Stone's River, Tennessee, and died the next day, 1 January 1863.

Hancock County Indiana Civil War Soldiers

Newspapers This N That

25 Sep 1861: "Mr. Samuel Marsh informs us that he now has more than a sufficient number of men enrolled to go into camp. All who have enrolled their names, are requested to meet at the Court House on Saturday next at 2 o'clock P.M. for the purpose of electing the officers of the Company. The Company has been reported, accepted, and will go into camp one day next week. Let every man able and willing to enter the service, embrace this opportunity. The Company will soon be in active service. Attached to the Company are quite a number of Capt. Riley's returned volunteers, who know just what to do and how to do it in the school of the soldier. among the number, we are glad to find our young friend, J. Term. Barrett, than whom, Capt. Riley informs us, he had no better man or soldier in his Company. In the selection of officers, the boys should look well to qualification. Experienced men, when they can be obtained are the ones to put in office." *Hancock Democrat*

14 May 1863: "A Deserter Exposed We have received a letter from John H. Brooks of Jackson Township, asking us to publish a private letter of M. S. Petit to his wife, a copy of which was enclosed. Under all the circumstances we do not deem it proper to publish the letter entirely. The pith of it is contained in these words. *'Give my best respects to all the peace men, and tell them to keep the ball rolling.'* Mr. Petit went into the army as a substitute and as a Union man, but he has been seduced into desertion and treasonable sentiments by the peace men of the Breckinridge order. He is not only their victim, other men have been induced to desert, and some who held commissions have resigned and now talk treason; and will yet be properly exposed if not arrested for their base perfidy to the people and Government, who too credulously confided in their oaths. Mr. Petit need give himself no uneasiness about the 'peace men' of

Hancock County Indiana Civil War Soldiers

the Breckinridge order in Hancock as they will not fail to take his advice, and 'keep the ball rolling.' Not the ball of the Government, but the ball of the party." *Hancock Democrat*

31 Dec 1863: "The 54th Indiana Regiment arrived from New Orleans last week, at which place they were mustered out of service. The members of the regiment from this county, Henry L. Dawson; John N. Leamon; Asa G. Sample; James M. Sample; Asa Smith; and John Wilson have arrived at home looking very well. They brought the remains of W.R. Barrett to his home, who was interred at Gilboa burying ground under the auspices of the Order of Odd Fellows, of which Mr. B. was an honored member. Wm. J. Scott, also the 54th, and from this county, reenlisted at New Orleans, in the 1st Indiana Heavy Artillery."

15 Dec 1864: "How To Send Letters South The following rules promulgated by General Butler for the transmission of letters across the lines, have been published several times before, but we reproduce them for the satisfaction of the many persons interested in the subject: 1) No letter must exceed one page of letter sheet, and must relate purely to domestic matters. 2) All letters, (including prisoners) must be sent with five cents postage enclosed, if to go to Richmond, and ten cents if beyond. 3) Every letter must be signed by the writer's name in full and post office address. 4) All letters must be enclosed to the Commanding General of the Department of Virginia and North Carolina, Fortress Monroe, endorsed 'via flag truce.' 5) No money will be forwarded except to prisoners of war. 6) All letters sent to Fortress Monroe without a strict compliance with these rules will be transmitted to the dead letter office." *Hancock Democrat*

4 May 1865: "Awful Calamity On the 27th day of April, the steamer Sultana, when about seven miles above Memphis having on board 2,176 souls, about 2,000 paroled prisoners, belonging to Ohio and Indiana, burst one of her boilers, took fire and burned to the water's edge. Only about 600 escaped instant death, and it is feared, a large number of those will die from injury and exposure. Kip (Christopher Hugh) Sears and B. F.

Hancock County Indiana Civil War Soldiers

Waller, of Company B, 9th Cavalry, were on the ill-fated boat, but succeeded in gaining the shore, and one of them, Sears, has arrived at home." *Hancock Democrat*

25 May 1865: "The Port Royal New South speaks on 6 May 1865, of the arrival at Jacksonville of squads of the 3,200 Andersonville prisoners who were coming in. The rebels finding it impossible to feed them, brought them to near our lines and turned them loose. Most of them have arrived, and they are being supplied. about twenty were left at Andersonville, too sick to be moved. The total number who have died at Andersonville since the establishment of that infernal pen exceeds 17,000." *Hancock Democrat*

7 Jul 1906: "Civil War Nurse Mrs. Mary Bell, of Greenfield, has experienced the horrors of war along with the veterans of '61-'65. She was a hospital nurse and can give interesting history of those four years. Mrs. Bell was formerly a resident of Ohio, but has lived on North State Street, Greenfield, for more than a year. She is a member of the Association of Army Nurses of the Civil War and a noble and interesting woman. The following is abstracted from a paper she wrote and presented by her before the Association of Army Nurses.

"When the dark clouds of war hovered over our land and darkened homes, then patriotism came to meet the emergency. Fathers, brothers, husbands and dearest friends were ready to go at their country's call, willing to fight its battles, and if necessary, sacrifice their lives upon the altar of their country.

"My interest in the war began with the departure of relatives and friends that were being sent to the 'front.' Weary days they were, not knowing what moment the sadness of news would come, and busy days they were, too. Teaching through the daytime and sewing with friends at the 'circles' evenings, knitting, scraping lint, getting supplies ready to be sent to our soldier boys that were out fighting for our country, our homes and our sacred rights. After I entered the service as an army nurse, my first work was at Covington Barracks, Kentucky, assisting my husband who was in the medical department.

Hancock County Indiana Civil War Soldiers

"We had so many die from the measles, mere boys in their teens, that I wearied seeing so much suffering and death, but realized their needs urgent and they were sorely in need of friends. We remained at the barracks until marching orders came The very sick must remain in the hospitals until well, many of them never again rejoining their regiments. There were sad and final partings.

"When our regiment reached its destination others were there in camp and when the tents were up it looked, indeed, a great city of tents beside the river. A post hospital was established and I entered upon my duties as matron. A large building, formerly a cotton factory, was appropriated, and was soon filled to overflowing, as the measles had broken out in camp, and every morning's 'sick call' brought us many patients.

"A pest house was soon a necessity, as there were cases of small pox, and they be isolated. It was my duty to prepare light diet for those patients and to write letters home to their families or friends, but under no condition was I to visit them, all orders coming to me from the 'surgeon in charge.' Many a soldier never came from that pest house only in a wooden box and a burial at night. Later the spotted fever broke out, claiming many victims. Regiments passing to the 'front' would leave us many sick to be cared for. Never at any time was there a scarcity of patients.

"The hospital could accommodate a hundred or more, and it seemed always to be filled to its utmost capacity. At times the gloom seemed to be almost impenetrable, many, very many dying. They seemed utterly without hope, and we could not cheer them. The mind wore upon the body until death claimed them, The doctor pronounced it homesickness.

"I was at the Jeffersonville hospital, a building that held twenty-four-hundred and often it was crowded, even out into the corridors. Here we were visited by Indiana's great War Governor. At this hospital were many soldiers resting on their homeward journey from the 'prison pens' of the South. They thought to rest and gain sufficient strength to take them the remainder of the journey to their Northern homes. I wrote scores

Hancock County Indiana Civil War Soldiers

of letters for them to their friends, always adding ; I will soon be there.' But many of the relatives and friends looked in vain. Death, the conqueror, came off victorious. The memory of their sunken eyes, hollow cheeks and ghastly forms will linger with me always.

"Comrades, these scenes came to me and to you in the morning of life. They come up before us all along the journey of life. With us the morning and noon-tide have passed, the shadows of evening are coming upon us. Soon 'marching orders' will come to pass over the River of Death, encamping on the other side, where I trust, I shall meet you again, not as of yore in hospitals filled with the sick and wounded, the dying and the dead, but in Heaven's bright clime." *Evening Star*

19 Jul 1906: "Hancock County Soldiers in Battles on Birthdays A.J. Bridges, of Greenfield, and William H, Power, of Wilkinson, met Monday morning at the shoe shop of Fred Beecher, on South State Street (Greenfield). In their greeting one said to the other (they are veterans of the Civil War), 'I believe I saw you at Kennesaw Mountain.' the other, Wm. H. Power, responded, 'Yes, I was there. It was on my birthday. Our company was repulsed on June 25th, which was my 16th birthday.' Mr. Bridges said, 'We fought the fiercest battle that I was in during the war, on June 27th at that place, which was my birthday also.' His company lost more than a man a minute during the struggle.

"The 27th was also the birthday of two soldiers of his company who went with him from this county. They were Joseph and Edward Martin, living four miles northeast of the city. Mr. Bridges said that the 26th day of last month he was sitting upon the street in this city when a stranger approached him and asked him if he knew A.J. Bridges. He answered that was his name. The stranger then said, 'Well, tomorrow is your birthday. It was 42 years tomorrow since I last saw you. We were then in the battles at Kennesaw Mountain and I was taken over the mountain as a prisoner.' The stranger was Harrison Berry, of Austin, Indiana, who had been visiting his son at

Hancock County Indiana Civil War Soldiers

Indianapolis and remembering that Greenfield was the home of his old comrade Bridges, he came over to see him. He had remembered through the forty-two years that the battle occurred on Mr. Bridges' birthday. The Kennesaw Mountain battle was the second one Mr. Bridges was in on his birthday. The previous year, on June 27th 1863, he was in the battle of Vicksburg." *Hancock Democrat*

16 August 1906: "Fifth Cavalry Annual Reunion And Camp Fire Will Be In This City The twenty-fourth annual reunion of the Fifth Cavalry will be held in this city September 12th and 13th. This is one of the fighting regiments of the Civil War and was attached to the army of the Cumberland a greater part of the time.

"Among the members of this regiment in this county are George Alford; Frank Brizendine; George W. Duncan; John Kiger; Almon Kiefer; Milton Morris; and Harrison Ridlen. The regiment was in the thickest of the fighting and there is an interest attached to the cavalry that is peculiarly appealing to the sentiments of the public. Some good stories are expected to be told at the camp fire" *Evening Star*

29 Sep 1906: "Ranks Thinning, Reunion Of Veterans Of War At Fortville: John B. Huston and other Greenfield people report an enjoyable day at the reunion of Company G, 12th Indiana Infantry in Fortville. The following is from the *Fortville Tribune*: At their last reunion there were about 47 living, and about one-half were present. Since last year their ranks have been thinned by death of several of the survivors, among whom were, Richard Allison; Henry Edmonds; and John T. Rash. The company originally consisted of 115 men, and was officered as follows, Captain James Huston; 1st Lieut. Eastley Helms; 2nd Lieut. Robert Alfont, who was during service promoted to 1st Lieut. and afterwards to the captaincy. Ralph Copper was orderly sergeant and afterwards promoted to 2nd and then to 1st Lieutenant.

"The following members were killed while in line of battle (See data on their respective pages): Ezekiel B. Cooper; Milton

Hancock County Indiana Civil War Soldiers

Curry; Archibald Gardner; George W. Kelly; James W. Moulden; Edward Pauly; William Shaffer; William Thomas; and Amos Wilson.

"The following died from wounds during service: Andrew Forgey; Hugh Forgey; James Lister; and Aaron Wright. The company's captain, James Huston, died of disease, 13 Oct 1864. The most of the company were discharged from service on 8 Jun 1865." *Evening Star, Greenfield*

19 August 1909: "Greenfield In It The Mexican War veterans of this State held their annual reunion at Indianapolis Tuesday. In the election of Officers, Greenfield fared pretty well, thank you. Capt. James H. Carr was elected vice-president; Dr. Robert Smith, treasurer; and Jerry Hendron of Greenfield was declared the baby of the organization. Of him the *Indianapolis Star* says: "there's the baby over there,' remarked a white-haired man with military bearing as he pointed out Jerry Hendron, 77 years old, from a crown of twenty-one veterans of the Mexican War who assembled at the State House. Henry M. Endsley, of Shelbyville, is the oldest at 87."

4 April 1912: "Almon Kiefer and John Stephens, of Greenfield, and Nathan Meek, of Indianapolis, old soldiers, will leave in a few days for the Dakotas, where they will take up soldier's claims for farm lands. Mr. Kiefer already has a large body of land which he drew from the Government a few months ago. They will remain on the lands for some time to prove up their claims." *Hancock Democrat*

25 April 1912: "Sinking of the Sultana Forty-two years ago on Saturday next the people of the North were shocked by the word that the Sultana, with 2,200 Union soldiers on board, had gone down and a large majority of the boys in blue had been lost. The soldiers were on their way home and were crowded on the Sultana. When near Memphis the boilers exploded and the Sultana went to the bottom of the Mississippi. Some two or three from this neighborhood were among the lost." *Hancock Democrat*

Hancock County Indiana Civil War Soldiers

_ **June 1912**: "Soldiers Report Happy Gathering; Thirty-One Helped Thomas Holland Celebrate Eighty-Eighth Birthday With Splendid Dinner And Good Time; The Civil War veterans from here who attended the birthday celebration of Thomas Holland at Maxwell, reported a grand, good time with their aged comrade who has now passed his eighty-eighth milestone in life's journey.

"There were thirty-one of the veterans who attended and enjoyed the day, and their average age was 72 ½ years. The oldest was Mr. Holland, the host, and the youngest was W.H. Power, who is 64 years old. Both were members of the 99th Indiana, Company B. A great feast was served at noon, and the soldiers attacked the good things to eat with the same energy and determination they attacked their enemies half a century ago. Although on this occasion the ranks of opposing forces were badly shattered, there was still more than a remnant left when the attacking forces had done their utmost. the soldiers say they never sat down to a better dinner. The company was entertained by different readings and stories, and with songs.

"The names and ages of all present are as follows: John Barr, age 67;Wm. Catt, age 77; T.H. Coffey, age 68; Jacob Davie, age 75; Wm. P. Denney, age 72; John H. Duncan, age 74; John K. Henby, age 72; Morris Hinchman, age 68; John Holliday, age 77; Adam Hutton, age 68; William Hutton, age 72; Stephen Jackson, age 69; George Johnson, age 69; Warren King, age 70; J.M. Larrimore, age 69; Edwin Martin, age 71; Joseph Martin, age 71; Jared C. Meek, age 84; Taylor Morford, age 64; J.P. Murphy, age 69; Wm. H. Payne, age 70; W.H. Power age 64; George W. Reed, age 69; Nevil Reeves, age 76; Wm. Reynolds, age 72; Albert T. Roberts, age 77; Lafayette Slifer, age 72; Henry Snow, age 74; H.C. Tibbetts, age 75; and David N. True, age 75." *Hancock Democrat*, Contributed by Bob Holland.

10 Jul 1913:"J.E. Hart Gives Some Gettysburg Observations J.E. Hart, of Greenfield, who was one of the two soldiers from Hancock County who attended the half century celebration of the battle of Gettysburg, has many interesting stories to tell of the battlefield. Mr. Hart was not in the battle, though his regiment

Hancock County Indiana Civil War Soldiers

was. He was off duty at the time, suffering from a wound received in the battle of Chancellorsville, Virginia.

"On the second day of the battle his regiment, which had only about 230 men left, was called out to reconnoiter and locate the enemy's lines, and were surprised by the enemy, losing 110 of their men in six minutes. In Company C, of the 27th Indiana Regiment, four color-bearers were killed and four were wounded in the fight. That was Mr. Hart's company and his location in the line was near the color-bearers.

"Mr. Hart says most of the fighting was in the wood-land, and the large trees are covered with knots, each knot being the location of a bullet which still remains in the tree. Spangler's Springs are still there, where the 'Yanks' and the 'Johnnies' drank together after the battle. Boy Scouts climbed down the cement steps and dipped water for the old soldiers at the reunion. The Boy Scouts who marched to the celebration over many miles of dust roads, did much service for the old soldiers in guiding them from place to place.

"A North Carolina Confederate bunked in the same tent with Mr. Hart. The old house in which Miss Wade was baking bread for the soldiers in the town of Gettsyburg when killed, and the bread tray and table on which she was working are still there. She was killed by a stray shot and was the only citizen killed in the town during the battle. The house is now used as a kind of museum.

"Six of the army nurses, now grown old, stood at their headquarters and sang patriotic songs for the soldiers, which were loudly cheered. There are many features of the battle marked by stones which bear inscriptions of the events. The right and left of Mr. Hart's 27th Indiana Regiment was marked by stone, and also the farthest point of their advance." *Evening Star, Greenfield* "Eventually the bitterness of the war abated to the point where the Grand Army of the Republic and the United Confederate Veterans began holding occasional joint encampments. In 1913, for the 50th anniversary of Gettsyburg, 54,000 veterans from both sides gathered. The high point of the

Hancock County Indiana Civil War Soldiers

event was when 180 veterans of the Philadelphia Brigade, which had defended the center of the Union line, met 120 survivors of Pickett's Division who had formed up 100 feet from the stone wall defending the line and marched under the original colors towards the wall. When they got there, the two sides clasped hands across the wall while spectators cheered." These soldiers were able to endure, fight, suffer, die, remember.....and forgive.

20 Oct 1921: "First Time They Met In 50 Years Three Comrades Of The Civil War Enjoy Sunday Together In This City Mr. and Mrs. Will Marsh entertained at dinner three comrades of Mr. Marsh's father, Elijah Marsh, in the Fifth Indiana Cavalry, John Vail, of Noblesville; William Sleeth, of Morristown; and Frank Gant, of Parsons, Kansas.

"The Fifth Indiana Cavalry was composed of a number of men from this county. Until a few years ago reunions were held annually, but now nearly all the members in this community have passed away. It is hoped to get all the survivors together soon in this city.

"Sunday was the first time since the close of the Civil War, fifty-six years ago, that Mr. Vail had met either Mr. Sleeth or Mr. Gant, the last named being present on a visit with relatives here. when Mr. Vail arrived Sunday his first remark was, 'There's Frank Gant, I'd know him anywhere.' The three comrades had a delightful day together. Mr. and Mrs. M.T. Willett also enjoyed the hospitality of Mr. and Mrs. Marsh on this occasion." *Greenfield Republican*

24 June 1924:"Answering the Last Call One by one the old veterans, who so gallantly and bravely offered up their lives that the Union might live, are passing to their reward. Of the millions, who in the pink and bloom of young manhood answered the call to arms, now, only a mere handful are left and they, with only few exceptions, are bent with age and former hardships of labor.

"Their ranks are rapidly thinning and in only a few more years none will be left to recount the deeds of valor and

Hancock County Indiana Civil War Soldiers

patriotism performed and to retell the tales of hardship and suffering endured in the terrible conflict.

"This week saw the passing away of two of this grand old army in this city. Mr. George W. Johnson and Alexander Derry, both of whom served three years or more in the Civil War and were in some of the most severe fighting in the war. Mr. Johnson also served on the western plains in the Indian campaigns following the Civil War.

:The Samuel H. Dunbar Post 92, G.A.R., in this city, has only twenty-eight members left, only about half of whom live in the city." *Hancock Democrat*

18 Jun 1925: "Mexican War veterans met in Greenfield in 1904. Jerry Hendren was last of the survivors in Hancock County who died in 1911. In March 1879, Hancock County Mexican War veterans formed an organization on the call of Alexander Andis; Robert Andis; Thomas Branham; John H. Childs; Jerry Hendren; Adams L. Ogg; Louis T. Osborn; Dr. E.W. Pierson; John Roberts; and Newton Scott.

"Jeremiah Hendren was the youngest of the Mexican War veterans in Hancock County. He was a Mason and presented to Hancock County lodge the sword he used in the war with Mexico. Mr. Hendren was the last survivor of the war in the county. He died 29 Oct 1911. Dr. Robert Smith and James H. Carr were next to Mr. Hendren, the last of the veterans in the county to die."

5 Jun 1930: "Veteran of the Civil War is 94 Years Old Frank Sanford Probably the Oldest Living Person Born in Greenfield Frank Sanford, age 94 years, one of Hancock County's oldest citizens, and perhaps the oldest living person who first saw the light of day in Greenfield, was down town this morning to greet friends.

"Mr. Sanford's home is in the northeast corner of Buck Creek Township, on a farm where he has lived continuously for seventy years and is here a few days as the guest of his son, Isaac Sanford.

Hancock County Indiana Civil War Soldiers

" 'I was born in Greenfield, my parents told me,' said Mr. Sanford, in August 1836, but was moved to Green Twosnhip when a small child. I can well remember when I was about seven years old, my mother took me and we walked to Greenfield from north of Eden. I recollect that there was a low spot about where the public square is now, which had quite a lot of water in it. We crossed the north branch over a foot log, on what is now State Street. The foot log had poles along it so that children wouldn't be afraid.

"I can think of lots of things and as people used to be then. I suppose there are few if any folks living can actually remember old Colonel Milroy, who was one of the early leaders in the community. I can remember distinctly and describe his appearance. I even remember the wen he had on the side of his face. The Colonel ran a tavern out on the top of Strawboard Hill (East Main Street, A Street going north and Morristiwn Pike going south) with a big gold-lettered sign out in front.

"I tell you things have greatly changed. The new things that have come along are wonderful. I paid on the ground three years during the Civil War, but it doesn't appear to me that that hurts much after all. If I'm still here next August for the Sanford reunion in Riley Park, I'm going to tell them lots of things about old times. Come on out and listen, if you care to." *Greenfield Reporter*

4 June 1931: The County's Living Civil War Veterans The following story of the living Civil War veterans is taken from the *Hancock Democrat*: Fourteen Civil War veterans represent the last remnant of the Grand Army of the Republic in Hancock County. Z.T. Morford, commander of the G.A.R. Post in Greenfield, has compiled a list of veterans living in the county and this list is believed to be correct.

"Although these men are not as spry as they formerly were, their hearts still hold the same spirit which they fought for in the early '60s. With the strength and number of Civil War veterans diminishing G.A.R. Posts in Fortville, New Palestine and Greenfield have been discontinued. Seven members are required

Hancock County Indiana Civil War Soldiers

for a quorum and as none of the three posts have that many members it is impossible to conduct a meeting.

"However, the local G.A.R. post holds together and retains a room on the first floor of the court house, which the county commissioners gave to the local unit a number of years ago. Although, this room could be used for other purposes, the commissioners desire that the veterans retain control of it as long as they wish. Commander Morford, who has served as commander of the Greenfield G.A.R. before, is the commander now. He and several other veterans occasionally meet in the post room. However, the burden of carrying on has been transferred to the shoulders of other patriotic organizations.

"Several interesting documents, pictures and other articles hang on the walls of the post room. A picture taken 31 May 1915, shows forty-nine members of the Samuel H. Dunbar Post No. 92, Commander Morford is the only living man today that appeared in the picture taken sixteen years ago.

"A picture of the old Andersonville Prison was removed from the walls several years ago. At the time Providence Springs is said to have sprung from the ground, three Hancock County soldiers were confined in the confederate prison. They were George Duncan; Frank Brizendine; and Jeff Willett, all of whom are dead now. The Civil War veterans who are living today are as follows:

"James M. Elliott, age 88. Mr. Elliott lives in New Palestine. He was born in Ohio 27 Oct 1842 and enlisted at Greenfield in August 1862, and served in Company B, 79th Indiana Regiment, until 1865, at which time he was discharged in Washington, D.C.

"Francis M. Hanes, age 87. Mr. Hanes was born in Marion County, 27 Nov 1843; and enlisted 8 Aug 1862, at Indianapolis, a member of Company B, 8th Indiana Infantry Regiment. Mr. Hanes was discharged as a Corporal at Hilton Head, South Carolina, 14 Jun 1865. He now lives at New Palestine.

" Z.T. Morford, age 83. Mr. Morford is commander of the Greenfield G.A.R. Post. He enlisted when sixteen years old in Company A, 148th Ohio, in Butler County, Ohio. Mr. Morford

Hancock County Indiana Civil War Soldiers

has two brothers who served in the Union army, one of them dying while in the service, Elisha Morford died of typhoid fever aboard a river steamer enroute to the siege of Vicksburg. The second brother, Daniel B. Morford, died at Memphis, Tennessee, about ten years ago... Z.T. Morford enlisted during the latter part of 1864 and was discharged at Edgefield, Teneessee, in October 1865. Mr. Morford lives in Greenfield.

Joseph Palmer, age 84. Mr. Palmer was born in Greensburg and at an early age moved to this county. He enlisted at Indianapolis, 14 Oct 1864, and was discharged at the end of the war. Mr. Palmer recalls riding beside Sherman on his march to the sea. 'On one occasion old Uncle Billy Sherman ordered me to turn two horses, which I was leading for him, loose because of their physical condition was such that they were practically unable to travel for lack of feed.' Mr. Palmer lives in Greenfield.

"William Power, age 83. Mr. Power was born at Pottsville, Pennsylvania, 25 Jun 1848. He enlisted at Warrington, Hancock County, 22 Mar 1864, as a member of Company B, 99th Indiana Regiment.

"The other seven Civil War veterans of the county are: Samuel L. Burk, of near Greenfield; Frank Clark, of New Palestine; J.E. Hart, of Greenfield; Martin Maily, of Eden; Freeman Murray, could this be Freeborn Murrer of Fortville; Frank Sanford, Route 4, Greenfield; and Scott Watts, of Greenfield. *Hancock Democrat* See data on soldiers respective pages.

Hancock County Indiana Civil War Soldiers

Bibliography

Hancock County, Indiana, Sources
Biographies, B.F. Bowen, 1902
Cemeteries, Sue Baker, 1993
Civil War Discharge Book, Recorder's Office
Court Records Index, Sue Baker, 2000
Death Records, official, 1882-1989
Marriage Records Index, 1828-1920
Historical Society newsletters
History, J.H. Binford, 1882
History, George Richman, 1916
Newspapers
  Democrat
  Evening Star
  Greenfield Republican
  Greenfield Reporter
The Pioneer, Samuel Harden, 1895
Veterans Burial List, Dr. C.M. Gibbs, 1940

Published Sources
A Sketchbook of Indiana History, Arville Funk, 1969
Boys in Blue, Samuel Harden, 1888
Civil War Dictionary, Mark Boatman III, 1959
Civil War Source Book, Philip Katcher, 1992
Class of 1846, West Point, John Waugh, 1994
Common Soldier, James Robertson, Jr.,
  National Park Civil War Series
Crossroads of Conflict, Civil War Sites in Georgia, 1993
Encyclopedia of the American Civil War, Vols., I-IV
Georgia Historic Sites
  Dallas

Hancock County Indiana Civil War Soldiers

Pickett's Mill
Resaca
Grand Army of the Republic, Indiana Archives
Guide to Indiana Civil War Manuscripts, Centennial Commission, 1965
Hallowed Ground, Allen Brier and Harrison Hunt, 1990
Handwriting of American Records, Kay Kirkham, 1973
Historical Data Systems
History of the Ram Fleet, Warren Crandall, 1907
Hoosiers in the Civil War, Arville Funk, 1967
History of 99th Regiment, D,.R. Lucas, 1900
_____ of 79th Regiment, 7 Member Committee, 1891
_____ of the 12th Regiment, State Archives
_____ of the 8th Regiment, State Archives
Indiana in the Civil War, Emma Thornbrough, 1965
Lightning Mule Brigade, Robert Willett, Jr. Guild Press
Morgan Raid in Indiana and Ohio, Arville Funk, 1971
National Park Service
   Andersonville Prison, Library, Database
   Chattanooga Cemetery
   Chickamauga/Chattanooga
   Kennesaw Mountain
   Marietta Cemetery
   Nashville Cemetery
Presidents, Soldiers, Statesmen, Vol. II, H. H. Hardesty, 1899
Report of Adjutant General of Indiana, W.H.H. Terrell, 1866
Sultana
   Disaster on the Mississippi, Gene Salecker, 1996
   Loss of the Sultana, Rev. Chester Berry, 1892
   Sultana Tragedy, Jerry Potter, 1992
   Transport to Disaster, James Elliott, 1962
The Rooster, John F. Mitchell, 1913
World Book Online, Civil War, Gabor Borritt
Yanks, Rebels, Rats and Rations, Patricia Mitchell, 1993

Hancock County Indiana Civil War Soldiers

Index

11th Indiana Regiment, 440
11th Indiana Zouaves, 8
121st Infantry Regiment, 426
12th Indiana Regiment, 442
13th Indiana Cavalry Regiment, 429
18th Indiana Regiment, 445
19th Indiana Regiment, 445
1st Cherokee Mounted Rifle Regiment, 437
1st Cherokee Mounted Rifles, 13
51st Indiana Regiment, 448
53rd Indiana Regiment, 449
57th Indiana Regiment, 9, 455
5th Indiana Cavalry, 423
79th Indiana Infantry Regiment, 457
8th Indiana Regiment, 430
90th Indiana Regiment, 423
99th Indiana Regiment, 461
9th Indiana Cavalry, 426
Abney, 29
Acker, 29
Adams, 29, 30
Adkins, 30
Akeman, 30, 430
Alexander, 21, 30, 31, 437, 438, 444

Alfont, 31, 516
Alford, 31, 32, 471, 474, 516
Alfrey, 32
Allee, 30
Allen, 32, 33, 461
Alley, 8, 33, 463
Allison, 18, 21, 33, 504, 505, 516
Allman, 34
Alyea, 34, 42, 430, 495
America's Devil's Island, 468
Amos, 36
Anderson, 21, 36, 430
Andersonville, 513
Andersonville Prison, 469
Andersonville Raiders, 470
Andis, 9, 17, 37, 43, 498, 521
Andrick, 38
Answering the Last Call, 520
Apple, 39, 506
Applegate, 39
Armstrong, 39, 508
Arnold, 40, 445
Asbury, 40
Ash, 40
Ashcraft, 40, 44
Askins, 41, 433

Hancock County Indiana Civil War Soldiers

Assassination, 12
Atkison, 41, 450
Ayres, 41
Bailey, 45
Baity, 9, 45, 318
Baker, 45
Baldwin, 46, 463, 507
Bales, 46, 434
Ball, 46, 47
Ballenger, 13, 47
Banks, 47
Bannon, 47, 444
Banta, 48
Bargoner, 505
Barnard, 48, 444
Barnett, 48, 445
Barr, 1, 48, 258, 518
Barrett, 21, 48, 49, 428, 461, 511
Bartlow, 50
Barton, 50, 471
Barwick, 50, 160, 425, 471
Basey, 50, 51
Beachman, 51
Beaver, 51
Bedford, 51
Bedgood, 1, 51, 442
Beeler, 51
Beeson, 51, 52, 461
Bell, 52, 504
Bellville, 52
Belville, 52, 425, 471
Bennett, 52, 504
Berry, 53, 453, 471, 515
Bevil, 53
Bills, 53, 505

Bird, 53
Bixler, 53
Black, 54, 438, 507
Blackledge, 30
Blakely, 54, 425, 462, 472
Blanton, 54
Blessinger, 54, 428, 473, 484
Bodkin, 55
Bogart, 55
Bogg, 55
Bolander, 55
Boles, 56
Boman, 56
Bond, 21, 56
Boone, 56
Bounty, 5
Bowers, 56, 434
Bowman, 463
Boyce, 56, 461, 507, 508
Boyer, 57, 509
Bracken, 57, 58, 75
Braddock, 58
Bragg, 58
Brandenburg, 58
Branham, 17, 18, 19, 24, 58, 70, 521
Branson, 59, 508
Brantlinger, 59
Breece, 59
Brewer, 60
Bridges, 60, 61, 515
Bright, 61
Brinegar, 18, 61, 461
Brizendine, 61, 116, 425, 471, 516

Hancock County Indiana Civil War Soldiers

Brock, 61
Brooks, 62, 63, 71, 457, 486, 488, 511
Brother vs Brother, 498
Brown, 19, 21, 63, 64, 444, 463, 506, 509
Brunson, 471
Buchanan, 21, 64, 431
Buchel, 18, 64, 507, 508
Buckley, 508, 509
Bucy, 65
Buglers, 8
Bundy, 65
Buntrum, 65
Burdette, 65
Burial of a soldier:, 4
Burk, 3, 65, 66, 504
Burke, 66, 457
Burns, 66, 507, 508
Burnwick, 67
Burris, 67, 68, 447, 490
Bush, 68, 437
Bussell, 69
Butcher, 69
Butterfield, 69
Butternuts, 434
Butts, 69, 72
Byers, 69, 457
Byfield, 69
Byrkitt, 69
Cady, 73, 428
Cahaba, Alabama, Prison, 472
Cahill, 73
Calder, 73, 508, 509
Caldwell, 73

Call To Arms, 1
Camp, 73
Camp Benton, 432
Camp Chase, Ohio, 475
Camp Joe Reynolds,, 461
Camp Morton, 441
Camp Oglethorpe, Macon, Georgia, 473
Campbell, 21, 74, 425, 471
Cannon, 74
Cantwell, 74
Card, 74
Carmichael, 75
Carr, 75, 453, 461, 507, 517
Carroll, 77
Carson, 77
Cartwright, 77
Cass, 10, 77, 463, 471
Casto, 78
Catlin, 78, 444
Catt, 3, 78, 79, 461, 518
Chambers, 79
Chancery, 80
Chandler, 80
Chapman, 21, 80
Chappel, 80, 484
Chappell, 80
Charles Ellett, 27
Charlottesville George Landis Post #545, 504
Childers, 81
Childs, 521
Chittenden, 21, 81, 425, 433, 471, 474
Chitwood, 82
Christian, 82

Hancock County Indiana Civil War Soldiers

Church, 82, 428, 473, 484
Civil War Pass, 140
Clampett, 82
Clapper, 82, 438
Clark, 82
Clayton, 21, 83
Clements, 83
Clevenger, 83
Cliff, 83
Clifford, 83, 446
Cline, 84
Cloud, 84, 508
Cly, 84
Cobler, 505
Cochran, 84
Coffey, 84, 518
Coffin, 85, 446
Cohee, 86
Colburn, 86
Cole, 86
Coleman, 86
Collins, 86, 87, 425, 430, 437, 446, 462, 471, 495
Collyer, 86
Colonel Lew Wallace's Zouaves, 440
Color bearer, 137
Combs, 509
Comstock, 87, 99
Confederate brothers, 9
Conger, 89, 504, 505
Conner, 89
Connett, 89
Cook, 89
Cooper, 90, 92, 258, 516
Copeland, 92

Copper, 92, 444, 505, 516
Cottrell, 92
County's Living Civil War Veterans, 522
Courtney, 92
Cox, 461
Craft, 18, 93
Craining, 93
Crane, 100, 509
Cravens, 94, 445
Crawford, 18, 19, 94, 445
Creviston, 94
Crews, 94
Crosley, 94, 442
Cross, 95, 448, 504
Crossley, 96
Crowder, 96, 445
Cummins, 96, 505, 508
Cunningham, 96
Curry, 96, 97, 98, 444, 462, 507, 517
Custer, 98
Dailey, 101, 504
Dangler, 101
Darter, 101
Davidson, 101, 102, 423, 433, 439, 442, 444
Davie, 518
Davis, 3, 18, 102, 103, 104, 109, 111, 504
Dawson, 105, 512
Day, 21, 105, 119, 120
Dearmin, 105
DeCamp, 106
Deck, 106
Deel, 106

Hancock County Indiana Civil War Soldiers

Delbert, 107
Denney, 318, 518
Dennis, 18, 107
Denny, 107, 179, 442
Deppery, 108
Derry, 108, 521
Deserter, 459
Deshong, 108
Despo, 108
Destruction Of The Sultana, 477
Dexter, 108
Dickerson, 108
Dickey, 109
Die from the measles, 514
Dille, 109
Dillman, 109, 434, 461
Dinkle, 109
Dipper, 21, 109
Disability, 7
Disastrous expedition, 424
Disease, 4
Dixon, 17, 109
Dobbins, 21, 109
Domanget, 110
Dorman, 110, 436
Doty, 110
Dougherty, 111
Dove, 111, 433, 507, 508
Dowling, 111
Downing, 111
Drake, 111
Drummer, 8
Drummer boy, 104, 440
Dubois, 111
Dugan, 111

Dunbar, 6, 17, 18, 19, 112, 242, 431, 433, 434, 436, 437, 438, 497, 507
Dunbar corner, 445
Dunbar House,, 6
Duncan, 17, 21, 24, 114, 116, 318, 425, 448, 471, 507, 516, 518
Dunham, 117
Dunlap, 117
Dunn, 21, 117
Dye, 21, 118, 431
Dye Jr, 21
Eakes, 121, 128, 461
Earl, 122, 442
Eastes, 122
Eastman, 434
Eaton, 122, 123, 145
Edmonds, 505, 516
Edmunds, 123
Edwards, 17, 21, 123, 444
Egger, 123
Eighth Regiment, 2
Eikman, 123, 306
Ellingwood, 124, 474
Elliott, 21, 124, 445, 461, 506, 509, 523
Ellis, 21, 125
Elmore, 125
Elsbury, 125
Ely, 125
Endicott, 125
England, 125, 126
Eskew, 507
Evans, 126, 471
Everett, 126

Hancock County Indiana Civil War Soldiers

Everson, 126, 439
Examining A Recruit, 2
Fair, 129
Fansler, 129
Farris, 129
Faulkenburg, 129
Faurot, 129, 130
Fausett, 130, 505
Ferren, 507
Ferrin, 130
Fetron, 130
Fifth Cavalry Annual Reunion, 516
First tailor shop, 242
Fisk, 130
Fletcher, 131, 462, 484, 509
Flowers, 131
Foley, 1, 131
Forbush, 131
Forgey, 132, 444, 517
Forman, 133
Fort, 133, 425, 457, 472, 509
Fortville Solomon D. Kempton Post No. 228, 505
Foster, 18, 60, 134, 160, 428, 473
Fountain, 17, 134
Fouty, 134
Fowler, 134
Frankenstine, 508
Franklin, 134
Franzman, 506
Frazier, 135
Fred, 135, 136, 139
Frederick, 136
Frost, 1, 136
Fry, 136
Fuller, 9, 137, 430, 438, 488, 497
Furry, 138
Galligher, 141
Galloway, 141
Gant, 116, 141, 425, 471, 520
Gapen, 17, 21, 143
Gappen, 21, 141, 142, 143, 155
Garberick, 143
Gard, 143
Gardner, 144, 444, 517
Garriott, 144, 508, 509
Gaskins, 18
Gates, 145, 471
Geary, 146
Gem William E. Hart Post G.A.R. No. 454, 506
George, 507
Gephart, 146
Gery, 507
Gettysburg Observations, 518
Gibbons, 146
Gibbs, 146
Gibson, 146
Gilbert, 146
Gillian, 146
Gilson, 147
Gimason, 147
Ginder, 147
Gipe, 147, 509

Hancock County Indiana Civil War Soldiers

Glass, 147
Goar, 147
Goble, 147
Gooding, 13, 18, 19, 24, 148, 150, 507
Gooding block, 242
Gooding Corner, 148, 162
Gordon, 150, 509
Gorham, 150
Grand Army of the Republic, 501
Grand Review, 14, 15, 79, 159, 177
Grand Review,, 14
Gray, 150, 484
Green, 151, 504
Greenfield Samuel Dunbar G.A.R. Post No. 92, 507
Greenfield Sax Horn Band, 445
Grenier, 442
Griener, 151
Griffith, 151, 445, 504
Grigsby, 69, 151, 152
Gross, 152
Groves, 152, 508
Gruder, 147
Grundon, 152
Gumden, 152
Gundrum, 152
Gunn, 152, 154, 156
Guymon, 76
Gwinn, 154
Hackleman, 157
Hafner, 24, 157
Hahn, 157

Haines, 157, 439
Hall, 157
Halley, 157
Ham, 157, 508, 509
Hamilton, 158, 428, 463
Hampton, 159
Handy, 159
Hanes, 159, 439, 506, 523
Hanley, 159
Hanna, 18
Hansing, 159
Hardin, 159, 160, 444
Harlan, 160
Harris, 160, 161, 507
Harrison, 21, 161, 461
Hart, 17, 18, 19, 24, 161, 162, 434, 445, 506, 518
Hartley, 163, 308, 447
Hartner, 21, 163
Harvey, 163, 428
Haskell, 163
Haskett, 163
Hasley, 163
Hatfield, 163
Hawk, 164
Hawkins, 164
Hays, 165
Heath, 165, 486
Heavenridge, 166
Hedges, 166
Hedrick, 166, 322
Heller, 167
Helms, 167, 507, 508, 516
Henby, 167, 448, 474, 518
Hendren, 167, 521
Hendricks, 168

Hancock County Indiana Civil War Soldiers

Hendron, 517
Henner, 168
Henon, 168
Henry, 18, 168, 190, 318
Herod, 168, 428, 473
Herrod, 426
Herron, 168, 169
Hervey, 169
Hiday, 3, 170, 171, 172
Higbee, 172
Higgenbotham, 172
Higgins, 172, 173
Hill, 3, 21, 173, 435, 438
Hinchman, 19, 30, 174, 175, 518
Hind, 175
Hinds, 175, 442
Hobbs, 176
Hodson, 439
Hogle, 176, 507, 508
Holden, 176, 446, 508
Holding, 177, 446
Holland, 177, 191
Holliday, 518
Holoway, 178
Holt, 178
Home Guards, 17
Hoobler, 178
Hook, 178, 179, 428, 442, 505, 506
Hooker, 179
Hoover, 180, 425, 471
Horton, 180
Hospital nurse, 513
Hough, 13
Hover, 180

How To Send Letters South, 512
Howard, 180, 181, 443
Hubbell, 182
Hudson, 11, 116, 182, 184, 185, 188, 425, 472
Hughes, 186
Huguneard, 186
Humbles, 186
Humphries, 186
Hunt, 186, 187, 509
Hunter, 187
Huntsinger, 187
Huston, 187, 188, 444, 506, 507, 516, 517
Hutson, 188, 425, 472
Hutton, 21, 188, 425, 428, 450, 452, 472, 518
Illness, 4
Invalid Corps, 5
Irish, 192
Jack, 192, 434
Jackson, 21, 192, 193, 518
Jacobs, 194
James, 194, 504
Jarrett, 121, 195, 196
Jeff, 196, 471
Jenkins, 196
Jennings, 196
John Hunt Morgan, 23
Johnson, 21, 196, 197, 198, 425, 471, 507, 508, 518, 521
Jonas, 198, 425, 471
Jones, 21, 198
Jordan, 200, 506

Hancock County Indiana Civil War Soldiers

Joseph Chapman, 161
Kappeler, 200
Kauble, 18, 19, 201
Kearns, 201
Keefer, 507
Keeley, 201
Keffer, 201
Keifer, 201
Keiser, 202
Kellenberger, 202
Keller, 203
Kelley, 203
Kellum, 203
Kelly, 203, 463, 517
Kempton, 203
Kennedy, 204
Kenyon, 204, 509
Kern, 205
Kesner, 205
Kessler, 205
Kiefer, 507, 516, 517
Kiger, 205, 516
Kimberlin, 12, 205, 471, 477, 478, 484
Kinder, 206, 504
King, 207, 506, 518
Kingen, 207, 464
Kingery, 208
Kinneman, 208
Kinsey, 208
Kirkhoff, 208, 428, 508
Kirkman, 208
Kiser, 208
Kitchen, 208, 506
Kite, 208
Klem, 208, 506

Knapsacks, 460
Knight, 17, 209, 509
Knights of the Golden Circle, 23
Knoop, 209
Knotts, 209
Knox, 209
Kowan, 210
Kraft, 6
Kreager, 210
Kreft, 6, 210
Kroening, 210
Kuntz, 210
Kunz, 210, 442
Kurtz, 210, 468, 471, 473, 474
Lace, 211
Lacey, 212
Lacy, 213
Lain, 213, 430, 497
Laird, 213
Lake, 213, 439
Lakin, 213
Lamb, 3, 214, 433, 438, 446
Lambertson, 214, 445
Landis, 214
Lane, 214
Langenberger, 215
Langford, 215
Lanham, 215
Lankford, 215
Laporte, 21, 215
Larimore, 215
Larkin, 216
Larrimore, 518
LaRue, 216

Hancock County Indiana Civil War Soldiers

Lawson, 216, 425, 484
Layman, 217
Layton, 217
Leakey, 217
Leamon, 218, 512
Ledmore, 219
Lee, 219
Lemay, 219
Leonard, 219, 461
Letters, 485
Lewis, 219
Libby Prison, 474
Lighter moments, 7
Lincolnfelter, 219, 430
Lindsey, 17, 18, 19
Lineback, 220
Lipscomb, 21, 221
Lister, 221, 444, 517
Lockwood, 221
Loder, 221
Loehr, 221, 428
Long, 222
Lonsberry, 222
Loomis, 223, 458
Low, 223
Lowder, 224, 225, 434, 438
Lowe, 225
Loy, 225
Lucas, 226, 461
Lummis, 223
Lunsford, 226, 471
Luntsford, 226
Lutes, 226
Lyman, 227
Lymon, 226
Lynam, 21, 226, 228, 507

Lynch, 227
Lyon, 227
Mack, 228, 425, 471
Madden, 228
Madison, 228
Magee, 228
Maley, 318
Manche, 228, 272
Mann, 229
Manning, 229
March to the Sea., 10
Marine disaster., 12
Market, 230
Marlin, 230
Marsh, 21, 230, 231, 425, 446, 453, 511, 520
Marshall, 231
Martin, 21, 232, 233, 234, 235, 438, 445, 454, 486, 515, 518
Mason, 13
Mavity, 235
Mayer, 235
Mays, 235, 438
McBane, 235, 430
McCole, 236
McCollum, 236
McConnell, 236, 485
McCord, 236, 461
McCorkhill, 236, 439
McCorkle, 428
McCrarey, 445
McCray, 237
McDaniel, 237
McDonald, 237, 438
McDuffey, 237

Hancock County Indiana Civil War Soldiers

McElvey, 21
McFadden, 237
McFall, 238
McFarland, 238
McGahey, 238
McGee, 238, 437, 509
McGuire, 238
McKelvy, 239
McKenzie, 239
McKinley, 239
McKinne, 239
McKown, 18
McMillen, 240
McNamee, 21, 240
McQuerry, 240
McQuery, 464
McRoberts, 240
Meek, 116, 240, 242, 243, 425, 471, 507, 509, 517, 518
Meek's Reserve, 242
Melton, 244, 507
Memphis wharf, 477
Mendenhall, 244
Merket, 21, 230
Mesler, 244
Mess Kit Utensils, 274
Messler, 244
Mexican War, 37, 46, 58, 60, 80, 254, 293, 308
Mexican War veterans, 521
Meyer, 244
Michael, 245
Millard, 254
Miller, 245, 247, 425, 438, 472, 507, 508, 509

Millikan, 247
Milner, 248, 273, 509
Milroy, 249
Mintz, 249
Mississippi Marine Brigade, 27
Mississippi Marines,, 27
Mitchell, 18, 249, 250, 447
Moncrief, 254
Mooney, 255, 484
Moore, 255, 256
Morford, 21, 256, 463, 518, 523
Morgan, 59, 258, 438
Morgan and his men, 25
Morgan's Raid, 23
Morical, 258
Morris, 258, 506, 516
Morrison, 259
Mosier, 259
Moulden, 259, 517
Mule brigade, 449
Mullen, 259
Mullin, 21
Munden, 259, 260
Murphy, 260, 261, 461, 518
Murrer, 261
Music, 3
Musician, 8
Muth, 262, 265, 275, 429
Myer, 270
Myers, 270
Nagley, 276
National Road, 241
Neal, 276
Nealis, 276

Hancock County Indiana Civil War Soldiers

Neff, 276
Nelson, 276
New Palestine Charles Kirkhoff Post No. 534, 507
News of the surrender, 13
Newspapers This 'N' That, 511
Nibarger, 276, 462, 464
Nicholas, 506
Nichols, 277, 507, 508
Nigh, 277
Niles, 278, 280, 504, 505
Nixon, 278
Noble, 278, 445
Noel, 278
Nogle, 279
Norman, 433
Nurse, Mrs. Mary Bell, 513
O'Donnell, 281
Oertel, 286
Offutt, 281, 282
Ogg, 282, 284, 289, 445, 491, 493, 494, 521
Old State Road, 241
Oldham, 284
Oliphant, 284
Oliver, 284
Olvey, 284, 285, 286, 444
O'Maley, 286
O'Neal, 509
Orear, 286
O'Reilly, 286
Ormsten, 286
Ormston, 505
Orr, 286

Ortle, 462
Osbon, 287
Osborn, 18, 287, 288, 521
Owens, 288, 504, 505
Owings, 288
Packard, 506
Palmer, 290, 506, 524
Pardee, 290
Pardue, 290
Paris, 291
Parker, 290
Parkhurst, 291
Parks, 291
Parole, 10
Parrish, 291
Parsons, 291
Patterson, 292, 505, 506
Pauley, 292, 444
Paullus, 293
Pauly, 517
Payne, 518
Peanut man, 103
Pennock, 293
Pension, 6
Perigo, 293, 505
Perkins, 293
Perman, 293, 428, 473, 484
Perry, 17, 242, 293, 294
Personett, 294
Pest house, 514
Petit, 511
Philpot, 21, 295, 504
Philpott, 437, 505
Pickard, 296
Pickle, 297
Pierce, 298

Hancock County Indiana Civil War Soldiers

Pierson, 298, 445, 521
Pierson's Grove, 431
Pilkington, 298
Pilkinton, 425
Pioneer Corps, 3
Pioneers, 435
Piper, 298
Poole, 299
Pope, 21, 299, 425, 471
Porter, 24, 300
Potts, 300
Powell, 300
Power, 11, 301, 305, 463, 465, 509, 515, 518, 524
Powers, 302, 505
Prather, 302
Pratt, 302, 504, 505
Price, 302, 425, 472
Prickett, 303
Priddy, 304
Prince, 304
Prisoners, 10
Prisons, 467
Pritchard, 304
Private's pay, 5
Probasco, 304
Pugh, 304
Purdue, 304
Pyeatte, 304
Pyle, 304
Pyles, 304
Rabe, 306
Ragan, 307, 454
Rains, 24, 307
Ram Fleet, 27
Ramsdell, 308

Ransdell, 308
Rardin, 18, 309, 428
Raridan, 21, 308
Rash, 309, 310, 509, 516
Rawlings, 310
Ray, 310
Read, 484
Reagan, 471
Reams, 310
Reamsheart, 311
Redman, 311
Redmire, 311
Reed, 311, 312, 445, 518
Reedy, 312
Reese, 313
Reeves, 3, 21, 313, 314, 315, 463, 508, 509, 518
Regimental Band, 445
Reitsell, 315
Remeshart, 21
Renan, 315
Renforth, 315
Rensford, 316
Reunion Of Veterans Of War At Fortville, 516
Reynolds, 316, 430, 444, 457, 505, 506, 518
Rhue, 317
Rice, 318
Richards, 318, 442
Richardson, 319, 445, 505, 506
Richey, 319
Richie, 319
Richman, 319, 464
Richmond, 320

Hancock County Indiana Civil War Soldiers

Ridlen, 321, 516
Rigney, 321, 334
Riley, 1, 13, 21, 323, 326, 423, 425, 426, 430, 471
Ringwalt, 326
Rittenhouse, 326
Robb, 326
Roberts, 326, 327, 506, 518, 521
Robertson, 328, 497
Robinson, 328
Robison, 430
Rock, 328, 335, 504, 505
Rockey, 329
Roland, 329, 505
Rollins, 21, 329
Romack, 329
Romola, 492
Roney, 3, 330, 437, 485
Ross, 506
Rowland, 330
Rozel, 330
Ruddick, 332, 442
Rudrick, 332, 442
Rumler, 330, 336
Rush, 332
Russell, 332
Ryan, 508, 509
Rynearson, 333
Rynierson, 21
Sample, 337, 512
Samuel Newton Shelby, 28
Samuels, 116, 337, 425, 471
Sanders, 337
Sandy, 337
Sanford, 338, 506, 521

Sapp, 338
Sargent, 338
Savage, 338
Schaub, 338
Schleter, 339
Schrieber, 339
Schultz, 339
Scott, 21, 339, 340, 342, 433, 437, 439, 454, 463, 471, 484, 494, 496, 505, 506, 512, 521
Scotten, 343
Scotton, 438
Sears, 10, 344, 345, 428, 473, 512
Seely, 345
Sellery, 346
Seward, 346
Sewell, 346
Shafer, 346
Shaffer, 347, 425, 444, 471, 517
Sharpshooter, 79, 314
Sharpshooters, 3
Shaw, 348, 463, 471
Sheets, 348
Shelby, 28, 348, 506
Shell, 350
Shellhouse, 17, 21, 350
Shelton, 351
Shepherd, 351
Sherf, 351
Sherman, 351, 352, 380
Sherrett, 352
Sherrill, 353
Shiloh Church,, 441

Hancock County Indiana Civil War Soldiers

Shipley, 353
Shipman, 353, 463, 505
Shirley, 353
Shirm, 354
Shorn, 21, 354
Short, 21, 354
Shroy, 354
Shull, 354
Shultz, 355, 457, 505
Shumway, 11, 355
Shutes, 356, 448
Siberry, 356
Siddell, 357
Siders, 357
Simcox, 357
Simmons, 357
Simpson, 357
Sinking of the Sultana, 517
Siplinger, 358
Sisson, 358
Sitton, 358
Sivey, 359
Skinner, 360
Sleeth, 21, 360, 425, 520
Slifer, 21, 360, 362, 484, 518
Sloan, 18
Smail, 363
Smith, 21, 363, 364, 365, 454, 471, 508, 512, 517
Snell, 366
Snider, 366, 472, 490, 506
Snodgrass, 366
Snow, 1, 21, 367, 368, 445, 471, 507, 518
Snyder, 368, 425, 433

Soldiers, 29
Soldiers' families, 6
Soldiers in Battles on Birthdays, 515
Soldiers Report Happy Gathering, 518
Soots, 368
Spangler, 368
Sparks, 368
Spilker, 369
Spillman, 241
Spurry, 369
Squire, 369
Staats, 369
Stanbrough, 369
Stanley, 369, 458
Stanridge, 369
Steele, 369, 461, 488
Steffey, 370
Steller, 370
Stephens, 370, 371, 517
Stephenson, 370, 431
Sterling, 370
Stevens, 370, 371, 437
Stevenson, 21
Steward, 428, 473, 484
Stewart, 371, 372, 445
Stineback, 17, 372
Stirk, 372
Stockdale, 372
Stokes, 373
Stoneman, 424
Stout, 373, 507, 508
Stowder, 373
Strahl, 373
Strawboard Hill, 522

Hancock County Indiana Civil War Soldiers

Strickland, 374, 381
Stuart, 374, 446, 506
Stump, 375
Sturges, 375, 427
Stutsman, 21, 375, 382, 431, 506
Substitute, 6
Sullivan, 21, 376
Sulphur Branch Trestle, 427
Sulphur Branch Trestle, Alabama,, 428
Sultana, 12, 78, 80, 429, 512
Sultana Explosion, 475
Surgeons, 3
Surrender, 12
Surrender terms, 11
Sutherland, 377, 378
Swift, 378
Swope, 17, 18, 19, 378
Tague, 60, 75, 383
Tattman, 383
Taylor, 383, 506
Terms of Surrender, 11
Teush, 383
Thayer, 19, 58, 179, 383, 384, 385, 440, 442
Theobald, 385
Thomas, 17, 18, 385, 386, 387, 397, 457, 487, 517
Thomas Certificate, 398
Thompson, 388, 389, 425, 471, 472
Thornburgh, 389, 445
Thornton, 389

Three Comrades Of The Civil War, 520
Tibbetts, 389, 449, 518
Titanic, 12
Toon, 390
Torrence, 390, 506
Travis, 21, 390
Troy, 391
Truce on Cheatham Hill., 457
True, 21, 41, 391, 393, 394, 399, 463, 518
Trueblood, 394
Turner, 395
Tuttle, 17, 21, 24, 395, 439, 486, 508
Tygart, 396
Tyner, 1, 101, 396, 439
Ulrey, 21, 400
Underwood, 400, 437, 438, 439
Union brothers, 9
Union Guard, 21, 430
Unwary dog, 469
Vail, 401, 520
Valentine, 401, 508, 509
Vandyke, 401
Vanhorn, 508, 509
Vanlangingham, 401
Vanzant, 401, 402, 444
Varner, 402
Vernon, 402, 463
Vest, 402
Vestal, 402
Veteran of the Civil War is 94, 521

Hancock County Indiana Civil War Soldiers

Veteran Reserve Corps, 5
Virgin, 402
Volmer, 402
Voorhees, 402
Vote, 11, 356
Wagoner, 402
Walker, 17, 18, 402, 403, 428, 444, 473, 505, 506
Wall, 21
Wallace, 18, 19, 405, 440
Waller, 405, 484, 513
Walls, 1, 405, 426, 433, 437, 488
Wallsmith, 406
Walters, 406, 407
War with Mexico, 75
Ward, 406, 447
Warner, 406, 484
Waterman, 406, 444
Watson, 407, 444, 453
Watts, 407, 463, 506
Weaver, 408
Webb, 408
Welling, 408, 438
Wellings, 491
Wellington, 408
Welsby, 408
Welsh, 408
Welt, 408
Werts, 408
West, 18, 19, 409, 505, 506
Whelchel, 409
Whetsel, 409
Whitaker, 409, 410
White, 13, 410
Whitecotton, 410

Whitehurst, 410, 463
Whiteside, 410
Whitesides, 411
Windell, 417
Whortle, 462
Whorton, 411, 449
Wiggins, 10, 411, 436
Wilborn, 412
Wilcoxen, 412
Wilkins, 412, 507, 508
Willett, 116, 412, 413, 425, 471
Williams, 413, 415, 425, 442, 471
Willis, 415, 430
Willow Branch Lorenzo Fort Post No. 438, 508
Wills, 415
Wilson, 415, 416, 417, 484, 485, 486, 488, 489, 497, 505, 512, 517
Windler, 417
Windsor, 417, 449
Wingfield, 241, 417
Winn, 418, 428, 462
Winslow, 418
Wirts, 507
Wiseman, 418
Wishmeier, 419
Witham, 419
Wolf, 21, 419
Women's Relief Corps, 502
Women's Relief Corps Grave Marker, 503
Wood, 419
Woodall, 419

Hancock County Indiana Civil War Soldiers

Woodhall, 419
Woods, 419, 446
Wort, 408
Wray, 419
Wright, 421, 444, 461, 463, 504, 505, 517
Wyant, 421
Wynn, 31, 418, 505, 506

Yancey, 421, 505, 506
York, 422, 505, 506
Young, 422
Youse, 422, 464
Youst, 422, 445
Zouaves, 440
Zumwalt, 422

www.ingramcontent.com/pod-product-compliance
Lightning Source LLC
Chambersburg PA
CBHW060908300426
44112CB00011B/1385